D1093295

PRENTICE HALL
WRITING COACH

Upper Saddle River, New Jersey
Boston, Massachusetts
Chandler, Arizona
Glenview, Illinois

WRITING COACH

WELCOME TO
Writing
COACH

Seven Great Reasons to Learn to Write Well

Acknowledgments appear on page R55, which constitute an extension of this copyright page.

PEARSON

0-13-253146-1

978-0-13-253146-7

8 9 10   V057 14

1 Writing is hard, but hard is **rewarding**.

2 Writing helps you **sort things out**.

3 Writing helps you **persuade** others.

4 Writing makes you a **better reader**.

5 Writing makes you **smarter**.

6 Writing helps you get into and through **college**.

7 Writing **prepares you** for the world of work.

AUTHORS

The contributing authors guided the direction and philosophy of *Prentice Hall Writing Coach*. Working with the development team, they helped to build the pedagogical integrity of the program and to ensure its relevance for today's teachers and students.

Program Authors

Jeff Anderson

Jeff Anderson has worked with struggling writers and readers for almost 20 years. His works integrate grammar and editing instruction into the processes of reading and writing. Anderson has written articles in NCTE's *Voices from the Middle, English Journal*, and *Educational Leadership.* Anderson won the NCTE Paul and Kate Farmer Award for his *English Journal* article on teaching grammar in context. He has published two books, *Mechanically Inclined: Building Grammar, Usage, and Style into Writer's Workshop* and *Everyday Editing: Inviting Students to Develop Skill and Craft in Writer's Workshop* as well as a DVD, *The Craft of Grammar.*

Grammar gives me a powerful lens through which to look at my writing. It gives me the freedom to say things exactly the way I want to say them.

Kelly Gallagher

Kelly Gallagher is a full-time English teacher at Magnolia High School in Anaheim, California. He is the former co-director of the South Basin Writing Project at California State University, Long Beach. Gallagher is the author of *Reading Reasons: Motivational Mini-Lessons for the Middle and High School, Deeper Reading: Comprehending Challenging Texts 4–12, Teaching Adolescent Writers,* and *Readicide.* He is also featured in the video series, *Building Adolescent Readers.* With a focus on adolescent literacy, Gallagher provides training to educators on a local, national and international level. Gallagher was awarded the Secondary Award of Classroom Excellence from the California Association of Teachers of English—the state's top English teacher honor.

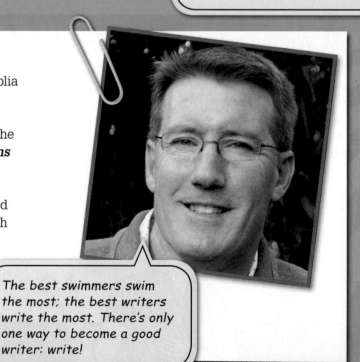

The best swimmers swim the most; the best writers write the most. There's only one way to become a good writer: write!

Contributing Authors

Evelyn Arroyo

Evelyn Arroyo is the author of **A+RISE,** Research-based Instructional Strategies for ELLs (English Language Learners). Her work focuses on closing the achievement gap for minority students and English language learners. Through her publications and presentations, Arroyo provides advice, encouragement, and practical success strategies to help teachers reach their ELL students.

> *Your rich, colorful cultural life experiences are unique and can easily be painted through words. These experiences define who you are today, and writing is one way to begin capturing your history. Become a risk-taker and fall in love with yourself through your own words.*

> *When you're learning a new language, writing in that language takes effort. The effort pays off big time, though. Writing helps us generate ideas, solve problems, figure out how the language works, and, above all, allows us to express ourselves.*

Jim Cummins, Ph.D.

Jim Cummins is a Professor in the Modern Language Centre at the University of Toronto. A well-known educator, lecturer, and author, Cummins focuses his research on bilingual education and the academic achievement of culturally diverse students. He is the author of numerous publications, including **Negotiating Identities: Education for Empowerment in a Diverse Society.**

Grant Wiggins, Ed.D.

Grant Wiggins is the President of Authentic Education. He earned his Ed.D. from Harvard University. Grant consults with schools, districts, and state education departments; organizes conferences and workshops; and develops resources on curricular change. He is the co-author, with Jay McTighe, of **Understanding By Design,** the award-winning text published by ASCD.

> *I hated writing as a student—and my grades showed it. I grew up to be a writer, though. What changed? I began to think I had something to say. That's ultimately why you write: to find out what you are really thinking, really feeling, really believing.*

> *Concepts of grammar can sharpen your reading, communication, and even your reasoning, so I have championed its practice in my classes and in my businesses. Even adults are quick to recognize that a refresher in grammar makes them keener— and more marketable.*

Gary Forlini

Gary Forlini is managing partner of the School Growth initiative **Brinkman—Forlini—Williams,** which trains school administrators and teachers in Classroom Instruction and Management. His recent works include the book **Help Teachers Engage Students** and the data system **ObserverTab** for district administrators, **Class Acts: Every Teacher's Guide To Activate Learning**, and the initiative's workshop **Grammar for Teachers**.

CONTENTS IN BRIEF
WRITING

WRITING GAME PLAN

1 You, the Writer

2 Types of Writing

3 The Writing Process

4 Sentences, Paragraphs, and Compositions

Writing without grammar only goes so far. Grammar and writing work together. To write well, grammar skills give me great tools.

CORE WRITING CHAPTERS

WRITING COACH
Online
www.phwritingcoach.com

**Interactive
Writing Coach™**

**Interactive
Graphic Organizer**

**Interactive
Model**

**Online
Journal**

Resources

Video

GRAMMAR

GRAMMAR GAME PLAN

Find It FIX IT 20 Major Grammatical Errors and How to Fix Them

> Grammar without writing is only a collection of rules, but when these rules are put into action as I write, the puzzle comes together.

CORE GRAMMAR CHAPTERS

STUDENT RESOURCES

Handbooks
Glossaries

WRITING COACH
Online

- Grammar Tutorials
- Grammar Practice
- Grammar Games

www.phwritingcoach.com

Writing COACH : How to Use This Program

This program is organized into two distinct sections: one for WRITING and one for GRAMMAR.

In the **WRITING** section, you'll learn strategies, traits, and skills that will help you become a better writer.

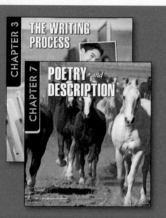

In the **GRAMMAR** section, you'll learn the rules and conventions of grammar, usage, and mechanics.

What DIGITAL writing and grammar resources are available?

The Writing Coach Online boxes will indicate opportunities to use online tools.

In **Writing,** use the **Interactive Writing Coach™** in two ways to get personalized guidance and support for your writing.
- Paragraph Feedback and
- Essay Scorer

WRITING COACH

Online

www.phwritingcoach.com

👍 **Interactive Writing Coach™**
- Choosing from the Topic Bank gives you access to the Interactive Writing Coach™.
- Submit your writing and receive instant personalized feedback and guidance as you draft, revise, and edit your writing.

WRITING COACH

Online

www.phwritingcoach.com

Grammar Tutorials
Brush up on your grammar skills with these animated videos.

Grammar Practice
Practice your grammar skills with Writing Coach Online.

Grammar Games
Test your knowledge of grammar in this fast-paced interactive video game.

In **Grammar,** view grammar tutorials, practice your grammar skills, and play grammar video games.

What will you find in the WRITING section?

Writing Genre

Each chapter introduces a different **writing genre.**

Learn about the key characteristics of the **genre** before you start writing.

Focus on a single form of the genre with the **Feature Assignment**.

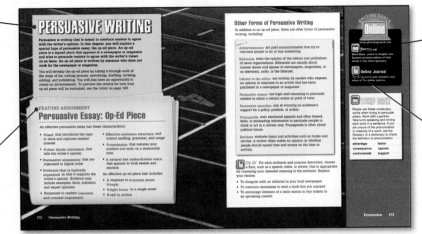

Writing Coach Online

- View the **Word Bank** words in the eText glossary, and hear them pronounced in both English and Spanish.

- Use your **Online Journal** to record your answers and ideas as you respond to *Try It!* activities.

Mentor Text and Student Model

The **Mentor Text** and **Student Model** provide examples of the genre featured in each chapter.

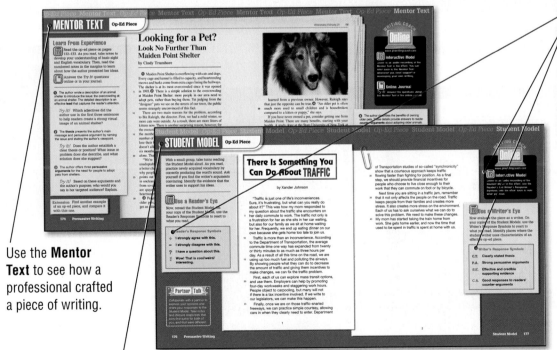

Writing Coach Online

- Use the **Interactive Model** to mark the text with Reader's and Writer's Response Symbols.

- Listen to an audio recording of the **Mentor Text** or **Student Model.**

Use the **Mentor Text** to see how a professional crafted a piece of writing.

Review the **Student Model** as a guide for composing your own piece.

The **Topic Bank** provides prompts for the **Feature Assignment.**

Choose from a bank of topics, or follow steps to find an idea of your own.

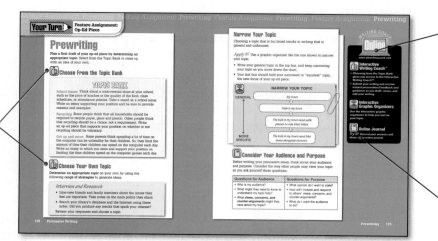

Writing Coach Online

- As you narrow your topic, get the right type of support! You'll find three different forms of graphic organizers—one model, one with step-by-step guidance, and one that is blank for you to complete.

- Use *Try It!* ideas to practice new skills. Use *Apply It!* activities as you work on your own writing.

Whether you are working on your essay drafts online or with a pen and paper, an **Outline for Success** can get you started.

Consult this **outline** for a quick visual specific to the writing task assigned in each chapter.

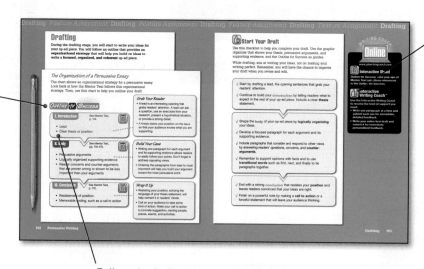

Writing Coach Online

- Start with just a paragraph and build up to your essay draft, or if you are ready, go straight to submitting your essay. The choice is yours!

Follow the bulleted suggestions for each part of your draft, and you'll be on your way to success.

You can use the **Revision RADaR** strategy as a guide for making changes to improve your draft.

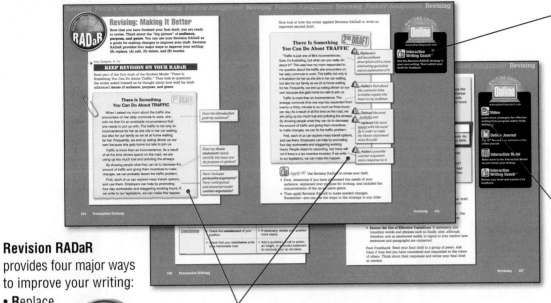

Check out these example drafts to see how to apply **Revision RADaR.**

Revision RADaR

provides four major ways to improve your writing:

- **R**eplace
- **A**dd
- **D**elete
- **R**eorder

Writing Coach Online

- With **Interactive Writing Coach™,** submit your paragraphs and essays multiple times. View your progress in your online writing portfolio. Feel confident that your work is ready to be shared in peer review or teacher conferencing.

- View **videos** with strategies for writing from program author **Kelly Gallagher.**

In the editing stage, **What Do You Notice?** and **Mentor Text** help you zoom in on powerful sentences.

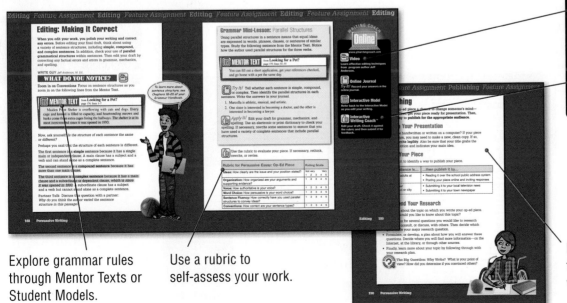

Writing Coach Online

- View **videos** with strategies for writing from program author **Jeff Anderson.**

- Submit your essay for feedback and a score.

Explore grammar rules through Mentor Texts or Student Models.

Use a rubric to self-assess your work.

Find the best way to share your writing with others.

How do end-of-chapter features help you apply what you've learned?

In **Make Your Writing Count** and **Writing for Media** you will work
on innovative assignments that involve the 21st Century life and
career skills you'll need for communicating successfully.

Make Your Writing Count
Work collaboratively on project-based
assignments and share what you have
learned with others. Projects include:

- Debates
- TV Talk Shows
- News Reports

Writing for Media
Complete an assignment on your own by exploring media
forms, and then developing your own content. Projects include:

- Blogs
- Storyboards
- Documentary Scripts
- Multimedia Presentations

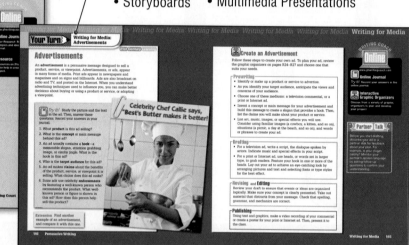

Test Prep

The **Writing for Assessment** pages help you prepare
for important standardized tests.

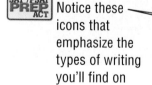
Notice these
icons that
emphasize the
types of writing
you'll find on
high-stakes tests.

Use **The ABCDs of
On-Demand Writing**
for a quick, memorable
strategy for success.

Writing Coach Online
Submit your essay for
feedback and a score.

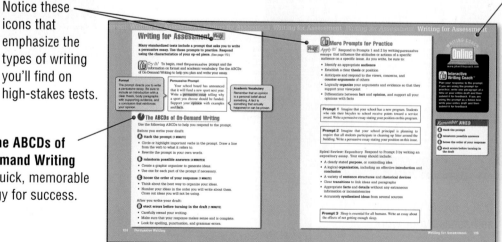

What will you find in the GRAMMAR section?

Grammar Game Plan

The **Find It/Fix It** reference guide helps you fix the **20** most common errors in student writing.

Study each of the 20 common errors and their corrections, which are clearly explained on each page.

Follow cross-references to more instruction in the grammar chapters.

Review the **Check It** features for strategies to help you avoid these errors.

Grammar Chapters

Each grammar chapter begins with a **What Do You Notice?** feature and **Mentor Text.**

Use the **Mentor Text** to help you zoom in on powerful sentences. It showcases the correct use of written language conventions.

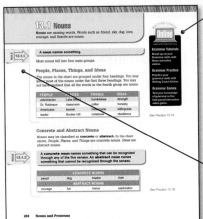

Writing Coach Online
The **Writing Coach Online** digital experience for Grammar helps you focus on just the lessons and practice you need.

Use the grammar section as a quick reference handbook. Each **grammar rule** is highlighted and numbered.

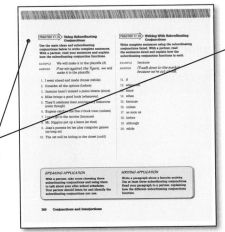

Try **Practice** pages and **Test Warm-Ups** to help you check your progress.

WRITING

WRITING GAME PLAN

CONTENTS

WRITING COACH

Online

www.phwritingcoach.com

All content available online

- Interactive Writing Coach™
- Interactive Graphic Organizer
- Interactive Models
- Online Journal
- Resources
- Video

WRITING

Connect to the Big Questions

- **What do you think?**
  What is the most important life event?

- **Why write?**
  What should we put in and leave out to be accurate and honest?

Connect to the Big Questions

- **What do you think?**
  How do our own stories shape us?

- **Why write?**
  What can fiction do better than nonfiction?

WRITING COACH

Online

www.phwritingcoach.com

All content available online

- Interactive Writing Coach™
- Interactive Graphic Organizer
- Interactive Models
- Online Journal
- Resources
- Video

WRITING

Connect to the Big Questions

- **What do you think?**
  What do music, art, and poetry best communicate?

- **Why write?**
  How do we best convey feelings through words on a page?

Connect to the Big Questions

THE BIG QUESTION

- **What do you think?**
  To what extent do computers change the way we learn?

- **Why write?**
  What should we tell and what should we describe to make information clear?

WRITING COACH

Online

www.phwritingcoach.com

All content available online
- Interactive Writing Coach™
- Interactive Graphic Organizer
- Interactive Models
- Online Journal
- Resources
- Video

WRITING

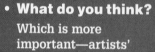

Connect to the Big Questions

- **What do you think?**
  Which is more important—artists' rights or community standards?

- **Why write?**
  What is your point of view? How will you know if you've convinced others?

WRITING

Connect to the Big Questions

• **What do you think?**
What should we learn from our history?

• **Why write?**
Do you understand a subject well enough to write about it? How will you find out what all the facts are?

Connect to the Big Questions

- **What do you think?**
  When is it most necessary to justify crucial workplace decisions?

- **Why write?**
  What do daily workplace communications require of format, content, and style?

WRITING COACH

Online

www.phwritingcoach.com

All content available online

- Interactive Writing Coach™
- Interactive Graphic Organizer
- Interactive Models
- Online Journal
- Resources
- Video

GRAMMAR

CHAPTER 15 Phrases and Clauses 355

CHAPTER 16 Effective Sentences 395

WRITING COACH

Online

www.phwritingcoach.com

All content available online

• Grammar Tutorials
• Grammar Practice
• Grammar Games

GRAMMAR

USAGE

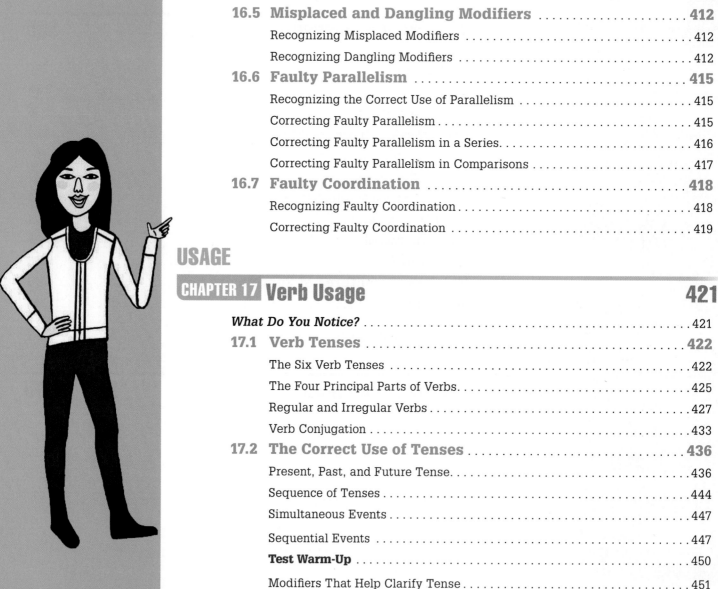

CHAPTER 17 | Verb Usage — 421

WRITING COACH.com

Online

www.phwritingcoach.com

All content available online
• Grammar Tutorials
• Grammar Practice
• Grammar Games

GRAMMAR

CHAPTER 20 Using Modifiers — 505

CHAPTER 21 Miscellaneous Problems in Usage — 519

MECHANICS

GRAMMAR

WRITING COACH

Online

www.phwritingcoach.com

All content available online
- Grammar Tutorials
- Grammar Practice
- Grammar Games

STUDENT RESOURCES

ONFICTION NARRATION *Memoir* FICTION NARRATION *Realistic Short*
UASION *Op-Ed Piece* RESPONSE TO LITERATURE *Comparison Essay* RES
roposal NONFICTION NARRATION *Memoir* FICTION NARRATION *Real.*
ssay PERSUASION *Op-Ed Piece* RESPONSE TO LITERATURE *Comparison*
ésumé, Proposal NONFICTION NARRATION *Memoir* FICTION NARRAT.
ation Essay PERSUASION *Op-Ed Piece* RESPONSE TO LITERATURE *Comp.*
etter, Résumé, Proposal NONFICTION NARRATION *Memoir* FICTION NA.
lassification Essay PERSUASION *Op-Ed Piece* RESPONSE TO LITERATURE
over Letter, Résumé, Proposal NONFICTION NARRATION *Memoir* FICTI.

POETRY *Sonnet and Free Verse Poem* EXPOSITION *Classification Essay*
Informational Research Report WORKPLACE WRITING *Cover Letter, Résumé*
Short Story POETRY *Sonnet and Free Verse Poem* EXPOSITION *Classification*
RESEARCH *Informational Research Report* WORKPLACE WRITING *Cover Le*
Realistic Short Story POETRY *Sonnet and Free Verse Poem* EXPOSITION *Cla*
Essay RESEARCH *Informational Research Report* WORKPLACE WRITING C
TION Realistic Short Story POETRY *Sonnet and Free Verse Poem* EXPOSIT
parison Essay RESEARCH *Informational Research Report* WORKPLACE WRI
ARRATION Realistic Short Story POETRY *Sonnet and Free Verse Poem* EX

Writing

CHAPTER 1

YOU, THE WRITER

What kind of writer are you?
Do you write easily and frequently,
or are you a bit reluctant, writing only
when you need to?

Why Do You Write?

Writing well is one of the most important life skills you can develop.
Being a good writer can help you achieve success in school and beyond.
Most likely, you write for many reasons. You write:

To Share

You probably often write to **share** your experiences with others. Writing
can be an easy way to **reach out** to people and connect with them.

To Persuade People

Writing can also be an effective way to **persuade** people to consider
your opinions. For example, you may find it's easier to convince someone
of your point of view when you've effectively organized your thoughts in
an essay or a letter.

To Inform

Another reason to write is to **inform**. Perhaps you want to tell an
audience how you built your computer network or how you finally got
your e-mail to function properly.

To Enjoy

Personal fulfillment is another important motivation for writing, since
writing enables you **to express** your thoughts and feelings. In addition,
writing can also help you recall an event, or let you escape from
everyday life.

Fortunately, writing well is a skill you can learn and one that you can
continue to improve and polish. This program will help you improve your
writing skills and give you useful information about the many types
of writing.

What Do You Write?

Writing is already an important part of your everyday life. Each day is full of opportunities to write, allowing you to capture, express, think through, and share your thoughts and feelings, and demonstrate what you know. Here are some ways you might write.

- Recording thoughts in a journal
- Texting friends or posting on social networking sites
- E-mailing thank-you notes to relatives
- Creating lists of things to do or things you like
- Writing research reports, nonfiction accounts, fiction stories, and essays in school

How Can You Find Ideas?

The good news is that ideas are all around you. You just need to be aware of the rich resources that are available.

By Observing

Observing is a good way to start to find ideas. Did you see anything interesting on your way to school? Was there something unusual about the video game you played last night?

By Reading

Reading is another useful option—look through newspaper articles and editorials, magazines, blogs, and Web sites. Perhaps you read something that surprised you or really made you feel concerned. Those are exactly the subjects that can lead to the ideas you want to write about.

By Watching

Watching is another way to get ideas— watch online videos or television programs, for example.

WRITING COACH

Online

www.phwritingcoach.com

 Online Journal

Try It! Record your notes, answers, and ideas in the online journal. You can also record and save your answers and ideas on pop-up sticky notes in the eText.

❝ Writer to Writer ❞

I write when I want to be heard or connect. Writing lets me be a vital part of my community and reach outside it as well. All the while, I get to be me—my unique self.

—Jeff Anderson

How Can You Keep Track of Ideas?

You may sometimes think of great writing ideas in the middle of the night or on the way to math class. These strategies can help you remember those ideas.

Start an Idea Notebook or a Digital Idea File

Reserving a small **notebook** to record ideas can be very valuable. Just writing the essence of an idea, as it comes to you, can later help you develop a topic or essay. A **digital idea file** is exactly the same thing—but it's recorded on your computer, cell phone, or other electronic device.

Keep a Personal Journal

Many people find that keeping a **journal** of their thoughts is helpful. Then, when it's time to select an idea, they can flip through their journal and pick up on the best gems they wrote—sometimes from long ago.

Maintain a Learning Log

A **learning log** is just what it sounds like—a place to record information you have learned, which could be anything from methods of solving equations to computer shortcuts. Writing about something in a learning log might later inspire you to conduct further research on the same topic.

Free Write

Some individuals find that if they just let go and write whatever comes to mind, they eventually produce excellent ideas. **Free writing** requires being relaxed and unstructured. This kind of writing does not require complete sentences, correct spelling, or proper grammar. Whatever ends up on the paper or on the computer screen is fine. Later, the writer can go back and tease out the best ideas.

How Can You Get Started?

Every writer is different, so it makes sense that all writers should try out techniques that might work well for them. Regardless of your personal writing style, these suggestions should help you get started.

Get Comfortable

It's important to find and create an environment that encourages your writing process. Choose a spot where interruptions will be minimal and where you'll find it easy to concentrate. Some writers prefer a quiet library. Others prefer to work in a room with music playing softly on their computer.

Have Your Materials Ready

Before starting to write, gather all the background materials you need to get started, including your notes, free writing, reader's journal, and portfolio. Make sure you also have writing tools, such as a pen and paper or a computer.

Spend Time Wisely

Budgeting your available writing time is a wise strategy. Depending on your writing goal, you may want to sketch out your time on a calendar, estimating how long to devote to each stage of the writing process. Then, you can assign deadlines to each part. If you find a particular stage takes longer than you estimated, simply adjust your schedule to ensure that you finish on time.

| | | ◄ October ► | | | | |
SUNDAY	MONDAY	TUESDAY	WEDNESDAY	THURSDAY	FRIDAY	SATURDAY
		1 Start Research	2 Finish Research	3 Write Outline	4	5
6	7	8 Finish First Draft	9 Finish Revising	10 Finish Proof-reading	11	12
13	14 DUE DATE	15	16	17	18	19
20	21	22	23	24	25	26
27	28	29	30	31		

How Do You Work With Others?

If you think of writing as a solitary activity, think again. Working with others can be a key part of the writing process.

Brainstorming

Brainstorming works when everyone in a group feels free to suggest ideas, whether they seem commonplace or brilliant.

Cooperative Writing

Cooperative writing is a process in which each member of a group concentrates on a different part of an assignment. Then, the group members come together to discuss their ideas and write drafts.

Peer Feedback

Peer feedback comes from classmates who have read your writing and offered suggestions for improvements. When commenting on a classmate's work, it's important to provide constructive, or helpful, criticism.

21st Century Learning

Collaborate and Discuss

In **collaborative writing,** each group member takes an assigned role on a writing project. A collaborative group may decide on such possible roles as leader, facilitator, recorder, and listener. The roles may change as the group discusses and works through the writing process. The goal, however, is to work and rework the writing until all members feel they have produced the best result.

Possible Roles in a Collaborative Writing Project

LEADER
Initiates the discussion by clearly expressing group goals and moderates discussions

FACILITATOR
Works to move the discussion forward and clarify ideas

COMPROMISER
Works to find practical solutions to differences of opinion

LISTENER
Actively listens and serves to recall details that were discussed

Using Technology

Technology allows collaboration to occur in ways that were previously unthinkable.

- By working together on the Internet, students around the world have infinite opportunities to collaborate online on a wide range of projects.

- Collaboration can range from projects that foster community cooperation, such as how to improve debates during local elections, to those that increase global awareness, such as focusing on how to encourage more recycling.

- Being able to log in and to contribute to media, such as journals, blogs, and social networks, allows you to connect globally, express your views in writing, and join a world-wide conversation.

Where Can You Keep Your Finished Work?

A **portfolio,** or growing collection of your work, is valuable for many reasons. It can serve as a research bank of ideas and as a record of how your writing is improving. You can create a portfolio on a computer or in a folder or notebook. You'll learn more about managing a portfolio in chapter 3.

A **Reader's Journal,** in which you record quotes and ideas from your reading, can also be used to store original ideas. Your journal can be housed on a computer or in a notebook.

Reflect on Your Writing

Analyzing, making inferences, and drawing conclusions about how you find ideas can help you become a better, more effective writer. Find out more about how you write by asking yourself questions like these:

- Which strategies have I found most effective for finding good ideas for writing?

- What pieces of writing represent my best work and my weakest work? What do the pieces in each group have in common?

Partner Talk

With a partner, talk about your collaborative writing experiences. Be sure to share your responses to such questions as these: What project did you work on as a collaborative effort? What did you learn that you might not have discovered if you were developing a writing project by yourself?

CHAPTER 2

TYPES *of* WRITING

Genres and Forms

Genres are types, or categories, of writing.

- Each genre has a specific **purpose,** or goal. For example, the purpose of persuasive writing is to convince readers to agree with the writer's point of view.
- Each genre has specific **characteristics.** Short stories, for example, have characters, a setting, and a plot.

In this chapter, you will be introduced to several genres: nonfiction narratives, fiction narratives, poetry and descriptive writing, expository writing, persuasive writing, responses to literature, and workplace writing.

Forms are subcategories of genres that contain all the characteristics of the genre plus some unique characteristics of their own. For example, a mystery is a form of short story. In addition to plot, characters, and setting, it has a mystery to be solved.

Selecting Genres

In some writing situations, you may need to select the correct genre for conveying your intended meaning.

- To **entertain,** you may choose to write a short story or a humorous essay.
- To **describe** an emotion, writing a poem may be best.
- To **persuade** someone to your point of view, you may want to write a persuasive essay or editorial.

Each genre has unique strengths and weaknesses, and your specific goals will help you decide which is best.

Nonfiction Narration

Nonfiction narratives are any kind of literary text that tells a story about real people, events, and ideas. This genre of writing can take a number of different forms but includes well-developed conflict and resolution, interesting and believable characters, and a range of literary strategies, such as dialogue and suspense. Examples include Samuel Pepys's "The Diary" and Nick Hornby's "Songbook."

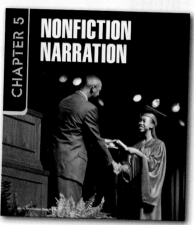

CHAPTER 5

NONFICTION NARRATION

Personal Narratives

Personal narratives tell true stories about events in a writer's life. These types of writing are also called **autobiographical essays.** The stories may tell about an experience or relationship that is important to the writer, who is the main character. They have a clearly defined focus and communicate the reasons for actions and consequences.

Biographical Narratives

In a **biographical narrative,** the writer shares facts about someone else's life. The writer may describe an important period, experience, or relationship in that other person's life, but presents the information from his or her own perspective.

Blogs

Blogs are online journals that may include autobiographical narratives, reflections, opinions, and other types of comments. They may also reflect genres other than nonfiction such as expository writing, and they may include other media, such as photos, music, or video.

Diary and Journal Entries

Writers record their personal thoughts, feelings, and experiences in **diaries** or **journals.** Writers sometimes keep diaries and journals for many years and then analyze how they reacted to various events over time.

Eyewitness Accounts

Eyewitness accounts are nonfiction writing that focus on historical or other important events. The writer is the narrator and shares his or her thoughts about the event. However, the writer is not the main focus of the writing.

Memoirs

Memoirs usually focus on meaningful scenes from writers' lives. These scenes often reflect on moments of a significant decision or personal discovery. For example, many modern U.S. presidents have written memoirs after they have left office. These memoirs help the public gain a better understanding of the decisions they made while in office.

Reflective Essays

Reflective essays present personal experiences, either events that happened to the writers themselves or that they learned about from others. They generally focus on sharing observations and insights they had while thinking about those experiences. Reflective essays often appear as features in magazines and newspapers.

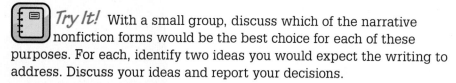 *Try It!* With a small group, discuss which of the narrative nonfiction forms would be the best choice for each of these purposes. For each, identify two ideas you would expect the writing to address. Discuss your ideas and report your decisions.

- To tell about seeing a championship kite-flying tournament
- To write about one of the first astronauts to walk in space
- To record personal thoughts about a favorite teacher

Fiction Narration

CHAPTER 6

FICTION NARRATION

Fiction narratives are literary texts that tell a story about imagined people, events, and ideas. They contain elements such as characters, a setting, a sequence of events, and often, a theme. As with nonfiction narratives, this genre can take many different forms, but most forms include well-developed **conflict** and **resolution**. They also include **interesting and believable elements** and a range of **literary strategies,** such as dialogue and suspense. Examples include Anton Chekhov's "An Upheaval" or Virginia Woolf's "The Lady in the Looking Glass: A Reflection."

Realistic Fiction

Realistic fiction portrays invented characters and events in everyday situations that most readers would find familiar. Although characters may be imaginary, writers sometimes use real individuals in their own lives as a basis for the fictional ones. Because the focus is on everyday life, realistic fiction often presents problems that many people face and solutions they devise to solve them.

Fantasy Stories

Fantasy stories stretch the imagination and take readers to unreal worlds. Animals may talk, people may fly, or characters may have superhuman powers. Good fantasy stories have the elements of narrative fiction and manage to keep the fantastic elements believable.

Historical Fiction

Historical fiction is about imaginary people living in real places and times in history. Usually, the main characters are fictional people who know and interact with famous people and participate in important historical events.

Mystery Stories

Mystery stories present unexplained or strange events that characters try to solve. These stories are popular, probably because they are often packed full of suspense and surprises. Some characters in mystery stories, such as Sherlock Holmes, have become so famous that many people think of them as real people.

Myths and Legends

Myths and **legends** are traditional stories, told in cultures around the world. They were created to explain natural events that people could not otherwise explain or understand. They may, for example, tell about the origin of fire or thunder. Many myths and legends include gods, goddesses, and heroes who perform superhuman actions.

Science Fiction

Science fiction stories tell about real and imagined developments in science and technology and their effects on the way people think and live. Space travel, robots, and life in the future are popular topics in science fiction.

Tall Tales

You can tell a **tall tale** from other story types because it tells about larger-than-life characters in realistic settings. These characters can perform amazing acts of strength and bravery. One very famous hero of tall tales is Pecos Bill, who could ride just about anything—even a tornado!

Try It! Think about what you've read about narrative fiction and narrative nonfiction genres. Then, discuss in a group which **genre** would be best if you were planning a first draft and had these purposes in mind. **Select the correct genre** for conveying your intended meaning to your audiences. Then, identify two or three ideas that you would expect to include in a first draft. Be sure to explain your choices.

- To tell about a Texas rancher who can lasso lightning
- To share a true story about a famous person
- To tell the story of your most exciting day at school

Poetry and Description

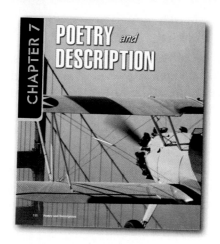

Poetry and other kinds of descriptive literature express ideas and feelings about real or imagined people, events, and ideas. They use rhythm, rhyme, precise language, and sensory details—words that appeal to the senses—to create vivid images. In addition, they use figurative language—writing that means something beyond what the words actually say—to express ideas in new, fresh, and interesting ways.

Structural elements, such as line length and stanzas, also help the poet express ideas and set a mood. Some examples of poetry include William Shakespeare's "Sonnet 29" and John Donne's "Song."

Ballad

A **ballad** is a form of lyric poetry that expresses the poet's emotions toward someone or something. Ballads rhyme, and some have refrains that repeat after each stanza, which makes them easy to translate into songs.

In many places, traditional folk ballads were passed down as oral poems or songs and then later written. Some ballads tell about cultural heroes. Other ballads tell sad stories or make fun of certain events.

Free Verse

Free verse is poetry that has no regular rhyme, rhythm, or form. Instead, a free verse poem captures the patterns of natural speech. The poet writes in whatever form seems to fit the ideas best. A free verse poem can have almost anything as its subject.

" Writer to Writer "

Writing fiction and poetry sharpens your creativity—a skill valued by universities and employers.

—Kelly Gallagher

Partner Talk

Think about an example of fiction that you've especially enjoyed reading. Then, choose a partner and report your choices to each other. Be sure to explain what made the fiction piece so enjoyable, interesting, or exciting.

Prose Poem

A **prose poem** shares many of the features of other poetry, since it has rhythm, repetition, and vivid imagery. However, it is different from other poetry in one important way: It takes the form of prose or non-verse writing. Therefore, a prose poem may look like a short story on a page.

Sonnet

The **sonnet** is a form of rhyming lyric poetry with set rules. It is 14 lines long and usually follows a rhythm scheme called iambic pentameter. Each line has ten syllables and every other syllable is accented.

Haiku

Haiku is a form of non-rhyming poetry that was first developed in Japan hundreds of years ago. Many poets who write haiku in English write the poems in three lines. The first line has seven syllables, the second line has five syllables, and the third line has seven syllables. Haiku poets often write about nature and use vivid visual images.

Other Descriptive Writing

Descriptive writing includes descriptive essays, travel writing, and definition essays.

- **Descriptive essays** often use words that involve the senses to create a clear picture of a subject. For example, a descriptive essay about a freshly grilled hamburger might use adjectives such as *juicy*, *spicy*, *steamy*, *fragrant*, *hot*, and *glistening* to paint a word picture.
- A **travel essay** uses sensory words to describe a place.
- A **definition essay** can draw on a writer's emotional experience to describe something abstract, like friendship or happiness.

The qualities of description can also be used in other types of writing. For example, a short story can be more realistic or compelling when it includes strong description.

Try It! Now that you've learned more about poetry and description, discuss which specific **genre** would be best for each of these purposes. **Select the correct genre** for conveying your intended meaning to your audiences. Then, identify two or three types of information that you would want to include in a first draft. Be ready to explain your thinking.

- To tell about a trip to a beach in Mexico
- To describe a drop of rain
- To tell the story of a character who lives in the wilderness

Exposition

Exposition is writing that seeks to communicate ideas and information to specific audiences and for specific purposes. It relies on facts to inform or explain.

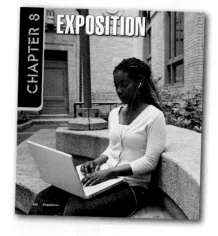

- Effective expository writing reflects an organization that is well planned—with effective introductory paragraphs, body paragraphs, and concluding paragraphs.

- In addition, good expository writing uses a variety of sentence structures and rhetorical devices—deliberate uses of language for specific effects.

Examples of expository writing include *The London Gazette's* "The Great Fire" and English Government's "Evacuation Scheme."

Analytical Essay

An **analytical essay** explores a topic by supplying relevant information in the form of facts, examples, reasons, and valid inferences to support the writer's claims.

- An **introductory paragraph** presents a thesis statement, the main point to be developed.

- The **body of the essay** provides facts about the topic, using a variety of sentence structures and transitions to help the writing flow.

- The **concluding paragraph** sums up ideas, helping readers understand why the topic is important.

Compare-and-Contrast Essay

A **compare-and-contrast** essay explores similarities and differences between two or more things for a specific purpose. As with other expository essays, the compare-and-contrast essay offers clear, factual details about the subject.

Cause-and-Effect Essay

A **cause-and-effect essay** traces the results of an event or describes the reasons an event happened. It is clearly organized and gives precise examples that support the relationship between the cause and effect.

" Writer to Writer "

Expository forms can shape my thinking and help my writing gel. I find the expository patterns clarifying my thoughts and filling in gaps that I may have otherwise missed.

—Jeff Anderson

Choose a different partner this time. Discuss a poem that you've read in class. Share your thoughts about the poem and describe what made the piece successful.

Classification Essay

In a **classification essay,** a writer organizes a subject into categories and explains the category into which an item falls.

- An effective classification essay **sorts** its subjects—things or ideas—into several categories.

- It then offers **examples** that fall into each category. For example, a classification essay about video games might discuss three types of video games—action, adventure, and arcade.

- The essay might conclude with a statement about how the items classified are different or about how they are similar.

Problem-Solution Essay

A **problem-solution essay** presents a problem and then offers solutions to that problem. This type of essay may contain opinions, like a persuasive essay, but it is meant to explain rather than persuade.

- An effective problem-solution essay presents a clear statement of the problem, including a summary of its causes and effects.

- Then, it proposes at least one realistic solution and uses facts, statistics, or expert testimony to support the solution.

- The essay should be clearly organized, so that the relationship between the problem and the solution is obvious.

Pro-Con Essay

A **pro-con essay** examines arguments for and against an idea or topic.

- It has a topic that has two sides or points of view. For example, you might choose the following as a topic: Is it right to keep animals in zoos?

- Then, you would develop an essay that tells why it's good to keep animals in zoos, as well as why it's harmful to keep animals in zoos.

- It's important to be sure to give a clear analysis of the topic.

Newspaper and Magazine Articles

Newspaper and **magazine articles** offer information about news and events. They are typically factual and do not include the writer's opinions. They often provide an analysis of events and give readers background information on a topic. Some articles may also reflect genres other than the analytical essay, such as an editorial that aims to persuade.

Internet Articles

Articles on the **Internet** can supply relevant information about a topic.

- They are often like newspaper or magazine articles but may include shorter sentences and paragraphs. In addition, they include more visuals, such as charts and bulleted lists. They may also reflect genres other than analytical essays.

- It's always wise to consider the source when reading Internet articles because only the most reputable sources should be trusted to present correct facts.

On-Demand Writing

Because essay questions often appear on school tests, knowing how to write to **test prompts**, especially under time limits, is an important skill.

Test prompts provide a clear topic with directions about what should be addressed. The effective response to an essay demonstrates not only an understanding of academic content but also good writing skills.

Try It! Think about what you've learned about expository writing and consider the other genres you've discussed. Then, discuss in a group which **genre** would be best if you were planning a first draft with these purposes in mind. **Select the correct genre** for conveying your intended meaning to your audiences. Then, identify two or three key ideas that you would want to include in a first draft. Be sure to explain your choices.

- To weigh the benefits of two kinds of pets
- To imagine what life would be like on the moon

Partner Talk

Share your experiences with writing expository essays with a partner. Talk about strategies that worked well for you, as well as those that weren't as successful. Be sure to include your analysis of why certain strategies worked better than others.

Persuasion

Persuasive writing aims to influence the attitudes or actions of a specific audience on specific issues. A strong persuasive text is logically organized and clearly describes the issue. It also provides precise and relevant evidence that supports a clear thesis statement. Persuasive writing may contain diagrams, graphs, or charts. These visuals can help to convince the reader. Examples include Gandhi's "Defending Nonviolent Resistance" or Lord John Russell's "Speech in Favor of Reform."

CHAPTER 9 PERSUASION

Persuasive Essays or Argumentative Essays

A **persuasive essay** or **argumentative essay** uses logic and reasoning to persuade readers to adopt a certain point of view or to take action. A strong persuasive essay starts with a clear thesis statement and provides supporting arguments based on evidence. It also anticipates readers' counter-arguments and responds to them as well.

Persuasive Speeches

Persuasive speeches are presented aloud and aim to win an audience's support for a policy, position, or action. These speeches often appeal to emotion and reason to convince an audience. Speakers sometimes change their script in order to address each specific audience's concerns.

Editorials

Editorials, which appear in newspapers, in magazines, or on television, radio, or the Internet, state the opinion of the editors and publishers of news organizations. Editorials usually present an opinion about a current issue, starting with a clear thesis statement and then offering strong supporting evidence.

Op-Ed Pieces

An **op-ed piece** is an essay that tries to convince the readers of a publication to agree with the writer's views on an issue. The writer may not work for the publication and is often an expert on the issue or has an interesting point of view. The writer is identified so that people can judge his or her qualifications.

Letters to the Editor

Readers write **letters to editors** at print and Internet publications to express opinions in response to previously published articles. A good letter to the editor gives an accurate and honest representation of the writer's views.

Reviews

Reviews evaluate items and activities, such as books, movies, plays, and music, from the writer's point of view. A review often states opinions on the quality of an item or activity and supports those opinions with examples, facts, and other evidence.

Advertisements

Advertisements in all media—from print to online sites to highway billboards—are paid announcements that try to convince people to buy something or do something. Good advertisements use a hook to grab your attention and support their claims. They contain vivid, persuasive language and multimedia techniques, such as music, to appeal to a specific audience.

Propaganda

Propaganda uses emotional appeals and often biased, false, or misleading information to persuade people to think or act in a certain way. Propaganda may tap into people's strongest emotions by generating fear or attacking their ideas of loyalty or patriotism. Because propaganda appears to be objective, it is wise to be aware of the ways it can manipulate people's opinions and actions.

Try It! Think about what you have learned about exposition, description, and persuasion. Form a group to discuss and draw conclusions about which **genres** would be best if you were planning a first draft with each of these intentions in mind. **Select the correct genre** for conveying your intended meaning to your audiences. Then, identify two or three types of information that you would want to include in a first draft.

- To explain how an event happened
- To describe a beautiful landscape
- To encourage teens to buy teeth-whitening toothpaste

Partner Talk

Share your experiences with various types of persuasive texts with a partner. Talk about the types of persuasive text that you think are most effective, honest, and fair. Be sure to explain your thinking.

Responses to Literature

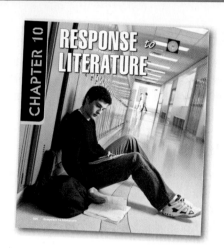

Responses to literature analyze and interpret an author's work. They use clear **thesis statements** and **evidence from the text using embedded quotations to support the writer's ideas.** They also evaluate how well authors have accomplished their goals. Effective responses to literature extend beyond literal analysis to evaluate and discuss how and why the text is effective or not effective. Examples include Anita Desai's "The English Language Takes Root in India" or Elizabeth McCracken's "Creating a Legend."

Critical Reviews

Critical reviews evaluate books, plays, poetry, and other literary works. Reviews present the writer's opinions and support them with specific examples. The responses may analyze the aesthetic effects of an author's use of language in addition to responding to the content of the writing.

Compare-and-Contrast Essays

Compare-and-contrast essays explore similarities and differences between two or more works of literature. These essays provide relevant evidence to support the writer's opinions.

Letters to Authors

Readers write **letters to authors** to share their feelings and thoughts about a work of literature directly.

Blog Comments

Blog comments on an author's Web site or book retailer pages let readers share their ideas about a work. Readers express their opinions and give interpretations of what an author's work means.

Try It! As a group, decide which **genre** would be most appropriate if you were planning a first draft for each of these purposes. **Select the correct genre** for conveying your intended meaning to your audiences. Then, identify two or three key questions that you would want to answer in a first draft.

- To tell an author why you think her book is excellent
- To write an opinion about a newspaper article
- To imagine how a certain landform came to be

> **Partner Talk**
>
> Interview your partner about his or her experiences writing interpretative responses. Be sure to ask questions such as these:
>
> - How did you support your opinion of the author's work?
> - How did you choose evidence, such as quotes, to support your analysis or opinion?

Research Writing

Research writing is based on factual information from outside sources. Research reports organize and present ideas and information to achieve a particular purpose and reach a specific audience. They present evidence in support of a clear thesis statement.

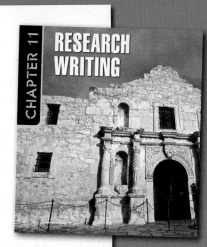

Research Reports and Documented Essays

Research reports and **documented essays** present information and analysis about a topic that the writer has studied. Start with a clear thesis statement. Research reports often include graphics and illustrations to clarify concepts. Documented essays are less formal research writings that show the source of every fact, quote, or borrowed idea in parentheses.

Experiment Journals and Lab Reports

Experiment journals and **lab reports** focus on the purposes, procedures, and results of a lab experiment. They often follow a strict format that includes dates and specific observation notes.

Statistical Analysis Reports

A **statistical analysis report** presents numerical data. Writers of this type of report must explain how they gathered their information, analyze their data, tell what significance the findings may have, and explain how these findings support their thesis statement.

Annotated Bibliographies

An **annotated bibliography** lists the research sources a writer used. It includes the title, author, publication date, publisher, and brief notes that describe and evaluate the source.

Try It! Discuss which kinds of reports you might write if you were planning a first draft for these purposes. **Select the correct form** for conveying your intended meaning to your audiences. Then, identify two or three key questions that you would want to answer in a first draft. Explain your choices.

- To accompany a project you plan to enter in a science fair
- To write about a poll taken to predict the results of a local election

Share with a partner the kinds of research writing you've done in school. Explain which projects you've enjoyed and why.

Workplace Writing

Workplace writing is writing done on the job or as part of a job, often in an office setting. It usually communicates details about a particular job or work project. This type of writing features organized and accurately conveyed information and should include reader-friendly formatting techniques, such as clearly defined sections and enough blank space for easy reading.

Business Letters and Friendly Letters

A **business letter** is a formal letter written to, from, or within a business. It can be written to make requests or to express concerns or approval. For example, you might write to a company to ask about job opportunities. Business letters follow a specific format that includes an address, date, formal greeting, and closing.

In contrast, a **friendly letter** is a form of correspondence written to communicate between family, friends, or acquaintances. For example, you might write a thank-you note for a gift.

Memos

Memos are short documents usually written from one member of an organization to another or to a group. They are an important means of communicating information within an organization.

E-mails

E-mail is an abbreviation for "electronic mail" and is a form of electronic memo. Because it can be transmitted quickly, allowing for instant long-distance communication, e-mail is a very common form of communication that uses a computer and software to send messages.

Forms

Forms are types of workplace writing that ask for specific information to be completed in a particular format. Examples include applications, emergency contact information forms, and tax forms.

Instructions

Instructions are used to explain how to complete a task or procedure. They provide clear, step-by-step guidelines. For example, recipes and user manuals are forms of instructions.

Project Plans

Project plans are short documents usually written from one member of an organization to another. They outline a project's goals and objectives and may include specific details about how certain steps of a project should be achieved.

Résumés

A **résumé** is an overview of a person's experience and qualifications for a job. This document lists a person's job skills and work history. Résumés can also feature information about a person's education.

College Applications

College applications are documents that ask for personal information and details about someone's educational background. College administrators use this information to decide whether or not to accept a student.

Job Applications

Job applications are similar to résumés in that they require a person to list work experience and educational background. Most employers will require a completed job application as part of the hiring process.

Try It! As a group, discuss which form of workplace writing would be best for each of these purposes. Select the correct form for conveying your intended meaning to your audiences. Identify two or three types of information you would expect to include in a first draft.

- To inform the company that made your cell phone that it does not work properly
- To prepare information about your qualifications for a job search
- To create a plan for your group assignment in science class

Partner Talk

Share with a partner your experience with workplace and procedural writing. For example, have you ever written instructions, created a résumé, or completed a job application? What do you find are particular challenges with this type of writing?

Writing for Media

The world of communication has changed significantly in recent years. In addition to writing for print media such as magazines and books, writers also write for a variety of other **media,** in forms such as:

- Scripts for screenplays, video games, and documentaries
- Storyboards for graphic novels and advertisements
- Packaging for every kind of product
- Web sites and blogs

Scripts

Scripts are written for various media, such as documentaries, theater productions, speeches, and audio programs. Movies, television shows, and video games also have scripts.

- A good script focuses on a clearly expressed or implied **theme** and has a specific **purpose.**
- It also contains interesting details, which contribute to a definite **mood or tone.**
- A good script also includes a clear **setting,** **dialogue,** and well-developed **action.**

Blogs

Blogs address just about every purpose and interest. For example, there are blogs about local issues, pets, or food.

Advertisements

Advertisements are designed to persuade someone to buy a product or service. Advertisements use images, words, and music to support their message. Writers write the content of advertisements. In addition, they may help create music and design the sound and the images in the ad.

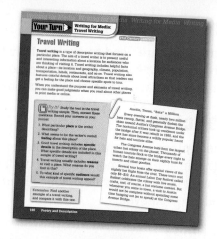

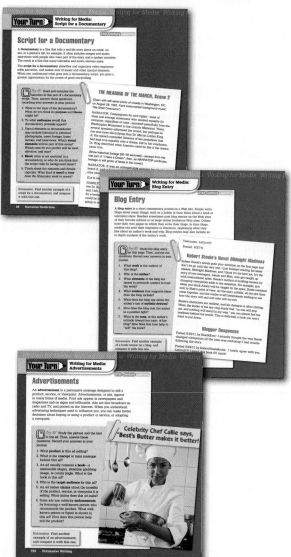

Creating Multimedia Projects

A **multimedia project** or presentation uses sound, video, and other media to convey a point or entertain an audience. No matter what type of project you choose as your own multimedia project, it is important to follow these steps:

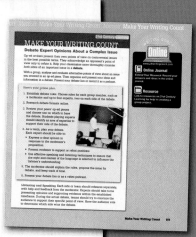

- Decide on the project's **purpose** and your target **audience.**

- Choose **media** that will effectively convey your **message.**

- **Plan** your presentation. Will you work alone or with a partner or group? If you work with others, how will you assign the tasks?

- What **equipment** will you need? Will you produce artwork, record audio, and take photographs? Should you produce a storyboard to show the sequence of details in your presentation? Be sure to allow enough time to produce the text and all the other elements in your project.

- Keep the **writing process** in mind. There should be working and reworking along the way.

- **Assess** the progress of the project as you work. Ask questions, such as: Does my project incorporate appropriate writing genres? Will the presentation interest my audience? Have I kept my purpose in mind?

- **Rehearse!** Before presenting your project, be sure to do several "practice runs" to weed out and correct any errors.

- Keep an electronic record of your presentation for future reference.

- After your presentation, have others assess the project. Their critique will help you to do an even better job next time!

Partner Talk

Share with a partner your experience with writing for media or multimedia projects. Have you created a Web site or contributed to one? Have you had to complete multimedia projects for a class assignment or for a personal project on which you worked? Talk about how writing for media presents different challenges from more traditional writing and how you have dealt with those challenges.

Reflect on Your Writing

Learning more about the different types of writing can help you focus on the characteristics of each type so you can keep improving your own writing. Think about what you've learned in Chapter 2 as you answer these questions:

- What type of writing most interests you?

- What type of writing do you think is most useful? Why?

CHAPTER 3

THE WRITING PROCESS

Writing Traits

Good writing has specific qualities, or traits. In this chapter you will learn about these traits and how to use rubrics to evaluate your writing in terms of them. You will also learn how to address them during the writing process.

Ideas

The best writing is built from strong ideas. It shows original thinking and provides readers with interesting, significant information. It also sends a strong message or presents a clear "angle" or point of view on a subject. In good writing, ideas are well developed, or explained and supported with examples and other details.

Organization

A well-organized paper has an obvious plan. Ideas move from sentence to sentence and paragraph to paragraph in a logical way. For example, events in a story often appear in chronological order, the order in which they occurred. Some expository writing presents ideas in order of importance. Descriptive writing may use a spatial organization, describing something from top to bottom or left to right.

Voice

Voice is the combination of word choice and personal writing style that makes your writing unique. It shows your personality or "take" on a story. Voice connects a reader to the writer. While the content of your writing is critical, effective writing features a strong voice.

Word Choice

To best achieve your purpose in writing, choose words carefully. When you choose precise words, you choose words that express your exact meaning. When you choose vivid words, you choose words that create pictures for readers, words that describe how a subject looks, sounds, smells, and so on. You may also use figures of speech (direct or indirect comparisons of unlike things) to create memorable images of your subject.

Sentence Fluency

Sentence fluency refers to the rhythm and flow of writing. Keep the rhythm of your writing fresh by varying sentence patterns, and create flow by choosing sentence structures that match your meaning. For example, you might show the connection between two ideas by joining them in one longer sentence, or you might create emphasis by breaking off a series of long sentences with one short sentence.

Conventions

By following the rules of spelling, capitalization, punctuation, grammar, and usage, you help readers understand your ideas.

WRITING COACH
Online
www.phwritingcoach.com

Online Journal

Try It! Record your answers and ideas in the online journal. You can also record and save your answers and ideas on pop-up sticky notes in the eText.

"Writer to Writer"

Good writing is a symphony of traits—all coming together to make the paper sing.

—Kelly Gallagher

Overview of Writing Traits	
Ideas	• Significant ideas and informative details • Thorough development of ideas • Unique perspective or strong message
Organization	• Obvious plan • Clear sequence • Strong transitions
Voice	• Effective word choice expressing personality or perspective • Attention to style
Word Choice	• Precise, not vague, words • Vivid, not dull, words • Word choices suited to audience and purpose
Sentency Fluency	• Varied sentence beginnings, lengths, and structures • Smooth sentence rhythms used to support meaning
Conventions	• Proper spelling and capitalization • Correct punctuation, grammar, usage, and sentence structure

Rubrics and How to Use Them

You can use rubrics to evaluate your writing. A rubric allows you to score your writing on a scale for each trait. You will use a six-point rubric like this to help evaluate your writing in chapters 5–12.

Writing Traits	Rating Scale
Ideas: How interesting, significant, or original are the ideas you present? How well do you develop, or explain, support, and extend, ideas?	Not very Very 1 2 3 4 5 6
Organization: How logically is your piece organized? How much sense do your transitions, or movements from idea to idea, make?	1 2 3 4 5 6
Voice: How authentic and original is your voice?	1 2 3 4 5 6
Word Choice: How precise and vivid are the words you use? How well does your word choice help achieve your purpose?	1 2 3 4 5 6
Sentence Fluency: How well do your sentences flow? How strong and varied is the rhythm they create?	1 2 3 4 5 6
Conventions: How correct is your punctuation? Your capitalization? Your spelling?	1 2 3 4 5 6

Each trait to be assessed appears in the first column. The rating scale appears in the second column. The higher your score for a trait, the better your writing exhibits that trait.

Using a Rubric on Your Own

A rubric can be a big help in assessing your writing while it is still in process. Imagine you are about to start writing a piece of narrative fiction. You consult a rubric, which reminds you that narrative fiction should have characters, a setting, and a conflict and resolution. As you write, you try to incorporate and develop each element. After drafting, you might check the rubric again to make sure you are on track. For example, after reviewing the rubric again, you might decide that you have not developed the conflict or its resolution well. You would then go back and revise to improve your writing and get a better score.

Narrative Fiction Elements	Rating Scale
	Not very Very
Interesting characters	1 2 3 4 5 6
Believable setting	1 2 3 4 5 6
Literary strategies	1 2 3 4 5 6
Well-developed conflict	1 2 3 4 5 6
Well-developed resolution	1 2 3 4 5 6

 Try It! If you checked your story against the rubric and rated yourself mostly 1s and 2s, what actions might you want to take?

Using a Rubric With a Partner

In some cases, building your own rubric can help you ensure that your writing will meet your expectations. For example, if your class has an assignment to write a poem, you and a partner might decide to construct a rubric to check one another's work. A rubric like the one shown here can help point out whether you should make any changes. Extra lines allow room for you to add other criteria.

Poetry Elements	Rating Scale
	Not very Very
Good sensory details	1 2 3 4 5 6
Colorful adjectives	1 2 3 4 5 6
	1 2 3 4 5 6
	1 2 3 4 5 6
	1 2 3 4 5 6

 Try It! What other elements might you add to the rubric?

Using a Rubric in a Group

It is also helpful to use a rubric in a group. That way you can get input on your writing from many people at the same time. If the group members' ratings of your piece are similar, you will probably have an easy time deciding whether to make changes. If the responses vary significantly, you might want to discuss the results with the group. Then, analyze what led to the differing opinions and make careful judgments about what changes you will make.

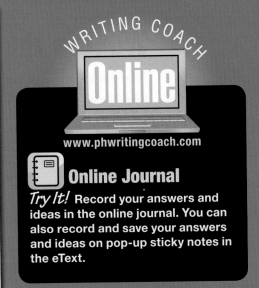

WRITING COACH

Online

www.phwritingcoach.com

Online Journal

Try It! Record your answers and ideas in the online journal. You can also record and save your answers and ideas on pop-up sticky notes in the eText.

What Is the Writing Process?

The five steps in the writing process are prewriting, drafting, revising, editing, and publishing. Writing is a process because your idea goes through a series of changes or stages before the product is finished.

Study the diagram to see how moving through the writing process can work. Remember, you can go back to a stage in the process. It does not always have to occur in order.

Prewriting

In prewriting, you will:
- Explore ideas
- Choose a purpose and an audience
- Gather details
- Sequence ideas

Drafting

In drafting, you will:
- Put ideas down
- Develop a thesis or controlling idea
- Structure ideas in a sustained way

Revising

In revising, you will:
- Re-read draft to see what works and what does not
- Use a rubric to evaluate
- Analyze what you want to change or improve
- Make changes

Editing

In the editing phase, you will:
- Check the accuracy of facts
- Correct errors in spelling, grammar, usage, and mechanics

Publishing

In publishing, you will:
- Produce a final polished copy of your writing
- Share your writing

Why Use the Writing Process?

Writing involves careful thinking, which means you will make changes as you write. Even professional writers don't just write their thoughts and call it a finished work of art. They use a process. For example, some writers keep going back to the revising stage many times, while others feel they can do the revision in just one step. It is up to each writer to develop the style that works best to produce the best results.

You might find that the writing process works best for you when you keep these tips in mind:

- Remember that the five steps in the writing process are equally important.
- Think about your audience as you plan your paper and develop your writing.
- Make sure you remember your topic and stick to your specific purpose as you write.
- Give your writing some time to "rest." Sometimes it can be good to work on a piece, walk away, and look at it later, with a fresh eye and mind.

The following pages will describe in more detail how to use each stage of the writing process to improve your writing.

WRITING COACH

Online

www.phwritingcoach.com

Online Journal

Try It! Record your answers and ideas in the online journal. You can also record and save your answers and ideas on pop-up sticky notes in the eText.

" Writer to Writer "

Writing process gives us the freedom to write like mad, tinker like an engineer, evaluate like a judge—playing different roles at different stages. Most importantly it gives us the freedom to get our words out of our heads and into the world.

—Jeff Anderson

Prewriting

Prewriting

Drafting

Revising

Editing

Publishing

No matter what kind of writing you do, planning during the prewriting stage is crucial. During prewriting, you determine the topic of your writing, its purpose, and its specific audience. Then, you narrow the topic and gather details.

Determining the Purpose and Audience

What Is Your Purpose?

To be sure your writing communicates your ideas clearly, it is important to clarify why you are writing. Consider what you want your audience to take away from your writing. You may want to entertain them, or you may want to warn them about something. Even when you write an entry in a private journal, you're writing for an audience—you!

Who Is Your Audience?

Think about the people who will read your work and consider what they may already know about your topic. Being able to identify this group and their needs will let you be sure you are providing the right level of information.

Choosing a Topic

Here are just a few of the many techniques you can use to determine an appropriate topic.

- **Brainstorm**
  You can brainstorm by yourself, with a partner, or with a group. Just jot down ideas as they arise, and don't rule out anything. When brainstorming in a group, one person's idea often "piggy-backs" on another.

- **Make a Mind Map**
  A mind map is a quick drawing you sketch as ideas come to you. The mind map can take any form. The important thing is to write quick notes as they come to you and then to draw lines to connect relationships among the ideas.

- **Interview**

  A fun way to find a writing topic is to conduct an interview. You might start by writing interview questions for yourself or someone else. Questions that start with *what*, *when*, *why*, *how*, and *who* are most effective. For example, you might ask, "When was the last time you laughed really hard?" "What made you laugh?" Then, conduct the interview and discover the answers.

- **Review Resources and Discuss Ideas**

  You can review resources, such as books, magazines, newspapers, and digital articles, to get ideas. Discussing your initial ideas with a partner can spark even more ideas.

Narrowing Your Topic

Once you have settled on a topic idea you really like, it may seem too broad to tackle. How can you narrow your topic?

- **Use Graphic Organizers**

  A graphic organizer can help narrow a topic that's too broad. For example, you might choose "Animals" as a topic. You might make your topics smaller and smaller until you narrow the topic to "The Habitat of Emperor Penguins."

WRITING COACH

Online

www.phwritingcoach.com

Online Journal

Try It! Record your answers and ideas in the online journal. You can also record and save your answers and ideas on pop-up sticky notes in the eText.

"Writer to Writer"

Put something down. Anything. Then, magic will happen.

—Jeff Anderson

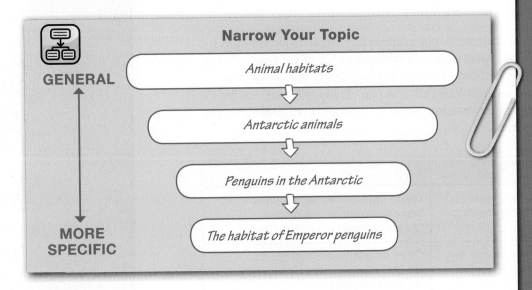

Narrow Your Topic

GENERAL

Animal habitats

Antarctic animals

Penguins in the Antarctic

The habitat of Emperor penguins

MORE SPECIFIC

Prewriting (continued)

Prewriting
Drafting
Revising
Editing
Publishing

- **Use Resource Materials**
  The resource materials you use to find information can also help you narrow a broad topic. Look up your subject online in an encyclopedia or newspaper archive. Scan the resources as you look for specific subtopics to pursue.

Gather Details

After you decide on a topic, you will want to explore and develop your ideas. You might start by looking through online resources again, talking with people who are knowledgeable about your topic, and writing everything you already know about the topic. It will be helpful to gather a variety of details. Look at these types:

- Facts
- Statistics
- Personal observations
- Expert opinions
- Examples
- Descriptions
- Quotations
- Opposing viewpoints

After you have narrowed your topic and gathered details, you will begin to plan your piece. During this part of prewriting, you will develop your essay's thesis or controlling idea—its main point or purpose. If you are writing a fiction or nonfiction story, you will outline the events of the story.

As you plan your piece, you can use a graphic organizer. Specific kinds of graphic organizers can help structure specific kinds of writing. For example, a plot map can help plot out the sequence of events in a mystery story. A pro-con chart like this one can clarify the reasons for and against an idea. It presents arguments for and against adding funds to a school music program.

Pro	Con
Adding funds to the school music budget would allow more students to learn to play instruments.	Giving more money to the music department would mean other programs would get less money.
Research shows that music helps the brain become more flexible.	Other programs, such as sports, are important in keeping students physically healthy.
Band members could stop selling gift-wrap materials at holiday time.	The school board has already approved the current budget allocations.

Drafting

In the drafting stage, you get your ideas down. You may consult an outline or your prewriting notes as you build your first draft.

The Introduction

Most genres should have a strong introduction that immediately grabs the reader's attention and includes the thesis. Even stories and poems need a "hook" to grab interest.

Prewriting
Drafting
Revising
Editing
Publishing

WRITING COACH

Online

www.phwritingcoach.com

Online Journal
Try It! Record your answers and ideas in the online journal. You can also record and save your answers and ideas on pop-up sticky notes in the eText.

Try It! Which of these first sentences are strong openers? Read these examples of first sentences. Decide which ones are most interesting to you. Explain why they grab your attention. Then, explain why the others are weak.

- Have you ever wondered what it would be like to wake up one morning to find you're someone else?
- There are many ways to paint a room.
- Yogi Berra, the famous baseball star, said, "You got to be careful if you don't know where you're going, because you might not get there."
- Autumn is a beautiful season.
- On Sunday, we went to the store.
- When I woke up that morning, I had no idea that it would be the best day of my life.

The Body

The body of a paper develops the main idea and details that elaborate on and support the thesis. As you tell your story or build an argument these details may include interesting facts, examples, statistics, anecdotes or stories, quotations, personal feelings, and sensory descriptions.

The Conclusion

The conclusion typically restates the thesis and summarizes the most important concepts of a paper.

Revising: Making It Better

Prewriting

Drafting

Revising

Editing

Publishing

No one gets every single thing right in a first draft. In fact, most people require more than two drafts to achieve their best writing and thinking. When you have finished your first draft, you're ready to revise.

Revising means "re-seeing." In revising, you look again to see if you can find ways to improve style, word choice, figurative language, sentence variety, and subtlety of meaning. As always, check how well you've addressed the issues of purpose, audience, and genre. Carefully analyze what you'd want to change and then go ahead and do it. Here are some helpful hints on starting the revision stage of the writing process.

Take a Break

Do not begin to revise immediately after you finish a draft. Take some time away from your paper. Get a glass of water, take a walk, or listen to some music. You may even want to wait a day to look at what you've written. When you come back, you will be better able to assess the strengths and weaknesses of your work.

Put Yourself in the Place of the Reader

Take off your writer's hat and put on your reader's hat. Do your best to pretend that you're reading someone else's work and see how it looks to that other person. Look for ideas that might be confusing and consider the questions that a reader might have. By reading the piece with an objective eye, you may find items you'd want to fix and improve.

Read Aloud to Yourself

It may feel strange to read aloud to yourself, but it can be an effective technique. It allows you to hear the flow of words, find errors, and hear where you might improve the work by smoothing out transitions between paragraphs or sections. Of course, if you're more comfortable reading your work aloud to someone else, that works, too.

Share Your Work to Get Feedback

Your friends or family members can help you by reading and reacting to your writing. Ask them whether you've clearly expressed your ideas. Encourage them to tell you which parts were most and least interesting and why. Try to find out if they have any questions about your topic that were not answered. Then, evaluate their input and decide what will make your writing better.

Use a Rubric

A rubric might be just what you need to pinpoint weaknesses in your work. You may want to think about the core parts of the work and rate them on a scale. If you come up short, you'll have a better idea about the kinds of things to improve. You might also use a rubric to invite peer review and input.

21st Century Learning

Collaborate and Discuss

When presenting and sharing drafts in the revision stage with a small group, it may be wise to set some ground rules. That way, the group is more likely to help each other analyze their work and make thoughtful changes that result in true improvements.

Here are some suggestions for reviewing drafts as a group:

- Cover the names on papers the group will review to keep the work anonymous.
- Print out copies for everyone in the group.
- Show respect for all group members and their writing.
- Be sure all critiques include positive comments.
- While it is fine to suggest ways to improve the work, present comments in a positive, helpful way. No insults are allowed!
- Plan for a second reading with additional input after the writer has followed selected suggestions.

WRITING COACH

Online

www.phwritingcoach.com

Online Journal

Try It! **Record your answers and ideas in the online journal. You can also record and save your answers and ideas on pop-up sticky notes in the eText.**

Partner Talk

After a group revision session, talk with a partner to analyze each other's feeling on how the session went. Discuss such issues as these: Did the group adhere to the ground rules? What suggestions could you and your partner make to improve the next session?

Revision RADaR

Prewriting
Drafting
Revising
Editing
Publishing

The Revision RADaR strategy, which you will use throughout this book, is an effective tool in helping you conduct a focused revision of your work.

You can use your Revision RADaR to revise your writing. The letters **R**, **A**, **D**, and **R** will help you remember to **r**eplace, **a**dd, **d**elete, and **r**eorder.

To understand more about the Revision RADaR strategy, study the following chart.

R	**A**	**D** and	**R**
Replace . . .	**Add . . .**	**Delete . . .**	**Reorder . . .**
• Words that are not specific • Words that are overused • Sentences that are unclear	• New information • Descriptive adjectives and adverbs • Rhetorical or literary devices	• Unrelated ideas • Sentences that sound good, but do not make sense • Repeated words or phrases • Unnecessary details	• So most important points are last • To make better sense or to flow better • So details support main ideas

 ## Replace

You can strengthen a text by replacing words that are not specific, words that are overused, and sentences that are unclear. Take a look at this before and after model.

BEFORE
As I ran to the finish line, my heart was beating.
AFTER
As I sprinted to the finish line, my heart was pounding in my chest.

Apply It! **How did the writer replace the overused verb *ran*? What other replacements do you see? How did they improve the text?**

Add

You can add new information, descriptive adjectives and adverbs, and rhetorical or literary devices to make your piece more powerful. Study this before and after model.

BEFORE
Shadows made the night seem scary.

AFTER
Ominous shadows made the dark night seem even more sinister.

Apply It! **How did the second sentence make you feel, compared with the first? Explain.**

 Delete

Sometimes taking words out of a text can improve clarity. Analyze this before and after model.

BEFORE
The candidates talked about the issues, and many of the issues were issues that had been on voters' minds.

AFTER
The candidates talked about the issues, many of which had been on voters' minds.

Apply It! **Describe the revision you see. How did taking out unnecessary repetition of the word *issues* help the sentence flow more naturally?**

 Reorder

When you reorder, you can make sentences flow more logically. Look at this example.

BEFORE
Put the sunflower seeds over the strawberries, which are on top of the pineapple in a bowl. You'll have a delicious fruit salad!

AFTER
To make a delicious fruit salad, cut pineapple into a bowl. Add strawberries and then sprinkle a few sunflower seeds over the top.

Apply It! **Which of the models flows more logically? Why?**

WRITING COACH

Online

www.phwritingcoach.com

Online Journal

Try It! Record your answers and ideas in the online journal. You can also record and save your answers and ideas on pop-up sticky notes in the eText.

« Writer to Writer »

Anyone can write a first draft, but revision is where the paper comes to life.

—Kelly Gallagher

USING TECHNOLOGY

Most word processing programs have a built-in thesaurus tool. You can use the thesaurus to find descriptive words that can often substitute for weaker, overused words.

Revision RADaR (continued)

Read the first draft of the Student Model—a review of the book
Technology Drives Me Wild! Think about how you might use your
Revision RADaR to improve the text in a second draft.

Kelly Gallagher, M. Ed.

KEEP REVISION ON YOUR RADAR

Prewriting
Drafting
Revising
Editing
Publishing

Technology Book Drives Reviewer Wild

As a technology fan, I always look for new books about the latest in
technology, as soon as they come out. So, when I bought *Technology
Drives Me Wild!* by James Frank, after reading other books by Mr.
Frank, I had high hopes this would be another winner that would
improve my life. Those high hopes were not met by reading this
disappointing book.

This book, which dashed my high hopes of learning some new stuff,
has many mistakes. One error is that computers were not invented in
the early 1800s. Did Thomas Jefferson use a computer when he was
president? I don't think so.

The one good thing about *Technology Drives Me Wild!* is the fact that
it is a very short book. That way, you won't waste too much time, if you
decide not to take my advice and read this boring book after all.

It would have helped to show more pictures when explaining how
computer chips work. Besides that, the text is boring and there are no
diagrams or photos to keep the text from being boring. In addition, the
boring text is very wordy and many of the explanations are unclear and
impossible to understand. Also, the photograph of Mr. Frank on the
book jacket is out of focus.

Here's a summary of my recommendation about this book: don't
read it! Use your time to find better information about technology in
other sources.

> *Does my **introduction grab reader interest?***

> *Are my word choices varied?*

After writing the first draft, the student used Revision RADaR and asked questions like these:

- What could I **replace**?
- What could I **add**?
- What words might I **delete**?
- Should I **reorder** anything?

The student writer created this second draft after using Revision RADaR.

Technology Book Drives Reviewer Wild

2ND DRAFT

There's no doubt about it. I find the expansion of technology fascinating. I'm always anxious to read the latest developments and to consider how they might enhance my own life. Having read James Frank's previous excellent books on technology, I rushed out to buy his latest—*Technology Drives Me Wild!* Unfortunately, this book turned out to be a be grave disappointment.

R *Replaced opening with more engaging sentences*

I'd hoped to glean new information and a fresh understanding of improvements in global positioning systems, netbooks, and cell phones from the book. What I discovered instead was a substandard account, fraught with errors. For example, I am quite certain that while some people may have dreamed of computers in the 1800s, I doubt any actually existed. Mr. Frank should have checked his facts.

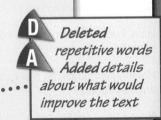

D *Deleted repetitive words*
A *Added details about what would improve the text*

Perhaps additional diagrams, photographs, and other visuals would have helped clarify the weak explanations of how, for example, computer chips work. The addition of lively text would have also helped.

It's fortunate that *Technology Drives Me Wild!* is a short book. That way, even if you pick it up in error, you will not have wasted much of your valuable time.

Try It! What other words did the writer replace? Add? Delete? Reorder?

Partner Talk

Work with a partner to write as many substitutions for the verb *walk* as possible. Remember to consider the different ways people walk. For example, how does a young child walk? How does a successful team captain walk? How might a very elderly person walk? Discuss the value of using more specific words in your writing.

Editing: Making It Correct

Prewriting

Drafting

Revising

Editing ▷

Publishing

Editing is the process of checking the accuracy of facts and correcting errors in spelling, grammar, usage, and mechanics. Using a checklist like the one shown here can help ensure you've done a thorough job of editing.

Editing Checklist	
Task	**Ask Yourself**
Check your facts and spelling	❑ Have I checked that my facts are correct? ❑ Have I used spell check or a dictionary to check any words I'm not sure are spelled correctly?
Check your grammar	❑ Have I written any run-on sentences? ❑ Have I used the correct verbs and verb tenses? ❑ Do my pronouns match their antecedents, or nouns they replace?
Check your usage	❑ Have I used the correct form of irregular verbs? ❑ Have I used object pronouns, such as *me*, *him*, *her*, *us*, and *them* only after verbs or prepositions? ❑ Have I used subject pronouns, such as *I*, *he*, *she*, *we*, and *they* correctly—usually as subjects?
Check for proper use of mechanics	❑ Have I used correct punctuation? ❑ Does each sentence have the correct end mark? ❑ Have I used apostrophes in nouns but not in pronouns to show possession? ❑ Have I used quotation marks around words from another source? ❑ Have I used correct capitalization? ❑ Does each sentence begin with a capital letter? ❑ Do the names of specific people and places begin with a capital letter?

Using Proofreading Marks

Professional editors use a set of proofreading marks to indicate changes in a text. Here is a chart of some of the more common proofreading marks.

Proofreader's Marks

(b.f.)	boldface
⅃	break text start new line
(Caps)	capital letter
⁀‿	clos e up
ℓ	deletes
a/	insert word
,/	insert comma
=/	insert hyphen
t/	insert leter
⊙/	insert period
(ital)	italic type
(Stet)	let stand as is
(l.f.)	lightface
(l.c.)	Lower case letter
[	move left
]	move right
¶	new paragraph
(rom)	roman type
	run text up
(sp)	spell out whole word
	transpoes

WRITING COACH Online

www.phwritingcoach.com

Online Journal

Try It! **Record your answers and ideas in the online journal. You can also record and save your answers and ideas on pop-up sticky notes in the eText.**

USING TECHNOLOGY

Many word processing programs have automatic spelling and grammar checks. While these tools can be helpful, be sure to pay attention to any suggestions they offer. That's because sometimes inappropriate substitutes are inserted automatically!

Editing: Making It Correct (continued)

Prewriting

Drafting

Revising

Editing

Publishing

WRITE GUY *Jeff Anderson, M. Ed.*

WHAT DO YOU NOTICE?

Using an editing checklist is a great way to check for correct grammar. However, using a checklist is not enough to make your writing grammatically correct. A checklist tells you what to look for, but not how to correct mistakes you find. To do that, you need to develop and apply your knowledge of grammar.

Looking closely at good writing is one way to expand your grammar know-how. The *What Do You Notice*? feature that appears throughout this book will help you zoom in on passages that use grammar correctly and effectively.

As you read this passage from "One Dog's Feelings," zoom in on the sentences in the passage.

> *Bo clearly shows when he is angry. He gnashes his teeth, growls, and sometimes even spits! On the other hand, Bo, who can simultaneously chew on two pairs of shoes, is usually content. When he's happy, he simply smiles.*

Now, ask yourself: *What do you notice about the sentences in this passage?*

Maybe you noticed that the writer uses sentences of varying lengths and with different structures. Or perhaps you noticed that the writer varies the way sentences begin.

After asking a question that draws your attention to the grammar in the passage, the *What Do You Notice*? feature provides information on a particular grammar topic. For example, following the passage and question, you might read about simple and complex sentences, which are both used in the passage.

The *What Do You Notice*? feature will show you how grammar works in actual writing. It will help you learn how to make your writing correct.

 Online Journal

Try It! Record your answers and ideas in the online journal. You can also record and save your answers and ideas on pop-up sticky notes in the eText.

One Dog's Feelings

Some people wonder if animals feel and show emotions. However, I am absolutely positive that dogs experience a full range of emotions. I owe this knowledge to my dog, Bo.

Bo clearly shows when he is angry. He gnashes his teeth, growls, and sometimes even spits! On the other hand, Bo, who can simultaneously chew on two pairs of shoes, is usually content. When he's happy, he simply smiles. The colors on his tan and white face seem to glow.

He and my cat often rest together on the mat near the door. When they are together, they both purr with happiness. Neither Bo nor the cat minds that cool air seeps under the door. They're just happy to be with one another.

If my brothers or I want to play fetch, Bo is always up for a game. We often throw a ball into the woods, where it sometimes gets buried under leaves and sticks. Bo always rushes for the ball. And running back to us with the stick in his mouth is obviously his great joy. As for the sticks, few are ever left unfound.

When I leave for school in the morning, Bo whimpers—an obvious sign of sadness. That makes me feel miserable. However, the big payoff comes when I return home. Then Bo jumps up on the door, his tail wagging enthusiastically with excitement. Everybody wants to be loved like that!

66 Writer to Writer 99

If I wonder how to write any kind of writing, I look at models— well-written examples of the kind of writing I want to do. Models are the greatest how-to lesson I have ever discovered.

—Jeff Anderson

Try It! Read "One Dog's Feelings." Then, zoom in on two more passages. Write a response to each question in your journal.

1 What do you notice about the pronouns (*he, they, one, another*) in the third paragraph?

2. How does the writer use transitions, such as the word *however*, to connect ideas in the last paragraph?

Publishing

Prewriting

Drafting

Revising

Editing

Publishing

When you publish, you produce a final copy of your work and present it to an audience. When publishing you'll need to decide which form will best reach your audience, exhibit your ideas, show your creativity, and accomplish your main purpose.

To start assessing the optimal way to publish your work, you might ask yourself these questions:

- What do I hope to accomplish by sharing my work with others?
- Should I publish in print form? Give an oral presentation? Publish in print form and give an oral presentation?
- Should I publish online, in traditional print, or both?
- What specific forms are available to choose from?

The answers to most of these questions will most likely link to your purpose for writing and your audience. Some choices seem obvious. For example, if you've written a piece to contribute to a blog, you'll definitely want to send it electronically.

Each publishing form will present different challenges and opportunities and each will demand different forms of preparation. For example, you may need to prepare presentation slides of your plan to give a speech, or you may want to select music and images if you will be posting a video podcast online.

Ways to Publish

There are many ways to publish your writing. This chart shows some of several opportunities you can pursue to publish your work.

Genre	Publishing Opportunities	
Narration: Nonfiction	• Blogs • Book manuscript • Audio recording	• Private diary or journal entries • Electronic slide show
Narration: Fiction	• Book manuscript • Film	• Audio recording • Oral reading to a group
Poetry and Description	• Bound collection • Visual display	• Audio recording • Oral reading to a group
Exposition and Persuasion	• Print or online article • Web site • Slide show • Visual display	• Film • Audio recording • Oral reading or speech
Response to Literature	• Print or online letters • Visual displays	• Blogs • Slide show
Research Writing	• Traditional paper • Print and online experiment journals	• Multimedia presentation

Reflect on Your Writing

Think about what you learned in Chapter 3 as you answer these questions:

- What did you learn about the writing process?
- What steps in the writing process do you already use in your writing?
- Which stage do you think is the most fun? Which one may be most challenging for you? Explain.

WRITING COACH

Online

www.phwritingcoach.com

 **Online Journal**

Try It! Record your answers and ideas in the online journal. You can also record and save your answers and ideas on pop-up sticky notes in the eText.

Partner Talk

Discuss the chart on this page with a partner. If there are ways to publish that neither of you has ever tried, talk about how you might go about experimenting with those forms.

SENTENCES, PARAGRAPHS, *and* COMPOSITIONS

Good writers know that strong sentences and paragraphs help to construct effective compositions. Chapter 4 will help you use these building blocks to structure and style excellent writing. It will also present ways to use rhetorical and literary devices and online tools to strengthen your writing.

The Building Blocks: Sentences and Paragraphs

A **sentence** is a group of words with two main parts: a subject and a predicate. Together, these parts express a complete thought.

A **paragraph** is built from a group of sentences that share a common idea and work together to express that idea clearly. The start of a new paragraph has visual clues—either an indent of several spaces in the first line or an extra line of space above it.

In a good piece of writing, each paragraph supports, develops, or explains the main idea of the whole work. Of course, the traits of effective writing—ideas, organization, voice, word choice, sentence fluency, and conventions—appear in each paragraph as well.

Writing Strong Sentences

To write strong paragraphs, you need strong sentences. While it may be your habit to write using a single style of sentences, adding variety will help make your writing more interesting. Combining sentences, using compound elements, forming compound sentences, and using subordination all may help you make your sentences stronger, clearer, or more varied.

Combine Sentences

Putting information from one sentence into another can make a more powerful sentence.

BEFORE
Video games can be effective educational tools. They can help teach many subjects.

AFTER
Video games, which can help teach many subjects, can be effective educational tools.

Use Compound Elements

You can form compound subjects, verbs, or objects to help the flow.

BEFORE
Students can play video games on their laptops. Students can also play video games on their cell phones.

AFTER
Students can play video games on their laptops and cell phones.

Form Compound Sentences

You can combine two sentences into a compound sentence.

BEFORE
Video games can motivate students to learn. They must have educational value.

AFTER
Video games can motivate students to learn, but they must have educational value.

Use Subordination

Combine two related sentences by rewriting the less important one as a subordinate clause.

BEFORE
Video games can take time away from exercise. That can be unhealthy.

AFTER
Video games can take time away from exercise, which can be unhealthy.

WRITING COACH

Online

www.phwritingcoach.com

Online Journal

Try It! Record your answers and ideas in the online journal. You can also record and save your answers on pop-up sticky notes in the eText.

LEARN MORE

- See Chapter 21, Miscellaneous Problems in Usage, pages 524–540
- See Writing Coach Online

Writing Strong Paragraphs

If all the sentences in a paragraph reflect the main idea and work together to express that idea clearly, the result will be a strong paragraph.

Express Your Main Idea With a Clear Topic Sentence

A **topic sentence** summarizes the main idea of a paragraph. It may appear at the beginning, middle, or end of a paragraph. It may even be unstated. When the topic sentence comes at the beginning of a paragraph, it introduces the main idea and leads the reader naturally to the sentences that follow it. When it appears at the end of a paragraph, it can draw a conclusion or summarize what came before it. If the topic sentence is unstated, the rest of the paragraph must be very clearly developed, so the reader can understand the main idea from the other sentences.

Think about the topic sentence as you read this paragraph.

> Without a doubt, hiking must be the best sport in the world. Hiking is good exercise and makes me feel totally free. When I'm out on the trail, I can think more clearly than anywhere else. Even solving problems that seemed totally unsolvable at home becomes possible. I also use all of my senses when I hike. I hear birds singing, I notice strange plants, and I feel the soft underbrush beneath my boots. Sometimes I even think I can smell and taste the fresh air.

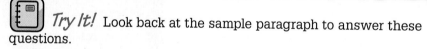 *Try It!* Look back at the sample paragraph to answer these questions.

1. What is the topic sentence?

2. Does the topic sentence introduce the main idea or draw a final conclusion? Explain.

3. What makes this topic sentence strong?

Write Effective Supporting Sentences

A clear topic sentence is a good start, but it needs to be accompanied by good details that support the paragraph's main idea. Your supporting sentences might tell interesting facts, describe events, or give examples. In addition, the supporting sentences should also provide a smooth transition, so that the paragraph reads clearly and logically.

Think about the topic sentences and supporting details as you read this paragraph.

What was life like before cell phones? It's barely imaginable! People were tied to land lines and could make and take calls only in homes, offices, or on pay phones. If there were an emergency, there could be unavoidable delays as people searched for an available phone. If they wanted to chat with friends, they usually had to wait until they got home. How ever did they live without being able to text? Some people send text messages to their friends about 50 times a day. What a different world it was way back then.

 Try It! Look at the paragraph and answer these questions.

1. What is the topic sentence of the paragraph?

2. Do you think it's an effective topic sentence? Why or why not?

3. What supporting details does the writer provide?

4. If you were the writer, what other supporting details might you add to strengthen the paragraph?

5. Which sentence in the paragraph breaks up the flow of ideas and does not provide a smooth transition to the next sentence?

WRITING COACH

Online

www.phwritingcoach.com

Online Journal

Try It! Record your answers and ideas in the online journal. You can also record and save your answers on pop-up sticky notes in the eText.

Include a Variety of Sentence Lengths, Structures, and Beginnings

To be interesting, a paragraph should include sentences of different lengths, types, and beginnings. Similarly, if every sentence has the same structure—for example, article, adjective, noun, verb—the paragraph may sound boring or dry.

Partner Talk

Work with a partner to take another look at the writing sample on this page. Talk about what you think the writer did well. Then, discuss what might make the paragraph even stronger.

21st Century Learning

Collaborate and Discuss

With a group, study this writing sample.

> The scene was tense as Carlos stepped to the plate. Looking confident, he took a few practice swings. Then he stopped and stared straight at the pitcher. The first pitch zoomed over home plate at about 90 miles an hour—right past Carlos. Strike one! The second pitch was high and outside. Ball one! Next Carlos took a deep breath; it was obvious he meant business now. He stared down the pitcher and raised his bat. Crack! Carlos hit that ball right over the fence behind second base and the game was over. It was a 4-2 victory for the home team, thanks to Carlos!

Discuss these questions about the paragraph.

1. What is the topic sentence? How does it draw in the reader?
2. What details support the topic sentence in each paragraph?
3. Point out some examples of varying sentence lengths and beginnings.
4. What examples can you find of sentences with a variety of sentence structures?
5. Which words help the transitions and flow of the paragraphs?

USING TECHNOLOGY

It's often better to use the tab key, rather than the space bar, to indent a paragraph. Using the tab key helps to ensure that the indents in all paragraphs will be uniform.

Composing Your Piece

You've learned that the building blocks of writing are strong sentences and paragraphs. Now it's time to use those building blocks to construct an effective composition. While the types of writing vary from short poems to long essays and research papers, most types have a definite structure with clearly defined parts.

The Parts of a Composition

Writers put together and arrange sentences and paragraphs to develop ideas in the clearest way possible in a composition. Some types of writing, such as poetry and advertisements, follow unique rules and may not have sentences and paragraphs that follow a standard structure. However, as you learned in Chapter 3, most compositions have three main sections: an introduction, a body, and a conclusion.

I. Introduction

The introduction of a composition introduces the focus of the composition, usually in a thesis statement. The introduction should engage the reader's interest, with such elements as a question, an unusual fact, or a surprising scene.

II. Body

Just as supporting statements develop the ideas of a topic sentence, the body of a composition develops the thesis statement and main idea. It provides details that help expand on the thesis statement. The paragraphs in the body are arranged in a logical order.

III. Conclusion

As the word implies, the conclusion of a composition concludes or ends a piece of writing. A good way to ensure the reader will remember your thesis statement is to restate it or summarize it in the conclusion. When restating the thesis, it's usually most effective to recast it in other words. Quotations and recommendations are other ways to conclude a composition with memorable impact. The conclusion should provide a parting insight or reinforce the importance of the main idea.

" Writer to Writer "

Strong, varied sentences and unified paragraphs are the building blocks of effective writing.

—Kelly Gallagher

Rhetorical and Literary Devices

Like any builders, good writers have a set of tools, or devices, at their
fingertips to make their writing interesting, engaging, and effective.
Writers can use the rhetorical devices of language and their effects to
strengthen the power of their style. This section presents some tools you
can store in your own writing toolbox to develop effective compositions.

Sound Devices

Sound devices, which create a musical or emotional effect, are most
often used in poetry. The most common sound devices include these:

- **Alliteration** is the repetition of consonant sounds at the
  beginning of words that are close to one another.

  Example: Bees buzzed by both bouquets.

- **Assonance** is the repetition of vowel sounds in words that
  are close to one another.

  Example: My kite flew high into the sky.

- **Consonance** is the repetition of consonants within or at the
  end of words.

  Example: Each coach teaches touch football
  after lunch.

Structural Devices

Structural devices determine the way a piece of writing is organized.
Rhyme and meter are most often used to structure poetry, as are
stanzas and many other structural devices.

- **Rhyme** is the repetition of sounds at the ends of words. Certain
  poetry forms have specific rhyme schemes.
- **Meter** is the rhythmical pattern of a poem, determined
  by the stressed syllables in a line.
- **Visual elements**, such as stanzas, line breaks, line length, fonts,
  readability, and white space, help determine how a piece of writing
  is read and interpreted. These elements can also affect the emotional
  response to a piece.

Other Major Devices

You can use these devices in many forms of writing. They help writers express ideas clearly and engage their readers.

Device	Example
Figurative language is writing that means something beyond what the words actually say. Common forms of figurative language include these: • A **simile** compares two things using the words *like* or *as*. • A **metaphor** compares two things by mentioning one thing as if it is something else. It does not use *like* or *as*. • **Personification** gives human characteristics to a non-human object.	*The fallen autumn leaves were like colorful jewels.* *Her smile was a beacon of good cheer.* *Shadows crawled over the sand just before dusk.*
Hyperbole is exaggeration used for effect.	*The elephant was as big as a house.*
Irony is a contradiction between what happens and what is expected.	In a famous story, a wife cuts her hair to buy her husband a watch fob, and he sells his watch to buy her combs for her hair.
Paradox is a statement that contains elements that seem contradictory but could be true.	George Orwell said, "Ignorance is strength."
An **oxymoron** is word or phrase that seems to contradict itself.	I had jumbo shrimp for dinner.
Symbolism is an object that stands for something else.	An owl is often used as a symbol for wisdom.
An **allegory** is a narrative that has a meaning other than what literally appears.	Some say that his sci-fi story is actually an allegory for the effects of war.
Repetition (or tautology) occurs when content is repeated, sometimes needlessly—for effect.	The forest was dense, dense and dark as coal.

Using Writing Traits to Develop an Effective Composition

You read about rubrics and traits in Chapter 3. Now it's time to look at how they function in good writing.

Ideas

In an excellent piece of writing, the information presented is significant, the message or perspective is strong, and the ideas are original. As you read the sample, think about the ideas it presents and how it develops them.

Leaves of Three

Leaves of three. Let them be! It's an old rhyme that warns against the dangers of poison ivy—a plant with three waxy-looking leaves. If you've ever had a poison ivy rash, you know that the itching and pain it can cause are nothing to sneeze at. You may not know that the rash is caused by a colorless oil called urushiol or that not all people are allergic to this substance. However, those who are allergic never forget its effects.

Contracting the rash is, unfortunately, all too easy. Perhaps you've been outside, pulling up weeds on a sunny weekend. Because of the way poison ivy leaves bend down, you might not have even noticed them. Then it might have taken 12 to 48 hours before you felt a sharp itch and saw the telltale red blisters caused by even a brief brush with the plant.

What can you do for the discomfort of poison ivy? Applying ice helps some people. Others need anti-itch medication, especially if the reaction is intense or covers a large area. However, the best idea is to keep that old rhyme in mind and to be careful not to let those leaves of three ever come close to thee!

 Try It! Think about ideas in the sample as you respond to these prompts.

1. List two details that help readers relate to the topic.

2. List two significant pieces of information the writer includes.

3. List two details that clearly convey the writer's perspective.

Organization

A well-organized composition flows easily from sentence to sentence and paragraph to paragraph. It smoothly progresses from one idea to the next, indicating the connections between ideas with transitions. The paper also avoids needless repetition.

Think about organization as you reread "Leaves of Three" on page 56.

 Try It! Answer the questions about the writing sample on page 56.

1. Identify the transition the writer uses to move from the ideas in the first paragraph to the ideas in the second.

2. List three details in the third paragraph. Explain how each detail supports the first sentence in the paragraph.

3. Identify the topic of each paragraph, and explain whether the topics are presented in logical order.

Voice

Voice is the individual "sound" of a writer's writing, reflecting the writer's personality and perspective. A well-written piece has a distinctive voice that expresses the writer's individuality.

Read the writing sample. Think about voice as you read.

> What is it like to know a person who looks exactly like you? As identical twins, my brother, Ben, and I can tell you that it's totally great. There are many reasons why.
>
> First, it's great to have a special non-verbal communication with another person. Sometimes it's even scary. Take this morning. Ben and I never dress alike, since we like to show that we're individuals. So, each of us got dressed in our own room and then skipped down the stairs for breakfast. You guessed it! We'd chosen exactly the same clothes—right down to our striped socks.
>
> Second, we can have fun fooling people by pretending to be each other. It's great fun to see Dad's expression when he finds he's treated the wrong twin to a reward.

 Try It! Consider the writer's voice as you answer these questions.

1. Describe the writer's tone—his attitude toward his subject.

2. Which words and phrases create a voice in this sample? Explain.

WRITING COACH

Online

www.phwritingcoach.com

Online Journal

Try It! Record your answers and ideas in the online journal. You can also record and save your answers on pop-up sticky notes in the eText.

Partner Talk

Analyze the composition about poison ivy on page 56 with a partner. Discuss how well it might score for the traits of ideas and organization—from ineffective (1), to somewhat effective (2), to fairly effective (3), to effective (4), to highly effective in parts (5), to highly effective throughout (6).

Word Choice

By choosing words with precision, and by using vivid words to create images, good writers give their writing energy and help readers understand their exact meaning.

Think about the writer's word choice as you read these two drafts:

> Sally and Alice ran until they reached a place to make a turn. They headed off to the left, where the flowers were pretty and smelled nice.

> Sally and Alice jogged at a steady pace on the dirt path along the lake until they reached a fork in the trail. Without breaking stride, the two turned in unison and headed left, bound by their silent understanding that left was best—left, where the cream-and-gold honeysuckle blossoms, drooping with fragrance, filled the air with a drowsy sweetness.

 Try It! Answer the question about the two drafts.

1. List two vague or imprecise words in the first draft.

2. Explain which words in the second draft replace the words you listed. What do the words in the second draft help you understand?

Sentence Fluency

When you read the best writing aloud, you will find that the sentences flow smoothly; they do not sound choppy or awkward. The meaning and the rhythm of the sentences work together. To create and control rhythm in writing, good writers use a variety of sentence structures and patterns. Think about the rhythm of the sentences as you read this draft:

> Since I first joined the student council in the ninth grade, I have been a tireless advocate for many important student causes. My experience makes me a good candidate for president of the council; my advocacy makes me a great one. No one else matches my record.

 Try It! Answer the question about the sample.

Describe the rhythm created by the sentences. How does the writer emphasize the final sentence?

Conventions

If a piece of writing reflects a good command of spelling, capitalization, punctuation, grammar, usage, and sentence structure, it is much more likely to communicate clearly to readers.

Pay attention to spelling, capitalization, punctuation, grammar, usage, and sentence structure in the following first draft.

Super-Hero III Doesn't Fly

If you're among the thousands who have been waiting for the latest installment of the popular Super-Hero movie series, you'are in for a big disappointment. This sequel misses the boat—literally.

Me and my companion couldn't believe it! At the very beginning of the movie, as usual, our "hero" runs for the ship on his quest to capture the evil warlord. However, this time he misreads, the schedule and it took off for asia without his assistant and he.

Now, read this section of the reviewer's second draft.

Super-Hero III Doesn't Fly

If you're among the thousands who have been waiting for the latest installment of the popular Super-Hero movie series, you're in for a big disappointment. This sequel misses the boat—literally.

My companion and I couldn't believe it! At the very beginning of the movie, as usual, our "hero" runs for the ship on his quest to capture the evil warlord. However, this time he misreads the schedule, and the ship takes off for Asia without his assistant and him.

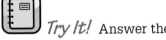 *Try It!* Answer these questions about both drafts.

1. What errors in convention did the writer correct in the second draft?
2. Why is the last sentence easier to read in the second draft?

www.phwritingcoach.com

Online Journal

Try It! Record your answers and ideas in the online journal. You can also record and save your answers on pop-up sticky notes in the eText.

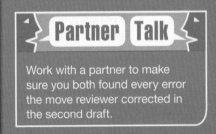 **Partner Talk**

Work with a partner to make sure you both found every error the move reviewer corrected in the second draft.

Using Interactive Writing Coach

As you learned in Chapter 3, you can use rubrics and your Revision RADaR to check how well your paragraphs and essays read. With Writing Coach, you also have another tool available to evaluate your work: the Interactive Writing Coach.

The Interactive Writing Coach is a program that you can use anywhere that you have Internet access. Interactive Writing Coach functions like your own personal writing tutor. It gives you personalized feedback on your work.

The Interactive Writing Coach has two parts: **Paragraph Feedback** and **Essay Scorer**.

- Paragraph Feedback gives you feedback on individual paragraphs as you write. It looks at the structure of sentences and paragraphs and gives you information about specific details, such as sentence variety and length.

- Essay Scorer looks at your whole essay and gives you a score and feedback on your entire piece of writing. It will tell you how well your essay reflects the traits of good writing.

This chart shows just a few questions that Paragraph Feedback and Essay Scorer will answer about your writing. The following pages explain Paragraph Feedback and Essay Scorer in more detail.

Sentences	• Are sentences varied in length? • Do sentences have varied beginnings? • Which sentences have too many ideas? • Are adjectives clear and precise? • Is the sentence grammatically correct? • Is all spelling correct in the sentence?
Paragraphs	• Does the paragraph support its topic? • Does the paragraph use transitions? • Does the paragraph contain the right amount of ideas and information?
Compositions	• Does the essay reflect characteristics of the genre? • Does it demonstrate the traits of good writing? • Is the main idea clear? • Is the main idea well supported? • Is the essay cohesive—does it hold together?

Interactive Writing Coach and the Writing Process

You can begin to use Essay Scorer during the drafting section of the writing process. It is best to complete a full draft of your essay before submitting to Essay Scorer. (While you are drafting individual paragraphs, you may want to use Paragraph Feedback.) Keep in mind, however, that your draft does not need to be perfect or polished before you submit it to Essay Scorer. You will be able to use feedback from Essay Scorer to revise your draft many times. This chart shows how you might use the Interactive Writing Coach and incorporate Essay Scorer into your writing process.

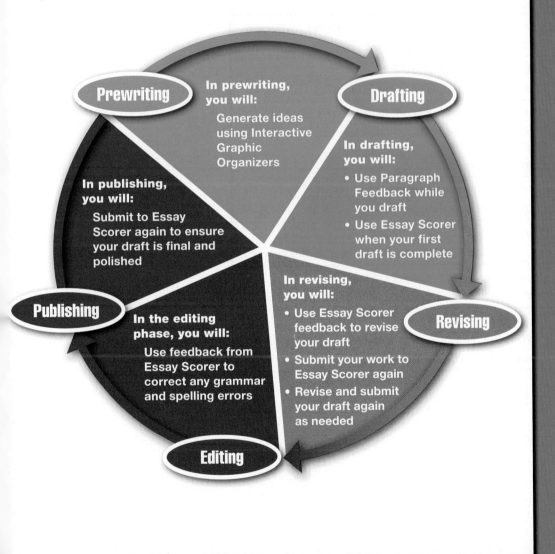

Prewriting

In prewriting, you will:

Generate ideas using Interactive Graphic Organizers

Drafting

In drafting, you will:

- Use Paragraph Feedback while you draft
- Use Essay Scorer when your first draft is complete

Revising

In revising, you will:

- Use Essay Scorer feedback to revise your draft
- Submit your work to Essay Scorer again
- Revise and submit your draft again as needed

Editing

In the editing phase, you will:

Use feedback from Essay Scorer to correct any grammar and spelling errors

Publishing

In publishing, you will:

Submit to Essay Scorer again to ensure your draft is final and polished

Paragraph Feedback With Interactive Writing Coach

The Paragraph Feedback assesses the ideas and topic support for each paragraph you write. You can enter your work into Paragraph Feedback one paragraph at a time. This makes it easy to work on individual paragraphs and get new feedback as you revise each one. Here are some things that Paragraph Feedback will be able to tell you.

Overall Paragraph Support	• Does the paragraph support the main idea? • Which sentences do not support the main idea?
Transitions	• Which sentences contain transition words? • Which words are transition words?
Ideas	• How well are ideas presented? • Which sentences have too many ideas?
Sentence Length and Variety	• Which sentences are short, medium, and long? • Which sentences could be longer or shorter for better sense or variety? • Are sentences varied?
Sentence Beginnings	• How do sentences begin? • Are sentence beginnings varied?
Sentence Structure	• Are sentence structures varied? • Are there too many sentences with similar structures?
Vague Adjectives	• Are any adjectives vague or unclear? • Where are adjectives in sentences and paragraphs?
Language Variety	• Are words repeated? • Where are repeated words located? • How can word choice be improved?

Essay Scoring With Interactive Writing Coach

Essay Scorer assesses your essay. It looks at the essay as a whole, and it also evaluates individual paragraphs, sentences, and words. Essay Scorer will help you evaluate the following traits.

Ideas	• Are the ideas original? Is a clear message or unique perspective presented? • Is the main idea clearly stated? • Is the main idea supported by informative details?
Organization	• Is the organization logical? • Is the introduction clear? Is the conclusion clear? • What transitions are used, and are they effective?
Voice	• Does the writer create a unique voice, expressing his or her personality or perspective? • Does the tone match the topic, audience, and purpose?
Word Choice	• Are precise words used? • Are vivid words used? • Do the word choices suit the purpose and audience?
Sentence Fluency	• Are sentence beginnings, lengths, and structures varied? • Do the sentences flow smoothly?
Conventions	• Is spelling correct? • Is capitalization used properly? • Is all punctuation (ending, internal, apostrophes) accurate? • Do subjects and verbs agree? • Are pronouns used correctly? • Are adjectives and adverbs used correctly? • Are plurals formed correctly? • Are commonly confused words used correctly?

www.phwritingcoach.com

Interactive Writing Coach™

Interactive Writing Coach provides support and guidance to help you improve your writing skills.
• **Select a topic to write about from the Topic Bank.**
• **Use the interactive graphic organizers to narrow your topic.**
• **Go to Writing Coach Online and submit your work, paragraph by paragraph or as a complete draft.**
• **Receive immediate, personalized feedback as you write, revise, and edit your work.**

Whenever you see the Interactive Writing Coach icon you can go to Writing Coach Online and submit your writing, either paragraph by paragraph or as a complete draft, for personalized feedback and scoring.

CHAPTER 5

NONFICTION NARRATION

What Do You Remember?

Why do we remember certain events more than others? What would make other people want to hear about special events? Good retelling of events often includes vivid details that build up to a conflict and end with a resolution.

In order to tell another person about a special event that happened in your life, you will need to remember details and to tell them in a way that builds interest by building conflict. You can do this by telling about your struggles to accomplish a goal.

Try It! Think about a special event that happened in your life. Think about details that would allow you to build interest in the story. Write those details in a list.

Consider these questions as you work on your list.

- What happened?
- Did the event almost not happen? If yes, why?
- What struggles did you experience?

Review the list you made, and then think about how you could use these details to build your story. Tell your memory to a partner. As you tell what happened, tell it so that the outcome is uncertain until the end.

What's Ahead

In this chapter, you will review two strong examples of a narrative nonfiction text: a Mentor Text and a Student Model. Then using the examples as guidance, you will write a narrative nonfiction memoir of your own.

WRITING COACH

www.phwritingcoach.com

 Online Journal

Try It! Record your answers and ideas in the online journal.

You can also record and save your answers and ideas on pop-up sticky notes in the eText.

 Connect to the Big Questions

Discuss these questions with a partner:

1 What do you think? What is the most important life event?

2 Why Write? What should we put in and leave out to be accurate and honest?

NARRATIVE NONFICTION

Narrative nonfiction is writing that tells a true story. In this chapter, you will explore a special type of narrative nonfiction, the memoir. A memoir is a narrative, or story, about you and your life. Every memoir has a plot (a series of events), characters, and a setting. It uses dialogue and sensory details to bring the story to life. A good memoir shares more than experiences—it allows the reader to see how experiences have shaped the writer's personality and attitudes.

You will develop your memoir by taking it through each of the steps of the writing process: prewriting, drafting, revising, editing, and publishing. You will also have an opportunity to write a script for a fictional interview with a famous person. To preview the criteria for how your memoir will be evaluated, see the rubric on page 83.

FEATURE ASSIGNMENT

Narrative Nonfiction: Memoir

An effective piece of narrative nonfiction has these characteristics:

- An **engaging true story** that holds readers' attention

- A **well-developed conflict,** or problem to be solved

- A **well-developed resolution,** the outcome of the conflict, that shows how the problem was solved

- **Literary strategies and devices,** such as dialogue and suspense, that make your narrative stand out and enhance the **plot**

- A specific **mood,** or emotion that the narrative conveys

- A unique **tone** that relays the writer's attitude toward events

- **Sensory details**—details related to the five senses of touch, taste, sight, sound, and smell— that help build the story's mood and tone

- A clear **theme,** or life lesson related to the topic

- **Effective sentence structure** and correct spelling, grammar, and usage

A memoir also includes:

- Specific detail about the writer's **personal experiences**

- Strong **characterization,** or full development of the personalities of real people to illustrate complex and non-stereotypical characters

Other Forms of Narrative Nonfiction

In addition to a memoir, there are other forms of narrative nonfiction, including:

Autobiographical narratives are stories written in the first person about the writer's own life. Some magazines publish short autobiographical narratives. Longer autobiographical narratives are published as books.

Biographical narratives are written in the third person about the life of someone other than the writer.

Blogs are online forums in which writers share autobiographical narratives, reflections, opinions, and other types of comments. Most blogs allow readers to post responses. Writing in a blog is not the same as publishing, since it is not considered a "permanent" form of writing.

Diary entries are intended only for the writer, unless the writer decides to share them. They include the writer's personal experiences, thoughts, and feelings. Sometimes the diaries of notable people are published after they pass away.

Narrative essays illustrate a theme with one or more biographical or autobiographical narratives.

Reflective essays, like narrative essays, tell about events that the writer experienced, witnessed, or heard about. Unlike narrative essays, reflective essays focus more on sharing the observations and insights that writers gained from these experiences. Magazines and newspapers often feature reflective essays.

Try It! For each audience and purpose described, choose a form, such as a diary, blog, or narrative essay, that is appropriate for conveying your intended meaning to the audience. Explain your choices.

- To privately record how you felt when your best friend moved away
- To tell how you have overcome adversity in your life
- To share a comment about your school's prom decorations

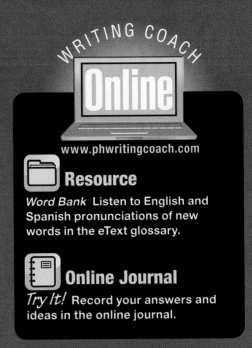

MENTOR TEXT   Memoir

Learn From Experience

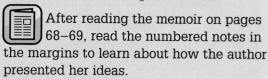 After reading the memoir on pages 68–69, read the numbered notes in the margins to learn about how the author presented her ideas.

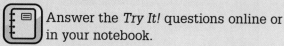 Answer the *Try It!* questions online or in your notebook.

---

❶ Sensory details help readers imagine the kit and the basement. They also help convey the **tone,** or the author's attitude toward her subject.

Try It! List three items that came with the microscope kit and three items the author supplied herself. What tone does this passage convey?

❷ The author **defines unfamiliar terms** to help readers understand her memoir.

Try It! How did the author define "hay infusion"? "Diatomaceous earth"? Were these definitions helpful to you? Explain.

❸ The **conflict,** or main struggle, is introduced in this paragraph.

Try It! How would you describe the conflict? Is it between the author and herself, another person, or an outside force?

Extension Find another example of a memoir, and compare it with this one.

From An American Childhood

by Annie Dillard

After I read *The Field Book of Ponds and Streams* several times, I longed for a microscope. Everybody needed a microscope. Detectives used microscopes, both for the FBI and at Scotland Yard. Although usually I had to save my tiny allowance for
5 things I wanted, that year for Christmas my parents gave me a microscope kit.

❶ In a dark basement corner, on a white enamel table, I set up the microscope kit. I supplied a chair, a lamp, a batch of jars, a candle, and a pile of library books. The microscope kit supplied
10 a blunt black three-speed microscope, a booklet, a scalpel, a dropper, an ingenious device for cutting thin segments of fragile tissue, a pile of clean slides and cover slips, and a dandy array of corked test tubes.

❷ One of the test tubes contained "hay infusion." Hay infusion
15 was a wee brown chip of grass blade. You added water to it and after a week it became a jungle in a drop, full of one-celled animals. This did not work for me. All I saw in the microscope after a week was a wet chip of dried grass, much enlarged.

❷ Another test tube contained "diatomaceous earth." This was,
20 I believed, an actual pinch of the white cliffs of Dover. On my palm it was an airy, friable chalk. The booklet said it was composed of the silicaceous bodies of diatoms—one-celled creatures that lived in, as it were, small glass jewelry boxes with fitted lids. Diatoms, I read, come in a variety of transparent geometrical shapes. Broken
25 and dead and dug out of geological deposits, they made chalk, and a fine abrasive used in silver polish and toothpaste. What I saw in the microscope must have been the fine abrasive—grit enlarged. It was years before I saw a recognizable, whole diatom. The kit's diatomaceous earth was a bust.
30 All that winter I played with the microscope. I prepared slides from things at hand, as the books suggested. I looked at the transparent membrane inside an onion's skin and saw the cells. I looked at a section of cork and saw the cells, and at scrapings from the inside of my cheek, ditto. . . .
35 **❸** All this was very well, but I wanted to see the wildlife I had read about. I wanted especially to see the famous amoeba who had eluded me. He was supposed to live in the hay infusion,

but I hadn't found him there. He lived outside in warm ponds and streams, too, but I lived in Pittsburgh, and it had been a cold winter.

40 Finally late that spring I saw an amoeba. The week before, I had gathered puddle water from Frick Park; it had been festering in a jar in the basement. This June night after dinner I figured I had waited long enough. In the basement at my microscope table I spread a scummy drop of Frick Park puddle water on a slide, peeked in, and lo, there was the famous amoeba. He

45 was as blobby and grainy as his picture; I would have known him anywhere.

Before I had watched him at all, I ran upstairs. My parents were still at table, drinking coffee. They, too, could see the famous amoeba. I told them, bursting, that he was all set up, that they should hurry before his water dried. It was the chance of a lifetime.

50 ❹ Father had stretched out his long legs and was tilting back in his chair. Mother sat with her knees crossed, in blue slacks. . . . The dessert dishes were still on the table. My sisters were nowhere in evidence. It was a warm evening; the big dining-room windows gave onto blooming rhododendrons.

Mother regarded me warmly. She gave me to understand that she was

55 glad I had found what I had been looking for, but that she and Father were happy to sit with their coffee, and would not be coming down.

She did not say, but I understood at once, that they had their pursuits (coffee?) and I had mine. She did not say, but I began to understand then, that you do what you do out of your private

60 passion for the thing itself.

I had essentially been handed my own life. In subsequent years my parents would praise my drawings and poems, and supply me with books, art supplies, and sports equipment, and listen to my troubles and enthusiasms, and supervise my hours, and discuss and

65 inform, but they would not get involved with my detective work, nor hear about my reading, nor inquire about my homework or term papers or exams, nor visit the salamanders I caught, nor listen to me play the piano, nor attend my field hockey games, nor fuss over my insect collection with me, poetry collection or stamp collection or

70 rock collection. My days and nights were my own to plan and fill.

❺ When I left the dining room that evening and started down the dark basement stairs, I had a life. I sat next to my wonderful amoeba, and there he was, rolling his grains more slowly now, extending an arc of his edge for a foot and drawing himself along

75 by that foot, and absorbing it again and rolling on. I gave him some more pond water.

I had hit pay dirt. For all I knew, there were paramecia, too, in that pond water, or daphniae, or stentors, or any of the many other creatures I had read about and never seen: volvox, the spherical algal colony; euglena

80 with its one red eye; the elusive, glassy diatom; hydra, rotifers, water bears, worms. ❺ Anything was possible. The sky was the limit.

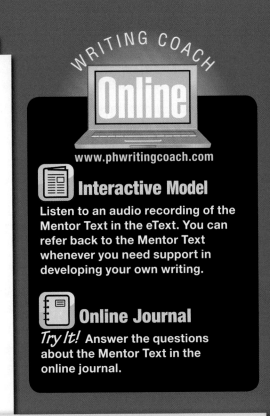

WRITING COACH

Online

www.phwritingcoach.com

Interactive Model

Listen to an audio recording of the Mentor Text in the eText. You can refer back to the Mentor Text whenever you need support in developing your own writing.

Online Journal

Try It! Answer the questions about the Mentor Text in the online journal.

❹ The author writes about three main **characters who are real people**—herself and her parents. This passage reveals more about the parents' personalities.

Try It! What insight into the parents does this passage give you? Are the parents complex characters or stereotypical parents? Explain.

❺ These sentences explore the **theme** of the memoir, or the message about life that the author wants to share.

Try It! What has the author learned? Restate the theme in your own words.

STUDENT MODEL — Memoir

With a small group, take turns reading this Student Model aloud. As you read, practice newly acquired vocabulary by correctly producing the word's sound. Also notice how the writer uses dialogue and creates suspense to strengthen the memoir.

Use a Reader's Eye

Now, reread the Student Model. On your copy of the Student Model, use the Reader's Response Symbols to react to what you read.

Reader's Response Symbols

+ **I like where this is going.**

− **This isn't clear to me.**

? **What will happen next?**

! **Wow! That is cool/weird/ interesting!**

Discuss the author's use of dialogue with a partner. Share your opinions about how effective the dialogue is in enhancing the plot, as well as whether or not you feel the dialogue is realistic. Take notes to describe specific examples in detail.

The Best GIFT

by Ariana Jordan

My grandmother always said that the best gift is the one you give away. I never understood what she meant by that. To me, the best gifts were the ones I got. That's why my family thoughtfully gave
5　me the nickname "Me-me." I was totally selfish, until a dog named Lucy changed my life.

I was on my way home from school when I saw a huge dog with filthy, matted fur. She looked at me, and I caught a flash of her bright blue eyes. I took off
10　my belt, put it around her neck, and pulled. The dog sat down and braced her legs. My dad trains dogs, so I know all the commands. "Come!" I ordered. The dog just looked at me. I found some crackers in my backpack. By holding the crackers in front of
15　her nose, I got the dog to walk home with me.

The first thing I did was give her a good scrubbing. Then, I brushed out her coat. By the time my mom came home, I had given her a name. "Mom, come meet Lucy!" I said.

20　Mom looked at the dog. "Oh, Me-me," she sighed. "You know we're selling the house and moving to an apartment. You can't keep her."

"Just for a week or two," I begged. "See how skinny she is?"

25　Over the next three weeks I fed, brushed, and trained Lucy. I taught her how to walk on a leash. I gently pulled her ears and tail and handled her paws to get her used to how children might touch her. I wanted to make sure she was well trained
30　so she never ended up on the street again.

1

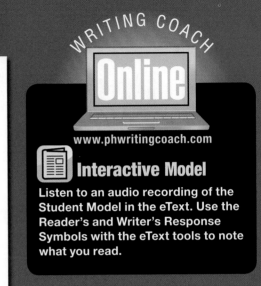

WRITING COACH

Online

www.phwritingcoach.com

Interactive Model

Listen to an audio recording of the Student Model in the eText. Use the Reader's and Writer's Response Symbols with the eText tools to note what you read.

One night my mom told me we had a contract to sell our house. She helped me place an online ad for a home for Lucy. That weekend, people started coming to see her. I didn't like any of them! Then Mr. Spindler

35 showed up with his eight-year-old daughter, Anna. Anna timidly reached out to Lucy. She stroked the dog's thick, reddish-brown fur and looked into her blue eyes. Then she threw her arms around Lucy's neck.

I had tears in my eyes when I handed Lucy's leash

40 to Anna, but I felt good, too. Because of my hard work, Lucy had a home and Anna had a new best friend. Now I volunteer at the animal shelter, getting dogs ready for their new homes, and no one calls me by my nickname anymore. Now I understand what my grandmother meant!

Use a Writer's Eye

Now, evaluate the piece as a writer. On your copy of the Student Model, use the Writer's Response Symbols to react to what you read. Identify places where the student writer uses characteristics of an effective memoir.

Writer's Response Symbols	
E.S.	**Engaging story**
C.R.	**Clear, well-developed conflict and resolution**
B.C.	**Believable characters**
S.D.	**Specific and vivid details**

2

Your Turn > Feature Assignment: Memoir

Prewriting

Plan a first draft of your memoir **by determining an appropriate topic.** You may select from the Topic Bank or come up with an idea of your own.

 Choose From the Topic Bank

TOPIC BANK

So Sorry Apologies can often be difficult to make. Select a memorable experience of regret and describe how you made your apology.

Kudos to Me Think about a time you had to overcome obstacles to achieve an important goal. Write a memoir that describes how you overcame obstacles to accomplish your goal and how you felt about yourself when you were successful.

The Test Taking tests is part of life as a high school student. Some people enjoy the challenge of taking a test, while others get nervous just thinking about it. Write a memoir about a test you remember taking. Describe the experience and how you felt about it.

 Choose Your Own Topic

Determine an appropriate topic on your own by using the following **range of strategies** to generate ideas.

Interview and Reflect

- Interview your family, asking them to tell stories about you when you were younger. Choose one of these stories and retell it from your point of view.

- Make a list of times when you have been surprised, either in a good or a bad way. Choose one of these times and write a memoir about it. Try to write it in such a way that the reader is surprised, too.

Narrow Your Topic

Choosing a topic that is too broad will prevent you from focusing on a clear theme in your memoir.

Apply It! Use a graphic organizer like the one shown to narrow your topic and help you to identify a topic for your memoir.

- Record your general topic—your broadest story idea—in the top box. Then, narrow your topic as you move down the chart.
- Your final box should hold your narrowest story idea, the new focus of your memoir.

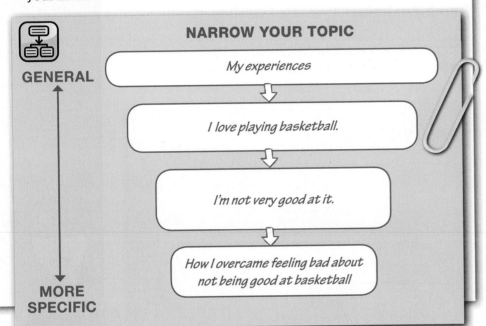

GENERAL

NARROW YOUR TOPIC

My experiences

I love playing basketball.

I'm not very good at it.

How I overcame feeling bad about not being good at basketball

MORE SPECIFIC

 ## Consider Multiple Audiences and Purposes

Before writing, consider how your writing will convey the intended meaning to multiple audiences. Consider the way others will perceive events as you ask yourself these questions.

Questions for Audience	Questions for Purpose
• Who are the people in my audiences? • Will the topic of my narrative engage each audience's interest? • What might each audience want to know about me—and why? • What literary devices might help me hold each audience's attention?	• What is my purpose for sharing this experience? Do I want to be humorous, thought-provoking, or something else? • As I develop my purpose, how much about myself do I want to share with each audience?

Record your answers in your writing journal.

Plan Your Piece

You will use a graphic organizer like the one shown to develop your conflict, theme, and resolution as well as organize your events and identify details. When it is complete, you will be ready to write a first draft that is well-organized and that structures ideas in a consistent and sustained way.

Develop Your Theme How did the experience you will narrate in your memoir change you? What new insights have you gained from reflecting on the experience? Use the answers to these questions to develop a **clear theme**, or controlling idea, for your memoir. Begin your graphic organizer by writing this idea.

Map Out Your Plot Events Continue filling out your plot diagram by noting the events that will lead to the highest point in the conflict and then reveal the resolution.

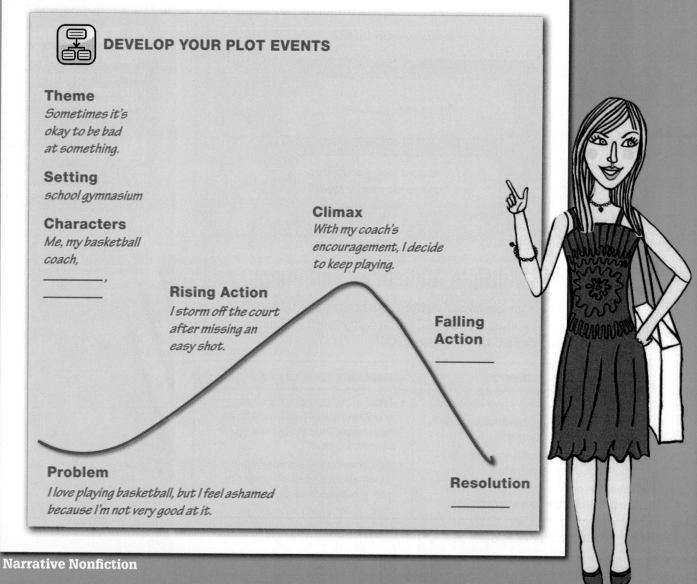

DEVELOP YOUR PLOT EVENTS

Theme
Sometimes it's okay to be bad at something.

Setting
school gymnasium

Characters
Me, my basketball coach,
_____,
_____

Rising Action
I storm off the court after missing an easy shot.

Climax
With my coach's encouragement, I decide to keep playing.

Falling Action
_____

Problem
I love playing basketball, but I feel ashamed because I'm not very good at it.

Resolution
_____

Gather Details

Writers of memoirs usually build upon the story elements of character and setting by using a range of **literary strategies and devices,** such as dialogue, sensory details, and suspense to develop and **enhance their plot.** Remember that sensory details appeal to the reader's five senses—touch, taste, sight, sound, and smell. Details like these can help pull readers into a story and create a definite mood or tone. Look at these examples of strategies writers use to develop their narratives:

- **Dialogue:** *"I stink at this! I'm going to quit for good."*
- **Sensory Details**: *The ball felt slick against my sweaty palms. I felt confident for once that I wouldn't miss. There was a dull thud as the ball hit the backboard and fell to the ground. The court was silent.*
- **Suspense:** *The next Saturday morning, my mom laid my basketball uniform out on my bed. I stood and looked at it for a long time, thinking of the frowns on my teammates' faces when I missed the shot. How could I face them?*

Good writers use a range of strategies to engage readers, to develop the theme, and to present a strong narrative.

Try It! Read the Student Model excerpt and identify which elements the author uses to develop the narrative.

 **STUDENT MODEL** from **The Best Gift**
page 70; lines 18–22

> "Mom, come meet Lucy!" I said.
>
> Mom looked at the dog. "Oh, Me-me," she sighed. "You know we're selling the house and moving to an apartment. You can't keep her."
>
> "Just for a week or two," I begged. "See how skinny she is?"

Apply It! Review the types of details writers of narrative nonfiction can use. Then, write notes about how you will use these elements in your memoir.

- Decide which **sensory details** are most likely to help you create an engaging story with the mood or tone you want.
- Determine which **literary strategies and devices,** such as suspense and dialogue, you will use to enhance the plot.

Add these elements to your graphic organizer, matching each detail to the right part of the story so that you create a well-developed **conflict** and **resolution** and set a definite mood and tone.

WRITING COACH

Online

www.phwritingcoach.com

Interactive Graphic Organizers

Use the interactive graphic organizers to help you create a plan for your writing.

Interactive Model

Refer back to the Interactive Model in the eText as you plan your writing.

Drafting

During the drafting stage, you will start to write your ideas for your memoir. You will follow an outline that provides an organizational strategy that will help you write an engaging memoir.

The Organization of a Nonfiction Narrative

The chart shows an organizational strategy for a nonfiction narrative. Look back at how the Mentor Text follows this organizational strategy. Then, use this chart to help you outline your draft.

I. Beginning   See Mentor Text, p. 68.

- Engaging opening
- Clear theme

II. Middle   See Mentor Text, pp. 68–69.

- Well-developed conflict
- Literary devices and strategies that enhance the plot
- Specific sensory details

III. End   See Mentor Text, p. 69.

- Well-developed resolution
- Ending that reflects the theme

Grab Your Reader

- An engaging opening will capture your readers' attention. Use a catchy phrase, an interesting quotation, or a personal observation to draw them into the story.
- Establishing a theme, or larger meaning, for your story tells readers your main idea.

Develop Your Plot

- A conflict can be presented by plotting events in chronological order. Use the action of the events to show why the main conflict presented a problem for you.
- A literary device like dialogue is one way to make characters true to life and connect readers to the plot.
- Providing vivid sensory details—about the characters, setting, and action—will let you define your mood or tone and help readers to feel as if they are a part of the story.

Wrap It Up

- A resolution shows how the problem was solved or how events ended and reminds readers of the beginning of your narrative.
- Reflecting on how the event affected you will leave readers with a memorable ending.

 # Start Your Draft

Use the checklist to help you complete your draft. Use the Plot Map that shows your conflict, resolution, and theme, and the Outline for Success as guides.

While drafting, keep in mind that this is an open-ended, or untimed situation. Take your time so you can develop a great story. However, aim at writing your ideas, not on making your writing perfect. Remember, you will have the chance to improve your draft when you revise and edit.

√ Start your **beginning** by drafting an attention-getting **opening sentence.** Make readers curious.

√ Continue by giving details that establish a clear **theme** for your narrative.

√ Introduce your main characters, setting, and the **conflict.**

√ To create a well-developed conflict to which readers can connect, develop the **middle** of your memoir by creating a series of **plot events** that show how you struggled with or learned more about the problem.

√ Use a range of **literary strategies and devices,** such as dialogue and suspense, to enhance the plot and keep your readers interested.

√ Focus on the craft of writing. Use **rhetorical devices,** such as hyperbole—exaggeration—or unusual comparisons to convey meaning in a clear but interesting way.

√ Remember that your **characters** are real people. Portray them as the complex and non-stereotypical individuals that they are.

√ Provide **sensory details** about the setting, characters, and characters' actions to define the mood or tone for your story.

√ At the **end** of your narrative, offer the readers a well-developed **resolution**—show how the conflict worked out. Finish in a way that is satisfying and that recalls the beginning of your true story.

√ Tie back to the theme by sharing an **insight** with your readers about how the events of your narrative affected you or your life.

WRITING COACH

Online

www.phwritingcoach.com

Interactive Model

Outline for Success View pop-ups of Mentor Text selections referenced in the Outline for Success.

Interactive Writing Coach™

Use the Interactive Writing Coach to receive the level of support you need:
- **Write one paragraph at a time and submit each one for immediate, detailed feedback.**
- **Write your entire first draft and submit it for immediate, personalized feedback.**

Revising: Making It Better

Now that you have finished your first draft, you are ready to revise. Think about the "big picture" of audience, purpose, and genre. You can use Revision RADaR as a guide for making changes to improve your draft. Revision RADaR provides four major ways to improve your writing: (R) replace, (A) add, (D) delete, and (R) reorder.

Kelly Gallagher, M. Ed.

KEEP REVISION ON YOUR RADaR

Read part of the first draft of the Student Model, "The Best Gift." Then look at questions the writer asked herself as she thought about how well her draft addressed issues of audience, purpose, and genre.

The Best Gift

1ST DRAFT

Over the next three weeks I fed, brushed, and trained Lucy. I taught her how to walk on a leash. I gently pulled her ears and tail and handled her paws.

> *Will readers understand why I did these things? Is my **meaning** clear?*

One night my mom told me we had a contract to sell our house. She helped me place an online ad for a home for Lucy. That weekend, people started coming to see her. I didn't like any of them! Then a man showed up with his daughter. Anna reached out to Lucy. She looked at Lucy. Then she held Lucy.

> *Have I included **sensory** details to define the mood of this moment in my story?*

I had tears in my eyes when I handed Lucy's leash to Anne, but I felt good too. Now I volunteer at the animal shelter, getting dogs ready for their new homes, and no one calls me by my nickname anymore. Because of my hard work, Lucy had a home and Anna had a new best friend.

> *Is this paragraph logically organized?*

> *Have I ended with a powerful thought that ties back to my **theme**?*

Now, look at how the writer applied Revision RADaR to write an improved second draft.

WRITING COACH

Online
www.phwritingcoach.com

Interactive Writing Coach™

Use the Revision RADaR strategy in your own writing. Then submit your paragraph or draft for feedback.

The Best Gift

2ND DRAFT

Over the next three weeks I fed, brushed, and trained Lucy. I taught her how to walk on a leash. I gently pulled her ears and tail and handled her paws to get her used to how children might touch her. I wanted to make sure she was well trained so she never ended up on the street again.

A *Added information about why I did these things to clarify my meaning to my audience*

One night my mom told me we had a contract to sell our house. She helped me place an online ad for a home for Lucy. That weekend, people started coming to see her. I didn't like any of them! Then Mr. Spindler showed up with his eight-year-old daughter, Anna. Anna timidly reached out to Lucy. She stroked the dog's thick, reddish-brown fur and looked into her blue eyes. Then she threw her arms around Lucy's neck.

R *Replaced general statements with more specific ones including sensory details*

I had tears in my eyes when I handed Lucy's leash to Anna, but I felt good, too. Because of my hard work, Lucy had a home and Anna had a new best friend. Now I volunteer at the animal shelter, getting dogs ready for their new homes, and no one calls me by my nickname anymore. Now I understand what my grandmother meant!

R *Reordered the information about my nickname to put it in a more logical spot*

A *Added a sentence to tie my resolution back to my theme*

 Apply It! Use the Revision RADaR strategy to revise your draft.

- First, determine if you have organized your memoir logically, made your meaning clear, and included the characteristics of the memoir form.
- Then apply the Revision RADaR strategy to make needed changes. Remember—you can use the steps in the strategy in any order.

Look at the Big Picture

Use the chart and your analytical skills to evaluate how well each section of your memoir addresses purpose, audience, and genre. When necessary, use the suggestions in the chart to revise your piece.

Section	Evaluate	Revise
Beginning	• Decide whether your **opening sentence** is engaging, making your audience want to read on.	• Add a catchy phrase, an interesting quotation, or a personal observation to draw readers into the story.
	• Make sure you have established a clear **theme.** Readers should know why you're writing, even if your theme is subtle.	• Sum up the point of your narrative in one sentence; then decide whether you want to include that sentence or hint at its idea.
Middle	• Review the plot of your narrative. Do you have a well-developed **conflict**? Do the events clearly present a problem that involves you?	• Add actions and details that develop the conflict. Reorder events to ensure logical organization in chronological, or time, order. Add, replace, or even delete details to keep readers in suspense about the conflict's outcome.
	• Underline details that show your characters in action in one or more settings. Do **sensory details** make the characters and settings interesting and believable? Do they define a mood or tone?	• Consider adding or revising dialogue to make the real-life characters more complex and less stereotypical. Also, to set a mood or tone, add vivid sensory details about characters and setting.
	• Look at the middle as a whole and evaluate your use of a range of **literary strategies and devices** to hold readers' interest and enhance the plot.	• Read dialogue in your story aloud to make sure it sounds realistic. Add text to enhance the sense of suspense. To add even more interest, experiment with rhetorical tropes, such as irony. (See page 81.)
End	• Check for a well-developed **resolution**—one that clearly reveals the conflict's outcome.	• Add or revise details to show how the problem was solved or how events ended it.
	• Evaluate your **closing** to see if it reflects the beginning and brings the narrative full circle.	• Add a sentence or information to connect the theme with the outcome of the conflict.

Focus on Craft: Tropes: Irony

Irony is a **trope,** or figure of speech, in which what is said is the opposite of what is meant. The writer emphasizes the real meaning by making an opposite, or ironic, statement that is clearly ridiculous in the context of the narrative. For instance, if a writer presents someone who is standing in a long line as saying, "This is exactly what I wanted to do today," the reader knows that the character is using irony to express his impatience.

 **STUDENT MODEL** from **The Best Gift**
page 70; lines 4–6

> That's why my family thoughtfully gave me the nickname "Me-me." I was totally selfish, until a dog named Lucy changed my life.

 Try It! Read the Student Model and ask yourself these questions. Record your answers in your journal.

- Do you think this sentence would have been stronger or weaker if the writer had left out the word *thoughtfully*? Explain.
- What feelings about her family does the writer's use of irony convey?

Fine-Tune Your Draft

Apply It! Use the revision suggestions to prepare your final draft after rethinking how questions of audience, purpose, and genre have been addressed.

- **Add Irony** If it would support your tone, use irony to express an emotional reaction or other information that means the opposite of what was written.
- **Use Transitions** Help readers understand how the events in your story are related by including appropriate transitions such as *therefore* or *however* to convey meaning and connect ideas.
- **Clarify Meaning** Make sure that all of your plot points are clearly explained and are organized in a logical manner. Add, replace, or delete details to ensure clarity of meaning.

Peer Feedback Read your final draft to a group of peers. Ask if they can identify the theme of your story, and whether or not they find the story interesting and engaging. Listen carefully to their comments and revise your draft as necessary.

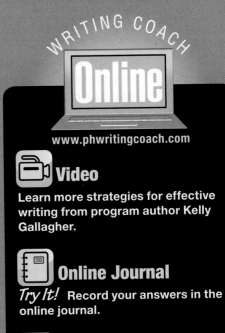

WRITING COACH

Online

www.phwritingcoach.com

Video
Learn more strategies for effective writing from program author Kelly Gallagher.

Online Journal
Try It! Record your answers in the online journal.

Interactive Model
Refer back to the Interactive Model as you revise your writing.

Interactive Writing Coach™
Revise your draft and submit it for feedback.

Editing: Making It Correct

To edit your draft, read it carefully to check for correct spelling and grammar. It can be helpful to read your story out loud to listen for places that need correction.

As you edit your draft, think about whether you have used **clauses** effectively. **Adverbial clauses,** subordinate clauses used as adverbs, can be used as transitions. A transition is a word, phrase, clause, or sentence that creates a relationship between ideas. Transitional adverbial clauses are usually **punctuated** with a comma. Also, edit your final draft for any errors in **grammar, mechanics, and spelling.**

WRITE GUY *Jeff Anderson, M. Ed.*

WHAT DO YOU NOTICE?

Zoom in on Conventions Focus on adverbial clauses used as transitions as you zoom in on these sentences from the Mentor Text.

> **MENTOR TEXT** from **An American Childhood**
> page 69; lines 44–46
>
> He was as blobby and grainy as his picture; I would have known him anywhere.
> Before I had watched him at all, I ran upstairs.

To learn more about adverbial clauses, see Chapter 15 of your Grammar Handbook.

Now, ask yourself: *What clause is used as a transition between the two paragraphs?*

Perhaps you said the **adverbial clause** *Before I had watched him at all.*

Notice that the adverbial clause begins with the subordinating conjunction *Before,* which stresses the time relationship between the two paragraphs.

Adverbial clauses can show a relationship of sequence or time order, comparison, contrast, or cause and effect. These clauses contain a subject and a verb and begin with subordinating conjunctions, such as *after, although, before, though,* and *where.*

Partner Talk Discuss this question with a partner: *What relationships can adverbial clauses create in a text?*

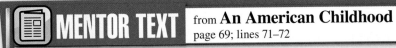

To learn more, see Chapter 23.

Grammar Mini-Lesson:
Commas With Transitions

Adverbial clauses used as transitions usually occur at the beginning of a sentence. Place a **comma** after an adverbial clause that precedes the sentence's main clause. Notice how a comma sets off the transitional adverbial clause in the Mentor Text.

 MENTOR TEXT from **An American Childhood**
page 69; lines 71–72

When I left the dining room that evening and started down the dark basement stairs, I had a life.

Try It! Rewrite this passage in your journal. Place a comma after any adverbial clauses used as transitions.

Chicago is really big. Before I moved there I had lived in a small town all my life. Since I had never lived in a big city I found Chicago very strange at first.

Apply It! Edit your draft for grammar, punctuation, capitalization, and spelling errors. Make sure that you have included adverbial clauses and other appropriate transitions for coherence between sentences and paragraphs. Check that you have **correctly punctuated** your adverbial clauses.

WRITING COACH
Online
www.phwritingcoach.com

Video
Learn effective editing techniques from program author Jeff Anderson.

Online Journal
Try It! Record your answers in the online journal.

Interactive Model
Refer back to the Interactive Model as you edit your writing.

Interactive Writing Coach™
Edit your draft. Check it against the rubric and then submit it for feedback.

 Use the rubric to evaluate your essay. If necessary, rethink, rewrite, or revise.

Rubric for Narrative Nonfiction: Memoir	Rating Scale
Ideas: How well do you narrate a single, important event?	Not very Very 1 2 3 4 5 6
Organization: How logically organized is your sequence of events?	1 2 3 4 5 6
Voice: How authentic and engaging is your voice?	1 2 3 4 5 6
Word Choice: How effectively do you use details to show characters and setting?	1 2 3 4 5 6
Sentence Fluency: How well do you build on each idea to create coherence?	1 2 3 4 5 6
Conventions: How correct are your commas with transitions?	1 2 3 4 5 6

Publishing

Share your experience and what it means to you by publishing your memoir. First, prepare your memoir for presentation. Then, choose ways to **publish it for appropriate audiences.**

Wrap Up Your Presentation

Is your memoir handwritten or written on a computer? If your memoir is handwritten, you may need to make a new, clean copy. If so, be sure to **write legibly.** Also be sure to add a title to your memoir that grabs the reader's attention and indicates the topic of the memoir.

Publish Your Piece

Use the chart to identify ways to publish your memoir.

If your audience is...	...then publish it by...
Classmates and teachers at school	• Submitting it to your school's literary magazine • Creating a Web page on your school's site for your and your classmates' memoirs. Add photographs to help bring the stories to life.
People outside of your school community	• Submitting your memoir to be read aloud on a local or national radio program • Posting it on a creative writing Web site

 Reflect on Your Writing

Now that you have finished your memoir, read it over and use your writing journal to answer these questions.

- How closely does the final product match your original goals?

- Which parts of your narrative are the strongest? Are any parts weak—dull, for example, or confusing? If so, how can you change this in your next writing assignment?

- Consider ways narrative nonfiction writing could be helpful to you in other classes. Why is knowing how to write narrative nonfiction an important skill?

 The Big Question: Why Write? What did you decide to put in or leave out to be accurate and honest?

MAKE YOUR WRITING COUNT

Staging a Game Show: What's My Line?

Memoirs provide details and insights about people's pasts and inner lives. Mine the rich details of your groups' memoirs to synthesize what you've learned into an entertaining and informative **game show** that invites contestants to question guests and guess who they are or what they did.

Your game will be **a multimedia presentation** with graphics, images, and sound that appeal to your audience. It will use questions with multiple points of view. Whether you present your game show live or video-record it, the rules of the game show should be logical and consistent so that participants know when to listen and when to speak.

Here's your action plan.

1. Choose group roles, such as host, contestants, panelists, and time-keeper, and set objectives.

2. As a group, decide on the object and the rules of the game. The game should involve quizzing contestants about the details of several memoirs.

3. For inspiration, look online at videos of old game shows like *What's My Line?*

4. Write questions that will help you develop a coherent presentation that conveys a clear and distinct perspective. Review your peers' memoirs to find details suited to questions.

5. In addition to a logical set of rules based on solid reasoning, your game show should include:

   - Stage design, such as props, desks, and buzzers or bells
   - Graphics, such as signs, nameplates, and flip charts
   - Theme music and sound effects

6. Make sure your video equipment is in good working order if you plan to record your show.

Listening and Speaking Rehearse with props, graphics, theme music, and sound effects before going "live." When you do go live, keep your rehearsal feedback in mind as you provide your contestants with a fresh challenge. Afterward, conduct a debriefing—viewing the videotape if available—to evaluate the merits and drawbacks of your game show format.

WRITING COACH

Online

www.phwritingcoach.com

Online Journal

Reflect on Your Writing Record your answers and ideas in the online journal.

Resource

Link to resources on 21st Century Learning for help in creating a group project.

Your Turn ▶ **Writing for Media: Script**

Script of a Fictional Interview

An **interview** is a formal conversation in which one person, the interviewer, tries to get specific information from another person, the interviewee. After the interviewer determines the focus, or theme, of the interview, he or she develops questions that will elicit the necessary information and details. For instance, the theme of an interview with a filmmaker might be how her latest work continues the stories of her earlier films.

A **script for a podcast or television interview** tells what viewers will see and hear and in what order. Of course, the interviewer does not know how the interviewee will respond to the questions, so the entire interview cannot be scripted. However, the scene, introduction, and initial question should be carefully mapped out.

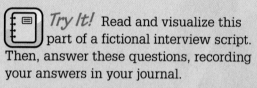

Try It! Read and visualize this part of a fictional interview script. Then, answer these questions, recording your answers in your journal.

1. What is the focus, or **theme,** of the interview? Is it explicit—stated directly—or is it implicit, or hinted at?

2. To what specific **audiences** would this interview probably appeal?

3. Interviews include **images,** usually of the interviewer and interviewee, and **sound,** usually the conversation between the two. They may also include graphics, film clips, audio recordings, and other elements. Which elements will be part of this scene?

4. What **literary techniques,** such as characterization and figures of speech, are used in the script?

Extension Find another example of an interview script, and compare it with this one.

INTERVIEW WITH NAIA JONES

(Open with footage of Jones's victory in the 600 meter butterfly race in the 2008 Beijing Olympics.)

(Zoom in on reporter Ross Reed at the University of Texas Swim Center in Austin, Texas. He is sitting in the bleachers. Accompany the cut with two seconds of ambient swim center noise, including splashing and whistles blowing. Then, fade the ambient noise.)

REED: We all remember that scene. Naia Jones, a U.S. swim team alternate, stunned the swimming world by blasting a full second off her best time and rocketing to victory. Since then, all eyes have been on Jones—and her performance has suffered. Now, many wonder whether her gold medal was a fluke.

(Naia Jones, dressed in warm-ups, enters the shot, and Reed rises to shake her hand.)

REED: Good morning, Ms. Jones.

JONES: Good morning, Ross.

REED: Like so many people, I was electrified by your victory in Beijing. Since then, though, you seem to have been struggling, and I was wondering if you could talk with us about how the pressures that came with that unexpected gold medal have affected you as an athlete and as a person…

Create a Script for a Fictional Interview

Follow these steps to create an introduction and initial question for your own script of a fictional interview with a famous person. To plan your script, you may want to create a storyboard to help you determine how and when you will incorporate different media elements.

Prewriting

- Choose a famous person you would like to interview. This person might be a recording artist, an actor, a scientist, a writer, a filmmaker, or anyone else who interests you.

- To choose a topic, think about what you would like to find out from your subject. Select a topic that would appeal to a specific audience of your choice.

- Decide on your purpose. Think about the information you hope to discuss and what your focus, or theme, will be. You may decide to state the theme explicitly and directly, or to suggest an implicit theme.

- Research your subject, gathering as much information about this person as you can. Synthesize information from multiple points of view into an insightful question that drives the interview.

- List the kinds of media elements that you might include—still photos, video, different kinds of camera shots, and audio clips.

Drafting

- Write a script that identifies the placement of each element in relation to the interview. Use the model on page 86 as a guide.

- As you draft, keep your purpose, audience, and theme in mind.

Revising and Editing

- Review your draft to ensure that your interview is informative and interesting; add or delete details that detract from this goal.

- Look for places where you can introduce a variety of literary techniques. For example, you might include figurative language or repetition for effect.

- Share your work with some classmates. Ask them whether your introduction gives them information and if your first question is clear and interesting. Revise your script after hearing their feedback.

- Check that spelling, grammar, and mechanics are correct.

Publishing

- Use your script to produce a podcast or video, asking classmates to play the roles of interviewer and interviewee. Practice the interview several times before filming so the actors read the lines convincingly.

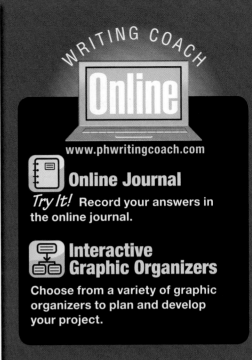

WRITING COACH

Online

www.phwritingcoach.com

Online Journal

Try It! Record your answers in the online journal.

Interactive Graphic Organizers

Choose from a variety of graphic organizers to plan and develop your project.

 ## Partner Talk

Before you start drafting, discuss your plan for your interview with a partner and ask for feedback. Use specific details to describe and explain your ideas. Increase the specificity of your details based on the type of information you are delivering.

Writing for Assessment

Many standardized tests include a prompt that asks you to write an essay about your personal experience. Use the prompts here to practice. Respond using the characteristics of a memoir. (See page 66.)

 Try It! Read the **narrative nonfiction** prompt and the information on format and academic vocabulary. Use the ABCDs of On-Demand Writing to help you plan and write your essay.

Format

The prompt directs you to write a *nonfiction narrative*. Be sure to include a beginning that introduces your main idea, a middle with a well-developed conflict, and an end that presents a resolution.

Narrative Nonfiction Prompt

Helping younger children is a rite of passage for teenagers that involves taking on adult responsibilities and setting an example. Write a nonfiction narrative about a time you helped someone younger, telling about a conflict that arose during the time and its resolution.

Academic Vocabulary

Remember that a *conflict* is a struggle between people or forces, and a *resolution* is the struggle's outcome.

The ABCDs of On-Demand Writing

Use the following ABCDs to help you respond to the prompt.

Before you write your draft:

Attack the prompt [1 MINUTE]

- Circle or highlight important words in the prompt. Draw a line from each word to what it refers to.
- Rewrite the prompt in your own words.

Brainstorm possible answers [4 MINUTES]

- Create a graphic organizer to generate ideas.
- Use one for each part of the prompt if necessary.

Choose the order of your response [1 MINUTE]

- Think about the best way to organize your ideas.
- Number your ideas in the order you will write about them. Cross out ideas you will not be using.

After you write your draft:

Detect errors before turning in the draft [1 MINUTE]

- Carefully reread your writing.
- Make sure that your response makes sense and is complete.
- Look for spelling, punctuation, and grammar errors.

 More Prompts for Practice

Apply It! Respond to Prompts 1 and 2 in timed or open-ended situations by writing **nonfiction narratives** that present an engaging story. As you write, be sure to:

- Identify an appropriate audience for your intended **purpose**
- Use a plot map to organize your ideas and develop a clear **theme**
- Give your narrative a well-developed **conflict** and **resolution**
- Avoid stereotypes and portray your real-life **characters** as complex people.
- Include a range of **literary strategies and devices,** such as suspense and dialogue, to enhance the plot
- Include **sensory details** that define the mood or tone
- Use appropriate **rhetorical devices,** such as metaphors, to keep the essay interesting and to convey meaning
- Include **transitions** to connect ideas

Prompt 1 What are your hopes for the future? Write a nonfiction narrative in which you tell what you've done so far to lay the groundwork for attaining these goals.

Prompt 2 Everyone encounters problems in life. Think of a problem that you have faced, and write a nonfiction narrative about how you handled the situation and what you learned from the experience.

More Strategies for Writing for Assessment

- Consider several possible topics and quickly list details that you might use in your response. Then, choose the topic for which you have the strongest ideas.
- If you do not understand any words in the prompt, use context clues to help you determine the meaning of any unfamiliar words.
- Be sure to follow the ABCDs of writing to a prompt. Planning is an important part of writing. Don't just start writing right away.
- Make sure to reread your piece after you have completed it. This will give you a chance to find and correct errors. If you are in a timed situation, be sure to leave enough time for this step.

WRITING COACH

Online

www.phwritingcoach.com

Interactive Writing Coach™

Plan your response to the prompt. If you are using the prompt for practice, write one paragraph at a time or your entire draft and then submit it for feedback. If you are using the prompt as a timed test, write your entire draft and then submit it for feedback.

Remember **ABCD**

Attack the prompt

Brainstorm possible answers

Choose the order of your response

Detect errors before turning in the draft

CHAPTER 6

FICTION NARRATION

What's the Story?

What story does this photograph tell? What more do you want to know about what is happening in the photograph? Could you make up a story of events that led up to this moment?

When people can relate to what is happening in the story, they are more likely to be interested in hearing the story. The key to telling a good story is to tell one that has believable setting and characters.

Try It! Think about the events that may have led up to this moment in this person's life. Make a list of the events. Consider these questions as you participate in an extended discussion with a partner. Take turns expressing your ideas and feelings.

- What struggles did this person have to get here?
- Did he have to work hard or not to get here?
- How do you think he feels about this moment?

Review your list. Use your list to tell a story about the events that led this person to this moment. Be sure to use many details to make your story believable.

What's Ahead

In this chapter, you will review two strong examples of a short story: a Mentor Text and a Student Model. Then, using the examples as guidance, you will write a short story of your own.

WRITING COACH

Online

www.phwritingcoach.com

 **Online Journal**

Try It! Record your answers and ideas in the online journal.

You can also record and save your answers and ideas on pop-up sticky notes in the eText.

 ## Connect to the Big Questions

Discuss these questions with a partner:

1 **What do you think?** How do our own stories shape us?

2 **Why Write?** What can fiction do better than nonfiction?

SHORT STORY

A short story is a brief work of fiction that presents characters and develops and resolves a single problem. In this chapter, you will explore a type of short story writing known as realistic fiction. While fictional stories tell about events that have not actually occurred, realistic fiction should seem like something that could happen in real life. The characters and settings need to be based in reality, unlike other forms of short stories, such as science fiction or fantasy.

You will develop the realistic fiction story by taking it through each of the steps of the writing process: prewriting, drafting, revising, editing, and publishing. You will also have an opportunity to write a realistic movie scene. To preview the criteria for how your realistic fiction will be evaluated, see the rubric on page 111.

FEATURE ASSIGNMENT

Short Story: Realistic Fiction

An effective short story has these characteristics:

- An **engaging** story with a well-developed **conflict,** or central problem, that reaches a **well-developed resolution**

- A clear **theme,** or central idea

- Complex and non-stereotypical **characters**

- A range of **literary strategies** and **devices,** such as dialogue and suspense, that enhance the **plot** and help to develop the characters' personalities

- **Sensory details** that involve one or more of the five senses of sight, touch, taste, sound, and smell **that define the mood** and **tone** of the story

- Effective **pacing,** or speed at which events happen in the story

- **Effective sentence structure** and correct spelling, grammar, and usage

A realistic fiction story also includes:

- Situations that could happen in real life

- Believable, current settings for the story that include time and place

Other Forms of Short Stories

In addition to realistic fiction, there are other forms of short stories, including:

Fantasy stories allow the writer to create imaginative worlds and characters. For example, the fantasy world may be home to non-human creatures, such as elves or fairies, or characters may have superhuman powers.

Historical fiction may be set during a real event in history or may involve real historic figures, but the plot and central characters are fictional.

Mystery stories focus on strange or unexplained occurrences. These stories are suspenseful. At least one of the main characters may be trying to unravel the mystery.

Myths and legends are stories meant to explain how the world works or to teach moral lessons. These stories often include gods or heroic humans whose deeds inspire others.

Science fiction stories focus on science and technology. Readers can visit other planets, co-exist with robots, travel backward in time, or experience life in the future.

Tall tales take place in realistic settings but revolve around a larger-than-life character. The stories show how the character can overcome obstacles using methods not available to ordinary humans.

Try It! For each audience and purpose described, choose a form, such as a tall tale, historical fiction story, or mystery story, that is appropriate for conveying your intended meaning to the audience. Explain your choices.

- To show what life might be like on Mars
- To discover the mastermind behind a series of unusual crimes
- To explain why Earth has seasons

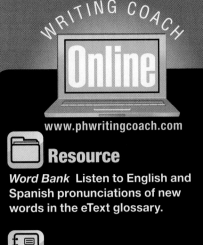

WRITING COACH

Online

www.phwritingcoach.com

Resource

Word Bank Listen to English and Spanish pronunciations of new words in the eText glossary.

Online Journal

Try It! Record your answers and ideas in the online journal.

WORD BANK

People often use these vocabulary words when they talk about short story writing. Work with a partner. Take turns saying each word aloud. Then write one sentence using each word. If you are unsure of the meaning of a word, use the Glossary or a dictionary to check the definition.

characterization	mood
develop	theme
dialogue	tone

MENTOR TEXT

Realistic Fiction

Learn From Experience

 Read the story on pages 94–97. As you read, take notes to develop your understanding of basic sight and English vocabulary. Then, read the numbered notes in the margins to learn how the author presented his ideas.

Answer the *Try It!* questions online or in your notebook.

---

❶ Sensory details define the **mood** of the story.

Try It! How would you describe the mood, or feeling, that the details convey? Which details convey this mood?

❷ The central **conflict** is introduced in a letter that the Captain has received.

Try It! Why does the letter cause conflict for the Captain?

❸ Descriptions reveal more information about the Captain, making him a more **complex character.**

Try It! What kind of person is the Captain? Briefly describe him.

❹ Details help clarify the **setting** of the story.

Try It! Where is the action taking place? During what historical period do you think the story takes place? Why? As you read look for details that reveal information about the cultural context of the time period.

October and June

by O. Henry

❶ The Captain gazed gloomily at his sword that hung upon the wall. In the closet near by was stored his faded uniform, stained and worn by weather and service. What a long, long time it seemed since those old days of war's alarms!

5 And now, veteran that he was of his country's strenuous times, he had been reduced to abject surrender by a woman's soft eyes and smiling lips. As he sat in his quiet room he held in his hand the letter he had just received from her—the letter that had caused him to wear that look of gloom. He re-read the fatal

10 paragraph that had destroyed his hope.

❷ In declining the honour you have done me in asking me to be your wife, I feel that I ought to speak frankly. The reason I have for so doing is the great difference between our ages. I like you very, very much, but I am

15 sure that our marriage would not be a happy one. I am sorry to have to refer to this, but I believe that you will appreciate my honesty in giving you the true reason.

The Captain sighed, and leaned his head upon his hand. Yes, there were many years between their ages. **❸** But he was strong

20 and rugged, he had position and wealth. Would not his love, his tender care, and the advantages he could bestow upon her make her forget the question of age? Besides, he was almost sure that she cared for him.

The Captain was a man of prompt action. In the field he had

25 been distinguished for his decisiveness and energy. He would see her and plead his cause again in person. Age!—what was it to come between him and the one he loved?

In two hours he stood ready, in light marching order, for his greatest battle. **❹** He took the train for the old Southern town in

30 Tennessee where she lived.

Theodora Deming was on the steps of the handsome, porticoed old mansion, enjoying the summer twilight, when the Captain entered the gate and came up the gravelled walk. She met him with a smile that was free from embarrassment. As the

35 Captain stood on the step below her, the difference in their ages

5 The author creates **suspense** by revealing Theodora's thoughts about the Captain.

Try It! What do Theodora's thoughts tell you about her feelings for the Captain?

did not appear so great. He was tall and straight and clear-eyed and browned. She was in the bloom of lovely womanhood.

"I wasn't expecting you," said Theodora; "but now that you've come you may sit on the step. Didn't you get my letter?"

40 "I did," said the Captain; "and that's why I came. I say, now, Theo, reconsider your answer, won't you?"

5 Theodora smiled softly upon him. He carried his years well. She was really fond of his strength, his wholesome looks, his manliness —perhaps, if—

45 "No, no," she said, shaking her head, positively; "it's out of the question. I like you a whole lot, but marrying won't do. My age and yours are—but don't make me say it again—I told you in my letter."

6 **Dialogue** brings the conflict to a head as Theodora voices her final decision.

Try It! What are Theodora's reasons for refusing to marry the Captain?

The Captain flushed a little through the bronze on his face. He was silent for a while, gazing sadly into the twilight. Beyond a line of woods that he could see was a field where the boys in blue had once bivouacked on their march toward the sea. How long ago it seemed now! Truly, Fate and Father Time had tricked him sorely. Just a few years interposed between himself and happiness!

Theodora's hand crept down and rested in the clasp of his firm, brown one. She felt, at least, that sentiment that is akin to love.

6 "Don't take it so hard, please," she said, gently. "It's all for the best. I've reasoned it out very wisely all by myself. Some day you'll be glad I didn't marry you. It would be very nice and lovely for a while—but, just think! In only a few short years what different tastes we would have! One of us would want to sit by the fireside and read, and maybe nurse neuralgia or rheumatism of evenings, while the other would be crazy for balls and theatres and late suppers. No, my dear friend. While it isn't exactly January and May, it's a clear case of October and pretty early in June."

"I'd always do what you wanted me to do, Theo. If you wanted to—"

70   "No, you wouldn't. You think now that you would, but you wouldn't. Please don't ask me any more."

    The Captain had lost his battle. But he was a gallant warrior, and when he rose to make his final adieu his mouth was grimly set and his shoulders were squared.

75   He took the train for the North that night. On the next evening he was back in his room, where his sword was hanging against the wall. He was dressing for dinner, tying his white tie into a very careful bow. And at the same time he was indulging in a pensive soliloquy.

80   "Pon my honour, I believe Theo was right, after all. Nobody can deny that she's a peach, but she must be twenty-eight, at the very kindest calculation."

    ❽ For you see, the Captain was only nineteen, and his sword had never been drawn except on the parade ground at

85 Chattanooga, which was as near as he ever got to the Spanish-American War.

❽ The **surprise ending** makes the story **engaging**.

Try It! What movies with engaging surprise endings have you seen? How might the tradition of surprise endings in literature have influenced these movies?

STUDENT MODEL

Realistic Fiction

With a small group, take turns reading this Student Model aloud. As you read, analyze, infer, and draw conclusions about the situation and characters in the story. Identify aspects of the story that make it seem realistic.

 ## Use a Reader's Eye

Now, reread the Student Model. On your copy of the Student Model, use the Reader's Response Symbols to react to what you read.

Reader's Response Symbols

+ **This is a good description.**

! **This is really cool/weird/interesting.**

— **This isn't clear to me.**

? **What will happen next?**

Participate in an extended discussion with a partner. Express your opinions and share your responses to the Student Model. Discuss the parts of the story that felt the most realistic.

The Acceptance Letter

by Kelly McMahon

Stacy looked at the text message from her best friend, Cassie. Cassie had gotten her acceptance letter from the university they had been planning to attend together since eighth grade. The phone beeped. Another message from
5 Cassie: this one asked if Stacy had received her letter yet.

She lied and typed back, "Not yet. I'm sure it will be fine." Stacy nervously wrung her hands so hard that they soon turned bright red and very hot.

Actually, the letter was sitting beside her on the porch
10 swing. It was a small envelope. She had known it was bad news without even opening it. Her mother, however, had insisted she open it and had remained hopeful until Stacy read the first line aloud: "We regret to inform you . . ."

She sighed loudly. All her future plans seemed to have
15 vanished like props in a magician's act.

"Hon, are you okay?" her mother asked, peeking around the screen door.

"I'm fine," she lied again. This was becoming an unusual habit; she'd been raised not to lie and to always tell the
20 truth. Now she was lying to her best friend and her mother.

"Just because you didn't get into that school doesn't mean your future is over," her mother said. She stepped out onto the porch and sat beside Stacy on the swing.

"Yeah, I know. But Cassie got in," she said softly, her
25 voice little more than a whisper.

"What did she say when you told her you didn't get in?"

"I didn't tell her. She was so happy."

Her mom patted her gently on the knee and stood up again.

30 "Come inside. Dinner is almost ready, and it's your night to set the table."

Stacy nodded her head.

1

After dinner, Stacy decided to call Cassie. It was time to tell her the truth.

35 "Did you get your acceptance letter?" Cassie asked immediately.

"No," Stacy said.

"Maybe it will come tomorrow."

"No, I got a letter today. It just wasn't an acceptance
40 letter."

"They didn't accept you?" Cassie asked, shocked.

"Nope. There goes our dream of going to school together," Stacy said.

"Just because we don't go to college together doesn't
45 mean we can't still be friends after graduation, you know. There's a really good community college near the university. Maybe you could go there for a while and we can still share an apartment. We'll make it work!" Cassie said.

Stacy hadn't thought about community college, but now
50 it was a good possibility. And if she could still be where Cassie was…. Stacy sat up straighter on the porch swing, feeling as if a huge weight had been lifted off her shoulders.

"You know," Stacy said to Cassie, "that just might work! I'll go talk to Mom about it!" She hit the "end" button on her
55 cell phone, and walked into the house, grinning.

2

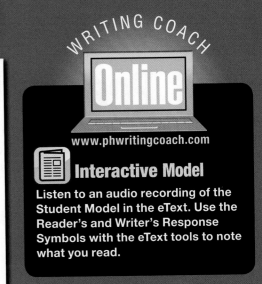

WRITING COACH

Online

www.phwritingcoach.com

 Interactive Model

Listen to an audio recording of the Student Model in the eText. Use the Reader's and Writer's Response Symbols with the eText tools to note what you read.

Use a Writer's Eye

Now evaluate the piece as a writer. On your copy of the Student Model, use the Writer's Response Symbols to react to what you read. Identify places where the student writer uses characteristics of an effective realistic fiction story.

Writer's Response Symbols	
R.D.	**Realistic and believable dialogue**
S.D.	**Vivid sensory details that create imagery and suggest mood**
W.C.	**Well-developed, interesting characters**
E.S.	**Engaging story**

Prewriting

Plan a first draft of your realistic fiction story by **determining an appropriate topic.** You can select from the Topic Bank or come up with an idea of your own.

Choose From the Topic Bank

TOPIC BANK

Lost! Think about how a person who is lost might feel. What kind of emotions would that person have? What would that person do to survive or to signal to rescuers, if possible? Write a realistic short story about a character or characters who are lost somewhere—in a city, at sea, in the wilderness, or a different place you can describe well.

May I Take Your Order? Teens today have many different kinds of jobs. Write a realistic short story about a teen character's first day at a new job. Your story can be funny or serious.

Oops! We all make mistakes; but some mistakes end up being pretty funny! Write a realistic short story about a character who makes a humorous mistake, show how it affects that person and how it is fixed.

Choose Your Own Topic

Determine an appropriate topic on your own using the following **range of strategies** to generate ideas.

Think and Discuss

- Think about things you or people you know have experienced. Draw up a list and consider if any of these experiences would make good stories.

- Jot down ideas based on the personalities of some people you know. Consider if any of them would make good traits for a character.

- Discuss with friends or other peers some of the situations affecting people in your age group. Consider if any of these situations would be the makings for a good short story.

Review your responses and choose a topic.

Narrow Your Topic

When your topic is too broad, you may have trouble creating a plot that is clear and easy for readers to follow.

Apply It! Use a graphic organizer like the one shown to narrow your topic.

- Write the main topic or general situation in the top box.
- Use the other boxes to narrow down your topic further.
- Your last box should hold your narrowest or "smallest" topic.

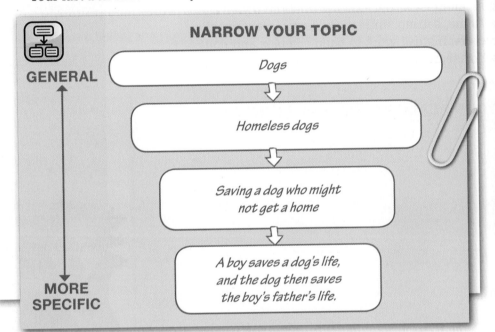

NARROW YOUR TOPIC

GENERAL

Dogs

↓

Homeless dogs

↓

Saving a dog who might not get a home

↓

A boy saves a dog's life, and the dog then saves the boy's father's life.

MORE SPECIFIC

WRITING COACH

Online

www.phwritingcoach.com

Interactive Graphic Organizers

Use the interactive graphic organizers to help you narrow your topic.

Online Journal

Try It! Record your answers and ideas in the online journal.

 ## Consider Multiple Audiences and Purposes

Before writing, think about your audiences and purposes. Consider the views of others as you ask yourself these questions.

Questions for Audience	Questions for Purpose
• Who is my audience? • What types of situations will they find familiar? • What types of characters will they be able to relate to the most?	• What theme or message will best serve the purpose of my story? • How will I create a well-developed conflict and resolution to keep my audience interested in the plot? • What techniques can I use to serve my purpose?

Record your answers in your writing journal.

Plan Your Piece

You will use a graphic organizer like the one shown to plan the plot of and identify details for your engaging short story. When it is complete, you will be ready to write your first draft.

Organize Your Realistic Fiction Use a graphic organizer to **structure** your ideas in a sustained way. Your plot should follow chronological, or time, order and contain a well-developed **conflict** and **resolution**.

Develop Important Story Elements Be sure to explain, with specifics and in detail, your general plot points, including the conflict, rising action, climax, falling action, and resolution. Add information to your plot map to create a clear **theme**, setting, and mood. As you plan, avoid creating predictable **characters**. Instead work to build complex and non-stereotypical characters who seem real.

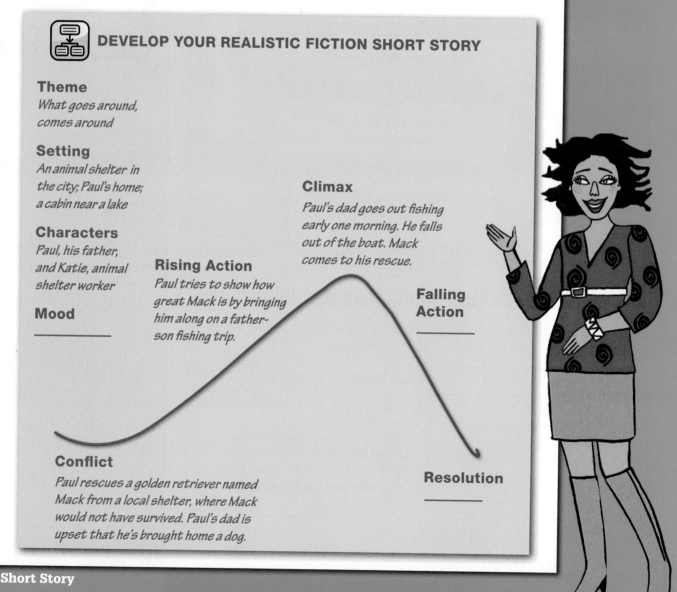

DEVELOP YOUR REALISTIC FICTION SHORT STORY

Theme
What goes around, comes around

Setting
An animal shelter in the city; Paul's home; a cabin near a lake

Characters
Paul, his father, and Katie, animal shelter worker

Mood
_____

Rising Action
Paul tries to show how great Mack is by bringing him along on a father-son fishing trip.

Climax
Paul's dad goes out fishing early one morning. He falls out of the boat. Mack comes to his rescue.

Falling Action
_____

Conflict
Paul rescues a golden retriever named Mack from a local shelter, where Mack would not have survived. Paul's dad is upset that he's brought home a dog.

Resolution
_____

Gather Details

To make their realistic fiction stories interesting and appealing, writers use many kinds of story elements. Look at these examples of literary devices and story elements:

- **Complex Characters:** *Paul knew his dad would be upset, but there was no way he could sit back and let that beautiful dog die. He had to rescue Mack and bring him home.*

- **A Central Conflict:** *Paul's father stood there, looking at him, with arms crossed and in stony silence; he wanted the dog to go back to the shelter immediately.*

- **Dialogue:** *"He's a great dog, Dad," Paul said. "He just needs some training. I can work with him!"*

- **Sensory Details:** *Mack's sharp, loud bark rang out like a gunshot in the still morning air.*

Try It! Read the Student Model excerpt and identify which elements the writer chose to use to create an effective story.

STUDENT MODEL from **The Acceptance Letter**
page 98; lines 24–27

"Yeah, I know. But Cassie got in," she said softly, her voice little more than a whisper.

"What did she say when you told her you didn't get in?"

"I didn't tell her. She was so happy."

 Apply It! Review the literary devices and elements that good writers use as they generate ideas and create realistic fiction.

- Identify details you can use in your story to establish the setting and create the **mood** or feeling your writing conveys. Remember that **sensory details**—details that appeal to the reader's senses of sight, smell, taste, touch, and hearing—are the most vivid.

- Decide which **literary strategies and devices** you can use to enhance your story's plot.

- Add these details and devices to your plot map.

WRITING COACH

Online

www.phwritingcoach.com

Interactive Graphic Organizers

Use the interactive graphic organizers to help you create a plan for your writing.

Interactive Model

Refer back to the Interactive Model in the eText as you plan your writing.

Drafting

During the drafting stage of an open-ended writing situation, you will start to write your ideas for your realistic fiction story. You will follow an outline that provides an organizational strategy that will help you structure your ideas in a sustained way to write a focused and organized realistic fiction story.

The Organization of a Short Story

The chart shows an organizational strategy for an engaging short story. Look back at how the Mentor Text follows this organizational strategy. Then, use this chart to help you outline your draft.

Outline for Success

I. Beginning

See Mentor Text, p. 94.

- Setting
- Introduction to characters
- Mood
- Introduce conflict and theme

Set the Scene

- The setting, main characters, and mood are established in the beginning through the use of word choice and sensory details.
- The conflict, or problem, is identified, and the theme, or the main idea of the story, may be suggested.

II. Middle

See Mentor Text, pp. 95–96.

- Well-paced plot
- Rise in action to develop the conflict
- Literary strategies and devices
- More sensory details

Build the Story

- A balance between action and dialogue will keep readers interested in the story.
- Further details and a logical rise in action create a well-developed conflict and show how the characters are affected by it.
- Literary strategies and devices, such as dialogue and suspense, move the plot forward.
- Further sensory details clearly define the mood and theme of the story.

III. End

See Mentor Text, p. 97.

- Resolution
- Effects of resolution on character

Reach a Resolution

- The resolution, or end to the conflict, must be believable and clear.
- A strong end explains what happens to characters after the resolution: Do things change for the better or worse? Are there unexpected consequences? What have characters and readers learned?

Start Your Draft

To complete your draft, follow each step in the process. Use the graphic organizer that shows your plot outline and details, and the *Outline for Success* as guides.

While drafting, aim at writing your ideas, not on making your writing perfect. Remember, you will have the chance to improve your draft when you revise and edit.

√ Draft the **beginning** of your story by introducing the setting and characters. Use **sensory details** to describe the mood.

√ Introduce the **theme** and **conflict,** but don't go into too much detail yet.

√ In the **middle,** develop conflict and theme by using **literary strategies and devices** to enhance the plot and bring characters closer to resolving their problem.

√ Make your **characters** complex and non-stereotypical; readers are interested in characters they can understand and relate to.

√ Continue to develop the characters through dialogue and actions. Let readers see their **motivations** and reactions to situations.

√ As you draft, include more **sensory details** to further establish the mood, or the feeling the reader gets from the story, and the tone, the way the writer feels about the topic.

√ Pay attention to the way you use language in your story. Include **rhetorical devices** to convey meaning to your audience. Rhetorical devices such as rhetorical questions, analogies, and metaphors will keep your writing lively and interesting.

√ Bring the story to an **end** by having the characters resolve the problem in a way that makes sense with the rest of the plot. Make sure that your **resolution** is well developed.

√ Be sure to clearly show how the **events** of the story have affected your characters by showing what the characters have learned or how they have grown or changed as a result of the events.

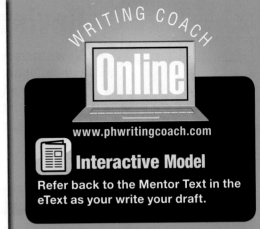

WRITING COACH

Online

www.phwritingcoach.com

Interactive Model

Refer back to the Mentor Text in the eText as your write your draft.

Revising: Making It Better

Now that you have finished your first draft, you are ready to revise. Think about the "big picture." You can use Revision RADaR as a guide for making changes to improve your draft. Revision RADaR provides four major ways to improve your writing: (R) replace, (A) add, (D) delete, and (R) reorder.

Kelly Gallagher, M. Ed.

KEEP REVISION ON YOUR RADaR

Read part of the first draft of the Student Model "The Acceptance Letter." Then look at questions the writer asked herself as she thought about how well her draft addressed issues of audience, purpose, and genre.

The Acceptance Letter

Cassie had gotten news about school. Stacy looked at the text message from her best friend. The phone beeped. Another message from Cassie: this one asked if Stacy had received her letter yet.

She typed back, "Not yet. I'm sure it will be fine."

Actually, the letter was sitting beside her on the porch swing. It was a small envelope. She had known it was bad news without even opening it. Her mother, however, had insisted she open it and had remained hopeful until Stacy read the first line aloud: "We regret to inform you . . ."

She sighed loudly.

"Stacey, what is the matter?" her mother asked, peeking around the screen door.

"Nothing is the matter, Mother. I am fine," she lied again. This was becoming an unusual habit; she'd been raised not to lie and to always tell the truth. Now she was lying to her best friend and her mother.

Does my opening introduce my theme and my conflict well? Have I used sensory details to set the mood for the story?

Have I used enough details to explain the conflict?

Does the dialogue sound realistic, like a real conversation?

Now look at how the writer applied Revision RADaR to write an improved second draft.

 ### The Acceptance Letter

Stacy looked at the text message from her best friend, Cassie. Cassie had gotten her acceptance letter from the university they had been planning to attend together since eighth grade. The phone beeped. Another message from Cassie: this one asked if Stacy had received her letter yet.

R **A** *Reordered the sentences and added further details to better establish both the conflict and the theme*

She lied and typed back, "Not yet. I'm sure it will be fine." Stacy nervously wrung her hands so hard that they soon turned bright red and very hot.

Actually, the letter was sitting beside her on the porch swing. It was a small envelope. She had known it was bad news without even opening it. Her mother, however, had insisted she open it and had remained hopeful until Stacy read the first line aloud: "We regret to inform you . . ."

A *Added sensory details to help set the mood for that moment in the story and to further develop Stacy's character*

She sighed loudly. All her future plans seemed to have vanished like props in a magician's act.

A *Added a rhetorical device—a simile, which compares two usually unrelated things—to clarify meaning and keep the writing interesting*

"Hon, are you okay?" her mother asked, peeking around the screen door.

"I'm fine," she lied again. This was becoming an unusual habit; she'd been raised not to lie and to always tell the truth. Now she was lying to her best friend and her mother.

R *Replaced unrealistic dialogue with more believable dialogue*

WRITING COACH

Online

www.phwritingcoach.com

Video

Learn more strategies for effective writing from program author Kelly Gallagher.

Apply It! Now, revise your draft to **clarify your meaning** to your audience and keep them fully engaged in the story.

- First, determine if you have engaged your audience, made the theme clear, and included a well-developed conflict and resolution.
- Then, apply your Revision RADaR to make needed changes in your story. Remember—you can use the steps in the strategy in any order.

Look at the Big Picture

Use the chart and your analytical skills to evaluate how well each section of your realistic fiction story addresses purpose, audience, and genre. When necessary, use the suggestions in the chart to revise your piece.

Section	Evaluate	Revise
Beginning	• Make sure you have introduced the main character(s) and the **conflict.**	• Use specific details and strong verbs to describe and clarify the problem that is bothering the main character.
	• Make sure your **theme** is clear.	• Ask yourself this question: Is the "big idea," or the most important idea I want my audience to learn, clearly set up? If not, revise as necessary.
Middle	• Check that the action is well paced, the conflict is well developed, and that the **plot** is logically organized.	• Reorder words, sentences, and paragraphs if necessary to make sure that the plot and conflict are clear. Add transitions wherever necessary to improve pacing and to connect ideas.
	• Make sure **literary strategies and devices,** such as dialogue, help you to create complex and non-stereotypical characters and to enhance the plot.	• Read dialogue aloud to make sure it sounds realistic and to make sure it accurately represents what your characters are thinking. Add other literary devices, such as suspense and foreshadowing, to improve the plot.
	• Make sure you can identify the **mood and tone** of the story.	• Add sensory details—those that affect sight, sound, touch, taste, and smell—to properly define the feelings you want to convey.
End	• Check your **resolution.** Is it well developed? Are all the loose ends of the story tied up?	• Reinforce the end of your story by answering questions such as: What happened then? How did the characters feel? What did they do after the problem was solved?
	• Make sure you clearly described the **results** of the main character's actions.	• Strengthen your theme by explaining how the resolution affected the character, and what lesson he or she might have learned from it.

Focus on Craft: Repetition

A **scheme** is a way that writers place emphasis or significance on a word or phrase. Authors sometimes use schemes such as **repetition**, or the repeating of words, phrases, or ideas, to emphasize certain elements in the story. When words and ideas are repeated, the reader appreciates that they are important and will pay more attention to these details.

Think about the use of repetition as you read these sentences from the Student Model.

 **STUDENT MODEL** | from **The Acceptance Letter**
page 98; lines 18–20

> "I'm fine," she lied again. This was becoming an unusual habit; she'd been raised not to lie and to always tell the truth. Now she was lying to her best friend and her mother.

 Try It! Now, ask yourself these questions:

- What word and idea from earlier in the Student Model are being repeated in the sample sentences?
- Why does the author repeat this idea and word?

Fine-Tune Your Draft

Apply It! Use the revision suggestions to prepare your final draft after rethinking how well questions of purpose, audience, and genre have been addressed.

- **Employ Schemes** Revise your draft to clarify meaning by rearranging words, sentences, and paragraphs to employ schemes, such as repetition.

- **Use Transitions** Transitions such as *next, as a result, finally,* and *on the other hand,* connect ideas between sentences and paragraphs. Be sure to add transitional words and phrases to your draft to connect ideas and convey meaning.

Peer Feedback Read your final draft to a group of peers. Ask if you have created an engaging story line. Mark any places in the text that the group tells you are strong or those that need more development. Think about their responses and revise your final draft as needed.

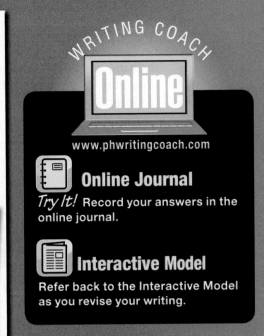

WRITING COACH

Online

www.phwritingcoach.com

Online Journal
Try It! Record your answers in the online journal.

Interactive Model
Refer back to the Interactive Model as you revise your writing.

Editing: Making It Right

Editing your draft means polishing your work and correcting errors. You may want to read through your work several times, looking for different errors and issues each time.

Before editing your final draft, consider using a **variety of sentence structures,** including **compound, complex, and compound-complex** sentences, and consistent **verb tenses** to establish setting and advance the plot. Then edit your final draft for any errors in **grammar, mechanics, and spelling.** Use a dictionary or other resource to check your spelling.

WRITE GUY *Jeff Anderson, M. Ed.*

WHAT DO YOU NOTICE?

Zoom in on Conventions Focus on verb tenses as you zoom in on this passage from the Student Model.

 **STUDENT MODEL** from **The Acceptance Letter**
page 98; lines 18–20

> "I'm fine," she lied again. This was becoming an unusual habit; she'd been raised not to lie and to always tell the truth.

> To learn more about verb tenses, see Chapter 17 of your Grammar Handbook.

Now, ask yourself: *Why are there different verb tenses in these sentences?*

Perhaps you said that the different verb tenses help show what has already happened and what is now happening in the narrative.

As in many narratives, the main action here is told in the **past tense,** with dialogue in the **present tense.** Stacy speaks to her mother in present tense: *I am (I'm).* However, the words describing what Stacy does are in past tense: *she lied.*

In this story, much of the conflict revolves around plans and expectations that have been ongoing for years. The author describes those plans and expectations using the **past perfect tense:** *she had (she'd) been.* Perfect tenses are formed by adding a form of the word *have* before the past participle of the main verb.

Verb tenses help establish consistency in a narrative by advancing the plot and letting readers know the sequence of events. Verb tenses may not always be consistent between sentences, but they should usually be consistent within sentences.

Partner Talk Discuss this question with a partner: *Why might a short story writer use different verb tenses?*

To learn more, see Chapter 17.

Grammar Mini-Lesson: Consistent Tenses

Narratives typically use a variety of verb tenses. For example, setting up dialogue and expressing a sequence of events usually require the use of different verb tenses. However, consistent use of verb tenses can help readers follow a plot through **compound, complex, and compound–complex sentence structures.** Notice how the Mentor Text author uses consistent verb tenses in a complex sentence.

 **MENTOR TEXT** from **October and June**
page 97; lines 75–77

On the next evening, he was back in his room, where his sword was hanging against the wall.

Try It! Notice whether each sentence is compound, complex, or compound-complex. Then rewrite each sentence to make the verb tenses consistent. Write the answers in your journal.

1. Arturo will write the letter, and Jan sends it. (compound)

2. After Lucy received the letter, she calls her friend, but her friend was not at home. (compound-complex)

3. The letter had included news that Lucy already knows. (complex)

Apply It! Edit your draft for **grammar, mechanics, capitalization, and spelling.** If necessary, rewrite sentences for consistent verb tense and to show a variety of correctly structured **compound, complex, and compound-complex sentences.**

 WRITING COACH
Online
www.phwritingcoach.com

 Video
Learn effective editing techniques from program author Jeff Anderson.

Online Journal
Try It! Record your answers in the online journal.

 Interactive Model
Refer back to the Interactive Model as you edit your writing.

Use the rubric to evaluate your piece. If necessary, rethink, rewrite, or revise.

Rubric for Short Story: Realistic Fiction	Rating Scale
Ideas: How well do you narrate a story with a clear characters and plot?	Not very Very 1 2 3 4 5 6
Organization: How clearly organized is the sequence of events?	1 2 3 4 5 6
Voice: How authentic and engaging is your voice?	1 2 3 4 5 6
Word Choice: How effective is your word choice in creating tone and style?	1 2 3 4 5 6
Sentence Fluency: How well have you used transitions to show connections among ideas?	1 2 3 4 5 6
Conventions: How consistent and correct are your verb tenses in a variety of sentence structures?	1 2 3 4 5 6

Publishing

Now you can share your realistic fiction with readers by publishing it. First, get your story ready for presentation. Then choose a way to **publish it for appropriate audiences.**

Wrap Up Your Presentation

Put the finishing touches on your story. Choose a readable font, with a type style that is simple and easy to read. Also be sure that the title of your story grabs the reader's attention and refers to your story's theme.

Publish Your Piece

Use this chart to identify a way to publish your written work.

If your audience is...	...then publish it by...
Students or adults at school	• Collecting classmates' short stories and publishing them together in a book. Add images to make the collection more appealing. • Posting your story on the school Web site and inviting responses
Younger children	• Turning your story into a play and having classmates play the roles of your characters • Reading the story to them at a local library

 ## Reflect on Your Writing

Once you are done with your realistic fiction story, read it over and use your writing journal to answer these questions. Use specific details to describe and explain your ideas. Increase the specificity of your details based on the type of information you are recording.

- Do you feel that you have created a realistic and exciting or otherwise interesting story? Explain. What can you focus on in future stories to make them better?

- How is knowing how to create a story plot a useful skill to have?

 The Big Question: Why Write? What can fiction do better than nonfiction?

Manage Your Portfolio You may wish to include your published realistic fiction story in your writing portfolio. If so, consider what this piece reveals about your writing and your growth as a writer.

MAKE YOUR WRITING COUNT

Explore the Real World in a Graphic Novel

Realistic fiction tells stories about life as it really is. Some of the most innovative realistic fiction can be found in graphic novels. Reveal your view of the world in a graphic novel based on a short piece of realistic fiction.

Work with a group to create a **graphic novel.** Study examples of the more realistic graphic novels in your local library, and analyze how graphics and text interact to tell a credible story. Create your graphic novel either with paper and ink or digitally, using illustration software.

Here's your action plan.

1. Choose roles, such as artist, writer, editor, and publisher.

2. Review graphic novels for format and style. Look online for tips on creating graphic novels. Then, review peers' short stories and choose one to adapt.

3. As a group, mark up the selected story for translation to graphic form. Decide how many panels to create and what images to show.

4. Work together to prepare the graphic novel. Each panel should include:

   - An illustration of the action
   - Dialogue for speech and thought bubbles
   - Narration below each panel

5. As a group, prepare to revise your work. First, generate a list of criteria to evaluate the draft. Then, revise the text and graphics.

6. Make copies of your final graphic novel to present to the class, or share it in an electronic slideshow.

Listening and Speaking With your group, discuss your production process. Think about what worked and what you would do differently in future productions. Share your insights as you present your final product to the class.

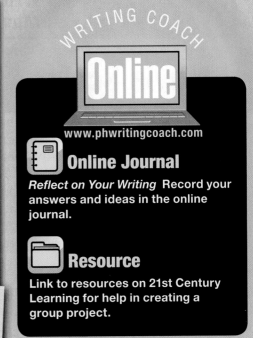

WRITING COACH

Online

www.phwritingcoach.com

Online Journal

Reflect on Your Writing Record your answers and ideas in the online journal.

Resource

Link to resources on 21st Century Learning for help in creating a group project.

**Writing for Media:
Movie Script**

Movie Script

Dramatic scenes are performed by actors in plays and movies. These scenes are meant to entertain or move audiences. Each scene is written in the form of a **movie script**, meaning each character's lines are listed along with the stage directions. These directions tell the actors how they should move or speak during the scene. Just like a short story, dramatic scenes have action, plot, dialogue, setting, and complex characters. They also convey a theme that is either directly or explicitly stated or just implicitly suggested through the actions of the plot.

Try It! Study the excerpt of a movie script that is based on one scene from the story described on page 102. Then answer these questions. Record your answers in your journal.

1. What is the **theme** of this script? Is it implicit or explicit? Explain.

2. What is the **conflict?** How do you think the conflict will be **resolved?**

3. Does Paul's **character** have depth and complexity, or is he stereotypical? Explain.

4. What are the **mood** and **tone** conveyed by this script?

5. How are the **speaking roles** of each actor identified?

6. Identify two examples of **stage directions** for movement. What kind of print indicates that the words are directions rather than dialogue?

7. Which information is an example of a direction that instructs the actor about the type of **emotion** he or she should show when speaking the line? Where could other similar directions be added to the script?

8. Identify two types of literary devices the author used to enhance the plot. Explain your choices.

The Lake

(Setting: A beautiful rural area with a cabin near a lake. A fishing boat is docked on the lake. Eighteen-year-old Paul and his father have just arrived for a fishing trip. Mack, a large golden retriever, jumps out of the car when Paul opens the door.)

DAD: *(surprised)* Wow, Paul! That dog is so energetic. I'm surprised he's made himself at home with us so quickly after coming home from the shelter.

PAUL: *(worried)* Me too, Dad. The shelter worker said that this was the last week he could stay there because he's been there so long. We were really lucky to find him! He's a great dog—he just needs a bit of training. I can work with him! Besides, you never know when we might need a dog around for help!

DAD: I just wonder how he'll behave when you go to college next month. He'll certainly miss you. Have you thought of that? *(Dad rubs his chest, as if he's in pain and then walks into the cabin.)*

PAUL: *(playfully petting Mack)* Mack, we'll figure something out! You're such a good boy!

DAD: *(walking back outside from the cabin)* Paul, please put the fishing gear in— *(Rubs his chest again.)*

PAUL: You okay, Dad?

DAD: *(lightly)* Yeah, I'm okay. I probably shouldn't be lifting all this heavy fishing gear. I am not feeling very well. Anyway, I want to go fishing early tomorrow, so please help me finish putting the gear in the boat.

(Mack races up to Dad and licks his hand.)

DAD: Hey, good boy! *(looks at Paul)* Paul, thanks for bringing this dog into the family!

Create a Movie Script

Follow these steps to create your own movie script. To plan your movie script, review the graphic organizers on pages R24–R27 and choose one that suits your needs.

Prewriting

- Decide on a theme to use in your story. How will you convey it— explicitly or implicitly?
- Identify and narrow a topic that will work well for a dramatic scene, such as a sporting event with lots of action, or an interpersonal conflict with lots of intense dialogue.
- Then, think about the people who will most likely enjoy your topic. What is their age group? What are their interests? Answering these questions will help identify your target audience.
- Brainstorm ideas for a conflict and resolution.
- Finally, invent a believable setting and complex, realistic characters for your scene.
- Then, outline the plot, writing notes for the beginning, middle, and end of your scene.
- List audio and visual elements you might want to address, such as sound effects, music, camera angles, and screen changes.

Drafting

- Make an outline to organize your plot elements, such as conflict and resolution and your dialogue. Consider ordering things in a way that is varied but still makes sense.

Revising and Editing

- Review your draft to make sure events are organized logically. Make sure the conflict, or problem, and the resolution are clear.
- Use Revision RADaR to improve your draft.
- Check that spelling, grammar, and mechanics are correct.

Publishing

- Read through your scene with classmates, and then rehearse the scene and perform it for the class.
- You may also want make a video recording of the performance.

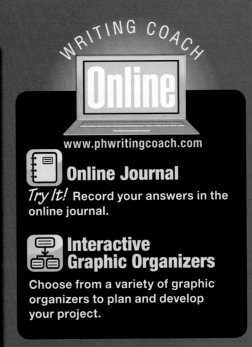

WRITING COACH

Online

www.phwritingcoach.com

Online Journal

Try It! Record your answers in the online journal.

Interactive Graphic Organizers

Choose from a variety of graphic organizers to plan and develop your project.

Partner Talk

Explain your ideas for your movie script to a partner. Ask your partner for feedback about your ideas, including ideas on how to make it more engaging for the audience. Monitor your partner's spoken language by asking follow-up questions to confirm your understanding.

Writing for Assessment

Now's your chance to demonstrate your creative writing ability. You can use the prompts on these pages to practice. Your responses should include the same characteristics as your realistic fiction story. Look back at page 92 to review these characteristics.

Try It! To begin, read the **short story** prompt and the information on format and academic vocabulary. Then, use the ABCDs of On-Demand Writing to help you plan and write your essay.

Format

The prompt directs you to write a *short story*. Start with a beginning that grabs readers' attention and introduces the theme and characters. Include a middle that develops an engaging story line with a well-developed conflict that leads to a resolution at the end.

Short Story Prompt

What might it be like to meet a famous person—an actor, a writer, or perhaps a sports star? Write a short story about a character your age who meets a famous person. Focus on creating a clear plot by using a range of literary strategies and devices to move the action along. Be sure to also use rhetorical devices to convey meaning.

Academic Vocabulary

Remember that a *literary device* is a technique or literary element, such as dialogue, suspense, and foreshadowing, that authors use to create an engaging plot. *Rhetorical devices,* such as rhetorical questions, analogies, and metaphors, enhance the text and help the reader connect to ideas in the story.

The ABCDs of On-Demand Writing

Use the following ABCDs to help you respond to the prompt.

Before you write your draft:

Attack the prompt [1 MINUTE]

- Circle or highlight important key phrases in the prompt. Draw a line from the key phrase to what it refers to.
- Rewrite the prompt in your own words.

Brainstorm possible answers [4 MINUTES]

- Create a graphic organizer to generate ideas.
- Use one for each part of the prompt if necessary.

Choose the order of your response [1 MINUTE]

- Think about the best way to organize your ideas.
- Number your ideas in the order you will write about them. Cross out ideas you will not be using.

After you write your draft:

Detect errors before turning in the draft [1 MINUTE]

- Carefully reread your writing.
- Look for spelling, punctuation, and grammar errors.
- Make sure that your response makes sense and is complete.

More Prompts for Practice

Apply It! Respond to Prompts 1 and 2 by writing engaging short stories that will appeal to your audience. As you write, be sure to:

- Establish a **theme** and a **conflict** that leads to a **resolution**
- Develop logical and well-paced action in a specific, believable **setting**
- Develop interesting and original **characters**
- Use **literary strategies and devices** to move the plot forward
- Include **sensory details** to set the mood or tone of the story
- Include **transitions** to connect ideas and **rhetorical devices** to keep your writing interesting

> **Prompt 1** Sports are often exciting and sometimes surprising. Write a short story in which a character takes part in an intense or somehow surprising sports event. Be sure to fully develop your character and the conflict.

> **Prompt 2** Sometimes life can be challenging, but people work hard to overcome challenges. Write a short story about a character who overcomes a personal obstacle. Be sure to develop a clear theme for the story.

Spiral Review: Narrative Respond to Prompt 3 by writing an **autobiographical narrative**. Make sure your narrative sets up an engaging story and reflects all of the characteristics described on page 66, including these elements:

- A well-developed **conflict** and **resolution** with a clear **theme**
- Complex and non-stereotypical **characters** who are real people
- A range of **literary strategies** and **devices** that enhance the plot
- **Sensory details** that define the **mood** or **tone** of your story

> **Prompt 3** We always remember the time when someone special came into our lives. Write an autobiographical narrative about the time you met someone who is a close friend today. Write your narrative in short story form, with dialogue and other devices to keep your writing interesting.

WRITING COACH

Online

www.phwritingcoach.com

👍 **Interactive Writing Coach**™

Plan your response to the prompt. If you are using the prompt for practice, write one paragraph at a time or your entire draft and then submit it for feedback. If you are using the prompt as a timed test, write your entire draft and then submit it for feedback.

Remember **ABCD**

Attack the prompt

Brainstorm possible answers

Choose the order of your response

Detect errors before turning in the draft

CHAPTER 7

POETRY *and* DESCRIPTION

What Do You See?

People see different things when they look at something. Some people may look at this photograph and see an airplane. Others might see excitement or freedom.

People use different words to describe what they see. Words can be a powerful way to capture experiences or feelings.

Try It! Take a few minutes to list what you see in the photograph. Remember, you might describe the actual image or you might describe how it makes you feel.

Consider these questions as you participate in an extended discussion with a partner. Take turns expressing your ideas and feelings.

- What do you actually see?
- What emotions does this photograph make you feel?
- What would you feel if you were flying this airplane?

Review the list you made. Use your list to describe to a partner what you see in this photograph. Think about how you would use these words to make a poem.

What's Ahead

In this chapter, you will review some strong examples of poems: Mentor Texts and Student Models. Then, using the examples as guidance, you will write a poem of your own.

x

POETRY AND DESCRIPTION

In this chapter, you will focus on writing a poem. Poetry is a concise form of writing that uses rhythm and sometimes rhyme to express a clear point of view. The organization of a poem depends on its specific form, such as a sonnet, a ballad, or free verse poem.

An important part of poetry—and other writing—is description. Sensory details, figurative language, and other poetic conventions contribute to imagery that helps readers picture what something looks like or imagine its aroma, sound, texture, or taste.

You will develop a poem by taking it through each of the steps of the writing process: prewriting, drafting, revising, editing, and publishing. You will also have an opportunity to use your descriptive writing skills to write a definition essay. To preview the criteria for how your poem will be evaluated, see the rubric on page 137.

FEATURE ASSIGNMENT

Poem

An effective poem has these characteristics:

- A clear **topic** or **theme**

- Careful attention to **word choice** and the **musical qualities** of language

- **Imagery** based on sensory language

- **Poetic traditions**, or organization and specific elements that reflect a specific poetic form, such as a sonnet or free verse poem

- **Poetic conventions,** or special poetic techniques, such as sound devices, sensory details, and figurative language

An English **sonnet** also includes:

- Usually, fourteen lines in four **stanzas**—three stanzas of four lines and one stanza of two

- A specific **meter** that includes a set rhythm and number of beats per line

- A **rhyme scheme** pattern of *abab cdcd efef gg*

A **free verse** poem also includes:

- Language meant to reflect the patterns of **natural speech**

- No specific rhyme pattern

- No specific meter

- No specific length

Other Forms of Poetry and Description

There are many forms of poetry and description, including:

Ballads are narrative poems and are meant to be sung. Ballads often contain repetition and have a simple, regular rhyme pattern and meter.

Descriptive essays use imagery and vivid details to help readers imagine the subject of the essay. Like all essays, they consist of an introduction, body, and conclusion. Descriptive forms include eyewitness accounts and travel writing.

Free verse is poetry that imitates the rhythms of everyday speech. Freed of set rhythm and rhyme patterns, free verse uses figurative language and sound devices to convey ideas and feelings.

Haiku are three-line poems that originated in Japan. Haiku consist of seventeen syllables divided into three lines of five, seven, and five syllables. Classic haiku are usually about nature.

Lyric poems express a speaker's feelings about a particular person, place, thing, or event. Unlike ballads, lyric poems do not tell a story. Sonnets and free verse poems are types of lyric poems.

Prose poems look like prose, or regular text you might find in a story or essay, but use poetic conventions to create a memorable description of a person, place, thing, or event.

Sonnets are 14-line poems written in a regular meter and pattern of rhyme. One kind of sonnet—the English sonnet—consists of three four-line stanzas and a final couplet, or two rhyming lines. In each stanza, alternating lines rhyme.

Try It! For each audience and purpose described, choose a form, such as a ballad or haiku, that is appropriate for conveying your intended meaning to the audience. Explain your choices.

- To share a travel experience with readers of a local newspaper
- To concisely describe for a teacher your impression of an upcoming storm
- To entertain your classmates with a song about a school event

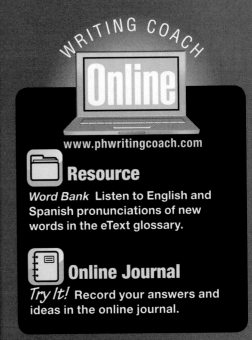

WRITING COACH

Online
www.phwritingcoach.com

Resource

Word Bank Listen to English and Spanish pronunciations of new words in the eText glossary.

Online Journal

Try It! Record your answers and ideas in the online journal.

People often use these basic and content-based vocabulary words when talking about poetry. Work with a partner. Take turns saying each word aloud. Then, write one sentence using each word. If you are unsure of the meaning of a word, use the Glossary or a dictionary to check the definition.

figurative	**sensory**
imagery	**stanza**
impression	**vivid**

MENTOR TEXT

Sonnets and Free Verse Poem

Learn From Experience

After reading the poems on pages 122–123, read the numbered notes in the margins to learn about how the poets presented their ideas.

Answer the *Try It!* questions online or in your notebook.

---

1 The sonnet has a strict **rhyme scheme,** or pattern.

Try It! Which words rhyme at the ends of lines 1–4? Which rhyme at the ends of lines 5–8? How does the change in the rhyme pattern beginning with line 5 help the reader to understand the poem?

2 The last two lines of the poem rhyme with each other, forming a **couplet** that concludes the poem.

Try It! In Shakespearean or English sonnets, the first twelve lines lead up to the last two lines. How do the last two lines sum up the theme of the poem? Put the theme in your own words.

3 Like Shakespeare, Moss uses **figurative language** to compare a woman to something else.

Try It! To what does Moss compare the woman in the first two lines? How is his comparison similar to that in the first two lines of Shakespeare's sonnet? How is it different?

Extension Find other examples of poems, and compare them with these poems.

In "Shall I Compare Thee to a Summer's Day?" Howard Moss puts a modern spin on William Shakespeare's classic sonnet—often to comic effect. Read and compare both sonnets. They say about the same thing, but in very different words and with very different tones.

Sonnet #18
by William Shakespeare

1 Shall I compare thee to a Summer's day?
Thou art more lovely and more temperate:
Rough winds do shake the darling buds of May,
And Summer's lease hath all too short a date:
5 Sometime too hot the eye of heaven shines,
And oft' is his gold complexion dimm'd;
And every fair from fair sometime declines,
By chance or nature's changing course untrimm'd:
But thy eternal Summer shall not fade
10 Nor lose possession of that fair thou owest;
Nor shall Death brag thou wanderest in his shade,
When in eternal lines to time thou growest:
2 So long as men can breathe, or eyes can see,
    So long lives this, and this gives life to thee.

Shall I Compare Thee to a Summer's Day?
by Howard Moss

3 Who says you're like one of the dog days?
You're nicer. And better.
Even in May, the weather can be gray,
And a summer sub-let doesn't last forever.
5 Sometimes the sun's too hot;
Sometimes it's not.
Who can stay young forever?
People break their necks or just drop dead!
But you? Never!
10 If there's just one condensed reader left
Who can figure out the abridged alphabet,
    After you're dead and gone,
    In this poem you'll live on!

WRITING COACH

Online

www.phwritingcoach.com

Interactive Model

Listen to an audio recording of the Mentor Text in the eText. You can refer back to the Mentor Text whenever you need support in developing your own writing.

Online Journal

Try It! Answer the questions about the Mentor Text in the online journal.

Trinity Place
by Phyllis McGinley

The pigeons that peck at the grain in Trinity
    Churchyard
    4 Are pompous as bankers. They walk with an air,
    5 they preen
Their prosperous feathers. They smugly regard
    their beauty
    They are plump, they are sleek. It is only the
    men who are lean.

5   The pigeons scan with disfavor the men who sit
    there,
    5 Listless in sun or shade. The pigeons sidle
Between the gravestones with shrewd, industrious
    motions.
    The pigeons are busy. It is only the men who are
    idle.

    5 The pigeons sharpen their beaks on stones, and
    they waddle
10   In dignified search of their proper, their daily
    bread.
Their eyes are small with contempt for the men on
    the benches.
    It is only the men who are hungry. The pigeons
    are fed.

4 The **simile,** or comparison, creates a vivid **image.**

Try It! What image of the pigeons does this simile create?

5 The poet uses **rhyme** to draw attention to the second and fourth lines in each stanza.

Try It! How does rhyme add to the musical qualities of the poem?

STUDENT MODEL

Sonnet and Free Verse Poems

With a small group, take turns reading these Student Models aloud. As you read, practice newly acquired vocabulary by correctly producing the word's sound. Also, think about the structure and elements of poetry. Review the Poet's Toolbox on page 129. Ask yourself how the poetic language informs and shapes your understanding of each poem.

 Use a Reader's Eye

Now, reread the Student Models. On your copies of the Student Models, use the Reader's Response Symbols to react to what you read.

Reader's Response Symbols

+ I can picture this.

– This image could be stronger.

? I wonder what this means.

! This is cool!

Express your ideas and feelings about the Student Models with a partner. How are your reactions similar? How do your feelings about the poems differ?

Winter's Approach

A Sonnet by Nancy Mundy

Leaves lose their lush green and briefly turn gold,
But spin to the ground in the first icy storm.
Frost is a blanket that spreads news of cold,
As birds of all feathers head South to get warm.

5 Some birds remain huddled, snug in their nests,
Chipmunks and squirrels fill their fat cheeks
    with seed.
Bears eat their fill and prepare for long rests,
And people wear woolens for warmth that they
    need.

Deer look for places to bed down in snow,
10 And icy engravings transform window panes.
On cold winter nights, the freezing winds blow.
Frogs hide in the mud and wait for spring rains.

When Spring fin'ly comes with its new budding
    blooms,
We'll all run out of our cold, lonely rooms.

Summer

A Free Verse Poem by Jeffrey Shu

Summer is freedom!
Mornings are warm now,
and the sun bakes our skin,
as sweat soaks our shirts.

5 Hooting and hollering,
we plunge into the cool lake,
soothing our sunburns,
tickling our toes.

Softball and picnics in the park
10 with family and friends;
smoky backyard barbeques,
long days at the beach.

In the late nights on the porch,
while we watch the stars,
15 the sweet spell of summer
seeps into our lives.

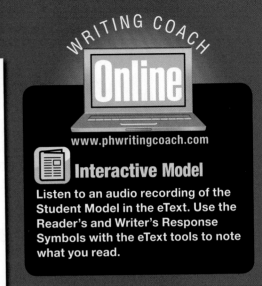

WRITING COACH

Online

www.phwritingcoach.com

Interactive Model

Listen to an audio recording of the Student Model in the eText. Use the Reader's and Writer's Response Symbols with the eText tools to note what you read.

 Use a Writer's Eye

Now, evaluate each poem as a writer. On your copies of the Student Models, use the Writer's Response Symbols to react to what you read. Identify places where the student writers use characteristics of an effective poem.

Writer's Response Symbols	
R.R.	**Rhythm or rhyme fits the poem's form**
S.D.	**Effective use of sound devices**
F.L.	**Figurative language conveys a mood**
I.D.	**Images and details appeal to the senses**

**Feature Assignment:
Sonnet or Free Verse Poem**

Prewriting

Plan a first draft of your poem **by determining an appropriate topic** and deciding on which form of poem you will write—a sonnet, free verse poem, or another form. Select a topic from the Topic Bank or come up with an idea of your own.

Choose From the Topic Bank

TOPIC BANK

A Place You Dislike Think of a place you dislike for any reason, such as the way it looks or makes you feel. Take notes on your impressions of the place. Use your notes to structure a poem about the place you have chosen.

Democracy Consider the concept of democracy and the images it conjures in your mind. Write a poem about democracy using sensory details, vivid images, and figurative language to express your ideas and impressions of democracy.

An Important Person Think about the people who have played major roles in your life. Choose one important person for the subject of a poem. Write a poem about the person and his or her importance in your life.

Choose Your Own Topic

Determine an appropriate topic on your own by using the following **range of strategies** to generate ideas.

Review and Reflect

- Review journals and photo albums to find important people, places, and ideas about which you might write.
- Reflect on important events in your life and identify the people involved.
- Reflect on concepts and ideals you find important and their effect on you.

Review your responses and choose a topic.

Narrow Your Topic

Narrow your topic to focus on specific details and images in order to write a carefully crafted poem.

Apply It! Use a graphic organizer to narrow your topic.

- Write your general topic in the top box and keep narrowing your topic as you move down the chart.
- Your last box should hold your narrowest or smallest topic.

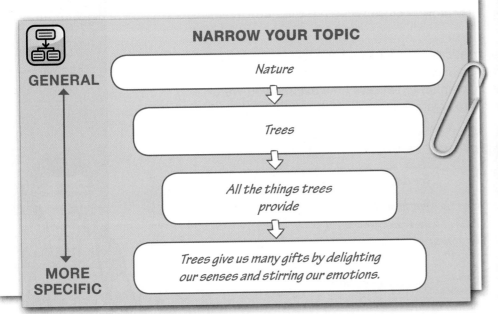

NARROW YOUR TOPIC

GENERAL

Nature

↓

Trees

↓

All the things trees provide

↓

Trees give us many gifts by delighting our senses and stirring our emotions.

MORE SPECIFIC

 # Consider Multiple Audiences and Purposes

Before writing, think about your audiences and purposes. Consider the ways others might view your topic as you ask yourself these questions.

Questions for Audience	Questions for Purpose
• Who will read my poem? • What will readers need to know to understand my poem's meaning? • What form of poetry will best convey my meaning to my audiences?	• What ideas, images, and feelings do I want to express in my poem? • How do I want to affect my readers? • What poetic conventions and traditions within different forms will help me achieve my purpose?

Record your answers in your writing journal.

Plan Your Piece

You will use a graphic organizer like the one shown to organize your poem and structure ideas in a sustained, or consistent, way. When it is complete, you will be ready to write your first draft.

Choose Your Topic and Form Decide on the topic of your poem and choose the best form for it. Will the structured nature of a sonnet fit your topic? Will free verse better reflect your ideas? Is there another poetic form you'd like to pursue? Add your topic and form to a graphic organizer like the one shown.

Develop Ideas and Details Use the graphic organizer to identify ideas, feelings, events, and sensory details—sights, sounds, tastes, smells, touch—related to your topic, theme, or controlling idea. Write whatever ideas come to you.

Consider how you will use poetic conventions and the traditions of your chosen poetic form to express the ideas, feelings, events, and sensory details. For instance, can you use a metaphor to express how excited you were? Could you use sound devices to create a musical quality for your poem?

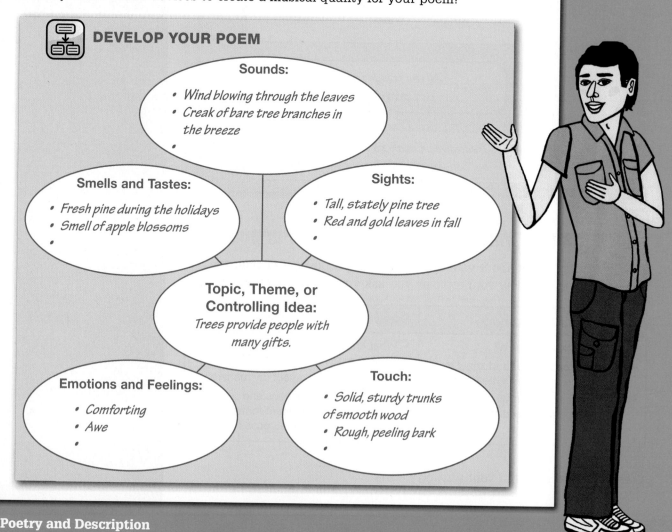

DEVELOP YOUR POEM

Sounds:
- Wind blowing through the leaves
- Creak of bare tree branches in the breeze
-

Smells and Tastes:
- Fresh pine during the holidays
- Smell of apple blossoms
-

Sights:
- Tall, stately pine tree
- Red and gold leaves in fall
-

Topic, Theme, or Controlling Idea:
Trees provide people with many gifts.

Emotions and Feelings:
- Comforting
- Awe
-

Touch:
- Solid, sturdy trunks of smooth wood
- Rough, peeling bark
-

Poet's Toolbox

Poets use a variety of poetic conventions to make their ideas vivid and clear. Here are some conventions you might use in your poem:

Figurative Language is writing that means something beyond what the words actually say.	
Simile: comparison using *like* or *as*	*The tree stood on the hill like a mast of a great ship.*
Metaphor: comparison made by saying that one thing is something else	*The leaves were a lacework through which we peered.*
Personification: human characteristics applied to non-human objects	*The oak cradled us in her shade.*
Symbols add depth and insight to poetry.	
An object that stands for something else	A tree could symbolize strength and power.
Sound Devices create a musical or emotional effect.	
Alliteration: repetition of consonant sounds at the beginning of nearby words	*The **t**owering **t**ree **t**oppled **t**o the ground.*
Assonance: repetition of vowel sounds in nearby words	*L**ea**fy tr**ee**s **ea**se the summer's h**ea**t.*
Consonance: repetition of consonants in the middle or at the end of words	*A**pp**le and ma**p**le trees give us fruit and sa**p**.*
Structural Elements help build the framework for poetic language.	
Rhyme: repetition of sounds at the ends of lines of poetry	*The leaves above danced and **played**; We sat below in the cool **shade**.*
Meter: rhythmical pattern of a poem. It is determined by stressed syllables in a line. Some forms of poetry have specific patterns of stressed syllables.	*We sat below in the cool shade.* (Stressed syllables in poetry are marked with a ´, while unstressed syllables are marked with a ˘.)
Graphic Elements position the words on the page.	
Arrangement of words on a page	capital letters, line spacing, and line breaks

Apply It! Review the ideas, feelings, and sensory details in the graphic organizer you created.

- First, confirm the poetic form you will develop.
- Then, decide which conventions from the Poet's Toolbox you would like to use in your poem. Keep in mind that some poetic conventions are used in specific forms.

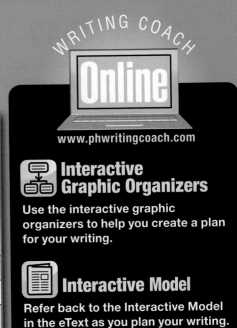

WRITING COACH

Online

www.phwritingcoach.com

Interactive Graphic Organizers

Use the interactive graphic organizers to help you create a plan for your writing.

Interactive Model

Refer back to the Interactive Model in the eText as you plan your writing.

Drafting

During the drafting stage, you will start to write your ideas for your sonnet or free verse poem. You will use the ideas you developed in prewriting and build on them to structure them in a sustained way according to the traditions required for the particular poetic form you chose.

Drafting a Free Verse Poem or Sonnet

Each poetic form has specific traditions, or characteristics. You will write your poem using these traditions, the conventions from the Poet's Toolbox, and the ideas, feelings, and sensory details you developed in your graphic organizer.

These charts show the traditions of each form. Review these characteristics. Then answer the questions in the right column as you draft your poem.

English Sonnet Characteristics	Questions to Answer While Drafting
• 14 lines • Three stanzas with four lines and one stanza with two lines • Rhyme scheme is *abab cdcd efef gg* • Specific meter • Poetic conventions used • Feelings or emotions conveyed • Vivid descriptions • Final two lines are a twist on or clarification of the first 12 lines	• What do I want to describe or express in each stanza? • What words will I rhyme in each stanza? **Tip:** Consult a rhyming dictionary and thesaurus. • Do my lines follow a set rhyme scheme? **Tip:** Read aloud as you write. Use a dictionary to determine syllabication. • What sound devices will I use? • What poetic conventions will I use? • What feelings or emotions will I express? • How will I make my descriptions vivid?

Free Verse Characteristics	Questions to Answer While Drafting
• Varied number of lines • Varied number of stanzas • No meter; follows natural speech patterns • Usually no rhyming is used • Poetic conventions used • Feelings or emotions conveyed • Vivid descriptions	• How long do I want my poem to be? **Tip:** You need not decide the *exact* number of stanzas and lines. • What sound devices will I use? • What poetic conventions will I use? • What feelings or emotions will I express? • How will I make my descriptions vivid?

Start Your Draft

Writing poetry is different from creating most other genres. The process is more open. Use the graphic organizer that shows your topic, ideas, and sensory details, and the Poet's Toolbox as guides, but be open to experimenting with your draft.

Remember, the most important part of drafting is just getting your ideas in writing. Because drafting is an open-ended situations you will have the chance to refine and improve your writing when you revise and edit.

WRITING COACH

Online

www.phwritingcoach.com

Interactive Model
Refer back to the Mentor Text in the eText as your write your draft.

Before You Write

√ Choose the **poetic form** you want to use—free verse, a sonnet, or another poetic form.

√ Review the **poetic traditions** of your poetic form that are listed in Drafting a Free Verse Poem or Sonnet. Make sure you use these characteristics when you write your draft.

√ Think of a striking image, figurative language, or other **poetic convention** to start your poem that will attract readers' attention.

While You Write

√ State or imply the **topic** or controlling idea. It does not have to be mentioned in each line, but should be sustained through the poem as a whole.

√ Include your **ideas** from prewriting. If a particular feeling, emotion, sensory detail, or other idea does not seem to work, try a different approach.

√ Review the **poetic conventions** in the Poet's Toolbox. Use some of these conventions to express your ideas. If you experiment with a convention and it does not seem to work, try another.

√ Include **rhetorical devices,** such as similes, metaphors, and personification, to convey meaning to your audience and to keep your writing interesting.

√ Make sure that you make careful word choices in your poem, including words that offer **sensory details** to ensure that your audience can fully experience the emotion in your poem.

√ Read your poem aloud to listen to the **sound devices** and evaluate their effects.

Revising: Making It Better

Now that you have finished your first draft, you are ready to revise. Think about the "big picture" of how well your audience will understand and connect to your poem. You can use your Revision RADaR as a guide for making changes to improve your draft. Revision RADaR provides four major ways to improve your writing: (R) replace, (A) add, (D) delete, and (R) reorder.

Kelly Gallagher, M. Ed.

KEEP REVISION ON YOUR RADAR

Read part of the first draft of the Student Model "Summer." Then look at questions the writer asked himself as he thought about how his draft will affect his audience.

Summer

1ST DRAFT

I feel free in the summer.
Mornings are warm now,
and the sun bakes our skin.
as sweat soaks our shirts.

Hooting and hollering,
we plunge into the cool lake,
relieving our sunburns,
soothing our toes.

Softball and picnics in at the park
with family and friends;
smoky backyard barbeques;
long days at the beach.

In the late nights on the porch,
while we watch the stars,
we enjoy our summer.

Does my first line grab my audience's attention, and does it accurately express my feelings?

Can I create a more musical sound in my poem here?

Does the end of my poem show powerful emotions and convey my controlling idea?

Now, look at how the writer applied Revision RADaR to write an improved second draft.

Summary

2ND DRAFT

Summer is freedom!
Mornings are warm now,
as the sun bakes our skin.
and sweat soaks our shirts.

Hooting and hollering,
we plunge into the cool lake,
soothing our sunburns,
tickling our toes.

Softball and picnics at parks
with family and friends;
smoky backyard barbeques;
long days at the beach.

In the late nights on the porch,
while we watch the stars,
the sweet spell of summer
seeps into our lives.

R *Reordered the words and ideas in this line to create a metaphor that better grabs my audience's attention and expresses my feelings*

R *Replaced "relieving" with "soothing" in line 7, and "soothing" with "tickling" in line 8 to create alliteration*

D *Deleted a boring, vague statement, and*
A *added sensory details and alliteration to clearly express my emotions and my controlling idea*

WRITING COACH

Online

www.phwritingcoach.com

Video

Learn more strategies for effective writing from program author Kelly Gallagher.

Apply It! Use your Revision RADaR to revise your draft.

- First, determine whether you have addressed the needs of your audience and purpose, and have included the poetic traditions, or characteristics, of a sonnet, free verse poem, or other poetic form you chose.
- Then, make sure you have included a variety of poetic conventions to make your writing interesting.
- Finally, apply your Revision RADaR to make needed changes. Remember—you can use the steps in Revision RADaR in any order.

Look at the Big Picture

Use the chart and your analytical skills to evaluate how well each section of your poem is organized and meets the needs of your audience. When necessary, use the suggestions in the chart to revise your poem.

Section	Evaluate	Revise
Topic and Sensory Details	• Make sure your controlling idea or **theme** is clear in the poem.	• Add information to clarify topic and theme.
	• Check that **sensory details** support the controlling idea or theme.	• Replace sensory details that do not support the controlling idea with new details that help paint a clearer picture.
Structural Elements	• Ensure the **poetic traditions** of your chosen form have been included in your poem.	• Review *Drafting a Free Verse Poem or Sonnet* to check the poetic traditions of your chosen poetic form. Revise your poem to include any missing characteristics.
	• For sonnets, check rhythm, rhyme, **meter,** and stanzas to match sonnet traditions.	• Use a rhyming dictionary to substitute rhymes. • Add or delete words or lines and reorder words to improve rhythm, rhyme, and meter.
	• For free verse, evaluate the natural sound of the **rhythm**.	• Read your free verse draft aloud to make sure that the rhythm sounds natural. If it doesn't, replace words to mimic natural speech patterns.
Poetic Conventions	• Make sure your **poetic conventions,** such as figurative language and word choice, create strong images for your readers.	• Replace boring or vague words with figurative language, vivid words, and sensory details.
	• Read aloud to check that your **sound devices** are effective and correct.	• Use a dictionary or thesaurus to find words that create better assonance or alliteration.

Focus on Craft: Metaphors

A **trope** is a deliberate use of language for effect. A **metaphor** is a type of trope that makes comparison between seemingly unlike things. In a metaphor, one thing is spoken about as if it were another. For example, *The children were bees, swarming around the basketball court* is a metaphor in which children are compared to bees—they swarm. Carefully chosen metaphors create vivid and original imagery.

Think about metaphors as you read these lines from the Student Model.

 **STUDENT TEXT** | from **Winter's Approach**
page 124; lines 1–4

Leaves lose their lush green and briefly turn gold,
But spin to the ground in the first icy storm.
Frost is a blanket that spreads news of cold,
As birds of all feathers head South to get warm.

Try It! Now, ask yourself these questions:

- Which line of the poem contains a metaphor?
- What things are compared in the metaphor? What do these items have in common? How are they different? What image does the metaphor create?

Fine-Tune Your Draft

Apply It! Use the revision suggestions to prepare your final draft after considering how well questions of audience and purpose have been addressed.

- **Employ Tropes** Use tropes, or figurative language such as metaphors, to help readers pull meaning from your poem.
- **Include Transitions** Use transitions, if necessary, to convey meaning to your audience and to help your ideas flow well. Transition words and phrases such as *then, next,* and *at last* can help you connect ideas.

Teacher or Family Feedback Read your final draft to your teacher or a family member. Think about the feedback you receive and revise your final draft as needed.

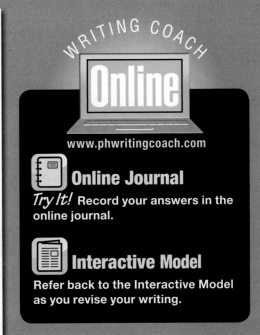

WRITING COACH

Online
www.phwritingcoach.com

Online Journal
Try It! Record your answers in the online journal.

Interactive Model
Refer back to the Interactive Model as you revise your writing.

Editing: Making It Correct

Editing your draft means polishing your work and correcting errors. You may want to read through your work several times when editing, looking for different errors each time.

As you edit your draft, consider using **different kinds of phrases,** such as **adjectival, adverbial, and verbal phrases.** A phrase is a group of words that act as a single part of speech. Then edit your final draft for errors in **grammar, mechanics, and spelling.**

WRITE GUY *Jeff Anderson, M. Ed.*

WHAT DO YOU NOTICE?

Zoom in on Conventions Focus on phrases as you zoom in on the lines from the Student Model.

> To learn more about phrases, see Chapter 15 of your Grammar Handbook.

STUDENT MODEL from **Winter's Approach**
page 124; lines 2–3

But spin to the ground in the first icy storm.
Frost is a blanket that spreads news of cold,

Now, ask yourself: *What does each highlighted phrase do?*

Perhaps you said that the first phrase modifies a verb and the last phrase modifies a noun.

Adjectival phrases are prepositional phrases that modify nouns or pronouns. The adjectival phrase *of cold* modifies the noun *news.*
Adverbial phrases are prepositional phrases that modify adjectives, adverbs, and verbs. The adverbial phrase *in the first icy storm* modifies the verb *spin.*

Verbal phrases function as adjectives, adverbs, and nouns. Participial phrases are made up of the past or present participle and its modifiers. They function as adjectives, as in: *Alarmed by the cold,* she turned on the heat. Gerund phrases are made up of the *-ing* verb form and its modifiers. They function as nouns, as in: *Turning on the heat* was necessary last night.

Infinitive phrases are a kind of verbal phrase that consist of *to,* the base form of a verb, and related modifiers. They function as nouns, adjectives, and adverbs. In the following example, the infinitive phrase acts as a noun: *To wait for spring* seems impossible.

Grammar Mini-Lesson: Commas and Phrases

To learn more, see Chapter 23.

Phrases are sometimes set off with a comma, especially introductory phrases. When a participial or infinitive phrase introduces a sentence, follow it with a comma. Place a comma after most introductory adjectival and adverbial phrases, too. However, you may choose not to place a comma after very short adjectival or adverbial phrases such as *in 2003*. Notice how the author of the Student Model uses a comma to set off an introductory participial phrase.

 STUDENT MODEL from **Summer** page 125; lines 5–6

> Hooting and hollering,
>
> we plunge into the cool lake,

Try It! Add commas to set off phrases in these sentences as needed. Then, identify the type or types of phrases used in each sentence. Write the answers in your journal.

1. Looking through the window he waited impatiently for his ride.

2. In school we studied biology.

Apply It! Edit your draft for **grammar, mechanics, and spelling.** Use a dictionary or other resource to check your spelling. If necessary, edit some sentences to use different types of phrases and **correct, consistent punctuation.**

WRITING COACH

Online

www.phwritingcoach.com

 Video
Learn effective editing techniques from program author Jeff Anderson.

 Online Journal
Try It! Record your answers in the online journal.

Interactive Model
Refer back to the Interactive Model as you edit your writing.

Use the rubric to evaluate your piece. If necessary, rethink, rewrite, or revise.

Rubric for Poetry: Sonnet or Free Verse Poem	Rating Scale
Ideas: How well is the poem's subject or controlling idea defined and developed?	Not very Very 1 2 3 4 5 6
Organization: How organized are your ideas?	1 2 3 4 5 6
Voice: How effectively do you use figurative language and poetic techniques to create a unique voice?	1 2 3 4 5 6
Word Choice: How well do the specific words you have chosen convey your meaning?	1 2 3 4 5 6
Sentence Fluency: How naturally does your writing flow in the form you've chosen?	1 2 3 4 5 6
Conventions: How correct is your use of commas with phrases?	1 2 3 4 5 6

Publishing

Publish your poem to share your insights, feelings, and ideas and make readers think, feel, and, possibly, laugh. First, get your poem ready for presentation. Then, choose a way to **publish your work for appropriate audiences.**

Wrap Up Your Presentation

If your poem is handwritten, you may need to make a new, clean copy. If so, be sure to **write legibly.** Add a title to your poem that will grab your readers' attention and that indicates the topic of your poem.

Publish Your Piece

Use this chart to identify a way to publish your poem.

If your audience is...	...then publish it by...
People attending a poetry reading	• Making a clean copy and submitting it for the program • Reading your poem aloud to the audience
Teenage readers	• Submitting your work to a poetry journal or teen magazine • Posting it on a blog and inviting readers to respond to the poem, making sure to also include an image or music that supports your controlling idea

 Reflect on Your Writing

Now that you are done with your poem, read it over and use your writing journal to answer these questions.

- Do you feel that your final poem contains enough descriptive detail to allow your readers to fully experience everything you describe? Explain.
- Are there any parts of the poem that are particularly strong? How can you build on these skills in future writing assignments?
- How does writing a poem help you appreciate the work of other poets?
- Find a published poem that conveys a theme similar to yours. What similarties and differences do you see?

The Big Question: Why Write? How do we best convey feelings through words on a page?

MAKE YOUR WRITING COUNT

Create an Advertisement Based on a Poem

Sonnets and free verse poems are expressive forms. They allow a writer to convey ideas that can't always be explained in ordinary language. Put your poetic language skills to the test and create an **advertisement** to sell an extraordinary product.

With a group, think about the different types of media messages that may contain poetic language. Discuss these messages and decide what their purposes are and how they are constructed. Then, produce an advertisement for television or the Internet that uses poetic language to interest people in a real or made-up product. Your final product should be a **multimedia presentation** with text, images, and sound.

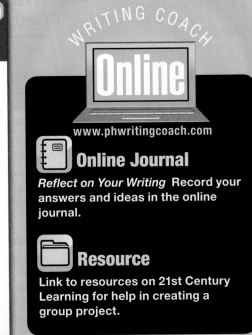

WRITING COACH

Online

www.phwritingcoach.com

Online Journal

Reflect on Your Writing Record your answers and ideas in the online journal.

Resource

Link to resources on 21st Century Learning for help in creating a group project.

Here's your action plan.

1. Choose group roles and set objectives. You will need a writer, an image manager, and a director.

2. Look online for examples of effective ads. Take notes about what makes them work well.

3. Review your peers' sonnets and free verse poems. Brainstorm for a list of products to match the language. Synthesize your viewpoints and choose one poem as the basis of an advertisement.

4. Work together to arrange the text on a poster or screen. Add appropriate images and make notes about sounds or animation effects you want to include.

5. Before presenting your advertisement, make sure that it contains:
   - A specific product
   - Poetic language expressing a positive point of view about the product
   - Text, images, and sound aimed at a particular audience

6. Rehearse your live presentation, or record and arrange the various media required for your TV or Web ad. Ensure that the presentation conveys the feeling you want to express about the product.

Listening and Speaking When you present your ad—whether live, online, or recorded—work as a team to highlight the various media that comprise your message.

**Writing for Media:
Definition Essay**

Definition Essay

A **definition essay** is an analytical essay that defines a word or concept. In a definition essay, the writer provides personal context and opinions to extend the dictionary definition of a term. Most definition essays focus on abstract terms, such as *democracy, prejudice,* or *love*. These essays follow the standard format of introduction, body, and conclusion. Definition essays are often found in literary and news magazines, as well as on the Internet.

Try It! Study the sample definition essay. Then, answer these questions. Record your answers in your journal.

1. What **concept** is defined in this essay?
2. What is the writer's **thesis statement**, or argument?
3. What literal, or dictionary, **definition** does the writer give?
4. What figurative definitions does the writer give that go beyond the literal definition?
5. What **personal context** or **opinion** does the writer include?

Extension Find another example of a definition essay, and compare it with this one.

How Do You Measure Success?

Recently, my parents told me that I should attend college so I can achieve great success. Didn't I want to become a big success like Bill Gates and make a billion dollars by creating something new and remarkable?

I'm sure my parents have good intentions, and I do plan to attend college, but success can be defined in many ways. I know that a lot of people define success by how much money they make and how much "stuff" they have. But accumulating wealth and expensive items doesn't make a person successful.

I think everyone can be successful in his or her own way. I may only have a minimum wage job and ride a bike to school, but I've been successful in making great friends and having a close relationship with my family. I have a solid grade point average, and I'm also pretty good at soccer. I know my coach would say I've had a successful season this year!

My college applications are almost complete, and I'm excited about what my future holds. Maybe I'll be like Bill Gates after all and invent a new gadget that'll be a huge success. But if not, I'll know that I'm a successful person in many other ways!

 **Create a Definition Essay**

Follow these steps to create your own definition essay. To plan your definition essay, review the graphic organizers on pages R24–R27 and choose one that suits your needs.

Prewriting

- Choose a concept that is important to you and about which you have a strong opinion.
- Identify your audience, their perspectives, and their knowledge of your topic.
- Gather information, including a literal, or dictionary, definition, from reference works and other sources. Construct a thesis statement that clearly expresses your central idea.
- Outline your definition, listing at least three main ideas as support for your view, as well as details to support those ideas.

Drafting

- Begin writing an introduction that grabs readers' attention, states your thesis, and prepares readers for the argument to come.
- Write the body of your essay, clearly explaining reasons for your views and including details that support those reasons. Be sure to logically organize your essay.
- Draft the conclusion by summing up your viewpoint and including a thought-provoking ending.

Revising and Editing

- Review your draft to make sure that your ideas are organized logically. Replace, add, delete, and reorder information as needed to improve your organization and make your meaning clear.
- Check for errors in spelling, grammar, and mechanics. Make corrections as needed.

Publishing

- Create a multimedia presentation that uses graphics, images, and sound to present the main ideas of your definition essay.
- Clearly show the literal definition of your concept and then explain how you feel about the idea. In the body of your presentation, stress your ideas and perspective.
- Then, share your presentation with your class.

WRITING COACH

www.phwritingcoach.com

Online Journal

Try It! Record your answers in the online journal.

 **Interactive Graphic Organizers**

Choose from a variety of graphic organizers to plan and develop your project.

Partner Talk

Before you start drafting, explain the literal and figurative meanings of the concept in your definition essay. Use specific details to describe and explain your ideas. Increase the specificity of your details based on the type of information you are delivering. Ask for feedback about your definitions.

Writing for Assessment

Writing a good poem can take a lot of practice. You can use these prompts to do just that—practice writing poems. Your responses should include the same characteristics as your sonnet or free verse poem. Look back at page 120 to review these characteristics.

Try It! To begin, read the **poetry** prompt and the information on format and academic vocabulary. Then, use the ABCDs of On-Demand Writing to help you plan and write your poem.

Format

The prompt directs you to write a *poem*. You may write either a sonnet, a free-verse poem, or another type of poem. Be sure to follow the poetic traditions of whichever form you choose.

Poetry Prompt

Think about a particular kind of music you enjoy. Write a poem about that music. Be sure to use poetic conventions to make your writing lively and interesting.

Academic Vocabulary

Remember that *poetic conventions* are the techniques poets use to create well-developed poems. Poetic conventions include elements such as figurative langauge, sound devices, and graphic elements.

 ## The ABCDs of On-Demand Writing

Use the following ABCDs to help you respond to the prompt.

Before you write your draft:

Attack the prompt [1 MINUTE]

- Circle or highlight important words in the prompt. Draw a line from the word to what it refers to.
- Rewrite the prompt in your own words.

Brainstorm possible answers [4 MINUTES]

- Create a graphic organizer to generate ideas.
- Use one for each part of the prompt if necessary.

Choose the order of your response [1 MINUTE]

- Think about the best way to organize your ideas.
- Number your ideas in the order you will write about them. Cross out ideas you will not be using.

After you write your draft:

Detect errors before turning in the draft [1 MINUTE]

- Carefully reread your writing.
- Make sure that your response makes sense and is complete.
- Look for spelling, punctuation, and grammar errors.

More Prompts for Practice

Apply It! Respond to Prompt 1 by writing a **poem** that reflects an awareness of poetic conventions and poetic traditions within different forms. As you write, be sure to:

- Identify your audience
- Consider your topic and the ideas about it you want to express
- Establish a clear topic, theme, or controlling idea
- Be sure to use the **poetic traditions,** or characteristics, of the **poetic form** you chose
- Include a variety of **poetic conventions,** such as figurative language and sound devices, to make your meaning clear to your audience

> **Prompt 1** Select a famous person from history, someone about whom you know a great deal. Write a poem about this person. Be sure to follow the poetic traditions of the poetic form you choose and use poetic conventions to create vivid images of your chosen historical figure.

Spiral Review: Narrative Respond to Prompt 2 by writing an **autobiographical narrative.** Make sure your narrative:

- Develops an engaging story, including a well-developed **conflict** that is resolved
- Has a clear and meaningful **theme**
- Presents interesting and believable real-life **characters**
- Uses a range of **literary strategies and devices** to enhance the plot
- Includes sensory details that define the **mood** and **tone**

> **Prompt 2** Think about how you met someone important in your life and how your friendship has developed over time. Write an autobiographical narrative about this meeting and your relationship. Be sure to explain what led up to your meeting, as well as describe the event itself and your resulting friendship.

WRITING COACH

Online

www.phwritingcoach.com

Interactive Writing Coach™

Plan your response to the prompt. If you are using the prompt for practice, write one paragraph at a time or your entire draft and then submit it for feedback. If you are using the prompt as a timed test, write your entire draft and then submit it for feedback.

Remember **ABCD**

Attack the prompt

Brainstorm possible answers

Choose the order of your response

Detect errors before turning in the draft

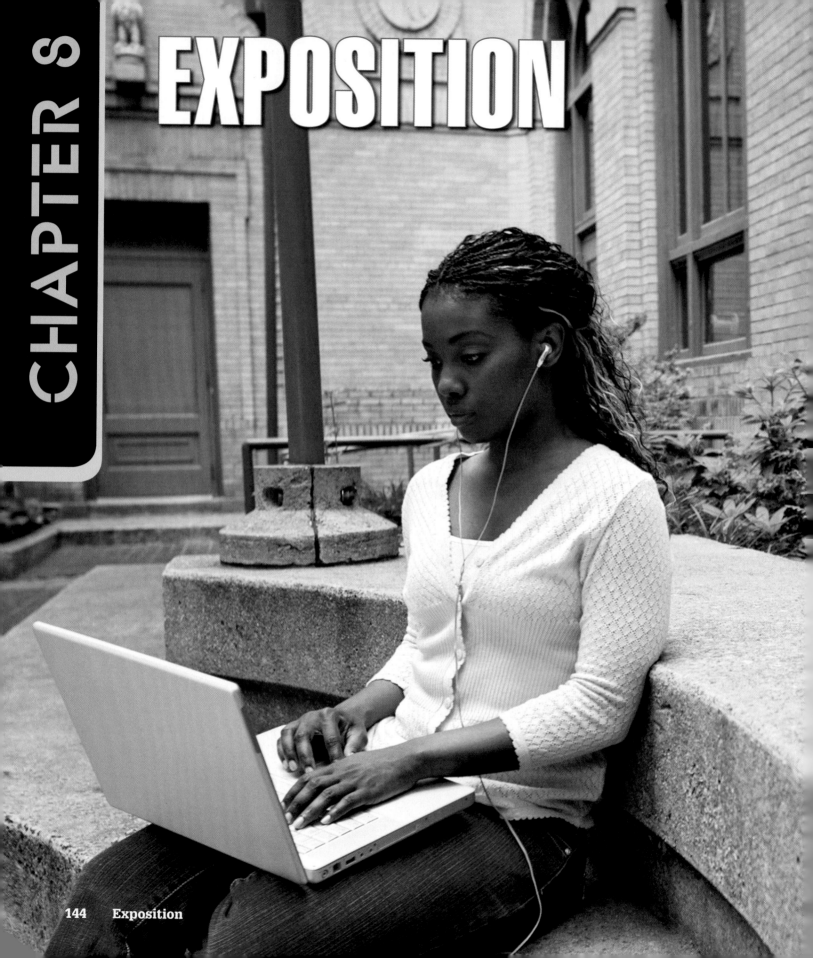

CHAPTER 8

EXPOSITION

How Can You Explain This?

What do you know about computers? What information and ideas about computers could you share with others?

Information can be presented many ways. For example, you can compare two things, you can discuss causes and effects, or you can present a problem and a solution.

Try It! Imagine that you wanted to explain different kinds of computers and their uses. How would you categorize them?

Consider these questions as you participate in an extended discussion with a partner. Take turns expressing your ideas and feelings.

- What is the purpose of computers?
- What different kinds of computers are used in businesses? At home?
- How would you describe different computers?

What's Ahead

In this chapter, you will review two strong examples of an analytical essay: a Mentor Text and a Student Model. Then, using the examples as guides, you will write an analytical essay in the classification form.

 Connect to the Big Questions

Discuss these questions with a partner:

1 **What do you think?** To what extent do computers change the way we learn?

2 **Why Write?** What should we tell and what should we describe to make information clear?

ANALYTICAL ESSAY

In an analytical essay, a writer explores a topic by breaking it into smaller pieces for study, decision, and explanation. In this chapter you will learn to write a special type of analytical essay known as a classification essay. In a classification essay, the writer organizes the topic into categories and provides examples that fit into each category. A classification essay begins with a clear thesis statement and gives details to support the categorization.

You will develop your classification essay by taking it through each of the steps of the writing process: prewriting, drafting, revising, editing, and publishing. You will also have an opportunity to write a script for a news interview. To preview the criteria for how your classification essay will be evaluated, see the rubric on page 163.

FEATURE ASSIGNMENT

Analytical Essay: Classification Essay

An effective analytical essay has these characteristics:

- A clear **thesis statement** or controlling idea

- A clear **organizational schema,** or way of organizing information, for conveying ideas

- **Relevant and substantial evidence** and **well-chosen details** that are clearly related to and strongly support the thesis

- A clear study, or **analysis** of views, information, and evidence presented for and against the thesis statement

- **Information** on **relevant perspectives,** or related points of view

- A careful **consideration** of the **validity, reliability,** and **relevance** of all **sources** before using them.

- A **variety of sentence structures** and **rhetorical devices,** such as rhetorical questions, that support the thesis

- Smooth and effective **transitions** between paragraphs and ideas

- **Effective sentence structure** and correct spelling, grammar, and usage

A classification essay also includes:

- A single **principle** by which the topic is sorted so that each category relates to the others

- **Examples** that illustrate each category

Other Forms of Analytical Essays

In addition to classification essays, there are other forms of analytical essays, including:

> Cause-and-effect essays trace the results of an event or the reasons an event happened.
>
> Compare-and-contrast essays explore similarities and differences between two or more things, people, places, or ideas.
>
> Newspaper and magazine articles supply relevant information about a particular topic by analyzing the topic's elements. They may also reflect genres other than analytical essays (for example, persuasive writing, or narrative nonfiction writing). These articles may appear in print or online.
>
> Problem-solution essays explore a particular problem and present one or more possible solutions to it.
>
> Pro-con essays explore two sides of an issue, presenting the arguments for and against a particular action or decision.

Try It! For each audience and purpose described, choose a form, such as a problem-solution essay, a newspaper article, or a pro-con essay, that is appropriate for conveying your intended meaning to the audience. Explain your choices.

- To present to a parent a way to solve a problem you are having with a pet
- To present to students the benefits and drawbacks of a candidate who is running for class president
- To critique a movie in the school newspaper

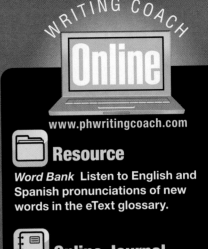

MENTOR TEXT

Analytical Essay

Learn From Experience

 After reading the analytical essay on pages 148–149, read the numbered notes in the margins to learn about how the author presented his ideas. Later you will read a Student Model, which shares these characteristics and also has the characteristics of a classification essay.

Answer the *Try It!* questions online or in your notebook.

❶ The essay begins with an **effective introductory paragraph** that includes an anecdote, or story that makes a point, and suggests the **thesis.**

Try It! How does the anecdote grab readers' attention? What do you think the thesis of the essay is?

❷ The author creates a **clear organizational structure** by using subheads to arrange **evidence.**

Try It! What other kinds of texts often have subheads? How do they compare with the subheads in the essay? How can subheads help you as a reader?

❸ The author supports the main idea with **relevant and substantial evidence and well-chosen details.**

Try It! What kind of evidence does the author provide? Do you think it is convincing? Explain.

Extension Find another example of an analytical essay, and compare it with this one.

Cats and Seniors:
A Loving and Healthy Relationship

by Brad Kollus

❶ Moochie, a cat who participated in an animal-assisted therapy program, visited a hospital where an elderly man with terminal cancer was in a coma and had not responded to any of his family's or caregivers' contacts. Donna Williamson,
5 Moochie's owner, put the cat on the comatose man's bed and rubbed the cat against his face. To everyone's astonishment the man awoke from the coma, pulled his arms from under the sheets and began petting Moochie. Can cats have a similar effect
10 on the health of seniors living within our society?

❷ Psychological Health
Unfortunately, many seniors in our society become lonely
15 and isolated as they retire and friends and family pass away. **❸** Pets, and especially cats, can play an important role in providing companionship and
20 love to people who are elderly, and many scientific studies have proven this to be true. One study of older adults found that cat owners had higher self-esteem and well being as compared to
25 non-cat owners. The same study found that men who owned cats had the lowest incidence of stress or anxiety while men who did not own cats had the highest level. The results of a study of elderly women found that pet owners had higher morale including less loneliness and agitation, more optimism, and levels of activity as
30 compared to those without pets.

Physical Health
It turns out that having a cat can also give seniors physical benefits. One study found that men who owned cats had fewer

physical illnesses than men without cats, who had 20% more
35 health problems. Another study found that seniors with pets
had fewer doctor's visits over a one year period than those
without. Researchers found in a study of Medicare recipients
that pet owning seniors had shorter hospital stays and had lower
health care costs than non-owners. The same study found that
40 pet owning seniors were shown to have lower triglyceride levels
than those without pets. High triglyceride levels can contribute
to heart disease.

How Cats Help

❹ A few researchers have looked at exactly how pets are
45 helping seniors stay healthy. In a study measuring the most
important benefits that seniors receive from their pets, two
factors stood out. The second most important was the need
to nurture. For most seniors, the combination of not having
children to care for and not having the responsibility of work led
50 them to feel unneeded. Having a cat to care for means they are
needed and gives them a sense of purpose and identity. The most
important benefit was attachment.

Many studies have found seniors' attachment to their pet to
be the essential factor to obtaining health benefits. When seniors
55 are highly attached to their cat or dog, the pet provides the same
social support and companionship as humans. In one study,
researchers discovered that seniors in general and particularly
widows who were highly attached to their pets had lower levels of
depression than pet owners who had lower levels of attachment.
60 Another study found that highly attached seniors were less
lonely and had less stress than owners with lower attachment.
Researchers found in another study that elderly owners were
physically healthier when they were highly attached to their cat
or dog.

65 One study demonstrates all of this research the best. Elderly
individuals who adopted cats were compared to those who
hadn't. The people with cats were less lonely, less anxious, and
less depressed. Physically those with cats had less hypertension,
lower blood pressure, and less need for medication. It turns
70 out those owners who were more attached to their cats had the
greatest health benefits. ❺ In the next 25 years, the percentage
of elderly persons is expected to grow to 1 out of 5 (60 million)
Americans. The important role cats can play in the lives of
seniors by helping them stay psychologically and physically
75 healthy by providing unconditional love will become even more
important in our society.

WRITING COACH

Online

www.phwritingcoach.com

Interactive Model

Listen to an audio recording of the
Mentor Text in the eText. You can
refer back to the Mentor Text
whenever you need support in
developing your own writing.

Online Journal

Try It! Answer the questions
about the Mentor Text in the
online journal.

❹ The author uses a **variety of sentence
structures,** including simple and complex sentences.

Try It! What information do the
simple sentences provide? Does the
sentence variety help you understand the
information better? Why or why not?

❺ In this **concluding paragraph,** the author makes
a prediction about the future importance of the role
of cats as pets.

Try It! Do you agree that this is a
reasonable prediction? Has the author
presented sufficient evidence to support
this prediction? Explain.

STUDENT MODEL

Classification Essay

With a small group, read and study this Student Model. Ask yourself if the categories or classifications make sense and if there are enough details to support the controlling idea.

Use a Reader's Eye

Now, reread the Student Model. On your copy of the Student Model, use the Reader's Response Symbols to react to what you have read.

Reader's Response Symbols

+   **Aha! That makes sense to me.**

−   **This isn't clear to me.**

?   **I have a question about this.**

!   **Wow! That is cool/weird/ interesting.**

Participate in an extended discussion with a partner. Express your opinions and share your responses to the Student Model. Identify the main purpose and likely audience of the Student Model, and decide whether or not the essay seems appropriate for that purpose.

You Need a SUMMER JOB... But What Kind?

by Navid Khan

Every spring, thousands of high school kids look forward to summer vacation with excitement… and dread. They feel excited because they know school will be out soon. But they dread looking for
5   a job. They don't know where to start. Before you begin your search for a summer job, it helps to think about what you like to do and about the different categories of jobs. Ask yourself these questions.

Are you a person who enjoys being outdoors even
10   when it rains or if you get dirty or wet? If you answer yes, the best jobs for you would be ones where you are outside a lot. For example, you could look for a job as a camp counselor, a lifeguard, or working for a gardening service or construction company.
15   However, some of these jobs require special skills or certification, and others are not available to high school students at all. For example, lifeguards need special training. Look for lifeguard training programs at pools or recreation centers in your town.

20   Do you enjoy dealing with different kinds of people? Are you able to handle a lot of things at once? If so, you may want to apply for a job waiting tables at a restaurant. Or you might try to get an office job in a business in your town. There, you will do things like
25   make copies, organize files, or answer phones. A job like this could help you learn more about the business world and maybe help you figure out a possible future career.

Do you work best on your own? Do you want to keep all the money you earn from your hard work? Do you
30   like to solve problems by yourself? If this describes

1

you, there are a lot of job possibilities for you. You can start your own small business. You could mow lawns, paint decks, or take care of pets. Maybe you could even start a babysitting business in your neighborhood.

35 There is more to finding a job than thinking about what you like to do. You have to make people want to hire you. According to recent information from the U.S. Bureau of Labor and Statistics, about 65 percent of young adults between the ages of 16 and 20 are out 40 hunting for summer jobs. So how can you stand out?

When you apply for a job, show the people in charge that you have a positive attitude. If you are applying for a job that you would really like to do, it should be easy. And if you are starting your own business, you should 45 have a lot of energy when telling people what you can do for them.

As the summer approaches, take charge of that dread! Think carefully about your skills and what you like to do. Use that information to help you find 50 a summer job that earns money, but is also a fun, worthwhile experience.

2

WRITING COACH
Online
www.phwritingcoach.com

Interactive Model

Listen to an audio recording of the Student Model in the eText. Use the Reader's and Writer's Response Symbols with the eText tools to note what you read.

Use a Writer's Eye

Now, evaluate the piece as a writer. On your copy of the Student Model, use the Writer's Response Symbols to react to what you have read. Identify places where the student writer uses characteristics of an effective classification essay.

Writer's Response Symbols

C.T. Clearly stated thesis

I.C. Effective introduction and conclusion

R.D. Good use of rhetorical devices

S.E. Effective supporting evidence

Your Turn **Feature Assignment: Classification Essay**

Prewriting

Choose from the Topic Bank, or plan a first draft of your classification essay by determining your own topic.

Choose From the Topic Bank

TOPIC BANK

Winter Olympic During the 1990s, four sports were added to the Winter Olympics: curling, freestyle skiing, short track speed skating, and snowboarding. Think about the origin of the sport, the equipment the athletes use, the setting, and the rules of the sport. Choose three of these sports and write a classification essay in which you describe the three sports and explain how they are played.

Green Packaging The choices for packaging consumer goods for shipment have evolved to include green or environmentally friendly products. Some of these choices are biodegradable packing peanuts, inflatable air pillows, corn-based poly bags, and containers made from recycled materials. Choose three of these products, and write a classification essay in which you describe these products, how they are produced and their environmental benefits.

Technology During the last part of the 20th century, technological advances have improved the lives of people around the world. Among these are the computer, the cell phone, and the global positioning system. Write a classification essay in which you describe each of these technologies and explain the effect they had on people around the world.

Choose Your Own Topic

Use the following range of strategies to determine a topic.

Observe and Research

- Note how various subjects are classified. For example, think about music, sports, or another topic of your choice. Then, think about unusual ways things might be connected.

- Search your library's database and the Internet using key words and phrases about a topic that interests you. Review the results to see patterns or categories that you could further research.

Review your responses and choose a topic.

Narrow Your Topic

Choosing a topic that is too broad for a classification essay results in an essay that is unfocused and disorganized—just the opposite of the true goal of this type of writing.

Apply It! Use a graphic organizer like the one shown to narrow your topic.

- Write your general topic in the top box and list the possible categories next to it. Keep narrowing the topic and categories as you move down the chart.

- Your last box should be a specific topic with a listing of three to five categories that fit under that topic.

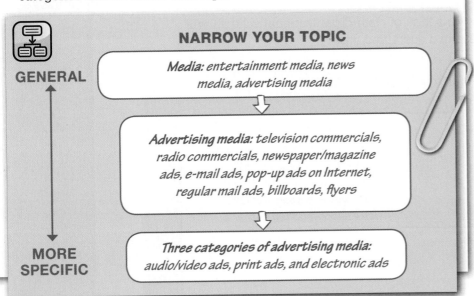

NARROW YOUR TOPIC

GENERAL

Media: entertainment media, news media, advertising media

Advertising media: television commercials, radio commercials, newspaper/magazine ads, e-mail ads, pop-up ads on Internet, regular mail ads, billboards, flyers

MORE SPECIFIC

Three categories of advertising media: audio/video ads, print ads, and electronic ads

www.phwritingcoach.com

Interactive Writing Coach™

- **Choosing from the Topic Bank gives you access to the Interactive Writing Coach™.**
- **Submit your writing and receive instant personalized feedback and guidance as you draft, revise, and edit your writing.**

Interactive Graphic Organizers

Use the interactive graphic organizers to help you narrow your topic.

Online Journal

Try It! **Record your answers and ideas in the online journal.**

Consider Multiple Audiences and Purposes

Before writing, think about your audiences and purposes. Consider how your writing will convey your intended meaning to multiple audiences. Consider the way others view your topic as you ask these questions.

Questions for Audience	Questions for Purpose
• Who are my various audiences? • How familiar are my audiences with the topic? • What questions might my audiences have about the way I have broken down the topic?	• What is my purpose for categorizing? What do I want my audiences to learn? • How might I best convey my ideas to my audiences? • How will I present the evidence and details within each category? • How will I provide multiple relevant perspectives about my topic?

Record your answers in your writing journal.

Plan Your Piece

You will use a graphic organizer like the one shown to state your thesis, organize and develop your arguments, and identify details. When it is complete, you will be ready to write your first draft.

Develop a Clear Thesis Evaluate your initial ideas and information to help you develop a thesis or controlling idea. Write a single sentence that clearly states the topic and the way you intend to classify the topic.

Organize Your Evidence Evaluate the categories for your topic and the evidence that you will use to support your thesis. Using your graphic organizer, name each category and then provide examples of how it relates to your thesis. Using this kind of clear organizational schema will help you structure your ideas in a sustained way.

DEVELOP YOUR CLASSIFICATIONS

Clear Thesis That States the Topic	*Advertisers send their messages to the public in many ways—through audio/video ads, print ads, and electronic ads—but some methods are more successful than others.*
First Category	*Audio/video ads*
Details	
Second Category	*Print ads*
Details	
Third Category	*Electronic ads*
Details	

Gather Details

To provide supporting evidence in a classification essay, writers use a variety of types of details. Look at these examples:

- **Examples:** *Television commercials can reach a wide audience.*
- **Facts:** *About 80 percent of computers have software to block pop-ups.*
- **Personal Observations:** *My mother is always annoyed at the amount of "junk mail" in our mailbox, especially ads.*
- **Analysis of Views:** *Although there are many categories of advertisements, some of these methods are more successful.*

As you research your topic, consult library and Internet resources:

- **Primary Sources:** *Newspaper articles, interviews, and photographs can provide first-hand accounts of events.*
- **Secondary Sources:** *Textbooks and commentaries provide analysis and perspective on events the author did not personally witness.*

Try It! Read the Student Model excerpt and identify and take notes about which kinds of supporting details the author used.

 STUDENT MODEL from **You Need a Summer Job... But What Kind?** page 150; lines 20-27

> Do you enjoy dealing with different kinds of people? Are you able to handle a lot of things at once? If so, you may want to apply for a job waiting tables at a restaurant. Or you might try to get an office job in a business in your town. There, you will do things like make copies, organize files, or answer phones. A job like this could help you learn more about the business world and maybe help you figure out a possible future career.

 Apply It! Review the types of support an analytical essay can use. Follow these steps:

- To make your writing thorough and accurate, choose your resources carefully. Be sure the sources you consult are valid, reliable, and relevant. Then, write an essay of sufficient length to meet your goals.
- You may find views and information that contradict the thesis statement or your evidence. If so, analyze and evaluate this information to determine its accuracy. You may decide to revise your thesis or to conduct further research.
- List well-chosen examples of each type of detail to include in your classification essay, and include them on your graphic organizer.

WRITING COACH

Online

www.phwritingcoach.com

Interactive Graphic Organizers

Use the interactive graphic organizers to help you create a plan for your writing.

Interactive Model

Refer back to the Interactive Model in the eText as you plan your writing.

Drafting

During the drafting stage, you will start to write your ideas for your analytical essay. You will follow an outline that provides an **organizational strategy** that will help you write a focused and organized classification essay.

The Organization of an Analytical Essay

The chart provides an organizing structure for an analytical essay. Look back at how the Student Model uses this organizational strategy. Then, use this chart to help you outline your draft.

Outline for Success

I. Introduction

See Student Model, p. 150.

- Strong opening
- Clear controlling idea or thesis that states your topic

Capture Attention

- A strong opening may ask a question, present a hypothetical situation, or use an interesting detail from your research.
- A clear statement of your controlling idea or thesis introduces your audience to your topic and point of view.

II. Body

See Student Model, pp. 150–151.

- Clear organizing schema for conveying ideas
- Supporting evidence about the categories
- Analysis of views and of information

Support Your Ideas

- Devoting a paragraph to each category and its supporting evidence keeps your information organized.
- Providing a variety of types of supporting details, such as facts, opinions, and anecdotes, will keep readers engaged and informed.
- Including information on all related views, even if they differ from or contradict your own, keeps your writing accurate and unbiased.
- Analyzing and discussing how differing or contradicting views relate to your thesis statement and supporting evidence keeps readers informed.

III. End

See Student Model, p. 151.

- Restatement of thesis
- Strong conclusion that summarizes how the classifications prove the thesis

Sum Up Strongly

- Restating your thesis and summing up your ideas brings readers back to the main point of the essay.
- Concluding with a rhetorical device, such as a rhetorical question, can help lead your audience to think further about your topic.

Start Your Draft

Use the graphic organizer with your categories and details and the Outline for Success as guides to help you write.

Remember the most important part of drafting is just getting your ideas in writing. Because you are drafting in an open-ended situation, you can always go back and refine your writing when you revise and edit.

√ Create an **effective introduction** by first drafting a strong introductory sentence that will catch your readers' attention.

√ Continue to build your introduction by telling readers what to expect in your classification essay. Include your **thesis statement.**

√ Before putting information into the body, carefully consider the validity, reliability, and relevance of **primary and secondary sources.** Use information from only the best, highly regarded sources.

√ For the **organizing schema** of the **body** of your essay, devote one or more paragraphs to each category. Use relevant and substantial evidence and well-chosen details in each paragraph to support the category. Make sure each paragraph is of sufficient length to explain your ideas.

√ Include information that represents all **relevant perspectives.** Carefully discuss and analyze views and information that contradict the thesis and supporting evidence.

√ Include **rhetorical devices**, such as analogies and a variety of sentence structures, to convey meaning and keep your writing interesting.

√ Use **transitions** between paragraphs to connect ideas.

√ To build an effective **conclusion, restate** your thesis and sum up the main points to remind readers of your controlling idea.

√ Reinforce your essay by leaving readers with a **thought-provoking point.** Be sure to tell readers why the classification you explain matters to them.

WRITING COACH

Online

www.phwritingcoach.com

Interactive Model

Outline for Success View pop-ups of Mentor Text selections referenced in the Outline for Success.

Interactive Writing Coach™

Use the Interactive Writing Coach to receive the level of support you need:

- Write one paragraph at a time and submit each one for immediate, detailed feedback.
- Write your entire first draft and submit it for immediate, personalized feedback.

Revising: Making It Better

Now that you have finished your draft, you are ready to revise. Think about the "big picture." You can use your Revision RADaR as a guide for making changes to improve your draft. Revision RADaR provides four major ways to improve your writing: (R) replace, (A) add, (D) delete, and (R) reorder.

Kelly Gallagher, M. Ed.

KEEP REVISION ON YOUR RADAR

Read part of the first draft of the Student Model "You Need a Summer Job...But What Kind?" Then look at questions the writer asked himself as he thought about how well his draft addressed issues of audience, purpose, and genre.

You Need a Summer Job...But What Kind?

1ST DRAFT

Many students can't wait for summer. They are excited about no school. But they also worry about finding work. They feel excited because they know school will be out soon. But they dread looking for a job. They don't know where to start. I have some information for you. Before you begin your search for a summer job, it helps to think about what you like to do and about the different categories of jobs. There are many different types of jobs. Ask yourself these questions.

Are you a person who enjoys being outdoors even when it rains or if you get dirty or wet? If you answer yes, the best jobs for you would be ones where you are outside a lot. The possibilities are endless.

Do you enjoy dealing with different kinds of people? If so, you may want to apply for a job waiting tables at a restaurant. Are you able to handle a lot of things at once? You could do things like make copies, organize files, or answer phones. So you might try to get an office job in a business in your town.

Does the introduction catch my readers' attention?

Does the thesis statement clearly identify the purpose of the essay?

Does the body include relevant details? Have I considered multiple relevant perspectives?

Is the information logically organized? Have I explained this category fully?

Now, look at how the writer applied Revision RADaR to write an improved second draft.

You Need a Summer Job... **2ND DRAFT**
BUT WHAT KIND?

Every spring, thousands of high school kids look forward to summer vacation with excitement...and dread. They feel excited because they know school will be out soon. But they dread looking for a job. They don't know where to start. Before you begin your search for a summer job, it helps to think about what you like to do and about the different categories of jobs. Ask yourself these questions.

Are you a person who enjoys being outdoors even when it rains or if you get dirty or wet? If you answer yes, the best jobs for you would be ones where you are outside a lot. For example, you could look for a job as a camp counselor, a lifeguard, or working for a gardening service or construction company. However, some of these jobs require special skills or certification, and others are not available to high school students at all. For example, lifeguards need special training. Look for lifeguard training programs at pools or recreation centers in your town.

Do you enjoy dealing with different kinds of people? Are you able to handle a lot of things at once? If so, you may want to apply for a job waiting tables at a restaurant. Or you might try to get an office job in a business in your town. There, you will do things like make copies, organize files, or answer phones.

R *Replaced dull words with lively ones to better pull readers into my essay*

D *Deleted unnecessary sentences to make thesis statement clear*

A *Added examples to include relevant details and added information on a different perspective, or a counter-argument*

R *Reordered sentences to build the category and to follow a more logical organization*

www.phwritingcoach.com

Interactive Writing Coach™

Use the Revision RADaR strategy in your own writing. Then submit your paragraph or draft for feedback.

Apply It! Use Revision RADaR to revise your draft.

- First, make sure you have established a **clear thesis** and have used an organizational **pattern that clearly conveys your meaning**.
- Finally, apply Revision RADaR to make needed changes.

Look at the Big Picture

Use the chart and your analytical skills to evaluate how well each section of your classification essay addresses audience, purpose, and genre. When necessary, use the suggestions in the chart to revise your essay.

Section	Evaluate	Revise
Introduction	• Check the **introductory sentence**. Make sure it catches the readers' attention.	• Make your first sentence more interesting by adding a question, anecdote, or strong detail.
	• To create an effective introduction, make sure your **thesis** clearly identifies the controlling idea for your essay.	• Write a thesis that clearly answers the question "How can I classify my topic, or divide it into categories, and describe it to readers?" Include information about why the classification is important.
Body	• Make sure your organizational schema presents your categories and evidence in a **logical** way.	• If your information appears to be out of order, reorder words, sentences, and paragraphs. Add transitions between paragraphs to show connections between ideas and to help organize the flow of information.
	• Check that you have used a variety of **sentence structures** to enhance readability.	• Avoid too many long sentences in a row. Combine or break apart existing sentences for clarity and an engaging writing style.
	• Check that you have included relevant and substantial **evidence** with well-chosen details to support your thesis.	• Add facts where needed to strengthen your controlling idea. Be sure to check the validity, reliability and relevance of primary and secondary sources before using them.
	• Check that you have included ample **evidence** that analyzes the thesis statement. Underline details that offer supporting evidence. Draw a line from each detail to the category with which it belongs.	• Delete details that do not support a category. Add details to create more support, represent all relevant perspectives, and address and analyze views that contradict the thesis statement.
Conclusion	• To create an effective **concluding paragraph,** make sure that you have restated your thesis or controlling idea.	• Replace words to state your main points clearly, and make sure you don't restate the thesis word for word.
	• Check that your conclusion ends with an **insight** or memorable note.	• Add a rhetorical device, such as a rhetorical question, to make your audience think further about your topic.

Focus on Craft: Transitional Words and Phrases

Your writing will be smoother when you use clear **transitional words and phrases** to show connections between ideas. Transitions can indicate different relationships among words, phrases, and sentences, and they help convey meaning.

- To indicate examples, use terms such as *for example* and *particularly*.
- To indicate additional information, use terms such as *in addition* and *moreover*.
- To compare and contrast, use words such as *although, however,* and *yet*.
- To show a sequence of events, use words such as *next, then,* and *finally*.

 STUDENT MODEL from **You Need a Summer Job... But What Kind?** page 150; lines 16–17

If you answer yes, the best jobs for you would be ones where you are outside a lot. For example, you could look for a job as a camp counselor, a lifeguard, or working for a gardening service or construction company. However, some of these jobs require special skills or certification, and others are not available to high school students at all.

 Try It! Now, ask yourself these questions. Record your answers in your journal.

- What does the transitional phrase *For example* signal?
- What does the transitional word *however* signal?
- What is the relationship between ideas in the second and third sentences? How do these transitions make that relationship clear?

Fine-Tune Your Draft

Apply It! Use the revision suggestions to prepare your final draft.

- **Choose Effective Transitions** Use transitions to convey meaning, clarify sequence, show comparisons or contrasts, and connect ideas.
- **Keep a Consistent Tone** The tone of your draft is how you present your attitude about the topic. Review your writing to evaluate your tone—is it formal and academic, or casual and light? Revise your manuscript to achieve consistency of tone.

Teacher or Family Feedback Share your final draft with your teacher or a family member. Revise it in response to the feedback you receive.

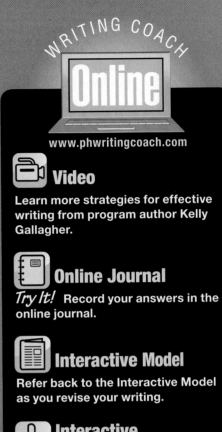

Editing: Making It Correct

When you edit your draft, you reread your work to check the spelling, grammar, and punctuation in each sentence.

As you edit your final draft, check that you have used a **variety of correctly structured sentences**, including simple, compound, complex, and compound-complex sentences. Use commas to **punctuate** each sentence structure correctly. Then correct other errors in **grammar, mechanics, and spelling.**

WRITE GUY *Jeff Anderson, M. Ed.*

WHAT DO YOU NOTICE?

Zoom in on Conventions Focus on sentence structures as you zoom in on the Mentor Text.

 **MENTOR TEXT** from **Cats and Seniors: A Loving and Healthy Relationship** pages 148–149; lines 17–22; 51–52; 62–64

> Pets… can play an important role in providing companionship and love to people…. and many scientific studies have proven this to be true…. The most important benefit was attachment…. Researchers found… that elderly owners were physically healthier when they were highly attached to their cat or dog….

Now, ask yourself: *How does the structure of each sentence differ?*

Perhaps you said that each sentence structure presents information in a different way.

The second sentence is a **simple** sentence because it has a single main clause. A main clause has a subject and a verb. A simple sentence expresses an idea concisely.

The first sentence is a **compound** sentence because it has two main clauses, which are joined by a comma and the conjunction *and*. This structure is often used to present ideas of equal weight.

The third sentence is a **complex** sentence because it has a main clause and a subordinate clause that cannot stand alone as a sentence. The subordinate clause is *when they were highly attached to their cat or dog.* Writers also use **compound-complex** sentences, which have two or more main clauses and at least one subordinate clause. The main and subordinate clauses show the relationship between ideas.

Partner Talk Discuss this question with a partner: *What would the Mentor Text be like if all its sentences had the same structure?*

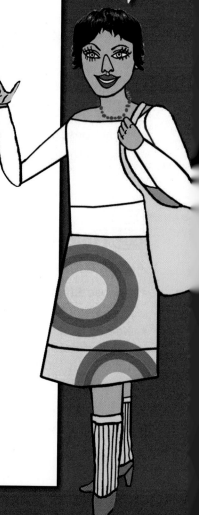

To learn more about different sentence structures, see Chapter 15.

To learn more, see Chapter 23.

Grammar Mini-Lesson: Commas in Sentence Structures

In **compound sentences,** commas separate the main clauses. In **complex sentences,** commas set off introductory subordinate clauses from the rest of the sentence. In **compound-complex sentences,** commas separate the main clauses and also set off introductory subordinate clauses. Notice the comma after the introductory clause in a complex sentence from the Mentor Text.

 MENTOR TEXT from **Cats and Seniors: A Loving and Healthy Relationship** page 149; lines 54–56

When seniors are highly attached to their cat or dog, the pet provides the same social support and companionship as humans.

 Try It! Tell whether each sentence is simple, compound, complex, or compound-complex. Then rewrite the sentences as needed to correct the use of commas. Write the answers in your journal.

1. When she got home she found an ad for the perfect job and she quickly applied.
2. Amber sent her résumé and the employer set up an interview.

Apply It! Edit your draft for **grammar, mechanics, and spelling.** If necessary, revise to use a variety of correctly structured compound, complex, and compound-complex sentences with the conventions of **correct punctuation.**

Use the rubric to evaluate your piece. If necessary, rethink, rewrite, or revise.

Rubric for Analytical Essay: Classification Essay	Rating Scale
Ideas: How clear are your categories and how well do you define them?	Not very Very 1 2 3 4 5 6
Organization: How well are your ideas organized?	1 2 3 4 5 6
Voice: How well have you engaged your reader?	1 2 3 4 5 6
Word Choice: How effective is your word choice in conveying a consistent tone?	1 2 3 4 5 6
Sentence Fluency: How well do you use transitions to create sentence fluency?	1 2 3 4 5 6
Conventions: How correct is your use of a variety of sentences?	1 2 3 4 5 6

Publishing

Share the information you've organized in your classification essay by getting it ready for a presentation. Then, choose a way to **publish it for appropriate audiences.**

Wrap Up Your Presentation

Is your essay handwritten or written on a computer? If your essay is handwritten, you may need to make a new, clean copy. Now that you have finished your draft, add the final details. Be sure to include page numbers on each page of your letter.

Publish Your Piece

Use the chart to identify a way to **publish** your essay.

If your audiences are...	...then publish it by...
Classmates or others at your school	• Submitting it to your school newspaper • Creating a multimedia presentation with images and sound that support the text and showing it to classmates
People in your neighborhood or city	• Posting it to a neighborhood Web site and inviting responses • Submitting it to a local newsletter or newspaper, or a print magazine targeted to your reading audience

 Extend Your Research

Think more about the topic on which you wrote your analytical essay. What else would you like to know about this topic? Use specific details to describe and explain your ideas. Increase the specificity of your details based on the type of information you are gathering.

- Brainstorm for several questions you would like to research and then consult, or discuss with others. Then, decide which question is your major research question.

- Formulate, or develop, a plan about how you will answer these questions.

- Decide where you will find more information—on the Internet, at the library, or through other sources.

- Finally, learn more about your topic by following through with your research plan.

 The Big Question: Why Write? What should we tell and what should we describe to make information clear?

MAKE YOUR WRITING COUNT

How to Classify

Classification is the process of analyzing a topic by breaking it into related categories. Help your classmates understand a complex topic by presenting an **informative lecture** based on a classification essay and supported by a classification chart.

Your lecture should take the form of a **multimedia presentation,** including images, graphics, and sound. Take advantage of available technology, such as presentation software or an overhead projector. Your lecture should appeal to a specific audience—your classmates. Present your lecture live or create a video podcast for students in your grade level.

WRITING COACH

Online

www.phwritingcoach.com

Online Journal

Extend Your Research Record your answers and ideas in the online journal.

Resource

Link to resources on 21st Century Learning for help in creating a group project.

Here's your action plan.

1. Choose roles, such as writer, graphics manager, and editor. Working back from your presentation date, set objectives for each group meeting.

2. Review your peers' classification essays. Select one on which to base your presentation. Assign parts for each member to cover in the lecture.

3. Research examples of classification charts and diagrams to find one that is best suited for the content you will present.

4. Plan the lecture and design the chart using available technology. Your lecture should contain:

   - Spoken text that informs your audience about the overarching principle and the characteristics of each category
   - A classification chart and bulleted list for each category
   - Images illustrating the unique properties of each category

5. Evaluate the content of your presentation to ensure you have effectively synthesized information from multiple viewpoints.

6. Then, present your lecture. Video-record it for a podcast if possible or post it online as a video.

Listening and Speaking As a group, practice delivering the lecture. Each speaker should refer to the graphics and images for support. While you rehearse, give each other feedback on effectively addressing your audience—by adjusting delivery and vocabulary, for example. Keep this feedback in mind as you present your lecture.

21st Century Learning

Script for a News Interview

Information in news articles can be presented in a variety of formats. Most articles are written as narratives, telling the true-life story of important or newsworthy events. In a **news interview script** format, the reporter's questions are presented and the subject's answers appear as a transcript of the discussion. A brief introduction often appears before the body of the interview, supplying readers with important context and background information.

In a news interview, the reporter pursues an angle on the story by following a line of questions that reveal a specific perspective or theme. This theme can be stated explicitly and directly, or it can be suggested implicitly, leaving readers to reach their own conclusions.

Try It! Study the text of the sample news interview script. Then answer these questions. Record your answers in your journal.

1. What is the **theme** of this interview? Is the theme explicit (clearly stated) or implicit (implied)?

2. Does the interviewer seem to have prepared for the interview? How do you know?

3. What information does the interviewer solicit from Ms. Parks?

4. Review the **introduction** to the interview. Does this introduction set up the circumstances behind the reason for the interview? Explain.

Extension Find another example of a script of a news interview, and compare it with this one.

A Local Hero

On Tuesday afternoon, Mary Parks, a retired schoolteacher and local adult literacy program volunteer, was in the right place at the right time. She was instrumental in helping authorities capture a mugger. Because of Ms. Parks's quick thinking, the mugger is now behind bars where he belongs, and our town's streets are safe again. One of our reporters sat down with Ms. Parks to discuss the events that took place that day.

Reporter: Ms. Parks, please tell us what you saw.

Parks: I was waiting outside of the bank for my friend Edith Wheeler. She was cashing a check.

Reporter: What happened when Ms. Wheeler came out of the bank?

Parks: It all happened so fast! A man ran up and grabbed her purse.

Reporter: Then what happened?

Parks: He was running so fast that he didn't see me. I stuck out my foot and tripped him.

Reporter: And eyewitness reports say the man dropped the purse?

Parks: It fell from his hand, and I grabbed it. Edith began shouting, and the bank guards ran outside. They caught him right away and called the police.

Reporter: How do you feel about being a local hero?

Parks: Oh, I don't think I'm a hero. I was just in the right place at the right time!

Create a Script for a News Interview

Follow these steps to create your own script for an interview. To plan your script, review the graphic organizers on R24–R27 and choose one that suits your needs.

Prewriting

- Identify a topic for the interview and an interviewee.
- Think about questions you have about the topic you've chosen. Consider both background questions and more in-depth questions.
- Research your topic and devise questions that will relay more information to the reader or viewer. Synthesize information from multiple points of view by collecting and compiling information from more than one source. Plan the angle or theme you will develop.
- Anticipate how the interviewee will respond to your questions.

Drafting

- Write a script using a question-and-answer format as its organizing structure. Include an introductory paragraph before the interview that provides background information about the topic and person being interviewed and grabs the audience's attention.
- Develop the theme for your interview. It can be implicit or explicit.
- Write the questions to ask during the interview, as well as the responses of the person being interviewed. As you draft, use a variety of literary techniques. For example, make sure that the dialogue sounds natural and include figurative language in your questions to emphasize key ideas.
- Include an attention-grabbing title for your interview script.

Revising and Editing

- Review your draft to make sure that your ideas are logically organized and that your theme has been clearly established.
- Make sure the questions and answers show knowledge of the topic. Remove any information that doesn't directly relate to the topic.

Publishing

- With a small group, create a video recording of your news interview. One person should be the narrator reading the introduction, another should be the reporter, and another should be the person being interviewed.
- Add graphics, images, and sound to enhance your work and appeal to your audience. In your video, show your audience that you have included information from multiple points of view. Present the recording to your class.

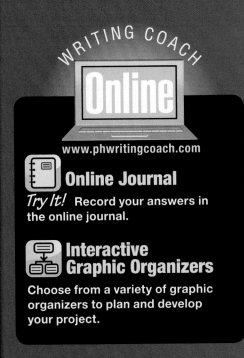

WRITING COACH

Online

www.phwritingcoach.com

Online Journal

Try It! Record your answers in the online journal.

Interactive Graphic Organizers

Choose from a variety of graphic organizers to plan and develop your project.

Partner Talk

Discuss your topic with a partner. Ask for ideas about the questions he or she might have. Monitor your partner's spoken language by asking follow-up questions to confirm your understanding.

Writing for Assessment

Many standardized tests include a prompt that asks you to write an analytical essay. Use the prompts here to practice. Respond using most of the characteristics of your classification essay. (See page 146.)

 Try It! To begin, read the **analytical essay** prompt and the information on format and academic vocabulary. Use the ABCDs of On-Demand Writing to help you plan and write your essay.

Format

The prompt directs you to write a *classification essay*. Be sure to include an introduction that clearly states your thesis, body paragraphs with main ideas supported by evidence, and a conclusion that restates your thesis.

Analytical Prompt

There are many different animals on Earth. Write a classification essay in which you classify two to three types of animals into categories, such as amphibian, mammal, and reptile. Be sure to offer evidence about why each animal belongs in the category to which you assigned it.

Academic Vocabulary

Remember that *categories* are the names of groups into which items with similar characteristics can be placed. Your *evidence* is the information you supply to support your ideas.

The ABCDs of On-Demand Writing

Use the following ABCDs to help you respond to the prompt.

Before you write your draft:

Attack the prompt [1 MINUTE]

- Circle or highlight important verbs in the prompt. Draw a line from the verb to what it refers to.
- Rewrite the prompt in your own words.

Brainstorm possible answers [4 MINUTES]

- Create a graphic organizer to generate ideas.
- Use one for each part of the prompt if necessary.

Choose the order of your response [1 MINUTE]

- Think about the best way to organize your ideas.
- Number your ideas in the order you will write about them. Cross out ideas you will not be using.

After you write your draft:

Detect errors before turning in the draft [1 MINUTE]

- Carefully reread your writing.
- Make sure that your response makes sense and is complete.
- Look for spelling, punctuation, and grammar errors.

More Prompts for Practice

Apply It! Respond to Prompts 1 and 2 in timed or open-ended situations by writing **analytical essays**. Follow these steps:

- Before gathering details, consider the validity, reliability, and relevance of your **primary and secondary sources.**

- Establish a clear **thesis** or controlling idea and then write an essay of sufficient lenght to develop the main point.

- Use an **organizing schema** that includes an effective **introduction**, logically organized **body** paragraphs, and an effective **conclusion.**

- Use **transitions** between paragraphs to connect your ideas.

- Use a variety of **sentence structures** and **rhetorical devices**.

- Include relevant and substantial **evidence** and well-chosen details, including information on all **relevant perspectives.**

- Analyze views and information that **contradict** the thesis statement and the evidence presented for it.

Prompt 1 Sometimes the food we love the most isn't very good for us. Write a classification essay in which you classify certain types of food as junk food or healthy food. Be sure to clearly explain why each type of food belongs in the category to which you assigned it.

Prompt 2 People today love a wide variety of types of movies. Write a classification essay that places three different movies into genre categories, such as drama, comedy, or horror. Explain why each movie belongs in the category to which you assigned it.

Spiral Review: Poetry Respond to Prompt 3 by writing a **poem**. Make sure your poem reflects all the characteristics described on page 120, including a specific **poetic form**, sensory details, figurative language, and other **poetic conventions** and **traditions.**

Prompt 3 Justice means "reasonableness and fairness." The concept of justice manifests in many forms and situations. Write a poem about your concept of justice. Use imagery, figurative language, and techniques such as alliteration and rhythm.

WRITING COACH

Online

www.phwritingcoach.com

Interactive Writing Coach™

Plan your response to the prompt. If you are using the prompt for practice, write one paragraph at a time or your entire draft and then submit it for feedback. If you are using the prompt as a timed test, write your entire draft and then submit it for feedback.

Remember **ABCD**

Attack the prompt

Brainstorm possible answers

Choose the order of your response

Detect errors before turning in the draft

CHAPTER 9

PERSUASION

What Do You Think?

Paying for digital music is a topic on which most people have an opinion. Some people think music should be free. Others think that people should pay for music so that artists get paid for their work.

You probably have an opinion on this topic. You may want to convince someone to share your opinion. In order to persuade someone to share your opinion, you must use facts and details to support your point of view.

Try It! Choose a side. List reasons why people should or should not be allowed to share digital music files for free. Consider these questions as you participate in an extended discussion with a partner. Take turns expressing your ideas and feelings.

- Why should music be free?
- Why should people pay for music?
- How is sharing music beneficial?
- What are the negatives of sharing digital music files for free?

Review the list you made. Choose a position on the issue by deciding which side to take. Write a sentence that states which position, or side, you will take. Then, take turns talking about your ideas and positions with a partner.

What's Ahead

In this chapter, you will review two strong examples of an argumentative essay: a Mentor Text and a Student Model. Then, using the examples as guidance, you will write an argumentative essay of your own.

WRITING COACH

www.phwritingcoach.com

Online Journal

Try It! Record your answers and ideas in the online journal.

You can also record and save your answers and ideas on pop-up sticky notes in the eText.

Connect to the Big Questions

Discuss these questions with a partner:

1 **What do you think?** Which is more important—artists' rights or community standards?

2 **Why Write?** What is your point of view? How will you know if you have convinced others?

ARGUMENTATIVE ESSAY

In this chapter, you will explore a kind of argumentative essay called an op-ed piece. An op-ed piece takes a position on an issue and tries to persuade an audience to agree with the writer's views. Op-ed pieces are found most commonly in the editorial sections of newspapers and magazines, although they may also be found online and even on TV and radio news programs, delivered as speeches.

You will develop the op-ed piece by taking it through each of the steps of the writing process: prewriting, drafting, revising, editing, and publishing. You will also have an opportunity to write an evaluative essay. To preview the criteria for how your op-ed piece will be evaluated, see the rubric on page 189.

FEATURE ASSIGNMENT

Argumentative Essay: Op-Ed Piece

An effective argumentative essay has these characteristics:

- A **lead** that introduces the topic or issue, captures readers' interest, and shows an awareness of the audience

- A **clear thesis** based on logical reasons supported by **precise and relevant evidence,** including facts, expert opinions, quotations, and/or commonly accepted beliefs

- **Information on the complete range of relevant perspectives,** including an honest and accurate representation of divergent views

- **An organizing structure** appropriate to the persuasive purpose, audience, and context

- Consideration of the validity and reliability of all **sources**

- Use of language, including **rhetorical devices** such as rhetorical questions, analogies, parallelism, and repetition, in order to appeal to an audience that doesn't care about the topic or has an opposite view

- An awareness of **possible audience response**

- Appropriate levels of **formality, style,** and **tone**

- **Effective sentence structure** and correct spelling, grammar, and usage

- A **conclusion** that restates the argument and encourages the audience to act

An effective op-ed piece also includes:

- A response to a **current event** or topic
- A tight **focus** on a single issue

Other Forms of Argumentative Essays

In addition to op-ed pieces, there are other forms of argumentative essays, including:

Advertisements are usually commercially-produced written, oral, or visual announcements intended to convince people to do or buy something.

Editorials state the opinion of editors and publishers employed by news organizations. Editorials are usually about current issues and appear in the editorial section of newspapers and magazines to distinguish them from news. Television, radio, and Internet sites may also present editorials.

Letters to the editor are written by readers who express an opinion in response to an article that has been published in the newspaper or magazine or on another topic of interest to the periodical's audience.

Persuasive essays use logic and reasoning to persuade readers to take a certain action or adopt a point of view.

Persuasive speeches try to win an audience's support for a policy, position, or action. Politicians, lobbyists, candidates for elected office, and policymakers deliver persuasive speeches.

Propaganda uses emotional appeals and often biased, false, or misleading information to persuade people to think or act in a certain way. Propaganda is often political in nature.

Reviews evaluate activities, products, and places. Many forms of media have critics who regularly contribute evaluations of things, such as books, movies, plays, computer software, video games, and restaurants. A review often advises whether people should spend time and money on something.

Try It! Imagine that you are to plan a draft for each audience and purpose described. Do preliminary draft planning by choosing a form, such as an editorial, letter to the editor, speech, or review, that is appropriate for conveying your intended meaning to multiple audiences. Explain your choices.

- To convince fellow club members to elect you president
- To discourage classmates from buying a band's new album
- To express disagreement with a decision made by your town's mayor that was described in a newspaper article

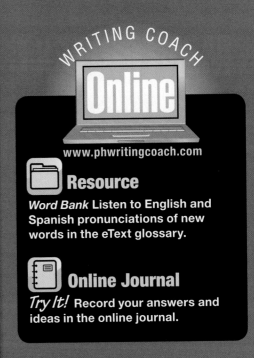

WORD BANK

People often use these basic and content-based vocabulary words when they talk about persuasive writing. Work with a partner. Take turns writing and saying each word in a sentence. If you are unsure of the meaning or pronunciation of a word, use the Glossary or a dictionary to check the definition or pronunciation.

divergent	relevant
importance	style
perspective	tone

MENTOR TEXT — Op-Ed Piece

Learn From Experience

 Read the op-ed piece on pages 174–175. As you read, take notes to develop your understanding of basic sight and English vocabulary. Then, read the numbered notes in the margins to learn how the author presented her ideas.

Answer the *Try It!* questions online or in your notebook.

1 The introduction captures readers' attention and **appeals to their sense of logic.**

Try It! According to the introduction, in what ways is a cheerleader like any other athlete? How do these similarities appeal to readers' sense of logic?

2 The author supports her assertions by providing **statistics** and quoting the **opinion of an expert.**

Try It! Is the support persuasive to you? Explain why or why not.

3 The author accurately and honestly represents a **differing view.**

Try It! With whom do you agree: the author or her opposition? Why?

Extension Find another example of an op-ed piece, and compare it with this one.

Competitive Cheerleading Is a Sport

by Tamra B. Orr

1 Every day in the United States, athletes pull on their uniforms, do stretches, lace up their shoes, and head off to practice. During their hours of training, they sweat profusely, breathe deeply, and concentrate fiercely. These athletes are not
5 in the middle of football fields, baseball diamonds, or basketball courts, however. They are on the sidelines. They are cheerleaders.

Cheerleaders have come a long way since the 1920s, when most cheerleaders were young men who did a few tumbles to entertain sports spectators. After World War II, young women
10 became involved, and by 1948, cheerleading had its own national organization. Once the first cheerleading competitions were televised in 1978, competitive cheerleading began to grow in popularity **2** It has been estimated that more than 330,000 people watch televised cheerleading competitions each year.

15 **The World of Competition 2** Currently in the United States, more than three million young men and women are involved in cheerleading. Though most of these young people perform solely for their high school or college, a significant number are involved in competitive cheerleading as well. They compete
20 against other schools in acrobatic high-pressure performances. To do so, they work as a team, memorize complicated moves, practice intensely—and risk major injury. In short, they are exactly like all athletes, except for one thing: The National Collegiate Athletic Association (NCAA) has not officially
25 recognized cheerleading as a sport. **2** "People who are older, they think back to what cheerleading was like in school and they cling to some of those stereotypes. But they don't see what's going on. They don't see the changes," said Lauren Gryskiewicz, head cheerleading coach at Georgia Tech, in an interview with
30 ESPN.com.

3 Among the arguments of those who "don't see the

changes" is that cheerleading is not competitive enough. These people argue that the primary purpose of cheerleading is to increase school spirit, whereas the primary purpose of a sport
35 is to compete. As the term "competitive cheerleading" implies, however, this type of cheerleading *is* competitive.

It is also extremely demanding. It requires the same levels of strength, skill, and mental toughness as any other sport. It also requires balance, coordination, and a sense of rhythm. **4**
40 Treating the sport as less than equal to others is an injustice. What is so important about NCAA approval? It paves the way for the funding of benefits such as sport-specific academic advisors, strength coaches, on-site training, and locker rooms. Equally important, it gives colleges the ability to offer
45 sports scholarships to cheerleaders and to recruit cheerleader athletes from high schools. In the eyes of many in the world of competitive cheerleading, NCAA approval would also give the sport the legitimacy it has already earned.

A Bigger Benefit 5 Perhaps the biggest indirect benefit
50 of NCAA acceptance is increased safety for all participants. Recruiting stronger team members would help, as would the extra funds for skilled coaches and first-rate medical care. Competitive cheerleading can be dangerous. Tricky lifts, tosses, and catches must be perfectly timed. If they aren't, landings
55 can be painful and involve anything from a temporary injury to permanent damage.

A recent report by the National Center for Catastrophic Sports Injury Research stated that cheerleading is the leading cause of sports injuries for women. Between 1980 and 2001,
60 emergency room visits for cheerleading injuries increased more than five times. "A major factor in this increase has been the change in cheerleading activity," states Dr. Frederick O. Mueller, lead researcher on the new report and a professor of exercise and sports science at Chapel Hill's University of North
65 Carolina. "If these cheerleading activities are not taught by a competent coach and keep increasing in difficulty, catastrophic injuries will continues to be a part of cheerleading."

Cheerleading is not just about standing on the sidelines and yelling support for the home team. It is also about practice,
70 hard work, skill, and stamina. In other words, it has the same requirements as any other team sport and should be recognized as such. **6** It is time for schools to join in the effort to give competitive cheerleading the recognition it deserves.

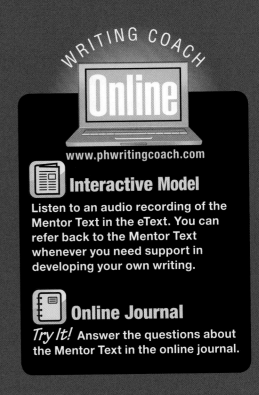

WRITING COACH

Online

www.phwritingcoach.com

Interactive Model

Listen to an audio recording of the Mentor Text in the eText. You can refer back to the Mentor Text whenever you need support in developing your own writing.

Online Journal

Try It! Answer the questions about the Mentor Text in the online journal.

4 The author **defines her position** in this **clear thesis statement.**

Try It! How does the author prepare readers for the thesis? What is her main message and purpose? Who do you think is her audience?

5 The author saves her strongest argument for last.

Try It! In the author's view, why is NCAA approval of cheerleading so important?

6 The author ends with a **call to action.**

Try It! What does the author ask schools to do?

STUDENT MODEL   Op-Ed Piece

With a small group, take turns reading this Student Model aloud. As you read, practice newly acquired vocabulary by correctly producing the word's sound. Also think about whether or not you are persuaded to agree with the author's position. Identify and provide evidence from the text to support your decision.

 ## Use a Reader's Eye

Now, reread the Student Model. On your copy of the Student Model, use the Reader's Response Symbols to react to what you read.

Reader's Response Symbols

+ I strongly agree with this.

− I strongly disagree with this.

? I have a question about this.

! Wow! That is cool/weird/interesting.

 ## Partner Talk

With a partner, share your opinions about the Student Model. Take notes and discuss responses that were the same for both of you, as well as responses that were different.

School and Community Safety—One Stop Away

by Julia Rogers

Last week's headline read "City's Most Dangerous Intersections: Central Ave and Broad Street Tops the List Again." The busy intersection at Central High's entrance presents a danger to all who pass through.
5   The four-way stop is not enough to keep pedestrians or drivers safe. A traffic light that directs cars and pedestrians is definitely and immediately needed.

The large number of drivers that pass through this intersection creates confusion, which raises the risk
10   of accident and injury. School teachers, teen drivers, public buses, and business people drive through this intersection every day. Vehicles make turns into, out of, and away from the school, as other drivers pass through on the way to work. Confusion about who has the right
15   of way causes accidents, as recent events have shown. Last month alone, three accidents happened here. No one was seriously injured, but the people involved were very lucky. According to Patrol Officer Warren, "A traffic light would greatly reduce drivers' risk of injury."

20   Accidents involving pedestrians are also a danger due to the intersection's traffic. Last week, Central High senior Ray Krantz was brushed by a car as he walked to school. His injuries were minor, but the next student hit may not be as lucky. As unclear as right of way is for
25   drivers, it is even more confusing for pedestrians. The crosswalk signs that accompany a traffic light would clearly let pedestrians know when it is all right to walk, making street crossing safe for both students and adults.

Some people argue that the new stoplight would
30   slow traffic and increase the amount of time it takes people to get to work. However, traffic studies of similar intersections have shown that this probably wouldn't happen. On average, a stoplight in this type of intersection actually lowered wait time by two minutes. "The benefits

1

35 don't end there," one Department of Transportation official explained. "Accidents decreased significantly, while driver and pedestrian confidence increased."

All in all, a new traffic light at the school intersection is a win-win situation: drivers and pedestrians would
40 both be safe. In order to achieve this, the students and community need your support. After all, would you want your child or parent to be injured at this intersection? Whoever supports local safety should contact the commissioner of the Department of Transportation.
45 E-mail him today to convince him of the importance of the stoplight!

WRITING COACH

Online

www.phwritingcoach.com

 **Interactive Model**

Listen to an audio recording of the Student Model in the eText. Use the Reader's and Writer's Response Symbols with the eText tools to note what you read.

Use a Writer's Eye

Now evaluate the piece as a writer. As you read, analyze the presentation of information by judging the coherence and logic of the writing. On your copy of the Student Model, use the Writer's Response Symbols to react to what you read.

Writer's Response Symbols	
C.T.	**Clearly stated thesis**
P.A.	**Strong persuasive arguments**
S.E.	**Effective supporting evidence**
C.A.	**Good responses to readers' counter-arguments**

Your Turn

**Feature Assignment:
Op-Ed Piece**

Prewriting

Plan a first draft of your op-ed piece **by determining an
appropriate topic.** You can select from the Topic Bank or come up
with an idea of your own.

Choose From the Topic Bank

TOPIC BANK

Mandatory Service Some people think that all 18-year-olds should perform
one year of national or community service (for example, the Peace Corps,
emergency medical services, Big Brother and Big Sister programs) before
they pursue college or a paying job. What is your position on this issue?
Write an essay in which you support your point of view with convincing
reasons and examples.

Animal Rights Some argue that animal protection laws should be
expanded. Research existing laws to protect animal rights and write an
op-ed piece for or against new laws to protect animals.

Voting Age Currently, the voting age is 18. Some people think the voting
age should be changed to 21. Write an op-ed piece in which you argue for
or against changing the voting age to 21.

Choose Your Own Topic

Determine an appropriate topic on your own by using the following **range
of strategies** to generate ideas.

Brainstorm and Research

- Generate ideas about issues that interest or concern you. With a
  partner, brainstorm for a list of issues. Take notes on your ideas and
  your partner's ideas.

- Search your library's database or the Internet to gather information on
  topics that interest you. Keep careful records of outside sources that
  you may use in your essay.

Review your notes. Choose your topic based on your interest and the
available information about your issue.

Narrow Your Topic

If your topic is too broad, you won't be able to cover it thoroughly, and your argument will be not be as persuasive as it could be.

Apply It! Use a graphic organizer like the one shown to narrow your topic.

- Write your general topic in the top box.
- Ask yourself, "Which element of this topic is most important?" Record your answer in the next box.
- Continue asking and answering questions until you identify a narrow, manageable topic for your op-ed piece.

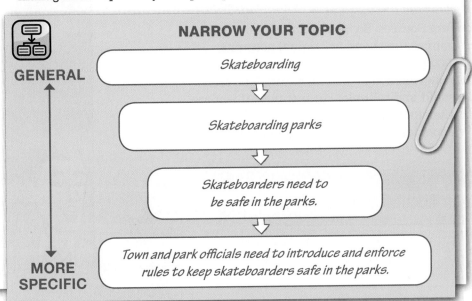

NARROW YOUR TOPIC

GENERAL

Skateboarding

Skateboarding parks

Skateboarders need to be safe in the parks.

Town and park officials need to introduce and enforce rules to keep skateboarders safe in the parks.

MORE SPECIFIC

Consider Multiple Audiences and Purposes

Before writing your argumentative essay, think about your audiences and purposes. Consider the views of others as you ask these questions, and record your answers in your journal.

Questions for Audience	Questions for Purpose
• Who are my audiences? • What do my readers already know about my topic? • What information will I need to include to help persuade my readers to agree with me?	• What attitude toward my position do I want my audiences to adopt? • What action do I hope to influence the audiences to take?

WRITING COACH

Online

www.phwritingcoach.com

Interactive Writing Coach™

- **Choosing from the Topic Bank gives you access to the Interactive Writing Coach™.**
- **Submit your writing and receive instant personalized feedback and guidance as you draft, revise, and edit your writing.**

Interactive Graphic Organizers

Use the interactive graphic organizers to help you narrow your topic.

Online Journal

Try It! **Record your answers and ideas in the online journal.**

Plan Your Piece

You will use the graphic organizer to state your thesis, organize your arguments, and identify details. When it is complete, you will be ready to write your first draft.

Develop a Clear Thesis Review and organize ideas and information you gathered to develop **a clear thesis**—one sentence that states your position. Write your thesis and add it to a graphic organizer like the one shown. All the points in your writing should contribute to this controlling idea.

Choose and Support Logical Reasons To support your thesis, list in the chart **logical reasons supported by evidence**. Record **information on the complete range of relevant perspectives** and a variety of evidence to support your arguments and respond to **divergent views**.

Consider Primary and Secondary Sources Some of your evidence will probably come from primary sources (firsthand or original accounts). Some details will come from secondary sources—those that analyze or discuss information found somewhere else. You must consider each source to make sure that it is **valid and reliable**. For instance, if you are writing an op-ed piece about the effects of video games, an article about the video games of ten years ago might not provide valid support for your point.

DEVELOP YOUR LOGICAL REASONS

Clear Thesis	*Town and park officials need to introduce and enforce rules to keep skateboarders safe in parks.*
First Logical Reason	*Injuries to skateboarders are less likely to occur if proper protective gear is worn.*
Supporting Evidence	
Second Logical Reason	*Designating specific areas based on skateboarders' expertise will protect less experienced skaters and provide a better experience for accomplished skaters.*
Supporting Evidence	
Reader's Divergent Views	*Many skateboarders cannot afford the proper protective gear.*
Response to Divergent Views	

Gather Details

To **support their logical reasons**, writers use a variety of types of details. Look at these examples:

- **Facts:** *Helmets, kneepads, and elbow pads provide protection against serious injury. Helmets guard against brain injury, and knee and elbow pads save skaters from scrapes, bruises, and even chipped bones.*

- **Expert Opinions:** *Park manager James Cellini believes that designating skating areas based on levels of expertise is sound.*

- **Quotations:** *"I learned the hard way that I should always wear knee pads," said expert skateboarder Gavin Jones. "I crashed and landed on my knee and had to wear a brace for months."*

Try It! Read the Student Model excerpt and identify which kinds of evidence the author used to support her argument. How does each type strengthen her writing?

 STUDENT MODEL from **School and Community Safety— One Stop Away** pages 176–177; lines 29–37

> Some people argue that the new stoplight would slow traffic and increase the amount of time it takes people to get to work. However, traffic studies of similar intersections have shown that this probably wouldn't happen. On average, a stoplight in this type of intersection actually lowered wait time by two minutes. "The benefits don't end there," one Department of Transportation official explained. "Accidents decreased significantly, while driver and pedestrian confidence increased."

 Apply It! Review the types of evidence a persuasive writer can use. Identify one piece of evidence for each of your logical reasons.

- Make sure your thesis uses a variety of supporting evidence. Add details to the graphic orgnizer to establish an **organizing structure** that is appropriate to your audience, persuasive purpose, and context. This plan will help you structure ideas in a sustained way.

- Be aware of your audience and avoid bias. Be sure to include an accurate and honest representation of **views** that are divergent, or different, from your own. Your response to those views should be respectful and use an appropriate level of **formality, style, and tone**.

- **Craft and keep a list of language to move an audience** that may be uninterested in or opposed to your view.

WRITING COACH

Online

www.phwritingcoach.com

Interactive Graphic Organizers

Use the interactive graphic organizers to help you create a plan for your writing.

Interactive Model

Refer back to the Interactive Model in the eText as you plan your writing.

Drafting

During the drafting stage, you will start to write your ideas for your op-ed piece. You will follow an outline that provides an **organizing structure appropriate to your persuasive purpose, audience, and context**. This will help you write a focused, organized, and coherent op-ed piece.

The Organization of an Argumentative Essay

The chart shows an organizational strategy for an argumentative essay. Look back at how the Mentor Text follows this organizational strategy. Then, use this chart to help you outline your draft.

Outline *for* Success

I. Introduction

See Mentor Text, p. 176.

- Lead
- Clear thesis or position

II. Body

See Mentor Text, p. 176–177.

- Logical reasons supported by evidence
- Organizing structure appropriate to persuasion
- An accurate and honest representation of divergent views, as well as information on the complete range of relevant perspectives

III. Conclusion

See Mentor Text, p. 177.

- Restatement of position
- Call to action

Formulate Your Thesis

- An effective opening should grab readers' interest. It can include a startling statistic, a relevant quotation, or a rhetorical question.
- A clear thesis identifies the topic or issue and states your position, or opinion, on the issue.

Structure Your Ideas

- The strongest arguments use a variety of types of evidence to directly support the position.
- One organizational structure appropriate to persuasion is ordering ideas from least to most important or from most to least, whichever will have the greater impact.
- Divergent views are those that differ from your own. Relevant perspectives are those that are directly related to the topic of your op-ed piece. Avoid bias by addressing these.

Wrap It Up

- A call to action asks your audience to do something specific and concrete, such as writing to an elected official.

Start Your Draft

Use the checklist to help complete your draft. Use the graphic organizer that shows your thesis, logical reasons, and precise and relevant evidence, as well as the Outline for Success as guides.

While drafting, aim at writing your ideas, not on making your writing perfect. Remember, you will have the chance to improve your draft when you revise and edit.

√ Draft your lead, the opening sentences that engage the audience. Your **opening** should set the tone for your essay, establishing your attitude toward the topic and the level of formality you will use.

√ Build your **introduction** by presenting a clear and **logical thesis**.

√ **Structure** the ideas in the **body** of your op-ed piece in a way that will persuade your audience and is appropriate to the context, or the environment in which you are sharing your op-ed piece.

√ Include a variety of support for your ideas and use counter-arguments to respond to opposing views. Develop a focused paragraph for each logical reason and its support. Include only evidence from **valid** and **reliable primary** and **secondary sources**.

√ Use specific **rhetorical devices**, such as an analogy, to back up your assertions. For example, draw a connection between your ideas and something familiar to readers: "If we don't hold people accountable, we are just like referees who don't call fouls."

√ Provide information on all **relevant perspectives.** When they differ from your own, accurately and honestly present each divergent view as fairly as you can. Report it without bias by using the author's own words when possible and avoiding taking ideas out of context.

√ Craft language that will move those who are uninterested in or opposed to your views. Adjust your levels of **formality, style, and tone** based on what is appropriate for your audience.

√ End with a strong **conclusion** that restates your position and presents a specific **call to action.**

WRITING COACH

Online

www.phwritingcoach.com

Interactive Model

Outline for Success View pop-ups of Mentor Text referenced in the Outline for Success.

Interactive Writing Coach™

Use the Interactive Writing Coach to receive the level of support you need:
- Write one paragraph at a time and submit each one for immediate, detailed feedback.
- Write your entire first draft and submit it for immediate, personalized feedback.

Revising: Making It Better

Now that you have finished your first draft, you are ready to revise. Think about the "big picture." You will consider the logical organization and clarity of meaning in your writing. You can use Revision RADaR as a guide for making changes to improve your draft. Revision RADaR provides four major ways to improve your writing: (R) replace, (A) add, (D) delete, and (R) reorder.

Kelly Gallagher, M. Ed.

KEEP REVISION ON YOUR RADAR

Read part of the first draft of the Student Model "School and Community Safety—One Stop Away." Then look at questions the writer asked herself as she thought about how well her draft addressed issues of logical organization and clarity of meaning.

School and Community Safety—One Stop Away

Last week's headline read "City's Most Dangerous Intersections: Central Ave and Broad Street Tops the List Again." The busy intersection at Central High's entrance is bad. Something should be done about this.

Last month alone, three accidents happened here. No one was seriously injured, but the people involved were very lucky. The large number of drivers that pass through this intersection creates confusion, which raises the risk of accident and injury. Teachers, teen drivers, school buses, and business people drive through this intersection every day. Vehicles make turns into, out of, and away from the school, as other drivers pass through on the way to work. Confusion about who has the right of way causes accidents, as recent events have shown. A police officer thinks that a traffic light would help.

Does my thesis statement precisely and effectively express my position and purpose?

Is my organization of ideas logical and fluid? Have I presented my main point first?

Is my idea expressed precisely and persuasively? Is the source of my information clear?

Now look at how the writer applied Revision RADaR to write an improved second draft.

School and Community Safety—One Stop Away

Last week's headline read "City's Most Dangerous Intersections: Central Ave and Broad Street Tops the List Again." The busy intersection at Central High's entrance presents a danger to all who pass through. The four-way stop is not enough to keep pedestrians or drivers safe. A traffic light that directs cars and pedestrians is definitely and immediately needed.

The large number of drivers that pass through this intersection creates confusion, which raises the risk of accident and injury. Teachers, teen drivers, school buses, and business people drive through this intersection every day. Vehicles make turns into, out of, and away from the school, as other drivers pass through on the way to work. Confusion about who has the right of way causes accidents, as recent events have shown. Last month alone, three accidents happened here. No one was seriously injured, but the people involved were very lucky. According to Patrol Officer Warren, "A traffic light would greatly reduce drivers' risk of injury."

R *Replaced the imprecise word bad with the word danger*

A *Added precise words to clarify meaning and to establish a clear thesis statement*

R *Reordered sentences to place my topic sentence first and to organize sentences more logically and fluidly*

R *Replaced general language with a quotation and identified the source of the information to clarify meaning*

Interactive Writing Coach™

Use the Revision RADaR strategy in your own writing. Then submit your paragraph or draft for feedback.

Apply It! Use Revision RADaR to revise your draft.

- First, determine if you have logically organized your essay, clearly expressed meaning, and included the characteristics of the op-ed form of the argumentative essay.
- Then apply Revision RADaR to make needed changes. Focus on **revising your draft to clarify meaning** by rearranging the words, sentences, and paragraphs. Remember—you can use the steps in Revision RADaR in any order.

Look at the Big Picture

Use the chart and your analytical skills to evaluate whether each section of your op-ed piece has clarity of meaning. Ensure that your writing reflects an awareness and anticipation of audience response through its **style, tone, and level of formality**. When necessary, use the suggestions in the chart to revise your piece.

Section	Evaluate	Revise
Introduction	• Check the **lead**. Will it grab readers' attention and draw them to the author's purpose?	• Add interest to your lead with rhetorical devices, such as rhetorical questions and hyperbole, or exaggeration.
	• Make sure you clearly and logically state your position in the **thesis**. Check that you use persuasive language here and throughout your writing.	• Use precise and carefully crafted language—vivid adjectives, strong opinion words, active verbs—to clarify the thesis and to move opposed or uninterested readers.
Body	• Check the logic of your reasons and underline details that offer **supporting evidence**. Draw a line from each detail to the reason it supports.	• Refine your key ideas by using precise language. Rearrange any detail that is not in the same paragraph as the reason it supports. If needed, delete or add details.
	• Make sure that your primary and secondary **sources** and the points you include are valid and reliable.	• Remove information from unrelated or untrustworthy sources.
	• Check that your **organizational structure** is appropriate to the audience, context, and purpose—persuasion.	• Rearrange arguments to make them more logical and fluid. Experiment to determine whether presenting the weakest or strongest argument first is more effective.
	• Make sure your representation of **divergent views** is accurate and honest and that all relevant perspectives are presented.	• Remove any bias or inaccuracies from descriptions of opposing views. Add any missing perspectives.
Conclusion	• Check the **restatement** of your position.	• Clarify meaning by changing words or rearranging sentences.
	• Make sure you include a clear **call to action.**	• Add specific and direct instructions to reinforce your call to action.

Focus on Craft: Rhetorical Questions

Employing **tropes, or rhetorical devices,** such as rhetorical questions allows you to achieve a specific rhetorical purpose in your essay. A rhetorical purpose is the intent of a piece of writing, such as to persuade or to explain. Rhetorical questions are asked for effect, not to be answered. For example, "When will this end?" is not asked to get information, but to express the speaker's impatience. Using carefully crafted and placed rhetorical questions in persuasion can help move an opposed audience.

Think about the rhetorical effect produced by this excerpt.

 STUDENT MODEL from **School and Community Safety— One Stop Away** page 177; lines 39-44

> All in all, a new traffic light at the school intersection is a win-win situation: drivers and pedestrians would both be safe. In order to achieve this, the students and community need your support. After all, would you want your child or parent to be injured at this intersection? Whoever supports local safety should contact the commissioner of the Department of Transportation.

Try It! Now, ask yourself these questions. Record your answers in your journal.

- What point does the author make with her rhetorical question?
- What rhetorical purpose does she hope to achieve?

 Fine-Tune Your Draft

Apply It! Use these suggestions to revise your draft to employ tropes and to achieve specific rhetorical purposes and consistency of tone.

- **Employ Tropes** Suggest ideas to your readers through rhetorical questions.
- **Achieve Rhetorical Purposes** Review your writing to ensure that you are using effective strategies to persuade your readers.
- **Maintain Consistency of Tone** Make sure your tone, the attitude toward your subject and audience, remains consistent throughout your op-ed piece. Revise your words and sentence structures to achieve a consistent and appropriate tone.

Peer Feedback Read your final draft to a group of peers. Ask if you have honestly and accurately represented and addressed divergent views. Think about your peers' responses and revise your final draft as needed.

WRITING COACH

Online

www.phwritingcoach.com

Video
Learn more strategies for effective writing from program author Kelly Gallagher.

Online Journal
Try It! Record your answers in the online journal.

Interactive Model
Refer back to the Interactive Model as you revise your writing.

 Interactive Writing Coach™
Revise your draft and submit it for feedback.

Editing: Making It Correct

To edit your draft, read it carefully to correct errors in spelling and grammar. It can be helpful to read your draft aloud to listen for where the writing needs correction.

Before editing your final draft, consider using **different types of clauses,** such as **adjectival, adverbial, and noun clauses.** Also consider using **parallel structures** within sentences and paragraphs. Then edit your final draft for any errors in **grammar, mechanics, and spelling.** Use a dictionary to check your spelling.

WRITE GUY *Jeff Anderson, M. Ed.*

WHAT DO YOU NOTICE?

Zoom in on Conventions Focus on the clauses— groups of words containing a subject and a verb— as you zoom in on the lines from the Student Model.

 **STUDENT MODEL** from **School and Community Safety– One Stop Away** pages 176-177; lines 25-27, 43-44

> The crosswalk signs that accompany a traffic light would clearly let pedestrians know when it is all right to walk.... Whoever supports local safety should contact the commissioner of the Department of Transportation.

To learn more about clauses, see Chapter 15.

Now ask yourself: *What does the first highlighted clause name or describe?*

Perhaps you said that *that accompany a traffic light* modifies the word *signs.* This clause is an **adjectival clause,** a subordinate clause that stands in for an adjective to modify a noun or pronoun. Adjectival clauses usually begin with a relative pronoun (e.g., *who, whom, whose, which, that*), which connects the clause to the word it modifies.

When it is all right to walk is a noun clause acting as a direct object of the verb *know. Whoever supports local safety* is also a noun clause acting as the subject of the second sentence. *Whoever supports local safety* is a noun clause. A **noun clause** is a subordinate clause that acts as a noun, naming a person, place, or thing. Noun clauses may function as the subject or object of a sentence and often begin with one of the following words: *how, that, what, when, where, whether, which, who, whom, whose, why.*

Partner Talk Discuss this question with a partner: *Why might a writer use clauses in place of adjectives, adverbs, and nouns?*

Grammar Mini-Lesson: Parallel Structures

Using **parallel structures** in a sentence means that equal ideas are expressed in words, phrases, clauses, or sentences of similar types. Parallel structure can add to the persuasive force of writing. Notice how the author uses parallel structure in the Student Model.

To learn more, see Chapter 16.

 STUDENT MODEL from **School and Community Safety– One Stop Away** page 176; lines 10–12

School teachers, teen drivers, public buses, and business people drive through this intersection every day.

 Try It! Tell whether each sentence includes an adjectival, adverbial, or noun clause. Then identify the sentence that has a parallel structure. Write the answers in your journal.

1. Reading a book, taking a nap, and baking a cake are my favorite things to do whenever it rains.
2. The traffic light that was desperately needed is living up to expectations.
3. Whatever you found should be returned to the owner.

 Apply It! Edit your draft for grammar, mechanics, and spelling. If necessary, rewrite some sentences to ensure that you have used **different types of clauses**, as well as complete sentences that include parallel structures.

 Use the rubric to evaluate your piece. If necessary, rethink, rewrite, or revise.

Rubric for Argumentative Essay: Op-Ed Piece	Rating Scale
Ideas: How clearly are the issue and your position stated?	Not very Very 1 2 3 4 5 6
Organization: How organized are your arguments and supporting evidence?	1 2 3 4 5 6
Voice: How authoritative is your voice?	1 2 3 4 5 6
Word Choice: How persuasive is the language you have used?	1 2 3 4 5 6
Sentence Fluency: How well have you used transitional words and phrases to show connections?	1 2 3 4 5 6
Conventions: How effective is your use of parallel structures?	1 2 3 4 5 6

 WRITING COACH

Online

www.phwritingcoach.com

 Video

Learn effective editing techniques from program author Jeff Anderson.

Online Journal

Try It! Record your answers in the online journal.

Interactive Model

Refer back to the Interactive Model as you edit your writing.

Interactive Writing Coach™

Edit your draft. Check it against the rubric and then submit it for feedback.

Publishing

Now you have the chance to change someone's mind—publish your op-ed piece. First, prepare your piece for publication. Choose a way to **publish** your **written work for appropriate audiences**.

Wrap Up Your Presentation

Is your piece handwritten or written on a computer? If your piece is handwritten, you may need to make a new, clean copy. If so, be sure to **write legibly.** Also be sure that your title grabs the reader's attention and indicates what your piece is about.

Publish Your Piece

Use the chart to identify a way to publish your piece.

If your audience is...	...then publish it by...
People in your community	• Submitting it to your local newspaper • Posting it on a community blog
School or community officials	• Presenting a multimedia presentation at a school board or community meeting • E-mailing it to the officials you want to persuade

 Extend Your Research

Think more about the topic on which you wrote your op-ed piece. What else would you like to know about this topic?

- Brainstorm for several questions you would like to research and then consult, or discuss with others. Then decide which question is your major research question.

- Formulate, or develop, a plan about how you will answer these questions. Decide where you will find more information—on the Internet, at the library, or through other sources.

- Finally, learn more about your topic by following through with your research plan.

 The Big Question: Why Write? What is your point of view? How will you know if you have convinced others?

MAKE YOUR WRITING COUNT

Debate Expert Opinions About a Complex Issue

Op-ed writers present their own points of view on controversial issues in the best possible terms. They acknowledge an opponent's point of view only to refute it. Help your classmates more thoroughly consider *both* sides of an important issue in a **debate**.

With a group, analyze and evaluate alternative points of view about an issue you covered in an op-ed piece. Then organize and present your ideas and information in a debate. Present your debate live or record it as a podcast.

Here's your action plan.

1. Establish debate rules. Choose roles for each group member, such as a moderator and up to four experts, two on each side of the debate.

2. Research debate formats online.

3. Review your peers' op-ed pieces and choose one on which to base the debate. Students playing experts should identify an area of expertise to support their side of the debate.

4. As a team, plan your debate. Each expert should be able to:

   - Express a clear opinion in response to the moderator's proposition

   - Present evidence to support or rebut positions

   - Use effective speaking and listening techniques to ensure that the style and content of the language is selected to influence the listener's understanding

5. The moderator should explain the rules, propose the issue for debate, and keep track of time.

6. Present your debate live or as a video podcast.

Listening and Speaking Each side or team should rehearse separately, with help and feedback from the moderator. Experts should take turns presenting opinions and supporting evidence within the established timeframe. During the actual debate, teams should try to convince the audience to support their specific point of view. Have the audience vote to determine which side wins the debate.

WRITING COACH

Online

www.phwritingcoach.com

Online Journal

Extend Your Research Record your answers and ideas in the online journal.

Resource

Link to resources on 21st Century Learning for help in creating a group project.

21st Century Learning

Evaluative Essay

An **evaluative essay** analyzes a subject, such as a book, a movie, or a political agenda, and expresses a judgment of or opinion about it. Evaluative essays appear in the forms of book and movie reviews, newspaper and magazine articles, and online publications.

Though the purpose of an evaluative essay is to make a judgment, it is important to avoid directly stating something is "great" or "horrible." An evaluative essay, instead, should explain why something has or lacks quality, using logical reasons and concrete evidence to support the writer's judgment or opinion.

Try It! Read the excerpt from the evaluative essay on this page. Then answer the questions. Record your answers in your writing journal.

1. Which sentence provides a **lead** that draws readers in and sets the stage for the argument?

2. The author presents a **clear thesis** that explains the author's evaluation of the restaurant without using generalities such as *good* or *bad*. How does the author feel about the restaurant?

3. What **logical reasons** does the writer include in the body of his evaluative essay to support his opinion?

4. What kind of **evidence** supports the reason?

5. Is the **organizational structure** of the information logical?

Extension Find another example of an evaluative essay, and compare it with this one

Heavenly Burgers

by Dave Preston

I couldn't believe it when I saw the sign outside of Burger Heaven on Main Street that read: "Under new management! Grand Reopening!" I wondered what kinds of changes had been made. Really, is there any way to improve the best burgers in Texas? I decided to have lunch there and soon realized that the answer to the question was undoubtedly yes.

I surveyed the menu and was shocked to discover an array of new and seemingly strange items on its glossy pages: Hawaiian burgers, avocado burgers, south-of-the-border burgers, and burgers topped with brie cheese and apple chutney. Although it was quite different from my usual choice at Burger Heaven, I decided to be adventurous and try the latter. The brie, chutney, and high-quality ground beef created a subtle yet lovely taste combination. The sweetness of the chutney was perfectly balanced by the savory meat. I suddenly did, indeed, find myself in heaven!

If you're a regular who chooses not to let your taste buds walk the wild side, you can still order any burger you did before the changes were made. Bob Killian, the new manager, told me, "We want to make sure we have a burger for everyone. Old Burger Heaven favorites mingle among the new burgers on the menu." And he's right—there's something for everyone here. I urge you to run—not walk—to the new and improved Burger Heaven!

Create an Evaluative Essay

Follow these steps to create your own evaluative essay. To plan your evaluative essay, review the graphic organizers on pages R24–R27 and choose one that suits your needs.

Prewriting

- Choose a familiar subject about which you have a strong opinion, such as a book you have recently read or a movie you have seen.
- Identify your audience and anticipate your audience's response.
- Choose your form—a review, a newspaper article, or an online publication, for example.
- Formulate a clear thesis that identifies not only your opinion or judgment but explains why the subject possesses or lacks quality.

Drafting

- Begin by crafting your introduction, including a clear thesis statement.
- Draft the body of your essay by developing well-organized paragraphs for each logical reason and including evidence as support. For instance, use each paragraph to discuss one reason that you recommend (or do not recommend) the thing you are evaluating. Be sure to respond to the views of those who might argue with your evaluation.
- Use language that will appeal to your audience. For instance, if you are reviewing a new documentary about skateboarding for your school newspaper, it might be appropriate to use an informal tone and jargon that teenagers would understand.
- Structure your ideas in a persuasive way, organizing them so that readers can easily follow your ideas.

Revising and Editing

- Review your draft to ensure that your writing demonstrates a clear focus, logically develops ideas in well-organized paragraphs, and uses language that will persuade your readers. Add any missing information and take out unnecessary words or unrelated evidence.
- Check that spelling, grammar, and mechanics are correct.

Publishing

- Make a final draft of your essay, being sure to give it a title. Share your essay with the class. Consider posting it on your school's Web site and inviting others to respond to your ideas.

WRITING COACH

Online

www.phwritingcoach.com

Online Journal

Try It! Record your answers in the online journal.

Interactive Graphic Organizers

Choose from a variety of graphic organizers to plan and develop your project.

 **Partner Talk**

Before you begin drafting, describe your ideas to a partner. Use specific details to describe and explain your ideas. Increase the specificity of your details based on the type of information you are delivering. Discuss if you have addressed divergent views.

Writing for Assessment ![SAT PREP ACT]

Many standardized tests include prompts that require you to write an argumentative essay. You can use the prompts on these pages to practice. Your responses should include the same characteristics as your op-ed piece. See page 172 to review these characteristics.

 Try It! Read the persuasive prompt and the information on format and academic vocabulary. Use the ABCDs of On-Demand Writing to help you plan and write your essay.

Format

The prompt directs you to write an *argumentative essay*. Be sure your thesis is clear, logical, and supported by evidence. Use an appropriate organizing structure, with an introduction, body, and conclusion.

Persuasive Prompt

Fiction and nonfiction are two distinctly different forms of literature. Identify which you prefer and why. Write an argumentative essay to advance your opinion. Be sure to include a clear thesis supported by logical reasons and relevant evidence.

Academic Vocabulary

Remember that a *thesis* is the statement of your position and is supported by *logical reasons*—your main arguments. Use *evidence*—facts, expert opinions, or quotations—to back up your reasons.

The ABCDs of On-Demand Writing

Use the following ABCDs to help you respond to the prompt.

Before you write your draft:

Attack the prompt [1 MINUTE]

- Circle or highlight important verbs in the prompt. Draw a line from the verb to what it refers to.
- Rewrite the prompt in your own words.

Brainstorm possible answers [4 MINUTES]

- Create a graphic organizer to generate ideas.
- Use one for each part of the prompt if necessary.

Choose the order of your response [1 MINUTE]

- Think about the best way to organize your ideas.
- Number your ideas in the order you will write about them. Cross out ideas you will not be using.

After you write your draft:

Detect errors before turning in the draft [1 MINUTE]

- Carefully reread your writing.
- Make sure that your response makes sense and is complete.
- Look for spelling, punctuation, and grammar errors.

More Prompts for Practice

Apply It! Respond to Prompt 1 by writing an **argumentative essay** **that includes a clear position.** As you write, be sure to:

- Formulate a clear **thesis** or position
- Include **divergent views** without bias and provide information on a complete range of **related perspectives**
- Use an appropriate **organizing structure** for persuasive writing
- Check that all your **sources, primary and secondary,** are valid and reliable
- Use language crafted to move **a disinterested or opposed audience**
- Include **rhetorical devices,** such as analogies or rhetorical questions, to back up assertions
- Show an awareness and anticipation of **audience response** by adjusting the level of formality, style, and tone as needed

> **Prompt 1** Write an argumentative essay to persuade your friends that the sport you love is the best one to play. Present a clear thesis based on logical reasons.

Spiral Review: Analytical Respond to Prompt 2 by writing an **analytical essay.** Make sure your essay reflects all of the characteristics described on page 146, including:

- Effective **introductions and conclusions**
- A variety of **sentence structures, rhetorical devices,** and **transitions** between paragraphs
- A clear **thesis statement** or controlling idea
- A clear **organizational schema** for conveying ideas
- Relevant and substantial **evidence** and well-chosen **details**
- Information on all **relevant perspectives**
- Consideration of the validity, reliability, and relevance of **primary and secondary sources**
- An analysis of views and information that **contradict the thesis statement** and the evidence presented for it

> **Prompt 2** Write an essay about the problem of childhood obesity and possible solutions to fix it. Support your ideas with ample evidence.

WRITING COACH

Online

www.phwritingcoach.com

Interactive Writing Coach™

Plan your response to the prompt. If you are using the prompt for practice, write one paragraph at a time or your entire draft and then submit it for feedback. If you are using the prompt as a timed test, write your entire draft and then submit it for feedback.

Remember **ABCD**

Attack the prompt

Brainstorm possible answers

Choose the order of your response

Detect errors before turning in the draft

CHAPTER 10

RESPONSE to LITERATURE

What Do You Think?

Authors have purposes for writing. Some authors write to inform. Some write to entertain. Others write to persuade.

Part of being an active reader is analyzing the author's purpose. You think about the author's purpose and use details to show how the author achieves that purpose.

Try It! Think about your favorite book. What do you think the author was trying to communicate by writing this book? Consider these questions as you participate in an extended discussion with a partner. Take turns expressing your ideas and feelings.

- How did you feel when reading this book?
- How did the author achieve his or her purpose?
- Do you think the author did a good job achieving his or her purpose? Why or why not?
- What details support your answer?

After your discussion, work with your partner to list several ideas to share with the class.

What's Ahead

In this chapter, you will review two strong examples of an interpretative response essay: a Mentor Text and a Student Model. Then, using the examples as guides, you will write an interpretative response essay of your own.

Connect to the Big Questions

Discuss these questions with a partner:

1 What do you think? What does the reader bring to a work of literature?

2 Why Write? What should you write about to make others interested in a text?

INTERPRETATIVE RESPONSE

An interpretative response is a brief analytic essay that presents the writer's ideas about an expository or literary work. In this chapter, you will explore a special kind of interpretative response: a comparison essay. When you write a comparison essay, you analyze two authors' works to identify similarities and differences in their treatment of a specific literary element. You provide evidence from the text, including quotations, as you analyze and explain your reactions to each work.

You will develop your comparison essay by taking it through each step of the writing process: prewriting, drafting, revising, editing, and publishing. You will also have an opportunity to write a music review of one of your favorite songs. To preview the criteria for how your comparison essay will be evaluated, see the rubric on page 215.

FEATURE ASSIGNMENT

Interpretative Response: Comparison Essay

An effective interpretative response has these characteristics:

- A **clear thesis** statement
- Writing that addresses the writing skills for an **analytical essay**
- References to and commentary on **evidence from the text,** including quotations, examples, and specific details
- Analysis of the **aesthetic,** or artistic **effects** of the authors' use of **stylistic or rhetorical devices,** such as symbolism, analogies, and rhetorical questions
- Analysis of **ambiguities**—uncertainties, **nuances**—slight differences in meaning, and **complexities** within the text

- Anticipation of and response to **readers' questions** and **contradictory,** or opposing, **information**
- **Effective sentence structure** and correct spelling, grammar, and usage

A comparison essay also includes:

- Analysis of a **specific element,** such as theme or character, and its treatment in two different works
- **Conclusions** that make the comparison valuable or important

Other Forms of Interpretative Response

In addition to a comparison essay, there are other forms of interpretative response, including:

Critical reviews evaluate books, plays, poetry, and other literary works. They appear in newspapers and magazines, on television and radio, and on the Internet. These kinds of interpretative works present the writer's opinions and support them with specific examples.

Letters to an author present an analysis of an author's work and the writer's reactions to it. The writer shares thoughts and feelings about what he or she has read and discusses what the work communicated. The writer also examines how the author's writing style added to the work. A letter includes a greeting and a closing and may ask the author questions or make requests of the author.

Response to literature essays analyze and interpret an author's work. These essays examine what an author states directly and indirectly and what those statements mean. Response to literature essays also evaluate how well an author has accomplished what he or she has set out to do.

Try It! For each audience and purpose described, select the correct form, such as a critical review or a comparison essay, that is appropriate for conveying your intended meaning to the audience. Explain your responses.

- To convince readers that a piece of literature is worth reading
- To demonstrate to a teacher how two pieces of literature are alike
- To explain to your classmates that a seemingly simple poem has a deeper meaning

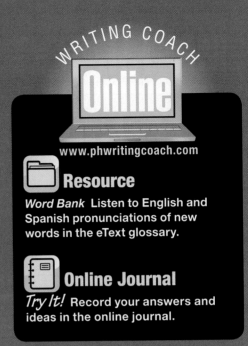

WRITING COACH

Online

www.phwritingcoach.com

Resource

Word Bank Listen to English and Spanish pronunciations of new words in the eText glossary.

Online Journal

Try It! Record your answers and ideas in the online journal.

WORD BANK

People often use these vocabulary words when they talk about interpretative response writing. Work with a partner. Take turns using each word in a sentence. If you are unsure of the meaning of a word, look at its affixes, or word parts—prefix, root, and suffix—for clues or use the Glossary or a dictionary to check the definition.

analyze	**interpret**
demonstrate	**style**
evaluate	**thematic**

MENTOR TEXT

Learn From Experience

 Read the comparison essay on pages 200–201. As you read, take notes to develop your understanding of basic sight and English vocabulary. Then, read the numbered notes in the margins to learn about how the author presented his ideas.

Answer the *Try It!* questions online or in your notebook.

---

1 The **introduction** makes a brief **analysis** of Arthur Conan Doyle's greatest achievement.

Try It! According to the author, what was Doyle's greatest achievement as an author?

2 The **controlling idea** makes it clear that the essay will show how Edgar Allan Poe's writing influenced Doyle's writing.

Try It! From the controlling idea, what main points about Poe's influence on Doyle do you think the essay will analyze?

3 This paragraph **compares and contrasts** the characters of Sherlock Holmes and C. Auguste Dupin.

Try It! How does the comparison and contrast support the controlling idea of the essay?

Extension Find another example of a comparison essay, and compare it with this one.

From Arthur Conan Doyle

by Robert W. Millett

1 In spite of his desire to be acknowledged as a writer of "serious" literature, Arthur Conan Doyle is destined to be remembered as the creator of a fictional character who has taken on a life separate from the literary works in which he appears.
5 Sherlock Holmes, as the prototype of almost all fictional detectives, has become a legend not only to his devotees but also to those who have not even read the works in which he appears. . . .

Doyle claimed that the character of Sherlock Holmes was based upon his memories of Dr. Joseph Bell, a teacher of anatomy
10 at the University of Edinburgh, whose diagnostic skills he had admired as a student of medicine. Bell, however, disclaimed the honor and suggested that Doyle himself possessed the analytical acumen that more closely resembled the skills of Sherlock Holmes. **2** Regardless of the disclaimers and acknowledgments,
15 there is little doubt that Doyle owed a large debt to Edgar Allan Poe and other predecessors in detective fiction. . . . It is the influence of Poe, however, that is most in evidence in the character of Holmes and in many of his plots.

Poe's character of C. Auguste Dupin bears remarkable
20 similarities to the Sherlock Holmes character. **3** Both Holmes and Dupin, for example, are eccentrics; both are amateurs in the detective field; both have little regard for the official police; and both enter into investigations not because of any overwhelming desire to bring a culprit to justice but out of the interest that
25 the case generates and the challenge to their analytical minds. In addition, both have faithful companions who serve as the chroniclers of the exploits of their respective detective friends. While Dupin's companion remains anonymous and the reader is unable to draw any conclusions about his personality, Dr.
30 Watson, on the other hand, takes on an identity (although always in a secondary role) of his own. The reader shares with Watson his astonishment at Holmes's abilities. In effect, Watson becomes a stand-in for the reader by asking the questions that need to be asked for a complete understanding of the situation.

WRITING COACH

Online

www.phwritingcoach.com

Interactive Model

Listen to an audio recording of the Mentor Text in the eText. You can refer back to the Mentor Text whenever you need support in developing your own writing.

Online Journal

Try It! Answer the questions about the Mentor Text in the online journal.

35 ❹ Generally, the Sherlock Homes stories follow a similar pattern: there is usually a scene at the Baker Street residence, at which time a visitor appears and tells his or her story. After Holmes makes some preliminary observations and speculates upon a possible solution to the puzzle, Holmes and Watson
40 visit the scene of the crime. Holmes then solves the mystery and explains to Watson how he arrived at the solution. "The Adventure of the Speckled Band" follows this formula, and it is apparent that Poe's "The Murders in the Rue Morgue" had a direct influence upon this "locked room" mystery. The murder,
45 the locked room, and the animal killer are all variations upon the ingredients in the first case in which C. Auguste Dupin appears. Even the reference to the orangutan on the grounds of the Manor House would appear to be an allusion to the murderer in Poe's story. . . .
50 Although Watson informs the reader that Holmes's knowledge of formal philosophy is nil, he is a philosopher in his own way. ❺ Holmes has probed the most abstract of understanding— ranging from the motivation of men to the nature of the universe—from the study of the physical world. He possesses
55 a peculiar morality akin to the John Stuart Mill variety: evil is doing harm to others. When he seeks justice, he inevitably finds it. . . . For him, the distinction between right and wrong is absolute and beyond debate. It was Doyle's skill in infusing such depth into his character that makes Holmes greater than Dupin.

❹ The author gives examples of similarities in Doyle's plots and Poe's plots. This **evidence** helps support the essay's **controlling idea.**

> *Try It!* How do the examples support the controlling idea? In your opinion, is this evidence convincing? Explain why or why not.

❺ The conclusion analyzes the **aesthetic effects** of Doyle's characterization of Sherlock Holmes.

> *Try It!* According to the author, how did Doyle make Sherlock Holmes such an extraordinary character?

Mentor Text **201**

STUDENT MODEL

Comparison Essay

With a small group, take turns reading the Student Model aloud. Look for evidence from the text that supports your understanding.

 Use a Reader's Eye

Reread the Student Model. On your copy of the Student Model, use the Reader's Response Symbols to react to what you read.

Reader's Response Symbols

+   **I agree with this point.**

−   **This isn't clear to me.**

?   **I have a question about this.**

!   **Well said!**

Participate in an extended discussion with a partner. Express your opinions and share your responses to the Student Model. Discuss the use of quotations to compare a specific element of the two poems.

Keats and Donne on Death

by Isaac Bergman

Death is a serious theme worthy of great poets. For example, John Keats's "When I Have Fears That I May Cease to Be" and John Donne's "Death, Be Not Proud" both discuss death in profound ways.
5 However, the imagery in these poems shows that while Keats believes that death can only destroy, Donne believes that death can be overcome.

Keats is afraid of death, because to him death means the loss of those things that make his life worth living:
10 "On the shore / of the wide world I stand alone, and think / Till Love and Fame to nothingness do sink." Earlier in the poem, Keats says that he hopes this "Love" will be a "high romance" with a "fair creature." He also says that he hopes the "Fame" he seeks will
15 be the result of the "high piled books" produced by his "teeming brain." In other words, Keats's fear is that death is a "nothingness" that will arrive before he can finish his life's work or find his true love.

Donne has a different attitude toward death,
20 and so the imagery in his poem is different, too. To Donne, death should "be not proud," because it is not "mighty and dreadful." Unlike Keats, Donne sees death as weak and merely a "slave to Fate, chance, kings, and desperate men." He also says that death
25 is like "rest and sleep," but not even a good sleep, because "charms can make us sleep as well, / and better than thy stroke." Donne believes that we will all wake from the sleep of death to eternal life, just as we wake from our normal sleep to our everyday
30 lives. In fact, Donne believes that it is death itself that

1

will die: "One short sleep past, we wake eternally, / And Death shall be no more; Death, thou shalt die."

35 Keats and Donne both know that death is a part of life, and both poets use powerful imagery to talk about that difficult theme. The differences in this imagery show two very different attitudes toward the subject, one of which is much more positive than the other. Which poet to believe is up to the reader to decide.

40 Not surprisingly, it is the reader's own experiences and attitudes that play a part in the way we respond to these poets' approaches. Like the two poets and their beliefs, contemporary readers also may be divided on the subject. This may explain why Keats's and Donne's poetry remains compelling years after their own deaths.

WRITING COACH

Online

www.phwritingcoach.com

Interactive Model

Listen to an audio recording of the Student Model in the eText. Use the Reader's and Writer's Response Symbols with the eText tools to note what you read.

Use a Writer's Eye

Now, evaluate the piece as a writer. On your copy of the Student Model, use the Writer's Response Symbols to react to what you read. Identify places where the student writer uses characteristics of an effective comparison essay.

Writer's Response Symbols

C.T. Clearly stated thesis

I.A. In-depth analysis

S.E. Effective supporting evidence

E.Q. Effective quotations

2

 **Feature Assignment:
Comparison Essay**

Prewriting

Plan your first draft. You can select from the Topic Bank or come up with an idea of your own.

 Choose From the Topic Bank

TOPIC BANK

Themes Read the two poems, "Sonnet #18" by William Shakespeare and "Shall I Compare Thee to a Summer's Day?" by Howard Moss on page 122. Consider the theme of each poem and write a comparison essay in which you discuss how effectively each author develops the theme.

Characters Think about two or more stories or poems that have similar types of characters. Write a comparison essay about two or more of these characters in which you discuss how effectively the authors have developed realistic or memorable characters.

Novel and Sequel Choose a novel that has been followed by a "spin off" or sequel. Write an essay in which you compare the author's use of stylistic and rhetorical devices in both works.

 Choose Your Own Topic

Determine an appropriate topic on your own by using the following **range of strategies** to generate ideas.

Consider and Discuss

- In a small group review the wide variety of texts you have read. Compare their positions, information, and themes.

- Consider how a particular story would change if it were set in a different time or place. Discuss your thoughts with a partner.

- Think about nonfiction and expository reading you have done on a single topic that interests you. List what the selections have in common, or how they are different. Discuss your ideas with a partner.

Review your responses and choose a topic.

Narrow Your Topic

Choosing a topic that is too broad results in writing that is too general. While you may want to compare the work of two authors, you will need to choose a specific element to keep your writing focused.

Apply It! Use a graphic organizer to narrow your topic.

- Write your general topic in the top box, and keep narrowing your topic as you move down the chart.
- Your last box should hold your narrowest or "smallest" topic, the new focus of your comparison essay.

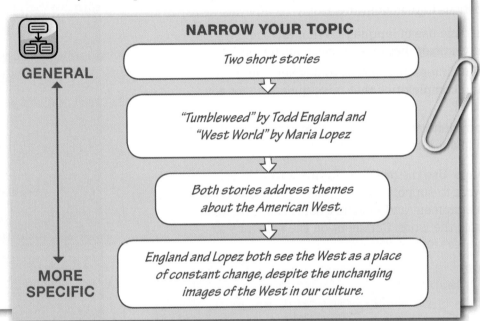

NARROW YOUR TOPIC

GENERAL

> Two short stories

> "Tumbleweed" by Todd England and "West World" by Maria Lopez

> Both stories address themes about the American West.

MORE SPECIFIC

> England and Lopez both see the West as a place of constant change, despite the unchanging images of the West in our culture.

Interactive Writing Coach™

- **Choosing from the Topic Bank gives you access to the Interactive Writing Coach™.**
- **Submit your writing and receive instant personalized feedback and guidance as you draft, revise, and edit your writing.**

Interactive Graphic Organizers

Use the interactive graphic organizers to help you narrow your topic.

Online Journal

Try It! **Record your answers and ideas in the online journal.**

Consider Multiple Audiences and Purposes

Think about your audiences and purposes. Consider the way others view your topic. As you plan to write an interpretation of an expository or literary text, anticipate the questions and contradictory information readers may have. Consider how you will respond to their ideas as you ask these questions.

Questions for Audience	Questions for Purpose
• Who will read my essay? My teacher? Classmates? Family members? • What will readers need to know to understand my ideas about the stories? What questions might they have?	• What do I want my readers to know about the stories? What do I want readers to take away from my piece? • What comparisons do I want to make? • What information might contradict my views?

Record your answers in your writing journal.

Plan Your Piece

You will use a graphic organizer like the one shown to state your thesis, organize your main points of analysis, and identify details. When it is complete, you will be ready to write your first draft.

Develop a Clear Thesis Think about your reaction to the works you have selected. Then state your ideas in a clear thesis. Add your thesis statement to a graphic organizer like the one shown.

Develop Your Analysis Think about what your thesis addresses in the text. Ask yourself these questions to thoroughly develop your analysis:

- Consider each author's artistic use of language. What are the **aesthetic effects** of the stylistic or rhetorical devices in the work?

- Look beyond the plot to find interesting points to develop. Note **ambiguities, nuances,** and **complexities** that raise questions for you. How do they affect the text?

- What **questions** and **contradictory**, or opposing, **information** might readers have as they read your ideas?

Gather Supporting Evidence Use the graphic organizer to help you gather **evidence** from the work to support your response. Your evidence should advance your thesis statement and include quotations, examples, and other specific details from the work. Comment on the evidence to analyze how it relates to the text and your thesis.

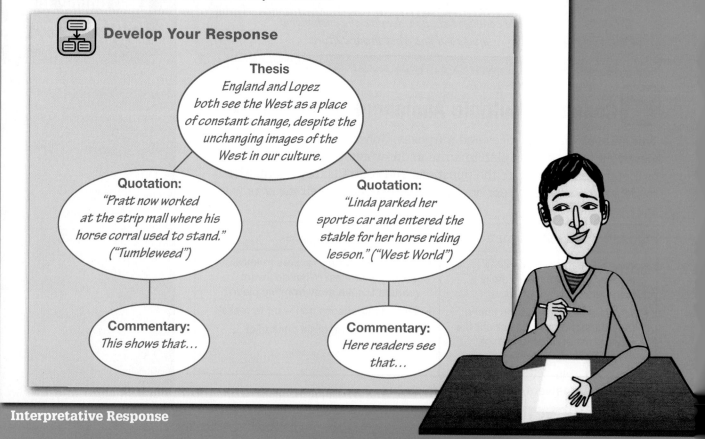

Develop Your Response

Thesis
England and Lopez both see the West as a place of constant change, despite the unchanging images of the West in our culture.

Quotation:
"Pratt now worked at the strip mall where his horse corral used to stand." ("Tumbleweed")

Quotation:
"Linda parked her sports car and entered the stable for her horse riding lesson." ("West World")

Commentary:
This shows that…

Commentary:
Here readers see that…

Gather Details

To support their opinions about expository or literary texts, writers use different kinds of details. Look at these examples:

- **Quotations From the Text:** *"The only cowboys Linda saw were on the town's postcards."*
- **Commentary on Quotations:** *Western symbols such as cowboys are used ironically by placing them on everyday items, like a postcard, to show how the West has changed over time.*
- **Examples of Stylistic Devices:** *Both authors use typical Western symbols, such as horses, cowboys, and wagon trains.*
- **Personal Observations:** *I've visited many Western states, and I've seen the changes that each author describes.*

Try It! Read the Student Model excerpt and identify the types of evidence that the author uses to support his ideas.

STUDENT MODEL from **"Keats and Donne on Death"**
pages 202–203; lines 27–32

> Donne believes that we will all wake from the sleep of death to eternal life, just as we wake from our normal sleep to our everyday lives. In fact, Donne believes that it is death itself that will die: "One short sleep past, / we wake eternally, / And Death shall be no more; Death, thou shalt die."

Apply It! Review the devices and strategies writers use to develop interpretative response drafts. Then, continue to gather details for your comparison essay.

- Review the text for **quotations** that provide evidence that supports your thesis statement.
- Write **commentary** to explain and further define your evidence.
- Then, add these quotations and commentary to your graphic organizer.
- Interpretative essays are a form of analytic writing—they state a thesis and then develop it. Ensure that your plan for writing will address the skills of an analytical essay. (See page 146.)

You will be able to use your completed graphic organizer to help you **structure your ideas** to build on each other in a **sustained way**.

WRITING COACH

Online

www.phwritingcoach.com

Interactive Graphic Organizers

Use the interactive graphic organizers to help you create a plan for your writing.

Interactive Model

Refer back to the Interactive Model in the eText as you plan your writing.

Drafting

During the drafting stage, you will start to write ideas for your comparison essay. You will follow an outline that provides a clear organizational strategy that will help you write a comparison essay that develops ideas based on a strong thesis statement.

The Organization of a Comparison Essay

The chart shows an organizational strategy for an interpretative response. Look back at how the Mentor Text follows this organizational strategy. Then, use this chart to help you outline your draft.

Outline for Success

I. Introduction

See Mentor Text, p. 200.

- Opening statement
- Titles and authors of literary works
- Clear thesis statement

Grab Your Reader

- A strong opening statement grabs your reader's attention. You can ask a question or refer to a character or event in the author's work.
- Identifying the titles and authors of the works you are comparing informs readers of the intent of your essay.
- A clear thesis statement expresses the controlling idea of your response and analysis.

II. Body

See Mentor Text, pp. 200–201.

- Evidence, including quotations, from text
- Commentary
- Characteristics of an analytical essay

Develop Your Ideas

- Supporting evidence from the text should explain and develop the controlling idea of your essay.
- Commentary introduces, explains, or further develops each piece of your evidence. You can also use commentary to state or refute opinions.
- Characteristics of an analytical essay, such as rhetorical devices and the use of reliable sources, will keep your comparison essay academic, formal, clear, and well organized.

III. Conclusion

See Mentor Text, p. 201.

- Restatement of thesis
- Memorable ending

Wrap It Up

- Restating or paraphrasing your thesis brings readers back to the controlling idea of your essay.
- A memorable ending offering insight can make readers think further about the text and can leave a lasting impression.

 Start Your Draft

Use the checklist to help you complete your draft. Use the graphic organizer that shows your thesis, analysis and interpretation of the work, and supporting evidence, and the Outline for Success as guides.

Remember the most important part of drafting is just getting your ideas in writing. Because you are drafting in an open-ended situation, you can always go back and refine your writing when you revise and edit.

√ Your **introduction** should start with an effective **opening statement**. Next, identify the titles and authors of the works you're analyzing.

√ Advance, or present, a clear **thesis statement** so that your reader understands the intent of your essay.

√ Use the **body** of your essay to clearly develop and advance your **ideas**. Use a variety of sentence patterns to express your thoughts.

√ Start a new paragraph for each new idea. **Organize** your paragraphs and structure your ideas in a logical way, and use the writing skills of an analytical essay. (See page 146.)

√ Support your ideas with specific and relevant **evidence** from the text, including quotations. Provide commentary to explain and develop your evidence or opinions.

√ Use **rhetorical devices,** such as analogies, to convey your meaning and establish your unique writing style.

√ In addition to analyzing the content of each selection, note the authors' use of stylistic or **rhetorical devices,** and analyze their aesthetic effects. For example, explain how symbolism expresses the authors' ideas and adds to the readers' enjoyment.

√ Address the challenges you find in each selection. Identify and analyze any **ambiguities,** nuances, and complexities within the text.

√ Anticipate and respond to **readers' questions** and contradictory information.

√ In your **conclusion**, restate or paraphrase your **thesis.**

√ Finish on a **memorable note** and leave your readers thinking about the importance of the comparison you have developed.

WRITING COACH

www.phwritingcoach.com

 Interactive Model

Outline for Success View pop-ups of Mentor Text selections referenced in the Outline for Success.

Interactive Writing Coach™

Use the Interactive Writing Coach to receive the level of support you need:

• Write one paragraph at a time and submit each one for immediate, detailed feedback.

• Write your entire first draft and submit it for immediate, personalized feedback.

Revising: Making It Better

Now that you have finished your first draft, you are ready to revise. Think about the "big picture" and consider the logical organization and clarity of meaning in your writing. You can use Revision RADaR as a guide for improving your draft. Revision RADaR provides four major ways to improve your writing: (R) replace, (A) add, (D) delete, and (R) reorder.

Kelly Gallagher, M. Ed.

KEEP REVISION ON YOUR RADaR

Read part of the first draft of the Student Model "Keats and Donne on Death." Then look at questions the writer asked himself as he thought about how well his draft addressed issues of logical organization and clarity of meaning.

Keats and Donne on Death

Death is a serious theme worthy of great poets. For example, John Keats's "When I Have Fears That I May Cease to Be" and John Donne's "Death, Be Not Proud" both discuss death in profound ways. However, these poems shows that while Keats believes that death can only destroy, Donne believes that death can be overcome.

Keats is afraid of death, because to him death means the loss of those things that make his life worth living. He doesn't want to let go of life. Early in the poem, Keats says that he hopes this "Love" will be a "high romance" with a "fair creature." In other words, Keats's fear is that death is a "nothingness" that will arrive before he can finish his life's work or find his true love. He also says that he hopes the "Fame" he seeks will be the result of the "high piled books" produced by his "teeming brain."

> *Does my thesis statement clearly express the controlling idea?*

> *Have I provided evidence here that supports my thesis statement?*

> *Does my organization let me present information logically?*

Now, look at how the writer applied Revision RADaR to write an improved second draft.

WRITING COACH

www.phwritingcoach.com

Interactive Writing Coach™

Use the Revision RADaR strategy in your own writing. Then submit your paragraph or draft for feedback.

Keats and Donne on Death

Death is a serious theme worthy of great poets. For example, John Keats's "When I Have Fears That I May Cease to Be" and John Donne's "Death, Be Not Proud" both discuss death in profound ways. However, the imagery in these poems shows that while Keats believes that death can only destroy, Donne believes that death can be overcome.

Keats is afraid of death, because to him death means the loss of those things that make his life worth living: "On the shore / of the wide world I stand alone, and think / Till Love and Fame to nothingness do sink." Earlier in the poem, Keats says that he hopes this "Love" will be a "high romance" with a "fair creature." He also says that he hopes the "Fame" he seeks will be the result of the "high piled books" produced by his "teeming brain." In other words, Keats's fear is that death is a "nothingness" that will arrive before he can finish his life's work or find his true love.

A Added "the imagery in" to make the thesis statement clearer

D Deleted unnecessary repetition
A Added a quotation

R Replaced <u>Early</u> with <u>Earlier</u> to accommodate new quotation

R Reordered the sentences in a logical order

Apply It! Use Revision RADaR to revise your draft to clarify the meaning you want to convey.

- First, determine if you have ordered your ideas logically, and if you have presented strong evidence in support of your comparisons.
- Then apply Revision RADaR to make needed changes. Remember—you can use the steps in the strategy in any order.

Look at the Big Picture

Use the chart and your analytical skills to evaluate how well each section of your comparison essay addresses purpose, audience, and genre. When necessary, use the suggestions in the chart to revise your piece.

Section	Evaluate	Revise
Introduction	• Check the **opening.** It should grab readers' attention and entice them to read on.	• Make your opening more interesting by connecting with the readers. Write a strong first sentence or pose a question.
	• Make sure the **thesis statement** clearly expresses the controlling idea of your response.	• Reread your essay. Does your thesis state the main idea your essay develops? If not, revise to include this information.
Body	• Check that you have presented information for each of the **compared works** that advances, or develops, your thesis.	• Add ideas as needed to support the works compared in your essay. Confirm that you present a balanced essay that discusses both selections in detail.
	• Make sure that you have supported each idea with **evidence,** including quotations from the text, and provided necessary commentary.	• Skim the authors' works to find relevant examples and quotations, and add them as necessary. Add explanatory commentary as needed.
	• Make sure your analysis addresses the **aesthetic effects** of the author's use of stylistic or rhetorical devices.	• Identify something that you think one author did especially well or in an interesting way. Then tell how the other author handled a similar situation.
	• Check that you have **logically organized** sentences and paragraphs to clearly convey your ideas.	• Reorder words, sentences, and paragraphs as needed to improve flow. Address the writing skills for an analytical essay. (See page 146.)
	• Make sure you have identified and analyzed any **ambiguities, nuances,** and **complexities** within the text.	• Stay focused on your thesis, but look for interesting elements in the works and add any analysis to explain or compare them.
	• Check that you have anticipated and responded to **readers' questions** and any contradictory information.	• Discuss your ideas with others. Revise to address any differing views or information they have.
Conclusion	• Check the **restatement** of your thesis.	• Add any missing information and delete irrelevant information.
	• Check that your **conclusion** leaves readers with a clear understanding of your ideas.	• Add a final statement that sums up your ideas about the two works or states why they are meaningful to you.

Focus on Craft: Analogies

Tropes are expressions or figures of speech that writers use to convey meaning. **Analogies** are tropes that draw comparisons in order to show similarity and help the reader or listener understand an idea. These comparisons can be unusual or startling. For example, you might not immediately see the connection between need and the solar system, but the narrator of a poem might express his or her longing for a companion by drawing an analogy that compares that desire to Earth's need for the sun.

Think about the effect of analogies as you read the following sentence from the Student Model.

 **STUDENT MODEL** from **Keats and Donne on Death**
page 202; lines 24–27

He also says that death is like "rest and sleep," but not even a good sleep, because "charms can make us sleep as well, / and better than thy stroke."

 Try It! Now, ask yourself these questions:

- What two things is the poet comparing?
- Would the writer's analysis of the poem be more or less effective without the analogy?

Fine-Tune Your Draft

Apply It! Use the revision suggestions to prepare your final draft.

- **Employ Tropes** Use analogies to make comparisons between ideas.
- **Use Transitions** If necessary, add transition words and phrases such as *therefore, however,* and *although* to show the relationships between paragraphs and sentences.
- **Achieve Rhetorical Purpose** A rhetorical purpose is the reason for a particular style of writing. In a comparison essay, the rhetorical purpose is to compare two or more things. Check that your essay truly compares two works. Add or delete information as needed.
- **Use Relevant and Substantial Evidence** Include references to quotations from the expository or literary texts you discuss. Include your commentary to identify and analyze the ambiguities, nuances, and complexities within the texts.

Teacher Feedback Share your final draft with your teacher. Ask if your writing clearly states a main idea and provides ample supporting evidence. Think about the response you receive and revise your final draft as needed.

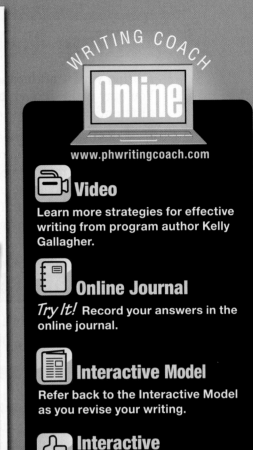

WRITING COACH

Online

www.phwritingcoach.com

Video
Learn more strategies for effective writing from program author Kelly Gallagher.

Online Journal
Try It! Record your answers in the online journal.

Interactive Model
Refer back to the Interactive Model as you revise your writing.

Interactive Writing Coach™
Revise your draft and submit it for feedback.

Editing: Making It Correct

Editing your draft means polishing your work and correcting errors. You may want to read through your work several times, looking for different errors and issues each time.

As you edit your draft, pay special attention to the **punctuation and capitalization** of quotations. Quotations are important in an interpretative response because they support your claims. Make sure that the quotations you use are smoothly integrated into your writing. Then, edit your final draft by correcting any factual errors and errors in **grammar, mechanics, and spelling.**

WRITE GUY *Jeff Anderson, M. Ed.*

WHAT DO YOU NOTICE?

Zoom in on Conventions Focus on the quotation as you zoom in on this passage from the Student Model.

 **STUDENT MODEL** from **Keats and Donne on Death**
page 202; lines 8–11

> Keats is afraid of death, because to him death means the loss of those things that make his life worth living: "On the shore / of the wide world I stand alone, and think / Till Love and Fame to nothingness do sink."

Now, ask yourself: *What part of these lines is quoted? How do you know?*

Quoted material is enclosed in quotation marks. This quotation is preceded by the introductory tagline beginning *Keats is afraid.* Introductory taglines are followed by a comma or a colon. The tagline helps create a smooth transition between the writer's analysis and the quotation that supports his analysis.

Some quotations have a concluding tagline (at the end of the quoted material) or a medial tagline (in the middle of the quotation). With a concluding tagline, replace a period at the end of the quotation with a comma (the comma goes inside the quotation mark), and then add the tagline. If the quotation ends with an exclamation point or question mark, do not change the end punctuation.

If your tagline falls in the middle of a sentence, end the first part of the quotation with a comma inside the quotation marks and place a comma after the tagline.

> To learn more about quotations, see Chapter 23.

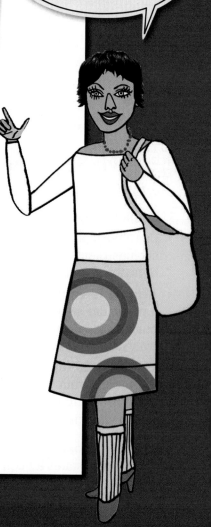

Grammar Mini-Lesson: Capitalization

To learn more, see Chapter 22.

In a quotation, keep the same **capitalization** that was in the original text.

- If the quotation could stand alone as a sentence, the beginning of the quotation should be capitalized, even though it comes in the middle of your sentence.

- If you quote a line of poetry that begins with a capital letter, retain the capitalization.

- If you quote a fragment that does not include the sentence's first word, do not capitalize the first word of the quotation. In the sentence from the Student Model, notice how the author does not capitalize the first word of the quoted fragments.

STUDENT MODEL from **Keats and Donne on Death**
page 202; lines 24–27

He also says that death is like "rest and sleep," but not even a good sleep, because "charms can make us sleep as well, / and better than thy stroke."

 Try It! Revise each sentence using the **correct capitalization and punctuation**. Write the answers in your journal.

1. In chapter one, the author states "the chef added a secret ingredient."
2. Amanda rarely liked spinach, says the narrator, and found it bitter.

 Apply It! Edit your draft for grammar, mechanics, and spelling, including correct punctuation and capitalization of quotations. If necessary, revise some sentences to improve the integration of quoted material.

Use the rubric to evaluate your piece. If necessary, rethink, rewrite, or revise.

Rubric for Interpretative Response: Comparison Essay	Rating Scale
Ideas: How well does your response present a focused statement about the works being compared?	Not very Very 1 2 3 4 5 6
Organization: How clearly organized is your analysis?	1 2 3 4 5 6
Voice: How well have you engaged the reader and sustained his or her interest?	1 2 3 4 5 6
Word Choice: How precisely do your word choices accurately reflect your purpose?	1 2 3 4 5 6
Sentence Fluency: How well have you varied sentence structure and length?	1 2 3 4 5 6
Conventions: How correct is your use of punctuation, quotation marks, and capitalization?	1 2 3 4 5 6

WRITING COACH

Online

www.phwritingcoach.com

Video
Learn effective editing techniques from program author Jeff Anderson.

Online Journal
Try It! Record your answers in the online journal.

Interactive Model
Refer back to the Interactive Model as you edit your writing.

Interactive Writing Coach™
Edit your draft. Check it against the rubric and then submit it for feedback.

Publishing

Share your thoughts and ideas in your comparison essay by publishing it. First, get your response ready for presentation. Then, choose a way to **publish it for the appropriate audience.**

Wrap Up Your Presentation

Now that you have finished your draft, add the final details. Be sure to include page numbers on each page of your essay. You can write them on each page or add them in the header or footer feature of your word-processing program. Also, be sure to add a title.

Publish Your Piece

Use the chart to identify a way to publish your comparison essay for multiple audiences.

If your audience is...	...then publish it by...
Readers of a particular writer	• Sending it to a magazine or online journal • Submitting it to the author's Web site
Students at school	• Reading it aloud in English class • Submitting it to your school newspaper • Posting your piece online and inviting responses

Extend Your Research

Think more about the topic on which you wrote your comparison essay. What else would you like to know about this topic? Use specific details to describe and explain your ideas. Increase the specificity of your details based on the type of information you are recording.

- Brainstorm for several questions you would like to research and then consult, or discuss with others. Then, decide which question is your major research question.

- Formulate, or develop, a plan about how you will answer these questions. Decide where you will find more information—on the Internet, at the library, or through other sources.

- Finally, learn more about your topic by following through with your research plan.

The Big Question: Why Write? What should you write about to make others interested in a text?

MAKE YOUR WRITING COUNT

Create a Literary Review Show

Interpretative responses to literature often compare themes and ideas across works and genres. Help classmates choose between a pair of books dealing with similar characters or themes.

With a group, plan a **literary review program.** Your program will be a **multimedia presentation,** including audio and visual elements, such as graphics, images, and sound. Although the critics will make different points about the book they discuss, they should arrive at a unified recommendation by the end of the program. Present your program live or video-record it for a specific audience—your class.

Here's your action plan.

1. Choose roles, such as director, storyboard illustrator, and two critics.

2. Review your peers' comparative essays. Choose a pair of stories to review. Read the stories together and hold a discussion to elaborate on the points made in the essay.

3. For inspiration, view online clips of book or film review shows.

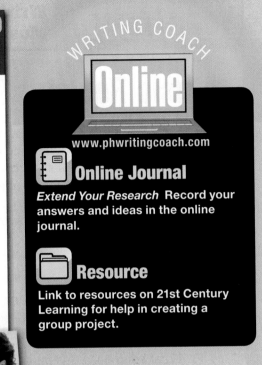

4. Create a storyboard, a scene-by-scene outline of a video presentation. The storyboard should include sketches and notes that break the program into a series of frames:

   - Identify and summarize a pair of stories

   - Note the critics' points about each story and synthesize those multiple points of view into a unified recommendation at the end

   - Incorporate notes on graphics, images, camera directions, and the reviewers' dialogue

5. Using your storyboard as a guide, rehearse and if possible, record, your presentation. Then, present your live or recorded program to the class.

Listening and Speaking During rehearsal, peers should provide feedback, and critics should adjust their delivery, vocabulary, and use of supporting sound and graphics accordingly. During the presentation, keep your peers' feedback in mind as you try to convince your classmates to read the story you recommend.

WRITING COACH

Online

www.phwritingcoach.com

Online Journal

Extend Your Research Record your answers and ideas in the online journal.

Resource

Link to resources on 21st Century Learning for help in creating a group project.

21st Century Learning

Music Review

In a **music review,** a listener provides his or her opinion about a piece of music, citing likes, dislikes, and comparisons with the artist's prior work. A music review is a short commentary about a musician, group, live performance, or new music release. It can be posted online or in print media. Readers sometimes post music reviews on their own Web sites, on the Web sites of their favorite musical artists, or in newspapers or magazines.

Try It! Study this music review. Then, answer the questions. Record your answers in your journal.

1. What **song** does this music review address?

2. What **artist,** musician, or band produced the song?

3. **Lyrics** are the words to a song. What does the reviewer say about the singer's use of stylistic or rhetorical devices in the song's lyrics?

4. What **comparisons** does the review make? How is the artist's current work similar to and different from his earlier work?

5. Music reviews often include **descriptions** of the song's rhythm, instruments, and overall sound. How does the review describe the sound of this song?

6. Music reviews may include a **recommendation,** or a statement about whether the reviewer thinks people should buy the song. Would this review encourage you to buy the piece of music? Why or why not?

Extension Find another example of a music review, and compare it with this one.

New Sound From an Old Pro

It took two long years, but finally Tim Russell has a hit song again. "Be Back Soon" is Russell's newest work, and it was well worth the wait. It's a completely new type of song for him and will not remind listeners of the fast beats of "Hold Back the Tide" or "It's Not Going to Be Today."

Instead of following his usual pattern, Russell has written a ballad and inserted hints of the happiness in his life. Most listeners know that he and his wife had a baby late last year. His song shows his feelings about being a new dad when he says, "I am beckoned to the road. His tiny smile always in my heart. I sing as fast as I can. Tell him I'll be back soon."

Listeners get the expected dose of guitar and some saxophone by Russell at the end of the song. It's a toned-down and mellow Tim Russell for his old fans—and new listeners—to sit back and enjoy.

Write a Music Review of a Song

Follow these steps to create your own music review of a song. To plan your review, scan the graphic organizers on pages R24–R27 and choose one that suits your needs.

Prewriting

- Identify a song with lyrics that you have recently heard and enjoyed.
- Decide the best audience for the song. Consider not only which listeners are sure to like the song, but also who else might enjoy it.
- Listen to the song several times. Identify important passages in the lyrics and note the instruments that contribute to the song's sound.
- If necessary, research the artist to find out more about his or her career. For example, has he or she had hit songs previously? Has he or she won any music awards?

Drafting

- Begin with a strong opening statement to grab your readers' attention.
- Write a brief description of the song's lyrics and sound. Include specific details that will help bring the music to life for readers. Consider using sensory details that appeal to taste, touch, sight, scent, and sound.
- Discuss particular elements of the song, including both the lyrics and the music. Consider making comparisons to other well-known songs.
- Address any concerns, questions, or arguments readers might have.
- End with a recommendation that sums up your ideas.

Revising and Editing

- Review your draft to ensure that your ideas flow logically and that you have presented them in a persuasive way.
- Be sure that you have used an appropriate tone and done all you can to describe the song's sound and lyrics.
- Check that spelling, grammar, and mechanics are correct.

Publishing

- Post your music review on a school Web site, and invite your classmates to read your entry.
- Turn your music review into a script for a video recording of a music critic's television show. Include graphics, images, and sounds to support you main points and to appeal to your specific audiance. To enhance your review, consider multiple points of view and synthesize that information into your taping.

WRITING COACH

Online

www.phwritingcoach.com

Online Journal

Try It! **Record your answers in the online journal.**

Interactive Graphic Organizers

Choose from a variety of graphic organizers to plan and develop your project.

⟨ Partner Talk ⟩

Before you start drafting, describe your planned music review to a partner, and ask for feedback. For example, you might ask whether your opening will grab readers' attention. Monitor your partner's spoken language by asking follow-up questions to confirm your understanding.

Writing for Assessment

You may see a prompt that asks you to write an essay in which you respond to, analyze, or interpret literature. Respond to this prompt using the characteristics of your comparison essay. (See page 198.)

 Try It! To begin, read the interpretative prompt and the information on format and academic vocabulary. Use the ABCDs of On-Demand Writing to help you plan and write your essay.

Format

The prompt directs you to write a *critical review*. Your essay should include a clear thesis statement, expressing the controlling idea of your response and evidence supporting your analysis.

Interpretative Prompt

Write an essay that is a critical review of a expository or literary text you have read. Analyze and evaluate the work. Support your ideas with specific evidence. [30 minutes]

Academic Vocabulary

When you *evaluate* a literary work, you give your opinion about its strengths and weaknesses. *Evidence* is the details and examples you use to support your opinion.

The ABCDs of On-Demand Writing

Use the following ABCDs to help you respond to the prompt.

Before you write your draft:

Attack the prompt [1 MINUTE]

- Circle or highlight important verbs in the prompt. Draw a line from the verb to what it refers to.
- Rewrite the prompt in your own words.

Brainstorm possible answers [4 MINUTES]

- Create a graphic organizer to generate ideas.
- Use one for each part of the prompt if necessary.

Choose the order of your response [1 MINUTE]

- Think about the best way to organize your ideas.
- Number your ideas in the order you will write about them. Cross out ideas you will not be using.

After you write your draft:

Detect errors before turning in the draft [1 MINUTE]

- Carefully reread your writing.
- Make sure that your response makes sense and is complete.
- Look for spelling, punctuation, and grammar errors.

More Prompts for Practice

Apply It! Respond to Prompt 1 in a timed or open-ended situation by writing an **interpretative response** that **advances a thesis statement**. As you write, be sure to:

- Include a clear **thesis statement**
- Address the **writing skills** for an analytical essay (See page 146.)
- Analyze the **aesthetic effects** of the author's use of stylistic or rhetorical devices
- Identify and analyze **ambiguities, nuances, and complexities**
- Respond to possible questions and **contradictory information**
- Support ideas with **evidence** from the text and explanatory **commentary**
- Use **transitions** between paragraphs and a variety of **rhetorical devices** to convey your meaning

> **Prompt 1** Write an essay that compares and contrasts two characters or the main idea or message in two expository or literary texts. Support your ideas and opinions with specific details and examples from the text.

Spiral Review: Persuasive Respond to Prompt 2 by writing a **persuasive essay.** Make sure your essay reflects all the characteristics described on page 172, including:

- A clear **thesis statement** based on logical reasons with various forms of support
- Accurate and honest representation of **divergent views** and information on the complete range of **relevant perspectives**
- An **organizing structure** appropriate to the purpose, audience, and context
- A consideration of the validity and reliability of all **primary and secondary sources**
- Language crafted to move a disinterested or opposed audience, using **rhetorical devices**
- An awareness and anticipation of audience response reflected in **formality, style, and tone**

> **Prompt 2** Write an essay to persuade a college admissions counselor why you should receive a particular type of scholarship.

WRITING COACH

Online

www.phwritingcoach.com

Interactive Writing Coach™

Plan your response to the prompt. If you are using the prompt for practice, write one paragraph at a time or your entire draft and then submit it for feedback. If you are using the prompt as a timed test, write your entire draft and then submit it for feedback.

Remember **ABCD**

Attack the prompt

Brainstorm possible answers

Choose the order of your response

Detect errors before turning in the draft

CHAPTER 11

RESEARCH WRITING

What Do You Want To Know?

How do people find out more information about interesting topics, such as the Alamo? They do research. Research is a way to gather, organize, and present information.

One of the first steps of research writing is to identify a topic that interests you and then formulate open-ended research questions. Open-ended research questions ask what you want to find out about the topic. For example, if you want to find out more about the Alamo, you would first decide what you want to know about it.

Try It! Take a few minutes to list some things you want to know about the Alamo.

Consider these questions as you participate in an extended discussion with a partner. Take turns expressing your ideas and feelings.

- What could I learn about where this building is located?
- What could I learn about what historical significance this building has?
- What can this building teach us about the past?

Review your list of questions with a partner. Then, discuss where you would go to research answers to your questions.

What's Ahead

In this chapter, you will review a strong example of an informational research report. Then, using the example as guidance, you will develop your own research plan and write your own informational research report.

WRITING COACH

Online

www.phwritingcoach.com

Online Journal

Try It! Record your answers and ideas in the online journal.

You can also record and save your answers and ideas on pop-up sticky notes in the eText.

THE BIG QUESTION

Connect to the Big Questions

Discuss these questions with your partner:

1 What do you think? What should we learn from our history?

2 Why write? Do you understand a subject well enough to write about it? How will you find out what all the facts are?

RESEARCH WRITING

Research writing is a way to gather information from various sources, and then evaluate, organize, and synthesize that information into a report for others to read. In this chapter, you will write an informational research report that conveys what you have learned about a topic that interests you. Before you write, you will search for information about your topic in different kinds of sources. You will evaluate the information you find, choose the best facts and details for your report, and organize your ideas so that you can clearly communicate them to your audience.

You will develop your informational research report by taking it through each of the steps of the writing process: prewriting, drafting, revising, editing, and publishing. You will also have an opportunity to use your informational research report in an oral or multimedia presentation that uses photos, charts, graphs, and other visuals to share what you have learned. To preview the criteria for how your research report will be evaluated, see the rubric on page 247.

FEATURE ASSIGNMENT

Research Writing: Informational Research Report

An effective informational research report has these characteristics:

- A specific **thesis statement** that states the report's main ideas

- **Evidence,** such as facts and the opinions of experts, to support the thesis

- An **analysis** of the topic that supports and develops **personal opinions**, is organized in a **logical progression**, and includes a clearly stated **point of view**

- An **argument** that incorporates the **complexities and discrepancies** of information from multiple sources and **anticipates and refutes counter-arguments**

- **Graphics** and **illustrations** that help explain important ideas when appropriate

- Proper **documentation of sources** to show where the author found information

- Correct **formatting,** or presentation, of written materials according to a style manual

- **Effective sentence structure** and correct spelling, grammar, and usage

Other Forms of Research Writing

In addition to an informational research report, there are other forms of research writing, including:

Annotated bibliographies list sources of information about a topic and provide a summary or evaluation of the main ideas of each source. Full publication information is given, including the title, author, date, and publisher of each source.

Biographical profiles give specific details about the life and work of a real person. The person may be living or dead, someone famous, or someone familiar to the writer.

Documentaries are filmed reports that focus on a specific topic or issue. These multimedia presentations use spoken and written text as well as photographs, videos, music, and other sound effects.

Health reports present the latest information, data, and research about a specific disease or health-related issue.

Historical reports give in-depth information about a past event or situation. These kinds of reports focus on a narrow topic and may discuss causes and effects.

Scientific reports analyze information and data concerning a current, past, or future scientific issue or problem. A lab report describes a scientific experiment, including observations and conclusions.

Try It! For each research report described, brainstorm possible topics with others. Then, consult with others to decide on and write a major research question for each topic. As you write, keep your audience and purpose in mind.

- A documentary about travelling in a foreign country
- A health report on Alzheimer's disease
- A historical report about the causes and effects of a past event

STUDENT MODEL

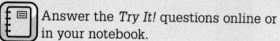**Use a Reader's Eye**

Read the Student Model on pages 226–229. On your copy of the Student Model, use the Reader's Response Symbols to react to what you read.

Reader's Response Symbols

√ **OK. I understand this. It's very clearly explained.**

? **I don't follow what the writer is saying here.**

+ **I think the writer needs more details here.**

− **This information doesn't seem relevant.**

! **Wow! That is cool/weird/interesting.**

Learn From Experience

Read the numbered notes in the margins as you reread the model to learn about how the writer presented his ideas.

Answer the *Try It!* questions online or in your notebook.

---

❶ The report uses **proper formatting** for heads and pagination.

❷ The **thesis statement** of a research paper explains the idea or reason for the research and how it will be supported with evidence.

❸ The **analysis** of how the Beatles affected American youth provides **evidence** that supports this thesis.

Try It! What main ideas will the report cover about the influence of the British in the United States? What is the writer's purpose? Who is the intended audience?

❶ O'Reilly 1

❶ William Sabourin O'Reilly
Professor F. E. Brockett
History 101
28 January 2010

❶ The British-American Cultural Connection

The success of the American Revolution in 1776 officially severed ties between the United States and Great Britain. Even so, the United States remained culturally attached to its colonial ruler. Military alliances in World War I and World War II further
5 cemented the friendship. Today, as the two English-speaking nations on the United Nations Security Council, Britain and the United States have a lot in common, politically and culturally. Examining popular culture reveals an enduringly powerful British influence. ❷ This report will use evidence from cultural critics
10 to demonstrate that many aspects of American culture have their origins in Great Britain and that Britain, in turn, takes many of its cultural cues from the United States.

Nowhere is British influence more pronounced than in twentieth-century popular music. In what has become known as
15 the British Invasion, the Beatles, a Liverpool rock band, changed the face of American pop music—and the country's youth culture. The picture (figure 1) shows the band members waving to thousands of adoring fans in New York City on February 7, 1964. For most of the decade, the Beatles were the most popular music
20 group in the United States.

❸ The Beatles were not an average British band; they were brilliant musicians and songwriters who inspired hysteria in millions of American teens. At the same time, the Beatles "managed to simultaneously mirror and to shape" youth culture
25 in the United States. (Farber 58). The Rock and Roll Hall of Fame credits them with "help[ing] confer self-identity upon a youthful, music-based culture" ("The Beatles"). Furthermore, the Beatles and their music spoke to American domestic issues of the

O'Reilly 2

Figure 1. The Beatles arriving at JFK, taken by United Press International (Library of Congress, [1964]).

1960s. According to cultural theorist Durwood Ball, the group's
30 optimism and positive energy "complemented the promise of the Civil Rights Act and the Great Society" (289). Their enormous popularity also compelled both critics and adults to take rock music seriously for the first time. Finally, their success opened American ears to subsequent waves of ground-breaking British
35 bands, including the Rolling Stones, The Who, and later, Pink Floyd. For this reason, the British bands popular in America today, such as Coldplay and M.I.A., owe a debt to the Beatles.

With the bands of the British invasion came revolutionary changes in fashion that also focused on American youth culture. Shortly after
40 the Beatles landed in New York City, British designer Mary Quant introduced the miniskirt. Quant's other designs, including baby-doll dresses, hot pants, and tights, "reflected a shift from the establishment to youth as the source of inspiration" ❹ ("Quant"). Rose Hardwick, manager of the Fashion Museum in Bath, England, points to the shift
45 dress and ankle boots as other examples of English-born fashions that made their way across the Atlantic. "Much of British fashion in this period," she said, "fits into the category of *mod*, short for modern." ❺ Innovative, bold, and fun, mod fashion, like music, put a new emphasis on self-expression. Inspired by pop art and minimalism,
50 British fashion embraced bright colors and geometrical patterns, the "streamlined and bold" style ("Mod Fashion").

WRITING COACH

Online

www.phwritingcoach.com

Interactive Model

Listen to an audio recording of the Student Model in the eText. You can refer back to the Student Model whenever you need support in developing your own writing. Use the Reader's and Writer's Response Symbols with the eText tools to note what you read.

Online Journal

Try It! Record your answers and ideas in the online journal.

❹ **Proper documentation** shows where the writer found information. The name in parentheses refers to a source on the Works Cited list.

Try It! How does using proper documentation make a research report more interesting to readers? Why might readers be curious about the sources used?

❺ Here and elsewhere, the writer provides an analysis that supports and develops **personal opinions.**

Try It! Drawing conclusions from the text, what would you say is the writer's opinion of mod fashion?

Informational Research Report (*continued*)

6 After detailing the British influence on American culture in the 1960s, the author discusses culture in the 1970s. This is a **logical progression** of ideas.

Try It! What type of order did the author use to create a logical progression? What other organizational strategies can authors use to help create logical progression?

7 In focusing on the American influence on British culture, the author addresses a **counter-argument**.

Try It! How does anticipating and addressing counter-arguments help demonstrate the complexities of a research topic?

8 A strong **conclusion** guides readers from the focus of the research report to a final, bold statement or a question for readers to ponder.

Try It! What final statement does the writer make? After reading this report, what conclusions can you draw about how readers will judge the British-American connection?

9 The Works Cited list provides proper **documentation** by listing publication information for each source used to write the report. The **formatting of the list** follows the MLA style manual.

Try It! Why might readers want to know what types of resources were used? How might readers use the Works Cited list to begin their own research?

Extension Locate one of the sources from the Works Cited page, and write a brief synopsis of it in your own words.

6 In the 1970s, the pattern of British influence in music and fashion repeated itself with British punk rock. The London band The Clash "played a major role in defining the punk movement" ("The Clash"). A video of The Clash performing its famous song "London Calling" illustrates the explosive excitement that defined the punk movement ("News"). British punk rock in turn fueled American punk bands. Punk rock "turned into Seattle grunge and then, into the alternative music scene that has become so popular today," said Denise Bonis, fiddle player for a New Orleans punk/zydeco band. Punk's distinctive fashion also found its way into the American mainstream. Band T-shirts, black leather, safety pins, spiked hair, and tight jeans all originated in punk rock.

7 The British-American cultural connection is a two-way street. American culture has affected British culture to an equal degree, particularly in the realm of popular music. The Beatles would not have existed were it not for the legendary American singer Elvis Presley, who borrowed from uniquely American musical forms, such as gospel, country, and African-American rhythm and blues (Brewster). The Beatles were well aware of Elvis' influence and often gave him credit for revolutionizing music. According to music historian James O'Donnell, Paul McCartney, singer and songwriter for the Beatles, learned to play the guitar by practicing Elvis' songs (65). John Lennon, another Beatle, remarked about his own musical influences: "Nothing really affected me until Elvis" (Ratcliffe 283). After Elvis, many other musical forms with American roots, such as disco and rap—and the clothing styles that developed around these types of music—made their way into British culture in the last half of the 20th century.

The British-American cultural influence is reciprocal, and it continues into the 21st Century. Indeed, examining any modern

Figure 2.
Mod dress; photo courtesy of Library of Congress.

O'Reilly 4

musical movement exposes powerful Anglo-American cultural
collaborations. Music television is a perfect example. The Beatles'
90 early films, *A Hard Day's Night, Help!,* and *Magical Mystery
Tour,* foreshadowed the advent of music television. Launched
in 1981, MTV was one of cable TV's first successes, yet many
of the channel's early videos came from Great Britain, "where
the tradition of making promo clips was fairly well-developed"
95 (Burns). Today's most wildly successful music television program,
American Idol, derived from a similar fusion of influences.

In the global age of mass communication, cultural influences
flow back and forth at lightning pace. American hip-hop can be
heard on deejays' turn-tables in London clubs, while most major
100 fashion designers exhibit their collections in both London and
New York City. **8** Fueled by a shared history and a common
language, the collaboration between Great Britain and the
United States advances the cultures of both, inspiring musicians,
designers, artists, and other connoisseurs of culture to new degrees
105 of creativity and self-expression.

9 Works Cited

Ball, Durwood. "Popular Music." *The Columbia Guide to America in the
1960s.* Ed. David Farber and Beth Bailey. New York: Columbia UP, 2001.
288-295. Print.

"The Beatles." *The Rock and Roll Hall of Fame and Museum.* Rock and Roll
Hall of Fame, n.d. Web. 21 Jan. 2010.

Bonis, Denise. Telephone interview. 12 Dec. 2009.

Brewster, Mike. "Elvis Presley: Birth of the Rock Star." *Business Week.* 24
Jan. 2004. Web. 23 Dec. 2009.

Burns, Gary. "Music Television." *The Museum of Broadcast Communications.*
MBC, n.d. Web. 21 Jan. 2010.

"The Clash." *The Rock and Roll Hall of Fame and Museum.* Rock and Roll
Hall of Fame, n.d. Web. 21 Jan. 2010.

Farber, David. "The American Sixties: A Brief History." *The Columbia
Guide to America in the 1960s.* Ed. David Farber and Beth Bailey. New
York: Columbia UP, 2001. 288-295. Print.

Hardwick, Rose. Message to the author. 13 Dec. 2009. E-mail.

"Mod Fashion." *Lucy and Lolita.* Lucy and Lolita, n.d. Web. 21 Jan. 2010.

"News." *The Clash.* Sony Music, 2008. Web. 21 Jan. 2010.

O'Donnell, James. *The Day John Met Paul: An Hour-By-Hour Account of
How the Beatles Began.* New York: Routledge, 2006. Print.

"Quant, Mary." *Encyclopedia Britannica Online.* Encyclopedia Britannica,
2010. Web. 21 Jan. 2010.

Ratcliffe, Susan, ed. *People on People: The Oxford Book of Biographical
Quotations.* New York: Oxford, 2001. Print.

WRITING COACH

Online

www.phwritingcoach.com

 Interactive Model

**Listen to an audio recording of the
Student Model in the eText. You can
refer back to the Student Model
whenever you need support in
developing your own writing. Use
the Reader's and Writer's Response
Symbols with the eText tools to note
what you read.**

Use a Writer's Eye

Now go back to the beginning of the Student
Model and evaluate the piece as a writer.
On your copy of the Student Model, use the
Writer's Response Symbols to react to what
you read. Identify places where the student
writer uses characteristics of an effective
informational research report.

Writer's Response Symbols	
T.S.	**Clear thesis statement**
S.E.	**Supporting evidence**
R.G.	**Relevant graphic**
D.S.	**Proper documentation of sources**

Your Turn

**Feature Assignment:
Informational Research Report**

Prewriting

Begin to plan a first draft of your research report by determining an appropriate topic. You can select from the Topic Bank or come up with an idea of your own.

 ## Choose From the Topic Bank

TOPIC BANK

Conserving Global Resources Which countries use or develop renewable resources (fleece, hardwoods, bamboo, recycled glass)? Identify a country that uses renewable resources and explain how the resources are used and maintained, as well as the costs and benefits of using renewable resources.

Island Societies Great Britain, Singapore, and Sri Lanka are island societies. How does geography influence the countries' economics, transportation, government, and culture? Alternatively, research a mountain society. What are advantages and disadvantages of this unique geography?

Global Spokespeople How have celebrities, such as Oprah or Bono, brought attention to social, environmental, and health issues? Do global spokespeople inspire others to become involved in solving difficult problems?

 ## Choose Your Own Topic

Determine an appropriate topic of your own by using the following **range of strategies** to generate ideas.

Brainstorm and Browse

- **Consult** with a partner to **brainstorm** for and decide upon a list of topics that interest you.
- **Formulate major research questions** about your topics. Circle key words in your questions. Use your key words and phrases to browse your library's research resources. Search the Internet, using the same key words and phrases. Work with your partner to decide which topics provide results that interest you most.
- Review your work and choose a topic.

Formulate Your Research Question

A broad, general topic is almost impossible to research well and cover thoroughly. Plan to do some preliminary research in order to narrow your topic and then formulate your major research question.

Apply It! Use a printed or online graphic organizer like the one shown to narrow your topic.

- Write your general topic in the top box, and keep narrowing your topic with research questions as you move down the chart.

- Your last box should hold your narrowest or "smallest" research question. This will be the focus of your informational research report.

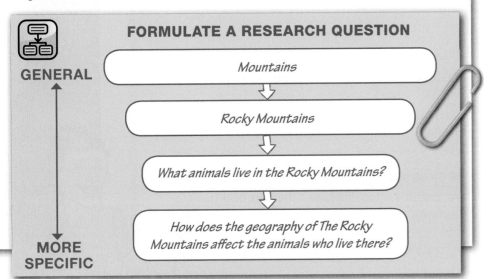

FORMULATE A RESEARCH QUESTION

GENERAL

Mountains

Rocky Mountains

What animals live in the Rocky Mountains?

How does the geography of The Rocky Mountains affect the animals who live there?

MORE SPECIFIC

Consider Multiple Audiences and Purposes

Before you begin researching your informational research report, think about your audiences and purposes. **Consider the views of others** as you ask yourself these questions.

Questions About Audiences	Questions About Purposes
• Who are my audiences? My teacher? My classmates? Outside professionals in the field? Someone else?	• Why am I writing this report? To inform? To inspire my audiences to learn more? Something else?
• What do my audiences need to know? What would interest my audiences?	• How do I want my audiences to react as they read?
• What degree of knowledge do my audiences already have about the topic?	• What is my point of view toward my topic?

Record your answers in your writing journal.

Make a Research Plan

Now that you have formulated an interesting research question, you are ready to develop a research plan. As part of your plan, you will create a timeline for finishing your report. You also will find and evaluate sources of information.

Find Authoritative, Objective Sources For your report, you will need to **gather evidence** from a variety of sources. Make sure the sources you plan to use are **reliable,** relevant, and accurate. Sources should be written or developed by experts on the topic for informed audiences in the field. Gather a variety of different sources to ensure that you avoid **over-reliance** on one source. Consider these tips:

Print Resources

- Find print resources in libraries and bookstores.
- Use encyclopedia articles, magazine articles, newspaper articles, trade books, and textbooks.
- Search for print resources using the library's electronic databases with help from a reference librarian.

Electronic Resources

- Find electronic resources using online search engines on the Internet.
- Choose only authoritative, reliable sites, such as those ending in:
  .edu (educational institution)
  .gov (government group)
  .org (not-for-profit organization; these may be biased toward a specific goal)
- If you are not sure that a site is reliable and unbiased, do not use it.

Interviews with Experts

- Ask questions of an expert on your topic.
- Set up a short in-person, e-mail, or telephone interview.
- Record the interview and take good notes.

Multimedia Resources

- Watch movies about your topic.
- Listen to podcasts or seminars related to the topic.
- Search for relevant photos, diagrams, charts, and graphs.

Evaluate Your Sources Do not assume that all sources of information on your topic are useful, good, or trustworthy. Use the checklist on page 233 to evaluate sources of information you find. The more questions that you can answer with a yes, the more likely you should use the source.

Checklist for Evaluating Sources

Does the source of information:

Contain **relevant** information that answers your research questions?

☐ Provide **strong evidence** to support **theories**?

☐ Give **facts** and **details** at a level you can understand?

☐ Tell all sides of a story, including **opposing viewpoints**?

☐ Provide **reliable, accurate** information written or compiled by experts for informed audiences?

☐ Have a recent **publication date**, indicating that it provides up-to-date information?

WRITING COACH

Online

www.phwritingcoach.com

Online Journal

Record your answers and ideas in the online journal.

Distinguish Between Types of Sources As you research, you will discover two kinds of sources: primary sources and secondary sources. Your teacher may require that you use both kinds of sources.

- A **primary source** is an original document, or a **text itself** without any interpretation by another person. For example, letters written by a soldier during the Korean War and financial records of U.S. Steel during the peak year of 1901 are primary sources.

- A **secondary source** is a source that provides an **interpretation** or understanding of a primary source. For example, a book about the history of steel production in the United States is a secondary source. Be aware that you are reading a writer's interpretation of a subject.

Apply It! Create a **research plan and timeline** for finishing your informational report. Avoid over-reliance on one source by listing at least four sources of information, including evidence from experts and texts written for audiences informed on the topic.

- Work with your teacher to determine the dates by which you need to finish your research, thesis statement, draft, and final report.

- For each of the print and electronic sources you plan to use, give full publication information.

- Evaluate whether each source is reliable by answering each question on the checklist. Reject unreliable sources.

Modify Your Plan After you begin to research a topic, you may find that you need to **modify**, or change, **your research questions**. If you cannot find answers to a research question, you may decide to **refocus**, or change the emphasis of, your topic. **Critique** your research plan at each step to evaluate it and make changes as the need occurs.

> **Partner Talk**
>
> Work with a partner to discuss your sources.
> - What theories do the sources present?
> - Do they provide supporting evidence for theories?
> - Is the evidence strong or weak?
> - How does the evidence help create a cogent—persuasive—argument?

Collect and Organize Your Data

For your informational research report, you will need to use **multiple sources** of information. Notes will help you remember and keep track of sources and information.

Organize Information From Multiple Sources Systematically organize relevant and accurate information so that it **supports central ideas, concepts, and themes** of your topic. Writing a heading that sums up the main idea of each group of notes will help you recognize the central ideas. Outlining central ideas will help you determine what further sources you need. Be sure to **think critically. Separate factual data from the analysis and complex inferences they produce.**

Keep Track of Multiple Sources Create a source card, with its own number, for each source. Then, note the full publishing information for the source, including the author, title, city of publication, publisher, and copyright date.

Take Notes When you take notes on a source, follow these guidelines.

- Note only facts and details you might use in your report.

- Be very careful to use your own words. You may use abbreviations at this stage.

- Separate facts from opinions and inferences.

- If you want to quote someone, enclose the exact words in large quotation marks. These marks will remind you that these are someone else's words—not your own.

Apply It! As you conduct research, record notes on information that is accurate and relevant to your research questions and topic. Effectively **organize the information** from different sources on note cards. Categorize the information to support your report's central ideas, concepts, and themes. You may also want to create **timelines or conceptual maps,** such as a web, to help you organize your ideas.

Paraphrase the information, or **summarize** it your own words. If you want to **quote**, copy the original, using large quotation marks.

Source 1

Ball, Durwood. "Popular Music." *The Columbia Guide to America in the 1960s*. Ed. David Farber and Beth Bailey. New York: Columbia University Press, 2001. 288-295. Print.

Notes From Source 1

Impact of Beatles on U.S. Youth

- Rock and Roll Hall of Fame
- British Invasion: Beatles, 4 musicians from Liverpool, arrived at JFK airport on Feb. 7th, 1964; greeted by fans
- "ignited the latent energy of youth"
- "helped confer self-identity upon a youthful, music-based culture"
- "announced the ascendency of youth"

Avoid Plagiarism

Plagiarism is using someone else's words or ideas as your own, without documenting the source of the information. Plagiarism is a serious error with severe consequences. Do not plagiarize. Teachers know when a paper you turn in isn't yours. They know your "voice."

Sometimes, students accidentally set themselves up to plagiarize by not taking good notes. The student who wrote this note card made two mistakes. He followed the original source too closely, and he forgot to include correct publication information. Even though he changed the sentence structure, he essentially used another writer's ideas without documenting the source.

WRITING COACH

Online

www.phwritingcoach.com

Online Journal

Record your answers and ideas in the online journal.

> Mary Quant was a British designer responsible for the miniskirt, baby-doll dresses, hot pants, and tights. Quant's designs reflected a shift in fashion from the establishment to youth as the source of inspiration.

Original Source

Notes From Source 5

British designer Mary Quant introduced miniskirt and other youthful designs (baby-doll dresses, hot pants, tights). Her designs "reflected a shift in fashion from the establishment to youth as the source of inspiration."

from <u>Encyclopedia Britannica</u>

Plagiarized Notes

Partner Talk

Review taking notes with a partner. Explain why each of these is essential:

- A source card for each source
- A heading that sums up the main idea in each group of notes
- A source card number on each note card
- Your own words to summarize ideas
- Large quotation marks for direct quotations

Use these strategies to avoid plagiarism.

- **Paraphrase** When you paraphrase information from a source, state the writer's idea in your own words. Read a passage and think about what it means. Then, write it as you might explain it to someone else.

- **Summarize** Use your own words to state the most important ideas in a long passage. A summary should be shorter than the original passage.

- **Quote** Enclose the writer's exact words in quotation marks, and identify the source.

Try It! Look at the Notes from Source 5 in the example. Highlight the parts that are plagiarizing the original. Now, write a new note based on the original source. Be sure to avoid plagiarizing the content.

Document Your Sources

When you write a research report, you need to **cite** all **researched information** that is not common knowledge, and cite it **according to a standard format.**

Works Cited On the Works Cited page at the end of your report, list all the sources that you used to write your report. Do not include sources you looked into but did not use. Follow the format shown in a standard style manual, such as that of the Modern Language Association (MLA) or American Psychological Association (APA). Your teacher will tell you which standard format style you should use.

Look at the example references shown. Use these and the MLA Styles for Sources chart on page R16 as a guide for writing your citations. Pay attention to formatting, including italics, abbreviations, and punctuation.

Book

Author's last name, author's first name followed by the author's middle name or initial (if given). *Full title of book.* City where book was published: Name of publisher, year of publication. Medium of publication.

O'Donnell, James. *The Day John Met Paul: An Hour-By-Hour Account of How the Beatles Began.* New York: Routledge, 2006. Print.

Interview

Interviewee's last name, interviewee's first name. Type of interview. Date of interview.

Bonis, Denise. Telephone interview. 12 Dec. 2009.

E-mail Message

Interviewee's last name, interviewee's first name. Message to the author. Date of message. Medium of message.

Hardwick, Rose. Message to the author. 13 Dec. 2009. E-mail.

Page from the Internet

Author's last name, author's first name followed by author's middle name or initial (if given) OR name of editor or compiler. "Name of page." *Title of Web site.* Publisher or N.p. if none given, date or n.d. if none given. Medium of publication. Date on which you accessed the page.

"The Clash." *The Rock and Roll Hall of Fame and Museum.* Rock and Roll Hall of Fame, n.d. Web. 21 Jan. 2010.

Parenthetical Citations A parenthetical citation is a quick reference to a source listed on the Works Cited page. These citations give the author's last name and the page number on which the information is located. If the author is mentioned in the sentence, only the page number is given in parentheses. Look at this sample citation from the Student Model.

 **STUDENT MODEL** from **"The British-American Cultural Connection"**
pages 226–227; lines 27–31

> Furthermore, the Beatles and their music spoke to American domestic issues of the 1960s. According to cultural theorist Durwood Ball, the group's optimism and positive energy "complemented the promise of the Civil Rights Act and the Great Society" (289).

When the author's name is not given in the source, use a title or a word from the title:

> A video of The Clash performing its famous song "London Calling" illustrates the explosive excitement that defined the punk movement ("News").

 Try It! Use MLA style to create a short Works Cited page based on the sources described.

- A book by Paul Hollander titled *Understanding Anti-Americanism: Its Origins and Impacts at Home and Abroad.* It was published in 2004 by the publisher Ivan R. Dee in Chicago.
- A Web page called "The Top 101 British Invasion Songs." The page is sponsored by New York radio station WCBS-FM. No information about the author is available. The writer looked at the page on December 20, 2009.
- A telephone interview with Eric Shaffer, the Beatles' press director for their 1964 American tour. The interview was done on November 13, 2009.

Critique Your Research Process

At every step in the research process, be prepared to modify or change your research question and refocus your plan. If you can't find enough information to write your thesis statement, try rewording your research question. Once you have enough evidence, you're ready to wrap up the prewriting part of your research paper and start drafting.

Apply It! Review your sources to ensure that you have included both **primary and secondary sources.** Make adjustments to your research if needed. Then, write an accurate entry for the Works Cited page for every source you have consulted for your informational research report. Format and document your sources correctly using a style manual.

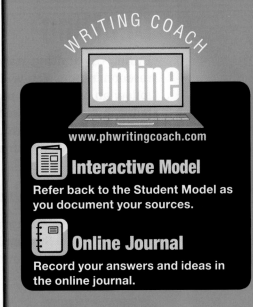

Partner Talk

Participate in an extended discussion with a partner to discuss research sources and express your ideas and opinions. Where have you looked for information on your topic? What sources do you like? What hasn't been reliable? How have you been keeping track of them?

Drafting

During the drafting stage, you will start to write your ideas for your research report. You will write a **clear thesis statement**. You will follow an outline that provides an **organizational strategy** that will help you write a **focused, organized, and coherent** research report. As you write your draft or prepare your notes for an oral presentation, remember to keep your audience in mind.

The Organization of an Informational Research Report

The chart shows an organizational strategy for a research report. Look back at how the Student Model follows this same strategy. Then, create a detailed outline for your research report. Use the template on page R26 to develop your outline. Also, refer to the Outline for Success as you work.

Outline for Success

I. Introduction

See Student Model, p. 226.

- Attention-grabbing introduction
- Clear thesis statement

Introduce Your Thesis Statement

- A **clear thesis statement** is often the last sentence in the introduction and answers your research question.

II. Body

See Student Model, pp. 226–228.

- Synthesis of information from multiple sources
- Presented as a logical progression of ideas
- Evidence that supports the thesis statement
- Anticipation of audience questions and counter-arguments
- Graphics and illustrations to explain concepts

Support Your Thesis Statement

- The headings on your notes have been grouped, and similar ideas that support your thesis are put into a logical order.
- Each paragraph states a major idea and supports it with evidence, such as facts, statistics, examples, and quotations.
- Relevant photos, charts, diagrams, or other visuals are included to help illustrate complicated information.

III. Conclusion

See Student Model, p. 229.

- Summary of findings and final conclusions
- Memorable ending with a final thought or insight

Add a Final Thought

- A conclusion pulls all the details together, reminding readers of the importance of the thesis.
- Your point of view about your topic is revealed or restated in the final paragraph.
- The reader may be asked to do something as a follow-up to the report, or the writer may take the conclusion to a deeper level.

👍 Start Your Draft

Use the checklist below to help complete your draft. Use your specific thesis statement; your detailed outline that shows your topic sentences and supporting evidence; your plan for the logical organization of the main ideas; and the Outline for Success as guides.

While drafting, aim at writing your ideas, not on making your writing perfect. Remember, you will have the chance to improve your draft when you revise and edit.

> √ Start your **introduction** by drafting attention-getting sentences.
>
> √ End with a clearly worded **thesis statement** that is based on your research question.

> √ Develop the **body** one paragraph at a time. Choose only the strongest supporting evidence for each major idea.
>
> √ Each paragraph should analyze evidence to **support and develop your opinions,** rather than just restating existing information.
>
> √ Develop your arguments using the **complexities, discrepancies,** and inconsistencies in information you've gathered from multiple sources and perspectives.
>
> √ Think like your readers might. Anticipate and refute counter-arguments.
>
> √ Use a variety of formats such as graphics and visuals to enhance your writing and support the thesis.
>
> √ Use a variety of **rhetorical strategies,** such as repetition and other deliberate uses of language, to reinforce your thesis and engage the audience.

> √ Draft a **conclusion** that sums up, restates, or adds a final thought.

WRITING COACH

Online

www.phwritingcoach.com

📰 Interactive Model

Outline for Success View pop-ups of Student Model selections referenced in the Outline for Success.

👍 Interactive Writing Coach™

Submit your draft one paragraph at a time and receive immediate, personalized feedback.

Provide and Document Evidence

While you are drafting, you will provide evidence to support your thesis and related claims. Your **claims** are an important part of your **analysis** of your topic. They are your opinions or understanding of information connected to your thesis, stated from your **point of view.** Be careful to differentiate between your opinions and ideas and those of other people. Document the words and ideas of other people when you provide evidence.

Give Facts and Statistics Facts are convincing evidence because they can be proven true. Statistics, or facts stated in numbers, are also convincing when they come from authoritative and up-to-date sources. Document facts and statistics that are not common knowledge or that could not be found in most sources about a topic.

Give Examples Make abstract or complicated ideas easier to understand by providing examples. You do not need to document examples from your own experience or observations. You do need to document examples from a particular source.

Quote Authorities Direct quotations from experts are also convincing evidence. Whenever you use a quotation, make sure to integrate it smoothly into your paragraph, and use your own words to identify the expert. After each quotation, provide an in-text citation to document your source, as shown in the Student Model excerpt.

 **STUDENT MODEL** from **"The British-American Cultural Connection"**
page 228; lines 62–66

> Punk rock "turned into Seattle grunge and then, into the alternative music scene that has become so popular today," said Denise Bonis, fiddle player for a New Orleans punk/zydeco band.

Try It! Use the Notes from Source 3 provided here to write a paragraph that supports the thesis *The Beatles revolutionized pop music.* Your paragraph should:

- Be a logically organized analysis of why the Beatles were brilliant musicians and songwriters
- Include at least one fact and one direct quotation
- Provide proper in-text citations to document sources of information

Notes From Source 3

Since Elvis Presley in the 1950s, rock and roll had gotten stale. The Beatles' arrival "introduced a modern sound and viewpoint" that was different than the previous decade. Broke sales records: forty-six Top Forty hits between 1964 and 1970. "For feats of sales and airplay alone, the Beatles are unquestionably the top group in rock and roll history." Innovations went beyond the sales figures: "The Beatles' legacy as a concert attraction...is distinguished primarily by the deafening screams of female fans more overcome by their appearance than the music they played." They also revolutionized how music was recorded—"layering sounds and crafting songs in a way that was experimental yet still accessible."—"The Beatles." The Rock and Roll Hall of Fame.

Use Graphics and Illustrations

You can present evidence to prove your thesis in graphics and other visuals as well as in words. While you are drafting, consider how you can use a diagram or these other types of graphics to help your audience understand ideas in your report. Be sure to refer to the figure in your text. Follow an accepted format to include a figure or table number, as well as a caption and source information. Use caution when copying an existing graphic because you will need permission from the copyright holder if you publish your work for use outside school.

- **Photographs** Use a photograph to help your audience picture how something looks. If you insert a photograph in your report, include a caption, or brief sentence explaining what the photo shows.

- **Maps** Maps can help show the location of where you are writing about. Be sure to include a legend with your map, in addition to the figure number, caption, and source.

- **Charts, Tables, and Graphs** Create a chart, table, or graph to provide information in a more visual or organized way. Give each a title that tells what it shows. If you include more than one, number them in numerical order. Include a complete citation for the source of information you used to create the chart, table, or graph. Put it below after the word *Source* and a colon.

Figure 3. The Beatles were originally from Liverpool, as shown in this map courtesy of Library of Congress.

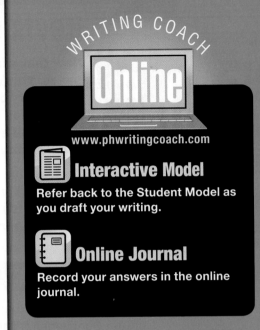

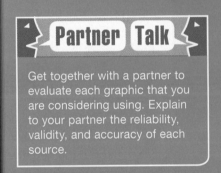

Partner Talk

Get together with a partner to evaluate each graphic that you are considering using. Explain to your partner the reliability, validity, and accuracy of each source.

Apply It! Brainstorm for two graphics that you might use in your informational research report. What information would each graphic explain? Find or create the two graphics, and add them to your report.

- Be sure to give your graphics titles.
- Use a style manual to correctly format and document your graphics and their sources.

Revising: Making It Better

Now that you have finished your draft, you are ready to revise. Think about the "big picture" of progression, analysis, and clarity of meaning. Your research paper should provide information in a logical progression. You should provide thoughtful analysis of your topic and you should develop your ideas clearly.

You can use the Revision RADaR strategy as a guide for making changes to improve your draft. Revision RADaR provides four major ways to improve your writing: (R) replace, (A) add, (D) delete, and (R) reorder.

Kelly Gallagher, M. Ed.

KEEP REVISION ON YOUR RADaR

Read part of the first draft of the Student Model "The British-American Cultural Connection." Then, look at questions the writer asked himself as he thought about how well his draft addressed issues of audience, purpose, and genre.

from The British-American Cultural Connection

American culture has affected British as well. As early as WWII, British parents worried about the negative effect of American movies. In 1943, Pearl Jephcott accused Hollywood of promoting "violence, vulgarity, sentimentality, and false psychology" (Savage 414). The American influence on Britain extends to music as well.

A brief look at music television will expose numerous Anglo-American cultural collaborations— from MTV to American Idol. The Beatles would not have existed were it not for Elvis Presley, who borrowed from uniquely American musical forms, such as gospel, country, and African-American rhythm and blues (Brewster).

> *Have I organized relevant and accurate information to support central ideas, concepts, and themes? Does all my information argue for my thesis? Have I anticipated counter-arguments?*

> *Is the information clearly and logically presented? Have I documented my sources according to a style manual?*

Now look at how the writer applied Revision RADaR to write an improved second draft.

from **The British-American Cultural Connection**

The British-American cultural connection is a two-way street. American culture has affected British culture to an equal degree, particularly in the realm of popular music. The Beatles would not have existed were it not for the legendary American singer Elvis Presley, who borrowed from uniquely American musical forms, such as gospel, country, and African-American rhythm and blues (Brewster). The Beatles were well aware of Elvis' influence and often gave him credit for revolutionizing music. According to music historian James O'Donnell, Paul McCartney, singer and songwriter for the Beatles, learned to play the guitar by practicing Elvis' songs (65). John Lennon, another Beatle, remarked about the musical influences of his youth: "Nothing really affected me until Elvis" (Ratcliffe 283). After Elvis, many other musical forms with American roots, such as disco and rap—and the clothing styles that developed around these types of music—made their way into British culture in the last half of the 20th century.

R *Replaced a vague topic sentence to support a personal opinion and anticipate a counter-argument*

D *Deleted the sentences about Hollywood that do not support thesis; also deleted main idea sentence about music that is now repetitive*

A *Added further evidence of Elvis' impact on the Beatles by citing a source. Used a direct quote by John Lennon to support my argument about cultural connections*

 Apply It! Use your Revision RADaR to revise your draft.

- First, determine if you have presented ideas in a logical progression, provided analysis of source material that goes beyond restating, and incorporated source material with your ideas to achieve clarity of meaning.
- Then, apply Revision RADaR to make needed changes. Remember— you can use the steps in the strategy in any order.

Look at the Big Picture

Use the chart and your analytical skills to evaluate how well each section of your informational research report addresses **purpose, audience, and genre.** When necessary, use the suggestions in the chart to revise your piece.

Section	Evaluate	Revise
Introduction	• Check that the **opening paragraphs** grab your readers' attention.	• Add a quotation, anecdote, or interesting fact that engages readers' interest.
	• Make sure you have a **clear thesis** statement.	• Clarify your thesis statement to indicate the major idea your report will explore.
Body	• Make sure each body paragraph uses a variety of formats and strategies to **argue for the thesis.**	• Add graphics or rhetorical devices that develop and support your thesis.
	• Do you provide an **analysis** that supports and develops personal opinions and **anticipates counter-arguments?**	• Use source material to develop your own opinions about the topic. Anticipate and answer reader questions. Add details to refute counter-arguments.
	• Use the complexities and discrepancies in information gathered from multiple sources to develop your argument.	• Delete irrelevant or biased information. Add new sources and perspectives to represent multiple views.
	• Make sure quotations and facts that are not common knowledge are **documented** and **formatted** according to a style manual.	• Identify the source of each quotation. Add parenthetical citations, following the style specified in a style manual.
	• Think about whether your readers can follow the **progression** of your **ideas.**	• Add transitional words, phrases, sentences, or even paragraphs to make connections clear.
Conclusion	• Ensure that your final paragraphs circle back to your thesis. • Make sure your research report ends with a new **insight** or leaves the reader with a final thought.	• Track your thesis through the points you develop in your report. Remind readers how those points support and prove your main idea. • Add a statement about what you learned.
Works Cited/ Bibliography	• Complete your **reference list** using a style manual.	• Accurately cite all researched information according to a standard format. Build a Works Cited page or bibliography. • Add footnotes where appropriate.

Focus on Craft: Schemes and Antithesis

In rhetoric, a **scheme** is a stylistic device that makes writing more interesting and therefore more persuasive. **Antithesis** is a type of scheme that juxtaposes contrasting words, phrases, sentences, or ideas in order to add emphasis. Antithesis can contrast opposites, as Charles Dickens did in *A Tale of Two Cities:* "It was the best of times, it was the worst of times...." Antithesis can also contrast degrees, as Neil Armstrong did when he landed on the moon: "That's one small step for a man, one giant leap for mankind." Notice how these contrasting words or ideas are always used in a balanced, parallel structure. Look at this model:

 **STUDENT MODEL** from **"The British-American Cultural Connection"** page 226; lines 21–23

> The Beatles were not an average British band; they were brilliant musicians and songwriters who inspired hysteria in millions of American teens.

 Try It! Now, ask yourself these questions:

- Why does the writer include the clause *The Beatles were not an average British band*?
- How does this addition add emphasis to the clauses that follows?

Fine-Tune Your Draft

Apply It! Use the revision suggestions to prepare your final draft. Make sure you keep your audience and purpose in mind as you focus on words to express exactly what you mean.

- **Employ Schemes** Use stylistic devices to achieve your **rhetorical purpose,** or writing reason. You are writing to inform your audience about your research topic. Look for places where you can add the scheme antithesis to emphasize, persuade, and reveal your opinion. Be sure the antithetical structures are parallel.

- **Use a Consistent Tone** Your tone, or attitude toward your subject, should remain the same throughout your report. Review your writing to ensure consistency.

Teacher and Family Feedback Share your draft with your teacher and/or family. Ask for feedback on your report's length and complexity. Are they sufficient to address the topic completely? Review the comments and revise your final draft as needed.

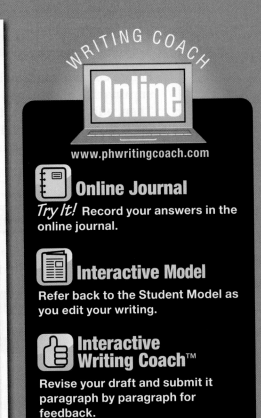

WRITING COACH

Online

www.phwritingcoach.com

Online Journal
Try It! Record your answers in the online journal.

Interactive Model
Refer back to the Student Model as you edit your writing.

Interactive Writing Coach™
Revise your draft and submit it paragraph by paragraph for feedback.

Editing: Making It Correct

Before editing your final draft, think about how you will **paraphrase, summarize, quote,** and **accurately cite** all researched information. Then, edit your draft using a **style manual,** such as *MLA Handbook for Writers of Research Papers,* to **document** sources and **format the materials,** including quotations.

WRITE GUY *Jeff Anderson, M. Ed.*

 **WHAT DO YOU NOTICE?**

Zoom in on Conventions Focus on quotations as you zoom in on these lines from the Student Model.

> **STUDENT MODEL** from **"The British-American Cultural Connection"** page 226–227; lines 27–31
>
> Furthermore, the Beatles and their music spoke to American domestic issues of the 1960s. According to cultural theorist Durwood Ball, the group's optimism and positive energy "complemented the promise of the Civil Rights Act and the Great Society" (289).

> To learn more about integrating quotations, see Grammar Game Plan, Error 18, page 290.

Now, ask yourself this question: *What techniques has the writer used to help integrate the quotation?*

Perhaps you noted these as good techniques that are surrounding the quote.

- The writer prepares the reader for the information in the quote by using an introductory phrase to identify the quote's author.
- Part of the introductory phrase ties the quote into the writer's flow of ideas and point of view.
- The writer used quotation marks at the beginning and end of the quotation.
- The writer has properly cited the source, using correct format and punctuation.

Partner Talk Discuss this question with a partner: *Does the quotation integrate well and flow smoothly with the sentences that surround it?* Monitor your partner's spoken language by asking follow-up questions to confirm your understanding.

Grammar Mini-Lesson: Punctuation

Punctuating Quotations With Citations Quotations follow specific rules for punctuation depending on the style manual you are using for your report. Study this sentence from the Student Model. For more on punctuation with a quotation, see Grammar Game Plan Error 6, page 278.

To learn more, see Chapter 23.

STUDENT MODEL from **"The British-American Cultural Connection"** page 227; lines 46–48

"Much of the British fashion of this period," she said, "fits into the category of *mod,* short for modern" (Hardwick).

Try It! Tell whether the quotations below are punctuated properly and follow correct citation formatting. Write the answers in your journal.

1. Launched in 1981, MTV was one of cable TV's first successes, yet many of the channel's early videos came from Great Britain, "Where the tradition of making promo clips was fairly well-developed (MBC)."

2. John Lennon, another Beatle, "remarked about his own musical influences: "nothing really affected me until Elvis." (Ratcliffe/283).

Apply It! **Edit your draft for grammar, mechanics, and spelling.** Use a style manual to check your formatting and documentation of sources. If necessary, rewrite sentences with quotations to ensure you've integrated them properly, as well as punctuated and cited them according to a standard format.

Use the rubric to evaluate your piece. If necessary, rethink, rewrite, or revise.

Rubric for Informational Research Report	Rating Scale
Ideas: How clearly have you expressed and developed your thesis statement?	Not very Very 1 2 3 4 5 6
Organization: How logical is the progression of your ideas?	1 2 3 4 5 6
Voice: How clearly have you expressed your point of view?	1 2 3 4 5 6
Word Choice: How well have you used precise language to develop your supporting evidence?	1 2 3 4 5 6
Sentence Fluency: How well have you used sentence variety in your report?	1 2 3 4 5 6
Conventions: How correct is the formatting of sources that you used?	1 2 3 4 5 6

WRITING COACH

Online

www.phwritingcoach.com

 Video

Learn effective editing techniques from program author Jeff Anderson.

 Online Journal

Try It! Record your answers in the online journal.

 Interactive Model

Refer back to the Student Model as you edit your writing.

 Interactive Writing Coach™

Edit your draft and check it against the rubric. Submit it paragraph by paragraph for feedback.

Publishing

Now that you worked through the writing process to create your report, find a way to share your knowledge. When you've finished your final draft, **publish** it **for an appropriate audience.**

Wrap Up Your Presentation

Your teacher may require you to turn in a typed final paper. Follow guidelines to make a cover sheet and table of contents before submitting your work.

Publish Your Piece

Use the chart to identify a way to **publish your informational research report for the appropriate audience.** You may be publishing a written report or presenting your report as an **oral** or **multimedia presentation.**

If your audience is...	...then publish it by...
Students or adults at school	• Displaying your written report in the school library or media center • Presenting your research at an assembly or to another English class
A local group or club with a special interest in your topic	• Presenting an oral or multimedia report at a club meeting; answering questions about your research • Posting your report online and inviting comments

 ## Reflect on Your Writing

Now that you are done with your informational research report, read it over and use your writing journal to answer these questions.

- Which parts of your research report do you like the most? Which parts would you like to improve if you could?
- What will you advise someone else about researching?
- What is something fun or interesting that you learned from your report?

 The Big Question Why Write? Do you understand a subject well enough to write about it? How did you find out what the facts were?

Manage Your Portfolio You may wish to include your published informational research report in your writing portfolio. If so, consider what this piece reveals about your writing and your growth as a writer.

MAKE YOUR WRITING COUNT

Communicate Ideas in a Class Newspaper

Research reports answer complex questions about the world by providing evidence from a variety of credible sources. Inform your schoolmates about a range of topics by using media-creation tools to prepare an issue of a **class newspaper.**

Newspapers contain articles about current and newsworthy events and topics of interest. With a group, create a newspaper with brief articles about the topics of your group members' research reports. Present the newspaper as a **multimedia presentation**, complete with text, images, and sound. Your newspaper may be printed or posted electronically.

Here's your action plan.

1. Meet in groups and select roles such as writer, editor, designer, and image researcher.

2. Review your research reports. Assign articles and discuss possible layout and visuals. Writers should prepare brief articles about each other's topics.

3. View online newspapers for ideas about formatting text and visuals. Locate appropriate images, graphics, and sound.

4. Edit and arrange the articles. Develop headlines that summarize their main ideas and add bylines that identify the writers. Choose a name for your paper.

5. Your newspaper should:

   - Incorporate a visually appealing layout
   - Synthesize information from multiple points of view
   - Include headlines, by-lines, and photo or image credits

6. Rehearse and then give your multimedia presentation.

7. Assemble all group newspapers into an electronic class newspaper.

Listening and Speaking Meet with your group to discuss how to present your group's newspaper to the class. Then, practice your multimedia presentation. Listeners should provide feedback. Presenters should adjust their delivery accordingly. During the presentation, work as a team to engage and inform your audience.

WRITING COACH
Online

www.phwritingcoach.com

 **Online Journal**

Reflect on Your Writing Record your answers and ideas in the online journal.

Resource

Link to resources on 21st Century Learning for help in creating a group project.

Writing for Media: Summary of Research Reports

21st Century Learning

Summary of Research Reports

There are many kinds of research reports, including biographical profiles, historical reports, analyses of cultural trends, and documentaries. You can find examples of all these research reports by searching the World Wide Web. In this assignment, you will create a **summary of research reports** about a specific aspect of the British-American cultural connection. You'll follow a research plan as you gather information from multiple sources. Then, you'll put it all together to inform your audience about the variety and content of research reports about your topic.

Try It! Study the excerpt from the **summary of research reports** shown on this page. Then, answer these questions. Record your answers in your journal.

1. What is the **subject** of the research reports summarized in this excerpt?

2. A summary of research reports gives an overview of the information available on a specific topic. What different **types of research reports** has the author summarized? What information is available?

3. Has the writer provided a good **variety** of research reports in this summary? What other types of research reports might have information on Beatlemania?

4. Is the writing **subjective**, presenting the writer's personal opinion, or **objective**, presenting only factual information? How can you tell?

5. What effect does the **photograph** have? How does it show the phenomenon of Beatlemania in a way that the text cannot?

6. What suggestions would you give the writer for **improving** this summary of research reports?

BEATLEMANIA!
WITH THE BEATLES

Beatlemania refers to the frantic, exuberant, almost hysterical adoration the Beatles inspired in their fans during the early years of their success (Larson 116). Research reports on Beatlemania suggest that it was one of the most exciting moments in 20th century pop culture, so exciting that it is still being analyzed today.

The best primary-source account of Beatlemania is the 1964 film *A Hard Day's Night*. The film stars the four Beatles and depicts several days in the life of the band. The movie, though a comedy, attempts to show how the Beatles had become trapped by their own enormous fame (IMDB).

In addition, numerous statistical reports provide facts and figures to demonstrate the overwhelming commercial rewards of Beatlemania. The Billboard Hot 100 singles chart from the years 1964 to 1970 reveals their dozens of top-selling singles, while Capitol and Apple Records show their record-breaking sales. To date, the Beatles have sold more than a billion records worldwide ("Hot 100").

Works Cited

"Hot 100." *Billboard.com*. N.p., n.d. Web. 16 Dec. 2009.
IMDB (Internet Movie Data Base). *A Hard Day's Night*.
    IMDB.com. N.p., n.d. Web. 16 Dec. 2009.
Larson, Thomas E. *The History of Rock and Roll*. Dubuque:
    Kendall, 2004. Print.

1

Create a Summary of Research Reports

Follow these steps to create your own online **summary of research reports.** To plan your summary, review the graphic organizers on pages R24–R27 and choose one that suits your needs.

Prewriting

- Consult with classmates and others to help you determine a topic for your summary of research reports. **Brainstorm** for a list of several ideas and choose the one that interests you most.

- Be sure to identify the target **audience** for your summary. Are you writing to inform a group of cultural theorists? A fan club?

- Formulate a **research plan** for engaging in the complex, multi-faceted topic you have selected. What specific research questions will you try to answer? You'll need to gather information from **multiple sources,** including experts on the topic and texts written for an audience informed about the topic. Your task is to summarize several research reports. Find at least three and avoid over-reliance on a single source.

- Evaluate the sources as you work, determining if they're **reliable,** relevant, and accurate. Unreliable sources should be rejected.

- Be sure to differentiate between theories and supporting evidence. Determine if supporting evidence is strong or weak and work to understand how the evidence supports a cogent, or persuasive, argument.

- Record information on note cards, in a learning log, or on the computer. As you take notes, **separate facts from inferences,** and use timelines or concept maps to organize your ideas. Document and cite your sources according to a standard format.

- As you take notes, paraphrase, summarize, and quote information. Look for patterns in the research you find.

- As you research, **systematically organize** relevant and accurate source material to support central ideas, concepts, and themes.

- Plan **graphics and illustrations** you can add to your report. Be sure to record source information for any graphics you intend to use. As you work, you may need to **modify** your research question to refocus your research plan.

WRITING COACH

Online

www.phwritingcoach.com

Online Journal

Try It! Record your answers in the online journal.

Interactive Graphic Organizers

Choose from a variety of graphic organizers to plan and develop your project.

Partner Talk

Ask a partner to critique your research plan. Does your partner have questions you haven't thought about asking? You may decide to modify your research questions to refocus your research plan.

Your Turn **Summary of Research Reports** (*continued*)

Drafting

- Keep your goal in mind as you draft. You are reporting on the type of information available on your subject.

- Organize your notes by the forms of research reports you are summarizing, such as documentaries, statistical reports, trend analyses, and so on. Then, start writing sentences and paragraphs.

- Provide an analysis that **develops and supports your personal opinions.** Do not just restate existing information—tell readers about the quality and depth of what you have found.

- Present your information in a logical order and use a variety of **formats, schemes, and rhetorical devices** to argue for your thesis in an engaging way.

- To convincingly refute anticipated counterarguments, incorporate the **complexities and discrepancies** of the information you have gathered from multiple sources and perspectives.

- Avoid **plagiarizing**. Use your own words, or enclose direct quotations in quotation marks.

- Acknowledge your sources as needed in context or in a credits section. Use a **style manual** to document your sources and format your report.

Revising

Use Revision RADaR techniques as you review your draft carefully.

- **Replace** general terms with vivid details and unclear explanations with precise ideas.

- **Add** specific details or missing information to support your argument.

- **Delete** information that does not support your thesis or develop your argument.

- **Reorder** sentences or paragraphs to present ideas clearly and logically.

- Read aloud your online report to make sure it reads smoothly. Check that it is of sufficient **length and complexity** to fully address your topic.

- Use an **evaluative tool,** such as a rubric or teacher feedback, to check the quality of your research.

Editing

Now take the time to check your Online Summary of Research Reports carefully before you post it online. Focus on each sentence and then on each word. Look for these common kinds of errors:

- Errors in subject-verb agreement
- Errors in pronoun usage
- Run-on sentences and sentence fragments
- Spelling and capitalization mistakes
- Omitted punctuation marks
- Problems with proper citations and quotations

Publishing

- If your school newspaper is published online, submit your online summary as an editorial or column.
- Search for online forums devoted to your topic.
- Post your summary as a blog entry. Search for a Web site that allows users to create a free blog.
- With your classmates, create an anthology of your summaries. Print it for classroom display or for your school library.

Extension Find another example of a research report summary and compare it with the one you are writing.

Writing for Assessment

Many standardized tests include a prompt that asks you to write or critique a research plan. Use these prompts to practice. Respond using the characteristics of your informational research report. (See page 224.)

 Try It! Read the prompt carefully. Then, create a detailed research plan. List all of the actions you will take to research this topic. Be as specific as you can. Use the ABCDs of On-Demand Writing to help you plan and write your research plan.

Format

Write your *research* plan in the form of an outline. List everything you would do in the order you would do it. Under some main headings, you may have subheadings.

Research Plan Prompt

Write a research plan for an informational report that discusses one of the Seven Wonders of the World. Your plan should include: a research topic and question, a list of possible sources, the audience, and the steps you'll take following a timeline. [30 minutes]

Academic Vocabulary

Potential *sources* are those print or online resources you might use if you were to develop a research report based on this plan. In your response, list reliable sources or search engines you might use.

The ABCDs of On-Demand Writing

Use these ABCDs to help you respond to the prompt.

Before you write your draft:

Attack the prompt [1 MINUTE]

- Circle or highlight important verbs in the prompt. Draw a line from the verb to what it refers to.
- Rewrite the prompt in your own words.

Brainstorm possible answers [4 MINUTES]

- Create a graphic organizer to generate ideas.
- Use one for each part of the prompt if necessary.

Choose the order of your response [1 MINUTE]

- Think about the best way to organize your ideas.
- Number your ideas in the order you will write about them. Cross out ideas you will not be using.

After you write your draft:

Detect errors before turning in the draft [1 MINUTE]

- Carefully reread your writing.
- Make sure that your response makes sense and is complete.
- Look for spelling, punctuation, and grammar errors.

 **More Prompts for Practice**

Apply It! Prepare a **written critique of the research plan** in Prompt 1. Make specific suggestions to improve each research plan. Consider these questions:

- Has the **research plan** covered all of the prewriting steps?
- Is there a limited **topic?** Is it appropriate for the audience and purpose?
- Is the writer planning to find enough **sources?** Are the sources varied?
- Does the research plan say anything about **evaluating** sources?

Prompt 1 Rosa wrote the following research plan. Explain what she did well and what needs improvement.

My Topic: I'll investigate the pyramids. I'll research ancient Egyptian religious beliefs as well as pharaohs that built pyramids.

My Research: I'll look in encyclopedias and visit a museum to get ideas for sources.

My Audience and Purpose: My audience will be my classmates.

My Writing: I'll set up a timeline for researching, revising, and editing. I think I'll give myself three days to visit the museum and library.

Spiral Review: Narrative Nonfiction If you choose to write a **personal narrative** in response to Prompt 2, make sure your story reflects the characteristics described on page 66.

Prompt 2 Think about a person or event that affected how you think or act. Use specific details to describe the experience and outcome.

Spiral Review: Response to Literature If you choose to write a **response to literature** in response to Prompt 3, make sure your response reflects all of the characteristics described on page 198. Your essay should:

- Advance a clear **thesis**
- Include **commentary** on **quotations** from the text
- Include **transitions** and **rhetorical devices** to convey meaning
- Analyze the **aesthetic effects** of the author's use of stylistic or rhetorical devices

---

Prompt 3 Write a comparison essay in which you analyze two authors' works and compare a specific element, such as theme or writing style. Consider both expository and literary texts. Explain your reactions to each work, providing evidence from the text as you develop your response.

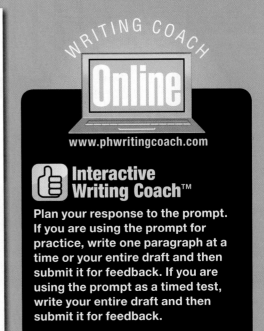

WRITING COACH

Online

www.phwritingcoach.com

Interactive Writing Coach™

Plan your response to the prompt. If you are using the prompt for practice, write one paragraph at a time or your entire draft and then submit it for feedback. If you are using the prompt as a timed test, write your entire draft and then submit it for feedback.

Remember **ABCD**

A ttack the prompt

B rainstorm for possible answers

C hoose the order of your response

D etect errors before turning in the draft

CHAPTER 12

WORKPLACE WRITING

What's Ahead

In this chapter, you will learn to write practical forms of writing, including a variety of work-related documents, procedural documents which explain how to perform a task, and research reports. All of these documents present organized information that is accurately conveyed in a reader-friendly format. The language used for these documents is clear, formal, and polite.

Characteristics of Writing

Effective workplace writing has these characteristics:

- A clear **purpose and audience**
- **Well-organized, accurate** information
- **Reader-friendly formatting techniques**
- Detailed and clear language that is **formal and polite**
- Correct **grammar, punctuation, and spelling** appropriate to the form of writing

Forms of Writing

Forms of workplace writing that you will learn are:

Cover letters are business letters. They can be written for various reasons. For example, job applicants include cover letters when sending a résumé to apply for a job.

Instructions are used to explain how to complete a task or procedure. These procedural texts are written in a step-by-step format.

Proposals are used in business to get approval for a project. They are broken into formal sections that address phases of the project and project funding.

Résumés are formal summaries of a person's job qualifications.

Other forms of workplace writing include:

College application essays are written in response to a prompt. They generally take the form of personal essays in which the applicant reveals his or her unique qualities.

Project plans are procedural texts that break down a project into phases, and outline what will be accomplished in each phase.

 Try It! For each audience and purpose described, select the correct form, such as a cover letter, instructions, or résumé that is appropriate for conveying your intended meaning to the audience. Explain your choices.

- To tell your parents how to find the Spanish Club's Web page
- To recommend a teacher for an award

Connect to the Big Questions

Discuss these questions:

1 What do you think? When is it most necessary to justify crucial workplace decisions?

2 Why write? What do daily workplace communications require of format, content, and style?

 **WORD BANK**

These vocabulary words are often used with workplace writing. Use the Glossary or a dictionary to check the definitions.

achievement	apply
application	technical

STUDENT MODEL Cover Letter

Learn From Experience

 After reading the cover letter on this page, read the numbered notes in the margin to learn about how the writer presented his ideas. As you read, practice newly acquired vocabulary by correctly producing the word's sound.

Try It! Record your answers and ideas in the online journal.

---

❶ The **return address** is **correctly formatted.** It lists the name of the writer, his address, and the date when the letter was written.

❷ The **inside address** is also correctly formatted. It lists the name of the recipient and her business address. The formal **salutation** is followed by a colon.

❸ The first paragraph **clearly states the letter's purpose** and the writer's **viewpoint.**

❹ The second paragraph provides detailed **evidence** that supports the writer's viewpoint.

❺ In the concluding paragraph, the writer provides contact information and steers the recipient toward an interview.

Try It!

- Summarize the cover letter.
- What assertion, or claim, does the writer make in the first paragraph?
- Does he support his assertion adequately with facts or other evidence?
- Do you find the cover letter persuasive?

Extension Take the role of the recipient of the letter and write a response to the sender.

---

❶ James Robinson
2103 Paseo Drive
Nacogdoches, TX 79961
May 1, 2010

❷ Sarah Hope
Hope Music Studio
677 Santos Road
Nacogdoches, TX 79961

❷ Dear Ms. Hope:

My guidance counselor, Mr. Young, told me that Hope Music Studio has an opening for a summer intern. **❸** I am writing to apply for that position. As my résumé shows, I am well prepared to work in a music studio.

❹ For more than six years, I have been taking guitar and piano lessons, as well as music theory. The lessons led me to write songs and play in a band in middle school. I coordinated sound equipment for the band's shows and learned a lot. Then, two years ago, I started my own band. We play coffee shops and private parties, and I coordinate our sound with a state-of-the-art sound board. I also run sound for other bands.

I will bring enthusiasm, energy, and a willingness to learn to your efforts at Hope Studios. **❺** Please contact me at 555-555-5578 to schedule a time when we can discuss my qualifications.

Sincerely,

James Robinson

James Robinson

Your Turn ➤ **Feature Assignment: Cover Letter**

Prewriting

- Plan a first draft of a work-related document—a **cover letter**. You can select from the Topic Bank or come up with an idea of your own.

TOPIC BANK

Computer Camp Counselor Imagine that you are applying for a summer job as a camp counselor at a computer camp. Write a cover letter in which you highlight your qualifications.

Résumé Cover Letter Write a cover letter to accompany a résumé for the job of your choice. Use a business format, and be sure to tell why you are a good candidate for the position.

- Brainstorm for facts and details, such as a list of experiences and qualities, to support your viewpoint that you're qualified for the job.
- Be sure to locate and use accurate contact information.

 ## Drafting

- Write a first paragraph that includes a clearly stated **purpose.** As you draft your second paragraph, ask and answer **relevant questions** that address readers' potential problems or misunderstandings. Also consider what your audience will find **engaging.** End with a paragraph suggesting a course of action.
- Use appropriate **formatting and organizational structures of business letters.**
- If you provide **technical information,** use accessible language to address the needs of the reader.

 ## Revising and Editing

Check that **questions of purpose, audience, and genre** have been addressed. Have you supported your point of view? Have you addressed questions your recipient is likely to ask? Have you followed standard business letter format?

Publishing

- If you plan to mail the letter, print it on suitable paper.
- If you plan to e-mail it, create a Portable Document Format (PDF) attachment of the letter.

WRITING COACH

Online

www.phwritingcoach.com

 Interactive Model
Listen to an audio recording of the Student Model.

 Online Journal
Try It! Record your answers and ideas in the online journal.

 Interactive Writing Coach™
Submit your writing and receive personalized feedback and support as you draft, revise, and edit.

 Video
Learn strategies for effective revising and editing from program authors Jeff Anderson and Kelly Gallagher.

 **Partner Talk**

Read your final draft to a partner. Ask if your letter addresses all of the concerns that your potential employer might have.

STUDENT MODEL 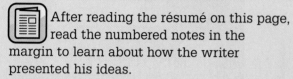 Résumé

Learn From Experience

After reading the résumé on this page, read the numbered notes in the margin to learn about how the writer presented his ideas.

Try It! Record your answers and ideas in the online journal.

❶ Résumés usually begin with **contact information:** the writer's name, address, telephone number, and e-mail address.

❷ In the Objective, the writer uses **precise, formal language** to state his job goal.

❸ **Appropriate format structures,** such as these **headings,** make it easy to find information. **Lists of facts and details** are organized in reverse chronological order, starting with the most recent experiences.

❹ Vivid, active verbs help to present the writer's experience in the most positive light.

❺ The writer **lists achievements** that are relevant to his objective and distinguish him from other applicants.

Try It!

- Why does the writer include dates on the résumé?
- Why does he refer to the attached music samples? Why do you think the writer attaches music samples to his résumé?
- What things did you learn about résumé-writing that you might use to write your own résumé?

Extension Find another example of a résumé and compare it with this one.

---

❶ James Robinson

2103 Paseo Drive
Nacogdoches, TX 79961
936-555-5578
E-mail: jdrobinson@example.com

❷ Objective

To get an internship at a music studio that will build on my experience and help me qualify for a career in music

❸ Education

Nacogdoches High School, Nacogdoches, TX
Expected graduation, May 2011

❸ Music Experience

2008–Present
Rhythm guitarist and songwriter for the Border Boys (samples attached)

2006–2008
Rhythm guitarist, lead singer, songwriter for the Echomaniacs

❸ Sound Experience

2009–Present
❹ Coordinate sound for local band

2008–Present
Coordinate sound for the Border Boys with digital sound board

2006–2008
Arranged sound for the Echomaniacs with simple equipment and in small spaces

❺ Achievements

2010 Best Local Band, High-School Division

2007–present Nacogdoches High School Honor Roll

Computer Skills

Word processing, spreadsheets, multimedia presentations, digital sound mixing

References are available on request.

Your Turn

Feature Assignment: Résumé

Prewriting

- Plan a first draft of your **résumé.** You can select from the topic bank or come up with an idea of your own.

TOPIC BANK

Résumé Write a résumé to accompany the cover letter you wrote in the previous assignment.

- Consider your audience and details they may find **engaging.** Because they know nothing about you, ask yourself what **questions** your readers will have. List and answer these questions to avoid potential problems and misunderstandings.

- Because you are just getting started in the work world, you should list items that demonstrate your responsibility and commitment. Show all work experience, volunteer experience, academic achievements, and computer skills you have—even if the information does not seem to relate to the position you are seeking. Brainstorm for these supporting **facts** and **details.**

 ## Drafting

- The first section should list your objective, or goal. This gives you a chance to show a **clearly stated purpose** and **viewpoint.** The rest of the résumé will provide **support** for your viewpoint.

- A résumé is a work-related document. Use appropriate **formatting** and **organizational structures.** Make sub-sections that include the headings *Education, Experience, Interests/Activities,* and *Computer Skills.* Include the date range for each activity.

 ## Revising and Editing

Evaluate how well you have addressed your **purpose, audience,** and **genre.** Whenever necessary, revise your draft to clarify meaning. Have you addressed questions your recipient is likely to ask? Have you followed résumé format? Make sure any **technical information** and **skills** are explained in **accessible language.** Finally, find and fix **spelling errors.**

Publishing

- If you plan to mail the résumé, print it on suitable paper. Stamp and mail it along with a cover letter.

- If you plan to e-mail it, create a PDF of the résumé and attach it to your message.

WRITING COACH

www.phwritingcoach.com

 Interactive Model

Listen to an audio recording of the Student Model.

 Online Journal

Try It! Record your answers and ideas in the online journal.

 Interactive Writing Coach™

Submit your writing and receive personalized feedback and support as you draft, revise, and edit.

 Video

Learn strategies for effective revising and editing from program authors Jeff Anderson and Kelly Gallagher.

Have a partner review your résumé. Ask whether you present information that makes you a good candidate for the job.

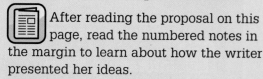

STUDENT MODEL Proposal

Learn From Experience

 After reading the proposal on this page, read the numbered notes in the margin to learn about how the writer presented her ideas.

Try It! Record your answers and ideas in the online journal.

---

❶ This **subhead** and the others are **appropriate formatting** techniques. They make it easy to understand the **organizational structure** of the proposal.

❷ Notice that the **purpose** of the proposal is clearly stated in the opening background section.

❸ The plan helps **support the writer's viewpoint** that she can start a babysitting business. **Numbered steps** are another **appropriate format structure.**

❹ The **facts** in the resources section **support the purpose** of the proposal—obtaining a loan from parents.

❺ The **summary** briefly restates the main ideas of the proposal.

Try It!

- How does the organization of the proposal meet readers' needs?
- What impression do you think the writer makes with her proposal? Why do you say so?

Proposal: Babysitting Business

Lynda Harper

❶ Background

I have four years of babysitting experience and more clients than I can serve alone. I also have Red Cross babysitting certification. I am ready to manage other babysitters to provide babysitting to a larger group of families. To do so, I need $500 for advertising and $500 to pay an accountant. **❷** This proposal outlines my plans for the business and addresses the funding issue.

❸ Project Plan

1. I will contact all families I have worked for to let them know about my business.
2. My staff will be experienced and Red Cross babysitter certified.
3. I will advertise in the local paper and with a magnetic car sign.
4. I will work with an accountant and learn about managing money.

❹ Resources

I have $450 in savings. Between now and the end of the school year, I will earn a minimum of another $150 by babysitting. The remaining $400 would be an investment from my parents, to be paid back at the rate of $100 a month.

❺ Summary

I believe that my business will be a success. I could repay the parental investment within four months. Most important, starting and running this business will contribute to my future success.

 **Feature Assignment: Proposal**

Prewriting

- Plan a first draft of your **proposal.** You can select from the Topic Bank or come up with an idea of your own.

> ### TOPIC BANK
>
> **Senior Lounge** The senior class has been given one thousand dollars to make the school a better place for students in the future. Write a proposal in which you suggest that the money be spent to establish a senior lounge in an empty classroom.
>
> **Community Garden** Write a proposal to your town's city council or mayor's office in which you suggest turning an empty lot into a community vegetable garden.

- Brainstorm for a list of things that your audience will need to know about the purpose of your proposal. List the steps necessary to accomplish your plan.
- Gather **accurate information** for the resources section. Back up your budget with research on what items or services cost.

Drafting

- As you draft this work-related document, ask and answer **relevant questions** that engage readers. Your goal is to persuade your audience to accept your ideas. Consider their needs to avoid potential problems and misunderstandings.
- Use appropriate **organizational and formatting structures,** including the section heads for proposals shown in the Student Model.
- Organize the information so that your first and last sections include a clearly stated **purpose and point of view.**
- Provide **technical information** in accessible language.

Revising and Editing

- Consider how well you have addressed questions of purpose and audience. Is your purpose clearly stated? Will your audience understand technical information? Is your proposal structured correctly?
- Then, revise your draft to clarify meaning.

Publishing

- Print the proposal on paper that is suitable for business correspondence.
- Deliver the proposal to the appropriate audience.

MAKE YOUR WRITING COUNT

Present a Research Report at a Job Fair

Proposals, letters, and résumés help people communicate important information to specific audiences. These workplace documents may involve the seeds for activities or ideas that will help classmates learn more. Make a **research report** and presentation to share at a Job Fair.

With a group, **brainstorm** for several topics from among your work in this chapter. Have a discussion with others to **decide upon a topic** that will be helpful to someone trying to make decisions about a future job. Work together to formulate **an open-ended research question** that will help you produce a research report about the topic. Consider topics such as careers in computers, careers in the music industry, and careers in landscaping.

As you develop your report, be sure to **modify research questions** and **evaluate collected information** as necessary. Group members should **consult** one another to **critique the process** as you work. Be prepared to refocus and implement changes. Focus on researching information related to interesting career paths. Remember that a research report should:

- State a clear thesis
- Consider audience and purpose
- Express a clear point of view
- Provide supporting evidence
- Present ideas in a logical way
- Document sources properly

Organize a Career Day to present your research to students in your school. Your report should be a **multimedia presentation** that uses graphics, images, and sound.

Here's your action plan.

1. Research takes time. In a group, make a plan for several group meetings. Set objectives and choose roles for each member.

2. Work together to develop a **research plan** involving:

   - Gathering evidence from **experts on the topic** and from **texts written for informed audiences**
   - Choosing reliable sources and strong evidence over unreliable sources and weak evidence
   - Using a variety of sources to avoid error due to over-reliance on one source
   - Separating inferences and theories from supporting evidence and factual data in your sources
   - Understanding how your sources use supporting evidence to develop a cogent—persuasive—argument

3. Discuss your findings. Use a system such as headings or sub-topics to organize the **relevant and accurate information** you have gathered to support your central ideas, concepts, and themes. Use **conceptual maps** and **timelines** to organize complex ideas. Differentiate between primary and secondary sources. Next, work together to create a clear thesis statement.

4. Outline the content of the report. Assign sections of the outline to each group member. You may need to research further before you write a draft. Be sure to **paraphrase, summarize, quote,** and **accurately cite sources** according to a standard format, such as MLA style.

5. Work together to compile data and write a rough draft. Develop an argument based on **complex information** gathered from multiple sources and perspectives. Use this data and any **discrepancies**— inconsistencies—to anticipate and refute counter-arguments.

6. As a group, revise the draft's language and style. Check that your **analysis** is original and that it supports and develops **personal opinions,** instead of simply restating existing information. Use a style manual for **documenting sources** and **formatting materials.**

7. Revise and edit to ensure that the thesis is supported by evidence presented through a variety of **formats** and **rhetorical strategies.** Check that the report **length and complexity** are sufficient to address the topic.

8. Finally, add audio-visual support, such as music and video clips.

9. Present your report to interested students, counselors, and teachers.

Listening and Speaking Practice the presentation in front of another group or each other. Listen to feedback and make improvements. At the Jobs Fair, speak clearly and confidently to your audience.

WRITING COACH

Online

www.phwritingcoach.com

Online Journal

Record your answers and ideas in the online journal.

Resource

Link to resources on 21st Century Learning for help in creating a group project.

Your Turn

**Writing for Media:
Set of Instructions**

Set of Instructions

Once you have applied to college or for a job or training program, you have accumulated considerable knowledge about a complex process. Share your knowledge with others through a **blog** posting that is a **set of instructions** on how to apply to college or for a job or training program.

A blog is a Web site that you create and update periodically. It is a multimedia forum that allows you to provide information using text, images, graphics, and audio.

If you don't have access to a computer, you can still make a multimedia presentation. Present your instructions orally, and accompany your speech with posters. In this portion of a blog, a student who explored a career in veterinary medicine created a set of instructions for others interested in applying to veterinary college.

Try It! Study the set of instructions on this page. Then, answer these questions. Record your answers in your journal.

1. How does the writer state the **purpose** of and **audience** for the instructions?

2. How does the writer use the **blog's format** and **organizational structures** to present information?

3. How do the photograph and audio links help show the writer's **viewpoint**? How do they appeal to the writer's audience?

4. Does the writer use **accessible language** for any **technical information**?

5. How does the writer include **relevant questions to engage readers?**

**Becoming Dr. Barkley, DVM
A Journal of My Journey Toward Becoming a Veterinarian**
September 15, 2010

So You Want to Be a Vet, Too?

The more I explore a career in veterinary medicine, the more people I encounter with a similar goal. Most of these people have no idea what's involved in becoming a vet. If you're one of those people, these guidelines, based on my experience, might help:

What Do I Need To Do To Get Into Vet School?
Here are some tips to help you on your way.

1. Be a great student—Bs are okay, but As are better! Do really well in science and math.

2. Practice good study habits and discipline in other parts of your life.

3. Get a job, or volunteer, working with animals.

4. Find a mentor, someone in the field, who can help you navigate the process. A practicing vet can answer your questions as you learn more about veterinary medicine. This person may be able to write a recommendation for you later.

5. Apply to 4-year colleges with excellent biology or pre-med programs.

About the Blogger
Ariel Barkley, a senior at West High School, has wanted to be a vet since she was four years old. She currently cares for two cats, a dog, a goat, and a heifer.

Audio Links
Links to Ariel's interviews with West's animal care professionals!

Blog Archive

Create a Set of Instructions

Follow these steps to create a blog featuring a **set of instructions** on how to pursue a particular educational path after high school. To plan your procedural presentation, review the graphic organizers on pages R24–R27 to select one best suited to your needs.

Prewriting

- Brainstorm for a list of the steps involved in obtaining the higher education goals of your choice. Conduct additional research as needed.
- Make a detailed list of the steps involved in completing the project.
- Consider the needs of your **specific audience.** What does your audience already know about the process? What does the audience need to know?

Drafting

- Create headings for each step in your procedure. Each heading will be a link on your blog. This is a **reader-friendly formatting technique** that will allow your audience to focus on steps of your presentation that interest them most.
- Describe each step in your **procedure.** Provide details, facts, and examples that support your explanations.
- **Organize the information** on the blog. Most blogging Web sites provide a template, allowing you to easily upload text.
- Choose additional media for your blog, such as **audio**, **photos**, and **links** to other Web sites.
- Choose fonts, colors, and backgrounds that will make it easy for your audience to read your blog.

Revising and Editing

Each step of your instructions should relate to your overall topic. Make sure that your media clips are well **synthesized to reflect your overall point of view.** Your supporting media—audio interviews, links to educational institutions, and images—should also support the topic.

Publishing

- Post your set of instructions on your blog.
- Present your blog, to the class or to another audience.
- As you describe your blog or share your information in a live presentation, speak clearly and allow time for your audience to ask questions.

WRITING COACH Online

www.phwritingcoach.com

Online Journal

Try It! Record your answers and ideas in the online journal.

Interactive Graphic Organizers

Use the graphic organizers to plan your multimedia presentation.

 ### Partner Talk

Before publishing, review your set of instructions with a partner. Ask for feedback about the effectiveness of your blog as well as the supporting graphics, images, or audio. Your partner should be able to tell you if your documents reflect a clearly stated purpose.

Writing for Assessment

Many standardized tests include a prompt that asks you to write a procedural text. Use these prompts to practice. Respond using the characteristics of your set of instructions or procedural text.

(See pages 266–267.)

 Try It! Read the **procedural text** prompt and the information on the format and academic vocabulary. Use the ABCDs of On-Demand Writing to help you plan and write your procedural text.

Format

Describe the purpose of the *procedural text* in the first section. Be sure to include steps that organize information using reader-friendly formatting techniques such as a numbered list or materials lists.

Procedural Text Prompt

Your friend wants to be the DJ at a graduation party. She needs to have written instructions about how to collect the music she will play. Write a procedural text that anticipates and answers your reader's questions.

Academic Vocabulary

A procedural text is a kind of text that tells somebody how to perform a task. *Anticipate* means to foresee something and deal with it in advance.

The ABCDs of On-Demand Writing

Use the following ABCDs to help you respond to the prompt.

Before you write your draft:

Attack the prompt [1 MINUTE]

- Circle or highlight important verbs in the prompt. Draw a line from the verb to what it refers to.
- Rewrite the prompt in your own words.

Brainstorm possible answers [4 MINUTES]

- Create a graphic organizer to generate ideas.
- Use one for each part of the prompt if necessary.

Choose the order of your response [1 MINUTE]

- Think about the best way to organize your ideas.
- Number your ideas in the order you will write about them. Cross out ideas you will not be using.

After you write your draft:

Detect errors before turning in the draft [1 MINUTE]

- Carefully reread your writing.
- Look for spelling, punctuation, and grammar errors.
- Make sure that your response makes sense and is complete.

More Prompts for Practice

Apply It! Respond to Prompt 1 by writing a **procedural text** in a timed or open-ended situation. As you write, be sure to follow these tips:

- Consider and answer what your **audience** finds engaging as well as what it knows and needs to know about the procedure to best anticipate potential problems and misunderstandings
- Develop a draft with **transitions** that clearly **convey meaning**
- Clearly state the **purpose** of the text you are writing and provide a well-supported **point of view**
- Use appropriate **formatting and organizational structures** to develop steps or paragraphs that have a clear purpose. Support your ideas with **facts** and **details**
- Accurately define any **technical terms** in language your audience will understand

Prompt 1 Your young nephew is looking for programs in culinary arts, but isn't sure how to go about finding a chef school. He has asked you for advice about online research. Write instructions outlining what steps he should take to do research into culinary arts academies on the Internet.

Spiral Review: Research Respond to Prompt 2 by writing a **critique of the research process**. Your critique should determine if the research plan:

- Addresses a major topic and **research question**
- Sets up to do research on a **complex, multifaceted topic**
- Contains plans for compiling data from **reliable sources**
- Mentions organizing information to include **graphics and forms**
- References using a **standard format** from an appropriate style manual

In your response, offer suggestions for improvement as needed.

Prompt 2 Emilio wrote this research plan. Evaluate it for what he did well and what needs improvement.
My Topic: Charlotte Brontë, the nineteenth-century author of *Jane Eyre;* I think she must have had a very exciting life.
My Research: I will begin by re-reading *Jane Eyre.* Then, I will look in newspapers and magazines for current articles about Charlotte Brontë.
My Writing: I think I'll need two weeks to research and write.

WRITING COACH

Online

www.phwritingcoach.com

Interactive Writing Coach™

Plan your response to the prompt. If you are writing the prompt for practice, write one paragraph at a time or your entire draft and submit it for feedback. If you are using the prompt for a timed test, write your entire draft and submit it for feedback.

Remember **ABCD**

Attack the prompt

Brainstorm possible answers

Choose the order of your response

Detect errors before turning in the draft

Grammar

Find It FIX IT

This handy guide will help you find and fix errors in your writing!

Grammar Game Plan

20

Major Grammatical Errors and How to Fix Them

GAME PLAN Use the right words to add clarity and forcefulness to your writing. Make sure your words say exactly what you mean them to say.

CLARIFY MEANING Do not confuse the meanings of words with similar spellings. Also, words with similar definitions can have important shades of meaning. Check that words you found in a thesaurus are used correctly.

She made my favorite ~~desert~~ dessert last night.

I ran ~~further~~ farther than I had run the previous day.

SPELL-CHECK ERRORS Computer spell-checkers often correct a misspelling with a different, similarly spelled word. Be sure to proofread your work carefully to catch these errors. In each of the following examples, the word with a strikethrough represents an inappropriate spell-checker correction.

I asked for a ~~class~~ glass of skim milk.

My doctor gave me ~~clutches~~ crutches after I broke my leg.

Tech Tip

Be your own "spell-checker"! Proofread! Your computer's spell-checker will not identify every misspelling or incorrectly used word.

LEARN MORE

• See Chapter 21, Miscellaneous Problems in Usage, pages 524–540
• See Writing Coach Online

Check It

Use a current or completed draft of your work to practice using words correctly.

✓ **READ carefully.** Take the time to read your draft closely. For a double-check, have someone else read your work.

✓ **IDENTIFY possible mistakes.** Mark any difficult or commonly misused words in your draft.

✓ **USE a dictionary.** If you are not sure of a word's meaning, consult a dictionary.

2

Missing Comma After Introductory Element

Tech Tip

Remember to add commas to introductory elements that you cut and paste from different parts of a sentence or paragraph.

LEARN MORE
- See Chapter 23, Punctuation, pages 574–577
- See Writing Coach Online

GAME PLAN Place a comma after the following introductory elements in your work.

WORDS Place a comma after introductory words of direct address, words of permission, and interjections.

Jared,ₐdid you turn in your book report?

Yes,ₐI turned it in yesterday.

Hey,ₐI thought you were sick today.

PHRASES Place a comma after introductory prepositional, participial, and infinitive phrases.

After the show,ₐwe drove home.

Surprised by the invitation,ₐMelissa accepted it.

To drive well,ₐshe will need to practice more.

CLAUSES Introductory adverbial clauses should be followed by a comma.

If she does well on the test,ₐshe will get an A in the class.

✓ Check It

Use a current or completed draft of your work to practice placing commas after introductory elements.

✓ **SCAN your draft.** Look for introductory words, phrases, and clauses.

✓ **IDENTIFY missing commas.** Mark sentence starters that might need a comma.

✓ **USE your textbook.** Consult the grammar section of your textbook if you are not sure whether or not to use a comma.

Incomplete or Missing Documentation

GAME PLAN Provide complete citations for borrowed words and ideas. Use the citation style (such as MLA) that your teacher recommends.

MISSING CITATIONS Cite sources of direct quotes and statistics. Remember—when in doubt, cite the source.

The president wrote, "It was the most challenging act of my presidency"∧(Douglas 12).

Mr. Shore reported that it created a divide between parties∧(Shore 14).

INCOMPLETE CITATIONS Make sure your citations include complete source information. This information will vary depending on the source and the citation style, but it may include the author's name, the source's title, and the page number or other location information.

The reviewer suggested that the play "was the best production" he had seen all year (Lee∧24).

All but eight employees have master's degrees (Brighten∧21).

Tech Tip

Be sure to include the citations attached to sentences when you cut and paste text.

LEARN MORE
- See Chapter 11, Research Writing, pages 234–237
- See Writing Coach Online

 *Check It*

Use a current or completed draft of your work to practice documenting your sources.

✓ **REVIEW your notes.** Look for introductory words, phrases, and clauses.

✓ **USE a style guide.** Check the appropriate format and contents for your citations in the style guide your teacher recommends.

4

Vague Pronoun Reference

LEARN MORE
- **See Chapter 19, Agreement, pages 500–504**
- **See Writing Coach Online**

GAME PLAN Create clear pronoun-antecedent relationships to make your writing more accurate and powerful.

VAGUE IDEA Pronouns such as *which, this, that,* and *these* should refer to a specific idea. Sometimes, changing a pronoun to an adjective that modifies a specific noun can avoid a vague reference.

Mrs. Adams was appointed director of the high school marching band. This∧appointment will allow the band to compete in competitions this year.

UNCLEAR USE OF *IT, THEY,* AND *YOU* Be sure that the pronouns *it, they,* and *you* have a clearly stated antecedent. Replacing the personal pronoun with a specific noun can make a sentence clearer.

Mr. Michaels is organizing a little league team at the park district this summer. It∧The team should be fun for my younger brother to join.

The coaches told the team members that ~~they need to change~~ the practice schedule∧will be changed.

To complete the course, ~~you~~∧students need to write a research report.

✓ Check It

Use a current or completed draft of your work to practice identifying vague pronoun references.

✓ **READ** carefully. Read your draft slowly to locate pronouns.

✓ **IDENTIFY** possible errors. Mark any vague pronoun references.

✓ **REVISE** your draft. Rewrite sentences with vague pronoun-antecedent relationships.

GAME PLAN Spelling errors can change the meaning of a sentence. Proofread your work after spell-checking to be sure you have used the correct words.

SPELL-CHECK ERRORS Computer spell-checkers often replace misspelled words with others close in spelling but different in meaning. Proofread your work carefully to correct these errors.

When I went to the department store, I ~~thought~~ ˄bought a new pillow for my bed.

The school announcements said that there is a ~~chores~~ ˄chorus concert tonight.

HOMOPHONES Words that are pronounced the same but have different spellings and meanings are called homophones. Check that you have used the correct homophones to convey your intended meaning.

The recipe calls for ~~flower~~ ˄flour, sugar, and eggs.

Roberto asked for a second ~~peace~~ ˄piece of lettuce to feed his rabbit.

Tech Tip

Proper nouns are not checked by a computer spell-checker. Proofread to make sure that you have spelled people's names correctly.

LEARN MORE

• See Chapter 21, Miscellaneous Problems in Usage, pages 524–540
• See Writing Coach Online

✔ *Check It*

Use a current or completed draft of your work to practice spelling words correctly.

✔ **READ** carefully. Read your draft word by word looking for spelling errors.

✔ **IDENTIFY** possible mistakes. Mark any incorrect words or words that are misspelled.

✔ **USE** a dictionary. If you are not certain how to spell a word or think a homophone has been used incorrectly, consult a dictionary.

6

Punctuation Error With a Quotation

GAME PLAN Quotation marks are used to identify direct quotations. Proper punctuation helps to identify quotations and relate them to your work.

DIRECT AND INDIRECT QUOTATIONS A direct quotation is enclosed in quotation marks. Indirect quotations do not need quotation marks.

Tyler's mom said, "Wash your dishes after you finish dinner."

Tyler's mom said to wash our dishes after dinner.

QUOTATION MARKS WITH OTHER PUNCTUATION When commas or periods end a quotation, the punctuation goes inside the quotation marks. Question marks and exclamation marks go either inside or outside the quotation marks, depending on the sentence structure. Colons and semicolons used after quoted material should be placed outside the quotation marks.

"I can collect the donations," said the volunteer.

The committee member asked, "Can you each bring in a donation for the clothing drive?"

Did she say, "You can donate hats, gloves, or scarves"?

The fundraising committee said, "We need people to volunteer their time to help with the fundraising event"; I participated last year.

Tech Tip

If you cut and paste quotations, remember to copy the taglines to make sure you have included all of the correct punctuation marks that accompany direct quotations.

LEARN MORE

- See Chapter 23, Punctuation, pages 593–599
- See Writing Coach Online

✔ Check It

Use a current or completed draft of your work to practice punctuating quotations correctly.

✔ **READ** carefully. If you used indirect quotations, make sure that they are not set in quotation marks.

✔ **IDENTIFY** direct quotations. Mark each direct quotation in your work. Is each quotation punctuated correctly?

✔ **REVISE** your sentences. Correct all punctuation errors in your quotations.

GAME PLAN Before you insert a comma, think about how your ideas relate to one another. Make sure the comma is necessary.

ESSENTIAL ELEMENTS Appositives, participial phrases, and adjectival clauses that are essential to the meaning of a sentence are not set off by commas.

The student council member, Bethany, is calling a brief meeting after school today.

The teacher, directing the school play, had to take a leave of absence.

The meeting, that the students are attending after school, is about assigning a replacement director for the school play.

COMPOUND PREDICATE Commas should not break apart a compound predicate.

She had baked bread, and was cooking dinner now.

The fire chief directed traffic, and helped extinguish the fire.

✔ *Check It*

Use a current or completed draft of your work to practice correctly punctuating essential elements.

✔ **SCAN** Mentor Texts. Notice how professional writers use commas.

✔ **IDENTIFY** essential elements. Did you use commas to indicate these elements?

✔ **REVISE** your sentences. Delete any commas that set off essential elements.

Tech Tip

As you restructure sentences by cutting and pasting from different parts of a sentence or paragraph, remember to add or delete commas.

LEARN MORE
- See Chapter 23, Punctuation, pages 576–577, 583–584
- See Writing Coach Online

8

Unnecessary or Missing Capitalization

Tech Tip

Sometimes word processors will automatically capitalize any word that follows a period, even if the period is part of an abbreviation. Proofread carefully for incorrectly capitalized words.

LEARN MORE
- See Chapter 22, Capitalization, pages 543–562
- See Writing Coach Online

GAME PLAN Follow the rules of capitalization, such as capitalizing proper nouns, the first word of a sentence, and titles of works of art.

PROPER NOUNS Names, geographical locations, and organizations are examples of nouns that should be capitalized.

Walt Disney is a famous American who created amusement parks in California and Florida, among other places.

He is a member of the Rotary Club.

TITLES OF WORKS OF ART The first word and all other key words in the titles of books, poems, stories, plays, paintings, and other works of art are capitalized.

Have you read the poem *Ode on a Grecian Urn*?

We're going to see the play *Macbeth* with my English class.

 *Check It*

Use a current or completed draft of your work to practice correctly capitalizing words.

✓ **SCAN** your draft. Look for words that are capitalized.

✓ **IDENTIFY** incorrect capitalization. Mark words that might be capitalized incorrectly.

✓ **USE** your textbook. Consult the grammar section of your textbook if you are not sure if a word should be capitalized.

9

Missing Word

GAME PLAN Make sure there are no missing words in a text. This will allow ideas to flow smoothly and will help readers understand the text.

ARTICLES In order to make sure that ideas follow smoothly and sentences are coherent, you must proofread your work. A missing word, even a missing article (*a, an, the*), is enough to confuse a reader.

Marnie asked for ∧an apple to be packed in her lunch, but she got an orange instead.

KEY IDEAS When copying and pasting text, you might miss moving a word in a sentence. If that word is central to the main idea of the sentence, the intended meaning could be lost.

When the votes were recounted, it was clear that ∧Tommy was the winner.

Some of Karen's friends went to a movie, but she stayed home to study for her ∧exams on Monday.

✔ Check It

Use a current or completed draft of your work to practice proofreading.

✔ **READ** carefully. Read your draft word by word to make sure that you did not omit a word.

✔ **IDENTIFY** unclear sentences. Mark any sentences you find that do not make sense. Are they unclear because of a missing word?

✔ **REVISE** your sentences. Add words to your sentences to make the meaning clear.

Tech Tip

When cutting and pasting sentences, you may accidentally insert the same word twice, one right after the other. While spell-checkers generally highlight duplicate words, proofread to be sure the sentence reads as you intended.

LEARN MORE

- See Editing sections in the writing chapters
- See Writing Coach Online

10

Faulty Sentence Structure

Tech Tip

When you cut one part of a sentence and paste it in another, remember to check that the new sentence structure is correct.

LEARN MORE

- See Chapter 16, Effective Sentences, pages 415–420
- See Writing Coach Online

GAME PLAN Sentences should express complex ideas using consistent tenses and similar structures.

FAULTY PARALLELISM When you express complex ideas, it is important that you use parallel grammatical structures to express ideas in phrases, clauses, or sentences of similar types.

Mrs. Barry's favorite activities are to read books, to talk about books, and ~~writes~~ to write in her journal.

I chose the school that has the best program, that is near my home, and that has the smallest classes.

FAULTY COORDINATION Ideas that are not of equal importance should not be connected with *and*. Instead, use multiple sentences or turn one idea into a subordinate clause.

Billy is attending the state university next year. ~~and his~~ His family thinks that he should study engineering, but ~~and~~ he wants to study physics.

Shira is hosting a dinner party tomorrow night for 15 people, ~~and~~ though only 12 of the 15 people sent in an RSVP.

✔ Check It

Use a current or corrected draft of your work to practice correctly structuring sentences.

✔ **SCAN** Mentor Texts. Notice how professional writers present complex ideas.

✔ **IDENTIFY** possible mistakes. Mark any sentences that have faulty parallelism or faulty coordination.

✔ **REVISE** your sentences. Rewrite any sentences that do not have correct sentence structure.

GAME PLAN Use commas to set off nonessential elements of sentences.

APPOSITIVE If an appositive is not essential to the meaning of a sentence, it should be set off by commas.

Antarctica, the coldest continent, is covered by a sheet of ice.

PARTICIPIAL PHRASE A participial phrase not essential to the meaning of a sentence is set off by commas.

Antarctica, covered by a sheet of ice, is the coldest continent.

ADJECTIVAL CLAUSE Use commas to set off an adjectival clause if it is not essential to the meaning of a sentence.

Penguins, which are flightless birds, are one of the animal species that can survive in the Antarctic climate.

 Check It

Use a current or completed draft of your work to practice using commas correctly with nonessential elements.

✔ **SCAN** Mentor Texts. Notice how professional writers use commas to set off nonessential elements.

✔ **IDENTIFY** nonessential elements. Did you use commas to indicate these words, phrases, or clauses?

✔ **REVISE** your sentences. Use commas to set off nonessential elements.

Tech Tip

When you cut part of a sentence and paste it to another, be sure to include the correct punctuation. Proofread these sentences carefully.

LEARN MORE
• See Chapter 23, Punctuation, pages 576–577
• See Writing Coach Online

12

Unnecessary Shift in Verb Tense

LEARN MORE
- See Chapter 17, Verb Usage, pages 444–450
- See Writing Coach Online

GAME PLAN Use consistent verb tenses in your work. Shift tenses only to show that one event comes before or after another.

SEQUENCE OF EVENTS Do not shift tenses unnecessarily when showing a sequence of events.

Ms. Jung will teach the class world history, and then she ~~quizzes~~ ∧will quiz the class.

His mom worked from home in the morning and ~~works~~ ∧worked from the office in the afternoon.

SUBORDINATE CLAUSE The verb in the subordinate clause should follow logically from the tense of the main verb. The verbs require a shift in tense if one event happens before or after another.

Mya wishes that she ~~sees~~∧had seen the play last week.

April suspects that they ~~went~~∧will go to the baseball game without her tomorrow.

✓ Check It

Use a current or completed draft of your work to practice using consistent tenses.

✓ **SCAN** Mentor Texts. Notice how professional writers use consistent tenses within a sentence.

✓ **IDENTIFY** possible mistakes. Mark any shift in verb tense within a sentence.

✓ **USE** your textbook. Consult the grammar section of your textbook if you are not sure that you have used consistent tenses.

GAME PLAN Use a comma before a coordinating conjunction to separate two or more main clauses in a compound sentence.

MAIN CLAUSES Place a comma before a coordinating conjunction (e.g. *and, but, or, nor, yet, so, for*) in a compound sentence.

My aunt is adding more chili powder to her pot of chili, but I already think it's too spicy.

BRIEF CLAUSES The main clauses in some compound sentences are brief and do not need a comma if the meaning is clear.

The roses bloomed and the trees flowered.

COMPOUND SUBJECTS AND VERBS Commas should *not* be used to separate compound subjects and compound verbs in a sentence.

The boys, and girls enjoyed the hike to the waterfall.

I always look left, and look right before crossing the street.

Tech Tip

Be careful when you create a compound sentence by cutting and pasting from different parts of a sentence or paragraph. Remember to include a comma to separate the main clauses.

LEARN MORE
- See Chapter 23, Punctuation, pages 569–573
- See Writing Coach Online

✔ *Check It*

Use a current or completed draft of your work to practice using commas in compound sentences.

✔ **SCAN** your draft. Look for compound sentences.

✔ **IDENTIFY** missing commas. Mark any compound sentences that should be punctuated with a comma.

✔ **REVISE** your sentences. Add commas before coordinating conjunctions to separate main clauses.

14

Unnecessary or Missing Apostrophe

Tech Tip

Proofread your draft carefully. Not all computer grammar checkers will point out incorrect uses of apostrophes.

LEARN MORE

- See Chapter 18, Pronoun Usage, pages 467–468
- See Chapter 23, Punctuation, pages 612–617
- See Writing Coach Online

GAME PLAN Use apostrophes correctly to show possession.

SINGULAR NOUNS To show the possessive case of most singular nouns, add an apostrophe and -*s*.

 The college's∧dorm rooms are smaller than I expected.

PLURAL NOUNS Add an apostrophe to show the possessive case for most plural nouns ending in -*s* or -*es*. For plural nouns that do not end in -*s* or -*es*, add an apostrophe and -*s*.

 The bunnies'∧ home appears to be in my backyard.

The dentist said my teeth's∧lack of cavities was good news.

POSSESSIVE PRONOUNS Possessive pronouns (e.g. *his, hers, its, our, their*) show possession without the use of an apostrophe. Remember that the word *it's* means "it is" while *its* shows possession.

 ∧Their car stands out among the rest on the block because∧its paint color is bright yellow.

 **Check It**

Use a current or completed draft of your work to practice showing possession.

✓ **SCAN** Mentor Texts. Notice when professional writers use apostrophes to indicate possession.

✓ **IDENTIFY** possible mistakes. Mark each apostrophe in your draft. Did you use them correctly to show possession?

✓ **REVISE** your sentences. Make sure to delete any apostrophes you used with possessive pronouns.

GAME PLAN Use correct punctuation to avoid run-on sentences, which are two or more sentences punctuated as if they were a single sentence.

FUSED SENTENCE A fused sentence contains two or more sentences joined with no punctuation. To correct a fused sentence, place a period (and capitalize the following word) or a semicolon between the main clauses.

My uncle used to take me fishing when I was younger ~~we~~. We had a good time even though we never caught a single fish.

While we were fishing, my aunt would bake with my younger sister; we would have fresh bread for dinner.

RUN-ON SENTENCE Make sure you place a comma before coordinating conjunctions that join main clauses to avoid run-on sentences.

I took gymnastics classes for eight years, and it paid off when I made the team!

Tech Tip

Remember to proofread your work. Not all grammar checkers identify run-on sentences.

LEARN MORE

- See Chapter 16, Effective Sentences, pages 410–411
- See Writing Coach Online

> ✓ *Check It*
>
> Use a current or completed draft of your work to practice correcting run-on sentences.
>
> ✓ **SCAN** your draft. Look for run-on sentences.
>
> ✓ **IDENTIFY** missing punctuation. Mark sentences that might need a period or a semicolon to separate main clauses.
>
> ✓ **REVISE** your sentences. When correcting fused sentences, vary your sentence structure.

16

Comma Splice

LEARN MORE

- See Chapter 16, Effective Sentences, pages 410–411
- See Chapter 23, Punctuation, page 570
- See Writing Coach Online

GAME PLAN Use correct punctuation to avoid comma splices. A comma splice happens when two or more complete sentences are joined only with a comma.

PERIOD Replace the comma with a period (and capitalize the following word) to separate two complete thoughts.

After we set up our tent, it started to rain, ~~we~~ . We all rushed into the tent to wait for the weather to clear.

SEMICOLON Replace the comma with a semicolon if the ideas are similar.

My family goes camping every summer, ; it is our favorite activity to do together.

COORDINATING CONJUNCTION A comma splice can be corrected by placing a coordinating conjunction (e.g. *and, or, but, yet, nor*) after the comma.

Mrs. Jared is driving to her mother's house, or maybe she is driving to her mother-in-law's house.

Use a current or completed draft of your work to practice correcting comma splices.

✓ **READ** carefully. Take time to read your draft carefully. Have someone else read your work for a double-check.

✓ **IDENTIFY** possible mistakes. Mark any comma splices you find.

✓ **REVISE** your sentences. Fix comma splices in different ways to vary your sentence structure.

GAME PLAN Check that pronouns agree with their antecedents in number, person, and gender. When the gender is not specified, the pronoun must still agree in number.

GENDER NEUTRAL ANTECEDENTS When gender is not specific, use *his or her* to refer to the singular antecedent.

<u>Each</u> volleyball player must submit ~~their~~ his or her permission slip by the end of the day tomorrow.

OR, NOR, AND When two or more singular antecedents are joined by *or* or *nor*, use a singular personal pronoun. Use a plural personal pronoun when two or more antecedents are joined by *and*.

My mom <u>or</u> my aunt will pick me up after ~~their~~ her class.

The twins Kevin <u>and</u> Derrick will buy a gift for ~~his~~ their dad.

INDEFINITE PRONOUNS A plural indefinite pronoun must agree with a plural personal pronoun. A singular indefinite pronoun must agree with a singular personal pronoun.

<u>All</u> of the students were rehearsing for ~~his~~ their choir concert at the nursing home next weekend.

<u>One</u> of the chaperones is in charge of making sure ~~their~~ her students arrive on time.

✔ Check It

Use a current or completed draft of your work to practice pronoun-antecedent agreement.

✔ **READ** carefully. Take time to read your draft carefully. For a double-check, have someone else read your work.

✔ **IDENTIFY** possible mistakes. Mark any pronouns that do not agree with their antecedents in a sentence.

✔ **USE** your textbook. Consult the grammar section of your textbook if you are not sure whether your pronouns and antecedents agree.

18

Poorly Integrated Quotation

LEARN MORE
- See Chapter 23, Punctuation, pages 593–599
- See Writing Coach Online

GAME PLAN Quotations should flow smoothly into the sentences that surround them. Add explanatory information to link quotes to the rest of your work.

QUOTE IN A SENTENCE Prepare the reader for the information contained in the quote by introducing the quote's idea.

Mr. Porter in his article∧wrote about community volunteering: "We have more volunteers signed up to help this month than we have ever had before" (2).

Jen∧says to win sectionals, her team must come together: "Now more than ever we need to focus on acting as one."

QUOTE AS A SENTENCE Place an introductory phrase before or after a quotation that stands alone. In most cases, this phrase should identify the quote's author or speaker.

∧According to the district representative, "The high school will have the funding to build a new pool by April of next year" (Bergdorf 17).

✓ Check It

Use a current or completed draft of your work to practice integrating quotations.

- ✓ **SCAN Mentor Texts.** Notice how professional writers integrate quotations into their work.
- ✓ **IDENTIFY quotes.** Mark each quote in your work. Does each quote flow smoothly with the surrounding sentence?
- ✓ **REVISE your sentences.** Add explanatory information and introductions as needed.

19

GAME PLAN Use hyphens correctly in your writing, including with compound words and compound adjectives.

COMPOUND WORDS Hyphens can connect two or more words that are used as one compound word. Some compound words do not require a hyphen. Check a current dictionary if you are unsure about hyphenating a word.

My ~~grand-mother~~ ∧grandmother always enters the town's ~~cookoff~~ ∧cook-off.

He has good ~~selfcontrol~~ ∧self-control because he always makes ~~him-self~~ ∧himself exercise when he'd rather watch television.

COMPOUND ADJECTIVES A compound adjective that appears before a noun should be hyphenated. Remember not to hyphenate a compound proper noun acting as an adjective.

My teachers say that internships will help me gain real-∧life experience.

In history class, we learned that the Iron Age culture in Europe and Asia was characterized by the use of iron.

Tech Tip

The automatic hyphenation setting in word processors causes words at the end of a line of text to hyphenate automatically. Be sure to turn off this setting when you are writing a standard essay.

LEARN MORE

- See Chapter 23, Punctuation, pages 605–609
- See Writing Coach Online

✓ Check It

Use a current or completed draft of your work to practice hyphenating words.

✓ **IDENTIFY** possible errors. Mark any compound adjectives before a noun that are not hyphenated.

✓ **REVISE** your sentences. Add a hyphen to words that should be hyphenated.

✓ **USE** a dictionary. Consult a dictionary if you are not sure if a word should be hyphenated.

20

Sentence Fragment

Tech Tip

Sometimes, when you cut text from a sentence and paste it to another, you may miss cutting the whole sentence. Make sure you have both a subject and a verb in the new sentences.

LEARN MORE

- See Chapter 14, Basic Sentence Parts, pages 339–342
- See Chapter 16, Effective Sentences, pages 407–411
- See Writing Coach Online

GAME PLAN Use complete sentences when writing. Make sure you have a subject and a complete verb in each and that each sentence expresses a complete thought.

LACKING A SUBJECT OR VERB A complete sentence must have a subject and a verb.

The class president was organizing a recycling program for the school. ~~And~~ She had a lot of help from the rest of her class!

Ryan's dog was yelping after a bee stung its nose.

SUBORDINATE CLAUSE A subordinate clause cannot stand on its own as a complete sentence because it does not express a complete thought.

Connor joined the track team. ~~After~~ after his coach told him he needed to stay in shape for the soccer season.

Jordan will be taking over as team captain. ~~Until~~ until the actual team captain returns from vacation.

✔ *Check It*

Use a current or completed draft of your work to practice writing complete sentences.

✔ **SCAN** your draft. Look for incomplete sentences.

✔ **IDENTIFY** missing words. Mark sentences that have missing subjects or verbs.

✔ **REVISE** your sentences. Rewrite any sentences that are missing subjects or verbs or that are subordinate clauses standing on their own.

CHAPTER 13

THE PARTS *of* SPEECH

Use each part of speech to help you improve the quality and clarity of your writing.

WRITE GUY *Jeff Anderson, M.Ed.*

WHAT DO YOU NOTICE?

Spot different parts of speech as you zoom in on these lines from the poem "Sonnet 39" by Sir Philip Sidney.

MENTOR TEXT

> O make in me those civil wars to cease;
> I will good tribute pay, if thou do so.

Now, ask yourself the following questions:

- What is the subordinating conjunction in these lines?
- Does the subordinate clause in these lines come before or after the main, or independent, clause?

The subordinating conjunction in these lines is the word *if*. The subordinate clause *if thou do so* comes after the main clause *I will good tribute pay*. Conjunctions play an important role in starting clauses and in connecting related clauses.

Grammar for Writers A conjunction is an essential part of speech because it has a variety of functions. Based on the conjunction you choose, you can completely change the relationship between ideas in your sentences.

How is a conjunction like a telephone operator?

That's easy. Both make connections!

13.1 Nouns and Pronouns

Nouns and pronouns make it possible for people to label everything around them.

WRITING COACH

Online

www.phwritingcoach.com

Grammar Practice
Practice your grammar skills with Writing Coach Online.

Grammar Games
Test your knowledge of grammar in this fast-paced interactive video game.

Nouns

The word *noun* comes from the Latin word *nomen*, which means "name."

RULE 13.1.1

> **A noun** is the part of speech that names a person, place, thing, or idea.

Nouns that name a *person* or *place* are easy to identify.

PERSON	Uncle Mike, neighbor, girls, Bob, swimmer, Ms. Yang, Captain Smith
PLACE	library, Dallas, garden, city, kitchen, James River, canyon, Oklahoma

The category *thing* includes visible things, ideas, actions, conditions, and qualities.

VISIBLE THINGS	chair, pencil, school, duck, daffodil, fort
IDEAS	independence, democracy, militarism, capitalism, recession, freedom
ACTIONS	work, research, exploration, competition, exercise, labor
CONDITIONS	sadness, illness, excitement, joy, health, happiness
QUALITIES	kindness, patience, ability, compassion, intelligence, drive

Concrete and Abstract Nouns

Nouns can also be grouped as *concrete* or *abstract*. A **concrete noun** names something you can see, touch, taste, hear, or smell. An **abstract noun** names something you cannot perceive through any of your five senses.

CONCRETE NOUNS	person, cannon, road, city, music
ABSTRACT NOUNS	hope, improvement, independence, desperation, cooperation

See Practice 13.1A

Collective Nouns

A **collective noun** names a *group* of people or things. A collective noun looks singular, but its meaning may be singular or plural, depending on how it is used in a sentence.

COLLECTIVE NOUNS			
army	choir	troop	faculty
cast	class	crew	legislature

Do not confuse collective nouns—nouns that name a collection of people or things acting as a unit—with plural nouns.

Compound Nouns

A **compound noun** is a noun made up of two or more words acting as a single unit. Compound nouns may be written as separate words, hyphenated words, or combined words.

COMPOUND NOUNS	
Separate	life preserver coffee table bird dog
Hyphenated	sergeant-at-arms self-rule daughter-in-law
Combined	battlefield dreamland porthole

Check a dictionary if you are not sure how to write a compound noun.

Common and Proper Nouns

Any noun may be categorized as either *common* or *proper*.
A **common noun** names any one of a class of people, places,
or things. A **proper noun** names a specific person, place, or thing.
Proper nouns are capitalized, but common nouns are not.
(See Chapter 22 for rules of capitalization.)

COMMON NOUNS	building, writer, nation, month, leader, place, book, war
PROPER NOUNS	Jones, Virginia, *Leaves of Grass*, Revolutionary War, White House, Mark Twain, France, June

A noun of direct address—the name of a person to whom you
are directly speaking—is always a proper noun, as is a family
title before a name. In the examples below, common nouns are
highlighted in yellow, and proper nouns are highlighted in orange.

COMMON NOUNS	My **sister** is a **teacher**.
	Our **doctor** always makes us wait.
	My favorite **person** is my **brother**.
DIRECT ADDRESS	Please, **Grandpa**, can you take us to the park?
	Mom, can you get the check?
	Analise, please bring your fruit cup when you come to the party.
FAMILY TITLE	**Uncle Mike** lived in **New York City**.
	Grandma makes salad with marshmallows, a favorite with the whole family.
	My favorite person is **Aunt Emma**.

See Practice 13.1B

PRACTICE 13.1A **Identifying and Labeling Nouns as Concrete or Abstract**

Read each item. Then label each item *concrete noun* or *abstract noun*, and write another similar abstract or concrete noun.

EXAMPLE   power

ANSWER   *abstract noun, authority*

1. timepiece
2. grace
3. maturity
4. petal
5. revenge
6. necklace
7. magazine
8. gallery
9. fear
10. restaurant

PRACTICE 13.1B **Recognizing Kinds of Nouns (Collective, Compound, Proper)**

Read each sentence. Then, write whether the underlined nouns are *collective*, *compound*, or *proper*. Answer in the order the words appear.

EXAMPLE   Marcia can't wait to rejoin her team.

ANSWER   *proper, collective*

11. Janice's car had a tune-up on Friday.
12. I think Scrappy is the best-behaved dog in the litter.
13. I hope Captain Martin makes me a part of his crew.
14. My mother-in-law just arrived from Greece.
15. There are some poisonous snakes in Arizona.
16. Some professionals believe fingerpainting is an art.
17. I watched a group of tourists enter the Natural History Museum.
18. Her favorite radio station plays jazz.
19. There is a host of sparrows in the tree.
20. Sam tells me there is good fishing in Lake Superior.

SPEAKING APPLICATION

Take turns with a partner. Describe a country you would like to visit and tell why. Include at least three abstract nouns in your response. Your partner should listen for and name the abstract nouns.

WRITING APPLICATION

Write a paragraph about what you plan to do during your next summer vacation. Include at least one common, one collective, one compound, and one proper noun.

Practice   297

Pronouns

Pronouns help writers and speakers avoid awkward repetition of nouns.

RULE 13.1.2

> **Pronouns** are words that stand for nouns or for words that take the place of nouns.

Antecedents of Pronouns Pronouns get their meaning from the words they stand for. These words are called **antecedents.**

RULE 13.1.3

> **Antecedents** are nouns or words that take the place of nouns to which pronouns refer.

The arrows point from pronouns to their antecedents.

EXAMPLES   Dad said that he had left his book at home.

When my **grandparents** moved, **they** gave **their** books to me.

Attending the senior prom was tiring, but **it** was fun!

Antecedents do not always appear before their pronouns, however. Sometimes an antecedent follows its pronoun.

EXAMPLE   Because of **its** weather, **San Diego**, California, is my favorite city.

There are several kinds of pronouns. Most of them have specific antecedents, but a few do not.

See Practice 13.1C

Personal Pronouns The most common pronouns are the **personal pronouns.**

> **Personal pronouns** refer to the person speaking (first person), the person spoken to (second person), or the person, place, or thing spoken about (third person).

13.1.4 | RULE

PERSONAL PRONOUNS		
	SINGULAR	**PLURAL**
First Person	I, me my, mine	we, us our, ours
Second Person	you your, yours	you your, yours
Third Person	he, him, his she, her, hers it, its	they, them their, theirs

In the first example below, the antecedent of the personal pronoun is the person speaking. In the second, the antecedent of the personal pronoun is the person being spoken to. In the last example, the antecedent of the personal pronoun is the thing spoken about.

FIRST PERSON **My** name is not Bonnie.

SECOND PERSON When **you** left, **you** forgot **your** briefcase.

THIRD PERSON The carpet is new, and **its** padding is soft.

Reflexive and Intensive Pronouns These two types of pronouns look the same, but they function differently in sentences.

> A **reflexive pronoun** ends in *-self* or *-selves* and indicates that someone or something in the sentence acts for or on itself. A reflexive pronoun is essential to the meaning of a sentence.
> An **intensive pronoun** ends in *-self* or *-selves* and simply adds emphasis to a noun or pronoun in the sentence.

13.1.5 | RULE

REFLEXIVE AND INTENSIVE PRONOUNS		
	SINGULAR	PLURAL
First Person	myself	ourselves
Second Person	yourself	yourselves
Third Person	himself, herself, itself	themselves

REFLEXIVE   The restaurant chefs prepared **themselves** for the dinner rush.

INTENSIVE   Joshua David **himself** wrote an account of what had taken place.

See Practice 13.1D

Reciprocal Pronouns **Reciprocal pronouns** show a mutual action or relationship.

RULE 13.1.6

The **reciprocal pronouns** *each other* and *one another* refer to a plural antecedent. They express a mutual action or relationship.

EXAMPLES   The two teachers shared the papers with **each other**.

The teachers shared their evaluations with **one another**.

See Practice 13.1E

Demonstrative Pronouns **Demonstrative pronouns** are used to point out one or more nouns.

RULE 13.1.7

A **demonstrative pronoun** directs attention to a specific person, place, or thing.

There are four demonstrative pronouns.

DEMONSTRATIVE PRONOUNS	
SINGULAR	PLURAL
this, that	these, those

Demonstrative pronouns may come before or after their antecedents.

BEFORE   **That** is the **car** I would like to purchase.

AFTER   I hope to visit **Greece** and **Italy** . **Those** are my first choices.

One of the demonstrative pronouns, *that*, can also be used as a relative pronoun.

Relative Pronouns

Relative pronouns are used to relate one idea in a sentence to another. There are five main relative pronouns.

> A **relative pronoun** introduces an adjective clause and connects it to the word that the clause modifies.

13.1.8 **RULE**

RELATIVE PRONOUNS				
that	which	who	whom	whose

EXAMPLES   We read a **biography** **that** contained an account of the officer's life.

The **soldier** **who** had written it described his experiences.

The hiking **trip** , **which** they knew would be long, was last weekend.

See Practice 13.1F

PRACTICE 13.1C **Identifying Pronouns and Antecedents**

Read each sentence. Then, write an appropriate pronoun to complete the sentence and write the antecedent.

EXAMPLE   I am planning a big party for _____ parents.

ANSWER   *my, I*

1. Patrick is someone who spends _____ money wisely.

2. The sauce was so spicy that _____ made my eyes water.

3. Neither Samantha nor Jacinta had any difficulty selecting _____ college.

4. The professor and her teaching aide have posted _____ research online.

5. Phillip hopes _____ submission will get to the magazine on time.

6. Lucas is watching _____ brother's basketball team play.

7. Several subscribers are voicing _____ opinions on the matter.

8. Mrs. Johnson, _____ dinner is now ready.

9. Cora has started babysitting to help with _____ car payments.

10. Either Frank or Nathaniel will offer _____ services as a volunteer.

PRACTICE 13.1D **Identifying Personal, Reflexive, and Intensive Pronouns**

Read each sentence. Then, identify the pronoun and label it *personal*, *reflexive*, or *intensive*.

EXAMPLE   Stacy played with the dog and gave him a biscuit.

ANSWER   *him — personal*

11. Please remember to bring all the equipment yourself.

12. I told him about the plans for the picnic.

13. They will wear costumes during the play.

14. Colin gave himself plenty of time to finish.

15. Who besides you can finish the project?

16. I have only myself to blame for the ruined plans.

17. I won, and the gold medal was mine!

18. The audience entered and found seats themselves.

19. They couldn't fasten their seat belts.

20. The monkeys looked at themselves in the mirror and started howling.

SPEAKING APPLICATION

Take turns with a partner. Describe your ideal employer. Include three or more pronouns that refer to him or her. Your partner should listen for and name the pronouns and their antecedents.

WRITING APPLICATION

Write a paragraph about a memorable event that you have attended. Use personal, reflexive, and intensive pronouns.

PRACTICE 13.1E **Identifying Reciprocal Pronouns**

Read each sentence. Then, write the reciprocal pronoun in each sentence.

EXAMPLE   The tennis partners were proud of each other.

ANSWER   *each other*

1. Tina and Bruce will never forget each other.

2. They write each other every month.

3. Alana, Stacey, and Rachel sent letters to one another.

4. Ben and Mei completely respect each other.

5. David, Miguel, and Sarah definitely care a lot for one another.

6. The group drew closer to one another.

7. It is understood that we like each other.

8. We are expected to like one another.

9. John and Ashley certainly cared for each other.

10. They talk to one another about current events.

PRACTICE 13.1F **Recognizing Demonstrative and Relative Pronouns**

Read each sentence. Then, write each underlined pronoun and label it *demonstrative* or *relative*.

EXAMPLE   <u>That</u> is the best part of the album.

ANSWER   *That* — *demonstrative*

11. The shirt <u>that</u> Daryl bought has a stain on the collar.

12. <u>These</u> belong to Kara and Jim.

13. The man <u>who</u> is standing near the entrance is a lawyer.

14. <u>Those</u> are the games I am going to buy.

15. It is hard to believe <u>that</u> he said it so loudly.

16. <u>This</u> tastes just like it did in the restaurant.

17. The chef <u>who</u> won the contest studied overseas.

18. The man, <u>whose</u> son is in the band, is clapping along with the music.

19. The house, <u>which</u> was bright green, was very noticeable.

20. Have you found the map <u>that</u> was missing?

SPEAKING APPLICATION

Describe to a partner a good friend of yours. Use reciprocal pronouns in your description. Your partner should listen for and name the reciprocal pronouns.

WRITING APPLICATION

Write a paragraph about your favorite movie. Use demonstrative and relative pronouns in your paragraph.

Interrogative Pronouns

Interrogative pronouns are used to ask questions.

RULE 13.1.9

> An **interrogative pronoun** is used to begin a question.

The five interrogative pronouns are *what*, *which*, *who*, *whom*, and *whose*. Sometimes the antecedent of an interrogative pronoun is not known.

EXAMPLE   **Which** team finished first?

See Practice 13.1G

Indefinite Pronouns

Indefinite pronouns sometimes lack specific antecedents.

RULE 13.1.10

> An **indefinite pronoun** refers to a person, place, or thing that may or may not be specifically named.

INDEFINITE PRONOUNS				
SINGULAR			**PLURAL**	**BOTH**
another	everyone	nothing	both	all
anybody	everything	one	few	any
anyone	little	other	many	more
anything	much	somebody	others	most
each	neither	someone	several	none
either	nobody	something		some
everybody	no one			

Indefinite pronouns sometimes have specific antecedents.

NO SPECIFIC ANTECEDENT   **Both** wore the same dress.

SPECIFIC ANTECEDENTS   **All** of the **employees** left early.

Indefinite pronouns can also function as adjectives.

ADJECTIVE   **Few** painters are as famous as this one.

See Practice 13.1H

PRACTICE 13.1G > Recognizing Interrogative Pronouns

Read each sentence. Then, write the interrogative pronoun needed to complete the sentence.

EXAMPLE _____ wants my help?

ANSWER *Who*

1. _____ of the two books was easier to understand?

2. _____ family brought all this terrific food?

3. With _____ are you going to the concert?

4. _____ of the tournaments do you plan to enter?

5. _____ inspired you to write this book?

6. To _____ did you deliver the package?

7. _____ found out about the surprise party?

8. _____ was the total price of the entertainment system?

9. _____ idea was it to show up late?

10. _____ have you encountered that is a problem?

PRACTICE 13.1H > Identifying Personal and Indefinite Pronouns

Read each sentence. Write the appropriate personal pronoun to complete the sentence. Then, write the indefinite pronoun used in the sentence.

EXAMPLE Few of my friends have sold _____ raffle tickets.

ANSWER *their, Few*

11. Many of the contestants brought noisemakers with _____.

12. Several of my colleagues turned in _____ reports before the meeting.

13. No one on the boys' soccer team wears _____ uniform during practice.

14. Everyone in the girl's choir brings _____ own style to the group.

15. Few of my classmates changed _____ minds after the council speeches.

16. Some of the tourists carried travel books with _____.

17. All of the drivers are revving _____ engines.

18. None of our luggage has scratches on _____.

19. Most of the students like _____ new teacher.

20. Each of the men raised _____ trophy to the spectators.

SPEAKING APPLICATION

Imagine you are applying for a job. Take turns with a partner interviewing each other. Use interrogative pronouns in your questions. Your partner should listen for and name the interrogative pronouns.

WRITING APPLICATION

Using three of the completed sentences above, replace the indefinite pronouns with your own. Make sure that the new sentences still make sense.

13.2 Verbs

Every complete sentence must have at least one **verb**, which may consist of as many as four words.

RULE 13.2.1

A **verb** is a word or group of words that expresses time while showing an action, a condition, or the fact that something exists.

Action Verbs and Linking Verbs

Action verbs express action. They are used to tell what someone or something does, did, or will do. **Linking verbs** express a condition or show that something exists.

RULE 13.2.2

An **action verb** tells what action someone or something is performing.

ACTION VERBS

Ricky **learned** about hockey rules.

The radio **blared** the broadcast from the weather station.

We **chose** two books about former presidents.

I **remember** the play about Dr. Jekyll.

The action expressed by a verb does not have to be visible. Words expressing mental activities—such as *learn, think,* or *decide*—are also considered action verbs.

The person or thing that performs the action is called the *subject* of the verb. In the examples above, *Ricky, radio, we,* and *I* are the subjects of *learned, blared, chose,* and *remember.*

> A **linking verb** is a verb that connects its subject with a noun, pronoun, or adjective that identifies or describes the subject.

LINKING
VERBS

That man **is** a famous author.

The window **seems** sparkly.

The verb *be* is the most common linking verb.

THE FORMS OF *BE*			
am	am being	can be	have been
are	are being	could be	has been
is	is being	may be	had been
was	was being	might be	could have been
were	were being	must be	may have been
		shall be	might have been
		should be	shall have been
		will be	should have been
		would be	will have been
			would have been

Most often, the forms of *be* that function as linking verbs express the condition of the subject. Occasionally, however, they may merely express existence, usually by showing, with other words, where the subject is located.

EXAMPLE   The yogurt **is** in the freezer.

Other Linking Verbs A few other verbs can also serve as linking verbs.

OTHER LINKING VERBS		
appear	look	sound
become	remain	stay
feel	seem	taste
grow	smell	turn

EXAMPLES

The lasagna **smelled** like garlic and tomatoes.

The music **sounds** too loud.

The house **smelled** delicious when we were done.

The situation at the school **remained** tense.

The drivers **grew** tired.

Some of these verbs may also act as action—not linking—verbs. To determine whether the word is functioning as an action verb or as a linking verb, insert *am*, *are*, or *is* in place of the verb. If the substitute makes sense while connecting two words, then the original verb is a linking verb.

LINKING VERB

The air **felt** damp. (The air **is** damp.)

ACTION VERB

The climbers **felt** the snowflakes.

LINKING VERB

The horseradish **tastes** bitter. (The horseradish **is** bitter.)

ACTION VERB

I **taste** the chili pepper.

See Practice 13.2A
See Practice 13.2B

PRACTICE 13.2A > **Identifying Action and Linking Verbs**

Read each sentence. Write the action verb in each sentence.

EXAMPLE   The speeding train raced through the station.

ANSWER   *raced*

1. Olivia negotiated extra time for her project.

2. The owls hooted all night.

3. Gloria represents her high school on the city volleyball team.

4. She thought about the problem.

5. For a science project, Duane constructed a sundial.

Read each sentence. Write the linking verb in each sentence.

EXAMPLE   It felt humid earlier this morning.

ANSWER   *felt*

6. David Beckham is a soccer player.

7. The children remained quiet.

8. Amy looked very pale and sick.

9. Some dog breeds are extremely active.

10. Everyone felt sorry about the misunderstanding.

PRACTICE 13.2B > **Distinguishing Between Action and Linking Verbs**

Read each sentence. Then, write the verb in each sentence, and label it *action* or *linking*.

EXAMPLE   Emma Grace seems unusually quiet.

ANSWER   *seems* — linking

11. The freighter sailed away in the morning.

12. The capital of Texas is Austin.

13. My sister grew tall in a short time.

14. The magician's assistant reached into the bag.

15. The speaker was extremely late for the assembly.

16. We slipped out the door unnoticed.

17. The blueberry cobbler smells delicious.

18. The trail was dangerous for hikers.

19. The coyote appeared from behind the bushes.

20. I tasted lots of garlic in the soup.

SPEAKING APPLICATION

Take turns with a partner. Describe the plot of your favorite movie. Your partner should listen for and identify the action and linking verbs that you use.

WRITING APPLICATION

Write three sentences with action verbs and underline the action verbs. Then, write three sentences with linking verbs and underline the linking verbs.

Practice   309

Transitive and Intransitive Verbs

All verbs are either **transitive** or **intransitive,** depending on whether or not they transfer action to another word in a sentence.

A **transitive verb** directs action toward someone or something named in the same sentence. An **intransitive verb** does not direct action toward anyone or anything named in the same sentence.

The word toward which a transitive verb directs its action is called the *object* of the verb. Intransitive verbs never have objects. You can determine whether a verb has an object by asking *whom* or *what* after the verb.

TRANSITIVE Mark **threw** the basketball.
(Threw what? basketball)

The lion **ate** the prey.
(Ate what? prey)

INTRANSITIVE The graduates **practiced** on the field.
(Practiced what? [no answer])

The kids **shouted** loudly.
(Shouted what? [no answer])

Because linking verbs do not express action, they are always intransitive. Most action verbs can be either transitive or intransitive, depending on the sentence. However, some action verbs can only be transitive, and others can only be intransitive.

TRANSITIVE I **wrote** a letter from Washington, D.C.

INTRANSITIVE The author **wrote** quickly.

See Practice 13.2C

ALWAYS TRANSITIVE	The Capulets **rival** the Montagues.
ALWAYS INTRANSITIVE	They **winced** at the sound of the gong.

Verb Phrases

A verb that has more than one word is a **verb phrase.**

> A **verb phrase** consists of a main verb and one or more helping verbs.

13.2.6 RULE

Helping verbs are often called auxiliary verbs. One or more helping verbs may precede the main verb in a verb phrase.

VERB PHRASES	I **will be taking** my car to the shop.
	I **should have been watching** when I tripped on the curb.

All the forms of *be* listed in this chapter can be used as helping verbs. The following verbs can also be helping verbs.

OTHER HELPING VERBS			
do	have	shall	can
does	has	should	could
did	had	will	may
		would	might
			must

A verb phrase is often interrupted by other words in a sentence.

INTERRUPTED VERB PHRASES	I **will** definitely **be taking** my car to the shop.
	Should I **take** my car to the shop?

See Practice 13.2D

PRACTICE 13.2C **Distinguishing Between Transitive and Intransitive Verbs**

Read each sentence. Identify each underlined verb as *transitive* or *intransitive*.

EXAMPLE   Derrick <u>greeted</u> the visitors.

ANSWER   *transitive*

1. When <u>will</u> Felicia <u>paint</u> her room?

2. The train <u>stopped</u> at the station.

3. The children <u>play</u> checkers.

4. Mr. Lopez <u>baked</u> bread.

5. Last night, we <u>ate</u> on the patio.

6. Alex <u>wrote</u> a research report.

7. Both Roland and Tracy <u>ran</u> in the race.

8. The kite <u>flew</u> overhead.

9. Sharika <u>returns</u> from her trip tomorrow.

10. Gabriel <u>drives</u> a minivan.

PRACTICE 13.2D **Recognizing Verb Phrases**

Read each sentence. Then, write the verb phrase in each sentence.

EXAMPLE   The astronauts are working in space.

ANSWER   *are working*

11. A tiny kitten was wandering around the yard.

12. His favorite movie is playing tonight.

13. The new computer chip is not recommended.

14. A funny costume will always make children laugh.

15. Fairy tales are sometimes called folktales.

16. We have used computers in math class before.

17. The magician is thinking of a number.

18. The firefighters had appeared uninjured.

19. We had heard the new song on the radio.

20. The refreshments will be welcomed after the game.

SPEAKING APPLICATION

Take turns with a partner. Tell about your favorite school trip, using transitive and intransitive verbs. Your partner should listen for and name each type of verb.

WRITING APPLICATION

Write three sentences with verb phrases. Underline the verb phrases in your sentences.

13.3 Adjectives and Adverbs

Adjectives and **adverbs** are the two parts of speech known as *modifiers*—that is, they slightly change the meaning of other words by adding description or making them more precise.

Adjectives

An **adjective** clarifies the meaning of a noun or pronoun by providing information about its appearance, location, and so on.

> An **adjective** is a word used to describe a noun or pronoun or to give it a more specific meaning.

RULE 13.3.1

An adjective answers one of four questions about a noun or pronoun: *What kind? Which one? How many? How much?*

EXAMPLES   **snow** boots (What kind of boots?)

that shoe (Which shoe?)

four pairs of shoes (How many pairs?)

six gallons of water (How much water?)

When an adjective modifies a noun, it usually precedes the noun. Occasionally, the adjective may follow the noun.

EXAMPLES   The student was **calm** about her low grade.

I considered the student **calm** .

An adjective that modifies a pronoun usually follows it. Sometimes, however, the adjective precedes the pronoun as it does in the example on the next page.

AFTER   She was **ashamed** when she didn't pass.

BEFORE   **Ashamed** that he broke the glass, he handed her a towel.

More than one adjective may modify a single noun or pronoun.

EXAMPLE   The school hired a **creative, experienced** art teacher.

Articles Three common adjectives—*a, an,* and *the*—are known as **articles.** *A* and *an* are called **indefinite articles** because they refer to any one of a class of nouns. *The* refers to a specific noun and, therefore, is called the **definite article.**

INDEFINITE EXAMPLES	DEFINITE EXAMPLES
a daisy	the stem
an orchid	the mask

Remember that *an* is used before a vowel sound; *a* is used before a consonant sound.

EXAMPLES   **a** once-clean house (*w* sound)

a unicycle (*y* sound)

an honest politician (no *h* sound)

See Practice 13.3A

Nouns Used as Adjectives Words that are usually nouns sometimes act as adjectives. In this case, the noun answers the questions *What kind?* or *Which one?* about another noun.

NOUNS USED AS ADJECTIVES	
flower	flower garden
lawn	lawn mower

See Practice 13.3B

Proper Adjectives Adjectives can also be proper. **Proper adjectives** are proper nouns used as adjectives or adjectives formed from proper nouns. They usually begin with capital letters.

PROPER NOUNS	PROPER ADJECTIVES
Monday	Monday morning
San Francisco	San Francisco streets
Europe	European roses
Rome	Roman hyacinth

Compound Adjectives Adjectives can be compound. Most are hyphenated; others are combined or are separate words.

HYPHENATED   **rain-forest** plants

water-soluble pigments

COMBINED   **airborne** pollen

evergreen shrubs

See Practice 13.3C   SEPARATE   **North American** rhododendrons

Pronouns Used as Adjectives Certain pronouns can also function as adjectives. The seven personal pronouns known as either **possessive adjectives** or **possessive pronouns** do double duty in a sentence. They act as pronouns because they have antecedents. They also act as adjectives because they modify nouns by answering *Which one?* The other pronouns become adjectives instead of pronouns when they stand before nouns and answer the question *Which one?*

A pronoun is used as an adjective if it modifies a noun.

13.3.2 RULE

Possessive pronouns, demonstrative pronouns, interrogative pronouns, and indefinite pronouns can all function as adjectives when they modify nouns.

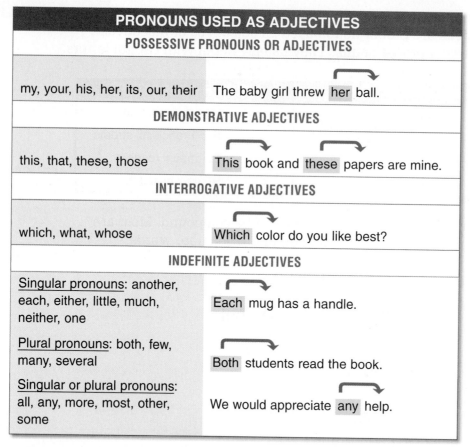

PRONOUNS USED AS ADJECTIVES	
POSSESSIVE PRONOUNS OR ADJECTIVES	
my, your, his, her, its, our, their	The baby girl threw her ball.
DEMONSTRATIVE ADJECTIVES	
this, that, these, those	This book and these papers are mine.
INTERROGATIVE ADJECTIVES	
which, what, whose	Which color do you like best?
INDEFINITE ADJECTIVES	
Singular pronouns: another, each, either, little, much, neither, one	Each mug has a handle.
Plural pronouns: both, few, many, several	Both students read the book.
Singular or plural pronouns: all, any, more, most, other, some	We would appreciate any help.

Verb Forms Used as Adjectives Verb forms used as adjectives usually end in -*ing* or -*ed* and are called **participles.**

EXAMPLE   I picked the **growing** vegetables.

Nouns, pronouns, and verb forms function as adjectives only when they modify other nouns or pronouns. The following examples show how their function in a sentence can change.

	REGULAR FUNCTION	AS AN ADJECTIVE
Noun	The road was curved.	The road surface was bumpy.
Pronoun	This was a fun party.	This party was fun.
Verb	I planted flowers in the garden.	The planted flowers needed sun.

See Practice 13.3D

PRACTICE 13.3A > **Recognizing Adjectives and Articles**

Read each sentence. Then, write the adjective(s) and the article(s) in each sentence.

EXAMPLE   A fish swam around a small reef.

ANSWER   *small; A, a*

1. Maya picked the perfect spot for the garden.

2. The Indian restaurant has delicious food.

3. In late spring, we see the beautiful flowers.

4. The story is funny and has a positive message.

5. The city has a dry climate.

6. Please set these bowls on the round table.

7. The explorers went to the frigid Alaskan wilderness.

8. Please bring me a blue shirt.

9. A beach ball bobbed up and down in the lake.

10. In many Japanese homes, the people sleep on futons.

PRACTICE 13.3B > **Identifying Nouns Used as Adjectives**

Read each sentence. Then, write the noun that is used as an adjective in each sentence.

EXAMPLE   The puppy slept on a feather pillow.

ANSWER   *feather*

11. She offered us some spinach casserole.

12. The baseball practice lasted until after dark.

13. The vegetable farmers planted corn.

14. Old photographs and a diamond ring filled her keepsake box.

15. I set my radio alarm for 7:00 A.M.

16. We went to the shore during our school holiday.

17. She donated the entire cash reward from the settlement.

18. The club organized a Sunday picnic.

19. Air bubbles give the fish oxygen.

20. The fisherman threw crab nets into the ocean.

SPEAKING APPLICATION

Take turns with a partner. Tell about a special holiday that you have spent with your family. Your partner should listen for and name the adjectives and articles that you use.

WRITING APPLICATION

Write three sentences that contain nouns used as adjectives.

> **PRACTICE 13.3C** **Recognizing Proper and Compound Adjectives**

Read each sentence. Then, write the adjective in each sentence, and label it *proper* or *compound*.

EXAMPLE   The meal began with a French soup.

ANSWER   *French — proper*

1. Do you enjoy Chinese food?
2. My dad built a four-foot table.
3. I am a part-time worker at the restaurant.
4. The speaker was a Buddhist priest.
5. Sean listens to Celtic music.
6. My grandmother is a kindhearted person.
7. Anne speaks with a British accent.
8. She lives in an area called the Old South neighborhood.
9. Ours is a breathtaking continent.
10. That's an Irish lullaby.

> **PRACTICE 13.3D** **Recognizing Pronouns and Verbs Used as Adjectives**

Read each sentence. Then, write the pronoun or verb used as an adjective in each sentence and the noun it modifies.

EXAMPLE   This drawing is mine.

ANSWER   *this, drawing*

11. That laptop is his.
12. These shoes are very comfortable.
13. The swaying trees moved gracefully.
14. Both squirrels disappeared behind a tree.
15. The last step is to trim those edges.
16. The bouncing kangaroo was everyone's favorite.
17. My wilting flowers could use water.
18. Each person wanted something different.
19. Which court will we play on?
20. This food is the best I have tasted in a long time.

SPEAKING APPLICATION

With a partner, name four adjectives that are proper or compound. Then, use these adjectives in a brief paragraph that tells how people can help others in their community.

WRITING APPLICATION

Write four sentences about your town. Include pronouns used as adjectives and verbs used as adjectives in your sentences.

Adverbs

Adverbs, like adjectives, describe other words or make other words more specific.

> **An adverb is a word that modifies a verb, an adjective, or another adverb.**

13.3.3 RULE

When an adverb modifies a verb, it will answer any of the following questions: *Where? When? In what way? To what extent?*

An adverb answers only one question when modifying an adjective or another adverb: *To what extent?* Because it specifies the degree or intensity of the modified adjective or adverb, such an adverb is often called an **intensifier.**

The position of an adverb in relation to the word it modifies can vary in a sentence. If the adverb modifies a verb, it may precede or follow it or even interrupt a verb phrase. Normally, adverbs modifying adjectives and adverbs will immediately precede the words they modify.

ADVERBS MODIFYING VERBS	
Where?	**When?**
The children ran outside.	She never picked the flowers.
The children ran there.	Later, we toured the flower show.
The boy ran around.	She waters the flowers daily in the yard.
In what way?	**To what extent?**
She officially sold flowers in the shop.	The puppy was still playing energetically.
She graciously made any kind of bouquet.	He always made the right choice.
Jane left quickly after the presentation.	Be sure to wash completely after gardening.

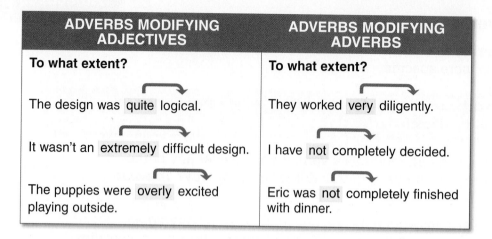

ADVERBS MODIFYING ADJECTIVES	ADVERBS MODIFYING ADVERBS
To what extent?	**To what extent?**
The design was quite logical.	They worked very diligently.
It wasn't an extremely difficult design.	I have not completely decided.
The puppies were overly excited playing outside.	Eric was not completely finished with dinner.

Adverbs as Parts of Verbs Some verbs require an adverb to complete their meaning. Adverbs used this way are considered part of the verb. An adverb functioning as part of a verb does not answer the usual questions for adverbs.

EXAMPLES   The garbage truck **backed up** along the side of the street.

Please **point out** which ship model is yours.

Daniel had to **run out** to pick up dinner for the team.

See Practice 13.3E

Nouns Functioning as Adverbs
Several nouns can function as adverbs that answer the questions *Where?* or *When?* Some of these words are *home, yesterday, today, tomorrow, mornings, afternoons, evenings, nights, week, month,* and *year.*

NOUNS USED AS ADVERBS	
NOUNS	**AS ADVERBS**
Nights seems to fly by.	I work out nights.
My year in Italy seems like so long ago.	Let's go on vacation this year.
Tomorrow will be a sunny day.	I am sure I will finish my book tomorrow.

Adverb or Adjective?
Adverbs usually have different forms from adjectives and thus are easily identified. Many adverbs are formed by the addition of *-ly* to an adjective.

ADJECTIVES   The forest was **beautiful**.

The baby looked through the **open** door.

ADVERBS   The forest was cared for **beautifully**.

The students discussed the test **openly**.

Some adjectives, however, also end in *-ly*. Therefore, you cannot assume that every word ending in *-ly* is an adverb.

ADJECTIVES   a **weekly** magazine

a **monthly** payment

a **stately** mansion

smelly socks

Some adjectives and adverbs share the same form. You can determine the part of speech of such words by checking their function in the sentence. An adverb will modify a verb, adjective, or adverb; an adjective will modify a noun or pronoun.

ADVERB   The presentation ran **late**.

ADJECTIVE   We enjoyed the **late** brunches on vacation.

ADVERB   The surfer glided **straight** through the wave.

See Practice 13.3F   ADJECTIVE   The horizon was **straight**.

Adjectives and Adverbs   321

PRACTICE 13.3E Recognizing Adverbs

Read each sentence. Then, write the adverb or adverbs in each sentence, and tell whether each one modifies a *verb*, an *adjective*, or an *adverb*.

EXAMPLE   My sister draws well.

ANSWER   *well — verb*

1. Is your dog still sick?
2. Our neighbor drives cautiously.
3. The parade route ended there.
4. Suze thinks they returned yesterday.
5. The goalie blocked every shot perfectly.
6. We already wrote our thank-you e-mails.
7. Seth always completes his assignments.
8. The mail is quite obviously late.
9. Mom speaks glowingly about her garden.
10. Our dog is very friendly.

PRACTICE 13.3F Identifying Adverbs and the Words They Modify

Read each sentence. Then, write the adverb or adverbs in each sentence and the word they modify.

EXAMPLE   We will be riding home on the bus.

ANSWER   *home, riding*

11. I am really sorry that I missed the party.
12. She gets up early to go to school.
13. Carla expects her team to finish first in the tournament.
14. Our new car arrived yesterday from the factory.
15. Serena rode fast, and we could not catch up with her.
16. The soup seems rather salty to me.
17. The plane will be landing very soon.
18. My sister works weekday afternoons at the college.
19. The warrior fought bravely.
20. He bought a car that was almost new.

SPEAKING APPLICATION

Take turns with a partner. Tell about something that you enjoy doing. Your partner should name adverbs that you use and whether each one modifies a verb, an adjective, or another adverb.

WRITING APPLICATION

Use sentence 16 as a model to write three similar sentences. Replace the adverb in sentence 16 with other adverbs.

13.4 Prepositions, Conjunctions, and Interjections

Prepositions and conjunctions function in sentences as connectors. **Prepositions** express relationships between words or ideas, whereas **conjunctions** join words, groups of words, or even entire sentences. **Interjections** function by themselves and are independent of other words in a sentence.

Prepositions and Prepositional Phrases

Prepositions make it possible to show relationships between words. The relationships may involve, for example, location, direction, time, cause, or possession. A preposition may consist of one word or multiple words. (See the chart on the next page.)

> A **preposition** relates the noun or pronoun that appears with it to another word in the sentence.

RULE 13.4.1

Notice how the prepositions below, highlighted in pink, relate to the words highlighted in yellow.

LOCATION   Jewelry **is made** **around** the **world**.

TIME   Classical music will **last** **for** **centuries**.

CAUSE   Kim is **late** **because of** the **traffic**.

> A **prepositional phrase** is a group of words that includes a preposition and a noun or pronoun.

RULE 13.4.2

The noun or pronoun with a preposition is called the **object of the preposition.** Objects may have one or more modifiers. A prepositional phrase may also have more than one object. In the example below, the objects of the prepositions are highlighted in blue, and the prepositions are in pink.

EXAMPLE   Thomas and Nick waited **on** the **corner** **for** a **bus**.

PREPOSITIONS			
aboard	before	in front of	over
about	behind	in place of	owing to
above	below	in regard to	past
according to	beneath	inside	prior to
across	beside	in spite of	regarding
across from	besides	instead of	round
after	between	into	since
against	beyond	in view of	through
ahead of	but	like	throughout
along	by	near	till
alongside	by means of	nearby	to
along with	concerning	next to	together with
amid	considering	of	toward
among	despite	off	under
apart from	down	on	underneath
around	during	on account of	until
aside from	except	onto	unto
as of	for	on top of	up
as	from	opposite	upon
atop	in	out	with
barring	in addition to	out of	within
because of	in back of	outside	without

See Practice 13.4A

Preposition or Adverb?

Many words may be used either as prepositions or adverbs. Words that can function in either role include *around, before, behind, down, in, off, on, out, over,* and *up.* If an object accompanies the word, the word is used as a preposition.

PREPOSITION The committee meets **around** a huge table.

ADVERB The discussion about the topic went **around and around** .

See Practice 13.4B

PRACTICE 13.4A **Identifying Prepositions and Prepositional Phrases**

Read each sentence. Then, write each prepositional phrase and underline each preposition.

EXAMPLE   In the evening, we went to the opera.

ANSWER   *In the evening, to the opera*

1. The girls asked for tickets to the play.

2. Please keep the information between you and me.

3. Their plane arrived from New York at midnight.

4. Across the lake is a village with a hotel.

5. We talked for hours about the past.

6. The price of this car is below its market value.

7. Enter through those doors and into the station.

8. With much nervousness, I walked across the bridge.

9. The singer received a standing ovation from the audience.

10. Your keys are under the mat near the front door.

PRACTICE 13.4B **Distinguishing Between Prepositions and Adverbs**

Read each sentence. Then, label each underlined word as a *preposition* or an *adverb*.

EXAMPLE   I will wait <u>near</u> the entrance.

ANSWER   *preposition*

11. A squirrel scurried <u>up</u> the tree.

12. The moon rose <u>up</u> above the clouds.

13. Someone left the radio <u>on</u> all day.

14. When Marty moved <u>away</u>, I wanted to go with him.

15. Becca turned <u>around</u> and waved at me.

16. Chuck stayed <u>behind</u> after the game ended.

17. A tassel on my parasol fell <u>off</u>.

18. A creek runs <u>below</u> the fields.

19. My grandfather is <u>in</u> good health again.

20. They went <u>out</u> and took a long walk in the garden.

SPEAKING APPLICATION

Take turns with a partner. Describe the locations of objects in the room. Your partner should listen for and identify the prepositional phrases that you use and the preposition in each phrase.

WRITING APPLICATION

Write a sentence using the word *down* as a preposition. Then, write a sentence using *down* as an adverb.

Conjunctions

There are three main kinds of conjunctions: **coordinating, correlative,** and **subordinating.** Sometimes a type of adverb, the **conjunctive adverb,** is also considered a conjunction.

RULE
13.4.3

> A **conjunction** is a word used to connect other words or groups of words.

Coordinating Conjunctions The seven coordinating conjunctions are used to connect similar parts of speech or groups of words of equal grammatical weight.

COORDINATING CONJUNCTIONS						
and	but	for	nor	or	so	yet

EXAMPLES Linda **and** Margaret ran the editorial meeting.

Linda left early, **so** Margaret left with her.

Correlative Conjunctions The five paired correlative conjunctions join elements of equal grammatical weight.

CORRELATIVE CONJUNCTIONS		
both . . . and	either . . . or	neither . . . nor
not only . . . but also	whether . . . or	

EXAMPLES She made **both** pasta **and** eggplant.

Neither Beth **nor** Fred liked the eggplant.

I don't know **whether** to meet them for brunch **or** dinner.

Subordinating Conjunctions Subordinating conjunctions join two complete ideas by making one of the ideas subordinate to, or dependent upon, the other.

SUBORDINATING CONJUNCTIONS			
after	because	lest	till
although	before	now that	unless
as	even if	provided	until
as if	even though	since	when
as long as	how	so that	whenever
as much as	if	than	where
as soon as	inasmuch as	that	wherever
as though	in order that	though	while

The subordinate idea in a sentence always begins with a subordinating conjunction and makes up what is known as a subordinate clause. A subordinate clause may either follow or precede the main idea in a sentence.

EXAMPLES   I lived in my parents' house **because** I was saving money.

After the rain ends, the flowers in the desert bloom.

Conjunctive Adverbs Conjunctive adverbs act as transitions between complete ideas by indicating comparisons, contrasts, results, and other relationships. The chart below lists the most common conjunctive adverbs.

CONJUNCTIVE ADVERBS		
accordingly	finally	nevertheless
again	furthermore	otherwise
also	however	then
besides	indeed	therefore
consequently	moreover	thus

Prepositions, Conjunctions, and Interjections   327

Punctuation With Conjunctive Adverbs Punctuation is usually required both before and after conjunctive adverbs.

EXAMPLES There was almost two feet of snow this weekend. **Therefore**, we shoveled our way out.

Felix was a very persuasive speaker; **indeed**, he could convince you to do almost anything.

We arrived on time; **otherwise**, the reservation would be canceled.

See Practice 13.4C
See Practice 13.4D
See Practice 13.4E

Interjections

Interjections express emotion. Unlike most words, they have no grammatical connection to other words in a sentence.

RULE 13.4.4

> An **interjection** is a word that expresses feeling or emotion and functions independently of a sentence.

Interjections can express a variety of sentiments, such as happiness, fear, anger, pain, surprise, sorrow, exhaustion, or hesitation.

SOME COMMON INTERJECTIONS				
ah	dear	hey	ouch	well
aha	goodness	hurray	psst	whew
alas	gracious	oh	tsk	wow

EXAMPLES **Ouch**! That knife is very sharp.

Wow! I can't believe that!

Oh! I can't go.

Whew! We worked hard at the gym.

See Practice 13.4F

PRACTICE 13.4C > **Identifying Different Conjunctions**

Read each sentence. Then, write the conjunction in each sentence, and label it *coordinating*, *correlative*, *subordinating*, or *conjunctive*.

EXAMPLE   Either you can visit me, or I will visit you.

ANSWER   *Either . . . or* — correlative

1. We are going skiing even though there is not much snow.

2. The applause was deafening; therefore, the speaker paused.

3. Not only is Max smart, but also he is a good watchdog.

4. Dad said we can have pasta or chicken for dinner.

5. Tricia and Maria are my closest friends.

6. Whether it rains or not, we will have fun.

7. I had planned to have a party, but I got sick.

8. Both Jill and Nguyen are having dinner with us.

9. We did our best; indeed, we practiced every day.

10. As soon as the mayor arrived, the speeches began.

PRACTICE 13.4D > **Supplying Conjunctions**

Read each sentence. Then, supply a conjunction of the kind indicated in parentheses. Some sentences have more than one possible answer. Be sure each finished sentence makes sense.

EXAMPLE   It was raining, _____ we canceled the picnic. (coordinating conjunction)

ANSWER   *so*

11. I want to go to the dance, _____ I'm grounded. (coordinating conjunction)

12. Luca longed to see the movie; _____, it opened. (conjunctive adverb)

13. Alex applied to schools in _____ Wisconsin _____ Michigan. (correlative conjunction)

14. Eat a big breakfast _____ we'll have no time for lunch. (subordinating conjunction)

15. We can choose to play volleyball _____ softball in gym class. (coordinating conjunction)

16. _____ Hannah forgot my birthday, I forgive her. (subordinating conjunction)

17. A juror spoke to the press; _____, the judge declared a mistrial. (conjunctive adverb)

18. _____ medication _____ meditation made Javier's headaches go away. (correlative conjunction)

19. _____ you read it, you'll see why I liked the book. (subordinating conjunction)

20. _____ you exercise now _____ later makes no difference. (correlative conjunction)

SPEAKING APPLICATION

Take turns with a partner. Tell about something that you did with a friend. Your partner should name conjunctions that you use and tell what kind of conjunction each one is.

WRITING APPLICATION

Write a paragraph about what you like to do after school. Use one coordinating conjunction, one subordinating conjunction, one correlative conjunction (both parts), and one conjunctive adverb.

PRACTICE 13.4E> **Using and Identifying Conjunctions**

For each blank, write a coordinating conjunction, subordinating conjunction, conjunctive adverb, or part of a correlative conjunction. Label each. Some blanks will have more than one possible answer.

EXAMPLE _____ you exit, watch the gap between the train _____ the platform.

ANSWER *As* (subordinating conjunction); *and* (coordinating conjunction)

1. _____ you wish on a star, be imaginative _____ somewhat realistic.

2. The Constitution _____ protects freedom of speech _____ safeguards other rights.

3. A balanced diet promotes good health; _____, exercise _____ rest are also necessary.

4. Choose _____ soup _____ salad, not both.

5. "To be _____ not to be," says Hamlet; _____ we learn his fate.

6. You get only three guesses, _____ think carefully _____ you answer.

7. Select _____ milk _____ juice to drink.

8. _____ the bus charges $70 roundtrip, the train charges only $20; _____, take the train.

9. Amy worried about _____ the ride was safe _____ not.

10. We canceled the picnic _____ we saw lightning _____ heard thunder.

PRACTICE 13.4F> **Supplying Interjections**

Read each sentence. Then, write an interjection that shows the feeling expressed in the sentence.

EXAMPLE _____, I spilled my drink!

ANSWER *Oops*

11. _____, what have you done now?

12. _____! I hit my thumb with the hammer!

13. _____, the prince would never see the princess again.

14. _____, I don't know what else to do.

15. _____! That's a beautiful sunset!

16. _____! Want to buy a used stereo?

17. _____, where do you think you're going?

18. _____! We are the champions!

19. _____, I can't find the map.

20. _____! I'm so glad that's over!

SPEAKING APPLICATION

With a partner, pick a coordinating conjunction, a correlative conjunction, a subordinating conjunction, and a conjunctive adverb. Then, take turns using each conjunction in a sentence.

WRITING APPLICATION

Write three sentences with interjections. With a partner, read your sentences aloud and discuss other interjections that would also make sense in your sentences.

Test Warm-Up

DIRECTIONS

Read the introduction and the passage that follows. Then, answer the questions to show that you can use and understand the function of conjunctions and interjections in reading and writing.

Kiran wrote this paragraph about competition in television. Read the paragraph and think about the changes you would suggest as a peer editor. When you finish reading, answer the questions that follow.

HBO Versus the Networks

(1) HBO differs from traditional networks. (2) When I discovered this, I exclaimed, "Whew! Maybe that's why it has been so successful." (3) HBO is a subscription service. (4) It earns money from subscribers. (5) It chooses not to fill as many hours as the networks. (6) HBO doesn't feel obligated to put all its new series on in the fall. (7) HBO asks for only 12 episodes instead of the usual 22.

---

1 What change, if any, should be made in sentence 2?

  A Change *Whew!* to **Aha!**

  B Change *Whew!* to **Hurray!**

  C Change *Whew!* to **Goodness!**

  D Make no change

2 What is the most effective way to combine sentences 3 and 4?

  F Since HBO is a subscription service, it earns money from subscribers.

  G HBO is a subscription service, but it earns money from subscribers.

  H HBO is a subscription service; however, it earns money from subscribers.

  J HBO is a subscription service, or it earns money from subscribers.

3 How should sentence 5 be revised to include a conjunctive adverb?

  A Aha! It chooses not to fill as many hours as the networks.

  B Well! It chooses not to fill as many hours as the networks.

  C Furthermore, it chooses not to fill as many hours as the networks.

  D But it chooses not to fill as many hours as the networks.

4 What is the most effective way to combine sentences 6 and 7 with a correlative conjunction?

  F HBO either puts all its new series on in the fall, or it asks for the usual 22.

  G HBO neither puts all its new series on in the fall, nor does it ask for 22 episodes.

  H HBO doesn't feel obligated; therefore, it asks for only 12 episodes instead of the usual 22.

  J HBO doesn't feel obligated to put all its new series on in the fall, though it asks for only 12 instead of 22 episodes.

13.5 Words as Different Parts of Speech

Words are flexible, often serving as one part of speech in one sentence and as another part of speech in another.

Identifying Parts of Speech

To *function* means "to serve in a particular capacity." The function of a word may change from one sentence to another.

> **The way a word is used in a sentence determines its part of speech.**

The word *well* has different meanings in the following sentences.

As a Noun	The well in the yard is made of stone.
As a Verb	During the graduation ceremony, tears welled in their eyes.
As an Adjective	Alia didn't feel well before class.

Nouns, Pronouns, and Verbs A **noun** names a person, place, or thing. A **pronoun** stands for a noun. A **verb** shows action, condition, or existence.

The chart below reviews the definition of each part of speech.

PARTS OF SPEECH	QUESTIONS TO ASK YOURSELF	EXAMPLES
Noun	Does the word name a person, place, or thing?	His visit to the Statue of Liberty awakened Mark's curiosity.
Pronoun	Does the word stand for a noun?	They shared some samples with her.

PARTS OF SPEECH	QUESTIONS TO ASK YOURSELF	EXAMPLES
Verb	Does the word tell what someone or something did? Does the word link one word with another word that identifies or describes it? Does the word show that something exists?	I played piano. That woman was a pianist. The soloist appeared nervous. The audience is getting impatient.

See Practice 13.5A

The Other Parts of Speech An **adjective** modifies a noun or pronoun. An **adverb** modifies a verb, an adjective, or another adverb. A **preposition** relates a noun or pronoun that appears with it to another word. A **conjunction** connects words or groups of words. An **interjection** expresses emotion.

PARTS OF SPEECH	QUESTIONS TO ASK YOURSELF	EXAMPLES
Adjective	Does the word tell *what kind, which one, how many, or how much?*	Those four muffins are an unusual texture.
Adverb	Does the word tell *where, when, in what way,* or *to what extent?*	Please go back. Run now. Sing very quietly. I am extremely overwhelmed.
Preposition	Is the word part of a phrase that includes a noun or pronoun?	Inside the library, the students were on the computers.
Conjunction	Does the word connect other words in the sentence or connect clauses?	Both Laura and I will bake because they need snacks; besides, it will be fun!
Interjection	Does the word express feeling or emotion and function independently of the sentence?	Hey, hold onto that. Wow! That's exciting!

See Practice 13.5B

PRACTICE 13.5A > Identifying Nouns, Pronouns, and Verbs

Read each sentence. Then, label the underlined word *noun*, *pronoun*, or *verb*.

EXAMPLE   I showed the <u>group</u> my outline.

ANSWER   *noun*

1. Sally <u>groups</u> the flowers in her garden by color.
2. <u>He</u> is learning to play a guitar.
3. The photographer <u>said</u>, "Please smile."
4. Liam always has a big <u>smile</u> on his face.
5. We <u>left</u> the store in a hurry.
6. <u>Dad</u> pulled out of the driveway and made a left turn.
7. <u>They</u> are coming over, and we will paint the house.
8. Bill, will <u>you</u> and Scarlet come here, please?
9. You must be careful about what you <u>post</u> online.
10. I helped Mom put up a new <u>post</u> for the fence.

PRACTICE 13.5B > Recognizing All the Parts of Speech

Read each sentence. Then, write which part of speech each underlined word is in the sentence.

EXAMPLE   I did my homework <u>before</u> dinner.

ANSWER   *preposition*

11. <u>She</u> had warned us <u>before</u> the storm hit.
12. Certain people <u>do</u> their chores too <u>fast</u>.
13. Theo made a <u>quick</u> trip to the grocery store.
14. <u>Many</u> of us voted to have school uniforms.
15. <u>Well</u>, I have <u>nothing</u> more to say.
16. Jake eats a <u>light</u> snack before a track <u>meet</u>.
17. <u>After</u> staying up all night, I was <u>exhausted</u>.
18. Charles <u>threw</u> the ball <u>low</u>, and I missed it.
19. Why are you sitting there <u>in</u> the dark?
20. They are leaving, <u>and</u> so am <u>I</u>.

SPEAKING APPLICATION

Take turns with a partner. Tell about something that you did earlier today. Your partner should identify some nouns, pronouns, and verbs that you use.

WRITING APPLICATION

Write the part of speech of each word in sentence 18.

CHAPTER 14

BASIC SENTENCE PARTS

Write high-quality sentences by pairing strong subjects and verbs in your writing and using complements and clauses to add description.

WRITE GUY *Jeff Anderson, M.Ed.*

WHAT DO YOU NOTICE?

Focus on different sentence parts as you zoom in on these lines from the poem "The Lake Isle of Innisfree" by William Butler Yeats.

MENTOR TEXT

> There midnight's all a glimmer, and noon a purple glow,
> And evening full of the linnet's wings.

Now, ask yourself the following questions:

- What is the subject and the verb in the clause *There midnight's all a glimmer*?
- How does recognizing subjects and verbs help you understand the poem?

The subject and verb in the clause *There midnight's all a glimmer* are *midnight's (midnight is)*. Recognizing subjects and verbs in the poem helps you group ideas, so you know who or what is giving or receiving action or being described. In the clause *There midnight's all a glimmer*, Yeats is describing how the night looks in Innisfree.

Grammar for Writers Poets use the special forms and devices of poetry, but they also depend on their understanding of subjects and verbs and other sentence parts to create lines that readers can follow. As you write, ask yourself questions like, *Will the subject of this sentence (or this line) be clear to my readers?*

In your poem about your dog, the subject of the first line is a bit fuzzy.

I agree. That dog needs a haircut!

14.1 Subjects and Predicates

A **sentence** is a group of words that expresses a complete unit of thought. *The cereal in the bowl* is not a complete unit of thought because you probably wonder what the writer wanted to say about the cereal. *The cereal in the bowl is soggy*, however, does express a complete unit of thought.

RULE 14.1.1

A **sentence** is a group of words that has two main parts: a complete subject and a complete predicate. Together, these parts express a complete thought or paint a complete picture.

The **complete subject** contains a noun, pronoun, or group of words acting as a noun, plus its modifiers. These words tell *who* or *what* the sentence is about. The **complete predicate** consists of the verb or verb phrase, plus its modifiers. These words tell what the complete subject is or does.

COMPLETE SUBJECTS	COMPLETE PREDICATES
Snakes	slither.
A bell-clanging streetcar	moved through the turn.
Wood or cellulose	makes a delicious meal for a termite.
The candidate's approach to fiscal problems	impressed the voters attending the rally.

Sometimes, part of the predicate precedes the complete subject.

EXAMPLES   **At noon** , **the cluster of waiters**
                complete   complete subject

served tea .
predicate

Tonight   **my English class**
complete   complete subject
visited a theater .
            predicate

See Practice 14.1A

Simple Subjects and Predicates

The most essential parts of a sentence are the **simple subject** and the **simple predicate.** These words tell you the basics of what you need to know about the topic of the sentence. All of the other words in the sentence give you information about the simple subject and simple predicate.

> The **simple subject** is the essential noun, pronoun, or group of words that acts as a noun in a complete subject. The **simple predicate** is the essential verb or verb phrase in a complete predicate.

RULE 14.1.2

Note: When sentences are discussed in this chapter, the term *subject* will refer to a simple subject, and the term *verb* will refer to a simple predicate.

SUBJECTS	VERBS
Small feet	fit nicely into ballet slippers.
Many schoolteachers	have used films in their lessons.
Jars of beads	were sitting on the craft table.
A colorful painting	covered the wall.
The student's counselor	reviewed all of her college applications.
Studies of other cultures	have certainly revealed much about their traditions.

In the last example, the simple subject is *studies,* not *cultures; cultures* is the object of the preposition *of.* Objects of prepositions never function as simple subjects. In this same example, the simple predicate is a verb phrase. In addition, the word *certainly* is not part of the simple predicate because it does not provide essential information.

See Practice 14.1B

PRACTICE 14.1A ▷ **Recognizing Complete Subjects and Predicates**

Read each sentence. Then, rewrite the sentence, and draw a vertical line between the complete subject and the complete predicate.

EXAMPLE   The man with the leash is looking for his dog.

ANSWER   *The man with the leash | is looking for his dog.*

1. The campground in New Mexico is close to Texas.

2. Spaghetti with meatballs is Dad's favorite dish.

3. The teacher responded enthusiastically to our suggestion.

4. Gathering up their books, the students left.

5. The twelve-person jury reached a unanimous verdict.

6. The classic holiday songs have been recorded in many arrangements and styles.

7. My uncle Jack has a secret recipe for barbeque sauce.

8. The field trips to the museum and the television station have been postponed.

9. The principal, a friendly, outgoing woman, began to converse with the students.

10. Many different kinds of tea are now available in stores.

PRACTICE 14.1B ▷ **Identifying Simple Subjects and Predicates**

Read each sentence. The complete subject is underlined. The rest of the sentence is the complete predicate. Write the simple subject and simple predicate.

EXAMPLE   The road to the cabin was blocked by snow.

ANSWER   *road, was blocked*

11. A basket of seasonal fruits makes a delightful gift.

12. The package had obviously been carefully addressed.

13. At eighteen, my sister got a part-time job.

14. Uncle Bill's movie collection is limited to westerns and mysteries.

15. The ancient coins at the museum are rare and valuable.

16. The entire city came to a halt during the power outage.

17. We talked to our old teacher at the library.

18. That old vacant warehouse may be renovated.

19. An increasing number of students are volunteering in the community.

20. Telltale pawprints on the floor pointed to our dog as the guilty party.

SPEAKING APPLICATION

Take turns with a partner. Tell about something interesting that has happened to you. Your partner should name the complete subject and complete predicate in each of your sentences.

WRITING APPLICATION

Write a paragraph about your favorite place to visit. In each sentence, underline the simple subject, and double underline the simple predicate.

Fragments

A **fragment** is a group of words that does not contain either a complete subject or a complete predicate, or both. Fragments are usually not used in formal writing. You can correct a fragment by adding the parts needed to complete the thought.

> A **fragment** is a group of words that lacks a subject or a predicate, or both. It does not express a complete unit of thought.

14.1.3 RULE

FRAGMENTS	COMPLETE SENTENCES
glass of water (complete predicate missing)	The glass of water was cold and delicious . (complete predicate added)
swim in the ocean (complete subject missing)	Sharks swim in the ocean. (complete subject added)
from the pot (complete subject and predicate missing)	Pasta from the pot was poured into the bowl . (subject and complete predicate added)

In conversations, fragments usually do not present a problem because tone of voice, gestures, and facial expressions can add the missing information. A reader, however, cannot ask a writer for clarification.

Fragments are sometimes acceptable in writing that represents speech, such as the dialogue in a play or short story. Fragments are also sometimes acceptable in elliptical sentences.

> An **elliptical sentence** is one in which the missing word or words can be easily understood.

14.1.4 RULE

EXAMPLES   Until tonight.

Why such a scared face?

Locating Subjects and Verbs

To avoid writing a fragment, look for the subject and verb in a sentence. To find the subject, ask, "Which word tells *what* or *who* this sentence is about?" Once you have the answer (the subject), then ask, "What does the subject do?" or "What is being done to the subject?" This will help you locate the verb.

In some sentences, it's easier to find the verb first. In this case, ask, "Which word states the action or condition in this sentence?" This question should help you locate the verb. Then ask, "*Who* or *what* is involved in the action of the verb?" The resulting word or words will be the subject.

EXAMPLE   Birds often feed on insects and seeds.

To find the subject first, ask, "Which word or words tell what or whom this sentence is about?"

ANSWER   Birds (*Birds* is the subject.)

Then ask, "What do birds do?"

ANSWER   feed (*Feed* is the verb.)

To find the verb first, ask, "Which word or words state the action or condition in the sentence?"

ANSWER   feed (*Feed* states the action, so it is the verb.)

Then ask, "Who or what feeds?"

ANSWER   Birds (*Birds* is the subject.)

To easily locate the subject and verb, mentally cross out any adjectives, adverbs, and prepositional phrases you see. These words add information, but they are usually less important than the simple subject and verb.

EXAMPLE   ~~The~~ **vegetables** **should grow** ~~rapidly~~
                  simple subject   verb phrase
            ~~in the next three weeks.~~

340   Basic Sentence Parts

Sentences With More Than One Subject or Verb

Some sentences contain a **compound subject** or a **compound verb,** or a subject or verb with more than one part.

> **A compound subject** consists of two or more subjects. These subjects may be joined by a conjunction such as *and* or *or*.

14.1.5 RULE

EXAMPLES   The **campers** and **hikers** found their way with a compass.

Sandals, towels, and **pails** are always found around the beach house.

Neither the **host** nor the **guests** were tired.

> **A compound verb** consists of two or more verbs. These verbs may be joined by a conjunction such as *and, but, or,* or *nor*.

14.1.6 RULE

EXAMPLES   I neither **saw** the movie nor **read** the book.

Laura **left** class and **ran** to the movies.

They **cried** and **laughed** throughout the entire movie.

Some sentences contain both a compound subject and a compound verb.

EXAMPLES   My **dad** and **uncle** **chased** after the squirrels but **ran** into each other instead.

The **mom** and **dad** **eyed** each other, **turned** warily, and then **jumped** in the pool.

See Practice 14.1C
See Practice 14.1D

PRACTICE 14.1C **Locating Subjects and Verbs**

Read each sentence. Then, write the simple subject(s) and the main verb(s) in each sentence. Underline the subject(s).

EXAMPLE   The state with the best weather is Hawaii.

ANSWER   *state, is*

1. We hiked uphill for more than an hour and then took a break.

2. Some trained birds have large vocabularies.

3. Serena Zambrano was the first girl from our school to win the state championship.

4. Students and teachers enjoyed competing on the softball field.

5. Both Roger and Ling wrote and performed original songs.

6. We built and painted our own bookshelves.

7. Both bats and owls are active at night.

8. Many of today's television shows feature real people, not actors.

9. Members of the community took the trash away from the waterfront.

10. People in unfamiliar surroundings may feel anxious and uncertain.

PRACTICE 14.1D **Fixing Sentence Errors**

Read each group of words. Decide if it is a sentence or a fragment. If it is a sentence, write *sentence*. If it is a fragment, rewrite it to make it a sentence.

EXAMPLE   In spite of not feeling well.

ANSWER   *Rosita continued in spite of not feeling well.*

11. His sister, a funny yet shy girl.

12. Stepped off the plane after a grueling flight.

13. She organized her locker before going to class.

14. Onto a street, lined with shops and restaurants.

15. The metal tabletop extremely cold after the freezing night.

16. Our class was winning the recycling contest.

17. Were playing happily in the snow fort.

18. Riding the subway to work that morning, Mr. Green.

19. I typed steadily from early in the morning until lunchtime.

20. On the bank of the creek sat.

SPEAKING APPLICATION

Take turns with a partner. Tell about your favorite possessions. Your partner should name the subject and the verb in each of your sentences.

WRITING APPLICATION

Write a fragment of your own. Use the fragment in three different sentences.

14.2 Hard-to-Find Subjects

While most sentences have subjects that are easy to find, some present a challenge.

Subjects in Declarative Sentences Beginning With *Here* or *There*

When the word *here* or *there* begins a declarative sentence, it is often mistaken for the subject.

> **Here and there are never the subject of a sentence.**

RULE 14.2.1

Here and *there* are usually adverbs that modify the verb by pointing out *where* something is located. However, *there* may occasionally begin a sentence simply as an introductory word.

In some sentences beginning with *here* or *there*, the subject appears before the verb. However, many sentences beginning with *here* or *there* are **inverted.** In an inverted sentence, the subject follows the verb. If you rearrange such a sentence in subject–verb order, you can identify the subject more easily.

INVERTED   There **are** the **tickets**. (verb–subject order)

REARRANGED   The **tickets** **are** there. (subject–verb order)

SENTENCES BEGINNING WITH *HERE* OR *THERE*	SENTENCES REARRANGED IN SUBJECT–VERB ORDER
There are the company's office buildings .	The company's office buildings are there.
Here is the ticket to get in.	The ticket to get in is here.
There is money stuck in the machine.	Money is stuck in the machine there.

> **In some declarative sentences, the subject is placed after the verb in order to give the subject greater emphasis.**

RULE 14.2.2

Because most sentences are written in subject–verb order, changing that order makes readers stop and think. Inverted sentences often begin with prepositional phrases.

SENTENCES INVERTED FOR EMPHASIS	SENTENCES REARRANGED IN SUBJECT–VERB ORDER
Toward the waiting taxi raced the anxious tourists .	The anxious tourists raced toward the waiting taxi.
Around the corner sped the police car .	The police car sped around the corner.

Subjects in Interrogative Sentences

Some interrogative sentences use subject–verb order. Often, however, the word order of an interrogative sentence is verb–subject.

EXAMPLES   Which **breeder** **has** the best puppies?
(subject–verb order)

       Are **we** going there?
(verb–subject order)

RULE 14.2.3

> In interrogative sentences, the subject often follows the verb.

An inverted interrogative sentence can begin with a verb, a helping verb, or one of the following words: *how, what, when, where, which, who, whom, whose,* or *why.* Some interrogative sentences divide the helping verb from the main verb. To help locate the subject, mentally rearrange the sentence into subject–verb order.

INTERROGATIVE SENTENCES	REARRANGED IN SUBJECT–VERB ORDER
Is the Seattle Space Needle open at night?	The Seattle Space Needle is open at night.
Do they own those puppies?	They do own those puppies.
Where will the game be held ?	The game will be held where?

Subjects in Imperative Sentences

The subject of an imperative sentence is usually implied rather than specifically stated.

> **In imperative sentences, the subject is understood to be *you*.**

IMPERATIVE SENTENCES	SENTENCES WITH *YOU* ADDED
First, visit the Space Needle.	First, [you] visit the Space Needle.
After the tour, come back here.	After the tour, [you] come back here.
Jane, introduce me to the tour guide.	Jane, [you] introduce me to the tour guide.

In the last example, the name of the person being addressed, *Jane*, is not the subject of the imperative sentence. Instead, the subject is still understood to be *you*.

Subjects in Exclamatory Sentences

In some **exclamatory sentences,** the subject appears before the verb. In others, the verb appears first. To find the subject, rearrange the sentence in subject–verb order.

> **In exclamatory sentences, the subject often appears after the verb, or it may be understood.**

EXAMPLES   What **do I know**!
(I do know what.)

Run now!
(Subject understood: [You] run now!)

In other exclamatory sentences, both the subject and verb may be unstated.

See Practice 14.2A
See Practice 14.2B

EXAMPLES   Tree! ([You watch out for the] tree!)
Smoke! ([I see] smoke!)

PRACTICE 14.2A Identifying Hard-to-Find Subjects

Read each sentence. Then, write the simple subject of each sentence.

EXAMPLE   There are many paths in the woods.

ANSWER   *paths*

1. Here is my phone number.
2. Where is the rest of your report?
3. What did you get for lunch?
4. Just outside of town is a little park.
5. There have been a number of questions about the schedule.
6. Between the gym and the locker rooms are some storage rooms.
7. Tell me in great detail about your wonderful trip.
8. There are three fascinating art classes for the seniors.
9. When did the accident occur?
10. Behind the garage are some chicken coops.

PRACTICE 14.2B Locating Hard-to-Find Verbs

Read each sentence. Then, write the verb(s) in each sentence.

EXAMPLE   High in the sky soared the eagle.

ANSWER   *soared*

11. Can you believe what that man just donated?
12. Why not taste a new type of food?
13. Outside the window gathered a noisy crowd.
14. Before the concert, play your favorite song for me.
15. In the warm water swam the graceful dolphin.
16. As a last resort, tug lightly on the dog's leash.
17. Hey, get our luggage out of the rain!
18. Where are the keys to the back door?
19. To whom did you give the book?
20. Please take your foot off the pedal.

SPEAKING APPLICATION

Take turns with a partner. Say sentences that describe someone doing something. Your partner should name the subject in each of your sentences.

WRITING APPLICATION

Write three imperative sentences. Underline the verb in each sentence.

14.3 Complements

Some sentences are complete with just a subject and a verb or with a subject, verb, and modifiers: *The crowd cheered.* Other sentences need more information to be complete.

The meaning of many sentences, however, depends on additional words that add information to the subject and verb. For example, although *The satellite continually sends* has a subject and verb, it is an incomplete sentence. To complete the meaning of the predicate—in this case, to tell *what* a satellite sends—a writer must add a **complement.**

> A **complement** is a word or group of words that completes the meaning of the predicate of a sentence.

There are five kinds of complements in English: **direct objects, indirect objects, object complements, predicate nominatives,** and **predicate adjectives.** The first three occur in sentences that have transitive verbs. The last two are often called **subject complements.** Subject complements are found only with linking verbs. (See Chapter 13 for more information about action and linking verbs.)

Direct Objects

Direct objects are the most common of the five types of complements. They complete the meaning of action verbs by telling *who* or *what* receives the action.

> A **direct object** is a noun, pronoun, or group of words acting as a noun that receives the action of a transitive verb.

EXAMPLES **I** **visited** the **Metropolitan Museum of Art** .
direct object

Snow and **sleet** **covered** the **driveway** .
direct object

Direct Objects and Action Verbs The direct object answers the question *Whom?* or *What?* about the action verb. If you cannot answer the question *Whom?* or *What?* the verb may be intransitive, and there is no direct object in the sentence.

EXAMPLES

Dogs **can see** in black and white.
(Ask, "Dogs can see *what*?" No answer; the verb is intransitive.)

The girl **spun** in a circle.
(Ask, "The girl spun *what*?" No answer; the verb is intransitive.)

RULE 14.3.3

In some inverted questions, the direct object may appear before the verb. To find the direct object easily, rearrange inverted questions in subject–verb order.

INVERTED QUESTION

Which **newspapers did they read** ?
       direct object

REARRANGED IN SUBJECT–VERB ORDER

They did read which **newspapers** ?
                             direct object

Some sentences have more than one direct object, known as a **compound direct object.** If a sentence contains a compound direct object, asking *Whom?* or *What?* after the action verb will yield two or more answers.

EXAMPLES

The surgeons **wore masks** and
                    direct object
gloves .
direct object

The team **has played** at **stadiums** and
                             direct object
arenas during the last six months.
direct object

In the last example, *months* is the object of the preposition *during*. The object of a preposition is never a direct object.

Indirect Objects

Indirect objects appear only in sentences that contain transitive verbs and direct objects. Indirect objects are common with such verbs as *ask*, *bring*, *buy*, *give*, *lend*, *make*, *show*, *teach*, *tell*, and *write*. Some sentences may contain a compound indirect object.

> An **indirect object** is a noun or pronoun that appears with a direct object. It often names the person or thing that something is given to or done for.

14.3.4 RULE

EXAMPLES   The **editor** **gave** the **author** a manuscript
                                                    indirect object
correction.
direct object

I **showed** my **mom** and **sister** the party
                        compound indirect object
invitation.
direct object

To locate an indirect object, make sure the sentence contains a direct object. Then, ask one of these questions after the verb and direct object: *To* or *for whom?* or *To* or *for what?*

EXAMPLES   The **coach** **taught** our **team** a new **play**.
(The coach taught a play *to whom*? ANSWER: our team)

We **made** our **mother** a **jewelry box**.
(Made a jewelry box *for whom*? ANSWER: our mother)

An indirect object almost always appears between the verb and the direct object. In a sentence with subject–verb order, the indirect object never follows the direct object, nor will it ever be the object of the preposition *to* or *for*.

EXAMPLES   **Jane** **sent** the **shoes** to **me**.
                                direct object object of preposition

Tina **sent** **me** the **book**.
                    indirect object   direct object

Tina **gave** **Jon** a **critique** of the book.
                    indirect object   direct object

See Practice 14.3A
See Practice 14.3B

Object Complements

While an indirect object almost always comes *before* a direct object, an **object complement** almost always *follows* a direct object. The object complement completes the meaning of the direct object.

RULE 14.3.5

> An **object complement** is an adjective or noun that appears with a direct object and describes or renames it.

A sentence that contains an object complement may seem to have two direct objects. However, object complements occur only with such verbs as *appoint, call, consider, declare, elect, judge, label, make, name, select,* and *think.* The words *to be* are often understood before an object complement.

EXAMPLES

The **organizers** of the concert **declared** **it** a
                                                         direct object
successful **benefit**.
     object complement

The **president** **appointed** **her** **chair**
                             direct   object
over the organization.   object complement

I **consider** **Christina** a caring **mother** and
                direct object   object complement
compassionate **sister**.
         object complement

Subject Complements

Linking verbs require **subject complements** to complete their meaning.

RULE 14.3.6

> A **subject complement** is a noun, pronoun, or adjective that appears with a linking verb and gives more information about the subject.

There are two kinds of subject complements: **predicate nominatives** and **predicate adjectives.**

Predicate Nominatives

The **predicate nominative** refers to the same person, place, or thing as the subject of the sentence.

> A **predicate nominative** is a noun or pronoun that appears with a linking verb and renames, identifies, or explains the subject. Some sentences may contain a compound predicate nominative.

RULE 14.3.7

EXAMPLES

Kevin Charles **is** an **officer** with the navy.
predicate nominative

The **winner** **will be** **Kelly**.
predicate nominative

Mark Cullen **was** a **teacher** and former **coach**.
compound predicate nominative

Predicate Adjectives

A **predicate adjective** is an adjective that appears with a linking verb. It describes the subject in much the same way that an adjective modifies a noun or pronoun. Some sentences may contain a compound predicate adjective.

> A **predicate adjective** is an adjective that appears with a linking verb and describes the subject of the sentence.

RULE 14.3.8

EXAMPLES

Your **action** **seems** **vindictive**.
predicate adjective

The **football player** **was** **strong**.
predicate adjective

The **sun** **felt** **warm** and **comforting**.
compound predicate adjective

See Practice 14.3C
See Practice 14.3D

The band **uniforms** **are** **green** and **black**.
compound predicate adjective

PRACTICE 14.3A > Identifying Direct and Indirect Objects

Read each sentence. Then, write and label each direct object and indirect object.

EXAMPLE The mail carrier delivered a letter to my father.

ANSWER *letter* — direct object

1. The neighbors planned a surprise party.
2. Mix the raisins into your oatmeal.
3. I wrote the city council a letter.
4. You can rent DVDs through the mail.
5. Nonfiction books give readers an alternative to novels.
6. Chase needs a knife and fork.
7. Mom's clothing designs may bring her fame and fortune.
8. I sent Alia a package.
9. Stores have sold customers thousands of these gadgets.
10. Sheila asked the singer for his autograph.

PRACTICE 14.3B > Distinguishing Between Indirect Objects and Other Words

Read each sentence. Then, identify each indirect object. If there are no indirect objects, write *no indirect object*.

EXAMPLE Doris gave me her last stamps.

ANSWER *me*

EXAMPLE Doris ran out of stamps just before the holidays.

ANSWER *no indirect object*

11. Give the principal the trophy for safekeeping.
12. Show the losing team some respect.
13. Don't wait for your cousins to extend you an invitation.
14. Practice the piano whenever and wherever you can.
15. The electric heater provided us warmth when we worked late last night.
16. The overnight delivery service charges too much for my budget.
17. Lonny used the delivery service to mail an application for me.
18. The company will give you the special rate for family and friends.
19. They saved my brother and me seats at the movie theater.
20. Give everyday people as much attention as you extend to celebrities.

SPEAKING APPLICATION

Take turns with a partner. Tell about a family event. Your partner should name the direct object and indirect object, if any, in each of your sentences.

WRITING APPLICATION

Focusing on your favorite season, write three sentences using only direct objects as complements. Then, write three sentences using both direct and indirect objects.

PRACTICE 14.3C > Locating Object and Subject Complements

Read each sentence. Then, write the complement and label it *object complement* or *subject complement*.

EXAMPLE   Our club named Vanessa president.

ANSWER   *president* — object complement

1. These shoes used to be tight.
2. We all declared the experiment a success.
3. Jen's best stroke is the butterfly.
4. Sanjay considers his music teacher brilliant.
5. This part of the country is rich in oil and gas.
6. With hard work, you can make your goals attainable.
7. My great-grandfather was famous for his photographs.
8. Most of that restaurant's food is too spicy for me.
9. Dad calls his new car The Chariot.
10. The students voted Lee Ann the most popular student.

PRACTICE 14.3D > Identifying Complements

Read each sentence. Then, identify the complement(s) as *direct object, indirect object, object complement, predicate nominative,* or *predicate adjective.*

EXAMPLE   The teacher considered us studious.

ANSWER   *us* — direct object;
          studious — object complement

11. Henry (Hank) Aaron is the first entry in my biographical dictionary.
12. Aaron hit 755 home runs in his baseball career.
13. Kareem Abdul-Jabbar is seven feet two inches tall.
14. Critics considered Marian Anderson (1897–1993) a great low-voiced singer.
15. Sherwood Anderson, no relation to Marian Anderson, wrote short stories.
16. The astronaut Neil Armstrong declared setting foot on the moon "a giant leap."
17. The dancer Fred Astaire's real name was Fredrick Austerlitz.
18. *Pride and Prejudice* (1813) may be Jane Austen's most famous novel.
19. *Persuasion* (1818) is Austen's best work.
20. The last film version I saw of an Austen novel was impressive.

WRITING APPLICATION

Use sentences 11 and 12 in Practice 14.3D as models to write similar sentences. Underline and label the complement in each sentence.

SPEAKING APPLICATION

Take turns with a partner. Describe one of your heroes. Your partner should point out each complement you use and tell whether it is a direct object, indirect object, object complement, predicate nominative, or predicate adjective.

Test Warm-Up

DIRECTIONS
Read the introduction and the passage that follows. Then, answer the questions to show that you can use and understand the function of complements in reading and writing.

Galil wrote the following paragraph about great books of the twentieth century. Read the paragraph and think about the changes you would suggest as a peer editor. When you finish reading, answer the questions that follow.

Great Book Recommendations

(1) The New York Public Library is a respected place worldwide. (2) To celebrate its hundredth anniversary in 1995, its librarians gave lists of influential books. (3) At the top of the list of modern literature, they placed the play *The Three Sisters* by Anton Chekhov. (4) Among works of protest, they named one by W. E. B. Du Bois. (5) Another work in this category was by Upton Sinclair. (6) One book listed under "Mind and Spirit" was *The Interpretation of Dreams* by Sigmund Freud. (7) That choice was interesting.

---

1 The meaning of sentence 1 can be clarified by changing the predicate nominative to —

  A area

  B educational resource

  C school of knowledge

  D tourist attraction

2 The meaning of sentence 2 can be clarified by adding which indirect object?

  F to readers

  G gladly

  H readers

  J best-selling

3 What is the most effective way of combining sentences 4 and 5 to create a compound direct object?

  A Books by W. E. B. Du Bois and by Upton Sinclair were among the works of protest named.

  B Works of protest on their list were by W. E. B. Du Bois and by Upton Sinclair, among others.

  C Among works of protest, they named one by W. E. B. Du Bois; also one by Upton Sinclair.

  D Among works of protest, they named one by W. E. B. Du Bois and one by Upton Sinclair.

4 The meaning of sentence 7 can be clarified by changing the predicate adjective to —

  F predictable

  G an honor

  H a mistake

  J a surprise

CHAPTER 15

PHRASES *and* CLAUSES

Use phrases and clauses to add important detail and dimension to your writing.

WRITE GUY *Jeff Anderson, M.Ed.*

WHAT DO YOU NOTICE?

Spot the clauses as you zoom in on these sentences from Act V of the play *Macbeth* by William Shakespeare.

MENTOR TEXT

> Doctor: This disease is beyond my practice. Yet I have known those which have walked in their sleep who have died holily in their beds.

Now, ask yourself the following questions:

- What is the first adjectival clause in the doctor's speech, and what noun or pronoun does it modify?
- What is the second adjectival clause in the speech, and what noun or pronoun does it modify?

The first adjectival clause is *which have walked in their sleep,* and the second adjectival clause is *who have died holily in their beds.* Both clauses modify the demonstrative pronoun *those.* Commas are not used to set off either of these restrictive clauses because each one adds essential meaning to the sentence.

Grammar for Writers Writers can use adjectival and adverbial clauses to add significant details to their sentences. Choose your words carefully so that they add to your writing in the way you intend.

What's a good adjectival phrase for the hamburger I ate for lunch?

Let's see. How about a burger with fries?

15.1 Phrases

When one adjective or adverb cannot convey enough information, a phrase can contribute more detail to a sentence. A **phrase** is a group of words that does not include a subject and verb and cannot stand alone as a sentence.

There are several kinds of phrases, including **prepositional phrases, appositive phrases, participial phrases, gerund phrases,** and **infinitive phrases.**

Prepositional Phrases

A **prepositional phrase** consists of a preposition and a noun or pronoun, called the object of the preposition. *Over their heads, until dark,* and *after the baseball game* are all prepositional phrases. Prepositional phrases often modify other words by functioning as adjectives or adverbs.

Sometimes, a single prepositional phrase may include two or more objects joined by a conjunction.

EXAMPLES
   between the **chair** and the **desk**
     preposition   object   object

   with the **moon** and the **stars**
     preposition object   object

   beside the **car** and **bike**
     preposition object   object

See Practice 15.1A

Adjectival Phrases

A prepositional phrase that acts as an adjective is called an **adjectival phrase.**

RULE 15.1.1

> An **adjectival phrase** is a prepositional phrase that modifies a noun or pronoun by telling *what kind* or *which one*.

ADJECTIVES	ADJECTIVAL PHRASES
A beautiful mural hung in the library.	A mural of great beauty hung in the library. (*What kind of mural?*)
I sent my college friend a photograph.	I sent my friend at college a photograph. (*Which friend?*)

Like one-word adjectives, adjectival phrases can modify subjects, direct objects, indirect objects, or predicate nominatives.

MODIFYING
A SUBJECT

The school **across the road** has been convenient.

MODIFYING
A DIRECT OBJECT

Let's take a picture **of the Statue of Liberty**.

MODIFYING AN
INDIRECT OBJECT

I gave the people **at the gardens** a tour.

MODIFYING
A PREDICATE
NOMINATIVE

Rome is a city **with many buildings**.

A sentence may contain two or more **adjectival phrases.** In some cases, one phrase may modify the object of the preceding phrase. In others, two phrases may modify the same word.

EXAMPLES

MODIFIES ⟶ MODIFIES ⟶

We bought tickets **for the game at Central**.

MODIFIES ⟶

The mural **in the hallway of the dance** was wonderful.

Adverbial Phrases

> An **adverbial phrase** is a prepositional phrase that modifies a verb, an adjective, or an adverb by pointing out *where, why, when, in what way,* or *to what extent*.

ADVERBS	ADVERBIAL PHRASES
We worked quickly. (Worked *in what way?*)	We worked with great speed .
I was happy then. (Happy *when?*)	I was happy after the dance .
The helicopter flew overhead. (Flew *where?*)	The helicopter flew over the garden .

Adverbial phrases can modify verbs, adjectives, or adverbs.

MODIFYING A VERB
The apples fell and rolled **across the barn** .

MODIFYING AN ADJECTIVE
Tom was happy **beyond belief** .

MODIFYING AN ADVERB
Her fear showed deep **in her eyes** .

An adverbial phrase may either follow the word it modifies or be located elsewhere in the sentence. Often, two adverbial phrases in different parts of a sentence can modify the same word.

EXAMPLES
MODIFIES
The beautiful flowers appeared **along the river** .

MODIFIES
Along the river , beautiful flowers appeared.

MODIFIES — MODIFIES
After breakfast , we gathered **in the garden** .   See Practice 15.1B

PRACTICE 15.1A Identifying Prepositional Phrases

Read each sentence. Write the prepositional phrase or phrases in each sentence. Then, write the word each phrase modifies. Finally, use the phrase in a sentence of your own.

EXAMPLE   She wanted tickets for the baseball game.

ANSWER   *for the baseball game; tickets*
We had good seats for the baseball game.

1. In the afternoon they traveled to the country.

2. They arrived at about nine in the morning.

3. We will go to the mountains tomorrow.

4. The gas station over the hill has the highest prices.

5. We planned our class reunion for months.

6. We clapped our hands with great joy.

7. The room is filled with antiques.

8. The flower shop is not far from the library.

9. I received recognition from the panel.

10. I walked to the store in about two hours.

PRACTICE 15.1B Identifying Adjectival and Adverbial Phrases

Read each sentence. Write the adjectival or adverbial phrase. Then, label the phrase *adjectival* or *adverbial*. Finally, use the phrase in a sentence of your own.

EXAMPLE   A seat on an airplane is inexpensive right now.

ANSWER   *on an airplane — adjectival*
The windows on an airplane are rather small.

11. After dinner Jody and I went to the beach.

12. The baseball coach was happy after the win.

13. We will tell you the story at a later time.

14. Which subway train will take me into Manhattan?

15. A team of professional actors visited the school today.

16. He spoke politely to the teacher.

17. The food in the cafeteria tasted good today.

18. The latch on the fence needs repair.

19. The potholes in the road worried drivers.

20. Will sat near Monisha.

SPEAKING APPLICATION

Take turns with a partner. Describe the location of an object in the room. Your partner should listen for the prepositional phrases that you use and indicate the function of each phrase (adjectival or adverbial) by telling the words that they modify.

WRITING APPLICATION

Show that you understand the function of adjectival and adverbial phrases. Write four sentences using adjectival and adverbial phrases. Explain the function of each phrase by identifying the word it modifies. Read your sentences to a partner who should identify the phrases as you speak.

Appositives and Appositive Phrases

The term *appositive* comes from a Latin verb that means "to put near or next to."

Appositives Using **appositives** in your writing is an easy way to give additional meaning to a noun or pronoun.

RULE 15.1.3

> An **appositive** is a word or group of words that identifies, renames, or explains a noun or pronoun.

As the examples below show, appositives usually follow immediately after the words they explain.

EXAMPLES

The breakfast staff, **Jerome and Mia**, cleared the dishes.

Janice's band, **Falling Leaves**, played at the charity event.

Notice that commas are used in the examples above because these appositives are **nonessential.** In other words, the appositives could be omitted from the sentences without altering the basic meaning of the sentences.

Some appositives, however, are not set off by any punctuation because they are **essential** to the meaning of the sentence.

EXAMPLES

The artist **Picasso** was a famous Spanish painter.
(The appositive is essential because it identifies which specific artist.)

My friend **Kris** is an excellent sketch artist.
(The appositive is essential because you might have several friends.)

Note About Terms: Sometimes, the terms *nonrestrictive* and *restrictive* are used in place of *nonessential* and *essential*.

Appositive Phrases When an appositive is accompanied by its own modifiers, it is called an **appositive phrase.**

> An **appositive phrase** is a noun or pronoun with modifiers that adds information by identifying, renaming, or explaining a noun or pronoun.

Appositives and appositive phrases may follow nouns or pronouns used in almost any role within a sentence. The modifiers within an appositive phrase can be adjectives, adjective phrases, or other groups of words functioning as adjectives.

EXAMPLES   Mr. Reid, **my gym teacher**, had us run laps around the field.

Bon explained horticulture, **the study of cultivating plants**.

ROLES OF APPOSITIVE PHRASES IN SENTENCES	
Identifying a Subject	Louis Pasteur, a famous scientist, conducted many experiments.
Identifying a Direct Object	The holistic nutritionist prepared a salad, a vegetarian meal.
Identifying an Indirect Object	I bought my friend, a girl of seventeen, a camera.
Identifying an Object Complement	I chose the color yellow, an unusual color for shoes.
Identifying a Predicate Nominative	My favorite sound is summer rain, a relaxing sound.
Identifying the Object of a Preposition	Plant the vegetables in the garden, a warm, sunny place.

Compound Appositives Appositives and appositive phrases can also be compound.

EXAMPLES The entire family—**grandparents**, **parents**, and **children**—went together.

All nuts, **cashews** and less expensive **varieties**, are on sale at the store today.

I used two herbs, **oregano** and **marjoram**, to flavor my stew.

See Practice 15.1C

Grammar and Style Tip When **appositives** or **appositive phrases** are used to combine sentences, they help to eliminate unnecessary words. One way to streamline your writing is to combine sentences by using an appositive phrase.

TWO SENTENCES	COMBINED SENTENCE
New York City is located on the Hudson River. It is an important U.S. seaport.	New York City, an important U.S. seaport, is located on the Hudson River.
Soccer is one of my favorite sports. It is a sport that is played all over the world.	Soccer, one of my favorite sports, is played all over the world.
Bordering Mexico, Texas is one of our largest states. It is also one of our richest oil states.	Texas, one of our largest states and richest oil states, borders Mexico.

Read aloud the pairs of sentences in the chart. Notice how the combined sentences, which began as two choppy sentences, include the same information. However, they flow much more smoothly once the information in both sentences is clearly linked.

See Practice 15.1D

PRACTICE 15.1C > **Identifying Appositives and Appositive Phrases**

Read each sentence. Then, write the appositive or appositive phrase in each sentence. Finally, identify the function of the phrase—explain which word it tells more about.

EXAMPLE   I read a good book, *Twilight*, by Stephenie Meyer.

ANSWER   *Twilight; a good book*

1. Brad has an unusual hobby, ventriloquism.

2. Playing her instrument, a cello, takes great concentration and skill.

3. I visited my sister's class, a group of four-year-olds.

4. I made my special dessert, a strawberry tart.

5. Have you spoken to your sister Josanna today?

6. Meryl Streep, a talented actress, is my pick to win the award.

7. My mom loves her job, writing children's books.

8. Leigh Leggett, a doctor, lives in Washington.

9. I planted my favorite tree, a crape myrtle.

10. Football, one of my favorite sports, is fun to watch.

PRACTICE 15.1D > **Using Appositive and Appositive Phrases**

Read each pair of sentences. Then, combine the sentences using an appositive or an appositive phrase.

EXAMPLE   The dog ran into the culvert. A culvert is a type of drainage ditch.

ANSWER   *The dog ran into the culvert, a type of drainage ditch.*

11. Greenland is a country. It is a Danish territory.

12. Richard I was Robin Hood's hero. Richard I was king of England.

13. Will you let me borrow your skirt? It is the one with the white flowers.

14. Deena drank chai. Chai is a black tea.

15. The schnauzer is a sturdy and active dog. It is my favorite.

16. He lives in a yurt. A yurt is a type of tent.

17. Alaska is the nation's forty-ninth state. It entered the Union in January 1959.

18. Surtsey is an island. It is uninhabited.

19. Sam is my friend. He lives in Portland.

20. The graduates were part of the Class of 1991. They discussed having a reunion.

SPEAKING APPLICATION

Take turns with a partner. Tell about three different family members. Use three appositives or appositive phrases in your sentences. Your partner should identify the appositives or appositive phrases.

WRITING APPLICATION

Write two sentences about the same subject. Then, combine the sentences with an appositive or an appositive phrase.

Verbal Phrases

When a verb is used as a noun, an adjective, or an adverb, it is called a **verbal.** Although a verbal does not function as a verb, it retains two characteristics of verbs: It can be modified in different ways, and it can have one or more complements. A verbal with modifiers or complements is called a **verbal phrase.**

Participles

Many of the adjectives you use are actually verbals known as **participles.**

> **A participle** is a form of a verb that can act as an adjective.

The most common kinds of participles are **present participles** and **past participles.** These two participles can be distinguished from one another by their endings. Present participles usually end in *-ing (frightening, entertaining).* Past participles usually end in *-ed (frightened, entertained),* but many have irregular endings, such as *-t* or *-en (burnt, written).*

PRESENT PARTICIPLES	PAST PARTICIPLES
The limping runner favored her aching leg.	Confused, they returned to their interrupted dinner.

Like other adjectives, participles answer the question *What kind?* or *Which one?* about the nouns or pronouns they modify.

EXAMPLES   Joe's **tearing** eyes betrayed the pain of his injury.
(*What kind* of eyes? Answer: *tearing* eyes)

The **splintered** floorboard needs to be replaced.
(*Which* floorboard? Answer: *splintered* floorboard)

Participles may also have a **present perfect** form.

EXAMPLES   **Having decided**, Joe jumped into the water.

Having greeted the staff, the couple checked in.

Verb or Participle? Because **verbs** often have endings such as *-ing* and *-ed,* you may confuse them with **participles.** If a word ending in *-ed* or *-ing* expresses the action of the sentence, it is a verb or part of a verb phrase. If it describes a noun or pronoun, it is a participle.

> A **verb** shows an action, a condition, or the fact that something exists. A **participle** acting as an adjective modifies a noun or a pronoun.

RULE 15.1.6

ACTING AS VERBS	ACTING AS ADJECTIVES
The baby is crying at the loud noise. (What is the baby doing?)	The crying baby sat in her crib. (Which baby?)
The doctor delighted the new parents. (What did the doctor do?)	Delighted, the new parents thanked the doctor. (What kind of parents?)

Participial Phrases
A participle can be expanded by adding modifiers and complements to form a **participial phrase.**

> A **participial phrase** is a participle modified by an adverb or adverbial phrase or accompanied by a complement. The entire participial phrase acts as an adjective.

RULE 15.1.7

The following examples show different ways that participles may be expanded into phrases.

WITH AN ADVERB	**Traveling quickly**, we made it in time for the delivery.
WITH AN ADVERB PHRASE	**Traveling at breakneck speed**, we made it in time for the delivery.
WITH A COMPLEMENT	**Avoiding stops**, we made it in time for the delivery.

A participial phrase that is nonessential to the basic meaning of a sentence is set off by commas or other forms of punctuation. A participial phrase that is essential is not set off by punctuation.

NONESSENTIAL PHRASES	ESSENTIAL PHRASES
There is Tim, waiting in the car.	The man waiting in the car is Tim.
Built in 1901, the building was innovative.	The building built in 1901 was innovative.

In the first sentence on the left side of the chart above, *waiting in the car* merely adds information about Tim, so it is nonessential. In the sentence on the right, however, the same phrase is essential because many different men might be in view.

In the second sentence on the left, *Built in 1901* is an additional description of *building,* so it is nonessential. In the sentence on the right, however, the phrase is essential because it identifies the specific building that is being discussed.

RULE 15.1.8

Participial phrases can often be used to combine information from two sentences into one.

TWO SENTENCES	We were exhausted from the flight to Greece. We rested at the airport.
COMBINED	**Exhausted from the flight to Greece**, we rested at the airport.
TWO SENTENCES	We ate brunch. We shared stories from our past.
COMBINED	**Eating brunch**, we shared stories from our past.

Notice how part of the verb in one sentence is changed into a participle in the combined sentence.

See Practice 15.1E
See Practice 15.1F

PRACTICE 15.1E > **Identifying Participles**

Read each sentence. Then, identify the underlined word as *present participle* or *past participle*, and write the word that is modified.

EXAMPLE   <u>Elated</u>, he phoned his parents.

ANSWER   *past participle, he*

1. <u>Grinning</u>, my cousin accepted her prize.

2. The old man, <u>moving</u> slowly, inched his way across the street.

3. <u>Confused</u>, the performer stopped the performance.

4. The lead actress, <u>overwhelmed</u>, took another bow.

5. <u>Disturbed</u> by her decision, Tisha lay awake.

6. The participant, <u>exhausted</u>, finished first in the race.

7. <u>Inspired</u>, she began to write her speech.

8. The river, <u>swollen</u>, began to overflow.

9. The <u>relieved</u> climber finally got back down.

10. Her <u>shining</u> eyes showed her pride in her son's achievement.

PRACTICE 15.1F > **Recognizing Participial Phrases**

Read each sentence. Write the participial phrase in each sentence. Then, write *E* for *essential* or *N* for *nonessential*. Finally, use the phrase in a new sentence of your own.

EXAMPLE   The wheat swaying in the wind was like waves.

ANSWER   *swaying in the wind — E; Swaying in the wind, the tree branches shed their leaves.*

11. The wall eroded by the wind will be repaired.

12. A balloon blowing back and forth rose slowly into the sky.

13. I listened to the mockingbirds imitating calls of other birds.

14. Boyd's expression, beaming with excitement, showed his enthusiasm.

15. The water, evaporating quickly, was soon at a very low level.

16. The document, crinkled with age, was sealed in a glass container.

17. Led by the coach, the team ran onto the field.

18. The parade participants, dancing in the streets, soon grew tired.

19. The boat sailing at top speed reached the shore quickly.

20. Overjoyed by the results, the crowd cheered.

SPEAKING APPLICATION

Take turns with a partner. Describe your plans for the future. Your partner should listen for and identify the participles that you use.

WRITING APPLICATION

Write two sentences using the participial phrase: *spending time with friends.* In the first sentence, the participial phrase should be essential. In the second sentence, the participial phrase should be nonessential.

Gerunds

Many nouns that end in *-ing* are actually **verbals** known as **gerunds.** Gerunds are not difficult to recognize: They always end in *-ing*, and they always function as **nouns.**

> A **gerund** is a form of a verb that ends in *-ing* and acts as a **noun.**

FUNCTIONS OF GERUNDS	
Subject	Painting is my favorite pastime.
Direct Object	I enjoy traveling.
Indirect Object	Mrs. Kim's recipes give home cooking a good name.
Predicate Nominative	My brother's favorite activity is swimming.
Object of a Preposition	The pilot's smooth flight showed signs of his extensive training.
Appositive	Tim's hobby, climbing, is very strenuous.

Verb, Participle, or Gerund? Words ending in *-ing* may be parts of verb phrases, participles acting as adjectives, or gerunds.

> Words ending in *-ing* that act as **nouns** are called **gerunds.** Unlike verbs ending in *-ing,* gerunds do not have helping verbs. Unlike participles ending in *-ing,* they do not act as adjectives.

VERB   Angela is **dancing** in the studio.

PARTICIPLE   The **dancing** girl is very good.

GERUND   **Dancing** is very exciting.

VERB   The class was **yawning**, and that distracted the teacher.

PARTICIPLE   **Yawning**, the class distracted the teacher.

GERUND   The class's **yawning** distracted the teacher.

Gerund Phrases Like participles, gerunds may be joined by other words to make **gerund phrases.**

> A **gerund phrase** consists of a gerund and one or more modifiers or a complement. The entire gerund phrase acts as a noun.

 RULE 15.1.11

GERUND PHRASES	
With Adjectives	Her constant, happy smiling made everyone around her joyful.
With an Adverb	Writing quickly does not always help.
With a Prepositional Phrase	Many hotels in the city prohibit pets sleeping in the beds.
With a Direct Object	Owen was incapable of remembering the list.
With an Indirect and a Direct Object	The history teacher tried giving her students praise.

Note About Gerunds and Possessive Pronouns: Always use the possessive form of a personal pronoun in front of a gerund.

INCORRECT	We never listen to **him** bragging.
CORRECT	We never listen to **his** bragging.
INCORRECT	**Them** refusing to drive slowly is dangerous.
CORRECT	**Their** refusing to drive slowly is dangerous.

See Practice 15.1G

Infinitives
The third kind of verbal is the **infinitive.** Infinitives have many different uses. They can act as nouns, adjectives, or adverbs.

> An **infinitive** is a form of a verb that generally appears with the word *to* in front of it and acts as a noun, an adjective, or an adverb.

RULE 15.1.12

EXAMPLE   The police officer asked them not **to speed** .

INFINITIVES USED AS NOUNS	
Subject	To converse requires careful listening.
Direct Object	The villagers decided to rebel .
Predicate Nominative	The couple's only option was to wait .
Object of a Preposition	I have no goal in life except to sing .
Appositive	There is only one choice, to leave !

Unlike gerunds, infinitives can also act as adjectives and adverbs.

INFINITIVES USED AS MODIFIERS	
Adjective	We have time to walk .
Adverb	The soldier was too tired to fight .

Prepositional Phrase or Infinitive? Although both **prepositional phrases** and **infinitives** often begin with *to*, you can tell the difference between them by analyzing the words that follow *to*.

A **prepositional phrase** always ends with a noun or pronoun that acts as the object of the preposition. An **infinitive** always ends with a verb.

PREPOSITIONAL PHRASE	INFINITIVE
The pilot listened to the command .	The president's purpose is to command .
We were told to go to the back of the house.	Please make sure to back up the supply list.

Note About Infinitives Without *to*: Sometimes infinitives do not include the word *to*. When an infinitive follows one of the eight verbs listed below, the *to* is generally omitted. However, it may be understood.

VERBS THAT PRECEDE INFINITIVES WITHOUT *TO*			
dare	help	make	see
hear	let	please	watch

EXAMPLES

He won't dare **[to] go** without a map.

Please help me **[to] find** the destination.

Spencer helped Alan **[to] climb** up the hill.

Infinitive Phrases Infinitives also can be joined with other words to form phrases.

> An **infinitive phrase** consists of an infinitive and its modifiers, complements, or subject, all acting together as a single part of speech.

15.1.14 RULE

INFINITIVE PHRASES	
With an Adverb	Kate's family likes to run early.
With an Adverb Phrase	To walk in high heels is not easy.
With a Direct Object	Quinn hated to leave Houston.
With an Indirect and a Direct Object	He promised to show us the slides from indirect direct his hiking trip. object object
With a Subject and a Complement	I want him to finish his speech. subject complement

See Practice 15.1H

PRACTICE 15.1G **Identifying and Using Gerunds and Gerund Phrases**

Read each sentence. Then, write the gerund or gerund phrase in each sentence. Tell how it functions in the sentence—as the *subject, direct object, subject complement*, and so on. Finally, use the gerund or gerund phrase in a sentence of your own.

EXAMPLE   Skateboarding is not allowed in certain areas of the park.

ANSWER   *Skateboarding* — subject
Skateboarding is what my brother enjoys most.

1. He spoke about gardening.

2. Cracking your knuckles is a bad habit.

3. My father doesn't recommend driving fast.

4. Collecting teapots is her favorite hobby.

5. He enjoys playing golf.

6. Olivia tried riding her bicycle for the first time.

7. Traveling is a big part of her job.

8. My fear, flying in an airplane, is shared by others.

9. She was praised for helping her sister.

10. My great joy is reading.

PRACTICE 15.1H **Identifying and Using Infinitives and Infinitive Phrases**

Read each sentence. Write the infinitive or infinitive phrase in each sentence. Tell how it functions in the sentence—as *subject, direct object, subject complement*, and so on. Finally, use the phrase in a sentence of your own.

EXAMPLE   Everyone wants to go swimming.

ANSWER   *to go swimming* — direct object
I hope to go swimming tomorrow.

11. Amy tries to eat healthy foods everyday.

12. To graduate from college is her main priority.

13. This is necessary information to know.

14. We hiked for three miles to reach the campsite.

15. The banker had money to invest.

16. The manager has asked to talk about your account at lunch.

17. His goal was to earn one million dollars before he retired.

18. To take the picture was proving difficult.

19. During the test, we were allowed to use our dictionaries.

20. The trail to take is about three miles from here.

SPEAKING APPLICATION

Take turns with a partner. Say sentences with the following gerunds: *running, climbing, reading, studying,* and *searching*.

WRITING APPLICATION

Write three sentences with infinitive phrases. Underline each infinitive phrase.

15.2 Clauses

Every **clause** contains a subject and a verb. However, not every clause can stand by itself as a complete thought.

> **A clause** is a group of words that contains a subject and a verb.

RULE 15.2.1

Independent and Subordinate Clauses

The two basic kinds of clauses are **independent** or **main clauses** and **subordinate clauses.**

> An **independent** or **main clause** can stand by itself as a complete sentence.

RULE 15.2.2

Every sentence must contain an independent clause. The independent clause can either stand by itself or be connected to other independent or subordinate clauses.

STANDING ALONE

Dr. Onevi teaches biology .
independent clause

WITH ANOTHER INDEPENDENT CLAUSE

Dr. Onevi teaches biology , and
independent clause

his wife teaches chemistry .
independent clause

WITH A SUBORDINATE CLAUSE

Dr. Onevi teaches biology , **while his wife**
independent clause   subordinate clause

teaches chemistry .

When you subordinate something, you give it less importance.

> **A subordinate clause,** although it has a subject and verb, cannot stand by itself as a complete sentence.

RULE 15.2.3

Subordinate clauses can appear before or after an independent clause in a sentence or can even split an independent clause.

LOCATIONS OF SUBORDINATE CLAUSES	
In the Middle of an Independent Clause	The man to whom I introduced you teaches technology courses.
Preceding an Independent Clause	Unless the ice melts soon, the road will be too slick.
Following an Independent Clause	Mike asked that he be excused.

Like phrases, subordinate clauses can function as adjectives, adverbs, or nouns in sentences.

See Practice 15.2A

Adjectival Clauses

One way to add description and detail to a sentence is by adding an **adjectival clause.**

RULE 15.2.4

An **adjectival clause** is a subordinate clause that modifies a noun or pronoun in another clause by telling *what kind* or *which one.*

An adjectival clause usually begins with one of the relative pronouns: *that, which, who, whom,* or *whose.* Sometimes, it begins with a relative adverb, such as *before, since, when, where,* or *why.* Each of these words connects the clause to the word it modifies.

RULE 15.2.5

An **adjectival clause** often begins with a **relative pronoun** or a **relative adverb** that links the clause to a noun or pronoun in another clause.

The adjectival clauses in the examples on the next page answer the questions *What kind?* and *Which one?* Each modifies the noun in the independent clause that comes right before the adjectival clause. Notice also that the first two clauses begin with relative pronouns and the last one begins with a relative adverb.

EXAMPLES I returned the CD **that you had loaned me** .

We gave eating salad, **which we thought was healthful** , a second try.

In Germany, we visited the town **where my grandfather was born** .

Adjectival clauses can often be used to combine information from two sentences into one. By using adjectival clauses, you can indicate the relationship between ideas as well as add detail.

TWO SENTENCES	COMBINED SENTENCES
The architect is ready to design the building. He is well known for unusual designs.	The architect, who is ready to design the building, is well known for unusual designs.
My sister writes music. She is a freshman in college.	My sister, who is a freshman in college, writes music.

Essential and Nonessential Adjectival Clauses Adjectival clauses are set off by punctuation only when they are not essential to the meaning of a sentence. Commas are used to indicate information that is not essential. When information in an adjectival clause is essential to the sentence, no commas are used.

NONESSENTIAL CLAUSES	ESSENTIAL CLAUSES
One of Shakespeare's best characters is Romeo, who is the main character in *Romeo and Juliet* .	The program that everyone must watch tonight promises to be very informative.
Bill Johnson, who trained really hard, won the state championship.	An athlete who trains faithfully usually finds winning to be easy.

See Practice 15.2B

PRACTICE 15.2A > **Identifying Independent and Subordinate Clauses**

Read each sentence. Identify the underlined clause in each sentence as *independent* or *subordinate*. Explain the function of each clause by telling whether it states a main idea all by itself or whether it adds more information to a main idea.

EXAMPLE   We didn't make plans <u>because we don't know the outcome</u>.

ANSWER   *subordinate — adds more information to a main idea*

1. Her plan, <u>that we improve the environment</u>, received much support.

2. Bill's reply, <u>that we remain firm</u>, upset us all.

3. <u>Even though he wondered about his choice</u>, he went ahead with the decision.

4. After the concert, <u>everyone was elated</u>.

5. <u>Whenever I am in Chicago</u>, I like to visit the Sears Tower.

6. The child <u>who plays the tambourine</u> is my niece.

7. <u>After I pay the bill</u>, I will drop it by the office.

8. Leaving the safety of the shore, <u>we swam out to sea</u>.

9. <u>For a person who dislikes dancing</u>, you certainly attend a lot of dance classes.

10. If you leave food out, <u>the food will attract bugs</u>.

PRACTICE 15.2B > **Identifying Adjectival Clauses**

Read each sentence. Write the adjectival clause in each sentence. Then, write *E* if it is essential or *N* if it is nonessential. Explain the function of each clause by telling which word it modifies.

EXAMPLE   The ability to speak to others, which is Greg's greatest strength, helped him win support easily.

ANSWER   *which is Greg's greatest strength — N; ability*

11. CD Warehouse, which is the best music store in town, is having a sale.

12. The office manager to whom we had written has not yet replied.

13. The movie, which I saw last night, was very long.

14. Hope McVey, whose father is in the military, has lived all over the world.

15. The song that I wanted to hear was playing on the radio.

16. This is the necklace that my mother wants.

17. The clown, who is in the parade, is funny.

18. The sweater that I am wearing is too heavy.

19. Our mayor, who is very powerful, lives in a large house.

20. My brother collects stamps that portray different presidents.

SPEAKING APPLICATION

With a partner, take turns saying sentences that have independent and subordinate clauses. Your partner should identify the clauses as either independent or subordinate.

WRITING APPLICATION

Write four sentences using adjectival clauses. Exchange papers with a partner and underline the adjectival clauses in each sentence.

Relative Pronouns **Relative pronouns** help link a subordinate clause to another part of a sentence. They also have a function in the subordinate clause.

> **Relative pronouns** connect adjectival clauses to the words they modify and act as subjects, direct objects, objects of prepositions, or adjectives in the subordinate clauses.

15.2.6 RULE

To tell how a relative pronoun is used within a clause, separate the clause from the rest of the sentence, and find the subject and verb in the clause.

FUNCTIONS OF RELATIVE PRONOUNS IN CLAUSES	
As a Subject	The plane that is engineered correctly is sure to stay subject in the air.
As a Direct Object	Pier, whom my sister met in France , is a good friend. direct object (Reworded clause: my sister met *whom* in France)
As an Object of a Preposition	This is the car about which I heard rave reviews . object of preposition (Reworded clause: I heard rave reviews about *which*)
As an Adjective	The child whose behavior was questionable spoke to adjective his parents.

Sometimes in writing and in speech, a relative pronoun is left out of an adjectival clause. However, the missing word, though simply understood, still functions in the sentence.

EXAMPLES   The heroes [**whom**] we studied were great leaders.

The suggestions [**that**] they made were implemented.

See Practice 15.2C

Relative Adverbs Like relative pronouns, **relative adverbs** help link the subordinate clause to another part of a sentence. However, they have only one use within a subordinate clause.

Relative adverbs connect adjectival clauses to the words they modify and act as adverbs in the clauses.

EXAMPLE Tom couldn't wait for the day **when** he could go on vacation.

In the example, the adjectival clause is *when he could go on vacation*. Reword the clause this way to see that *when* functions as an adverb: *he could go on vacation when.*

Adverbial Clauses

Subordinate clauses may also serve as adverbs in sentences. They are introduced by subordinating conjunctions. Like adverbs, **adverbial clauses** modify verbs, adjectives, or other adverbs.

Subordinate **adverbial clauses** modify verbs, adjectives, adverbs, or verbals by telling *where, when, in what way, to what extent, under what condition,* or *why.*

An adverbial clause begins with a subordinating conjunction and contains a subject and a verb, although they are not the main subject and verb in the sentence. In the chart that follows, the adverbial clauses are highlighted in orange. Arrows point to the words they modify.

ADVERBIAL CLAUSES	
Modifying a Verb	After you've been in Italy, you should begin your cooking class. (Begin *when*?)
Modifying an Adjective	Angela is taller than her sisters are. (Taller *to what extent*?)
Modifying a Gerund	I like eating ice cream while I walk. (Eating *under what condition*?)

> **Adverbial clauses** begin with **subordinating conjunctions** and contain subjects and verbs.

EXAMPLE

Even though it rained, we still had a picnic.

subordinating
conjunction

Recognizing the subordinating conjunctions will help you identify adverbial clauses. The following chart shows some of the most common subordinating conjunctions.

SUBORDINATING CONJUNCTIONS			
after	because	so that	when
although	before	than	whenever
as	even though	though	where
as if	if	unless	wherever
as long as	since	until	while

Where an adverbial clause appears in a sentence can affect meaning.

EXAMPLES

Before she moved , Anne planned to visit Rome.

Anne planned to visit Rome **before she moved** .

Like adjectival clauses, adverbial clauses can be used to combine the information from two sentences into one. The combined sentence shows a close relationship between the ideas.

See Practice 15.2D
See Practice 15.2E
See Practice 15.2F
See Practice 15.2G
See Practice 15.2H

TWO SENTENCES

It was icy . They did not drive home.

COMBINED

Because it was icy, they did not drive home.

subordinating
conjunction

PRACTICE 15.2C **Identifying Relative Pronouns and Adjectival Clauses**

Read each sentence. Then, write the adjectival clause in each sentence, and underline the relative pronoun that introduces the clause. Finally, explain the function of each clause by telling which word it modifies.

EXAMPLE   The book, which you requested, is unavailable.

ANSWER   *which you requested — book*

1. This is the play that was reviewed in the newspaper.

2. The story that he told is unbelievable.

3. It is Sarah whose watch was stolen.

4. Is this the moment that we have been waiting for?

5. A team that doesn't play well together should be reorganized.

6. Here are the concert tickets that we ordered.

7. He applied to the university that his father graduated from.

8. We saw the coastline, which was rocky.

9. My brother, who arrived during the game, won't be leaving soon.

10. The low-pressure system that is approaching could produce tornadoes.

PRACTICE 15.2D **Recognizing Adverbial Clauses**

Read each sentence. Then, write the adverbial clause in each sentence. Finally, explain the function of each clause by telling which word it modifies.

EXAMPLE   She developed a cough whenever she caught a cold.

ANSWER   *whenever she caught a cold — developed*

11. Your hair looks better since you had it cut.

12. We had hoped to put in a pool when the weather became warmer.

13. Talking on the phone while she is cooking dinner is hard for my mother.

14. She is happier today than she was yesterday.

15. Nia didn't have her purse when we left the restaurant.

16. The meeting ended much earlier than we expected.

17. When I start my project, my father will help me buy the materials.

18. I am unable to join you while I am on vacation.

19. Faster than the meteorologist predicted, the storm descended upon us.

20. We decided to take action when we heard the news.

SPEAKING APPLICATION

Take turns with a partner. Tell about something funny that happened to you. Use at least two adjectival clauses beginning with relative pronouns. Your partner should listen for and identify the relative pronouns that you use.

WRITING APPLICATION

For each of the relative adverbs *when*, *while*, and *than*, write a sentence using the relative adverb in an adverbial clause.

PRACTICE 15.2E > **Using Adjectival Clauses and Identifying Their Function**

Read each sentence and identify the adjectival clause and the word it modifies. Then, use the same relative pronoun or relative adverb to create a new clause in an original sentence.

EXAMPLE The noise that I heard came from the basement.

ANSWER *adjectival clause:* **that I heard**; *modifies:* **noise**
The music that I prefer doesn't entertain my parents.

1. Please return the CD that you borrowed.

2. The soup recipe, which was my grandmother's, has a secret ingredient.

3. The place where we live is actually a historic village.

4. That news program, which airs for a whole hour, seems biased.

5. The journalism teacher, who is retiring this year, has influenced thousands of students.

6. The teacher to whom I owe the most is the music teacher.

7. The author, whose book everyone is reading, will speak this afternoon.

8. The soldiers, whom we e-mailed, were grateful for our chatty notes.

PRACTICE 15.2F > **Using Adjectival Clauses and Identifying Their Function**

Combine each pair of sentences by turning one into an adjectival clause and adding it to the other. Then, underline the adjectival clause and explain which word(s) the adjectival clause modifies.

EXAMPLE The news program's main host is Jim Lehrer. He has outstanding colleagues.

ANSWER *The news program's main host is Jim Lehrer, who has outstanding colleagues.* (modifies: *Jim Lehrer*)

9. The workers postponed their strike. It was scheduled during the World Series.

10. My friend Jacques knows a lot about animals. His father is a veterinarian.

11. Susanna seems to know her way around computers. Susanna is in her sixties.

12. I downloaded the podcasts from an online store. The store has more than music.

13. Block Island lies off the coast of Rhode Island. It has miles of walking trails.

14. They were born in 1946, after World War II. A lot of babies were born then.

15. Last summer, the Northeast had excess rain. The rain may account for dull autumn leaves.

16. The community college has higher enrollment this year. The community college has a low tuition.

SPEAKING APPLICATION

With a partner, take turns discussing a favorite movie. Use an adjectival clause in each of your spoken sentences. Have your partner identify the adjectival clauses you use.

WRITING APPLICATION

Write three sentences about computers. Use an adjectival clause in each sentence. Underline each adjectival clause and circle the noun or pronoun it modifies.

PRACTICE 15.2G **Using Adverbial Clauses and Identifying Their Function**

Read each sentence and identify the adverbial clause and the word it modifies. Then, use the same subordinating conjunction in a new clause for an original sentence.

EXAMPLE   When I heard the noise, I ran into the kitchen.

ANSWER   adverbial clause: *When I heard the noise*; modifies: *ran*

When Tom lost his balance, he fell.

1. Most library books are due before the end of the semester.

2. They raised no children, though they would have made great parents.

3. Since you now know your way around Chicago, you should visit more often.

4. While you wait for my train to arrive, enjoy the shops in the station.

5. Suki is happy whenever she gets to a big city.

6. Bob makes friends wherever he travels.

7. Even though she got into four out of the five colleges to which she applied, she was disappointed.

8. He travels from Ohio to California often because his mother lives there.

9. He fell into her arms as if she were the last woman on Earth.

10. The show isn't over unless I've finished my popcorn.

PRACTICE 15.2H **Using Adverbial Clauses and Identifying Their Function**

Combine each pair of sentences by turning one into an adverbial clause and adding it to the other. Then, underline the adverbial clause and explain which word(s) the adverbial clause modifies.

EXAMPLE   The workers postponed their strike. Then, the World Series ended.

ANSWER   *The workers postponed their strike until the World Series ended.* (modifies: *postponed*)

11. He is at work. He has access to the Internet.

12. Bob telephones. I can't get him to stop talking and hang up.

13. She savored the meal slowly. Every bite was delicious.

14. Leo is always easygoing. I see him all the time.

15. You study and rest. You'll do well on the test.

16. It isn't safe to walk home alone. The streets are not deserted.

17. Ceci drank eight glasses a day. She read an article about the benefits of water.

18. They work at two jobs each. They are living paycheck to paycheck.

19. Nancy became concerned about me. My report was two weeks late.

20. You finish your essay first. Then you can go hang out with your friends.

SPEAKING APPLICATION

Use the sentences in Practice 15.2G as a model. Say three sentences, each with an adverbial clause, to a partner. Your partner should identify each clause.

WRITING APPLICATION

Write a paragraph, without adverbial clauses, about winter activities. Then, rewrite the paragraph, adding three adverbial clauses. Discuss differences between the paragraphs.

Elliptical Adverbial Clauses Sometimes, words are omitted in adverbial clauses, especially in those clauses that begin with *as* or *than* and are used to express comparisons. Such clauses are said to be *elliptical.*

> An **elliptical clause** is a clause in which the verb or the subject and verb are understood but not actually stated.

RULE 15.2.10

Even though the subject or the verb (or both) may not appear in an elliptical clause, they make the clause express a complete thought.

In the following examples, the understood words appear in brackets. The sentences are alike, except for the words *he* and *him.* In the first sentence, *he* is a subject of the adverbial clause. In the second sentence, *him* functions as a direct object of the adverbial clause.

VERB
UNDERSTOOD
She resembles their aunt more **than he [does]** .

SUBJECT
AND VERB
UNDERSTOOD
She resembles their aunt more **than [she resembles] him** .

See Practice 15.2l

When you read or write elliptical clauses, mentally include the omitted words to clarify the intended meaning.

Noun Clauses

Subordinate clauses can also act as nouns in sentences.

> A **noun clause** is a subordinate clause that acts as a noun.

RULE 15.2.11

A noun clause acts in almost the same way a one-word noun does in a sentence: It tells what or whom the sentence is about.

RULE 15.2.12 In a sentence, a noun clause may act as a subject, direct object, indirect object, predicate nominative, object of a preposition, or appositive.

EXAMPLES   **Whatever you lost** can be found in your
                          subject
messy room!

My grandparents remembered **what food I liked**
when I visited.
                                         direct object

The chart on the next page contains more examples of the functions of noun clauses.

Introductory Words

Noun clauses frequently begin with the words *that, which, who, whom,* or *whose*—the same words that are used to begin adjective clauses. *Whichever, whoever,* or *whomever* may also be used as introductory words in noun clauses. Other noun clauses begin with the words *how, if, what, whatever, where, when, whether,* or *why.*

RULE 15.2.13 **Introductory words** may act as subjects, direct objects, objects of prepositions, adjectives, or adverbs in noun clauses, or they may simply introduce the clauses.

| SOME USES OF INTRODUCTORY WORDS IN NOUN CLAUSES ||
FUNCTIONS IN CLAUSES	EXAMPLES
Adjective	He could not determine which puppy he wanted most.
Adverb	They wanted to know how we knew French.
Subject	I want the design from whoever built their house.
Direct Object	Whatever my parents advised, I obeyed.
No Function	The doctor determined that he had broken his arm.

Note that in the following chart the introductory word *that* in the last example has no function except to introduce the clause.

FUNCTIONS OF NOUN CLAUSES IN SENTENCES	
Acting as a Subject	Whoever leaves last must close the garage.
Acting as a Direct Object	Please tell whomever you want about the reunion.
Acting as an Indirect Object	His terse manner gave whoever worked for him a case of nerves.
Acting as a Predicate Nominative	Our choice is whether to buy a cat or dog.
Acting as an Object of a Preposition	As long as you clean, you can use the house for whatever you like.
Acting as an Appositive	The team embraced the offer that they receive new uniforms before the game.

Some words that introduce noun clauses also introduce adjectival and adverbial clauses. It is necessary to check the function of the clause in the sentence to determine its type. To check the function, try substituting the words *it, you, fact,* or *thing* for the clause. If the sentence retains its smoothness, you probably replaced a noun clause.

NOUN CLAUSE   I knew **that they wouldn't bring it** .

SUBSTITUTION   I knew it.

In the following examples, all three subordinating clauses begin with *where,* but only the first is a noun clause because it functions in the sentence as a direct object.

NOUN CLAUSE   Mr. Santos told the students **where they would be during the fire drill** .
(Told the students *what?*)

ADJECTIVAL CLAUSE   They took the tiger out of the cage, **where the lock was broken** .
(*Which* cage?)

ADVERBIAL CLAUSE   They live **where the weather is cold all year** .
(Live *where?*)

Note About Introductory Words: The introductory word *that* is often omitted from a noun clause. In the following examples, the understood word *that* is in brackets.

EXAMPLES   The manager suggested **[that] you leave the application** .

After the band had chosen him for the show, Ben knew **[that] he was going to have a very busy month** .

They remembered **[that] you wanted to use the black guitar** .

See Practice 15.2J

PRACTICE 15.2I ▷ Identifying Elliptical Adverbial Clauses

Read each sentence. Then, write the adverbial clause in each sentence. For the adverbial clauses that are elliptical, add the understood words in parentheses. Finally, explain the function of each adverbial clause by telling which word it modifies.

EXAMPLE   My report received a higher grade than Mike's report.

ANSWER   *than Mike's report (did) or than Mike's report (received) — higher*

1. Eric knows my brother better than I.
2. Lydia's outfit is as colorful as Carolyn's outfit.
3. George's cousin is as tall as George.
4. The train station is closer to my house than to Jeff's.
5. The oak tree is taller than the house.
6. Lousia can run faster than Joe.
7. My desserts taste better than Maria's desserts.
8. The cat ran as fast as the dog.
9. Claude's hair is as short as Ron's hair.
10. My errors are worse than Timmy's errors.

PRACTICE 15.2J ▷ Recognizing Noun Clauses

Read each sentence. Then, write the noun clause and label it with its function— *subject, direct object, indirect object, predicate nominative, object of a preposition,* or *appositive.*

EXAMPLE   A good quality, affordable education is what everyone wants.

ANSWER   *what everyone wants* — predicate nominative

11. The new rules curbed whatever freedom I had.
12. We gave whoever stopped by a free meal.
13. Our petition, that the team be reinstated, needed signatures.
14. We decided that his stubborness could no longer be ignored.
15. Whoever fails this test must quit the team.
16. My brother asked someone about what time the shuttle was launched.
17. The factory sent whoever had pending business an invoice.
18. His fear is that he will have to give an acceptance speech.
19. Whatever friends Sandy invites to our home will be welcomed.
20. Pay whoever is behind the counter.

SPEAKING APPLICATION

Take turns with a partner. Say sentences that include adverbial clauses. Your partner should listen for and identify what each adverbial clause modifies.

WRITING APPLICATION

Show that you understand the function of noun clauses. Write four sentences with noun clauses. Then, trade sentences with a partner. Identify the noun clauses in each other's sentences, and explain the part of speech it functions as.

15.3 The Four Structures of Sentences

Independent and subordinate clauses are the building blocks of sentences. These clauses can be combined in an endless number of ways to form the four basic sentence structures: **simple, compound, complex,** and **compound-complex.**

WRITING COACH

Online

www.phwritingcoach.co

Grammar Practic
Practice your grammar skills with Writing Coach Onli

Grammar Games
Test your knowledg of grammar in this fast-paced interact video game.

RULE 15.3.1

A **simple sentence** contains a single independent or main clause.

Although a simple sentence contains only one main or independent clause, its subject, verb, or both may be compound. A simple sentence may also have modifying phrases and complements. However, it cannot have a subordinate clause.

In the following simple sentences, the subjects are highlighted in yellow, and the verbs are highlighted in orange.

ONE SUBJECT AND VERB	The **ballerina danced**.
COMPOUND SUBJECT	**Trish** and **Faith cooked** Thanksgiving dinner.
COMPOUND VERB	The **bonfire crackled** and **burned**.
COMPOUND SUBJECT AND VERB	Neither the **pilot** nor the **passengers saw** or **heard** the engine fire.

RULE 15.3.2

A **compound sentence** contains two or more main clauses.

The main clauses in a compound sentence can be joined by a comma and a coordinating conjunction (*and, but, for, nor, or, so, yet*) or by a semicolon (;). Like a simple sentence, a compound sentence contains no subordinate clauses.

EXAMPLE	The **student carried** books to class, and **she started** taking notes in her notebook.

See Practice 15.3A

> **A complex sentence** consists of one independent or main clause and one or more subordinate clauses.

15.3.3 RULE

The independent clause in a complex sentence is often called the main clause to distinguish it from the subordinate clause or clauses. The subject and verb in the independent clause are called the subject of the sentence and the main verb. The second example shows that a subordinate clause may fall between the parts of a main clause. In the examples below, the main clauses are highlighted in blue, and the subordinate clauses are highlighted in pink.

EXAMPLES   No one reacted to the pager when it vibrated .

The garden that she waters daily was full of flowers .

Note on Complex Sentences With Noun Clauses: The subject of the main clause may sometimes be the subordinate clause itself.

EXAMPLE   That they were very late upset them .

> **A compound-complex sentence** consists of two or more independent clauses and one or more subordinate clauses.

15.3.4 RULE

In the example below, the independent clauses are highlighted in blue, and the subordinate clause is highlighted in pink.

See Practice 15.3B
See Practice 15.3C
See Practice 15.3D

EXAMPLE   Sparky barked when he saw a cat , and he ran through the park chasing it .

PRACTICE 15.3A **Distinguishing Between Simple and Compound Sentences**

Read each sentence. Then, label each sentence *simple* or *compound*.

EXAMPLE   His speech was both short and poignant.

ANSWER   *simple*

1. Either Laurel plays, or we forfeit the game.

2. At this juncture, there are several good routes that are accessible.

3. Tito's in Cleveland is known for its sandwiches.

4. The playoff victory was the Panthers' last impressive showing of the season.

5. Neither did the brush fire die, nor did the strong winds calm.

6. The waiter wrapped our leftovers, and then he gave us our bill.

7. We found the exit to the museum easily, but it was locked.

8. The cows wandered out to pasture, and they munched on the grass.

9. Either Kyle or Marcus will arrive at noon.

10. The police car arrived at the scene, and it left within one hour.

PRACTICE 15.3B **Identifying the Four Structures of Sentences**

Read each sentence. Then, label each sentence *simple, compound, complex,* or *compound-complex*.

EXAMPLE   At this time, there are many dates available.

ANSWER   *simple*

11. The bluff was covered with hanging vines.

12. Though the partners worked tirelessly, they could not finish the project.

13. After the actors performed the play, the audience gave them a standing ovation.

14. The quarterly meeting was held on Thursday, and those who were in attendance, the shareholders, asked many questions about the company's future.

15. Ruby bought decorative stationery and spent all day writing letters.

16. If you leave lights on, you're wasting energy.

17. The dogs were barking, so Clarence stopped cleaning his room and fed them.

18. Would you rather see a movie or a play?

19. As soon as I have some free time, I will take down the tent and store it in the attic.

20. For a girl who doesn't like sports, you go to a lot of football games.

SPEAKING APPLICATION

Take turns with a partner. Tell about something fun that you did with a family member. Use both simple and compound sentences. Your partner should listen for and identify each sentence as simple or compound.

WRITING APPLICATION

Write a paragraph about what you think you will be doing twenty years from now. Your paragraph should include a variety of correctly structured sentences: simple, compound, complex, and compound-complex.

PRACTICE 15.3C Creating Correctly Structured Simple and Compound Sentences

Identify each sentence as simple or compound. Change compound sentences into simple sentences by dividing main clauses; change simple sentences into compound sentences by adding an original independent clause.

EXAMPLE   Aphrodite is the goddess of love, and Ares is the god of war.

ANSWER   *compound; simple sentences:* **Aphrodite is the goddess of love. Ares is the god of war.**

EXAMPLE   Aphrodite is also known as Venus.

ANSWER   *simple; compound sentence:* **Aphrodite is also known as Venus, and she is the goddess of love.**

1. Many people enjoy reading Greek myths.

2. Apollo symbolizes order, but Dionysus represents the irrational.

3. Another name for Ares is Mars, and another name for Artemis is Diana.

4. My favorite mythological figure is Cupid.

5. Hermes wears a winged helmet and winged sandals, for he is the messenger god.

6. Some myths have existed for thousands of years.

PRACTICE 15.3D Creating Correctly Structured Complex and Compound-Complex Sentences

Identify each sentence as simple or compound. Then, add an original subordinate clause to change simple sentences into complex sentences and compound sentences into compound-complex sentences.

EXAMPLE   I'm going to sleep.

ANSWER   *simple; complex sentence:* **Since it's late, I'm going to sleep.**

EXAMPLE   It's getting late, but I'm still awake.

ANSWER   *compound; compound-complex sentence:* **It's getting late, but I'm still awake even though I had very little sleep.**

7. There was a ceremony for the opening of the new library, but I couldn't go.

8. I promised to be home at midnight, but the buses weren't running.

9. Julia babysits for five different families in her neighborhood.

10. The lake is beautiful, so I go back every year.

11. Fairy tales with their gory details can sometimes frighten children.

12. Most states allow people to apply for a driving license at age 16.

SPEAKING APPLICATION

Discuss superheroes with a partner by saying four sentences with a variety of structures. Your partner should identify the structures you used.

WRITING APPLICATION

Write a paragraph about music, using only simple and compound sentences. Then, rewrite the paragraph, incorporating subordinate clauses. Compare differences between the paragraphs.

Practice   391

Test Warm-Up

DIRECTIONS

Read the introduction and the passage that follows. Then, answer the questions to show you can use and understand the function of different sentence structures in reading and writing.

Levi wrote this paragraph about museums. Read the paragraph and think about the changes you would suggest as a peer editor. When you finish reading, answer the questions that follow.

Museums Here and There

(1) Many people know of major museums. (2) They include the Smithsonian and the Met. (3) Other museums are less well-known. (4) The Royal Terrell Museum in Alberta, Canada, has the world's largest exhibit of complete dinosaur skeletons. (5) Philadelphia boasts the Please Touch Museum. (6) It is a children's museum. (7) The United States has about 90 museums for children. (8) Sometimes you are in a city for the first time. (9) Plan to visit one of its museums then.

1 What is the most effective way to combine sentences 1 and 2?

  A Many people know of major museums; include the Smithsonian and the Met.

  B Many people know of major museums, which include the Smithsonian and the Met.

  C Many people know of the Smithsonian and the Met.

  D Major museums include the Smithsonian and the Met.

2 What change, if any, should be made in sentence 3 to make it a simple sentence?

  F Insert **and they are rarely mentioned** after *well-known*

  G Insert **which is unfortunate** after *well-known*

  H Insert **because they are smaller** after *well-known*

  J Make no change

3 What is the most effective way to combine sentences 5 and 6?

  A Philadelphia boasts the Please Touch Museum; a children's museum.

  B Philadelphia boasts the Please Touch Museum, which is a children's museum.

  C Philadelphia boasts the Please Touch Museum, and a children's museum.

  D Philadelphia, a children's museum, boasts the Please Touch Museum.

4 What is the most effective way to combine sentences 8 and 9?

  F Sometimes in a city for the first time, you plan to visit one of its museums.

  G You are in a city for the first time; you plan to visit one of its museums.

  H When you visit one of the city museums, be there for the first time.

  J When you are in a city for the first time, plan to visit one of its museums.

PRACTICE 1 ⟩ **Identifying Nouns**

Read the sentences. Then, label each underlined noun *concrete* or *abstract*. If the noun is concrete, label it *collective, compound, common,* or *proper*.

1. The crew <u>team</u> stayed after practice to work on their <u>strategy</u> for the next meet.

2. My mother told me that she left my <u>geometry book</u> on the <u>coffee table</u>.

3. <u>People</u> often asked if we were sisters because we looked so much alike.

4. <u>Lauren</u> did not like physics class because the <u>theories</u> were difficult to understand.

5. The <u>train</u> is departing for <u>Wyoming</u> in half an hour.

PRACTICE 2 ⟩ **Identifying Pronouns**

Read the sentences. Then, label each underlined pronoun *reciprocal, demonstrative, relative, interrogative,* or *indefinite*.

1. <u>These</u> people generally don't agree on much.

2. The contest, <u>which</u> we knew would be challenging, was in March.

3. <u>Most</u> of the students dissected a frog last year in biology class.

4. <u>Whose</u> turn is it to read aloud?

5. The children enjoyed playing with <u>one another</u>.

PRACTICE 3 ⟩ **Classifying Verbs and Verb Phrases**

Read the sentences. Then, write the verb or verb phrase in each sentence. Label each *action* or *linking verb,* and *transitive* or *intransitive*.

1. The crowd cheered the band on with thunderous applause.

2. Eric's singing sounds magnificent in the empty auditorium.

3. Rebecca left the game begrudgingly.

4. Every spring, Matthew cleans the garage.

5. This chicken tastes delicious.

PRACTICE 4 ⟩ **Identifying Adjectives and Adverbs**

Read the sentences. Then, label the underlined word as an *adverb* or *adjective*. Write the word that is modified.

1. She felt <u>sincere</u> gratitude for the help.

2. The flowers on the table smelled <u>divine</u>.

3. I was <u>immensely</u> happy to see such a turnout.

4. Conrad was the <u>oldest</u> player on the squad.

5. We <u>greatly</u> appreciated her kindness.

PRACTICE 5 ⟩ **Using Prepositions, Conjunctions, and Interjections**

Read the sentences. Then, write the preposition(s), conjunction(s), and/or interjection(s). Label conjunction *coordinating, correlative,* or *subordinating*.

1. Wow! The stars are brilliant tonight.

2. Before we can leave the house, Sarah needs to put her shoes on.

3. Both Randy and Jorge wanted to win the competition.

4. Stop! Don't sit on the bench with the wet paint sign on it!

5. Erin wanted to meet early, so I had to make sure that I left on time.

Continued on next page ▶

Cumulative Review Chapters 13–15

PRACTICE 6 ▷ **Recognizing Direct and Indirect Objects and Object of a Preposition**

Identify the underlined items as *direct object, indirect object,* or *object of a preposition.*

1. My mother gave <u>us</u> another <u>chance</u> to tell the truth.

2. Was Matilda running into the <u>school</u>?

3. Before leaving, Molly told us the <u>itinerary</u> for her <u>trip</u>.

4. The soldiers walked up <u>hills</u> and along <u>riverbeds</u>.

5. Dad promised <u>Irene</u> and <u>me</u> that he would take us to the planetarium next Wednesday.

6. The principal proposed new <u>hours</u> to the <u>faculty</u>.

7. Across from my <u>house</u> sat two stray cats.

8. Caroline recalled how calm the town looked before it was hit by the <u>hurricane</u>.

9. During the <u>play</u>, the students remained quiet.

10. Have you commended <u>Walt</u> and <u>Brian</u> for their excellent behavior?

PRACTICE 7 ▷ **Identifying Phrases**

Read the sentences. Then, write the phrases, and label them *prepositional, appositive, participial, gerund,* or *infinitive.*

1. Over the course of three months, we studied twentieth-century U.S. history.

2. The teacher decided to postpone the exam for one week.

3. The howling wind blew the windows in the front rooms shut.

4. My dog, a German shepherd, has lived with us for nine years.

5. Running every day after school allowed him to gain energy and stamina.

6. It is important to stand up for your beliefs.

7. Theodore Roosevelt, a dedicated Progressive, fought to lessen the power of big business.

8. We stayed until midnight, when the game was officially over.

9. Thinking it over, Jaime decided to take decisive action.

10. Reading aloud is a good way to understand difficult texts.

PRACTICE 8 ▷ **Recognizing Clauses**

Label the underlined clauses in the following sentences *independent* or *subordinate.* Identify any subordinate clause as *adjectival, adverbial,* or *noun clause.* Then, label any adjectival clauses *essential* or *nonessential.*

1. We will go to the beach <u>if it is warm enough</u>.

2. My mom, <u>who was born in Florida</u>, has never seen snow.

3. <u>Even though I can't come to your birthday party</u>, I would like to help you set up for it.

4. <u>When the next storm will hit</u> has not yet been forecasted.

5. <u>I think of my grandmother</u> whenever I hear this song.

6. Sammy, <u>who traveled the farthest to get</u> here, set up her exhibit next to mine.

7. <u>Danielle walked up and down the aisles</u>, searching for the earring she lost.

8. You can set up the display <u>wherever you can find room</u>.

9. The real problem is <u>how to settle this dispute</u>.

10. My aunt <u>who never talks much</u> is coming to visit us next week.

394 **Cumulative Review**

CHAPTER 16

EFFECTIVE SENTENCES

Vary your sentence length and structure to add interest and surprise to your writing.

WRITE GUY *Jeff Anderson, M.Ed.*

WHAT DO YOU NOTICE?

Analyze phrasing as you zoom in on this sentence from the story "The Lady in the Looking Glass: A Reflection" by Virginia Woolf.

MENTOR TEXT

> She was thinking, perhaps, that she must order a new net for the strawberries; that she must send flowers to Johnson's widow; that it was time she drove over to see the Hippesleys in their new house.

Now, ask yourself the following questions:

- How does the author use parallel, or similar, phrasing in the sentence?
- In addition to words and punctuation, what else is parallel?

The author repeats the relative pronoun *that* at the start of each of the three subordinate clauses in the series. She also uses semicolons to separate them. Beyond words and punctuation, the author repeats similar ideas in each clause to help create a sense of how the character's thoughts flow from one proposed action to the next.

Grammar for Writers Parallel structure does more than clarify ideas. Writers can also use it to create a sense of lively, repetitive rhythm in their prose—much like meter in poetry.

We listened carefully, studied hard, and learned well.

You're right. We came, we saw, we conquered parallel structure.

16.1 The Four Functions of a Sentence

Sentences can be classified according to what they do—that is, whether they state ideas, ask questions, give orders, or express strong emotions.

WRITING COACH

Online

www.phwritingcoach.com

Grammar Practice
Practice your grammar skills with Writing Coach Online.

Grammar Games
Test your knowledge of grammar in this fast-paced interactive video game.

Declarative sentences are used to declare, or state, ideas.

> **RULE 16.1.1**
>
> A **declarative sentence** states an idea and ends with a period.

DECLARATIVE   Paris is a city in France.

To *interrogate* means "to ask." An **interrogative sentence** is a question.

> **RULE 16.1.2**
>
> An **interrogative sentence** asks a question and ends with a question mark.

INTERROGATIVE   In which country are people the healthiest?

Imperative sentences give commands or directions.

> **RULE 16.1.3**
>
> An **imperative sentence** gives an order or a direction and ends with either a period or an exclamation mark.

Most imperative sentences start with a verb. In this type of imperative sentence, the subject is understood to be *you*.

IMPERATIVE   Follow my instructions word for word.

Exclamatory sentences are used to express emotions.

> **RULE 16.1.4**
>
> An **exclamatory sentence** conveys strong emotion and ends with an exclamation mark.

EXCLAMATORY   Congratulations on your acceptance!

See Practice 16.1A
See Practice 16.1B

PRACTICE 16.1A Identifying the Four Types of Sentences

Read each sentence. Then, label each sentence *declarative*, *interrogative*, *imperative*, or *exclamatory*.

EXAMPLE How much did the ticket cost?

ANSWER *interrogative*

1. My favorite pizza topping is mushrooms.
2. Who knows where I can find a locksmith?
3. Take all the tools out of the truck.
4. What an absolutely wonderful occasion!
5. The game this weekend should be competitive.
6. Do you remember how many paintings we sold last year?
7. Make certain that you proofread your essay thoroughly.
8. What a strange coincidence!
9. Which movie would you recommend?
10. Watch out!

PRACTICE 16.1B Punctuating the Four Types of Sentences

Read each sentence. Label each sentence *declarative*, *interrogative*, *imperative*, or *exclamatory*. Then, in parentheses, write the correct end mark.

EXAMPLE There are many pieces to this puzzle

ANSWER *declarative (.)*

11. What a frightful mess
12. Is there a way out of this cave
13. Please deliver these to your brother
14. I always considered myself to be independent
15. Are you sure he went that way
16. Close all the windows before you leave
17. Beware
18. Which car do you prefer to drive
19. This visit will more than likely be a different experience
20. How many times do we have to go over this scene

SPEAKING APPLICATION

Take turns with a partner. Say declarative, interrogative, imperative, and exclamatory sentences. Your partner should identify each type of sentence.

WRITING APPLICATION

Write an intriguing first paragraph to a mystery novel, using at least one declarative, interrogative, imperative, and exclamatory sentence in your paragraph.

16.2 Sentence Combining

Too many short sentences can make your writing choppy and disconnected.

One way to avoid the excessive use of short sentences and to achieve variety is to combine sentences.

WRITING COACH

Online

www.phwritingcoach.com

Grammar Practice
Practice your grammar skills with Writing Coach Online.

Grammar Games
Test your knowledge of grammar in this fast-paced interactive video game.

RULE 16.2.1 > Sentences can be combined by using a **compound subject,** a **compound verb,** or a **compound object.**

TWO SENTENCES	Tara enjoyed the vacation to Mexico. Heather enjoyed the vacation to Mexico.
COMPOUND SUBJECT	Tara and Heather enjoyed the vacation to Mexico.
TWO SENTENCES	Mike worked hard. Mike was promoted.
COMPOUND VERB	Mike worked hard and was promoted.
TWO SENTENCES	Kelly saw the college. Kelly saw the professor.
COMPOUND OBJECT	Kelly saw the college and the professor.

See Practice 16.2A

RULE 16.2.2 > Sentences can be combined by joining two **main** or **independent clauses** to create a **compound sentence.**

Use a compound sentence when combining ideas that are related but independent. To join main clauses, use a comma and a coordinating conjunction (*for, and, but, or, nor, yet,* or *so*) or a semicolon.

EXAMPLE	The boy looked for his books. He did not notice them under the bed.
COMPOUND SENTENCE	The boy looked for his books, but he did not notice them under the bed.

16.2.3 RULE

Sentences can be combined by changing one into a subordinate clause to create a complex sentence.

To show the relationship between ideas in which one depends on the other, use a **complex sentence.** The subordinating conjunction will help readers understand the relationship. Some common subordinating conjunctions are *after, although, because, if, since, when,* and *while.*

EXAMPLE	We were excited. We thought the trip to Florida would be fun.
COMBINED WITH A SUBORDINATE CLAUSE	We were excited **because we thought the trip to Florida would be fun** .

16.2.4 RULE

Sentences can be combined by changing one of them into a phrase.

See Practice 16.2B
See Practice 16.2C
See Practice 16.2D
See Practice 16.2E

EXAMPLE	My team plays softball today. We play on the new field.
COMBINED WITH PREPOSITIONAL PHRASE	My team plays softball **on the new field** today.

EXAMPLE	My mom will leave for Florida today. She is a frequent traveler.
COMBINED WITH APPOSITIVE PHRASE	My mom, **a frequent traveler** , will leave for Florida today.

PRACTICE 16.2A **Combining Sentences Using Compound Subjects, Verbs, and Objects**

Read each set of sentences. Then, write one sentence that combines them.

EXAMPLE   Tanya is a good sister. She is also a model student.

ANSWER   *Tanya is a good sister and a model student.*

1. Cara is a gifted tennis player. Alan also plays tennis very well.

2. The performers picked up their instruments. The performers picked up their sheet music.

3. Heath Farnsworth is an army captain. He is a career military officer.

4. Jermaine Collins is an accomplished actor. He is also a volunteer firefighter.

5. The university's lacrosse team won their division. The basketball team won their division, too.

PRACTICE 16.2B **Combining Sentences Using Phrases**

Read each set of sentences. Combine each set by turning one sentence into a phrase that adds detail to the other.

EXAMPLE   Luke easily passed the exam. It was a biology test.

ANSWER   *Luke easily passed the exam, a biology test.*

6. The homecoming dance took place this weekend. It was attended by all the juniors and seniors.

7. Thyme is a flavorful herb. It is often used in gourmet cooking.

8. She had trouble tying the knot. Her name is Ellen Stewart.

9. Our team captains were Viktor Shah and Kenneth Mooney. They were seniors.

10. The tourists noticed a taxi as it appeared near the intersection. The intersection is a busy corner.

SPEAKING APPLICATION

Take turns with a partner. Say two related sentences about graduating high school. Your partner should combine these two sentences into one.

WRITING APPLICATION

Write two sentences about your school that relate to each other. Then, combine the sentences by turning one into a phrase. Repeat with two new related sentences.

PRACTICE 16.2C **Combining Sentences**

Read each pair of sentences. Then, combine the sentences, using a coordinating or subordinating conjunction and indicate which kind of conjunction you have used.

EXAMPLE   Dave was thirsty. He went to the water fountain.

ANSWER   *Dave was thirsty, so he went to the water fountain.; coordinating*

1. Fresh gumbo simmered in the pot. Rion set the table for dinner.

2. There was a terrible storm brewing. I decided to take an umbrella.

3. John is considering taking a job in Houston. His wife has family where they live now.

4. Thalia was eating her lunch. Her friend stopped by.

5. I could make pasta. We could order out.

6. Gregory and Hugh both earn good grades. They compete to see who can score higher.

7. The temperature was rising. Clouds covered the sky.

8. I was hired for the job. I have an extensive background in information technology.

9. Mr. Wu grows prize-winning roses. He is thinking about photographing them for a book.

10. I commit my afternoons to studying in the library. Mark spends his time practicing the saxophone.

PRACTICE 16.2D ▷ **Combining Sentences**

Combine each pair of sentences in two ways to get two different correctly structured compound or complex sentences. Discuss differences in meaning between the two sentences.

EXAMPLE   Ann wanted to pay this time.
            Rick always pays.

ANSWER   *Ann wanted to pay this time because Rick always pays.*

            Ann wanted to pay this time, but Rick always pays.

1. Tom heard the fire alarm. He exited the building.

2. Babette was excited. She was on her way to the airport.

3. The child had a tantrum. The parent developed a headache.

4. The city was not crowded. It was a holiday.

5. The performer's contact lens popped out. She didn't miss a beat.

6. The weather was very windy. The elderly couple worried about being blown over.

7. The team had won the World Series many years ago. They stood no chance now.

8. You broke it. Now you'll have to fix it.

9. The driver arrived early. The person needing the taxi wasn't ready.

10. The storm raged all day. The river overflowed.

PRACTICE 16.2E ▷ **Combining Sentences**

Revise the paragraph by combining sentences into compound or complex sentences. You should produce a paragraph of five sentences.

EXAMPLE   (1) The flu is not a new ailment.
            (2) The flu has existed for centuries.

ANSWER   *The flu is not a new ailment since it has existed for centuries.*

(1) The condition called influenza was named that in the 1400s by Italians. (2) The Italians blamed the condition on the influence of the stars and planets. (3) Today we know the real cause. (4) The cause is a virus. (5) Symptoms of the flu include aches and pains and a fever up to 104 degrees Fahrenheit. (6) The patient can also feel chills and fatigue. (7) Bed rest, analgesics, and warm fluids help a flu patient feel better. (8) It never hurts to have chicken soup. (9) Generally, patients should stay home from school or work. (10) At home, they cannot infect colleagues or classmates.

SPEAKING APPLICATION

To a partner, tell a brief story about an experience at school. Have your partner listen and suggest which sentences you may combine. Follow your partner's suggestions, and retell the story.

WRITING APPLICATION

Write a paragraph on the topic of comfort foods. Then, revise the paragraph by combining two pairs of adjacent sentences. Comment on the difference between the original and the revised paragraphs.

Test Warm-Up

DIRECTIONS
Read the introduction and the passage that follows. Then, answer the questions to show that you can use and understand sentence combining in reading and writing.

Naftali wrote this paragraph about a sleep disorder. Read the paragraph and think about the changes you would suggest as a peer editor. When you finish reading, answer the questions that follow.

Insomnia: What It Is and How to Fix It

(1) Insomnia is the inability to fall or stay asleep. (2) The result of insomnia is drowsiness. (3) Another result is fatigue. (4) One remedy for insomnia is to exercise. (5) Do not exercise close to bedtime. (6) Another remedy is to eat a snack before bedtime. (7) Recommended snacks include bananas, figs, milk, and turkey. (8) These foods are rich in tryptophan. (9) Tryptophan is an amino acid. (10) This amino acid makes people sleepy.

---

1 What is the most effective way to combine sentences 1, 2, and 3?

A Insomnia is the inability to fall or stay asleep; so drowsiness or fatigue result.

B Insomnia is the inability to fall or stay asleep, drowsiness or fatigue results.

C Insomnia is the inability to fall or stay asleep, resulting in drowsiness or fatigue.

D Resulting in drowsiness and fatigue is the inability to fall or stay asleep.

2 What is the most effective way to combine sentences 4 and 5?

F One remedy for insomnia is to exercise, but do not exercise close to bedtime.

G One remedy for insomnia is to not exercise close to bedtime.

H When close to bedtime, one remedy for insomnia is to exercise.

J One remedy for insomnia, not close to bedtime, is to exercise.

3 What is the most effective way to combine sentences 6 and 7?

A Another remedy is to eat a snack before bedtime, including bananas, figs, milk, and turkey.

B Another remedy is to eat a snack before bedtime; bananas, figs, milk, and turkey.

C Another remedy is to eat a snack, such as bananas, figs, milk, or turkey, before bedtime.

D Another remedy is to eat a snack of bananas, figs, milk, and turkey.

4 What is the most effective way to combine sentences 8, 9, and 10?

F These foods are rich in tryptophan, an amino acid that makes people sleepy.

G These foods are rich in tryptophan, an amino acid; this makes people sleepy.

H These foods are rich in amino acid since amino acid makes people sleepy.

J These foods are rich in tryptophan, an amino acid.

16.3 Varying Sentences

Vary your sentences to develop a rhythm, to achieve an effect, or to emphasize the connections between ideas. There are several ways you can vary your sentences.

Varying Sentence Length

To emphasize a point or surprise a reader, include a short, direct sentence to interrupt the flow of long sentences. Notice the effect of the last sentence in the following paragraph.

EXAMPLE   The Jacobites derived their name from *Jacobus,* the Latin name for King James II of England, who was dethroned in 1688 by William of Orange during the Glorious Revolution. Unpopular because of his Catholicism and autocratic ruling style, James fled to France to seek the aid of King Louis XIV. In 1690, James, along with a small body of French troops, landed in Ireland in an attempt to regain his throne. His hopes ended at the Battle of the Boyne.

Some sentences contain only one idea and can't be broken. It may be possible, however, to state the idea in a shorter sentence. Other sentences contain two or more ideas and might be shortened by breaking up the ideas.

LONGER SENTENCE   Many of James II's predecessors were able to avoid major economic problems, but James had serious economic problems.

MORE DIRECT   Unlike many of his predecessors, James II was unable to avoid major economic problems.

LONGER SENTENCE   James tried to work with Parliament to develop a plan of taxation that would be fair and reasonable, but members of Parliament rejected his efforts, and James dissolved the Parliament.

SHORTER SENTENCES   James tried to work with Parliament to develop a fair and reasonable taxation plan. However, because members of Parliament rejected his efforts, James dissolved the Parliament.

Varying Sentence Beginnings

Another way to create sentence variety is to start sentences with different parts of speech.

WAYS TO VARY SENTENCE BEGINNINGS	
Start With a Noun	Formal gardens are difficult to create.
Start With an Adverb	Naturally, formal gardens are difficult to create.
Start With an Adverbial Phrase	Because of their complexity, formal gardens are difficult to create.
Start With a Participial Phrase	Having tried to create formal gardens, I know how hard it is.
Start With a Prepositional Phrase	For the average person, formal gardens are very difficult to create.
Start With an Infinitive Phrase	To create a beautiful and functional formal garden was my goal.

See Practice 16.3A

Using Inverted Word Order

You can also vary sentence beginnings by reversing the traditional subject–verb order to create verb–subject order. You can reverse order by starting the sentence with an **adverb,** a **participial phrase,** or a **prepositional phrase.** You can also move a complement to the beginning of the sentence.

SUBJECT–VERB ORDER

A cry for help came out of the darkness.

The rules of the game are listed here.

I was never so angry.

A dark cloud was there over the lake.

VERB–SUBJECT ORDER

Out of the darkness came a cry for help.
prepositional phrase

Listed here are the rules of the game.
participial phrase

Never was I so angry.
adverb

There was a dark cloud over the lake.
adverb

See Practice 16.3B

PRACTICE 16.3A **Revising to Vary Sentence Beginnings**

Read each sentence. Rewrite each sentence to begin with the part of speech or phrase indicated in parentheses. You may need to add a word or phrase.

EXAMPLE Bob left the office; he was finished for the day. (participial phrase)

ANSWER *Finished for the day, Bob left the office.*

1. Barbara checked the telephone directory to get the number. (infinitive phrase)

2. My CD player is an older model, but it has excellent speakers. (prepositional phrase)

3. The committee approved the plan; the vote was overwhelming. (adverb phrase)

4. Joey accepted the award; he was grinning happily. (participial phrase)

5. The child drank lemonade at the fair. (prepositional phrase)

6. He framed the picture. (infinitive phrase)

7. They rested on the sidelines. (adverb)

8. The dog watched me through the window. (prepositional phrase)

9. Dinner was served at the hotel. (prepositional phrase)

10. The lion attacked the deer with agility. (prepositional phrase)

PRACTICE 16.3B **Inverting Sentences to Vary Subject-Verb Order**

Read each sentence. Rewrite each sentence by inverting subject-verb order to verb-subject order. Use the word in parentheses to start the new sentence.

EXAMPLE The falcon soared in the sky. (In)

ANSWER *In the sky soared the falcon.*

11. The cruise ship moved toward the shore. (Toward)

12. The skier raced away from the starting gate. (Away)

13. The results of the audition are posted here. (Posted)

14. Students are rarely so well prepared. (Rarely)

15. The little baby lamb pranced at the back of the herd. (At)

16. The cavalry stormed down the treacherous mountainside. (Down)

17. The bunny hopped into the meadow. (Into)

18. The bride sat inside the long, black car. (Inside)

19. The buried treasure was beneath the rock. (Beneath)

20. The only person I ever loved was here beside me. (Here)

SPEAKING APPLICATION

Take turns with a partner. Choose three sentences from Practice 16.3A. Say each sentence, but change the directive in the parentheses. Your partner should follow the directive to revise how the sentence begins.

WRITING APPLICATION

Write three sentences about any subject of your choice. Then, exchange papers with a partner. Your partner should invert the order of your sentences from subject-verb order to verb-subject order.

16.4 Avoid Fragments and Run-ons

Hasty writers sometimes omit crucial words, punctuate awkwardly, or leave their thoughts unfinished, causing two common sentence errors: **fragments** and **run-ons**.

Recognizing Fragments

Although some writers use them for stylistic effect, **fragments** are generally considered errors in standard English.

> **Do not capitalize and punctuate phrases, subordinate clauses, or words in a series as if they were complete sentences.**

16.4.1 RULE

Reading your work aloud to listen for natural pauses and stops should help you avoid fragments. Sometimes, you can repair a fragment by connecting it to words that come before or after it.

> **One way to correct a fragment is to connect it to the words in a nearby sentence.**

16.4.2 RULE

PARTICIPIAL FRAGMENT	inspired by the knowledge of the professor
ADDED TO A NEARBY SENTENCE	**Inspired by the knowledge of the professor ,** Peri sat through the lecture again.
PREPOSITIONAL FRAGMENT	before her assistant
ADDED TO A NEARBY SENTENCE	The professor entered the class **before her assistant** .
PRONOUN AND PARTICIPIAL FRAGMENT	the one filled with apples
ADDED TO NEARBY SENTENCE	The basket I want is **the one filled with apples** .

RULE 16.4.3

> **Another way to correct a fragment is to add any sentence part that is needed to make the fragment a complete sentence.**

Remember that every complete sentence must have both a subject and a verb and express a complete thought. Check to see that each of your sentences contains all of the parts necessary to be complete.

NOUN FRAGMENT   **the van of happy young teenagers**

COMPLETED SENTENCES

The van of happy young teenagers
          subject

parked **at the field.**
verb

We quietly **listened** to
subject   verb

the van of happy young teenagers .
      direct object

Notice what missing sentence parts must be added to the following types of phrase fragments to make them complete.

	FRAGMENTS	COMPLETED SENTENCES
Noun Fragment With Participial Phrase	the other team beaten by us	The other team was beaten by us.
Verb Fragment	will be at the game tomorrow	I will be at the game tomorrow.
Prepositional Fragment	in the locker room	I put the helmets in the locker room.
Participial Fragment	found under the bench	The water bottle found under the bench is mine.
Gerund Fragment	teaching children to play hockey	Teaching children to play hockey is rewarding.
Infinitive Fragment	to meet the new coach	I expect to meet the new coach.

You may need to attach a **subordinate clause** to a main clause to correct a fragment.

A **subordinate clause** contains a subject and a verb but does not express a complete thought and cannot stand alone as a sentence. Link it to a main clause to make the sentence complete.

ADJECTIVAL CLAUSE FRAGMENT	which was being held inside
COMPLETED SENTENCE	I enjoyed watching the basketball game, **which was being held inside** .
ADVERBIAL CLAUSE FRAGMENT	after she practiced her graduation speech
COMPLETED SENTENCE	**After she practiced her graduation speech** , she was ready for the commencement.
NOUN CLAUSE FRAGMENT	whatever food is served for breakfast
COMPLETED SENTENCE	We always enjoy **whatever food is served for breakfast** .

Series Fragments A fragment is not always short. A long series of words still needs to have a subject and a verb and express a complete thought. It may be a long fragment masquerading as a sentence.

SERIES FRAGMENT	COMPLETE SENTENCE
after studying modern dance, with its infrequent steps and movements, in the style typical of present-day theater	After studying modern dance, with its infrequent steps and movements, in the style typical of present-day theater, I was able to prepare for the show thoroughly .

See Practice 16.4A

Avoiding Run-on Sentences

A **run-on** sentence is two or more sentences capitalized and punctuated as if they were a single sentence.

> **Use punctuation and conjunctions to correctly join or separate parts of a run-on sentence.**

There are two kinds of **run-ons: fused sentences**, which are two or more sentences joined with no punctuation, and **comma splices**, which have two or more sentences separated only by commas rather than by commas and conjunctions.

FUSED SENTENCE	The employee worked late every day he was the employee of the month.
COMMA SPLICE	Only one dog was at the show, the others never came.

As with fragments, proofreading or reading your work aloud will help you find run-ons. Once found, they can be corrected by adding punctuation and conjunctions or by rewording the sentences.

FOUR WAYS TO CORRECT RUN-ONS		
	RUN-ON	**CORRECTION**
With End Marks and Capitals	The snow fell heavily in the living room the family huddled by the fireplace.	The snow fell heavily. In the living room, the family huddled by the fireplace.
With Commas and Conjunctions	The button needed to be sewn we could not locate the thread.	The button needed to be sewn, but we could not locate the thread.
With Semicolons	Our town has many patriotic events, for example, it hosts picnics and fireworks on July 4th.	Our town has many patriotic events; for example, it hosts picnics and fireworks on July 4th.
By Rewriting	The class began late, the professor wasn't there on time.	The class began late because the professor wasn't there on time.

See Practice 16.4B

PRACTICE 16.4A **Identifying and Correcting Fragments**

Read each sentence. If an item contains a fragment, rewrite it to make a complete sentence. If an item contains a complete sentence, write *correct*.

EXAMPLE   Adjusting the turntable again.

ANSWER   *Adjusting the turntable again, I finally got it right.*

1. The panel discussing a school-wide celebration.

2. Unfortunately, the flowers delivered to the wrong address.

3. Between you and me.

4. The mirror that Mother wanted.

5. After we left the music store went to eat lunch.

6. Please be quiet.

7. Their eyes met.

8. Their faces shining with awe at seeing the famous portrait.

9. Working with children.

10. Classified ads filling the pages of the newspaper.

PRACTICE 16.4B **Revising to Eliminate Run-on Sentences**

Read each sentence. Correct each run-on by correctly joining or separating the sentence parts.

EXAMPLE   I play first base, Sasha is the catcher.

ANSWER   *I play first base, and Sasha is the catcher.*

11. There are two choices, I don't like either.

12. The new mall will have over one hundred shops enclosed parking will be attached.

13. Eggs can be prepared in many ways, my favorite is scrambled eggs.

14. It rains a lot in the spring, it rained all last week.

15. I want to become a doctor I want to help people.

16. The couple just got married, their guests showered them with rose petals.

17. Some plants have medicinal properties, for example, mint leaves can aid in digestion.

18. Sherlock Holmes is a fictional detective, who also plays the violin.

19. A category 1 hurricane has the lowest wind speeds, a category 5 has the highest.

20. I prefer summer days, I do not enjoy cold weather.

SPEAKING APPLICATION

Take turns with a partner. Say sentence fragments. Your partner should make each fragment a complete sentence.

WRITING APPLICATION

Find and read a newspaper or magazine article. Choose one paragraph and change several correct sentences into run-on sentences. Then, exchange papers with a partner, and have your partner correct the run-ons.

16.5 Misplaced and Dangling Modifiers

Careful writers put modifiers as close as possible to the words they modify. When modifiers are misplaced or left dangling in a sentence, the result may be illogical or confusing.

WRITING COACH

www.phwritingcoach.com

Grammar Tutorials
Brush up on your Grammar skills with these animated videos.

Grammar Practice
Practice your grammar skills with Writing Coach Online.

Grammar Games
Test your knowledge of grammar in this fast-paced interactive video game.

Recognizing Misplaced Modifiers

A **misplaced modifier** is placed too far from the modified word and appears to modify the wrong word or words.

RULE 16.5.1 ▷ A **misplaced modifier** seems to modify the wrong word in the sentence.

MISPLACED MODIFIER
The woman ran over a rock **riding on the bike trail**.

CORRECTION
The woman **riding on the bike trail** ran over a rock.

MISPLACED MODIFIER
We heard the radio playing **while driving home**.

CORRECTION
While driving home, we heard the radio playing.

Recognizing Dangling Modifiers

With **dangling modifiers,** the word that should be modified is missing from the sentence. Dangling modifiers usually come at the beginning of a sentence and are followed by a comma. The subject being modified should come right after the comma.

RULE 16.5.2 ▷ A **dangling modifier** seems to modify the wrong word or no word at all because the word it should modify has been omitted from the sentence.

See Practice 16.5A

DANGLING PARTICIPIAL PHRASE	Estimating carefully, the school loan was paid off accurately. (*Who* did the estimating?)
CORRECTED SENTENCE	Estimating carefully, **the student** accurately paid off the school loan.

Dangling participial phrases are corrected by adding missing words and making other needed changes.

Dangling infinitive phrases and elliptical clauses can be corrected in the same way. First, identify the subject of the sentence. Then, make sure each subject is clearly stated. You may also need to change the form of the verb.

DANGLING INFINITIVE PHRASE	To get on the plane, the ticket must be presented. (*Who* is getting on the plane?)
CORRECTED SENTENCE	To get on the plane, **the travelers** must present their tickets.
DANGLING ELLIPTICAL CLAUSE	While floating down the canal, houses, boats, and other buildings were sighted. (*Who* was floating and sighted the other buildings?)
CORRECTED SENTENCE	While floating down the canal, **we** saw houses, boats, and other buildings.

A dangling adverbial clause may also occur when the antecedent of a pronoun is not clear.

DANGLING ADVERBIAL CLAUSE	When she graduated from high school, Amy's mother planned a picnic in the park. (*Who* graduated from high school, Amy or her mother?)
CORRECTED SENTENCE	**When Amy graduated from high school**, her mother planned a picnic in the park.

See Practice 16.5B

PRACTICE 16.5A **Identifying and Correcting Misplaced Modifiers**

Read each sentence. Then, rewrite each sentence, putting the misplaced modifiers closer to the words they should modify. If a sentence is correct, write *correct*.

EXAMPLE The horse gallops around the paddock with white hooves.

ANSWER *The horse with white hooves gallops around the paddock.*

1. Oranges are juicy that come from Florida.

2. Olivia gave her bike to her younger sister with a gel seat.

3. The pecan tree was hit by lightning with a forked trunk.

4. The woman crossed the street walking her dog.

5. The coat is in the hall closet that you need.

6. Emilio wants a hamburger and coffee cooked medium well.

7. Stephanie bought new glasses in the city with bifocals.

8. Carolyn called her parents elated by the good news.

9. Gloria purchased a necklace in Austin with a gold clasp.

10. The dog was groomed with a curly tail.

PRACTICE 16.5B **Identifying and Correcting Dangling Modifiers**

Read each sentence. Then, rewrite the sentences, correcting any dangling modifiers by supplying missing words or ideas.

EXAMPLE Reading the first page, the book was too difficult.

ANSWER *Reading the first page, I realized the book was too difficult.*

11. Turning the corner, a beautiful sunset could be seen.

12. While opening the box, a mistake had been made.

13. Closing the car door, her keys were still in the ignition.

14. To play baseball, a glove is needed.

15. Having finished the book, it was very late.

16. While eating breakfast, the phone rang.

17. Reaching the stop sign, an accident blocked the right lane.

18. Working too fast, an error was made.

19. While speaking on the phone, her dog ran out the door.

20. When he turned four, his brother was born.

SPEAKING APPLICATION

Take turns with a partner. Tell about an exciting experience that you have had. Use modifiers in your sentences. Your partner should listen for and identify the modifiers, and tell whether they are correctly placed.

WRITING APPLICATION

Use sentences 12, 14, and 16 as models to write your own sentences with dangling modifiers. Then, rewrite each sentence to correct the dangling modifiers.

16.6 Faulty Parallelism

Good writers try to present a series of ideas in similar grammatical structures so the ideas will read smoothly. If one element in a series is not parallel with the others, the result may be jarring or confusing.

Recognizing the Correct Use of Parallelism

To present a series of ideas of equal importance, you should use parallel grammatical structures.

> **Parallelism** involves presenting equal ideas in words, phrases, clauses, or sentences of similar types.

16.6.1 RULE

PARALLEL WORDS	The doctor looked **calm**, **focused**, and **determined**.
PARALLEL PHRASES	The greatest feeling I know is **to teach a skill to someone** and **then to see that person apply the skill**.
PARALLEL CLAUSES	The sunscreen **that you recommended** and **that my son needs** is on sale.
PARALLEL SENTENCES	**It couldn't be**, of course. **It could never, never be**. –Dorothy Parker

Correcting Faulty Parallelism

Faulty parallelism occurs when a writer uses unequal grammatical structures to express related ideas.

> Correct a sentence containing faulty parallelism by rewriting it so that each parallel idea is expressed in the same grammatical structure.

16.6.2 RULE

Faulty parallelism can involve words, phrases, and clauses in a series or in comparisons.

Nonparallel Words, Phrases, and Clauses in a Series

Always check for parallelism when your writing contains items in a series.

Correcting Faulty Parallelism in a Series

NONPARALLEL STRUCTURES

Marking, **sewing**, and **alteration** are three
gerund   gerund   noun
steps in the tailoring process.

CORRECTION

Marking, **sewing**, and **altering** are three
gerund   gerund   gerund
steps in the tailoring process.

NONPARALLEL STRUCTURES

I could not wait **to try my new skis**, **to ski**
infinitive phrase
down the slope, and **visiting the cozy lodge**.
infinitive phrase   participial phrase

CORRECTION

I could not wait **to try my new skis**, **to ski**
infinitive phrase
down the slope, and **to visit the cozy lodge**.
infinitive phrase   infinitive phrase

NONPARALLEL STRUCTURE

Some people feel **that badminton is**
noun clause
not a sport, but **it requires practice and**
independent clause
dedication.

CORRECTION

Some people feel **that badminton is not**
noun clause
a sport, but **that it requires practice and**
noun clause
dedication.

Another potential problem involves correlative conjunctions, such as *both ... and* or *not only ... but also*. Though these conjunctions connect two related items, writers sometimes misplace or split the first part of the conjunction. The result is faulty parallelism.

NONPARALLEL	Sue **not only** won the "Best Pie" competition **but also** the county title.
PARALLEL	Sue won **not only** the "Best Pie" competition **but also** the county title.

Nonparallel Words, Phrases, and Clauses in Comparisons

As the saying goes, you cannot compare apples with oranges. In writing comparisons, you generally should compare a phrase with the same type of phrase and a clause with the same type of clause.

Correcting Faulty Parallelism in Comparisons

NONPARALLEL STRUCTURES

Many people prefer **baseball** to **watching golf**.
                   noun
gerund phrase

CORRECTION

Many people prefer **baseball** to **golf**.
           noun   noun

NONPARALLEL STRUCTURES

I left my class **at 2:00 P.M.** rather than
          prepositional phrase
walking out at 3:00 P.M.
      gerund phrase

CORRECTION

I left my class **at 2:00 P.M.** rather than
          prepositional phrase
at the usual 3:00 P.M.
     prepositional phrase

NONPARALLEL STRUCTURES

Tate delights **in busy days** as much as
subject   prepositional phrase
relaxing days delight other **people**.
      subject   direct object

CORRECTION

Tate delights **in busy days** as much as
subject   prepositional phrase
other **people** delight **in relaxing days**.
     subject   prepositional phrase

See Practice 16.6A

16.7 Faulty Coordination

When two or more independent clauses of unequal importance are joined by *and*, the result can be faulty **coordination**.

Recognizing Faulty Coordination

To *coordinate* means to "place side by side in equal rank." Two independent clauses that are joined by the coordinating conjunction *and*, therefore, should have equal rank.

  **16.7.1**

> Use *and* or other coordinating conjunctions only to connect ideas of equal importance.

CORRECT COORDINATION	Phil designed a house, **and** Morgan built it.

Sometimes, however, writers carelessly use *and* to join main clauses that either should not be joined or should be joined in another way so that the real relationship between the clauses is clear. Faulty coordination puts all the ideas on the same level of importance, even though logically they should not be.

FAULTY COORDINATION	Production of aircraft accelerated in World War II, **and** aircraft became a decisive factor in the war.
	I didn't do well, **and** the test was easy.
	Will Rogers was from Oklahoma, **and** he died in an airplane crash.

Occasionally, writers will also string together so many ideas with *and's* that the reader is left breathless.

STRINGY SENTENCE	The fighter jet that flew over the airstrip did a few dips and turns, **and** the people on the ground craned their necks to watch, **and** everyone applauded and cheered.

Correcting Faulty Coordination

Faulty coordination can be corrected in several ways.

> **One way to correct faulty coordination is to put unrelated ideas into separate sentences.**

When faulty coordination occurs in a sentence in which the main clauses are not closely related, separate the clauses and omit the coordinating conjunction.

FAULTY COORDINATION	Production of aircraft accelerated in World War II, **and** aircraft became a decisive factor in the war.
CORRECTION	Production of aircraft accelerated in World War II. Aircraft became a decisive factor in the war.

> **You can correct faulty coordination by putting less important ideas into subordinate clauses or phrases.**

If one main clause is less important than, or subordinate to, the other, turn it into a subordinate clause. You can also reduce a less important idea to a phrase.

FAULTY COORDINATION	I didn't do well, **and** the test was easy.
CORRECTION	I didn't do well, **even though** the test was easy.
FAULTY COORDINATION	Will Rogers was from Oklahoma, **and** he died in an airplane crash.
CORRECTION	Will Rogers, a native of Oklahoma, died in an airplane crash.

Stringy sentences should be broken up and revised using any of the three methods just described. Following is one way that the stringy sentence on the previous page can be revised.

REVISION OF A STRINGY SENTENCE	The fighter jet that flew over the airstrip did a few dips and turns. Craning their necks, the people on the ground applauded and cheered.

See Practice 16.6B

PRACTICE 16.6A ▷ **Revising to Eliminate Faulty Parallelism**

Read each sentence. Then, rewrite the sentence to correct any nonparallel structures.

EXAMPLE   She not only plays golf but also soccer.

ANSWER   *She plays not only golf but also soccer.*

1. The new employee was energetic, helpful, and often arrived early.

2. I hate cleaning as much as medicine.

3. Going there is better than to stay home.

4. The picture is old, torn, and looks fragile.

5. Katy not only will go to the parade but also to the science fair.

6. I would choose reading a book over a movie.

7. I see trees swaying, ducks swimming, and flying birds.

8. He both wanted to stay in his house and to move to the country.

9. I think I sang well because I practiced a lot rather than because the nerves weren't there.

10. Laughing, telling jokes, and to play games make the time go by faster.

PRACTICE 16.6B ▷ **Revising to Eliminate Faulty Coordination**

Read each sentence. Then, rewrite each sentence to correct the faulty coordination.

EXAMPLE   It was true the Clays needed a babysitter, and they had five kids.

ANSWER   *It was true that the Clays, who had five kids, needed a babysitter.*

11. I have read many biographies, and all of them have been popular for years.

12. I plan to study chemistry in college, and biology is another course I'd like to take.

13. Eduardo bought a bike and it has 15 speeds.

14. Learning to parallel park was difficult for me, and I finally mastered the technique.

15. The car is a minivan, and has room for eight.

16. The truck had a full load, and it slowed going uphill.

17. There are guided tours and we will join them.

18. Oak trees lined the street, and it was called Grand Avenue.

19. Kit is attending an Ivy League university and she graduated from high school with honors.

20. Australia is a country as well as a continent and is located in the Southern Hemisphere.

SPEAKING APPLICATION

Take turns with a partner. Tell several things you plan to do with your family or friends. Your partner should listen for and correct any faulty parallelism in your description.

WRITING APPLICATION

Use sentences 14, 15, and 16 as models to write three sentences that contain faulty coordination. Exchange papers with a partner, and correct each other's work.

CHAPTER 17

VERB USAGE

Use strong verbs to set the stage of the action in your writing.

WRITE GUY *Jeff Anderson, M.Ed.*

WHAT DO YOU NOTICE?

Uncover the verbs as you zoom in on these sentences from the novel *Hard Times* by Charles Dickens.

MENTOR TEXT

> "We hope to have, before long, a board of fact, composed of commissioners of fact, who will force the people to be a people of fact, and of nothing but fact."

Now, ask yourself the following questions:

- What tense is the verb *hope* in the first clause? What tense is the verb in the second clause, *who will force the people to be a people of fact?*
- Why did the author use two different verb tenses in the same sentence?

The verb *hope* in the first clause is written in the present tense. The verb *will force* in the clause *who will force the people to be a people of fact* is written in the future tense. Dickens used the present tense of the verb *hope* to indicate that the speaker was expressing his wishes at the time he was speaking. He used *will force,* the future tense of the verb *force,* to explain how the speaker expected the commissioners to act in the future.

Grammar for Writers Although there are subtle differences between verb tenses, the variations are important. Think of tenses as a time travel tool you can use to help guide readers through the sequence of action in your writing.

How can I help my verbs to relax?

Try adjusting their tenses!

421

17.1 Verb Tenses

Besides expressing actions or conditions, verbs have different **tenses** to indicate when the action or condition occurred.

RULE 17.1.1 A **tense** is the form of a verb that shows the time of an action or a condition.

The Six Verb Tenses

There are six tenses that indicate when an action or a condition of a verb is, was, or will be in effect. Each of these six tenses has at least two forms.

RULE 17.1.2 Each tense has a **basic** and a **progressive** form.

The chart that follows shows examples of the six tenses.

THE BASIC FORMS OF THE SIX TENSES	
Present	Sandy acts in plays.
Past	She acted in last year's school musical.
Future	She will act in a play this spring.
Present Perfect	She has acted since she was a young child.
Past Perfect	She had acted in the high school's holiday musical.
Future Perfect	She will have acted in many plays by the time she gets to college.
Present	We go to the beach on summer vacation.
Past	We went to the beach last summer.
Future	We will go to the beach next summer.
Present Perfect	We have gone to other places, too.
Past Perfect	We had gone to the lake in July.
Future Perfect	We will have gone to different beaches during summer vacations.

See Practice 17.1A

Basic Verb Forms or Tenses

Verb tenses are identified simply by their tense names.
The **progressive tenses,** however, are identified by their tense names plus the word *progressive.* Progressive tenses show that an action is or was happening for a period of time.

The chart below shows examples of the six tenses in their progressive form or tense. Note that all of these progressive tenses end in *-ing.* (See the section on verb conjugation later in this chapter for more about the progressive tense.)

THE PROGRESSIVE TENSES	
Present Progressive	Sandy is acting in a play.
Past Progressive	She was acting in elementary school.
Future Progressive	She will be acting in the spring.
Present Perfect Progressive	She has been acting in many different kinds of plays.
Past Perfect Progressive	She had been acting only in small parts, but she now plays lead roles.
Future Perfect Progressive	Next season, she will have been acting for a decade.

The Emphatic Form

There is also a third form or tense, the **emphatic,** which exists only for the present and past tenses. The **present emphatic** is formed with the helping verb *do* or *does,* depending on the subject. The **past emphatic** is formed with *did.* The purpose of the emphatic tense is to put more emphasis on, or to stress, the action of the verb.

THE EMPHATIC TENSES OF THE PRESENT AND THE PAST	
Present Emphatic	The president does speak about issues that I think are important. The student council does act on students' complaints.
Past Emphatic	My dad did get a promotion to vice-president of his company. My mom did insist that I finish my homework before I could meet my friends.

See Practice 17.1B

PRACTICE 17.1A Identifying Verb Tenses

Read each sentence. Then, write the verb used in each sentence, and the tense of the verb.

EXAMPLE   Lucy has crossed the parking lot.

ANSWER   *has crossed* — *present perfect*

1. I often swim in the pool.

2. The plane took off right on time.

3. Abe has toured the Texas State Capitol.

4. By the end of the week, the competition will have hosted over three hundred athletes.

5. Sea scavengers will eat almost any detritous on the ocean floor.

6. By next week, I will have seen that movie three times.

7. Victor had visited his grandparents all summer.

8. My sister will enter all four skateboard competitions.

9. Andie and I wait at the intersection.

10. Bruce spoke to Natalia about the meeting.

PRACTICE 17.1B Recognizing Tenses or Forms of Verbs

Read each sentence. Then, write the verb, and the tense of the verb.

EXAMPLE   We have been climbing.

ANSWER   *have been climbing* — *present perfect progressive*

11. I did formulate a hypothesis.

12. Gary was sledding all afternoon.

13. Ruth had been studying for days.

14. Chisom will be hiding the presents.

15. We had been driving through three states.

16. They have been preparing for the science fair.

17. Damon does concede graciously.

18. Francine is paddling down the river.

19. I do recommend that restaurant.

20. Pedro will have been rehearsing for weeks.

SPEAKING APPLICATION

Take turns with a partner. Using complete sentences, describe the objects around you. Your partner should repeat each sentence, changing the tense of the verb that you used. Be sure to use all six verb tenses.

WRITING APPLICATION

Using at least three progressive tenses, write a paragraph, describing a fictional action scene. Underline each verb or verb phrase and write the form of each verb.

The Four Principal Parts of Verbs

Every verb in the English language has four **principal parts** from which all of the tenses are formed.

> A verb has four principal parts: the **present**, the **present participle**, the **past**, and the **past participle.**

17.1.3 RULE

The chart below shows the principal parts of the verbs *leave, present,* and *run.*

THE FOUR PRINCIPAL PARTS			
PRESENT	PRESENT PARTICIPLE	PAST	PAST PARTICIPLE
leave	leaving	left	(have) left
present	presenting	presented	(have) presented
run	running	ran	(have) run

The first principal part, the present, is used for the basic forms of the present and future tenses, as well as for the emphatic forms or tenses. The present tense is formed by adding an -*s* or -*es* when the subject is *he, she, it,* or a singular noun. The future tense is formed with the helping verb *will. (I will leave. Mary will present. Carl will run.)* The present emphatic is formed with the helping verb *do* or *does. (I do leave. Mary does present. Carl does run.)* The past emphatic is formed with the helping verb *did. (I did leave. Mary did present. Carl did run.)*

The second principal part, the present participle, is used with helping verbs for all of the progressive forms. *(I am leaving. Mary is presenting. Carl is running.)*

The third principal part, the past, is used to form the past tense. *(I left. Mary presented. Carl ran.)* As in the example *ran,* the past tense of a verb can change its spelling. (See the next section for more information.)

The fourth principal part, the past participle, is used with helping verbs to create the perfect tenses. *(I have left. Mary had presented. Carl had run.)*

See Practice 17.1C
See Practice 17.1D

PRACTICE 17.1C Recognizing the Four Principal Parts of Verbs

Read each sentence. Then, write the principal part and label as *present*, *present participle*, *past*, or *past participle*.

EXAMPLE   The Rangers are winning at halftime.

ANSWER   *winning* — present participle

1. I never eat alone in the cafeteria.

2. Our manager is driving to the other branches today.

3. The bus departed ahead of schedule.

4. Every student grasped the meaning of the story.

5. She is using an ointment to rub on her sore knee.

6. Bobby has completed his workout already.

7. By the end of the month, the proposal gained much support.

8. Some of my classmates find the assignment challenging.

9. Most applicants have submitted a cover letter with their resumes.

10. I am taking extra classes to get additional credits.

PRACTICE 17.1D Identifying the Four Principal Parts of Verbs

Read each sentence. Then, write the verb or verb phrase in each sentence, and the principal part used to form each verb.

EXAMPLE   You have passed the test.

ANSWER   *have passed* — past participle

11. Maria found the lost wallet.

12. The plane had risen above the clouds.

13. Armand is announcing his desire to run for class president.

14. Ray and Benjamin completed their entrance exams.

15. I am joining a gym to work out more often.

16. Roger stored all his belongings in his car.

17. Jack attempts to train his new puppy.

18. We vacationed the entire month of August.

19. I am looking for my camera.

20. Marta buys herself a necklace.

SPEAKING APPLICATION

Take turns with a partner. Tell a fictional short story about a day in the life of a pet dog. Use each of the four principal parts of a verb in your story.

WRITING APPLICATION

Use sentence 18 as the first sentence in a short essay about your dream vacation. Be sure to include the four principal parts of some verbs in your essay.

Regular and Irregular Verbs

The way the past and past participle forms of a verb are formed determines whether the verb is **regular** or **irregular.**

Regular Verbs The majority of verbs are regular. Regular verbs form their past and past participles according to a predictable pattern.

> **A regular verb is one for which the past and past participle are formed by adding *-ed* or *-d* to the present form.**

RULE 17.1.4

In the chart below, notice that a final consonant is sometimes doubled to form the present participle, the past, and the past participle. A final *e* may also be dropped to form the participle.

PRINCIPAL PARTS OF REGULAR VERBS			
PRESENT	PRESENT PARTICIPLE	PAST	PAST PARTICIPLE
advance	advancing	advanced	(have) advanced
grip	gripping	gripped	(have) gripped
predict	predicting	predicted	(have) predicted

See Practice 17.1E
See Practice 17.1F

Irregular Verbs Although most verbs are regular, many of the most common verbs are irregular. Irregular verbs do not use a predictable pattern to form their past and past participles.

> **An irregular verb is one whose past and past participle are *not* formed by adding *-ed* or *-d* to the present form.**

RULE 17.1.5

Usage Problems Remembering the principal parts of irregular verbs can help you avoid usage problems. One common usage problem is using a principal part that is not standard.

INCORRECT My mom **teached** me how to cook.

CORRECT My mom **taught** me how to cook.

A second usage problem is confusing the past and past participle when they have different forms.

INCORRECT   Mike **done** his chores before he went to school.

CORRECT   Mike **did** his chores before he went to school.

Some common irregular verbs are shown in the charts that follow. Use a dictionary if you are not sure how to form the principal parts of an irregular verb.

IRREGULAR VERBS WITH THE SAME PRESENT, PAST, AND PAST PARTICIPLE			
PRESENT	PRESENT PARTICIPLE	PAST	PAST PARTICIPLE
burst	bursting	burst	(have) burst
cost	costing	cost	(have) cost
cut	cutting	cut	(have) cut
hit	hitting	hit	(have) hit
hurt	hurting	hurt	(have) hurt
let	letting	let	(have) let
put	putting	put	(have) put
set	setting	set	(have) set
shut	shutting	shut	(have) shut
split	splitting	split	(have) split
spread	spreading	spread	(have) spread

Note About *Be:* *Be* is one of the most irregular of all of the verbs. The present participle of *be* is *being.* The past participle is *been.* The present and the past depend on the subject and tense of the verb.

CONJUGATION OF *BE*		
	SINGULAR	PLURAL
Present	I am. You are. He, she, or it is.	We are. You are. They are.
Past	I was. You were. He, she, or it was.	We were. You were. They were.
Future	I will be. You will be. He, she, or it will be.	We will be. You will be. They will be.

IRREGULAR VERBS WITH THE SAME PAST AND PAST PARTICIPLE			
PRESENT	PRESENT PARTICIPLE	PAST	PAST PARTICIPLE
bring	bringing	brought	(have) brought
build	building	built	(have) built
buy	buying	bought	(have) bought
catch	catching	caught	(have) caught
fight	fighting	fought	(have) fought
find	finding	found	(have) found
get	getting	got	(have) got or (have) gotten
hold	holding	held	(have) held
keep	keeping	kept	(have) kept
lay	laying	laid	(have) laid
lead	leading	led	(have) led
leave	leaving	left	(have) left
lose	losing	lost	(have) lost
pay	paying	paid	(have) paid
say	saying	said	(have) said
sell	selling	sold	(have) sold
send	sending	sent	(have) sent
shine	shining	shone or shined	(have) shone or (have) shined
sit	sitting	sat	(have) sat
sleep	sleeping	slept	(have) slept
spend	spending	spent	(have) spent
stand	standing	stood	(have) stood
stick	sticking	stuck	(have) stuck
sting	stinging	stung	(have) stung
strike	striking	struck	(have) struck
swing	swinging	swung	(have) swung
teach	teaching	taught	(have) taught
win	winning	won	(have) won
wind	winding	wound	(have) wound

IRREGULAR VERBS THAT CHANGE IN OTHER WAYS

PRESENT	PRESENT PARTICIPLE	PAST	PAST PARTICIPLE
arise	arising	arose	(have) arisen
become	becoming	became	(have) become
begin	beginning	began	(have) begun
bite	biting	bit	(have) bitten
break	breaking	broke	(have) broken
choose	choosing	chose	(have) chosen
come	coming	came	(have) come
do	doing	did	(have) done
draw	drawing	drew	(have) drawn
drink	drinking	drank	(have) drunk
drive	driving	drove	(have) driven
eat	eating	ate	(have) eaten
fall	falling	fell	(have) fallen
fly	flying	flew	(have) flown
give	giving	gave	(have) given
go	going	went	(have) gone
grow	growing	grew	(have) grown
know	knowing	knew	(have) known
lie	lying	lay	(have) lain
ride	riding	rode	(have) ridden
ring	ringing	rang	(have) rung
rise	rising	rose	(have) risen
run	running	ran	(have) run
see	seeing	saw	(have) seen
sing	singing	sang	(have) sung
sink	sinking	sank	(have) sunk
speak	speaking	spoke	(have) spoken
swim	swimming	swam	(have) swum
take	taking	took	(have) taken
tear	tearing	tore	(have) torn
throw	throwing	threw	(have) thrown
wear	wearing	wore	(have) worn
write	writing	wrote	(have) written

See Practice 17.1G
See Practice 17.1H

PRACTICE 17.1E > **Recognizing Principal Parts of Regular Verbs**

Read each group of regular verbs. Then, write the missing principal part of the verb.

EXAMPLE   named, naming, named

ANSWER   *name*

1. balance, balanced, (have) balanced
2. permitting, permit, permitted
3. matched, match, matching
4. interrupting, (have) interrupted, interrupt
5. fastened, (have) fastened, fasten
6. promised, promising, (have) promised
7. (have) removed, remove, removing
8. slap, slapped, slapping
9. tugging, tugged, (have) tugged
10. claimed, (have) claimed, claim

PRACTICE 17.1F > **Using the Correct Form of Regular Verbs**

Read each sentence. Then, choose the correct verb form from those given in parentheses to complete each sentence.

EXAMPLE   Harry (damaging, damaged) his car in the accident.

ANSWER   *damaged*

11. Mr. Wayne (stay, stayed) at a five-star hotel.
12. I have (stopped, stop) spending so much money on video games.
13. I am (filled, filling) my tank with gas.
14. Shana and Joe are (smiling, smile) at us from the bus.
15. Sunblock (protect, protected) her skin from harmful rays.
16. Zac is (explained, explaining) what happened during the fire drill.
17. Both my parents (admire, admiring) my independent spirit.
18. Mr. Fitch (demand, demanded) the attention of the entire class.
19. Silvio's food always (smelling, smells) really good.
20. Depak and Tony have (apologize, apologized) for being late.

SPEAKING APPLICATION

Take turns with a partner. Tell about your last summer vacation. Use as many principal parts of verbs as you can in your description.

WRITING APPLICATION

Write a paragraph about an idea for a movie. Use at least three regular verbs and different principal parts of those verbs.

PRACTICE 17.1G ▶ **Recognizing Principal Parts of Irregular Verbs**

Read each verb. Then, write the present participle, past, and past participle of each verb.

EXAMPLE   steal

ANSWER   *stealing, stole, (have) stolen*

1. hide
2. get
3. do
4. forget
5. understand
6. write
7. split
8. overdo
9. begin
10. let

PRACTICE 17.1H ▶ **Supplying the Correct Form of Irregular Verbs**

Read each sentence. Then, write the correct form of the irregular verb that is italicized. If the sentence is correct, write *correct*. Do not add or change any helping verbs.

EXAMPLE   I have *ate* a delicious dinner.

ANSWER   *eaten*

11. The news *spreaded* all over the country.
12. The sun *rising* well before I was out of bed.
13. Peter *drawed* the short straw, so he went first.
14. The truck was *drove* by an experienced driver.
15. My mother *forbidden* me to leave dirty dishes in the sink.
16. I have *forgave* Gino for being late to dinner.
17. Angelina *strove* to be the fastest runner on the field.
18. Beatrice has *shook* the bottle of salad dressing.
19. I have *forgot* his gift in the car.
20. Albert *lended* me his jacket.

SPEAKING APPLICATION

Take turns with a partner. Tell what you did during your free time yesterday and what you plan to do during that time today. Use irregular verbs in your description. Your partner should listen for and identify each irregular verb that you use.

WRITING APPLICATION

Write a paragraph about a happy time in your life. Use four different irregular verbs, using four different principal parts of that verb in your paragraph.

Verb Conjugation

The **conjugation** of a verb displays all of its different forms.

> **A conjugation** is a complete list of the singular and plural forms of a verb in a particular tense.

The singular forms of a verb correspond to the singular personal pronouns (*I, you, he, she, it*), and the plural forms correspond to the plural personal pronouns (*we, you, they*).

To conjugate a verb, you need the four principal parts: the present (*choose*), the present participle (*choosing*), the past (*chose*), and the past participle (*chosen*). You also need various helping verbs, such as *has, have,* or *will.*

Notice that only three principal parts—the present, the past, and the past participle—are used to conjugate all six of the basic forms.

CONJUGATION OF THE BASIC FORMS OF *CHOOSE*		SINGULAR	PLURAL
Present	First Person Second Person Third Person	I choose. You choose. He, she, or it chooses.	We choose. You choose. They choose.
Past	First Person Second Person Third Person	I chose. You chose. He, she, or it chose.	We chose. You chose. They chose.
Future	First Person Second Person Third Person	I will choose. You will choose. He, she, or it will choose.	We will choose. You will choose. They will choose.
Present Perfect	First Person Second Person Third Person	I have chosen. You have chosen. He, she, or it has chosen.	We have chosen. You have chosen. They have chosen.
Past Perfect	First Person Second Person Third Person	I had chosen. You had chosen. He, she, or it had chosen.	We had chosen. You had chosen. They had chosen.
Future Perfect	First Person Second Person Third Person	I will have chosen. You will have chosen. He, she, or it will have chosen.	We will have chosen. You will have chosen. They will have chosen.

See Practice 17.1I

Conjugating the Progressive Tense With *Be*

As you learned earlier, the **progressive tense** shows an ongoing action or condition. To form the progressive tense, use the present participle form of the verb (the *-ing* form) with a form of the verb *be*.

CONJUGATION OF THE PROGRESSIVE FORMS OF *CHOOSE*		SINGULAR	PLURAL
Present Progressive	First Person Second Person Third Person	I am choosing. You are choosing. He, she, or it is choosing.	We are choosing. You are choosing. They are choosing.
Past Progressive	First Person Second Person Third Person	I was choosing. You were choosing. He, she, or it was choosing.	We were choosing. You were choosing. They were choosing.
Future Progressive	First Person Second Person Third Person	I will be choosing. You will be choosing. He, she, or it will be choosing.	We will be choosing. You will be choosing. They will be choosing.
Present Perfect Progressive	First Person Second Person Third Person	I have been choosing. You have been choosing. He, she, or it has been choosing.	We have been choosing. You have been choosing. They have been choosing.
Past Perfect Progressive	First Person Second Person Third Person	I had been choosing. You had been choosing. He, she, or it had been choosing.	We had been choosing. You had been choosing. They had been choosing.
Future Perfect Progressive	First Person Second Person Third Person	I will have been choosing. You will have been choosing. He, she, or it will have been choosing.	We will have been choosing. You will have been choosing. They will have been choosing.

See Practice 17.1J

PRACTICE 17.1I ▷ Conjugating the Basic Forms of Verbs

Read each word. Then, conjugate each verb using the subject indicated in parentheses. Write the verbs in the past, future, present perfect, past perfect, and future perfect forms.

EXAMPLE   grabs (he)

ANSWER   *he grabbed, he will grab, he has grabbed, he had grabbed, he will have grabbed*

1. informs (she)

2. hide (I)

3. shake (they)

4. deliver (we)

5. chases (it)

6. grow (you)

7. pretends (he)

8. give (I)

9. get (you)

10. fit (we)

PRACTICE 17.1J ▷ Conjugating the Progressive Forms of Verbs

Read each sentence. Then, conjugate the progressive form of each verb indicated in parentheses.

EXAMPLE   I manage. (past progressive, future perfect progressive)

ANSWER   *I was managing. I will have been managing.*

11. He holds. (past progressive, future progressive)

12. We keep. (present perfect progressive, future perfect progressive)

13. They sink. (past perfect progressive, past progressive)

14. I fall. (future progressive, present perfect progressive)

15. She bites. (past perfect progressive, past progressive)

16. You prepare. (past progressive, future progressive)

17. I offer. (present perfect progressive, past perfect progressive)

18. They remove. (future perfect progressive, past progressive)

19. We scream. (past perfect progressive, future progressive)

20. He unites. (past progressive, future perfect progressive)

SPEAKING APPLICATION

Take turns with a partner. Say five verbs. Your partner should conjugate each verb for all six basic forms.

WRITING APPLICATION

Choose three verbs not used in Practice 17.1J and conjugate each verb for all six progressive forms.

17.2 The Correct Use of Tenses

The basic, progressive, and emphatic forms of the six tenses show time within one of three general categories: **present, past,** and **future.** This section will explain how each verb form has a specific use that distinguishes it from the other forms.

Present, Past, and Future Tense

Good usage depends on an understanding of how each form works within its general category of time to express meaning.

Uses of Tense in Present Time

Three different forms can be used to express present time.

RULE 17.2.1

> The three forms of the **present tense** show present actions or conditions as well as various continuing actions or conditions.

EXPRESSING PRESENT TENSE	
Present	I explore .
Present Progressive	I am exploring .
Present Emphatic	I do explore .

The main uses of the basic form of the present tense are shown in the chart below.

EXPRESSING PRESENT TENSE	
Present Action	Two dogs play in the park.
Present Condition	They are both excited.
Regularly Occurring Action	They go to the dog run on weekends.
Regularly Occurring Condition	The dog run is open all day.
Constant Action	Dogs pant when they run.
Constant Condition	Dogs are good pets.

See Practice 17.2A

Historical Present The present tense may also be used to express historical events. This use of the present, called the **historical present tense,** is occasionally used in narration to make past actions or conditions sound more lively.

THE HISTORICAL PRESENT TENSE	
Past Actions Expressed in Historical Present Tense	Michelangelo sits quietly and thinks about the block of marble in front of him.
Past Condition Expressed in Historical Present Tense	The people of Renaissance Italy appreciate Michelangelo's artistic genius and love his work.

The **critical present tense** is most often used to discuss deceased authors and their literary achievements.

THE CRITICAL PRESENT TENSE	
Action Expressed in Critical Present	Shakespeare writes plays about historical figures and about fictional ones.
Condition Expressed in Critical Present	Shakespeare is also a writer of sonnets.

The **present progressive tense** is used to show a continuing action or condition of a long or short duration.

USES OF THE PRESENT PROGRESSIVE TENSE	
Long Continuing Action	We are working on a group project.
Short Continuing Action	We are researching the ecology of our area.
Continuing Condition	We are enjoying working together.

USES OF THE PRESENT EMPHATIC TENSE	
Emphasizing a Statement	Marco does enjoy sculpting figures.
Denying a Contrary Assertion	No, he does not enjoy painting.
Asking a Question	Does he sculpt with clay?
Making a Sentence Negative	He does not want people to watch him work.

See Practice 17.2B

PRACTICE 17.2A > **Identifying Tense in Present Time**

Read each sentence. Then, label the verb form *present*, *present progressive*, or *present emphatic*.

EXAMPLE   I give Lisa my attention.

ANSWER   *present*

1. Rachel is training for a marathon.

2. Carlos is wrapping the presents for the celebration.

3. High tide occurs twice a day.

4. We do run the risk of losing our turn.

5. Nathan is cooking steaks on the grill.

6. Despite his tight schedule, Ralph finds time to exercise.

7. Jonathan does study very hard for exams.

8. Sagan grows stronger every year.

9. Catie is hoping for another chance to complete.

10. I do e-mail her whenever I get the chance.

PRACTICE 17.2B > **Supplying Verbs in Present Time**

Read each sentence. Then, rewrite each sentence, using the tense indicated in parentheses.

EXAMPLE   Becky puts the chair in the basement. (present progressive)

ANSWER   *Becky is putting the chair in the basement.*

11. Hassan is thinking about attending college after high school. (present)

12. Constance felt elated after winning the close game. (present emphatic)

13. Clarence reaches for the top of the cupboard. (present progressive)

14. Kelly keeps up with current events. (present emphatic)

15. Upon reflection, Warren does remember the event. (present)

16. Anya is keeping a close watch on her younger brother. (present)

17. Jackie loves babysitting. (present emphatic)

18. We do recommend learning about different cultures. (present)

19. Walter is helping those in need. (present emphatic)

20. Jose dives off the dock into the cold water. (present progressive)

SPEAKING APPLICATION

Take turns with a partner. Describe what is happening in your classroom right now, using present, present progressive, and present emphatic forms of verbs.

WRITING APPLICATION

Write a humorous short story, describing, in present tense, a fictional character's encounter with an alien from outerspace. Use the different forms of present-tense verbs in your short story.

Uses of Tense in Past Time

There are seven verb forms that express past actions or conditions.

> The seven forms that express **past tense** show actions and conditions that began at some time in the past.

FORMS EXPRESSING PAST TENSE	
Past	I teach .
Present Perfect	I have taught .
Past Perfect	I had taught .
Past Progressive	I was teaching .
Present Perfect Progressive	I have been teaching .
Past Perfect Progressive	I had been teaching .
Past Emphatic	I did teach .

The uses of the most common form, the past, are shown below.

USES OF THE PAST TENSE	
Completed Action	Barbara checked Lynn's grammar.
Completed Condition	Barbara was thorough in her review.

Notice in the chart above that the time of the action or the condition could be changed from indefinite to definite if such words as *last week* or *yesterday* were added to the sentences.

See Practice 17.2C

Present Perfect The **present perfect tense** always expresses indefinite time. Use it to show actions or conditions continuing from the past to the present.

USES OF THE PRESENT PERFECT TENSE	
Completed Action (Indefinite Time)	I have taken ballet lessons.
Completed Condition (Indefinite Time)	I have been in the ballet studio.
Action Continuing to Present	I have practiced for many hours.
Condition Continuing to Present	I have performed for others.

Past Perfect The **past perfect tense** expresses an action that took place before another action.

USES OF THE PAST PERFECT TENSE	
Action Completed Before Another Action	I had found a job with a veterinarian before the school year ended .
Condition Completed Before Another Condition	The job had been a great experience, and I was sad to leave.

These charts show the **past progressive** and **emphatic tenses.**

USES OF THE PROGRESSIVE TENSE TO EXPRESS PAST TIME	
Past Progressive	LONG CONTINUING ACTION Bob was going to run for office. SHORT CONTINUING ACTION He was talking to the current president. CONTINUOUS CONDITION He was being very proactive in his discussions.
Present Perfect Progressive	CONTINUING ACTION Bob has been working on his campaign for several weeks.
Past Perfect Progressive	CONTINUING ACTION INTERRUPTED He had been attending meetings, but he wanted to do more for the school.

USES OF THE PAST EMPHATIC TENSE	
Emphasizing a Statement	The test did seem easy when I first read it over.
Denying a Contrary Assertion	I didn't do as well as I'd hoped.
Asking a Question	Why did I feel so overconfident?
Making a Sentence Negative	He did not go out the night before the test.

See Practice 17.2D

PRACTICE 17.2C > **Identifying Tense in Past Time**

Read each sentence. Then, write the verb in each sentence that shows past time and identify the form of the tense.

EXAMPLE   After sleeping for hours, I had awoken to the sound of wind chimes.

ANSWER   *had awoken — past perfect*

1. All morning, the actor had been attempting to learn his lines.

2. I had finished the adventure novel in only fourteen hours!

3. The hesitant girl did ride the roller coaster.

4. We had been searching for the perfect pet.

5. Despite my attempts to stay organized, my homework vanished under a pile of papers.

6. The disappointed cheerleader has decided to try out for the gymnastics team.

7. We did not comprehend the importance of the occasion.

8. Todd had been surfing at the same beach since the age of sixteen.

9. The student was hoping for good grades and lots of college acceptance letters.

10. I stopped being concerned about what other people thought of my artwork.

PRACTICE 17.2D > **Supplying Verbs in Past Time**

Read each sentence. Then, rewrite each sentence and change the verb to the tense indicated in parentheses.

EXAMPLE   Before the storm, everyone *bought* canned goods. (past perfect)

ANSWER   *Before the storm, everyone had bought canned goods.*

11. Getting ready for college requires careful planning and preparation. (past emphatic)

12. The high school athletes receive the trophy, grinning all the while. (past progressive)

13. The dog climbed into the back seat of my car. (past perfect progressive)

14. By eight o'clock, everyone goes home. (past emphatic)

15. The students listen carefully to the two-hour lecture. (past perfect progressive)

16. After a long, difficult week, Karan groaned whenever she sat down. (past progressive)

17. The students work cooperatively. (past perfect progressive)

18. Joe lifts heavy weights every day. (past emphatic)

19. All day long, Pax gnaws on a bone. (past)

20. The corn pops loudly, attracting puzzled looks from the cat. (past perfect progressive)

SPEAKING APPLICATION

Take turns with a partner. Tell about a time you helped another person. Use verbs in at least four of the past tense forms. Your partner should listen for and identify the past-tense verbs.

WRITING APPLICATION

Write a paragraph about your most memorable birthday. Include at least four verbs in different forms of the past tense, and underline each past-tense verb.

Uses of Tense in Future Time

The **future tense** shows actions or conditions that will happen at a later date.

> **The future tense expresses actions or conditions that have not yet occurred.**

FORMS EXPRESSING FUTURE TENSE	
Future	I will work .
Future Perfect	I will have worked .
Future Progressive	I will be working .
Future Perfect Progressive	I will have been working .

USES OF THE FUTURE AND THE FUTURE PERFECT TENSE	
Future	I will paint with watercolors. I will work this afternoon.
Future Perfect	I will have painted every day this week. By the time of the art exhibition, I will have painted for two years.

Notice in the next chart that the **future progressive** and the **future perfect progressive tenses** express only future actions.

USES OF THE PROGRESSIVE TENSE TO EXPRESS FUTURE TIME	
Future Progressive	Ling will be gardening all weekend.
Future Perfect Progressive	By Monday, she will have been gardening for three days, and her knees will be sore.

The basic forms of the present and the present progressive tense are often used with other words to express future time.

EXAMPLES   My favorite band **plays** in town next month.

I **am going** to be in line for tickets.

See Practice 17.2E

See Practice 17.2F

PRACTICE 17.2E Identifying Tense in Future Time

Read each sentence. Then, write the future-tense verbs in each sentence and identify the form of the tense.

EXAMPLE Everyone will be hungry tonight.

ANSWER *will be* — future

1. The concert will be starting in a few minutes.
2. The clerk will have mailed your tickets by tomorrow.
3. In January, we will have been living in this house for seven years.
4. The committee will have made its decision by next week.
5. This time next month, we will have been collecting shells on a beach in Mexico all day.
6. A heavy rain will soak the area tonight.
7. The travel agent will make the reservations.
8. Thomas will be photographing the wedding.
9. The sun will rise in the east.
10. Caryn will be putting the baby to bed.

PRACTICE 17.2F Supplying Verbs in Future Time

Read each sentence. Then, rewrite each sentence, filling in the blank with the future tense of the verb indicated in parentheses.

EXAMPLE Those tight shoes _____ your feet later. (hurt, future)

ANSWER *Those tight shoes will hurt your feet later.*

11. I _____ all the seeds. (plant, future perfect)
12. I _____ disappointed if all my friends are away this summer. (be, future)
13. Ginger _____ from college next year. (graduate, future perfect)
14. I _____ to London for the weekend. (fly, future perfect)
15. By the time we stop, we _____ over thirteen hours. (travel, future perfect progressive)
16. The coach told us that we _____ this weekend. (practice, future progressive)
17. By tomorrow, I _____ all of the details. (memorize, future perfect)
18. My instructor _____ his lectures to be recorded. (allow, future progressive)
19. The new teacher _____ able to meet her students. (be, future perfect)
20. Someone _____ the package on the table. (leave, future)

SPEAKING APPLICATION

Take turns with a partner. Tell about your plans for the upcoming weekend. Use future-tense verbs in your sentences. Your partner should listen for and name the future-tense verbs that you use.

WRITING APPLICATION

Rewrite your corrections for sentences 13, 16, and 17, changing the verbs to include other future-tense verbs. Make sure your sentences still make sense.

Sequence of Tenses

A sentence with more than one verb must be consistent in its time sequence.

17.2.4

> When showing a sequence of events, do not shift tenses unnecessarily.

EXAMPLES   Jose **will run** track, and then he **will take** a shower.

Kima **has studied** for her test, and she **has finished** her research paper.

I **swam** and **surfed** in the ocean.

Sometimes, however, it is necessary to shift tenses, especially when a sentence is complex or compound-complex. The tense of the main verb often determines the tense of the verb in the subordinate clause. Moreover, the form of the participle or infinitive often depends on the tense of the verb in the main clause.

Verbs in Subordinate Clauses It is frequently necessary to look at the tense of the main verb in a sentence before choosing the tense of the verb in the subordinate clause.

17.2.5

> The tense of a verb in a subordinate clause should follow logically from the tense of the main verb.

INCORRECT   I **will know** that Dad **fixed** the car.

CORRECT   I **know** that Dad **fixed** the car.

As you study the combinations of tenses in the charts on the next pages, notice that the choice of tenses affects the logical relationship between the events being expressed. Some combinations indicate that the events are **simultaneous**—meaning that they occur at the same time. Other combinations indicate that the events are **sequential**—meaning that one event occurs before or after the other.

SEQUENCE OF EVENTS		
MAIN VERB	**SUBORDINATE VERB**	**MEANING**
MAIN VERB IN PRESENT TENSE		
I understand...	**PRESENT** that he drives a car. **PRESENT PROGRESSIVE** that he is driving a car. **PRESENT EMPHATIC** that he does drive a car.	Simultaneous events: All events occur in present time.
I understand...	**PAST** that he drove a car. **PRESENT PERFECT** that he has driven a car. **PAST PERFECT** that he had driven a car. **PAST PROGRESSIVE** that he was driving a car. **PRESENT PERFECT PROGRESSIVE** that he has been driving a car. **PAST PERFECT PROGRESSIVE** that he had been driving a car. **PAST EMPHATIC** that he did drive a car.	Sequential events: The driving comes before the understanding.
I understand...	**FUTURE** that he will drive a car. **FUTURE PERFECT** that he will have driven a car. **FUTURE PROGRESSIVE** that he will be driving a car. **FUTURE PERFECT PROGRESSIVE** that he will have been driving a car.	Sequential events: The understanding comes before the driving.

SEQUENCE OF EVENTS		
MAIN VERB	**SUBORDINATE VERB**	**MEANING**
MAIN VERB IN PAST TENSE		
I understood…	**PAST** that he drove a car. **PAST PROGRESSIVE** that he was driving a car. **PAST EMPHATIC** that he did drive a car.	Simultaneous events: All events take place in the past.
I understood…	**PAST PERFECT** that he had driven a car. **PAST PERFECT PROGRESSIVE** that he had been driving a car.	Sequential events: The driving came before the understanding.
MAIN VERB IN FUTURE TENSE		
I will understand…	**PRESENT** if he drives a car. **PRESENT PROGRESSIVE** if he is driving a car. **PRESENT EMPHATIC** if he does drive a car.	Simultaneous events: All events take place in future time.
I will understand…	**PAST** if he drove a car. **PRESENT PERFECT** if he has driven a car. **PRESENT PERFECT PROGRESSIVE** if he has been driving a car. **PAST EMPHATIC** if he did drive a car.	Sequential events: The driving comes before the understanding.

Time Sequence With Participles and Infinitives

Frequently, the form of a participle or infinitive determines whether the events are simultaneous or sequential. Participles can be present (*winning*), past (*won*), or perfect (*having won*). Infinitives can be present (*to win*) or perfect (*to have won*).

> **The form of a participle or an infinitive should logically relate to the verb in the same clause or sentence.**

To show simultaneous events, you will generally need to use the present participle or the present infinitive, whether the main verb is present, past, or future.

Simultaneous Events

IN PRESENT TIME	**Winning** the game, the team **celebrates**.
	present present
IN PAST TIME	**Winning** the game, the team **celebrated**.
	present past
IN FUTURE TIME	**Winning** the game, the team **will celebrate**.
	present future

To show sequential events, use the perfect form of the participle and infinitive, regardless of the tense of the main verb.

Sequential Events

IN PRESENT TIME	**Having won** the game, the team **is celebrating**.
	perfect present progressive
	(They won *before* they celebrated.)
IN PAST TIME	**Having won** the game, the team **celebrated**.
	perfect past
	(They won *before* they celebrated.)
SPANNING PAST AND FUTURE TIME	**Having won** the game, the team **will celebrate**.
	perfect future
	(They will celebrate *after* winning.)

See Practice 17.2G
See Practice 17.2H
See Practice 17.2I
See Practice 17.2J

PRACTICE 17.2G> **Identifying the Time Sequence in Sentences With More Than One Verb**

Read each sentence. Write the verb of the event that happens second in each sentence.

EXAMPLE   We will go to school after we have eaten breakfast.

ANSWER   *will go*

1. John feels that he did his job correctly.

2. The group wished that they had completed the project ahead of time.

3. I wrote a letter after I finished my homework.

4. Troy sat down and thought about his writing assignment.

5. After seeing John play basketball, the coach added him to the team.

6. When she heard what the plan was, she became excited.

7. When I woke up, I realized the solution.

8. Because we played with the friendly dog, he came back every afternoon.

9. You will see that you have chosen well.

10. I admired the mural that she had painted on the wall.

PRACTICE 17.2H> **Recognizing and Correcting Errors in Tense Sequence**

Read each sentence. Then, if a sentence has an error in tense sequence, rewrite it to correct the error. If a sentence is correct, write *correct*.

EXAMPLE   The squirrel stuffed the acorn into its mouth and scampers up the tree.

ANSWER   *The squirrel stuffed the acorn into its mouth and scampered up the tree.*

11. All of the students studied hard and learn the material.

12. Have you read the book and discuss it with the teacher?

13. The violinist listens carefully and imitated her instructor.

14. Last night, the wind blew hard and knocks down the fence.

15. Fernando wore his favorite jacket to the dance and enjoyed himself.

16. I took the rotten apple and throw it away.

17. Has she written and edit her paper yet?

18. Ice burst the pipes and floods the basement.

19. Have you seen and driven the model car?

20. I went to the mall to buy a shirt and ate Chinese food.

SPEAKING APPLICATION

Take turns with a partner. Tell about something fun that you like to do. Use two verbs in your sentences. Your partner should listen to and identify the sequence of events in your sentences.

WRITING APPLICATION

Use sentences 11, 14, and 18 as models to write your own sentences with incorrect tense sequence. Then, exchange papers with a partner. Your partner should rewrite your sentences, using the correct sequence in tense.

> **PRACTICE 17.2I** **Sequencing Tenses in Subordinate Clauses**

Read each sentence. Then, for each subordinate clause, fill in the blank with the correct tense of the verb specified in parentheses.

EXAMPLE   I see that she _____ the tango. (dance; present progressive)

ANSWER   *is dancing*

1. I hear that she _____ the science prize. (win; present perfect)

2. I figure that the car _____. (age; future)

3. I realize that the president _____. (speak; present progressive)

4. I understood that her feelings _____. (change; past progressive)

5. I realized that he _____ to the party. (walk; past perfect)

6. I will know if I _____ more supplies. (need; present)

7. I will know if she _____ my favorite sweater. (borrow; present perfect progressive)

8. I realize that he _____ to turn in his essay. (forget; present perfect)

9. I realize that they _____ all day. (travel; future perfect progressive)

10. I knew that he _____ at them. (look; past progressive)

> **PRACTICE 17.2J** **Sequencing Tenses in Main Clauses**

Read each sentence. Then, add a verb to finish the main clause attached to each phrase. Show whether events are simultaneous or sequential by putting the verb in the tense indicated in parentheses.

EXAMPLE   Finishing their lunch, they _____. (clean; past)

ANSWER   *Finishing their lunch, they **cleaned up their mess**.*

11. Setting the table, he _____. (sit; present)

12. Singing in the rain, she _____. (get; present progressive)

13. Having tiptoed up the stairs, he _____. (walk; present perfect)

14. Having sung at the top of their voices, they _____. (finish; past progressive)

15. Having laughed out loud, she _____. (tell; past perfect)

16. Waiting their turn, they _____. (stand; present progressive)

17. Wishing on a shooting star, I _____. (hope; past)

18. Listening to my sister snore, I _____. (sleep; future perfect)

19. Having reached their goals, they _____. (try; present progressive)

20. Having finished the project, she _____. (start; past perfect)

SPEAKING APPLICATION

Take turns with a partner. Say each sentence in Practice 17.2I. Have your partner identify the tense of the verb in each main clause.

WRITING APPLICATION

Write a brief paragraph about what you know about a sporting event. Use a variety of tenses to suggest sequence of events. Begin at least one sentence with a participial phrase.

Practice   449

Test Warm-Up

DIRECTIONS
Read the introduction and the passage that follows. Then, answer the questions to show that you can use and understand the function of sequence of tenses in reading and writing.

Mei wrote this paragraph about her cousin Regina. Read the paragraph and think about the changes you would suggest as a peer editor. When you finish reading, answer the questions that follow.

My Cousin's Thanksgiving Invitation

(1) Regina texts to invite me to Thanksgiving dinner, and I courteously declined. (2) She immediately wrote again to say that I could stay in her guest room. (3) I replied again that I already had accepted another invitation. (4) Then, she wrote, "But it would be so nice to have you." (5) Now I was annoyed. (6) She couldn't take rejection. (7) To end the conversation, I wrote, "Thanks, but I can't make it. Now I have to run." (8) Having gotten in the last word, she texted one more time. (9) She wrote, "I will understand if you changed your mind and show up at the last minute."

1 What change, if any, should be made in sentence 1?

 A Change *declined* to **will have declined**

 B Change *invite* to **invited**

 C Change *texts* to **texted**

 D Make no change

2 What change, if any, should be made in sentence 2?

 F Change *wrote* to **has written**

 G Change *say* to **said**

 H Change *stay* to **be staying**

 J Make no change

3 What change, if any, should be made in sentence 8?

 A Change *Having gotten* to **Getting**

 B Change *texted* to **texts**

 C Change *texted* to **is texting**

 D Make no change

4 What change, if any, should be made in sentence 9?

 F Change *wrote* to **has written**

 G Change *will understand* to **understood**

 H Change *changed* to **change**

 J Make no change

Modifiers That Help Clarify Tense

The time expressed by a verb can often be clarified by adverbs such as *often*, *sometimes*, *always*, or *frequently* and phrases such as *once in a while*, *within a week*, *last week*, or *now and then*.

> **Use modifiers when they can help clarify tense.**

17.2.7 RULE

In the examples below, the modifiers that help clarify the tense of the verb are highlighted in orange. Think about how the sentences would read without the modifiers. Modifiers help to make your writing more precise and interesting.

EXAMPLES Julia **works** **every afternoon** at the store.

She **rearranges** the sale racks **once a day**.

She **rearranges** the sale racks **now and then**.
(These two sentences have very different meanings.)

Occasionally, she **buys** something at the store.

She **always** **uses** her employee discount.

By next month, Julia **will have worked** at the store for two years.

Julia also **talks** to her friends **every night**.

Talking on the phone **is** **now** one of her favorite pastimes.

Sometimes, two friends **attempt** to call her at once.

She **always** **tries** not to keep them waiting too long.

See Practice 17.2K
See Practice 17.2L

PRACTICE 17.2K ▷ **Identifying Modifiers That Help Clarify Tense**

Read each sentence. Then, write the modifier in each sentence that helps clarify the verb tense.

EXAMPLE   My parents are going to Europe next week.

ANSWER   *next week*

1. Pamela has asked me to help her with her math homework tonight.

2. The Bearcats won the game yesterday.

3. My English class is always very interesting.

4. Occasionally, we receive a heavy downpour.

5. Sometimes, my father wakes up at 5:00 A.M.

6. Suddenly, the showers stopped and a rainbow appeared.

7. Last Thursday, we watched a film about Earth Day.

8. Each weekday, he works at the store after school.

9. Last summer, we did not receive much rain.

10. Mom seldom returns from her office before 6:00 P.M.

PRACTICE 17.2L ▷ **Supplying Modifiers to Clarify Meaning**

Read each sentence. Then, fill in the blank with a modifier that will clarify the meaning of each sentence.

EXAMPLE   Whitney _____ sings at parties.

ANSWER   *always*

11. _____, I will work at the garden supply store.

12. _____, we listened to my father tell a story.

13. _____, Tory walks five miles to the park.

14. The barred owl is _____ seen in the woods.

15. We will _____ meet the new principal.

16. I take piano lessons _____.

17. The tone of the drama class is _____ uplifting.

18. Mr. Roberts _____ lets everyone give his or her opinion.

19. We _____ eat healthy meals.

20. My mom _____ likes to invite our relatives to the house.

SPEAKING APPLICATION

Take turns with a partner. Tell each other about trips that you have taken. Use modifiers that help clarify tense in your sentences. Your partner should listen for and identify the modifiers in your sentences.

WRITING APPLICATION

Use your answers for sentences 11, 17, and 20 as models to write your own sentences. Rewrite the sentences to include different modifiers that clarify meaning.

17.3 The Subjunctive Mood

There are three **moods,** or ways in which a verb can express an action or condition: **indicative, imperative,** and **subjunctive.** The **indicative** mood, which is the most common, is used to make factual statements (*Karl is helpful.*) and to ask questions (*Is Karl helpful?*). The **imperative** mood is used to give orders or directions (*Be helpful.*).

Using the Subjunctive Mood

There are two important differences between verbs in the **subjunctive** mood and those in the indicative mood. First, in the present tense, third-person singular verbs in the subjunctive mood do not have the usual *-s* or *-es* ending. Second, the subjunctive mood of *be* in the present tense is *be*; in the past tense, it is *were*, regardless of the subject.

INDICATIVE MOOD	SUBJUNCTIVE MOOD
I want to be sure that she drives slowly.	I suggest that she drive slowly.
She is not punctual.	I insist that she be punctual.
I was angry that she was late.	If she were late, I'd be angry.

> Use the subjunctive mood (1) in clauses beginning with *if* or *that* to express an idea that is contrary to fact or (2) in clauses beginning with *that* to express a request, a demand, or a proposal.

17.3.1 RULE

Expressing Ideas Contrary to Fact Ideas that are contrary to fact are commonly expressed as wishes or conditions. Using the subjunctive mood in these situations shows that the idea expressed is not true now and may never be true.

EXAMPLES
Tracy wishes that she **were** better at piano.

She wishes that her fingers **were** more agile.

She could have performed in the recital if she **were** a better pianist.

Some *if* clauses do not take a subjunctive verb. If the idea expressed may be true, an indicative form is used.

EXAMPLES   I told my mom that **if** I **was** finished with my homework, I'd go shopping with her.

If we **are** to avoid the crowds, we should go now.

Expressing Requests, Demands, and Proposals Verbs that request, demand, or propose are often followed by a *that* clause containing a verb in the subjunctive mood.

REQUEST   We request that people **be** silent during the show.

DEMAND   It is required that people **be** silent during the show.

PROPOSAL   He proposed that people **be** silent during the show. See Practice 17.3A

Auxiliary Verbs That Express the Subjunctive Mood

Because certain helping verbs suggest conditions contrary to fact, they can often be used in place of the subjunctive mood.

RULE
17.3.3

Could, would, or *should* can be used with a verb to express the subjunctive mood.

The sentences on the left in the chart below have the usual subjunctive form of the verb *be: were.* The sentences on the right have been reworded with *could, would,* and *should.*

THE SUBJUNCTIVE MOOD WITH AUXILIARY VERBS	
WITH FORMS OF *BE*	**WITH *COULD, WOULD,* OR *SHOULD***
If the car **were** working, I'd drive.	If the car **would** work, I'd drive.
If I **were** to learn to drive, I'd go anywhere.	If I **would** learn to drive, I'd go anywhere.
If you **were** to learn to drive, could I ride with you?	If you **should** learn to drive, could I ride with you?

See Practice 17.3B

PRACTICE 17.3A **Identifying Mood (Indicative, Imperative, Subjunctive)**

Read each sentence. Then, identify whether each sentence expresses the *indicative, imperative,* or *subjunctive* mood.

EXAMPLE   I wish that today were Friday.

ANSWER   *subjunctive*

1. If I were an actor, I'd like to work on Broadway.

2. Walk the dog right now.

3. They requested that the flowers be delivered.

4. I demand that the package be ready by noon.

5. The caterers arrived just in time.

6. Turn over the pancakes so they don't burn.

7. If you were to help me, I would finish sooner.

8. Did Carol volunteer at the rummage sale all day?

9. If you were to open the windows, the paint would dry faster.

10. I wish that I were going with you.

PRACTICE 17.3B **Supplying Auxiliary Verbs to Express the Subjunctive Mood**

Read each sentence. Then, rewrite each sentence and complete it by supplying an auxiliary verb to express the subjunctive mood.

EXAMPLE   If I were in your place, I _____ be so happy.

ANSWER   *If I were in your place, I would be so happy.*

11. If I were stronger, I _____ lift heavier objects.

12. If you _____ leave, I _____ be sad.

13. If I were an inch taller, I _____ be the same height as my father.

14. The house _____ be cooler if you were to turn off the oven.

15. If you were to go to San Antonio, what _____ you see?

16. If I were at home, I _____ make a roast for dinner tonight.

17. We _____ not be so rushed if the deadline were extended.

18. If I could learn to throw a curve ball, I _____ be a better pitcher.

19. This meeting _____ run more smoothly if they weren't so many interruptions.

20. If I _____ get home earlier, I _____ exercise more often.

SPEAKING APPLICATION

Take turns with a partner. Say sentences that express the indicative, imperative, and subjunctive moods. Your partner should listen for and identify which mood each of your sentences expresses.

WRITING APPLICATION

Use the auxiliary verbs that you used to rewrite sentences 15, 16, and 17 to write sentences of your own. Be sure that your sentences still express the subjunctive mood.

17.4 Voice

This section discusses a characteristic of verbs called **voice**.

RULE 17.4.1

> **Voice or tense is the form of a verb that shows whether the subject is performing the action or is being acted upon.**

In English, there are two voices: **active** and **passive.** Only action verbs can indicate voice; linking verbs cannot.

Active and Passive Voice or Tense

If the subject of a verb performs the action, the verb is active; if the subject receives the action, the verb is passive.

Active Voice Any action verb can be used in the active voice. The action verb may be transitive (that is, it may have a direct object) or intransitive (without a direct object).

RULE 17.4.2

> **A verb is active if its subject performs the action.**

In the examples below, the subject performs the action. In the first example, the verb *telephoned* is transitive; *team* is the direct object, which receives the action. In the second example, the verb *developed* is transitive; *pictures* is the direct object. In the third example, the verb *gathered* is intransitive; it has no direct object. In the last example, the verb *worked* is intransitive and has no direct object.

ACTIVE VOICE

The captain **telephoned** the **team**.
transitive verb / direct object

Bill **developed** twenty-five **pictures** of the ocean.
transitive verb / direct object

Telephone messages **gathered** on the desk while she was away.
intransitive verb

Bill **worked** quickly.
intransitive verb

See Practice 17.4A
See Practice 17.4B

Passive Voice Most action verbs can also be used in the passive voice.

> **A verb is passive if its action is performed upon the subject.**

In the following examples, the subjects are the receivers of the action. The first example names the performer, the captain, as the object of the preposition *by* instead of the subject. In the second example, no performer of the action is mentioned.

PASSIVE
VOICE
The **team** **was telephoned** by the captain.
receiver of action   verb

The **messages** **were gathered** into neat piles.
receiver of action   verb

> **A passive verb is always a verb phrase made from a form of *be* plus the past participle of a verb. The tense of the helping verb *be* determines the tense of the passive verb.**

The chart below provides a conjugation in the passive voice of the verb *affect* in the three moods. Notice that there are only two progressive forms and no emphatic form.

THE VERB *AFFECT* IN THE PASSIVE VOICE	
Present Indicative	He is affected.
Past Indicative	He was affected.
Future Indicative	He will be affected.
Present Perfect Indicative	He has been affected.
Past Perfect Indicative	He had been affected.
Future Perfect Indicative	He will have been affected.
Present Progressive Indicative	He is being affected.
Past Progressive Indicative	He was being affected.
Present Imperative	(You) be affected.
Present Subjunctive	(if) he be affected
Past Subjunctive	(if) he were affected

See Practice 17.2C

Using Active and Passive Voice

Writing that uses the active voice tends to be much more lively than writing that uses the passive voice. The active voice is usually more direct and economical. That is because active voice shows someone doing something.

RULE 17.4.5

> **Use the active voice whenever possible.**

| ACTIVE VOICE | Melissa **created** a clay sculpture. |
| PASSIVE VOICE | A clay sculpture **was created** by Melissa. |

The passive voice has two uses in English.

RULE 17.4.6

> **Use the passive voice when you want to emphasize the receiver of an action rather than the performer of an action.**

EXAMPLE   Andrew **was given** the highest grades by the gymnastics judges.

RULE 17.4.7

> **Use the passive voice to point out the receiver of an action whenever the performer is not important or not easily identified.**

EXAMPLE   The T-shirts in the store **were marked** down, so we bought three.

The active voice lends more excitement to writing, making it more interesting to readers. In the example below, notice how the sentence you just read has been revised to show someone doing something, rather than something just happening.

EXAMPLE   The store manager **marked** down the T-shirts, so we bought three.
(*Who* marked down the shirts so that we could buy three?)

See Practice 17.4D

PRACTICE 17.4A > **Recognizing Active Voice (Active Tense)**

Read each sentence. Write the active verb(s) in each sentence and identify them as *transitive* or *intransitive*.

EXAMPLE   The early frost damaged and ruined the crops.

ANSWER   *damaged*— transitive
ruined— transitive

1. The new law protects consumers.

2. Shelly agreed to edit and rewrite the last part of the play.

3. The heavy wind blew down several trees.

4. Everyone enjoyed the festival.

5. The delivery truck comes once a week.

6. Fry the eggs on both sides.

7. Maddie tilled the soil and planted the seeds in the ground.

8. The soldiers prepared themselves for any kind of situation.

9. They ate dinner and discussed their mutual interests.

10. We called Alana and asked her to be a part of our group.

PRACTICE 17.4B > **Using Active Verbs**

Read each item. Then, write different sentences, using the items as active verbs.

EXAMPLE   created, gave

ANSWER   *Bill created a fictional character and gave it a funny name.*

11. delivered, signed

12. writes, erases

13. slept, woke

14. answered, wept

15. opened, flew

16. laugh, cry

17. bought, sold

18. winks, waves

19. toured, sang

20. adores, spoils

SPEAKING APPLICATION

Take turns with a partner. Say sentences in the active voice. Your partner will listen to and identify the active verbs in each of your sentences.

WRITING APPLICATION

Write a short paragraph about your dream vacation. Use active verbs in your description.

PRACTICE 17.4C Forming the Tenses of Passive Verbs

Read each verb. Then, using the subject indicated in parentheses, conjugate each verb in the passive voice for the present indicative, past indicative, future indicative, present perfect indicative, past perfect indicative, and future perfect indicative.

EXAMPLE   reword (it)

ANSWER   *it is reworded, it was reworded, it will be reworded, it has been reworded, it had been reworded, it will have been reworded*

1. borrow (it)

2. promise (I)

3. ask (she)

4. earn (it)

5. maintain (we)

6. lift (he)

7. follow (she)

8. buy (it)

9. tell (she)

10. carry (it)

PRACTICE 17.4D Supplying Verbs in the Active Voice

Read each sentence. Then, complete each sentence by suppling a verb in the active voice.

EXAMPLE   Politics _____ the conversation all evening.

ANSWER   *dominated*

11. Guests from several nations _____ freely at the reception.

12. Charlotte _____ the numerous compliments.

13. They _____ the winning essay today.

14. These pants _____ two sizes in the dryer.

15. The wind _____ waves across the water.

16. Preston _____ new flowers in his garden.

17. Olivia _____ her bike for the first time today.

18. I _____ the towels and swimsuits to take to the beach.

19. The dog _____ his tail back and forth.

20. The committee _____ to adjourn for the evening.

SPEAKING APPLICATION

Take turns with a partner. Say six verbs. Your partner should say the basic forms of each verb in the passive voice.

WRITING APPLICATION

Choose three of your corrected sentences for Practice 17.4D and rewrite each of them to show the passive voice.

CHAPTER 18

PRONOUN USAGE

Use each case of pronoun correctly to help create a smooth flow and rhythm in your writing.

WRITE GUY *Jeff Anderson, M.Ed.*

WHAT DO YOU NOTICE?

Discover pronouns as you zoom in on lines from the poem "Lines Composed a Few Miles Above Tintern Abbey" by William Wordsworth.

MENTOR TEXT

> . . . And I have felt
> A presence that disturbs me with the joy
> Of elevated thoughts; a sense sublime
> Of something far more deeply interfused,
> Whose dwelling is the light of setting suns . . .

Now, ask yourself the following questions:

- Which two forms of the first-person pronoun *I* are used in this verse?
- Why does the poet use the word *whose* in the final line?

The poet uses the nominative form *I* in the opening words *I have felt* because it performs the action of the verb. He uses the objective case *me* in the next line because *me* is the object of the verb *disturbs*. The poet uses *whose*—the possessive form of the pronoun *who*—to show ownership of the noun *dwelling*.

Grammar for Writers Look for commonly misspelled pronouns when you edit your writing. For example, the possessive pronoun *whose* is sometimes confused with the contraction *who's*, which is the shortened form of the words *who is* or *who has*.

Is that your nominative or possessive case?

My mom is on my case again.

461

18.1 Case

Nouns and pronouns are the only parts of speech that have **case**.

RULE **18.1.1**

Case is the form of a noun or a pronoun that shows how it is used in a sentence.

The Three Cases

Nouns and pronouns have three cases, each of which has its own distinctive uses.

RULE **18.1.2**

The three cases of nouns and pronouns are the nominative, the objective, and the possessive.

CASE	USE IN SENTENCE
Nominative	As the Subject of a Verb, Predicate Nominative, or Nominative Absolute
Objective	As the Direct Object, Indirect Object, Object of a Preposition, Object of a Verbal, or Subject of an Infinitive
Possessive	To Show Ownership

Case in Nouns
The case, or form, of a noun changes only to show possession.

NOMINATIVE   The **key** had been hidden for weeks.

(*Key* is the subject of the verb *had been hidden*.)

OBJECTIVE   We tried to find the **key**.
(*Key* is the object of the infinitive *to find*.)

POSSESSIVE   The **key's** location could not be determined.
(The form changes when 's is added to show possession.)

Case in Pronouns

Personal pronouns often have different forms for all three cases. The pronoun that you use depends on its function in a sentence.

NOMINATIVE	OBJECTIVE	POSSESSIVE
I	*me*	*my, mine*
you	*you*	*your, yours*
he, she, it	*him, her, it*	*his, her, hers, its*
we, they	*us, them*	*our, ours*
		their, theirs

EXAMPLES   **I** read the magazines about cars.

Martha sent the tickets to **me**.

The magazine about cars is **mine**.

See Practice 18.1A

The Nominative Case in Pronouns

The **nominative case** is used when a personal pronoun acts in one of three ways.

> Use the **nominative case** when a pronoun is the subject of a verb, a predicate nominative, or part of a nominative absolute.

18.1.3 | RULE

A **nominative absolute** consists of a noun or nominative pronoun followed by a participial phrase. It functions independently from the rest of the sentence.

EXAMPLE   **We having opened our history books,** our

teacher assigned us to read about the Civil War

and its outcome.

NOMINATIVE PRONOUNS	
As the Subject of a Verb	I will consult the book while she looks up the author.
As a Predicate Nominative	The owners were she and he.
In a Nominative Absolute	We having finished the soup, the server cleared and washed the dishes.

Nominative Pronouns in Compounds

When you use a pronoun in a compound subject or predicate nominative, check the case either by mentally crossing out the other part of the compound or by inverting the sentence.

COMPOUND
SUBJECT

The pilot and **I** inspected the flight plan.

(**I** inspected the flight plan.)

She and her sister swam in the pool.

(**She** swam in the pool.)

COMPOUND
PREDICATE
NOMINATIVE

The fastest swimmers were Dan and **he**.

(Dan and **he** were the fastest swimmers.)

The supervisors were Rae and **I**.

(Rae and **I** were the supervisors.)

Nominative Pronouns With Appositives

When an appositive follows a pronoun that is being used as a subject or predicate nominative, the pronoun should stay in the nominative case. To check that you have used the correct case, either mentally cross out the appositive or isolate the subject and verb.

SUBJECT

We coaches use clipboards.

(**We** use clipboards.)

PREDICATE
NOMINATIVE

The supervisors were **we** seniors.

(**We** were the supervisors.)

APPOSITIVE
AFTER NOUN

The team racers, **he** and **I**, won the trophy cup.

(**He** and **I** won the trophy cup.)

See Practice 18.1B

PRACTICE 18.1A **Identifying Case**

Read each sentence. Then, label the underlined pronoun *nominative*, *objective*, or *possessive*.

EXAMPLE   The dappled horse is <u>ours</u>.

ANSWER   *possessive*

1. Did she buy this sweater or did she knit <u>it</u>?

2. The train let <u>its</u> passengers off at Union Station.

3. <u>She</u> followed the directions on the back of the box.

4. Can <u>you</u> tell me which helmet is for sale?

5. Carlos bought <u>her</u> a necklace for graduation.

6. <u>We</u> promise not to let you down!

7. The investment made <u>them</u> a lot of money.

8. Are <u>you</u> the winner of the contest?

9. According to the law, the house should be <u>hers</u>.

10. The woman in the photograph is <u>she</u>.

PRACTICE 18.1B **Supplying Pronouns in the Nominative Case**

Read each sentence. Then, supply the correct pronoun from the choices in parentheses to complete each sentence.

EXAMPLE   When Lena left the store, (she, her) forgot her keys.

ANSWER   *she*

11. It was (he, him) whom the director chose.

12. Both my brother and (me, I) plan to go to the graduation ceremony.

13. My aunt and (she, her) used the same recipe.

14. (Them, They) are panning for gold in California.

15. The man sitting on the bench is (he, him).

16. (She, her) was eager to get the voyage underway.

17. Keisha and (her, she) finished before anyone else.

18. (Us, We) began to wonder if the scent was coming from the garden.

19. As Jason sat waiting in the lobby, (him, he) became more calm.

20. The losers of the tournament were (they, them).

SPEAKING APPLICATION

Take turns with a partner. Tell about a television show you saw recently. Your partner should listen for pronouns in your sentences and tell whether each one is possessive, nominative, or objective.

WRITING APPLICATION

Write a paragraph about a trip that you have taken. Underline all pronouns in the nominative case in your paragraph.

The Objective Case

Objective pronouns are used for any kind of object in a sentence as well as for the subject of an infinitive.

RULE 18.1.4

> Use the **objective case** for the object of any verb, preposition, or verbal or for the subject of an infinitive.

OBJECTIVE PRONOUNS	
Direct Object	The hockey puck hit him in the jaw.
Indirect Object	My sister sent me many beautiful pictures from Israel.
Object of Preposition	The coach stood in front of us on the new soccer field.
Object of Participle	The basketball coach addressing them seemed aggravated.
Object of Gerund	Confronting them at the party will make a big scene.
Object of Infinitive	I am required to meet her at the airport.
Subject of Infinitive	The teacher wanted her to stay after class.

Objective Pronouns in Compounds

As with the nominative case, errors with objective pronouns most often occur in compounds. To find the correct case, mentally cross out the other part of the compound.

EXAMPLES
The loud sirens alarmed Bill and **her**.
(The loud sirens alarmed **her**.)

Laura painted Alex and **me** a picture of my house.
(Laura painted **me** a picture of my house.)

Note About *Between*: Be sure to use the objective case after the preposition *between*.

INCORRECT   This password is between you and **I**.

CORRECT   This password is between you and **me**.

Objective Pronouns With Appositives

Use the objective case when a pronoun that is used as an object or as the subject of an infinitive is followed by an appositive.

EXAMPLES

The contest recipe intimidated **us** bakers.

My uncle brought **us** nieces rabbits.

The captain asked **us** troops to march forward.

See Practice 18.1C

The Possessive Case

One use for the **possessive case** is before gerunds. A **gerund** is a verbal form ending in *-ing* that is used as a noun.

> **Use the possessive case before gerunds.**

18.1.5 RULE

EXAMPLES

Your storytelling was very exciting.

We considered **his** storytelling to be exciting and fun.

Ryan consents to **our** attending the meeting.

Common Errors in the Possessive Case

Be sure not to use an apostrophe with a possessive pronoun because possessives already show ownership. Spellings such as *her's*, *our's*, *their's*, and *your's* are incorrect.

In addition, be sure not to confuse possessive pronouns and contractions that sound alike. *It's* (with an apostrophe) is the contraction for *it is* or *it has*. *Its* (without the apostrophe) is a possessive pronoun that means "belonging to it." *You're* is a contraction of *you are*; the possessive form of *you* is *your*.

POSSESSIVE PRONOUNS

The garden has served **its** purpose.

Don't forget **your** flowers.

CONTRACTIONS

It's likely we will see you again.

You're the only senior in your group this afternoon.

See Practice 18.1D
See Practice 18.1E
See Practice 18.1F

Find It/ FIX IT

14

Grammar
Game Plan

PRACTICE 18.1C > **Supplying Pronouns in the Objective Case**

Read each sentence. Then, write the correct pronoun from the choices in parentheses to complete each sentence.

EXAMPLE   Please ask (him, he) to join us for dinner.

ANSWER   *him*

1. We bought Rhiannon and (she, her) some potted flowers.
2. The soldier ordered (he, him) to stand at attention.
3. The incident was between Neil and (her, she).
4. Please tell (us, we) another joke.
5. We ordered (he, him) a new pair of boots.
6. I have to choose between (they, them).
7. The teacher asked Julie and (she, her) to comment on the essay.
8. Will you allow George and (he, him) to revise their essays?
9. My father gave (I, me) a ring that belonged to my grandmother.
10. Have you asked (her, she) to show you how to use the computer program?

PRACTICE 18.1D > **Recognizing Pronouns in the Possessive Case**

Read each sentence. Then, write the correct pronoun from the choices in parentheses to complete each sentence.

EXAMPLE   Everyone agreed with (us, our) inviting them to the dance.

ANSWER   *our*

11. Mom agreed to (their, they) painting the fence.
12. The deed proved that the house was (his, him).
13. (They, Their) treehouse is six feet off the ground.
14. My sister was happy about (my, me) learning to swim.
15. We thought (she, her) story was the best.
16. (His, Him) being so happy was due to the puppy in the yard.
17. (Us, Our) whistling caused several birds to respond.
18. The colorful garden with the orange lilies is (my, mine).
19. (Their, they) request has been fulfilled.
20. I appreciate you for always bringing (you, your) camera to the games.

SPEAKING APPLICATION

Take turns with a partner. Tell about an upcoming school event. Use three or more objective pronouns in your description. Your partner should listen for and identify each objective pronoun that you use.

WRITING APPLICATION

Write four sentences using the following possessive pronouns: *your, our, my,* and *her.*

PRACTICE 18.1E > **Supplying Pronouns in the Correct Case**

Read each sentence. Then, write a pronoun in the correct case to complete each sentence. More than one pronoun may be correct.

EXAMPLE   I brought my notebook; where's _____? (your's, yours)

ANSWER   *yours*

1. Many passengers got on the train at _____ starting point, Grand Central (it's, its).

2. She answered the question "Who's there?" with "It's _____, Sara." (I, me)

3. This confidential material is just for _____. (he, him)

4. _____ singing gives me a headache. (He, His)

5. Of all the entries, _____ deserves to win; it's the biggest tomato. (our's, ours)

6. The crowd pushed in front of _____ when the store opened. (we, us)

7. It was sunny the day _____ went to the baseball game. (we, us)

8. Having finished the test, the teacher let _____ leave. (us, we)

9. It is _____ who is the main character in the novel. (he, him)

10. Did you send the package to _____ yet? (she, her)

PRACTICE 18.1F > **Selecting the Correct Pronoun**

Read each sentence. Then, write the pronoun from the choices in parentheses that correctly completes the sentence.

EXAMPLE   Hannah was his first grandchild; now his grandchildren are (her, she) and Alex.

ANSWER   *she*

11. Roger and (I, me) submitted a joint science project.

12. The judges gave Roger and (I, me) second place.

13. We get a lot of ideas from (they, them).

14. After the race, we wanted the winners, (he and she, him and her), to rest.

15. The winners, who were (he and she, him and her), set records.

16. We wanted (them, they) to stay as our house guests.

17. Are you impressed or puzzled by (him, his) weight lifting?

18. The air conditioner annoys me; (its, it's) humming never stops.

19. How many chances are you going to give to Debbie and (she, her)?

20. I like all the drawings, but (yours, your's) are my favorite.

SPEAKING APPLICATION

With a partner, take turns choosing a set of pronouns—for example, *I, me, my, mine* or *she, her, her, hers*—and using them to speak about musicians. Your partner should listen for each pronoun and decide if it is used correctly.

WRITING APPLICATION

Write a brief paragraph about an actor—what you like about him or her and what you don't like. Use each of the masculine pronouns *he, him,* and *his* or each of the feminine pronouns *she, her,* and *hers* at least once.

Practice   469

Test Warm-Up

DIRECTIONS
Read the introduction and the passage that follows. Then, answer the questions to show that you can use and understand the function of pronoun case in reading and writing.

Amiri wrote this paragraph about a presentation on nutrition. Read the paragraph and think about the changes you would suggest as a peer editor. When you finish reading, answer the questions that follow.

Learning Nutrition Facts

(1) A nutritionist spoke at our school, presenting important information to we students. (2) Her and her assistant reviewed the six nutrients that we humans need: proteins, carbohydrates, fats, vitamins, minerals, and water. (3) Clearly, the nutritionist wanted the others and I to make more informed choices, not only in the kinds of foods we eat but also in portion size. (4) She handed out a chart titled "How Long Does It Take to Burn Off Calories?" (5) I'll need some time to absorb all of it's data.

---

1 What change, if any, should be made in sentence 1?

A Change *our* to **ours**

B Change *we* to **them**

C Change *we* to **us**

D Make no change

2 What change, if any, should be made in sentence 2?

F Change *Her and her assistant* to **She and her assistant**

G Change *her assistant* to **hers assistant**

H Change *we humans* to **us humans**

J Make no change

3 What change, if any, should be made in sentence 3?

A Change *the others* to **they**

B Change *I* to **me**

C Change *we* to **us**

D Make no change

4 What change, if any, should be made in sentence 5?

F Change *it's* to **my**

G Delete *it's*

H Change *it's* to **its**

J Make no change

18.2 Special Problems With Pronouns

Choosing the correct case is not always a matter of choosing the form that "sounds correct," because writing is usually more formal than speech. For example, it would be incorrect to say, "John is smarter than *me*" because the verb is understood in the sentence: "John is smarter than *I [am].*"

Using *Who* and *Whom* Correctly

In order to decide when to use *who* or *whom* and the related forms *whoever* and *whomever*, you need to know how the pronoun is used in a sentence and what case is appropriate.

Who is used for the nominative case. **Whom** is used for the objective case.

18.2.1 RULE

CASE	PRONOUNS	USE IN SENTENCES
Nominative	*who* *whoever*	As the Subject of a Verb or Predicate Nominative
Objective	*whom* *whomever*	As the Direct Object, Object of a Verbal, Object of a Preposition, or Subject of an Infinitive
Possessive	*whose* *whosever*	To Show Ownership

EXAMPLES   I know **who** cooked that lasagna.

Kate took **whoever** was off for vacation to the beach.

Ken did not know **whom** the teacher chose.

Whose car is sitting in the driveway?

The nominative and objective cases are the source of certain problems. Pronoun problems can appear in two kinds of sentences: direct questions and complex sentences.

In Direct Questions

Who is the correct form when the pronoun is the subject of a simple question. *Whom* is the correct form when the pronoun is the direct object, object of a verbal, or object of a preposition.

Questions in subject–verb word order always begin with *who*. However, questions in inverted order never correctly begin with *who*. To see if you should use *who* or *whom*, reword the question as a statement in subject–verb word order.

EXAMPLES   **Who** wants to go to the skateboard park?

                    Whom did you go with yesterday?

                    (You did go with whom yesterday.)

In Complex Sentences

Follow these steps to see if the case of a pronoun in a subordinate clause is correct. First, find the subordinate clause. If the complex sentence is a question, rearrange it in subject–verb order. Second, if the subordinate clause is inverted, rearrange the words in subject–verb word order. Finally, determine how the pronoun is used in the subordinate clause.

EXAMPLE   **Who ,** may I ask, has read the play?

REARRANGED   I may ask **who** has read the play.

USE OF PRONOUN   (subject of the verb *has read*)

EXAMPLE   Alicia is the one **whom** they chose to speak.

REARRANGED   They chose **whom** to speak.

USE OF PRONOUN   (object of the verb *chose*)

Note About Whose: The word *whose* is a possessive pronoun; the contraction *who's* means "who is" or "who has."

POSSESSIVE PRONOUN   **Whose** book is this?

CONTRACTION   **Who's** [who has] taken my book?

See Practice 18.2A

Pronouns in Elliptical Clauses

An **elliptical clause** is one in which some words are omitted but still understood. Errors in pronoun usage can easily be made when an elliptical clause that begins with *than* or *as* is used to make a comparison.

> In **elliptical clauses** beginning with *than* or *as*, use the form of the pronoun that you would use if the clause were fully stated.

18.2.2 RULE

The case of the pronoun is determined by whether the omitted words fall before or after the pronoun. The omitted words in the examples below are shown in brackets.

WORDS OMITTED BEFORE PRONOUN

You made more for Brent than **me**.

(You made more for Brent than for [you made] **me**.)

WORDS OMITTED AFTER PRONOUN

Blake is as determined as **he**.

(Blake is as determined as **he** [is].)

Mentally add the missing words. If they come *before* the pronoun, choose the objective case. If they come *after* the pronoun, choose the nominative case.

CHOOSING A PRONOUN IN ELLIPTICAL CLAUSES
1. Consider the choices of pronouns: nominative or objective.
2. Mentally complete the elliptical clause.
3. Base your choice on what you find.

The case of the pronoun can sometimes change the entire meaning of the sentence.

NOMINATIVE PRONOUN

He liked jogging more than **I**.

He liked jogging more than **I** [did].

OBJECTIVE PRONOUN

He liked jogging more than **me**.

He liked jogging more than [he liked] **me**.

See Practice 18.2B

PRACTICE 18.2A > Choosing *Who* or *Whom* Correctly

Read each sentence. Then, write *who* or *whom* to complete each sentence.

EXAMPLE (Who, Whom) did she think would be here?

ANSWER *Who*

1. (Who, Whom) did the teacher choose to be the school representative?

2. Meghan chose the person (who, whom) she believed was best qualified for the job.

3. From (who, whom) were you expecting a call?

4. Marshall was the person (who, whom) called early this morning.

5. (Who, Whom) was the last person chosen?

6. To (who, whom) should I address my letter?

7. (Who, Whom) did they trust with their important documents?

8. That man is the one (who, whom) received the award.

9. With (who, whom) did you travel to Venice?

10. Jorge is the student (whom, who) can best play the part of Romeo.

PRACTICE 18.2B > Identifying the Correct Pronoun in Elliptical Clauses

Read each sentence. Then, complete each elliptical clause by choosing the correct pronoun in parentheses and adding the missing words in brackets.

EXAMPLE Kendra tried as hard as (she, her) could.

ANSWER *Kendra tried as hard as she could [try].*

11. Due to her insightful remarks, Carly impressed Rosa as much as (we, us).

12. This year, Henry sank more foul shots than (he, him).

13. More praise was given to my sister than (I, me).

14. Petra has a newer car than (he, him).

15. She was as close to the exit as (I, me).

16. I have trained as hard as (they, them).

17. My brother is a better drummer than (I, me).

18. More work was given to me than (her, she).

19. You are better prepared than (she, her).

20. During the tryouts, more catches were made by Wai than (he, him).

SPEAKING APPLICATION

Take turns with a partner. Tell the name of a favorite book. Then, have your partner ask questions, using the pronouns *who* and *whom*, to obtain information about the book's characters.

WRITING APPLICATION

Write six comparisons using correct pronouns in elliptical phrases, and add the missing words in brackets.

CHAPTER 19

AGREEMENT

Recognizing the importance of subject-verb and pronoun-antecedent agreement will help you craft clear sentences.

WRITE GUY *Jeff Anderson, M.Ed.*

WHAT DO YOU NOTICE?

Find evidence of agreement as you zoom in on this sentence from the introduction to *Frankenstein* by Mary Wollstonecraft Shelley.

MENTOR TEXT

> At first we spent our pleasant hours on the lake or wandering on its shores; and Lord Byron, who was writing the third canto of *Childe Harold,* was the only one among us who put his thoughts upon paper.

Now, ask yourself the following questions:

- Why does the author use the singular verb *was*?
- What is the antecedent of the pronoun *his*?

The verb *was* in the second main clause is singular because the subject is one person—Lord Byron. The author uses *was* in the interrupting adjective clause because its subject, *who*, refers to one person, Lord Byron. The singular, masculine noun *Lord Byron* is the antecedent of the singular, masculine pronoun *his*, so they agree in number and gender.

Grammar for Writers Writers often use multiple clauses or phrases to craft complex sentences. When you write complex sentences, determine the subject and make sure the predicate and any pronouns that follow agree in number and gender.

Do your subjects and predicates always agree?

I don't know. I'll have to ask them.

19.1 Subject–Verb Agreement

For a subject and a verb to agree, both must be singular, or both must be plural. In this section, you will learn how to make sure singular and plural subjects and verbs agree.

WRITING COACH

Online

www.phwritingcoach.com

Grammar Tutorials
Brush up on your Grammar skills with these animated videos.

Grammar Practice
Practice your grammar skills with Writing Coach Online.

Grammar Games
Test your knowledge of grammar in this fast-paced interactive video game.

Number in Nouns, Pronouns, and Verbs

In grammar, **number** indicates whether a word is singular or plural. Only three parts of speech have different forms that indicate number: nouns, pronouns, and verbs.

RULE 19.1.1

> **Number** shows whether a noun, pronoun, or verb is singular or plural.

Recognizing the number of most nouns is seldom a problem because most form their plurals by adding -s or -es. Some, such as *mouse* or *ox*, form their plurals irregularly: *mice, oxen*.

Pronouns, however, have different forms to indicate their number. The chart below shows the different forms of personal pronouns in the nominative case, the case that is used for subjects.

PERSONAL PRONOUNS		
SINGULAR	PLURAL	SINGULAR OR PLURAL
I	*we*	*you*
he, she, it	*they*	

The grammatical number of verbs is sometimes difficult to determine. That is because the form of many verbs can be either singular or plural, and they may form plurals in different ways.

SINGULAR   He **helps**.

He **has helped**.

PLURAL   We **help**.

We **have helped**.

Some verb forms can be only singular. The personal pronouns *he*, *she*, and *it* and all singular nouns call for singular verbs in the present and the present perfect tense.

ALWAYS SINGULAR

She **speaks**.

She **has spoken**.

Allie **speaks**.

Kurt **has spoken**.

She **sees**.

She **has seen**.

The verb *be* in the present tense has special forms to agree with singular subjects. The pronoun *I* has its own singular form of *be*; so do *he*, *she*, *it*, and singular nouns.

ALWAYS SINGULAR

I **am** seventeen.

She **is** beautiful.

Ricky **is** home.

She **is** healthy.

All singular subjects except *you* share the same past tense verb form of *be*.

ALWAYS SINGULAR

I **was** going on vacation.

He **was** company chairman.

Laura **was** early to class.

He **was** getting into the cab.

See Practice 19.1A

A verb form will always be singular if it has had an *-s* or *-es* added to it or if it includes the words *has*, *am*, *is*, or *was*. The number of any other verb depends on its subject.

The chart on the next page shows verb forms that are always singular and those that can be singular or plural.

VERBS THAT ARE ALWAYS SINGULAR	VERBS THAT CAN BE SINGULAR OR PLURAL
(he, she, Jane) sees	(I, you, we, they) see
(he, she, Jane) has seen	(I, you, we, they) have seen
(I) am	(you, we, they) are
(he, she, Jane) is	(you, we, they) were
(I, he, she, Jane) was	

Singular and Plural Subjects

When making a verb agree with its subject, be sure to identify the subject and determine its number.

RULE 19.1.2

A singular subject must have a singular verb. A plural subject must have a plural verb.

SINGULAR SUBJECT AND VERB	PLURAL SUBJECT AND VERB
The police officer works in New York City.	These police officers work in New York City.
He was being cryptic about their vacation destination.	They were being cryptic about their vacation destination.
Brent looks through a dictionary for the correct spelling.	Brent and Emmett look through a dictionary for the correct spelling.
Texas is a large state in the United States.	Texas and California are large states in the United States.
Ricky takes first aid and health.	Ricky and Nick take first aid and health.
Thomas is planning a vacation to go see the Alamo in Texas.	Thomas and Gene are planning a vacation to go see the Alamo in Texas.
Christy plays piano for the church choir.	Christy and Amy play piano for the church choir.
She looks through the microscope.	They look through the microscope.
Terrance has been studying how to prevent diseases.	They have been studying how to prevent diseases.

See Practice 19.1B

PRACTICE 19.1A **Identifying Number in Nouns, Pronouns, and Verbs**

Read each word or group of words. Then, write whether the word or words are *singular*, *plural*, or *both*.

EXAMPLE   he

ANSWER   *singular*

1. table
2. knows
3. mice
4. us
5. are
6. you see
7. boxes
8. exposes
9. children
10. it

PRACTICE 19.1B **Identifying Singular and Plural Subjects and Verbs**

Read each sentence. Then, write the subject and verb in each sentence and label them *plural* or *singular*.

EXAMPLE   The note was left on the coffee table.

ANSWER   subject: *note*; verb: *was left*—*singular*

11. Recent weather reports indicate record-breaking snow this year.
12. Her strong legs come from her daily hour of running.
13. A cared-for flowerbed provides a great deal of beauty to a home.
14. This sport coat is very versatile.
15. My cats provide me with great companionship.
16. Our teacher grades our midterms on a curve.
17. The stained-glass windows have adorned the old building.
18. From a distance, the oil painting looks exactly like the tranquil lake.
19. Tommy has run the mile faster than anyone else on the team.
20. Is Arnie next up at bat?

SPEAKING APPLICATION

Take turns with a partner. Tell about a time when you overcame a fear that you had. Your partner should listen for and name the plural and singular nouns and verbs that you use.

WRITING APPLICATION

For each sentence in Practice 19.1B, change the subject from singular to plural or plural to singular. Make sure that the verb in each sentence agrees with your new subject.

Intervening Phrases and Clauses

When you check for agreement, mentally cross out any words that separate the subject and verb.

A phrase or clause that separates a subject and its verb does not affect subject–verb agreement.

In the first example below, the singular subject *discovery* agrees with the singular verb *interests* despite the intervening prepositional phrase *of hidden jewels,* which contains a plural noun.

EXAMPLES   The **discovery** of hidden jewels **interests** many people.

The **fundraisers**, whose goal is nearly reached, **require** more donations.

Intervening parenthetical expressions—such as those beginning with *as well as, in addition to, in spite of,* or *including*—also have no effect on the agreement of the subject and verb.

EXAMPLES   Your **presentation**, in addition to the data gathered by others, **is helping** to generate new ideas.

Francisco's **trip**, including visits to England, France, and Italy, **is lasting** three months.

See Practice 19.1C
See Practice 19.1D

Relative Pronouns as Subjects

When *who, which,* or *that* acts as a subject of a subordinate clause, its verb will be singular or plural depending on the number of the antecedent.

The antecedent of a relative pronoun determines its agreement with a verb.

EXAMPLES   He is the only **one** of the tourists **who has** the ability to speak Spanish.

(The antecedent of *who* is *one*.)

He is one of several **tourists who have** the ability to speak Spanish.

See Practice 19.1E   (The antecedent of *who* is *tourists*.)

Compound Subjects

A **compound subject** has two or more simple subjects, which are usually joined by *or* or *and*. Use the following rules when making compound subjects agree with verbs.

Subjects Joined by *And*
Only one rule applies to compound subjects connected by *and*: The verb is usually plural, whether the parts of the compound subject are all singular, all plural, or mixed.

> **A compound subject joined by *and* is generally plural and must have a plural verb.**

19.1.5 RULE

TWO SINGULAR SUBJECTS

A **snowstorm** and a **rainstorm hit** the state.

TWO PLURAL SUBJECTS

Puppies and **kittens chase** the ball across the yard.

A SINGULAR SUBJECT AND A PLURAL SUBJECT

The brown **puppy** and the gray **kittens chase** the ball across the yard.

There are two exceptions to this rule. The verb is singular if the parts of a compound subject are thought of as one item or if the word *every* or *each* precedes the compound subject.

EXAMPLES **Bacon and eggs was** all she could cook for breakfast.

Every weather center and emergency network in the United States **issues** warnings for severe weather.

Singular Subjects Joined by *Or* or *Nor*
When both parts of a compound subject connected by *or* or *nor* are singular, a singular verb is required.

> **Two or more singular subjects joined by *or* or *nor* must have a singular verb.**

EXAMPLE An **ice storm** or **rainstorm makes** driving difficult.

Plural Subjects Joined by *Or* or *Nor*
When both parts of a compound subject connected by *or* or *nor* are plural, a plural verb is required.

> **Two or more plural subjects joined by *or* or *nor* must have a plural verb.**

EXAMPLE Neither **rainstorms** nor **windstorms cause** as much mess as sandstorms.

Subjects of Mixed Number Joined by *Or* or *Nor*
If one part of a compound subject joined by *or* or *nor* is singular and the other is plural, the verb agrees with the subject closer to it.

> **If one or more singular subjects are joined to one or more plural subjects by *or* or *nor*, the subject closest to the verb determines agreement.**

EXAMPLES Neither **Katherine** nor my **sisters have packed**.

Neither my **sisters** nor **Katherine has packed**.

See Practice 19.1F

PRACTICE 19.1C **Identifying Intervening Phrases and Clauses**

Read each sentence. Then, write the intervening phrase or clause between the subject and verb in each sentence.

EXAMPLE The students in my class work hard on the project.

ANSWER *in my class*

1. The neighborhood where I live has many new homes.

2. Sap, which comes from trees, is used to make deliciously sweet syrup.

3. Her favorite book, a classic piece of literature, sits on her nightstand.

4. These dribbling drills, along with the sprints, are really exhausting.

5. The collection of films, which was critically acclaimed, won several awards.

6. The cake, with its three layers, served 100 people at the party.

7. The rock band, popular with everyone, will play at the pavilion tonight.

8. Jasmine, who is the smartest student in our class, always answers the questions.

9. The discovery of gold in Alaska in the 1800s led to a gold rush.

10. The smoke alarm in the kitchen was just replaced.

PRACTICE 19.1D **Correcting Agreement Errors With Intervening Phrases**

Read each sentence. Identify the subject, and check for subject-verb agreement. Rewrite sentences to correct errors in subject-verb agreement. If there is no error, write *correct*.

EXAMPLE The library lions greeting each visitor seems to stand guard eternally.

ANSWER *The library lions greeting each visitor* **seem** *to stand guard eternally.*

11. The kids in front of the audience seem tense.

12. The author, taking many questions from readers, look exhausted.

13. The film, praised in most newspapers, has attracted a wide audience.

14. Dinner for adults are being served in the main dining room.

15. An author often write about a subject with which he or she is familiar.

16. The clown who will entertain the children enjoy the parties.

17. He enjoys sunny days as well as enjoy rainy days.

18. Some people is fooled by the magician's trick.

19. The cars in the garage needs a major overhaul.

20. Many shows on Broadway is musicals.

SPEAKING APPLICATION

Take turns with a partner. Use sentences with intervening clauses to tell about a trip you would love to take someday. Your partner should listen for and identify the intervening clauses in your sentences.

WRITING APPLICATION

Using the sentences in Practice 19.1D as a model, write two sentences about a favorite restaurant. Your first sentence should have a singular subject, an intervening phrase, and a present-tense verb. In your second sentence, follow the same pattern but use a plural subject.

PRACTICE 19.1E > **Making Verbs Agree With Relative Pronouns**

Read each sentence. Then, write the singular or plural verb that agrees with the relative pronoun based on the number of its antecedent.

EXAMPLE   She is the only one of the counselors who (has worked, have worked) in this camp before.

ANSWER   *has worked*

1. He is one among many students who (wants, want) to study abroad.

2. She is the only one of the applicants who (has been accepted, have been accepted).

3. Virginia is one of 100 destinations that (ranks, rank) high on a prestigious list.

4. Watson is the only dog I know that (swallows, swallow) gloves.

5. Watson is one of many dogs that (has been adopted, have been adopted) by Debbie.

6. Grape is the only flavor that (is, are) always available here.

7. *Pride and Prejudice* is the only one of Austen's novels that (is, are) on the list.

8. *Pride and Prejudice* is among several novels that (belongs, belong) on the list.

9. France is the only one of Europe's countries that (appeals, appeal) to me.

10. France is one of the countries that (attracts, attract) me.

PRACTICE 19.1F > **Making Verbs Agree With Singular and Compound Subjects**

Read each sentence. Then, fill in the blank with the form of a verb that agrees with the singular or compound subject.

EXAMPLE   Either tomato sauce or tomato paste _____ used in this recipe.

ANSWER   *is*

11. The hikers _____ from their long excursion.

12. Neither Yen nor I _____ horror movies.

13. Either roses or a tree _____ planted in front of the house.

14. Neither she nor he _____ Spanish.

15. The cost of replacing the windows _____ covered by my insurance.

16. Neither Kathy nor the children _____ anywhere near the window.

17. A nice card _____ a person's day.

18. Shovels and plows _____ the streets after a blizzard.

19. Studying or reading _____ a productive way to spend a rainy afternoon.

20. Every Saturday, Chico and I _____ chess.

SPEAKING APPLICATION

Take turns with a partner. Say three present tense sentences about popular music. Each sentence must include the relative pronoun *that* to describe a musical group. Your partner should listen for subject-verb agreement.

WRITING APPLICATION

Write three original sentences about foods you enjoy. Each sentence should have a compound subject and a present tense verb.

Test Warm-Up

DIRECTIONS
Read the introduction and the passage that follows. Then, answer the questions to show that you can use and understand the function of subject-verb agreement in reading and writing.

Dahlia wrote this paragraph about Sunday breakfast. Read the paragraph and think about the changes you would suggest as a peer editor. When you finish reading, answer the questions that follow.

Many Helpers

(1) Sunday morning breakfast is an event in our family. (2) Bacon and eggs are my father's specialty at the stove, but my mother as well as my brother prefer to make pancakes. (3) I don't like eggs, so the only option among breakfast possibilities that appeal to me is hot oatmeal sprinkled with cinnamon. (4) Sometimes we have guests for Sunday breakfast. (5) My cousins or their mother whip up waffles or makes omelets. (6) Cleaning up the pots and pans—the only part of cooking that annoys me—go fast with so many helpers.

1 What change, if any, should be made in sentence 2?

A Change *are* to **is**

B Change *are* to **is** and *prefer* to **prefers**

C Change *prefer* to **prefers**

D Make no change

2 What change, if any, should be made in sentence 3?

F Change *like* to **likes**

G Change *is* to **are**

H Change *appeal* to **appeals**

J Make no change

3 What change, if any, should be made in sentence 5?

A Change *whip* to **whips** and *makes* to **make**

B Change *whip* to **whips**

C Change *makes* to **make**

D Make no change

4 What change, if any, should be made in sentence 6?

F Change *annoys* to **annoy**

G Change *go* to **goes**

H Change *annoys* to **annoy** and *go* to **goes**

J Make no change

Confusing Subjects

Some kinds of subjects have special agreement problems.

Hard-to-Find Subjects and Inverted Sentences

Subjects that appear after verbs are said to be **inverted.**
Subject–verb order is usually inverted in questions. To find out
whether to use a singular or plural verb, mentally rearrange the
sentence into subject–verb order.

> A verb must still agree in number with a subject that comes after it.

EXAMPLE	On the board **are** two dinner **specials**.
REARRANGED IN SUBJECT–VERB ORDER	Two dinner **specials are** on the board.

The words *there* and *here* often signal an inverted sentence.
These words never function as the subject of a sentence.

EXAMPLES	There **are** the news **photographs**.
	Here **is** the current **information**.

Note About *There's* and *Here's*: Both of these contractions
contain the singular verb *is: there is* and *here is*. They should be
used only with singular subjects.

CORRECT	**There's** only one **class** scheduled.
	Here's a name **tag** to pin on your shirt.

See Practice 19.1G

Subjects With Linking Verbs

Subjects with linking verbs may also cause agreement problems.

> A linking verb must agree with its subject, regardless of the number of its predicate nominative.

EXAMPLES   The **branches are** just flimsy sticks.

The big **flood was** the motivation for building the new dam.

In the first example, the plural verb *are* agrees with the plural subject *branches.* In the next example, the singular subject *flood* takes the singular verb *was.*

Collective Nouns

Collective nouns name groups of people or things. Examples include *audience, class, club,* and *committee.*

> **A collective noun takes a singular verb when the group it names acts as a single unit. A collective noun takes a plural verb when the group acts as individuals.**

19.1.11 RULE

SINGULAR   The plane **crew leaves** in December.

(The members act as a unit.)

PLURAL   The plane **crew were going** on separate routes.

(The members act individually.)

Nouns That Look Like Plurals

Some nouns that end in *-s* are actually singular. For example, nouns that name branches of knowledge, such as *civics,* and those that name illnesses, such as *mumps,* take singular verbs.

> **Use singular verbs to agree with nouns that are plural in form but singular in meaning.**

19.1.12 RULE

SINGULAR   **Mathematics is** my easiest subject.

When words such as *ethics* and *politics* do not name branches of knowledge but indicate characteristics, their meanings are plural. Similarly, such words as *eyeglasses, pants,* and *scissors* generally take plural verbs.

PLURAL The **acoustics** in the theater **are** excellent.

Indefinite Pronouns

Some indefinite pronouns are always singular, some are always plural, and some may be either singular or plural. Prepositional phrases do not affect subject–verb agreement.

RULE 19.1.13

Singular indefinite pronouns take singular verbs. Plural indefinite pronouns take plural verbs.

SINGULAR *anybody, anyone, anything, each, either, everybody, everyone, everything, neither, nobody, no one, nothing, somebody, someone, something*

PLURAL *both, few, many, others, several*

SINGULAR **Everyone** on the rescue mission **has arrived**.

PLURAL **Many** of the windows **were replaced**.

RULE 19.1.14

The pronouns *all, any, more, most, none,* and *some* usually take a singular verb if the antecedent is singular, and a plural verb if it is plural.

SINGULAR **Some** of the building **was ruined** by the wind.

PLURAL **Some** of the alliances **are** stronger than in the past.

Titles of Creative Works and Names of Organizations

Plural words in the title of a creative work or in the name of an organization do not affect subject–verb agreement.

RULE 19.1.15

A title of a creative work or name of an organization is singular and must have a singular verb.

EXAMPLES **Doctors without Borders is** a helpful group in the event of a disaster.
(organization)

The ***Mona Lisa*** by Leonardo da Vinci **is** a famous painting.
(creative work)

Amounts and Measurements

Although they appear to be plural, most amounts and measurements actually express single units or ideas.

> **A noun expressing an amount or measurement is usually singular and requires a singular verb.**

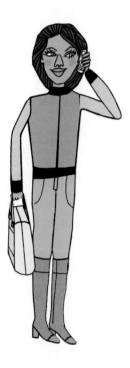

19.1.16 RULE

EXAMPLES **Five hundred million dollars is** the cost to build new highways in the state.

(*Five hundred million dollars is one sum of money.*)

Five blocks was our distance from the nearest coffee shop.

(*Five blocks is a single distance.*)

Three quarters of the town **votes** in the school board election.

(*Three quarters is one part of a town.*)

Half of the flowers **were uprooted**.

(*Half refers to a number of individual flowers, and not part of an individual flower, so it is plural.*)

See Practice 19.1H

PRACTICE 19.1G > Identifying Subjects and Verbs in Inverted Sentences

Read each sentence. Then, identify the subject and verb in each sentence.

EXAMPLE   These are the best players on the team.

ANSWER   subject: *players*; verb: *are*

1. Here are all the possible paint colors.
2. There is only one viable option to choose.
3. Can she be trusted?
4. There is no one here at the moment.
5. At the bottom of the laundry basket is your favorite pair of running shorts.
6. Along the route were various gas stations and visitor centers.
7. Where did you put my keys?
8. Among the contestants is a girl from Burundi.
9. Here is my favorite story from my childhood.
10. Are two cups of flour enough for this recipe?

PRACTICE 19.1H > Making Verbs Agree With Confusing Subjects

Read each sentence. Then, write the correct verb from the choices in parentheses to complete each sentence.

EXAMPLE   The film series (begins, begin) next week.

ANSWER   *begins*

11. The distance of the race (is, are) 5 kilometers.
12. Two thirds of the meal (was, were) consumed by the guests.
13. The senior class (was, were) visiting separate sites.
14. His pants (were, was) torn when he leapt over the fence.
15. *Sense and Sensibility* (is, are) a great work of literature.
16. American studies (was, were) her minor in college.
17. Several of the animals (was, were) released from captivity.
18. Everyone (agrees, agree) that the fundraiser was a huge success.
19. The least of your concerns (is, are) how to get the house ready in time.
20. Neither Charles nor Yvette (have, has) the folder.

SPEAKING APPLICATION

Take turns with a partner. Say five inverted sentences. Your partner should identify the subject and verb in each of your sentences.

WRITING APPLICATION

Write three sentences that include confusing subjects. Underline the subject in each sentence, and make sure that the verb agrees with the subject.

19.2 Pronoun–Antecedent Agreement

Like a subject and its verb, a pronoun and its antecedent must agree. An **antecedent** is the word or group of words for which the pronoun stands.

Agreement Between Personal Pronouns and Antecedents

While a subject and verb must agree only in number, a personal pronoun and its antecedent must agree in three ways.

> **A personal pronoun must agree with its antecedent in number, person, and gender.**

The **number** of a pronoun indicates whether it is singular or plural. **Person** refers to a pronoun's ability to indicate either the person speaking (first person), the person spoken to (second person), or the person, place, or thing spoken about (third person). **Gender** is the characteristic of nouns and pronouns that indicates whether the word is *masculine* (referring to males), *feminine* (referring to females), or *neuter* (referring to neither males nor females).

The only pronouns that indicate gender are third-person singular personal pronouns.

GENDER OF THIRD-PERSON SINGULAR PRONOUNS	
Masculine	*he, him, his*
Feminine	*she, her, hers*
Neuter	*it, its*

In the example below, the pronoun *her* agrees with the antecedent *First Lady* in number (both are singular), in person (both are third person), and in gender (both are feminine).

EXAMPLE   The First Lady shared **her** dreams with the

reporter.

Agreement in Number

There are three rules to keep in mind to determine the number of compound antecedents.

RULE 19.2.2

Use a singular personal pronoun when two or more singular antecedents are joined by *or* or *nor*.

EXAMPLES Either Kate **or** Brianna will bring **her** sample of a casserole to the sale.

Neither Bianca **nor** Belinda will wear **her** new dress tonight.

RULE 19.2.3

Use a plural personal pronoun when two or more antecedents are joined by *and*.

EXAMPLE Bobby **and** I are training for **our** marathon.

An exception occurs when a distinction must be made between individual and joint ownership. If individual ownership is intended, use a singular pronoun to refer to a compound antecedent. If joint ownership is intended, use a plural pronoun.

SINGULAR **Ben and Adie** read **her** favorite book.

PLURAL **Ben and Adie** bought **their** favorite books.

SINGULAR Neither **Alice nor Rosalie** let me use **her** cellphone.

PLURAL Neither **Alice nor Rosalie** let me use **their** cellphone.

The third rule applies to compound antecedents whose parts are mixed in number.

RULE 19.2.4

Use a plural personal pronoun if any part of a compound antecedent joined by *or* or *nor* is plural.

See Practice 19.2A

EXAMPLE	If either the **agent** or the **actresses** arrive, take **them** to the VIP lounge.

Agreement in Person and Gender Avoid shifts in person or gender of pronouns.

> As part of pronoun–antecedent agreement, take care not to shift either person or gender.

RULE 19.2.5

SHIFT IN PERSON	**Vincent** is planning to visit Italy because **you** can taste authentic Italian food.
CORRECT	**Vincent** is planning to visit Italy because **he** wants to taste authentic Italian food.

SHIFT IN GENDER	The **lion** threw **its** head back, roared, and stood on **his** hind legs.
CORRECT	The **lion** threw **its** head back, roared, and stood on **its** hind legs.

Generic Masculine Pronouns Traditionally, a masculine pronoun has been used to refer to a singular antecedent whose gender is unknown. Such use is called *generic* because it applies to both masculine and feminine genders. Many writers now prefer to use *his or her, he or she, him or her,* or to rephrase a sentence to eliminate the situation.

> When gender is not specified, either use *his or her* or rewrite the sentence.

RULE 19.2.6

EXAMPLES	Each **player** found a useful playbook in which to record **his or her plays** during the game.
	Players found useful playbooks in which to record **their plays** during the game.

See Practice 19.2B

Read each sentence. Then, rewrite each sentence to include the correct personal pronoun. If the sentence is correct, write *correct*.

EXAMPLE   My brothers and I are planning a surprise for their parents.

ANSWER   *My brothers and I are planning a surprise for our parents.*

1. Neither of the birds ate their seeds.

2. Joe and Laura's sister can't find their toothbrush.

3. Neither Sean nor John had any trouble choosing their topic.

4. The doctor and his assistant published her discoveries.

5. The boy used his hands to make shadow animals.

6. Danielle and her brother are coaching her sister's soccer team.

7. When my parents and my brother ski, he always wear a helmet.

8. Either Julio or Pete will shave their beard.

9. The Brady twins rode their bikes home.

10. Boris and Leo improved his performance by practicing more often.

Read each sentence. Then, revise each sentence so that the personal pronoun agrees with the antecedent.

EXAMPLE   With a gleam in his eyes, the baby shook its rattle.

ANSWER   *With a gleam in his eyes, the baby shook his rattle.*

11. Each girl must submit their report.

12. Those hikers will soon realize that you cannot walk for miles in unsturdy shoes.

13. Either Jerome or Ralph can use their ticket for the ride.

14. We learned in chemistry that you should record all of your observations.

15. All of the team members washed his or her uniform.

16. Meghan's doll looks as if she is real.

17. Their mother accompanied each athlete.

18. The welders wear goggles so that your eyes will be protected.

19. As the car pulled away, it left a trail of smoke in his wake.

20. A bee's sting is her defense.

SPEAKING APPLICATION

Take turns with a partner. Tell each other about a family pet or a favorite relative. Use several different pronouns in your sentences. Your partner should name the personal pronouns you use and tell if they agree with their antecedents.

WRITING APPLICATION

Use sentences 14, 15, and 19 as models to write similar sentences. Then, exchange papers with a partner. Your partner should revise each sentence to make the personal pronoun agree with the antecedent.

Agreement With Indefinite Pronouns

When an indefinite pronoun, such as *each, all,* or *most,* is used with a personal pronoun, the pronouns must agree.

> **Use a plural personal pronoun when the antecedent is a plural indefinite pronoun.**

RULE 19.2.7

EXAMPLES **Many** of the graduates were excited about **their** college choices.

All the graduates remembered to bring **their** caps.

When the indefinite pronoun is singular, a similar rule applies.

> **Use a singular personal pronoun when the antecedent is a singular indefinite pronoun.**

RULE 19.2.8

In the first example, the personal pronoun *his* agrees in number with the singular indefinite pronoun *one.* The gender (masculine) is determined by the word *boys.*

EXAMPLES Only **one** of the boys studied **his** class notes.

One of the boys remembered to bring **his** notes.

If other words in the sentence do not indicate a gender, you may use *him or her, he or she, his or her* or rephrase the sentence.

EXAMPLES **Each** of the politicians practiced **his or her** stump speech.

The **politicians** practiced **their** stump speeches.

For indefinite pronouns that can be either singular or plural, such as *all, any, more, most, none,* and *some,* agreement depends on the antecedent of the indefinite pronoun.

Most of the trip had lost **its** excitement.
(The antecedent of *most* is *trip,* which is singular.)

Most of the customers wanted **their** accounts credited.
(The antecedent of *most* is *customers,* which is plural.)

Some of the book had **its** pages torn.
(The antecedent of *some* is *book,* which is singular.)

All of the rackets had lost **their** name tags.
(The antecedent of *all* is *rackets,* which is plural.)

In some situations, strict grammatical agreement may be illogical. In these situations, either let the meaning of the sentence determine the number of the personal pronoun, or reword the sentence.

ILLOGICAL When **each of the pagers** buzzed, I answered **it** as quickly as possible.

MORE LOGICAL When **each of the pagers** buzzed, I answered **them** as quickly as possible.

MORE LOGICAL When **all of the pagers** buzzed, I answered **them** as quickly as possible.

See Practice 19.2C

Agreement With Reflexive Pronouns

Reflexive pronouns, which end in *-self* or *-selves,* should only refer to a word earlier in the same sentence.

RULE 19.2.9

A reflexive pronoun must agree with an antecedent that is clearly stated.

EXAMPLES **Benjamin** threw a party for **himself**.

You should consider **yourself** special.

Efficient **workers** would rather handle things **themselves**.

See Practice 19.2D
See Practice 19.2E
See Practice 19.2F

PRACTICE 19.2C **Making Personal and Indefinite Pronouns Agree**

Read each sentence. Then, fill in the blanks with an appropriate personal pronoun that agrees with the indefinite pronoun to complete each sentence.

EXAMPLE   Each of the girls has sold _____ quota of cookies.

ANSWER   *her*

1. Most of the fans brought blankets with _____.

2. No one on the girls' team wears _____ cap at a meet.

3. Much of the glass has smudges on _____.

4. Few of the voters changed _____ minds after the debate.

5. I think some of the tourists brought cameras with _____.

6. None of the students handed in _____ assignments late.

7. Most of the furniture has scratches on _____.

8. Everyone in the club brings _____ own opinions to the meetings.

9. Has any boy decided on _____ project yet?

10. All of the musicians are tuning _____ instruments.

PRACTICE 19.2D **Supplying Reflexive Pronouns**

Read each sentence. Then, fill in the blanks by writing the correct reflexive pronoun that agrees with the antecedent in each sentence.

EXAMPLE   Carlos wrote _____ a message.

ANSWER   *himself*

11. Christina and he left by _____.

12. Myra bought _____ a new jacket.

13. Pablo and I can handle the nominations committee's work by _____.

14. Steve made _____ a costume.

15. Grandma's stories about how she got _____ into sticky situations are very amusing.

16. Mom knitted _____ a sweater.

17. The babies look at _____ in the mirror.

18. Please make _____ comfortable in the living room.

19. Gina helped _____ to some mashed potatoes.

20. The lady fanned _____ to cool down.

SPEAKING APPLICATION

Take turns with a partner. Choose three indefinite pronouns. Your partner should say sentences, using a personal pronoun that agrees with each indefinite pronoun.

WRITING APPLICATION

Use sentences 11, 12, and 18 as models to write three similar sentences. Then, exchange papers with a partner. Your partner should rewrite each sentence, using the correct reflexive pronoun that agrees with the antecedent.

PRACTICE 19.2E > **Correcting Problems in Pronoun-Antecedent Agreement**

Read each sentence. Then, fill in the blank with an appropriate personal pronoun that agrees with its antecedent and completes each sentence.

EXAMPLE   My neighbor's male dog, Watson, likes _____ new home.

ANSWER   *his*

1. All of us want to go skiing for the holidays, but _____ can't count on the weather.

2. We couldn't tell the gender of the goldfish, so we called _____ Pat.

3. Both of my female cousins want _____ parents to extend curfew.

4. Most of the people in this town value _____ right to vote.

5. Some of the cake remained on _____ plate by noon, but most had been eaten.

6. They should consider _____ fortunate to have you as a daughter.

7. A doctor has to inform as well as comfort _____ patients.

8. Everyone in this girls' school wants _____ essay to win first prize.

9. Both parents work, so the twins look after _____ after school.

10. The conductor, James Levine, raised _____ baton.

PRACTICE 19.2F > **Using Pronouns Correctly**

For each of the given antecedents, write a sentence that includes a pronoun agreeing with the antecedent.

EXAMPLE   Each of the girls

ANSWER   *Each of the girls raised her hand.*

11. Everyone at the camp for boys and girls

12. One of the mothers

13. Neither of the fathers

14. Helene

15. Helene and Felix

16. The team (Treat the antecedent as singular.)

17. Every U.S. president to date

18. A police officer in the United States

19. Most of the audience

20. The team (Treat the antecedent as plural.)

SPEAKING APPLICATION

Choose three personal pronouns. Have your partner use one pronoun at a time in a sentence. Listen for pronoun-antecedent agreement.

WRITING APPLICATION

Write two sentences in which a personal pronoun agrees with the antecedent *some*. The first sentence should make clear that *some* is singular; the second sentence should make clear that *some* is plural.

Test Warm-Up

DIRECTIONS
**Read the introduction and the passage that follows. Then, answer the
questions to show that you can use and understand the function of
pronoun-antecedent agreement in reading and writing.**

*Muhammed wrote this paragraph about fans of pro sports. Read the
paragraph and think about the changes you would suggest as a peer
editor. When you finish reading, answer the questions that follow.*

One Favorite Sport? Or Four?

(1) In the course of a year, each of the four major professional
sports—baseball, basketball, football, and hockey—gets its moment in
the spotlight. (2) Fans claim that their favorite sport gives you more
enjoyment than the other three. (3) Of course, some of the fans enjoy
themselves no matter which sport he or she is watching. (4) Can the
same be said of a sportswriter? (5) Does a sportswriter enjoy whatever
sport he is writing about at the time?

---

1 What change, if any, should be made in
sentence 1?

  A Change *its* to **our**

  B Change *its* to **your**

  C Change *its* to **their**

  D Make no change

2 What change, if any, should be made in
sentence 2?

  F Change *their* to **his or her**

  G Change *you* to **your**

  H Change *you* to **them**

  J Make no change

3 What change, if any, should be made in
sentence 3?

  A Change *themselves* to
himself or herself

  B Change *themselves* to **themself**

  C Change *he or she is* to **they are**

  D Make no change

4 What change, if any, should be made in
sentence 5?

  F Change *he* to **she**

  G Change *he* to **he or she**

  H Change *he* to **they**

  J Make no change

19.3 Special Problems With Pronoun Agreement

This section will show you how to avoid some common errors that can obscure the meaning of your sentences.

WRITING COACH

Online

www.phwritingcoach.com

Grammar Tutorials

Brush up on your Grammar skills with these animated videos.

Grammar Practice

Practice your grammar skills with Writing Coach Online.

Grammar Games

Test your knowledge of grammar in this fast-paced interactive video game.

Vague Pronoun References

One basic rule governs all of the rules for pronoun reference.

RULE 19.3.1

> **To avoid confusion, a pronoun requires an antecedent that is either stated or clearly understood.**

The pronouns *which, this, that,* and *these* should not be used to refer to a vague or overly general idea.

In the following example, it is impossible to determine exactly what the pronoun *these* stands for because it may refer to three different groups of words.

Find It/ FIX IT

4

Grammar Game Plan

VAGUE REFERENCE	Kay was singing, the guests were happy, and the catered food was delicious. **These** made our birthday party a joyful occasion.

This vague reference can be corrected in two ways. One way is to change the pronoun to an adjective that modifies a specific noun. The second way is to revise the sentence so that the pronoun *these* is eliminated.

CORRECT	Kay was singing, the guests were happy, and the catered food was delicious. **These pleasures** made our birthday party a joyful occasion.
CORRECT	Kay's singing, the guests' happiness, and the delicious catered food made our birthday party a joyful occasion.

The personal pronouns *it, they,* and *you* should always have a clear antecedent.

In the next example, the pronoun *it* has no clearly stated antecedent.

VAGUE REFERENCE	Winnie is studying medical advancements next month. **It** should be very educational.

Again, there are two methods of correction. The first method is to replace the personal pronoun with a specific noun. The second method is to revise the sentence entirely in order to make the whole idea clear.

CORRECT	Winnie is studying medical advancements next month. **The experience** should be very educational.
CORRECT	**Winnie's study** of medical advancements should be very educational.

In the next examples, the pronoun *they* is used without clear antecedents.

VAGUE REFERENCE	I enjoyed reading the book about Shakespeare, but **they** never explained his symbolism in tragedy.
CORRECT	I enjoyed reading the book about Shakespeare, but **the authors** never explained Shakespeare's symbolism in tragedy.
VAGUE REFERENCE	When we arrived at the game, **they** told us which player was about to throw the opening pitch.
CORRECT	When we arrived at the game, **the announcer** told us which player was about to throw the opening pitch.

RULE 19.3.3

Use *you* only when the reference is truly to the reader or listener.

VAGUE REFERENCE **You** couldn't understand a word the musician sang.

CORRECT **We** couldn't understand a word the musician sang.

VAGUE REFERENCE In the school my grandfather went to, **you** were expected to be polite to everyone.

CORRECT In the school my grandfather went to, **students** were expected to be polite to everyone.

Note About *It*: In many idiomatic expressions, the personal pronoun *it* has no specific antecedent. In statements such as "It is late," *it* is an idiom that is accepted as standard English.

See Practice 19.3A

Ambiguous Pronoun References

A pronoun is **ambiguous** if it can refer to more than one antecedent.

RULE 19.3.4

A pronoun should never refer to more than one antecedent.

In the following sentence, *he* is confusing because it can refer to either *Wilson* or *Jason*. Revise such a sentence by changing the pronoun to a noun or rephrasing the sentence entirely.

AMBIGUOUS REFERENCE Wilson told Jason about the dolphins **he** spotted.

CORRECT Wilson told Jason about the dolphins **Wilson** spotted.
(Wilson knew about the dolphins.)

RULE 19.3.5

Do not repeat a personal pronoun in a sentence if it can refer to a different antecedent each time.

AMBIGUOUS REPETITION	When Tina asked her mother if **she** could borrow the earrings, **she** said that **she** needed them.
CLEAR	When Tina asked her mother if **she** could borrow the earrings, **Tina** said that **she** needed them.
CLEAR	When Tina asked her mother if **she** could borrow the earrings, her **mother** said that **she** needed them **herself**.

Notice that in the first sentence above, it is unclear whether the second *she* is referring to Tina or to her mother. To eliminate the confusion, Tina's name was used in the second sentence. In the third sentence, the reflexive pronoun *herself* helps to clarify the meaning.

Avoiding Distant Pronoun References

A pronoun should be placed close to its antecedent.

> **A personal pronoun should always be close enough to its antecedent to prevent confusion.**

19.3.6 RULE

A distant pronoun reference can be corrected by moving the pronoun closer to its antecedent or by changing the pronoun to a noun. In the example below, *it* is too far from the antecedent *knee*.

DISTANT REFERENCE	Betty shifted her weight from her injured knee. Three days ago, she had slipped and fallen down the stairs. Now **it** was in a brace.
CORRECT	Betty shifted her weight from her injured knee. Three days ago, she had slipped and fallen down the stairs. Now her **knee** was in a brace.
	(*Knee* replaces the pronoun *it*.)

See Practice 19.3B

PRACTICE 19.3A > **Correcting Vague Pronouns**

Read each sentence. Then, rewrite each sentence to avoid the use of vague pronouns.

EXAMPLE   At the annual picnic, they always feature fried chicken.

ANSWER   *The annual picnic always features fried chicken.*

1. It was past midnight when the snow stopped.

2. In that game, you can only reach "home" with an exact roll of the dice.

3. In Boston, they often drop their *r*'s.

4. It isn't fun going to a party alone.

5. It suggests in the article that Andrews is running for office.

6. The boys promptly wrote thank-you notes, which shocked their mother.

7. During the fire drill, they spoke about safety.

8. They can't do anything to prevent the crops from freezing.

9. She heard that they had discovered a new type of fuel.

10. To make a claim on the frontier, you had to live there.

PRACTICE 19.3B > **Recognizing Ambiguous Pronouns**

Read each sentence. Then, rewrite each sentence to avoid the use of ambiguous pronouns.

EXAMPLE   Phillippe told Jack that he would wait until after his football practice.

ANSWER   *Phillippe told Jack that he would wait until after Jack's football practice.*

11. Siobhan and Barbara shared her lunch.

12. After Nancy had spoken to Rebecca, she felt much calmer.

13. Mr. Patel asked Tate to repeat the experiment he had just completed.

14. The approaches to the bridges were clogged, as they often were at rush hour.

15. The window looked out over the garden, but it was overgrown with weeds.

16. While Bert wheeled his small son around the park, he was very content.

17. Kumar informed Hank that he would have to leave soon.

18. The coach told James that he would not renew his contract.

19. Alice told Bella that she was getting a promotion.

20. Plant the bulbs by the new bushes and water them.

SPEAKING APPLICATION

Take turns with a partner. Use sentences from Practice 19.3A as models to say similar sentences that contain vague pronoun references. Your partner should reword each sentence to make it clearer.

WRITING APPLICATION

Use sentences 11, 13, and 15 as models to write similar sentences. Then, exchange papers with a partner. Your partner should rewrite each sentence, correcting the ambiguous pronoun references.

USING MODIFIERS

Knowing how to use modifiers to make comparisons will help you write vivid descriptions.

CHAPTER 20

WRITE GUY *Jeff Anderson, M.Ed.*

WHAT DO YOU NOTICE?

Focus on comparisons as you zoom in on these lines from the poem "Song" by John Donne.

MENTOR TEXT

> Sweetest love, I do not go,
> For weariness of thee,
> Nor in hope the world can show
> A fitter love for me . . .

Now, ask yourself the following questions:

- Which degrees of comparison does the poet use?
- What comparisons are made?

The adjective *sweetest* is in the superlative degree, as shown by the ending *-est,* and the *-er* ending on the adjective *fitter* shows the comparative degree. The speaker of the poem compares the person he loves to all others when he says *sweetest.* By using the adjective *fitter,* the poet compares his love to the love the world could show him.

Grammar for Writers Writers can use different degrees of comparison to create more interesting and dynamic descriptions. Check how many items you are comparing to figure out which degree to use.

How can I compare thee to a summer's day?

You could say I was cooler.

20.1 Degrees of Comparison

In the English language, there are three degrees, or forms, of most adjectives and adverbs that are used in comparisons.

Recognizing Degrees of Comparison

In order to write effective comparisons, you first need to know the three degrees.

RULE 20.1.1

The three degrees of comparison are the **positive**, the **comparative**, and the **superlative.**

The following chart shows adjectives and adverbs in each of the three degrees. Notice the three different ways that modifiers are changed to show degree: (1) by adding -*er* or -*est*, (2) by adding *more* or *most*, and (3) by using entirely different words.

DEGREES OF ADJECTIVES		
POSITIVE	COMPARATIVE	SUPERLATIVE
funny	funnier	funniest
pleasant	more pleasant	most pleasant
bad	worse	worst
DEGREES OF ADVERBS		
slowly	more slowly	most slowly
pleasantly	more pleasantly	most pleasantly
badly	worse	worst

See Practice 20.1A

Regular Forms

Adjectives and adverbs can be either **regular** or **irregular,** depending on how their comparative and superlative degrees are formed. The degrees of most adjectives and adverbs are formed regularly. The number of syllables in regular modifiers determines how their degrees are formed.

RULE 20.1.2

Use -*er* or *more* to form the comparative degree and -*est* or *most* to form the superlative degree of most one- and two-syllable modifiers.

EXAMPLES	silly	sillier	silliest
	careful	more careful	most careful

> **All adverbs that end in *-ly* form their comparative and superlative degrees with *more* and *most*.**

20.1.3 RULE

EXAMPLES	cleverly	more cleverly	most cleverly
	cowardly	more cowardly	most cowardly

> **Use *more* and *most* to form the comparative and superlative degrees of all modifiers with three or more syllables.**

20.1.4 RULE

EXAMPLES	delicate	more delicate	most delicate
	dependable	more dependable	most dependable

Note About Comparisons With *Less* and *Least*: *Less* and *least* can be used to form another version of the comparative and superlative degrees of most modifiers.

EXAMPLES	delicate	less delicate	least delicate
	dependable	less dependable	least dependable

See Practice 20.1B

Irregular Forms

The comparative and superlative degrees of a few commonly used adjectives and adverbs are formed in unpredictable ways.

> **The irregular comparative and superlative forms of certain adjectives and adverbs must be memorized.**

20.1.5 RULE

In the chart on the following page, the form of some irregular modifiers differs only in the positive degree. The modifiers *bad*, *badly*, and *ill*, for example, all have the same comparative and superlative degrees *(worse, worst)*.

IRREGULAR MODIFIERS		
POSITIVE	**COMPARATIVE**	**SUPERLATIVE**
bad, badly, ill	worse	worst
far (distance)	farther	farthest
far (extent)	further	furthest
good, well	better	best
late	later	last or latest
little (amount)	less	least
many, much	more	most

RULE

20.1.6

Bad is an adjective. Do not use it to modify an action verb. *Badly* is an adverb. Use it after an action verb but not after a linking verb.

INCORRECT   The chorus sang its program **bad**.

CORRECT   The chorus sang its program **badly**.

INCORRECT   Our team feels **badly** about losing the game.

CORRECT   Our team feels **bad** about losing the game.

Note About *Good* and *Well*: *Good* is always an adjective and cannot be used as an adverb after an action verb. It can, however, be used as a predicate adjective after a linking verb.

INCORRECT   My band played **good** at last night's concert.

CORRECT   My band sounded **good** at last night's concert.

Well is generally an adverb. However, when *well* means "healthy," it is an adjective and can be used after a linking verb.

CORRECT   Marnie plays chess **well**.

CORRECT   Marnie should be **well** soon.

See Practice 20.1C
See Practice 20.1D

PRACTICE 20.1A > **Recognizing Positive, Comparative, and Superlative Degrees of Comparison**

Read each sentence. Then, identify the degree of comparison of the underlined word or words as *positive, comparative,* or *superlative.*

EXAMPLE   They have been waiting <u>longer</u> than we have.

ANSWER   *comparative*

1. The room will look <u>brighter</u> with a fresh coat of paint.

2. We congratulated the <u>proud</u> parents.

3. That was the <u>heaviest</u> rainfall to date.

4. Greta was voted <u>most likely</u> to succeed.

5. If I had been <u>more careful</u>, I wouldn't have made that mistake.

6. Luviano's serves the <u>spiciest</u> food in town.

7. The cat moved <u>stealthily</u> along the side of the house.

8. Surely the koala bear is one of the <u>laziest</u> animals.

9. An ice pack may make you feel <u>more comfortable</u>.

10. The stubborn child shook his head <u>vigorously</u>.

PRACTICE 20.1B > **Forming Regular Comparative and Superlative Degrees of Comparison**

Read each sentence. Then, rewrite each sentence with the correct comparative or superlative degree of the modifier indicated in parentheses.

EXAMPLE   My uncle was _____ than I expected. (generous)

ANSWER   *My uncle was more generous than I expected.*

11. This chair is _____ than that one. (comfortable)

12. Anthony made the mistake of wearing the _____ of his shirts. (itchy)

13. That shirt is the _____ of all the shirts on display. (bright)

14. I am _____ than I was yesterday. (sleepy)

15. Carly is _____ now than ever before. (happy)

16. These apples will ripen _____ if they are put in a paper bag. (quickly)

17. Please let me try on the _____ size. (small)

18. I was _____ by her attitude than by her lateness. (disappointed)

19. I am never _____ than when I relax on the swing. (tranquil)

20. That picture is the _____ of them all. (stunning)

SPEAKING APPLICATION

Take turns with a partner. Compare the size of objects found in your classroom. Use comparative, superlative, and positive degrees of comparison. Your partner should listen for and identify which degree of comparison you are using.

WRITING APPLICATION

Rewrite sentences 13, 15, and 17, changing the modifiers in parentheses. Then, exchange papers with a partner. Your partner should write the correct degree of the modifiers you provided.

PRACTICE 20.1C ▷ **Supplying Irregular Comparative and Superlative Forms**

Read each modifier. Then, write its irregular comparative and superlative forms.

EXAMPLE   good

ANSWER   *better, best*

1. much
2. ill
3. badly
4. many
5. well
6. late
7. bad
8. little (amount)
9. far (extent)
10. far (distance)

PRACTICE 20.1D ▷ **Supplying Irregular Modifiers**

Read each sentence. Then, fill in the blank with the form of the modifier in parentheses that best completes each sentence.

EXAMPLE   I delivered my monologue in the play _____ than I ever had before. (good)

ANSWER   *better*

11. Cheryl was clearly the _____ player in the game tonight. (good)
12. Denora was the _____ student in the class to hand in her paper. (late)
13. Six miles is the _____ I have ever run. (far)
14. I felt terrible yesterday, but I'm feeling _____ today. (well)
15. According to the poll, _____ people favor the independent candidate. (many)
16. My dad said that buying a new television was the _____ thing from his mind at the time. (far)
17. The doctor was treating the _____ case of hiccups that she had ever encountered. (bad)
18. Hudson plays the clarinet really _____ . (good)
19. Scottie feels lightheaded, but Ilene seems even _____. (bad)
20. The lid will probably fit better if you apply _____ pressure. (little)

SPEAKING APPLICATION

Take turns with a partner. Say sentences with irregular comparative and superlative forms. Your partner should listen for and identify the irregular comparative and superlative forms.

WRITING APPLICATION

Write pairs of sentences using the following modifiers correctly: *more* and *most*, *better* and *best*, *less* and *least*, *farthest* and *furthest*.

20.2 Making Clear Comparisons

The comparative and superlative degrees help you make comparisons that are clear and logical.

Using Comparative and Superlative Degrees

One basic rule that has two parts covers the correct use of comparative and superlative forms.

> Use the **comparative degree** to compare two persons, places, or things. Use the **superlative degree** to compare three or more persons, places, or things.

RULE 20.2.1

The context of a sentence should indicate whether two items or more than two items are being compared.

COMPARATIVE   Driving a car is **harder** than it looks.

I'm **less confident** than I thought I'd be.

Gas **costs more** than I thought it would.

SUPERLATIVE   Driving a car is the **hardest** thing I've done.

I'm the **least confident** driver in the class.

Gas is **most expensive** at the station on Broadway.

In informal writing, the superlative degree is sometimes used just for emphasis, without any specific comparison.

EXAMPLE   Ella was **most treacherously** betrayed.

Note About Double Comparisons: A double comparison is caused by using both *-er* and *more* or both *-est* and *most* to form a regular modifier or by adding an extra comparison form to an irregular modifier.

See Practice 20.2A

See Practice 20.2B

INCORRECT   Jane is **more younger** than my sister Meg.

CORRECT   Jane is **younger** than my sister Meg.

PRACTICE 20.2A Supplying the Comparative and Superlative Degrees of Modifiers

Read each sentence. Then, fill in the blank with the correct form of the underlined modifier.

EXAMPLE   The film is <u>good</u>, but the book is _____.

ANSWER   *better*

1. The old line of cars is selling <u>well</u>, but we hope the new line will sell even _____.

2. We drove <u>far</u> to reach the store and even _____ to reach a restaurant.

3. Marilyn looks <u>better</u> in green than in blue, but she looks _____ in red.

4. Jonas has <u>little</u> patience for board games and even _____ for word games.

5. Camilla has <u>much</u> interest in chemistry and even _____ in physics.

6. I ran quite <u>far</u> yesterday, but I intend to run even _____ today.

7. There were <u>many</u> guests at Hakim's party, but there were _____ at Marshall's.

8. I still feel <u>ill</u> this morning, but I felt _____ last night after I ate.

9. He arrived <u>late</u>, but I arrived even _____.

10. She is <u>shy</u>, but Yen is the _____ in the class.

PRACTICE 20.2B Revising Sentences to Correct Errors in Modifier Usage

Read each sentence. Then, rewrite each sentence, correcting any errors in the usage of modifiers to make comparisons. If a sentence contains no errors, write *correct*.

EXAMPLE   Adam is tallest than his friend Harry.

ANSWER   *Adam is taller than his friend Harry.*

11. Which of your parents is most likely to drive us to school?

12. The movie was worst than we expected.

13. Which of the two campsites is farthest?

14. Sean arrived at the library more later than Tommy.

15. Jeremy's plan is most viable than Katie's plan.

16. Edgar is the better player on the football team.

17. Kairi is the more talented of her three sisters.

18. Winston is the funnier student in our class.

19. This road will be the muddiest in town after the snow melts.

20. Wear a warmest coat and leave the other in the closet.

SPEAKING APPLICATION

Take turns with a partner. Compare two movies. Your partner should listen for and identify the comparisons in your sentences.

WRITING APPLICATION

Write three sentences with errors in modifier usage. Then, exchange papers with a partner. Your partner should correct your sentences.

Using Logical Comparisons

Two common usage problems are the comparison of unrelated items and the comparison of something with itself.

Balanced Comparisons

Be certain that things being compared in a sentence are similar.

> **Your sentences should only compare items of a similar kind.**

20.2.2 RULE

The following unbalanced sentences illogically compare dissimilar things.

UNBALANCED	I prefer **Monet's paintings** to **Renoir**.
CORRECT	I prefer **Monet's paintings** to **Renoir's**.

UNBALANCED	The **length of the sofa** is longer than the **wall**.
CORRECT	The **length of the sofa** is longer than the **length of the wall**.

Note About *Other* and *Else* in Comparisons

Another illogical comparison results when something is inadvertently compared with itself.

> **When comparing one of a group with the rest of the group, make sure that your sentence contains the word *other* or the word *else*.**

20.2.3 RULE

Adding *other* or *else* when comparing one person or thing with a group will make the comparison clear and logical.

ILLOGICAL	Dad's meals are tastier than anybody's.
	(Dad's meals cannot be tastier than themselves.)

See Practice 20.2C
See Practice 20.2D

LOGICAL	Dad's meals are tastier than anybody **else's**.

PRACTICE 20.2C **Revising to Make Comparisons Balanced and Logical**

Read each sentence. Then, rewrite each sentence, correcting the unbalanced or illogical comparison.

EXAMPLE   Andre's car is newer than his mother.

ANSWER   *Andre's car is newer than his mother's.*

1. My grandmother is older than anyone in the family.

2. The damage from yesterday's snowstorm is greater than last month.

3. Katya's dress is prettier than Jennifer.

4. Teddy's bowl of noodles was bigger than his father.

5. The test Freddie took is harder than Sonny.

6. Mr. Cassar lived longer than anyone in his family.

7. The boy who sits next to me speaks Spanish more fluently than anyone.

8. Your bonsai plant looks healthier than my sister.

9. At that store, shoes are less expensive than this store.

10. The Bulldogs are better than any football team.

PRACTICE 20.2D **Writing Clear Comparisons**

Read each sentence. Then, rewrite each sentence, filling in the blanks to make a comparison that is clear and logical.

EXAMPLE   John's voice is deeper than _____.

ANSWER   *John's voice is deeper than Pete's.*

11. Dionne's work is more legible than _____.

12. The storm we had on Saturday night was worse than _____.

13. Feeding the whales is more fun than _____.

14. Contact with poison ivy can hurt as much as _____.

15. Listening to music is more relaxing than _____.

16. A moose's antlers are bigger than _____.

17. His report on the history of Japan was more fascinating than _____ report.

18. Ask Margie to check the records because she is more thorough than _____.

19. The colors in that painting are similar to _____.

20. Wing's paper is longer than _____ in the class.

SPEAKING APPLICATION

Take turns with a partner. Say sentences that have unbalanced or illogical comparisons. Your partner should restate your sentences, using balanced and logical comparisons.

WRITING APPLICATION

Use sentences 11, 13, and 17 as models to write similar sentences. Then, exchange papers with a partner. Your partner should fill in the blanks to make the comparison in each sentence clear and logical.

Avoiding Comparisons With Absolute Modifiers

Some modifiers cannot be used logically to make comparisons because their meanings are *absolute*—that is, their meanings are entirely contained in the positive degree. For example, if a line is *vertical*, another line cannot be *more* vertical. Some other common absolute modifiers are *dead, entirely, fatal, final, identical, infinite, opposite, perfect,* and *unique*.

> **Avoid using absolute modifiers illogically in comparisons.**

RULE 20.2.4

| INCORRECT | The leaves on the trees look **more dead** in winter. |
| CORRECT | The leaves on the trees look **dead** in winter. |

Often, it is not only the word *more* or *most* that makes an absolute modifier illogical; sometimes it is best to replace the absolute modifier with one that expresses the intended meaning more precisely.

| ILLOGICAL | Some people believe that the stock exchange is the **most perfect** way to set prices. |
| CORRECT | Some people believe that the stock exchange is the **best** way to set prices. |

Sometimes an absolute modifier may overstate the meaning that you want.

| ILLOGICAL | The soccer loss to the rival team was the **most fatal** to our record this year. |
| CORRECT | The soccer loss to the rival team was the **most severe** to our record this year. |

See Practice 20.2E
See Practice 20.2F
See Practice 20.2G
See Practice 20.2H

In the preceding example, *most fatal* is illogical because something is either fatal or it is not. However, even *fatal* is an overstatement. *Most severe* better conveys the intended meaning.

PRACTICE 20.2E Revising Sentences to Correct Comparisons Using Absolute Modifiers

Read each sentence. Then, correct each illogical comparison by using more precise words.

EXAMPLE   The universe may be very infinite.

ANSWER   *The universe may be infinite.*

1. Jason's opinions are the most opposite of mine.

2. This model comes in a more infinite number of colors than that one.

3. Be sure the two poles are most perpendicular.

4. The judge's decision is extremely absolute.

5. The two lines in the figure on this page are more parallel.

6. Mom should treat us more equally.

7. His report was more complete than mine.

8. This step is more irrevocable than the last one.

9. A scorpion's sting is more fatal than the bite of a brown recluse spider.

10. The flowers I picked yesterday are less dead than the ones you picked.

PRACTICE 20.2F Revising Overstated Absolute Modifiers

Read each sentence. Then, rewrite each sentence, revising the overstated absolute modifier.

EXAMPLE   He has a very unique personality.

ANSWER   *He has a unique personality.*

11. Those two movies are the most identical films I have ever seen.

12. Luis executed the jump shot with a very perfect throw.

13. Turtles can live a long time, but they are not extremely immortal.

14. Juan was determined to do his very absolute best on the test.

15. That pile of papers is more unequal to this one.

16. The results of the election are extremely final.

17. The need for food and shelter is a very universal requirement of all living things.

18. After the storm, the electricity in our house went completely dead.

19. Love can be more eternal than beauty.

20. Roger's new portrait is the most perfect.

SPEAKING APPLICATION

Take turns with a partner. Say sentences that incorrectly use absolute modifiers. Your partner should restate your sentences correctly.

WRITING APPLICATION

Write three sentences with overstated absolute modifiers. Then, exchange papers with a partner. Your partner should revise the overstated absolute modifiers in your sentences.

PRACTICE 20.2G ▷ Correcting Problems in Comparison

Read each sentence. Then, rewrite each, correcting incorrect use of comparative and superlative degree, double comparisons, unbalanced and illogical comparisons, and comparisons with absolute modifiers.

EXAMPLE   My mother's cooking is worser than my father's.

ANSWER   *My mother's cooking is **worse** than my father's.*

1. The linen fabric is delicater than the hemp fabric.

2. After I crashed Erin's computer, I felt badly.

3. Comparing the old and the new mattresses, I felt the new one was the most comfortable.

4. Chip plays the drums good.

5. His drums are more pricier than mine.

6. The weather in Boulder is sunnier than Buffalo.

7. Grandma's memory is better than anyone's.

8. The new ring fit me more perfectly than the one I lost.

9. This year's first snow came earlier than last year.

10. The Crowne Plaza hotel in Pittsfield is taller than any building there.

PRACTICE 20.2H ▷ Making Correct Comparisons

Based on the directions in each numbered item, write a new sentence in which you make a comparison.

EXAMPLE   Compare Picasso with all other artists.

ANSWER   *Compared with all other artists, Picasso is the most inventive.*

11. Compare the winter weather in Florida with that in New Hampshire.

12. Compare biking with all other forms of transportation.

13. Compare the color red with all other colors.

14. Compare dogs with all other pets.

15. Compare bottled water with bottled soda.

16. Compare an Olympic-sized pool with a wading pool.

17. Compare the size of 12-inch and 16-inch pizzas.

18. Compare drinking water with all other drinks.

19. Compare two pairs of identical twins.

20. Compare two perfectly pitched baseball games.

SPEAKING APPLICATION

Take turns with a partner. Decide to say a sentence about the weather with a correct or incorrect comparison. Your partner should tell you why the sentence is correct or incorrect.

WRITING APPLICATION

Write a brief paragraph that logically compares TV shows. In your paragraph, use each of the following adjectives correctly: *perfect, unique, equal.*

Test Warm-Up

DIRECTIONS
Read the introduction and the passage that follows. Then, answer the questions to show that you can use and understand the function of modifiers in reading and writing.

Sebastian wrote this paragraph comparing New Hampshire and Vermont. Read the paragraph and think about the changes you would suggest as a peer editor. When you finish reading, answer the questions that follow.

New Hampshire vs. Vermont

(1) New Hampshire and Vermont share a border; how do they compare? (2) A good map shows that they are exactly equal in area. (3) New Hampshire has been a state longest, since 1788 (three years ahead of Vermont), and is more populous with 1,275,000 people versus 617,000. (4) Both states boast mountains, but New Hampshire's highest peak (Mount Washington, 6,288 feet) is more high than Vermont's (Mount Mansfield, 4,393 feet). (5) New Hampshire's state tree is the white birch; Vermont's, the sugar maple. (6) Some folks might say the maple, which yields sap for maple syrup, is more valuable, but other folks say birches are the best of all trees for climbing.

1 What change, if any, should be made in sentence 2?

  A Delete *good*

  B Delete *equal*

  C Delete *exactly*

  D Make no change

2 What change, if any, should be made in sentence 3?

  F Change *longest* to **longer**

  G Delete *more*

  H Delete *longest*

  J Make no change

3 What change, if any, should be made in sentence 4?

  A Change *highest* to **most high**

  B Change *more high* to **higher**

  C Delete *more*

  D Make no change

4 What change, if any, should be made in sentence 6?

  F Change *more valuable* to **most valuable**

  G Change *valuable* to **valuabler**

  H Change *the best* to **better**

  J Make no change

CHAPTER 21

MISCELLANEOUS PROBLEMS *in* USAGE

To make your writing clearer and more precise, learn the rules for avoiding common problems in usage.

WRITE GUY *Jeff Anderson, M.Ed.*

WHAT DO YOU NOTICE?

Look for pronouns as you zoom in on lines from the poem "The Prelude" by William Wordsworth.

MENTOR TEXT

> And the errors into which I fell, betrayed
> By present objects, and by reasonings false
> From their beginnings, inasmuch as drawn
> Out of a heart that had been turned aside . . .

Now, ask yourself the following questions:

- To what do the pronouns *which* and *that* refer?
- To what does the pronoun *their* refer?

The relative pronouns *which* and *that* are used to refer to things. In the lines above, *which* refers to the noun *errors* and *that* refers to the noun *heart*. The possessive pronoun *their* shows ownership and refers to the noun *reasonings*.

Grammar for Writers Writers can choose from a variety of pronouns to make their writing less repetitive and more interesting. You can avoid some common usage problems by carefully selecting the pronouns that you use in your writing.

Who is a relative pronoun.

To whose relatives are you referring?

21.1 Negative Sentences

In English, only one *no* is needed in a sentence to deny or refuse something. You can express a negative idea with words such as *not* or *never* or with contractions such as *can't, couldn't,* and *wasn't.* (The ending *-n't* in a contraction is an abbreviation of *not.*)

WRITING COACH

www.phwritingcoach.com

Grammar Practice
Practice your grammar skills with Writing Coach Online.

Grammar Games
Test your knowledge of grammar in this fast-paced interactive video game.

Recognizing Double Negatives

Using two negative words in a sentence when one is sufficient is called a **double negative.** While double negatives may sometimes be used in informal speech, they should be avoided in formal English speech and writing.

> **Do not use double negatives in formal writing.**

The following chart provides examples of double negatives and two ways each can be corrected.

DOUBLE NEGATIVE	CORRECTIONS
I haven't seen no new movies.	I haven't seen any new movies. I have seen no new movies.
I don't have no money for tickets.	I don't have any money for tickets. I have no money for tickets.
I never see nothing when I'm saving money.	I never see anything when I'm saving money. I see nothing when I'm saving money.

Sentences that contain more than one clause can correctly contain more than one negative word. Each clause, however, should contain only one negative word.

EXAMPLES   Because the ball **didn't** go through the goalposts, it **wasn't** a field goal.

When a ball **isn't** properly centered, the kicker **can't** kick it accurately.

Forming Negative Sentences Correctly

There are three common ways to form negative sentences.

Using One Negative Word The most common ways to make a statement negative are to use one **negative word,** such as *never, no,* or *none,* or to add the contraction *-n't* to a helping verb.

> Use only one **negative word** in each clause.

21.1.2 RULE

DOUBLE NEGATIVE	Michael **isn't never** going to beat that time.
PREFERRED	Michael **isn't ever** going to beat that time.
	Michael **is never** going to beat that time.

Using *But* in a Negative Sense When *but* means "only," it usually acts as a negative. Do not use it with another negative word.

DOUBLE NEGATIVE	My paper **didn't** need **but** one more source.
PREFERRED	My paper needed **but** one more source.
	My paper needed **only** one more source.

Using *Barely, Hardly,* and *Scarcely* Each of these words is negative. If you use one of these words with another negative word, you create a double negative.

> Do not use *barely, hardly,* or *scarcely* with another negative word.

21.1.3 RULE

DOUBLE NEGATIVE	Our class **hasn't hardly** begun to study space.
PREFERRED	Our class **has hardly** begun to study space.
DOUBLE NEGATIVE	It was cloudy, so the stars **weren't barely** visible.
PREFERRED	It was cloudy, so the stars **were barely** visible.
DOUBLE NEGATIVE	I **couldn't scarcely** even see the moon.
PREFERRED	I **could scarcely** even see the moon.

See Practice 21.1A

Using Negatives to Create Understatement

Sometimes a writer wants to express an idea indirectly, either to minimize the importance of the idea or to draw attention to it. One such technique is called **understatement.**

> Understatement can be achieved by using a negative word and a word with a negative prefix, such as *un-, in-, im-, dis-,* and *under-.*

EXAMPLES   That new movie is **hardly uninteresting**.

I **wasn't uninvolved** with the characters, particularly the leads.

I did **not underestimate** my interest in the plot.

These examples show that the writer is praising the people or things he or she is discussing. In the first example, the writer states that the movie is interesting. In the second example, the writer states that he or she was involved with the characters, especially the leads. In the third example, the writer states that he or she was interested in the plot.

If you choose to use understatement, be sure to use it carefully so that you do not sound critical when you wish to praise.

EXAMPLES   Although the plot sounded familiar, her short story **wasn't uninvolving**.

She had published the story, so I guess I **shouldn't underestimate** her talent.

In both examples above, the writer is actually making a negative statement. In the first example, the writer thinks the plot is familiar, but still involving. In the second example, the writer seems to think that, because the story was published, the writer must have some talent.

See Practice 21.1B

PRACTICE 21.1A **Revising Sentences to Avoid Double Negatives**

Read each sentence. Then, rewrite each sentence to correct the double negative.

EXAMPLE   I won't never tell.

ANSWER   *I won't ever tell.*

1. Miss Conklin had not heard nothing about a special program.

2. We don't have no tickets for tonight's concert.

3. Carlos won't never make that mistake again.

4. Don't hide the keys nowhere obvious.

5. The witness hadn't seen no one suspicious.

6. The professor wouldn't accept no late papers.

7. Paul never did nothing to antagonize the crew members.

8. You should not drive that car nowhere without snow tires.

9. Hardly no one knew the answers on the exam.

10. I can't find my address book nowhere.

PRACTICE 21.1B **Using Negatives to Create Understatement**

Read each item. Then, use each item to create understatement.

EXAMPLE   impervious

ANSWER   *Adam isn't impervious to delicious desserts.*

11. incorrect

12. unaffected

13. immature

14. underfed

15. improbable

16. disowned

17. uninterested

18. uninsured

19. indescribable

20. immaterial

SPEAKING APPLICATION

Take turns with a partner. Say sentences that contain double negatives. Your partner should listen to and correct your sentences to avoid the double negatives.

WRITING APPLICATION

Use items 13, 16, and 18 to write other sentences that contain double negatives. Then, exchange papers with a partner. Your partner should correct your sentences.

21.2 Common Usage Problems

Find It/ FIX IT

1

Grammar
Game Plan

Find It/ FIX IT

5

Grammar
Game Plan

WRITING COACH

Online

www.phwritingcoach.com

Grammar Practice
Practice your
grammar skills with
Writing Coach Online.

Grammar Games
Test your knowledge
of grammar in this
fast-paced interactive
video game.

(1) a, an The use of the article *a* or *an* is determined by the sound of the word that follows it. *A* is used before consonant sounds, while *an* is used before vowel sounds. Words beginning with *h-, o-,* or *u-* may have either a consonant or a vowel sound.

EXAMPLES	**a** high mountain (*h* sound)
	a one-time offer (*w* sound)
	a unicycle (*y* sound)
	an honorable person (no *h* sound)
	an opening (*o* sound)
	an understanding smile (*u* sound)

(2) accept, except *Accept,* a verb, means "to receive." *Except,* a preposition, means "to leave out" or "other than."

VERB	The settlers **accepted** the harsh climate.
PREPOSITION	They had everything they needed **except** wool.

(3) adapt, adopt *Adapt* means "to change." *Adopt* means "to take as one's own."

EXAMPLES	Immigrants **adapt** to life in their new land.
	They often **adopt** new customs, too.

(4) affect, effect *Affect* is almost always a verb meaning "to influence." *Effect,* usually a noun, means "a result." Sometimes, *effect* is a verb meaning "to bring about" or "to cause."

VERB	The president's speech **affected** me deeply.
NOUN	Its **effect** was to get me to volunteer to help others.
VERB	The speech **effected** a change in my behavior.

(5) aggravate *Aggravate* means "to make worse." Avoid using this word to mean "annoy."

INCORRECT	The thieves **aggravated** the police.
PREFERRED	Their crimes **are aggravating** the town's problems.

(6) ain't *Ain't*, which was originally a contraction for
am not, is no longer considered acceptable in standard English.
Always use *am not*, and never use *ain't*. The exception is in
certain instances of dialogue.

(7) all ready, already *All ready*, which consists of two separate
words used as an adjective, means "ready." *Already*, which is an
adverb, means "by or before this time" or "even now."

ADJECTIVE   Michael is **all ready** to learn to drive.

ADVERB   He has started studying the manual **already** .

(8) all right, alright *Alright* is a nonstandard spelling. Make
sure you use the two-word form.

INCORRECT   With some help from conservationists, the rain forest may
be **alright** .

PREFERRED   With some help from conservationists, the rain forest may
be **all right** .

(9) all together, altogether *All together* means "together as a
single group." *Altogether* means "completely" or "in all."

EXAMPLES   The crew worked **all together** to get the job done.

They were **altogether** happy to have such good sailors.

(10) among, between Both of these words are prepositions.
Among shows a connection between three or more items.
Between generally shows a connection between two items.

EXAMPLES   Orchids may be found **among** the many varieties of
plants in the rain forest.

Small plants grow in the few rays of sunshine that
filter **between** the larger plants and the trees.

See Practice 21.2A

(11) anxious This adjective implies uneasiness, worry, or fear.
Do not use it as a substitute for *eager*.

INCORRECT   I was **anxious** for the exam period to be over.

PREFERRED   I was **anxious** about how well I'd perform.

(12) anyone, any one, everyone, every one   *Anyone* and *everyone* mean "any person" or "every person." *Any one* means "any single person (or thing)"; *every one* means "every single person (or thing)."

EXAMPLES
Anyone can appreciate art.

You can choose **any one** of the art media to explore and learn about.

Everyone might not be able to paint or sculpt.

However, **every one** of us can enjoy some form of art.

(13) anyway, anywhere, everywhere, nowhere, somewhere   These adverbs should never end in *-s*.

INCORRECT
We looked up in the sky; the stars seemed to be **everywheres** we looked.

PREFERRED
We looked up in the sky; the stars seemed to be **everywhere** we looked.

(14) as   Do not use the conjunction *as* to mean "because" or "since."

INCORRECT
I think we should stay indoors today **as** the weather is going to be terrible.

PREFERRED
I think we should stay indoors today **because** the weather is going to be terrible.

(15) as to   *As to* is awkward. Replace it with *about*.

INCORRECT
I'm worried **as to** whether I'll be able to learn to drive my dad's car.

PREFERRED
I'm worried **about** whether I'll be able to learn to drive my dad's car.

(16) at   Do not use *at* after *where*. Simply eliminate *at*.

INCORRECT
I don't know **where** my dog is **at**.

PREFERRED
I don't know **where** my dog is.

(17) at, about Avoid using *at* with *about*. Simply eliminate *at* or *about*.

INCORRECT	On weekends, I have to be home **at about** 11:00.
PREFERRED	On weekends, I have to be home **at** 11:00.

(18) awful, awfully *Awful* is used informally to mean that something is "extremely bad." *Awfully* is used informally to mean "very." Both words are overused and should be replaced with more descriptive words. In standard English speech and writing, *awful* should only be used to mean "inspiring fear or awe in someone."

OVERUSED	The heat in the desert was **awful**.
PREFERRED	The heat in the desert was **extreme**.
OVERUSED	Dad was **awfully** angry that I'd stayed out late.
PREFERRED	Dad was **very** angry that I'd stayed out late.
OVERUSED	The thunderclouds looked **awful**.
PREFERRED	The thunderclouds looked **threatening**.

(19) awhile, a while *Awhile* is an adverb that means "for a short time." *A while,* which is a noun, means "a period of time." It is usually used after the preposition *for* or *after*.

ADVERB	I waited **awhile** for Sarah to call back.
	Marty practiced his foul shot **awhile**, and finally he could make it easily.
NOUN	After **a while**, we discussed our problem.
	It did take **a while**, but Marty's form improved.

(20) beat, win When you *win*, you "achieve a victory in something." When you *beat* someone or something, you "overcome an opponent."

INCORRECT	My dad was surprised when I **won** him in tennis.
PREFERRED	My dad was surprised when I **beat** him in tennis.
	I was surprised I could **win** against my dad.

See Practice 21.2B

PRACTICE 21.2A Recognizing Usage Problems 1–10

Read each sentence. Then, choose the correct item to complete each sentence.

EXAMPLE   Getting enough sleep should have a good (affect, effect) on your health.

ANSWER   *effect*

1. Some animals (adapt, adopt) quickly to changes in their environment.

2. The president (accepted, excepted) the challenge to debate with his opponent.

3. My cousin received (a, an) honorable discharge from the navy.

4. They should have (all ready, already) left by now.

5. I (ain't, am not) taking my little brother to the park today.

6. We should shout the cheer (all together, altogether).

7. One black orchid grew (among, between) many white ones.

8. My parents said it was (alright, all right) to hold the meeting at our house.

9. Perfumes (annoy, aggravate) my sinus problems.

10. We were (all ready, already) to play the game.

PRACTICE 21.2B Recognizing Usage Problems 11–20

Read each sentence. Then, choose the correct item to complete each sentence.

EXAMPLE   (Anyone, Any one) with a driver's license is eligible for the contest.

ANSWER   *Anyone*

11. It had been quite (a while, awhile) since we had seen the ocean.

12. Several horses escaped (as, because) the gate was left open.

13. We had some questions (as to, about) the validity of the experiment.

14. We discovered where the best pizza restaurant (was, was at) in our new town.

15. What could be causing that (awful, terrible) smell?

16. I've been practicing, so I know I can (beat, win) you in a game of chess.

17. The students were (anxious, eager) about taking three tests in one day.

18. I have seen (everyone, every one) of the movies showing at the movie theater.

19. I hope you are going (somewhere, somewheres) nice for your birthday.

20. The guests arrived (at, at about) noon.

SPEAKING APPLICATION

Take turns with a partner. Choose any pair of words from Practice 21.2A (except from #8), and tell your partner your choices. Your partner should say two sentences, using both words correctly.

WRITING APPLICATION

Write two sentences that include usage problems. Then, exchange papers with a partner. Your partner should correct your sentences.

(21) because   Do not use *because* after the phrase
the reason. Say "The reason is that" or reword the sentence.

INCORRECT   One **reason** to learn another language **is because**
it's good to understand how others think.

PREFERRED   One **reason** to learn another language **is that** it's
good to understand how others think.

(22) being as, being that   Avoid using either of these
expressions. Use *because* instead.

INCORRECT   **Being as** I was leaving work late, I went right home.

PREFERRED   **Because** I was leaving work late, I went right home.

(23) beside, besides   *Beside* means "at the side of" or "close to."
Besides means "in addition to."

EXAMPLES   In many books, photographs appear **beside** the text.

Besides being pretty, they complement the text.

(24) bring, take   *Bring* means "to carry from a distant place to
a nearer one." *Take* means "to carry from a near place to a far
one."

EXAMPLES   Jake will **bring** his uniform home today.

He can **take** it back after he's washed it.

(25) can, may   Use *can* to mean "have the ability to." Use *may* to
mean "have permission to" or "to be likely to."

ABILITY   My dad **can** fix almost any mechanical thing.

PERMISSION   He said I **may** work with him on the car.

POSSIBILITY   He **may** even show me how to change the oil.

(26) clipped words   Avoid using clipped or shortened words,
such as *gym* and *photo* in formal writing.

INFORMAL   I'm going to buy the **photo** taken at the prom.

FORMAL   I'm going to buy the **photograph** taken at the prom.

(27) different from, different than   *Different from* is preferred in standard English.

INCORRECT   That college in Iowa is **different than** the one in Ohio.

PREFERRED   That college in Iowa is **different from** the one in Ohio.

(28) doesn't, don't   Do not use *don't* with third-person singular subjects. Instead, use *doesn't.*

INCORRECT   Margaret **don't** have to babysit this evening.

PREFERRED   Margaret **doesn't** have to babysit this evening.

(29) done   *Done* is the past participle of the verb *do*. It should always take a helping verb.

INCORRECT   I **done** the rest of the semester's work.

PREFERRED   I **did** the rest of the semester's work.

(30) due to   *Due to* means "caused by" and should be used only when the words *caused by* can be logically substituted.

INCORRECT   **Due to** a lack of studying, I failed my history test.

PREFERRED   My failing grade on my history test was **due to** a lack of studying.

See Practice 21.2C

(31) each other, one another   These expressions usually are interchangeable. At times, however, *each other* is more logically used in reference to only two and *one another* in reference to more than two.

EXAMPLES   Sandra, Jane, and Patti appreciated **one another's** artistic skill.

The partners relied on **each other** for honest appraisals of their work.

(32) farther, further   *Farther* refers to distance. *Further* means "additional" or "to a greater degree or extent."

EXAMPLES   Africa is **farther** away than South America.

I'd like to do some **further** study on African customs.

(33) fewer, less   Use *fewer* with things that can be counted. Use *less* with qualities and quantities that cannot be counted.

EXAMPLES   **fewer** resources, **less** experience

(34) get, got, gotten   These forms of the verb *get* are acceptable in standard English, but a more specific word is preferable.

INCORRECT   **get** a license, **got** a car, **have gotten** car repairs

PREFERRED   **earn** a license, **bought** a car, **repaired** the car

(35) gone, went   *Gone* is the past participle of the verb *go* and is used only with a helping verb. *Went* is the past tense of *go* and is never used with a helping verb.

INCORRECT   My mom and dad **gone** to work already.

                They could **have went** later this morning.

PREFERRED   My mom and dad **went** to work already.

                They could **have gone** later this morning.

(36) good, lovely, nice   Replace these overused words with a more specific adjective.

WEAK   **good** music, **lovely** decorations, **nice** dance

BETTER   **rhythmic** music, **colorful** decorations, **exciting** dance

(37) in, into   *In* refers to position. *Into* suggests motion.

EXAMPLES   The tourists are **in** the history museum.

                They walked **into** the documents room.

(38) irregardless   Avoid this word in formal speech and writing. Instead, use *regardless*.

(39) just   When you use *just* as an adverb to mean "no more than," place it immediately before the word it modifies.

INCORRECT   My paper **just** needed one more draft.

PREFERRED   My paper needed **just** one more draft.

See Practice 21.2D

(40) kind of, sort of   Do not use these phrases in formal speech. Instead, use *rather* or *somewhat*.

PRACTICE 21.2C ▶ Recognizing Usage Problems 21–30

Read each sentence. Then, choose the correct item to complete each sentence.

EXAMPLE   Who (beside, besides) you is planning to attend?

ANSWER   *besides*

1. The game's cancellation was (due to, because of) rain.

2. How is an alligator different (from, than) a crocodile?

3. Please remember to (bring, take) your jacket home from school today.

4. The reason that the cat ran is (because, that) a dog came into our yard.

5. My new computer (can, may) do more than my old one.

6. The principal announced that we could pick up our (photos, photographs) after school.

7. I sat (besides, beside) the stream and began baiting my fishing line.

8. (Being as, Because) it is after five, the store is closed and will not reopen until tomorrow.

9. I know the right answers, but Thomas (don't, doesn't).

10. We (done, have done) most of the cleaning and should be finished soon.

PRACTICE 21.2D ▶ Revising Sentences to Correct Usage Problems 31–40

Read each sentence. Then, rewrite each sentence, correcting the errors in usage.

EXAMPLE   They canceled the contest because less than 100 people entered.

ANSWER   *They canceled the contest because fewer than 100 people entered.*

11. I consider Victoria to be a nice person.

12. Nathan is kind of excited about taking acting lessons.

13. There was fewer excitement about the party after we found out that it was taking place in the gymnasium.

14. We need to get supplies for the picnic.

15. After he had went only five miles, Brad was ready to quit the race.

16. The rescue team was determined to go irregardless of the risks.

17. She stepped in the room quietly.

18. Many of the football players helped each other learn the new plays.

19. I am confident of just the answers to questions 7 and 8.

20. If you travel just a little further, you will come to Willow Springs.

SPEAKING APPLICATION

Take turns with a partner. Say sentences with usage problems. Your partner should correct each of your sentences.

WRITING APPLICATION

Write a paragraph about a topic of your choice. Include sentences that contain usage problems. Then, exchange papers with a partner. Your partner should correct the usage problems in your paragraph.

(41) lay, lie The verb *lay* means "to put or set (something) down." Its principal parts—*lay, laying, laid, laid*—are followed by a direct object. The verb *lie* means "to recline." Its principal parts—*lie, lying, lay, lain*—are not followed by a direct object.

LAY

Lay your tools on the table.

The crew **is laying** down its tools for the evening.

Sally **laid** the hammer and the saw in the toolbox.

She **had laid** them in a dry place so they wouldn't rust.

LIE

After a long day, the mountain climbers **lie** down to rest.

Their climbing tools **are lying** on the ground.

The lead climber **lay** down after planning the next climb.

The trail map **has lain** in his backpack all day.

(42) learn, teach *Learn* means "to receive knowledge." *Teach* means "to give knowledge."

EXAMPLES

It is difficult to **learn** to scuba dive.

An experienced diver can **teach** you the skills.

(43) leave, let *Leave* means "to allow to remain." *Let* means "to permit."

INCORRECT

Leave me come along with you to the store.

PREFERRED

Let me come along with you to the store.

(44) like, as *Like* is a preposition meaning "similar to" or "such as." It should not be used in place of the conjunction *as*.

INCORRECT

A smart worker is valued **like** a prized possession is valued.

PREFERRED

A smart worker is valued **as** a prized possession is valued.

A smart worker is valued **like** a prized possession.

(45) loose, lose *Loose* is usually an adjective or part of such idioms as *cut loose, turn loose,* or *break loose. Lose* is always a verb and usually means "to miss from one's possession."

EXAMPLES

The torn pocket in your jeans looks **loose**.

If you're not careful, you could **lose** your wallet.

(46) maybe, may be   *Maybe* is an adverb meaning "perhaps."
May be is a helping verb connected to a main verb.

ADVERB   **Maybe** we can schedule the dance for next month.

VERB   It **may be** too late to schedule it for this month.

(47) of   Do not use *of* after a helping verb such as *should, would,
could,* or *must.* Use *have* instead. Do not use *of* after *outside,
inside, off,* and *atop.* Simply eliminate *of.*

INCORRECT   We **should of** tried to work together more closely.

PREFERRED   We **should have** tried to work together more closely.

(48) OK, O.K., okay   In informal writing, *OK, O.K.,* and *okay* are
acceptably used to mean "all right." Do not use them in standard
English speech or writing, however.

INFORMAL   We thought the new eligibility rules were **okay** .

PREFERRED   We thought the new eligibility rules were **fair** .

(49) only   *Only* should be placed immediately before the word it
modifies. Placing it elsewhere can lead to confusion.

EXAMPLES   **Only** the settlers used wagons to travel west.
          (No one else used wagons.)

          The settlers used **only** wagons to travel west.
          (They didn't travel in any other way.)

(50) ought   Do not use *ought* with *have* or *had.*

INCORRECT   Dave **hadn't ought** to have raised the membership fee.

PREFERRED   Dave **ought not** to have raised the membership fee.

(51) outside of   Do not use this expression to mean "besides"
or "except."

INCORRECT   There are no more classes today **outside of** physics.

PREFERRED   There are no more classes today **except** physics.

(52) plurals that do not end in -s The English plurals of certain nouns from Greek and Latin are formed as they were in their original language. Words such as *criteria, media,* and *phenomena* are plural. Their singular forms are *criterion, medium,* and *phenomenon.*

INCORRECT	The **media** is an important tool for raising environmental awareness.
PREFERRED	The **media** provide important tools for raising environmental awareness.
	Important tools for raising environmental awareness are available from the **media** .

See Practice 21.2E

(53) precede, proceed *Precede* means "to go before." *Proceed* means "to move or go forward."

EXAMPLES	Final exams will **precede** graduation.
	After graduation, we will **proceed** to celebrate with our families.

(54) principal, principle As an adjective, *principal* means "most important" or "chief." As a noun, it means "a person who has controlling authority," as in a school. *Principle* is always a noun that means "a fundamental law."

ADJECTIVE	My **principal** goal is to graduate with a good average.
NOUN	The student council reports to the **principal** .
NOUN	The **principles** of Project Graduation are to help students safely celebrate their graduation.

(55) real *Real* means "authentic." In formal writing, avoid using *real* to mean "very" or "really."

INCORRECT	In Miami, it is **real** hot during August.
PREFERRED	In Miami, it is **very** hot during August.

(56) says *Says* should not be used as a substitute for *said.*

INCORRECT	Last week, May **says** for me to wait on the corner.
PREFERRED	Last week, May **said** for me to wait on the corner.

(57) seen   *Seen* is a past participle and must be used with a helping verb.

INCORRECT   They **seen** the documentary on life in China.

PREFERRED   They **had seen** the documentary on life in China.

(58) set, sit   *Set* means "to put (something) in a certain place." Its principal parts—*set, setting, set, set*—are usually followed by a direct object. *Sit* means "to be seated." Its principal parts—*sit, sitting, sat, sat*—are never followed by a direct object.

SET   Please **set** the DVR to record my favorite show.

I **have set** it many times.

Do you need help **setting** it?

Dad **will set** the recorder for his show later.

SIT   Sometimes, it's nice to just **sit** and watch the ocean.

I **am sitting** on a blanket on the sand.

I **can sit** for hours watching the waves.

In fact, I **would sit** here all summer if I could.

(59) so   Avoid using *so* when you mean "so that."

INCORRECT   Some animals keep watch **so** others can eat safely.

PREFERRED   Some animals keep watch **so that** others can eat safely.

(60) than, then   Use *than* in comparisons. Use *then* as an adverb to refer to time.

EXAMPLES   Tropical climates are hotter **than** temperate climates.

Mornings are cool; **then**, the temperature rises quickly.

(61) that, which, who   Use these relative pronouns in the following ways: *that* and *which* refer to things; *who* refers only to people.

EXAMPLES   Weeds **that** have long roots are hard to pull up.

The roots, **which** can extend far underground, often break before I can pull the whole root.

My mom, **who** is a gardener, tells me to dig them out.

(62) their, there, they're   *Their,* a possessive pronoun, always modifies a noun. *There* can be used either as an expletive at the beginning of a sentence or as an adverb showing place or direction. *They're* is a contraction of *they are.*

PRONOUN   The spectators in the stadium will cheer for **their** favorite players.

EXPLETIVE   **There** will be a great deal of noise when the home team takes the field.

ADVERB   The bleachers are over **there** , to the left and right of the scoreboard.

CONTRACTION   **They're** big enough to fit several hundred fans each.

(63) them   Do not use *them* as a substitute for *those.*

INCORRECT   **Them** boats look close, but they're miles away.

PREFERRED   **Those** boats look close, but they're miles away.

(64) to, too, two   *To* begins a prepositional phrase or an infinitive. *Too,* an adverb, modifies adjectives and other adverbs and means "excessively" or "also." *Two* is a number.

PREPOSITION   **to** the boat, **to** the ocean

INFINITIVE   **to** see dolphins, **to** look for whales

ADVERB   **too** many to count, **too** big to be believed

NUMBER   **two** sea birds, **two** whales jumping

(65) when, where   Do not use *when* or *where* immediately after a linking verb. Do not use *where* in place of *that.*

INCORRECT   Winter is **when** skiers are happiest.
               They go to **where** there are steep slopes.

See Practice 21.2F
See Practice 21.2G   PREFERRED   Winter is **the time** skiers are happiest.
See Practice 21.2H   They go to **places with** steep slopes.

PRACTICE 21.2E > **Recognizing Usage Problems 41–52**

Read each sentence. Then, choose the correct item to complete each sentence.

EXAMPLE   Boris's grandfather (learned, taught) him to play chess.

ANSWER   *taught*

1. (Leave, Let) that poor cat alone!

2. My boss (okayed, approved) my new work schedule.

3. Do you have any idea where I may (have, of) left my keys?

4. I (laid, lay) on the sofa for almost four hours.

5. There (had ought, ought) to be a rule against so much noise across from the library.

6. (Only admit, Admit only) those students who have a ticket.

7. If you don't stop making that sound, I'm going to (lose, loose) my patience!

8. I don't have any plans after school (outside of, except for) doing homework.

9. I waited for (maybe, may be) five seconds, and then I burst out laughing.

10. I began acting (like, as if) I didn't care about the dance, even though I really did care.

PRACTICE 21.2F > **Revising Sentences to Correct Usage Problems 53–65**

Read each sentence. Then, rewrite each sentence, correcting the errors in usage.

EXAMPLE   Kareem is the only person which has been friendly to me.

ANSWER   *Kareem is the only person who has been friendly to me.*

11. Marian, please sit the book on the table.

12. Do you want to set downstairs or outside?

13. Daily, at four o'clock, is when I visit my aunt.

14. The principle also teaches history.

15. I have two leave now.

16. Did you pick up them socks that were on the floor in your room?

17. I brought an extra sweater so I wouldn't get cold.

18. I don't know why their not going too the zoo.

19. Keiko seen her sister playing soccer.

20. Marco is more athletic then his brother.

SPEAKING APPLICATION

Reread each sentence in Practice 21.2E. Discuss with a partner which usage errors you've made in past writing assignments.

WRITING APPLICATION

Write four sentences that include usage problems. Then, exchange papers with a partner. Your partner should correct your sentences.

PRACTICE 21.2G **Additional Practice With Usage Problems 1–30**

Read each sentence. Then, choose the correct item to complete each sentence.

EXAMPLE   We visited (a, an) historic house, dating back to revolutionary days.

ANSWER   *a*

1. What (affect, effect) will the ice storm have on your trip?

2. Todd liked sitting (beside, besides) the guest of honor.

3. (Among, Between) all ten of us, no one spoke Latvian.

4. I'm (anxious, eager) about my score on the test that will determine if I get into that school.

5. I have nothing to say (about, as to) the incident.

6. Talia can stay for (awhile, a while) but not overnight.

7. Howie (did, done) remarkably well on the placement exam.

8. Babies seem able to (adapt, adopt) to new surroundings.

9. When you leave the post office, please (bring, take) the mail back here.

10. The reason I won't drive is (because, that) I'm underage.

PRACTICE 21.2H **Additional Practice With Usage Problems 31–65**

Read each sentence. Then, choose the correct item to complete each sentence.

EXAMPLE   Lianna got (farther, further) in her research project today than she'd expected to.

ANSWER   *further*

11. Eleazer (gone, went) from rags to riches.

12. Steven eats meals with (fewer, less) calories than he used to.

13. (Lay, Lie) down on the examination table, and the doctor will be right in.

14. The inexperienced traveler thought he might (loose, lose) his wallet.

15. The teenager (should have, should of) known better than to speak without being called upon.

16. My cousin said, "I (hadn't ought to, ought not) tell you this, but I will."

17. The flower girl will (precede, proceed) the bride by ten paces.

18. The dictator's (principals, principles) will keep the citizens living under tyranny.

19. I was upset when I (had seen, seen) my best friend in the hospital.

20. Eat less, and exercise more; (than, then) you'll lose weight.

SPEAKING APPLICATION

Take turns with a partner. On the topic of funny experiences, say sentences that contain usage errors. Your partner should correct each of your sentences.

WRITING APPLICATION

Write a paragraph on the advantages and disadvantages of birthday parties. Include usage errors. Then, exchange papers with a partner. Your partner should correct the usage errors in your paragraph.

Test Warm-Up

DIRECTIONS
Read the introduction and the passage that follows. Then, answer the questions to show that you can recognize and correct usage problems in reading and writing.

Yvonne wrote this paragraph about shopping for clothes. Read the paragraph and think about the changes you would suggest as a peer editor. When you finish reading, answer the questions that follow.

Give Me That Old-Time Shopping

(1) Shopping for clothes online seemed awfully easy to adapt to after a while. (2) Just imagine boxes of clothing arriving at your door and a system for returning the ones you don't want—postage free. (3) Being as I don't have much spare time, shopping from home struck me as all together sensible. (4) After a while, though, when I realized I was spending a lot of time taking returns from my house to the post office, I became anxious to quit. (5) Besides, I miss going in my local shops and seeing the salespeople who help me shop and accept my returns.

1 What change, if any, should be made in sentence 1?

  A Change *awfully* to **very**

  B Change *adapt* to **adopt**

  C Change *a while* to **awhile**

  D Make no change

2 What change, if any, should be made in sentence 3?

  F Change *Being as* to **Because**

  G Change *all together* to **altogether**

  H Change *Being as* to **Because** and *all together* to **altogether**

  J Make no change

3 What change, if any, should be made in sentence 4?

  A Change *a while* to **awhile**

  B Change *taking* to **bringing**

  C Change *anxious* to **eager**

  D Make no change

4 What change, if any, should be made in sentence 5?

  F Change *Besides* to **Beside**

  G Change *in* to **into**

  H Change *accept* to **except**

  J Make no change

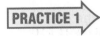

PRACTICE 1 ▷ **Combining and Varying Sentences**

Read the sentences. Then, rewrite each sentence according to the instructions in parentheses.

1. Peace was ushered in at the end of World War II. Prosperity was also ushered in. (Create a compound subject and end with a phrase.)

2. The clothes that I would need for my long journey were in my suitcase. (Invert the subject-verb order.)

3. Steven's group discussed politics to prepare their report. They also discussed the economy. (Create a compound direct object and start with an infinitive.)

4. Susan glanced over her shoulder. She heard a strange sound and wanted to see what had caused it. (Combine the sentences using the conjunction *because*.)

5. We took the shortcut to school even though I much preferred the longer, more scenic way. (Start with an adverb clause.)

6. Jason and Lisa run together every day after school. They are training for the marathon next month. (Combine the sentences using the conjunction *since*.)

7. Karen responded to the suggestion from the group to be flexible. She moved the meeting to another day. (Create a compound verb and start with an infinitive.)

8. The chairman spoke at length during the board meeting last Tuesday. (Start with a prepositional phrase.)

9. A pile of dust and deteriorating pipes were underneath the house. (Invert the subject-verb order.)

10. Styles of dress changed dramatically in the 1960s. Social norms also changed. (Create a compound subject and start with a prepositional phrase.)

PRACTICE 2 ▷ **Revising Pronoun and Verb Usage**

Read the sentences. Then, revise each sentence to fix problems in pronoun and verb usage. You may need to reorder, add, or eliminate words.

1. Someone left their jacket in the theater.

2. Whom is in charge of cleaning up the mess?

3. Both Jessica and me am going to the movies.

4. He losed his algebra book for the third time.

5. The person in charge is me.

6. She chasing that dog around the park, but she can't catch him.

7. Them is the first two picked for the team.

8. The novel was really well written, and his plot was very compelling.

9. Him and her sat next to each other.

10. To who should I submit this application?

PRACTICE 3 ▷ **Revising for Correct Use of Active and Passive Voice**

Read the sentences. Then, rewrite each sentence in the active voice. You may need to reorder, add, or delete words.

1. Poetry from this collection was beloved by people throughout the world.

2. This winter is being ranked by meteorologists as the coldest winter in decades.

3. Eating fruits and vegetables is believed by many to reduce the risk of heart disease.

4. Its fur is being licked by the cat.

5. Lunch is being served by cafeteria workers from 11:30 until 1:30.

Continued on next page ▶

Correcting Errors in Pronoun and Verb Usage

Read the sentences. Then, revise each sentence to correct agreement, verb usage, and pronoun usage. If a sentence is already correct, write *correct*.

1. The conductor requested that Sandra and me played the last few bars again.

2. The constant movement of the car caused him to get motion sickness.

3. Us is going to the basketball game on Wednesday night.

4. Henry had went all the way to the soccer game before realizing him had forgets his cleats.

5. Neither Ida nor Jesse had sings the song before.

 Using Comparative and Superlative Forms Correctly

Read the sentences. Then, write the appropriate comparative or superlative degree of the modifier in parentheses.

1. The rock concert we went to last night was the (loud) event I have ever attended.

2. Carson completed the exam (fast) than anyone else in the class.

3. Each math problem is (complex) than the next.

4. Shellie is the (strict) of the three of us when it comes to following the rules.

5. This is the (lengthy) book I have ever read.

 Avoiding Double Negatives

Read the sentences. Then, choose the word in parentheses that makes each sentence negative without forming a double negative.

1. The farmer wouldn't want (no, any) locusts damaging his crop this year.

2. Velma was extremely stubborn; she didn't want (no one, anyone) telling her what to do.

3. She had done (nothing, anything) like that before.

4. They weren't (nowhere, anywhere) that they had ever been before.

5. Ella would (never, ever) go near the abandoned house.

PRACTICE 7 **Avoiding Usage Problems**

Read the sentences. Then, choose the correct expression to complete each sentence.

1. Expecting to (loose, lose) the game, Ingrid just went out there and had fun playing.

2. Scott was (accepted, excepted) into his first-choice college.

3. The teacher said we (can, may) try out this plan of ours for a week.

4. Staying up all night can have a bad (effect, affect) on you the next day.

5. There are (less, fewer) people at this track meet (than, then) there were at the previous one.

6. (Since, As) it was not polite to linger, we left immediately after the show.

7. He announced that he was (already, all ready) to go, so we followed him out the door.

8. (Among, Between) the two of us, we can figure out the answer.

9. I (accept, except) your help gratefully; you (can, may) feed the baby.

10. How is today's weather any different (from, than) last week's?

CHAPTER 22

CAPITALIZATION

Use correct conventions of capitalization to shape how you present ideas for your readers.

WRITE GUY *Jeff Anderson, M.Ed.*

WHAT DO YOU NOTICE?

Keep track of capitalization as you zoom in on these lines from the poem "London, 1802" by William Wordsworth.

MENTOR TEXT

> Milton! thou should'st be living at this hour:
> England hath need of thee: she is a fen
> Of stagnant waters: altar, sword, and pen,
> Fireside, the heroic wealth of hall and bower,
> Have forfeited their ancient English dower . . .

Now, ask yourself the following questions:

- Why is the first word in each line capitalized?
- Which words are proper nouns? Which word is a proper adjective? Why are they capitalized?

The first word in each line of a traditional poem is capitalized even if the line starts in the middle of a complete thought. The words *Milton* and *England* are proper nouns naming a specific person and place, so they would be capitalized regardless of their position. Proper adjectives are capitalized because they are derived from proper nouns. The proper adjective *English* in the last line is formed from *England*.

Grammar for Writers Writers use capitalization to help their readers navigate and understand text. Therefore, checking for correct capitalization is an essential step in the writing process.

There are no capitals in your short story.

Maybe I just write small.

22.1 Capitalization in Sentences

Just as road signs help to guide people through a town, capital letters help to guide readers through sentences and paragraphs. Capitalization signals the start of a new sentence or points out certain words within a sentence to give readers visual clues that aid in their understanding.

Using Capitals for First Words

Always capitalize the first word in a sentence.

RULE 22.1.1 ▷ Capitalize the first word in **declarative, interrogative, imperative,** and **exclamatory** sentences.

DECLARATIVE	**J**ack told me all about it.
INTERROGATIVE	**H**ow old are you?
IMPERATIVE	**B**e careful on the steps.
EXCLAMATORY	**H**eads up!

RULE 22.1.2 ▷ Capitalize the first word in **interjections** and **incomplete questions.**

INTERJECTIONS	**F**antastic!
INCOMPLETE QUESTIONS	**W**ho said? **W**hen?

The word *I* is always capitalized, whether it is the first word in a sentence or not.

RULE 22.1.3 ▷ Always capitalize the pronoun *I*.

EXAMPLE	Bob, Fred, and **I** went fishing.

22.1.4 RULE

Capitalize the first word after a colon only if the word begins a complete sentence. Do not capitalize the word if it begins a list of words or phrases.

SENTENCE FOLLOWING A COLON | He asked for a ride: **H**e could not take another step.

LIST FOLLOWING A COLON | I will leave the following items for you: **m**y toolbox, the saw, and some tape.

22.1.5 RULE

Capitalize the first word in each line of traditional poetry, even if the line does not start a new sentence.

EXAMPLE | **I** think that I shall never see
A poem lovely as a tree. – Joyce Kilmer

See Practice 22.1A

Using Capitals With Quotations

There are special rules for using capitalization with **quotations.**

22.1.6 RULE

Capitalize the first word of a **quotation.** However, do not capitalize the first word of a continuing sentence when a quotation is interrupted by identifying words or when the first word of a quotation is the continuation of a speaker's sentence.

EXAMPLES | Margaret shouted, "**S**top the bus!"

"**A**s I was counting them," she said, "**h**e started to wrap them."

She said that he is "**t**he strongest person she knows."

See Practice 22.1B

PRACTICE 22.1A **Capitalizing Words**

Read each sentence. Then, rewrite each sentence, using correct capitalization.

EXAMPLE   oh no! this can't be happening!

ANSWER   *Oh no! This can't be happening!*

1. should we go somewhere this weekend?

2. i have everything that we need for the party: food, decorations, music, and games.

3. stop hovering by the door and come inside.

4. do not go gentle into that good night, old age should burn and rave at close of day. —Dylan Thomas

5. have you ever seen such an entertaining school musical?

6. what? when did you say we need to leave?

7. great news! the debate team finished first in their competition!

8. the mayor announced the outcome: all groups reached an agreement on the site of the new recreation center.

9. this novel has given me some great insights into life during the early twentieth century.

10. i wondered if i had packed enough clothes for my trip.

PRACTICE 22.1B **Using Capitals With Quotations**

Read each sentence. Then, write the word or words in each sentence that should be capitalized and correctly capitalize them.

EXAMPLE   the actor exclaimed, "wow! the theater is full tonight!"

ANSWER   *The, Wow, The*

11. "my understanding," Juliet said, "was that you would make the presentation."

12. Miranda asked, "does anyone know which is the most direct route to the mall?"

13. "i agree," James replied. "the characters in the story are complex and well-developed."

14. "i am not sure," Roger said, "but i think there is a great place to camp in that wooded area."

15. my mother always said that "time heals all wounds."

16. Michelle wondered, "will you be looking for a new job in April?"

17. "i really feel," Finula said, "that spending time with family should be a priority."

18. cindy remarked that she had "never seen such a crowd of people before."

19. "how do you know that?" he asked. "the announcement was never made."

20. "it wasn't entirely clear to me whether Karla was attending the party," Vinnie said.

SPEAKING APPLICATION

Take turns with a partner. Tell funny stories, using a variety of sentences. Your partner should identify the letters that should be capitalized in your sentences.

WRITING APPLICATION

Write a brief dialogue between you and a friend in which you discuss your interests. Be sure to use capitalization correctly in your quotations.

22.2 Proper Nouns

Capitalization makes important words stand out in your writing, such as the names of people, places, countries, book titles, and other proper names. Sometimes proper names are used as nouns and sometimes as adjectives modifying nouns or pronouns.

Find It / FIX IT

8

Grammar
Game Plan

Using Capitals for Proper Nouns

Nouns, as you may remember, are either **common** or **proper.**

Common nouns, such as *sailor*, *brother*, *city*, and *ocean*, identify classes of people, places, or things and are not capitalized.

Proper nouns name specific examples of people, places, or things and should be capitalized.

Capitalize all **proper** nouns.

RULE 22.2.1

EXAMPLES	**W**endy	**R**everend **B**rown	**G**overnor **J**ohnson
	Atlanta	**T**hird **S**treet	**B**lair **H**ouse
	Elizabeth	**M**oby **D**ick	RMS **Q**ueen

Names

Each part of a person's name—the given name, the middle name or initial standing for that name, and the surname—should be capitalized. If a surname begins with *Mc* or *O'*, the letter following it is capitalized (McAdams, O'Reilly).

Capitalize each part of a person's name even when the full name is not used.

RULE 22.2.2

EXAMPLES	**H**al **C**urry	**V. R. S**mall	**T**homas **H. P**erry

Capitalize the proper names that are given to animals.

EXAMPLES	**T**ippy	**L**assie	**P**epper

Proper Nouns 547

Geographical and Place Names

If a place can be found on a map, it should generally be capitalized.

RULE
22.2.3

Capitalize geographical and place names.

Examples of different kinds of geographical and place names are listed in the following chart.

GEOGRAPHICAL AND PLACE NAMES	
Streets	Madison Avenue, First Street, Green Valley Road
Towns and Cities	Dallas, Oakdale, New York City
Counties, States, and Provinces	Champlain County, Texas, Quebec
Nations and Continents	Austria, Kenya, the United States of America, Asia, Mexico, Europe
Mountains	the Adirondack Mountains, Mount Washington
Valleys and Deserts	the San Fernando Valley, the Mojave Desert, the Gobi
Islands and Peninsulas	Aruba, the Faroe Islands, Cape York Peninsula
Sections of a Country	the Northeast, Siberia, the Great Plains
Scenic Spots	Gateway National Park, Carlsbad Caverns
Rivers and Falls	the Missouri River, Victoria Falls
Lakes and Bays	Lake Cayuga, Gulf of Mexico, the Bay of Biscayne
Seas and Oceans	the Sargasso Sea, the Indian Ocean
Celestial Bodies and Constellations	Mars, the Big Dipper, moon, Venus
Monuments and Memorials	the Tomb of the Unknown Soldier, Kennedy Memorial Library, the Washington Monument
Buildings	Madison Square Garden, Fort Hood, the Astrodome, the White House
School and Meeting Rooms	Room 6, Laboratory 3B, the Red Room, Conference Room C

Capitalizing Directions

Words indicating direction are capitalized only when they refer to a section of a country.

EXAMPLES   Cotton was a major crop of the **S**outh.

Columbus sailed **w**est to find the New World.

Capitalizing Names of Celestial Bodies

Capitalize the names of celestial bodies except *moon* and *sun.*

EXAMPLE   **S**aturn is the sixth planet from the **s**un, and it has at least 31 **m**oons.

Capitalizing Buildings and Places

Do not capitalize words such as *theater, hotel, university,* and *park,* unless the word is part of a proper name.

EXAMPLES   She went to Yellowstone **P**ark last summer.

I love to walk in the **p**ark.

Events and Times

Capitalize references to historic events, periods, and documents as well as dates and holidays. Use a dictionary to check capitalization.

> **Capitalize the names of specific events and periods in history.**

22.2.4   RULE

SPECIAL EVENTS AND TIMES	
Historic Events	the Battle of Waterloo, World War I
Historical Periods	the Manchu Dynasty, Reconstruction
Documents	the Bill of Rights, the Magna Carta
Days and Months	Monday, June 22, the third week in May
Holidays	Labor Day, Memorial Day, Veterans Day
Religious Holidays	Rosh Hashanah, Christmas, Easter
Special Events	the World Series, the Holiday Antiques Show

Capitalizing Seasons

Do not capitalize seasons unless the name of the season is being used as a proper noun or adjective.

EXAMPLES   We are going to the lake this **s**ummer.

The **R**ye **S**ummer **F**estival is held each August.

Capitalize the names of organizations, government bodies, political parties, races, nationalities, languages, and religions.

VARIOUS GROUPS	
Organizations	Rotary, Knights of Columbus, the Red Cross
Institutions	the Museum of Fine Arts, the Mayo Clinic
Schools	Kennedy High School, University of Texas
Businesses	General Motors, Prentice Hall
Government Bodies	Department of State, Federal Trade Commission, House of Representatives
Political Parties	Republicans, the Democratic party
Nationalities	American, Mexican, Chinese, Israeli, Canadian
Languages	English, Italian, Polish, Swahili
Religions and Religious References	Christianity: God, the Holy Spirit, the Bible Judaism: the Lord, the Prophets, the Torah Islam: Allah, the Prophets, the Qur'an, Mohammed Hinduism: Brahma, the Bhagavad Gita, the Vedas Buddhism: the Buddha, Mahayana, Hinayana

See Practice 22.2A
See Practice 22.2B

References to Mythological Gods When referring to mythology, do not capitalize the word *god* (the *gods* of Olympus).

Capitalize the names of awards; the names of specific types of air, sea, and spacecraft; and brand names.

EXAMPLES   the **G**andhi **P**eace **P**rize   the **S**ilver **S**tar

Smooth & **C**lean soap   **A**pollo **X**

PRACTICE 22.2A **Identifying Proper Nouns**

Read each sentence. Then, write the proper noun or nouns in each sentence.

EXAMPLE   Mount Rushmore is located in South Dakota.

ANSWER   *Mount Rushmore, South Dakota*

1. The Oceans Cruise Line travels through the Mediterranean Sea, making stops in Spain, Italy, and Greece.
2. The Republican candidate gave a speech in Little Rock, Arkansas, today.
3. We took a family vacation to the Grand Canyon with Aunt Esther.
4. My friend, Nathan, enjoys playing songs on his Superstar electric guitar.
5. Mr. Gonzalez, the exchange teacher from Spain, also speaks Portuguese.
6. The reporter received a Pulitzer Prize.
7. The Constitution was ratified by most of the states by 1788.
8. Sacagawea guided Lewis and Clark on their westward expedition.
9. In Pompeii, Mount Vesuvius erupted and destroyed the entire city.
10. Governor Fields became a member of the cabinet; he was the head of the Department of Agriculture.

PRACTICE 22.2B **Capitalizing Proper Nouns**

Read each sentence. Then, write the word or words in each sentence that should be capitalized, and capitalize them, using conventions of capitalization correctly and consistently.

EXAMPLE   What event caused the start of world war I?

ANSWER   *World War I*

11. The terra-cotta warriors guarded the tomb of shi huangdi, china's first emperor.
12. Write to the board of health if you have some concerns about penelope's restaurant.
13. We mapped marco polo's travels through china.
14. In science class, I learned about the sun, mercury, venus, earth, and mars.
15. Mrs. o'neill gave us the task of planning the girl scouts of america camping trip this year.
16. The renaissance is a period of history with advances in art, science, and literature.
17. Sue marched in the memorial day parade.
18. Many african americans, from the northeast to the southwest, voted in the election.
19. The new comic book store, bookorama, is located on the corner of main street and green avenue.
20. In greek mythology, the goddess artemis was the twin sister of the god apollo.

SPEAKING APPLICATION

Take turns with a partner. Tell about an organization that you belong to or would like to belong to someday. Your partner should identify the proper nouns that you use.

WRITING APPLICATION

Use sentence 17 as a model to write three similar sentences. Replace the proper nouns in sentence 17 with other proper nouns, correctly and consistently using conventions of capitalization.

Using Capitals for Proper Adjectives

A **proper adjective** is either an adjective formed from a proper noun or a proper noun used as an adjective.

RULE

22.2.7

> Capitalize most **proper adjectives**.

PROPER ADJECTIVES FORMED FROM PROPER NOUNS	**A**ustrian choir	**E**lizabethan play
	Afghan hound	**N**ordic countries
	German ambassador	**R**ussian food

PROPER NOUNS USED AS ADJECTIVES	the **S**enate floor	the **K**ennedy speeches
	Shakespeare festival	a **B**ible class
	the **S**miths' house	**S**icilian pizza

Some proper adjectives have become so commonly used that they are no longer capitalized.

EXAMPLES	**h**erculean effort	**d**iesel engine
	pasteurized milk	**q**uixotic hope
	venetian blinds	**t**eddy bear

Brand names are often used as proper adjectives.

RULE

22.2.8

> Capitalize a **brand name** when it is used as an adjective, but do not capitalize the common noun it modifies.

EXAMPLES	**T**imo **w**atches	**S**witzles **c**hewy bars
	Super **C**ool **j**eans	**L**onglasting **f**reezers

Multiple Proper Adjectives

When you have two or more proper adjectives used together, do not capitalize the associated common nouns.

> **Do not capitalize a common noun used with two proper adjectives.**

22.2.9 **RULE**

ONE PROPER ADJECTIVE	TWO PROPER ADJECTIVES
Hudson River	Niagara and Hudson rivers
Wilson Street	Wilson, Main, and Lakewood streets
Shinnecock Canal	Shinnecock and Chemung canals
Banking Act	Banking and Civil Rights acts
Atlantic Ocean	Atlantic and Pacific oceans
Somerset County	Somerset and Camden counties
Galapagos Islands	Galapagos and Solomon islands

Prefixes and Hyphenated Adjectives

Prefixes and hyphenated adjectives cause special problems. Prefixes used with proper adjectives should be capitalized only if they refer to a nationality.

> **Do not capitalize prefixes attached to proper adjectives unless the prefix refers to a nationality. In a hyphenated adjective, capitalize only the proper adjective.**

22.2.10 **RULE**

EXAMPLES
all-American   Anglo-American

German-speaking   pro-Russian

American Italian-language newspaper

pre-Renaissance   Sino-Japanese

pre-Christian architecture   Indo-Greeks

See Practice 22.2C
See Practice 22.2D

PRACTICE 22.2C **Capitalizing Proper Adjectives**

Read each sentence. Then, write the word or words in each sentence that should be capitalized and capitalize them correctly.

EXAMPLE Nina and David are in the same french class.

ANSWER *French*

1. St. mark's basilica in Venice is an example of byzantine architecture.

2. kenyan long-distance runners have won many olympic medals.

3. We spent a relaxing day along the lake michigan shore.

4. He subscribes to a spanish-language newspaper.

5. Both african elephants and asian elephants are endangered species.

6. Damien exchanged his musicala brand trumpet for a kingly.

7. My house is across from sheila young's house.

8. His family went to the irish festival last month.

9. Bonnie has a french bull dog and a german shepherd.

10. During summer, I attend shakespeare plays performed in davidson's park.

PRACTICE 22.2D **Revising Sentences to Correct Capitalization Errors**

Read each sentence. Then, rewrite each sentence, using the conventions of capitalization correctly and consistently.

EXAMPLE My grandparents like to listen to italian operas on the radio.

ANSWER *My grandparents like to listen to Italian operas on the radio.*

11. Meshaun's favorite baseball team is the texas rangers.

12. ulysses s. grant led the union forces during the civil war.

13. The chinatown restaurants serve excellent chinese soups and entrees.

14. I have seen travel express buses all over the country, from miami to seattle.

15. The all-american athletes enjoyed the white house luncheon.

16. I never saw such adorable french poodles as the ones in the park.

17. In russian history, nicholas II was the last tsar, or emperor.

18. Many european immigrants arrived at ellis island in new york harbor.

19. Will you take german or french next year?

20. Last monday was rosh hashanah, the jewish new year.

SPEAKING APPLICATION

Discuss with a partner the importance of capitals. Suggest three ways capitalization makes reading and comprehension easier.

WRITING APPLICATION

Write a brief paragraph that contains proper adjectives and proper nouns. Be sure to use conventions of capitalization correctly and consistently.

Find It/ FIX IT

8

Grammar Game Plan

22.3 Other Uses of Capitals

Even though the purpose of using capital letters is to make writing clearer, some rules for capitalization can be confusing. For example, it may be difficult to remember which words in a letter you write need to start with a capital, which words in a book title should be capitalized, or when a person's title—such as Senator or Reverend—needs to start with a capital. The rules and examples that follow should clear up the confusion.

WRITING COACH

Online

www.phwritingcoach.com

Grammar Practice

Practice your grammar skills with Writing Coach Online.

Grammar Games

Test your knowledge of grammar in this fast-paced interactive video game.

Using Capitals in Letters

Capitalization is required in parts of personal letters and business letters.

Capitalize the first word and all nouns in letter salutations and the first word in letter closings.

RULE

22.3.1

SALUTATIONS

Dear **W**endy,

Dear **D**octor:

Dear **M**rs. **P**arson:

My **d**ear **S**ister,

CLOSINGS

With **d**eep **r**espect,

Yours with **m**uch **l**ove,

Sincerely and **f**orever **y**ours,

Best **r**egards,

Using Capitals for Titles

Capitals are used for titles of people and titles of literary and artistic works. The charts and rules on the following pages will guide you in capitalizing titles correctly.

Capitalize a person's title only when it is used with the person's name or when it is used as a proper name by itself.

WITH A PROPER NAME **S**enator **P**ilter was reelected for a second term.

AS A PROPER NAME I'm glad you can join us, **G**randfather.

IN A GENERAL REFERENCE The **c**ongressman followed the results of the election.

The following chart illustrates the correct form for a variety of titles. Study the chart, paying particular attention to compound titles and titles with prefixes or suffixes.

SOCIAL, BUSINESS, RELIGIOUS, MILITARY, AND GOVERNMENT TITLES	
Commonly Used Titles	Sir, Madam, Miss, Professor, Doctor, Reverend, Bishop, Sister, Father, Rabbi, Corporal, Major, Admiral, Mayor, Governor, Ambassador
Abbreviated Titles	*Before names*: Mr., Mrs., Ms., Dr., Hon. *After names*: Jr., Sr., Ph.D., M.D., D.D.S., Esq.
Compound Titles	Vice President, Secretary of State, Lieutenant Governor, Commander in Chief
Titles With Prefixes or Suffixes	ex-Congressman Randolph, Governor-elect Loughman

Some honorary titles are capitalized. These include First Lady of the United States, Speaker of the House of Representatives, Queen Mother of England, and the Prince of Wales.

> **Capitalize certain honorary titles even when the titles are not followed by a proper name.**

22.3.3 RULE

EXAMPLE

The **p**resident and **F**irst **L**ady visited with the **q**ueen of England.

Occasionally, the titles of other government officials may be capitalized as a sign of respect when referring to a specific person whose name is not given. However, you usually do not capitalize titles when they stand alone.

EXAMPLES

We thank you, **G**overnor, for taking us on this guided tour.

Twelve **s**enators voted to block the bill.

> **Relatives are often referred to by titles. These references should be capitalized when used with or as the person's name.**

22.3.4 RULE

WITH THE PERSON'S NAME

In the spring, **U**ncle **B**ill would take us hiking.

AS A NAME

Bob said that **G**randmother showed him how to do it.

> **Do not capitalize titles showing family relationships when they are preceded by a possessive noun or pronoun.**

22.3.5 RULE

EXAMPLES

our **a**unt   his **f**ather   Evan's **m**other

> **Capitalize the first word and all other key words in the titles of books, periodicals, poems, stories, plays, paintings, and other works of art.**

The following chart lists examples to guide you in capitalizing titles and subtitles of various works. Note that the articles (*a, an,* and *the*) are not capitalized unless they are used as the first word of a title or subtitle. Conjunctions and prepositions are also left uncapitalized unless they are the first or last word in a title or subtitle or contain four letters or more. Note also that verbs, no matter how short, are always capitalized.

TITLES OF WORKS	
Books	*The Red Badge of Courage* *Profiles in Courage* *All Through the Night* *John Ford: The Man and His Films* *Heart of Darkness*
Periodicals	*International Wildlife, Allure,* *Better Homes and Gardens*
Poems	"The Raven" "The Rime of the Ancient Mariner" "Flower in the Crannied Wall"
Stories and Articles	"Editha" "The Fall of the House of Usher" "Here Is New York"
Plays and Musicals	*The Tragedy of Macbeth* *Our Town* *West Side Story*
Paintings	*Starry Night* *Mona Lisa* *The Artist's Daughter With a Cat*
Music	*The Unfinished Symphony* "Heartbreak Hotel" "This Land Is Your Land"

22.3.7 RULE

Capitalize titles of educational courses when they are language courses or when they are followed by a number or preceded by a proper noun or adjective. Do not capitalize school subjects discussed in a general manner.

WITH CAPITALS	Honors Biology	Math 3
	History 105	Economics 313
	Latin	French

WITHOUT CAPITALS	geology	psychology
	algebra	biology
	history	math

EXAMPLES

This year, I will be taking woodworking, English, Honors Chemistry, and world history.

Mary's favorite classes are art history, French, and chemistry.

She does not like math and physical education as much.

See Practice 22.3A
See Practice 22.3B
See Practice 22.3C
See Practice 22.3D

After Russian class, I have to rush across the building to biology.

Read each item. Then, rewrite each item, correcting the errors in capitalization.

EXAMPLE   Dear aunt Rosanne,

ANSWER   Aunt

1. Ms. Barbara o. Doctrow
2. lenox, MA 01240
3. Dear sir:
4. best wishes,
5. yours truly,
6. 12 sherwood drive
7. Forest hills, NY 11375
8. Dearest brother,
9. november 12, 2010
10. Millburn, nj 07041

Read each sentence. Then, rewrite the word or words in each sentence that should be capitalized.

EXAMPLE   I have never met dr. Branson.

ANSWER   *Dr.*

11. Pardon my saying so, senator, but mayor Harding is right.
12. I agree that mr. Felt is fully recovered.
13. queen Elizabeth I ruled when sir Francis Drake defeated the Spanish Armada.
14. A colonel without a captain is useless according to general Campbell.
15. I voted for congressman Moore because he had more experience than his opponent.
16. In my opinion, *a day apart* is a fantastic title for the book.
17. In the movie *one flew over the cuckoo's nest*, nurse Ratchet plays the antagonist.
18. I noticed sergeant Smithers with the commander this morning.
19. The nurse asked dr. Blithe to clarify his prescription for mr. Bloomberg.
20. When will professor Jackson return our papers on Homer's *the odyssey*?

WRITING APPLICATION

Write examples of letter parts: recipient's address, sender's return address, date of letter, salutation, closing. Be sure to correctly use conventions of capitalization.

SPEAKING APPLICATION

Discuss with a partner the importance of capitalization in names and titles. Together, answer the following question: How does capitalizing a title show respect?

PRACTICE 22.3C **Using All of the Rules of Capitalization**

Read each sentence. Then, rewrite each sentence, using the conventions of capitalization correctly and consistently.

EXAMPLE   Kelly is an american citizen; her father, mr. borge, is danish-born.

ANSWER   *Kelly is an American citizen; her father, Mr. Borge, is Danish-born.*

1. the president of the united states both works and lives in the white house.

2. It is ironic that general "stonewall" jackson was killed by his own troops.

3. The great wall of china impressed mr. cheng so much that he wrote a book about it.

4. robert louis stevenson's book *kidnapped* is an adventure story set in scotland.

5. ms. malone was appointed the new head of the english department at the university.

6. "Her royal majesty queen elizabeth II recently visited the united states," said the british reporter.

7. I think senator McVittie made strong arguments during the debate.

8. *The star-spangled banner* was written in baltimore harbor by francis scott key.

9. mr. and mrs. lane hosted the memorial day picnic.

10. Did you read the latest issue of *stars*?

PRACTICE 22.3D **Revising Using All of the Rules of Capitalization**

Read the paragraph. For each item in bold type, rewrite any word that has an error in capitalization. If the numbered item is correct, write *correct*.

EXAMPLE   The (1) **Trip to Washington** is scheduled for (2) **thursday, November 19.**

ANSWER   (1) *trip*
          (2) *Thursday*

With only two days to see the sights and do some (1) **Research in washington, d.c.,** we'll have to plan carefully. My wish list includes the following: (2) **Several of the Museums** at the Smithsonian Institution, (3) **the Lincoln Memorial,** and the memorial to those lost in Vietnam. I hope there's also time to visit the (4) **library of congress,** where I'd like to see the (5) **declaration of independence,** and to visit the (6) **Headquarters** of the (7) **Environmental Protection Agency.** Maybe our first stop should be (8) **a tourism office** or Web site to ask the following: (9) **should we start** on one side of the city—(10) **say, the East**—and work our way west, or can we take subways back and forth?

WRITING APPLICATION

Write four sentences. Each sentence should contain a title such as "Professor." Two sentences should demonstrate when the title is capitalized, and the other two sentences should demonstrate when it is not capitalized.

SPEAKING APPLICATION

Dictate four sentences with words that require capitalization to a partner. Your partner should write the sentences using correct conventions of capitalization. Read the sentences and discuss if the words are correctly capitalized.

Test Warm-Up

DIRECTIONS
Read the introduction and the passage that follows. Then, answer the questions to show that you can use and understand the function of capitalization in reading and writing.

Manolo wrote this paragraph about Thanksgiving. Read the paragraph and think about the changes you would suggest as a peer editor. When you finish reading, answer the questions that follow.

The Origin of Thanksgiving

(1) The U.S. holiday known as Thanksgiving goes back to the autumn of 1621, long before the Nation was founded. (2) The governor of Plymouth, Leader of one of the first British settlements here, invited nearby Native Americans to celebrate with him and the other Pilgrims. (3) They held a three-day Festival of recreation and food to express thanks for the settlers' harvest. (4) In 1863, the celebration became an official national holiday, observed on the fourth Thursday of november.

1 What change, if any, should be made in sentence 1?

  A Change *Thanksgiving* to **thanksgiving**

  B Change *autumn* to **Autumn**

  C Change *Nation* to **nation**

  D Make no change

2 What change should be made in sentence 2?

  F Change *Leader* to **leader**

  G Change *British* to **british**

  H Change *Native Americans* to **native Americans**

  J Change *Pilgrims* to **pilgrims**

3 What change, if any, should be made in sentence 3?

  A Change *Festival* to **festival**

  B Change *recreation* to **Recreation**

  C Change *settlers'* to **Settlers'**

  D Make no change

4 What change, if any, should be made in sentence 4?

  F Change *national holiday* to **National Holiday**

  G Change *fourth* to **Fourth**

  H Change *november* to **November**

  J Make no change

PUNCTUATION

Follow the conventions of punctuation to craft clear sentences
that readers can follow with ease.

CHAPTER 23

WRITE GUY *Jeff Anderson, M.Ed.*

WHAT DO YOU NOTICE?

Keep track of punctuation as you zoom in on lines from *Beowulf*,
translated by Burton Raffel.

MENTOR TEXT

> Now Grendel and I are called
> Together, and I've come. Grant me, then,
> Lord and protector of this noble place,
> A single request!

Now, ask yourself the following questions:

- What purpose does the apostrophe serve in the second line?
- What does the exclamation mark tell you about the request
  being made?

In the second line, the apostrophe in *I've* shows that the letters
h and *a* have been deleted from the word *have* to form the
contraction. Writers also use apostrophes to show possession, such
as in the phrase *Beowulf's request*. The exclamation mark shows
that the speaker is making his single request with great emotion.

Grammar for Writers Writers who understand how
to correctly use punctuation can be creative while
knowing that readers will still understand their
ideas. Punctuation serves many purposes, so use
it in a variety of ways to make your writing more
interesting.

Do you always check your punctuation?

Yes! Of course! Especially the exclamation marks!

23.1 End Marks

End marks tell readers when to pause and for how long. They signal the end or conclusion of a sentence, word, or phrase. There are three end marks: the **period (.)**, the **question mark (?)**, and the **exclamation mark (!)**.

Using Periods

A **period** indicates the end of a declarative or imperative sentence, an indirect question, or an abbreviation. The period is the most common end mark.

RULE 23.1.1 Use a **period** to end a declarative sentence, a mild imperative sentence, and an indirect question.

A **declarative sentence** is a statement of fact, idea, or opinion.

DECLARATIVE SENTENCE	This is an interesting painting.

An **imperative sentence** gives a direction or command. Often, the first word of an imperative sentence is a verb.

MILD IMPERATIVE SENTENCE	Finish cooking the meal.

An **indirect question** restates a question in a declarative sentence. It does not give the speaker's exact words.

INDIRECT QUESTION	Bill asked me whether it would rain.

Other Uses of Periods

In addition to signaling the end of a statement, periods can also signal that words have been shortened, or abbreviated.

RULE 23.1.2 Use a period after most abbreviations and after initials.

PERIODS IN ABBREVIATIONS	
Titles	Dr., Sr., Mrs., Mr., Gov., Maj., Rev., Prof.
Place Names	Ave., Bldg., Blvd., Mt., Dr., St., Ter., Rd.
Times and Dates	Sun., Dec., sec., min., hr., yr., A.M.
Initials	E. B. White, Robin F. Brancato, R. Brett

Some abbreviations do not end with periods. Metric measurements, state abbreviations used with ZIP Codes, and most standard measurements do not need periods. The abbreviation for inch, *in.,* is the exception.

EXAMPLES mm, cm, kg, L, C, CA, TX, ft, gal

The following chart lists some abbreviations with and without periods.

ABBREVIATIONS WITH AND WITHOUT END MARKS	
approx. = approximately	misc. = miscellaneous
COD = cash on delivery	mph = miles per hour
dept. = department	No. = number
doz. = dozen(s)	p. or pg. = page; pp. = pages
EST = Eastern Standard Time	POW = prisoner of war
FM = frequency modulation	pub. = published, publisher
gov. or govt. = government	pvt. = private
ht. = height	rpm = revolutions per minute
incl. = including	R.S.V.P. = please reply
ital = italics	sp. = spelling
kt. = karat or carat	SRO = standing room only
meas. = measure	vol. = volume
mfg. = manufacturing	wt. = weight

Sentences Ending With Abbreviations When a sentence ends with an abbreviation that uses a period, do not put a second period at the end. If an end mark other than a period is required, add the end mark.

EXAMPLES	Please call Bob Fans Sr**.**
	Is that Sam Bents Jr**. ?**

RULE 23.1.3

> Do not use periods with acronyms, words formed with the first or first few letters of a series of words.

See Practice 23.1A

ACRONYMS	USA (United States of America)
	DOB (Date of Birth)

RULE 23.1.4

> Use a period after numbers and letters in outlines.

EXAMPLE

I**.** Maintaining your pet's health

   A**.** Diet

      1**.** For a puppy

      2**.** For a mature dog

   B**.** Exercise

Using Question Marks

A **question mark** follows a word, phrase, or sentence that asks a question. A question is often in inverted word order.

RULE 23.1.5

> Use a **question mark** to end an interrogative sentence, an incomplete question, or a statement intended as a question.

INTERROGATIVE SENTENCE	Does grass grow from seed **?**
	What time do you want to meet for brunch **?**
INCOMPLETE QUESTION	Many birds fly south for the winter. Why **?**
	I will take you home. When **?**

Use care, however, in ending statements with question marks. It is better to rephrase the statement as a direct question.

STATEMENT WITH A QUESTION MARK	The puppies haven't been born yet **?**
	We are going home **?**
REVISED INTO A DIRECT QUESTION	Haven't the puppies been born yet **?**
	Are we going home **?**

Use a period instead of a question mark with an **indirect question**—a question that is restated as a declarative sentence.

| EXAMPLE | Ken wanted to know when the take-out food he ordered would come **.** |

Using Exclamation Marks

An **exclamation mark** signals an exclamatory sentence, an imperative sentence, or an interjection. It indicates strong emotion and should be used sparingly.

See Practice 23.1B

> **Use an exclamation mark to end an exclamatory sentence, a forceful imperative sentence, or an interjection expressing strong emotion.**

RULE 23.1.6

| EXCLAMATORY SENTENCE | Look at the great weather **!** |
| FORCEFUL IMPERATIVE | Don't drop the packages **!** |

An interjection can be used with a comma or an exclamation mark. An exclamation mark increases the emphasis.

EXAMPLES	Wow **!** The day was wonderful **.**
	Oh **!** The action was great **.**
WITH A COMMA	Wow **,** the day was wonderful **.**

PRACTICE 23.1A > Using Periods Correctly in Sentences

Read each sentence. Then, rewrite the sentence, adding periods where needed. If the sentence is correct, write *correct*.

EXAMPLE   Socrates, who was born in 469 BC, was a philosopher.

ANSWER   *Socrates, who was born in 469 B.C., was a philosopher.*

1. I found a 5-kt gold earring on the ground.

2. Mail the letter to Dr Hugo Rivera, 9 Main St, Ft Worth, Tex, before Wednesday.

3. J R R Tolkien wrote the *Lord of the Rings* trilogy.

4. Kylie asked if Thurgood Marshall had been a supreme court judge.

5. Her flight is scheduled for arrival on Tues, Mar 12, at 7:14 PM.

6. Capt Mattson led the parade down Grant Blvd before turning onto Fifth St.

7. It took 6 m of string to tie all the newspapers.

8. Dr Sanchez asked me if I brushed my teeth after every meal

9. Tang finally woke up at 9:50 AM.

10. Franklin M. Martin Jr gave me this book.

PRACTICE 23.1B > Using Question Marks and Exclamation Marks Correctly in Sentences

Read each item. Then, write the correct end mark for each item.

EXAMPLE   What time does the museum open

ANSWER   ?

11. What a lovely card

12. Great work

13. How long have I been asleep

14. How often does the train stop at this station

15. Will you help at the car wash

16. Don't slam the door

17. Do you know how to change a flat tire

18. Thank you for these sweet-smelling flowers

19. I'm glad that's over

20. When did Jacinta call

SPEAKING APPLICATION

Take turns with a partner. Say sentences that contain initials and abbreviations for titles, place names, times, and dates. Your partner should tell where periods would be inserted if your sentences were written.

WRITING APPLICATION

Write two sentences that use question marks correctly and two sentences that use exclamation marks correctly. Label each sentence as *interrogative*, *exclamatory*, or *forceful imperative*.

23.2 Commas

A **comma** tells the reader to pause briefly before continuing
a sentence. Commas may be used to separate elements in a
sentence or to set off part of a sentence.

Commas are used more than any other internal punctuation mark.
To check for correct comma use, read a sentence aloud and note
where a pause helps you to group your ideas. Commas signal to
readers that they should take a short breath.

WRITING COACH

Online

www.phwritingcoach.com

Grammar Practice

Practice your
grammar skills with
Writing Coach Online.

Grammar Games

Test your knowledge
of grammar in this
fast-paced interactive
video game.

Using Commas With Compound Sentences

A **compound sentence** consists of two or more main or
independent clauses that are joined by a coordinating
conjunction, such as *and, but, for, nor, or, so,* or *yet.*

> Use a **comma** before a conjunction to separate two or more
> independent or main clauses in a **compound sentence**.

23.2.1 RULE

Use a comma before a conjunction when there are complete
sentences on both sides of the conjunction.

EXAMPLE

Jane is getting ready to compete**,** but I won't
independent clause
be able to see her perform.
independent clause

In some compound sentences, the main or independent clauses
are very brief, and the meaning is clear. When this occurs, the
comma before the conjunction may be omitted.

EXAMPLES

Polly read the chapter but she didn't understand it.

Laura would like to come for dinner but she is too

busy today.

In other sentences, conjunctions are used to join compound
subjects, objects, appositives, verbs, prepositional phrases,
or subordinate clauses. When the conjunction joins only two
elements, the sentence does not take a comma before the
conjunction.

CONJUNCTIONS WITHOUT COMMAS	
Compound Subject	Tim and Mike met at camp for the hike.
Compound Verb	The team laughed and reminisced as they remembered their season.
Two Prepositional Phrases	The player ran down the field and past the goalie.
Two Subordinate Clauses	I enjoy hiking trips only if they are short and if we camp outside.

A **nominative absolute** is a noun or pronoun followed by a participle or participial phrase that functions independently of the rest of the sentence.

Use a comma after a nominative absolute.

EXAMPLE   Important people being present, I decided to dress appropriately.

Grammar Game Plan

Avoiding Comma Splices

Remember to use both a comma and a coordinating conjunction in a compound sentence. Using only a comma can result in a **run-on sentence** or a **comma splice**. A **comma splice** occurs when two or more complete sentences have been joined with only a comma. Either punctuate separate sentences with an end mark or a semicolon, or find a way to join the sentences. (See Section 23.3 for more information on semicolons.)

Avoid comma splices.

INCORRECT   The snow clumped on the house, some of the gutters snapped under the weight.

CORRECT   The snow clumped on the house. Some of the gutters snapped under the weight.

Using Commas in a Series

A **series** consists of three or more words, phrases, or subordinate clauses of a similar kind. A series can occur in any part of a sentence.

> **Use commas to separate three or more words, phrases, or clauses in a series.**

23.2.4 RULE

Notice that a comma follows each of the items except the last one in these series. The conjunction *and* or *or* is added after the last comma.

SERIES OF WORDS	The pet store sold birds, cats, dogs, fish, and pet products.
SERIES OF PREPOSITIONAL PHRASES	The sign showed the way through the city, over the bridge, and past the river.
SUBORDINATE CLAUSES IN A SERIES	The critic wrote that the food was great, the atmosphere was exceptional, and the music was beautiful.

If each item (except for the last one) in a series is followed by a conjunction, do not use commas.

EXAMPLE	I rented comedies and romances and horror movies.

A second exception to this rule concerns items such as *salt and pepper*, which are paired so often that they are considered a single item.

EXAMPLES	On the platter were peanut butter and jelly, ham and cheese, and turkey and cheese sandwiches.
	Tim's favorite breakfast foods are toast and juice, oatmeal and raisins, and bacon and eggs.

Using Commas Between Adjectives

Sometimes, two or more adjectives are placed before the noun they describe.

RULE 23.2.5

> Use commas to separate **coordinate adjectives,** also called **independent modifiers,** or adjectives of equal rank.

EXAMPLES   a dark, long tunnel

a long, tiring, challenging race

An adjective is equal in rank to another if the word *and* can be inserted between them without changing the meaning of the sentence. Another way to test whether or not adjectives are equal is to reverse their order. If the sentence still sounds correct, they are of equal rank. In the first example, *a long, dark tunnel* still makes sense.

If you cannot place the word *and* between adjectives or reverse their order without changing the meaning of the sentence, they are called **cumulative adjectives.**

RULE 23.2.6

> Do not use a comma between cumulative adjectives.

EXAMPLES   a new life jacket
(*a life new jacket* does not make sense)

many long days
(*long many days* does not make sense)

RULE 23.2.7

> Do not use a comma to separate the last adjective in a series from the noun it modifies.

INCORRECT   The bright, sunny, day felt wonderful.

CORRECT   The bright, sunny day felt wonderful.

See Practice 23.2A
See Practice 23.2B

PRACTICE 23.2A ► **Using Commas Correctly in Sentences**

Read each sentence. Then, rewrite each sentence, adding commas where needed. Write the reason(s) for the comma usage.

EXAMPLE We requested the change months ago yet it hasn't happened.

ANSWER *We requested the change months ago, yet it hasn't happened.—compound sentence*

1. The camping trip was fun but it rained a lot.

2. Chili the mockingbird the pecan tree and the rodeo are all symbols of Texas.

3. The soft cushiony chair is so comfortable.

4. Sam is a sweet mild-tempered dog.

5. She took her jacket but she forgot her gloves.

6. His arm tired and sore the pitcher retired to the dugout.

7. Smiles cheers and thunderous clapping welcomed the new team to the field.

8. George flipped his hat into the air caught it and then put it on his head.

9. Dark green vegetables red meat beans and nuts are excellent sources of iron.

10. Their hands up in the air the thieves surrendered to the police.

PRACTICE 23.2B ► **Revising to Correct Errors in Comma Use**

Read each sentence. Then, rewrite each sentence, adding or deleting commas as necessary.

EXAMPLE I wanted to play, basketball, but the ball was deflated.

ANSWER *I wanted to play basketball, but the ball was deflated.*

11. Our clients, enjoyed the presentation, but didn't like the lunch.

12. During the flight I read my book.

13. Join us for the rally because, it's going to be a wild exciting gathering!

14. Mrs. Ramos has a collection of fancy, teapots.

15. No one is better than Leslie at buying designer-like expensive-looking outfits.

16. Frowns marring their faces the audience, protested the delay.

17. The ski instructor, was a young energetic teenager.

18. Mr. Harper took great care, with planning his garden, and selecting plants for it.

19. We took the boat out to go fishing, water-skiing and swimming.

20. Elizabeth took many pictures of the city, and the country, and the people she met.

SPEAKING APPLICATION

With a partner, read sentences 2 and 7 aloud. Discuss why commas are needed in those sentences.

WRITING APPLICATION

Write four sentences that use commas incorrectly. Exchange papers with a partner. Your partner should correct your sentences.

Using Commas After Introductory Material

Most material that introduces a sentence should be set off with a comma.

> **Use a comma after an introductory word, phrase, or clause.**

KINDS OF INTRODUCTORY MATERIAL	
Introductory Words	Yes, we do expect to meet with them soon.
	No, there has not been a time set to meet.
	Well, I was definitely surprised by his remark.
Nouns of Direct Address	Mia, will you answer the phone?
Introductory Adverbs	Hurriedly, they collected the money for the pizza.
	Patiently, the coach explained the play again.
Participial Phrases	Moving quickly, she avoided a potential disaster.
	Working next to each other in the office, we introduced ourselves and started to chat.
Prepositional Phrases	On the snowy mountain, the family went skiing together.
	After the lengthy flight, we were all exhausted.
Infinitive Phrases	To choose the right gift, I reviewed their housewarming list.
	To finish her test on time, Addie will have to use fewer details.
Adverbial Clauses	When he asked for a permit for the house, he was sure it would be denied.
	If you play baseball, you may be interested in going to a game.

Commas and Prepositional Phrases Only one comma should be used after two prepositional phrases or a compound participial or infinitive phrase.

EXAMPLES   In a pocket in the backpack, he found his cellphone.

Wandering in the crowd and looking for their parents, the children asked a firefighter for help.

It is not necessary to set off short prepositional phrases. However, a comma can help avoid confusion.

CONFUSING   In the rain puddles covered the road.

CLEAR   In the rain, puddles covered the road.

Using Commas With Parenthetical Expressions

A **parenthetical expression** is a word or phrase that interrupts the flow of the sentence.

> **Use commas to set off parenthetical expressions from the rest of the sentence.**

23.2.9 RULE

Parenthetical expressions may come in the middle or at the end of a sentence. A parenthetical expression in the middle of a sentence needs two commas—one on each side; it needs only one comma if it appears at the end of a sentence.

KINDS OF PARENTHETICAL EXPRESSIONS	
Nouns of Direct Address	Will you have breakfast with us, Cathy? I wonder, Mr. Colette, where they'll go for breakfast.
Conjunctive Adverbs	Someone had already bought them glasses, however. We could not, therefore, buy them.
Common Expressions	I listened to Ellie's report as carefully as everyone else did, I think.
Contrasting Expressions	Dena is twenty, not nineteen. Eva's personality, not her beauty, won Frank's heart.

Using Commas With Nonessential Expressions

To determine when a phrase or clause should be set off with commas, decide whether the phrase or clause is *essential* or *nonessential* to the meaning of the sentence. The terms *restrictive* and *nonrestrictive* may also be used.

An **essential, or restrictive, phrase** or **clause** is necessary to the meaning of the sentence. **Nonessential, or nonrestrictive, expressions** can be left out without changing the meaning of the sentence. Although the nonessential material may be interesting, the sentence can be read without it and still make sense. Depending on their importance in a sentence, appositives, participial phrases, and adjectival clauses can be either essential or nonessential. Only nonessential expressions should be set off with commas.

NONESSENTIAL APPOSITIVE	The meal was prepared by Christopher, the newest young chef.
NONESSENTIAL PARTICIPIAL PHRASE	The mountain, rising majestically in the distance, is the largest in the state.
NONESSENTIAL ADJECTIVAL CLAUSE	The river, which freezes in the winter, is popular with canoers in the summer.

Do not use commas to set off essential expressions.

ESSENTIAL APPOSITIVE	The part was played by the famous actress Katharine Hepburn.
ESSENTIAL PARTICIPIAL PHRASE	The man wearing the coat is my father.
ESSENTIAL ADJECTIVAL CLAUSE	The article that Laura suggested would change my conclusions.

See Practice 23.2C
See Practice 23.2D

PRACTICE 23.2C ▶ Placing Commas Correctly in Sentences

Read each sentence. Then, rewrite each sentence, adding commas where they are needed.

EXAMPLE   Before Monica could react the dishes had fallen to the floor.

ANSWER   *Before Monica could react, the dishes had fallen to the floor.*

1. Once the storm was over the snow melted quickly in the sun.

2. To win at chess I usually take my opponent's queen first.

3. Janice not Fernando will take the girls to the mall.

4. In addition the city has many accessible walking tours.

5. I am without a doubt the tallest person in the room.

6. Molly please make your bed.

7. Growing up we never had a treehouse.

8. Laura Ingalls Wilder who had three sisters wrote nine books in the *Little House* series.

9. Tomatoes are in fact fruits not vegetables.

10. To prevent a fire check that the toaster is unplugged.

PRACTICE 23.2D ▶ Revising Sentences for Proper Comma Use

Read each sentence. Then, rewrite each sentence, adding or deleting commas as necessary.

EXAMPLE   To ensure accuracy we counted the ballots, three times.

ANSWER   *To ensure accuracy, we counted the ballots three times.*

11. Warned by the radio announcer Mom took that alternate route, to avoid the accident not, because she was lost.

12. Please return this book to the library, for me Pru.

13. If you think you're going to sneeze, have a tissue, ready.

14. The meat, was overcooked, and too salty.

15. Moving much more slowly, than usual, Caleb showed us the dance steps.

16. Mr. Bailey who used to be a member of the Coast Guard, took in the lost kitten.

17. He must nevertheless, take the exam before Wednesday.

18. The keys, will turn up soon we hope.

19. I always use yellow mustard, not, ketchup on my hot dogs.

20. Happily she took the project home, with her.

SPEAKING APPLICATION

Take turns with a partner. Say sentences with appositives, participial phrases, and adverbial clauses. Your partner should tell where commas would be inserted if your sentences were written.

WRITING APPLICATION

Write a short story that includes at least six different ways to use commas, including introductory material, parenthetical expressions, and nonessential expressions.

Using Commas With Dates, Geographical Names, and Titles

Dates usually have several parts, including months, days, and years. Commas separate these elements for easier reading.

> When a date is made up of two or more parts, use a comma after each item, except in the case of a month followed by a day.

EXAMPLES The engagement took place on February 10, 2009, and they were married on June 6, 2010.

Our vacation started on April 15 and ended eight days later.
(no comma needed after the day of the month)

Commas are also used when the month and the day are used as an appositive to rename a day of the week.

EXAMPLES Friday, June 12, was the first trial flight of our new plane.

Beth will arrive on Monday, December 5, and will stay until Friday.

When a date contains only a month and a year, commas are unnecessary.

EXAMPLES I will run for office in November 2012.

Tom will visit South Africa in April 2011.

If the parts of a date have already been joined by prepositions, no comma is needed.

EXAMPLE The city's new street lighting was first turned on in May of 1935.

See Practice 23.2E

> **When a geographical name is made up of two or more parts, use a comma after each item.**

〈23.2.11〉 RULE

EXAMPLES   My parents, who moved to Dallas, Texas,

missed their old friends but like their new friends.

They're going to Ottawa, Ontario, Canada, for

their spring choir trip.

> **When a name is followed by one or more titles, use a comma after the name and after each title.**

〈23.2.12〉 RULE

EXAMPLE   John Chang, P.T., works with the football team.

A similar rule applies with some business abbreviations.

EXAMPLE   BookQual, Inc., publishes books about travel.

Using Commas in Numbers

Commas make large numbers easier to read by grouping them.

> **With large numbers of more than three digits, use a comma after every third digit starting from the right.**

〈23.2.13〉 RULE

EXAMPLES   1,000,000 dollars, 2,500 cars, 1,400 cups

> **Do not use a comma in ZIP Codes, telephone numbers, page numbers, years, serial numbers, or house numbers.**

〈23.2.14〉 RULE

See Practice 23.2F

ZIP CODE	07481	YEAR NUMBER	2010
TELEPHONE NUMBER	(201) 555-0748	SERIAL NUMBER	603-528-919
PAGE NUMBER	Page 2343	HOUSE NUMBER	12581 Rivers Road

PRACTICE 23.2E > **Using Commas With Dates and Geographical Names**

Read each sentence. Then, rewrite each sentence to show where to correctly place commas in dates and geographical names.

EXAMPLE   His golf vacation is in Yona Guam.

ANSWER   *His golf vacation is in Yona, Guam.*

1. The Declaration of Independence was not actually signed on July 4 1776.

2. On September 17 1998, we visited our friends in Helena Montana.

3. Tuesday February 21 is a holiday in China.

4. Anika was born in Brisbane Queensland Australia.

5. Many students in Anne Arundel County Maryland apply to the Naval Academy in Annapolis.

6. February 29 2000 was a leap day.

7. Terrance graduated at the top of his class on June 3 2004 in Alexandria Virginia.

8. We left for Santa Fe New Mexico on November 15 2005.

9. Abraham Lincoln was born on February 12 1809 and died on April 15 1865.

10. Mr. Wong visited London England in July 2009.

PRACTICE 23.2F > **Editing Sentences for Proper Comma Usage**

Read each sentence. Then, rewrite each sentence, adding or deleting commas as necessary.

EXAMPLE   Did Jane Carrie and Jean go to Lincoln Nebraska last summer?

ANSWER   *Did Jane, Carrie, and Jean go to Lincoln, Nebraska, last summer?*

11. Taylor Paul Ph.D. will be teaching this class, and Ms. Tiffany Lloyd will assist.

12. My favorite beaches were in Santa Monica California and Cape Cod Massachusetts.

13. Each box contains 185000 plastic cups.

14. My neighbor bought the house on, Saturday April 20 and he built that fence on April 25.

15. The quote by Edgar Allan Poe is found on page 1501.

16. Lionel Blaire M.D. lives in Boise Idaho during the summer and Dallas Texas in the winter.

17. Despite the traffic, we made it to Wilmington Delaware by Saturday July 9.

18. Neville Ward Sr. opened Kiddie Toys Ltd. in March 2002.

19. Karen lives at 1,394, Livingston Street.

20. If my printer breaks, I won't be able to finish the assignment by Friday October 9.

SPEAKING APPLICATION

Reread sentences 4 and 10. Discuss with a partner the necessity of commas in geographical names, especially in the names of foreign locations.

WRITING APPLICATION

Write six sentences with misused commas in dates, geographical names, titles, and numbers. Exchange papers with a partner. Your partner should correct your sentences.

Using Commas With Addresses and in Letters

Commas are also used in addresses, salutations of friendly letters, and closings of friendly or business letters.

> **Use a comma after each item in an address made up of two or more parts.**

Commas are placed after the name, street, and city. No comma separates the state from the ZIP Code. Instead, insert an extra space between them.

EXAMPLE   Send a card to the Santana family, 350 Ocean Lane, Brooklyn, New York 11201.

Fewer commas are needed when an address is written in a letter or on an envelope.

EXAMPLE   Ms. Wanda Smith

85 Tribute Street

Scranton, PA 18501

> **Use a comma after the salutation in a personal letter and after the closing in all letters.**

See Practice 23.2G

SALUTATIONS   Dear Aunt Sarah,   Dear Will,

CLOSINGS   Your friend,   Cordially,

Using Commas in Elliptical Sentences

In **elliptical sentences,** words that are understood are left out. Commas make these sentences easier to read.

> **Use a comma to indicate the words left out of an elliptical sentence.**

EXAMPLE   The Brinks celebrate their holidays formally;
the Blanes **,** casually.

The words *celebrate their holidays* have been omitted from the
second clause of the sentence. The comma has been inserted in
their place so the meaning is still clear. The sentence could be
restated in this way: *The Brinks celebrate their holidays formally;
the Blanes celebrate their holidays casually.*

Using Commas With Direct Quotations

Commas are also used to indicate where **direct quotations** begin
and end. (See Section 23.4 for more information on punctuating
quotations.)

> **Use commas to set off a direct quotation from the rest of a
> sentence.**

EXAMPLES   "You're here late **,** " commented Jake's brother.

She said **,** "The orientation ran longer than
expected **.** "

"I hope **,** " Anna's mother said **,** "the professor
doesn't forget the test **.** "

Using Commas for Clarity

Commas help you group words that belong together.

> **Use a comma to prevent a sentence from being misunderstood.**

UNCLEAR   Near the auditorium builders were constructing
new dorms.

CLEAR   Near the auditorium **,** builders were constructing
new dorms.

Misuses of Commas

Because commas appear so frequently in writing, some people are tempted to use them where they are not needed. Before you insert a comma, think about how your ideas relate to one another.

Find It/ FIX IT
7
Grammar
Game Plan

MISUSED WITH AN ADJECTIVE AND A NOUN After a walk, I enjoy a hot, hearty, snack.

CORRECT After a walk, I enjoy a hot, hearty snack.

MISUSED WITH A COMPOUND SUBJECT After their vacation, my friend John, and his friend Steve, were invited to the reunion.

CORRECT After their vacation, my friend John and his friend Steve were invited to the reunion.

MISUSED WITH A COMPOUND PREDICATE He peeked over the wall, and found his book.

CORRECT He peeked over the wall and found his book.

MISUSED WITH A COMPOUND OBJECT He chose a jacket with pockets, and a hood.

CORRECT He chose a jacket with pockets and a hood.

MISUSED WITH PHRASES Reading the book, and wondering about the author, she read the back cover.

CORRECT Reading the book and wondering about the author, she read the back cover.

MISUSED WITH CLAUSES She discussed what sources are useful in writing an essay, and which sources are reliable.

CORRECT She discussed what sources are useful in writing an essay and which sources are reliable.

PRACTICE 23.2G Adding Commas to Addresses and Letters

Read each item. Then, add commas where needed.

EXAMPLE   Dear Uncle Steve

ANSWER   *Dear Uncle Steve,*

1. Dear Cousin Debbie

2. Send an invitation to Theodore Keyes 112 Jackson Lane Miami Florida 33126.

3. Yours truly
   Mason West

4. My best friend moved to Fort Meyers Texas.

5. All the best
   Aunt Tilda

6. Dear Lynn Sharyn and Andrew

7. Douglas Frey
   4 Main Street
   Hastings-on-Hudson NY 10706

8. Sincerely
   Uncle Cory

9. With love
   Mom and Dad

10. My penpal lives at 135 E. River Street Lake Winnipesaukee New Hampshire 03245.

PRACTICE 23.2H Revising Sentences With Misused Commas

Read each sentence. Then, if a sentence contains a misused comma(s), rewrite the sentence with the comma(s) placed correctly. If the sentence is correct, write *correct*.

EXAMPLE   Last year I traveled, to Montevideo Uruguay for my job.

ANSWER   *Last year, I traveled to Montevideo, Uruguay, for my job.*

11. As of November, 16 2008, the district no longer served juice with school lunches.

12. I enjoy, ice cold, sweet yet sour lemonade.

13. Kemau, and his sister, ski every weekend.

14. Nobel prizes are presented in Stockholm Sweden every December, 10th.

15. Marlene, the spelling bee winner, is a good writer, too.

16. Austin Texas, and Salem Oregon are state capitals.

17. On February, 14 a special day to many people, I always give my mother a dozen roses.

18. Thinking about his next vacation, and where it would be, Mike drank his sweet herbal tea.

19. Greta shook my hand, and thanked me.

20. The inventor's notebook filled with diagrams, and illustrations, showed his innovative ideas.

SPEAKING APPLICATION

After correcting the items in Practice 23.2G, discuss with a partner the use of the comma or commas in each item.

WRITING APPLICATION

Write three compound-complex sentences, using as many commas as you can.

PRACTICE 23.2I > Revising Sentences for Missing Commas

Reach each sentence. Then, rewrite each sentence, adding commas wherever they are needed.

EXAMPLE   Do you agree with the proverb that says "The end justifies the means"?

ANSWER   *Do you agree with the proverb that says, "The end justifies the means"?*

1. I met Sue when we both lived at 1324 Second Avenue fifth floor.

2. Charles got his acceptance letter in February; Regina in March.

3. The letter ended with "Your friend Rory."

4. Who said "To go beyond is as wrong as to fall short"?

5. Next I went to college and studied literature.

6. Marilyn and John live on Wells Hill Road in Lakeville Connecticut.

7. Address the note *Dear Brother* and get directly to the point.

8. Above the door a horseshoe was hung.

9. "To go beyond" he said "is as wrong as to fall short."

10. Before you left without saying goodbye.

PRACTICE 23.2J > Identifying and Revising Comma Errors

Read each sentence. Then, rewrite each sentence, adding or deleting commas as necessary. If a sentence is correct as written, write *correct*.

EXAMPLE   I look forward to a scoop of delicious, creamy, ice cream.

ANSWER   *I look forward to a scoop of delicious, creamy ice cream.*

11. Barbara from camp, and her sister are traveling to Yellowstone National Park.

12. Lila wants to walk along the beach, and swim in the Caribbean at night.

13. In heavy rain puddles tend to form in the driveway.

14. Margaret Mead said "We won't have a society if we destroy the environment."

15. In exchange for helping him with math, he'll teach me the tango, and introductory Italian.

16. Send the invitation to Jeffrey at 320 Riverside Drive New York NY 10025.

17. Did the closing of the letter really say, "Love Denny"?

18. I was honored to win the award but nervous about giving a speech.

19. Neither Lawrence, nor Erin, will visit on Saturday.

20. English is a language of science; Italian of food.

SPEAKING APPLICATION

Take turns with a partner. Dictate a letter to a friend or relative. Include a salutation, brief body, and closing. As you dictate, tell your partner where to insert commas.

WRITING APPLICATION

Using the sentences in Practice 23.2J as a model, write four sentences with misused commas. Exchange your paper with a partner and correct each other's errors.

Test Warm-Up

DIRECTIONS
Read the introduction and the passage that follows. Then, answer the questions to show that you can use and understand the function of commas in reading and writing.

Nidal wrote an e-mail to his friend Lev. Read the piece and think about the changes you would suggest as a peer editor. When you finish reading, answer the questions that follow.

Subject: Your Upcoming Visit

Dear Lev,

(1) I can't believe that Saturday, June, 6, 2011, is finally only a week away. (2) We started planning your visit here so long ago—in the summer of 2010. (3) I'm going to the library today so I was wondering if there are any DVDs I should borrow for us to watch together. (4) Any ideas? (5) Of course we'll be outside more than in front of a television or computer. (6) I can't wait to introduce you to friends, neighbors, and other folks in the neighborhood. (7) I've been telling them about you forever.

See you soon
Nidal

---

1 What change should be made in sentence 1?

A Delete the commas after *June* and after *2011*

B Delete only the comma after *June*

C Put commas before and after *finally*

D Delete all the commas

2 What change, if any, should be made in sentence 3?

F Insert a comma after *library*

G Insert a comma after *DVDs*

H Insert a comma after *today*

J Make no change

3 What change, if any, should be made in sentence 5?

A Insert a comma after *Of course*

B Insert a comma after *outside*

C Insert a comma after *television*

D Make no change

4 What change, if any, should be made in the closing?

F Add a comma after *soon*

G Add a period after *soon*

H Change *See you soon* to **Yours truly**

J Make no change

23.3 Semicolons and Colons

The **semicolon (;)** is used to join related independent clauses. Semicolons can also help you avoid confusion in sentences with other internal punctuation. The **colon (:)** is used to introduce lists of items and in other special situations.

Using Semicolons to Join Independent Clauses

Semicolons establish relationships between two independent clauses that are closely connected in thought and structure. A semicolon can also be used to separate independent clauses or items in a series that already contain a number of commas.

> Use a semicolon to join related independent clauses that are not already joined by the conjunctions *and, but, for, nor, or, so, or yet.*

23.3.1 RULE

EXAMPLE We explored the country together **;** we were amazed at all the different kinds of people we met.

Do not use a semicolon to join two unrelated independent clauses. If the clauses are not related, they should be written as separate sentences with a period or another end mark to separate them.

Note that when a sentence contains three or more related independent clauses, they may still be separated with semicolons.

EXAMPLE The sky grew dark **;** the wind picked up **;** the storm rolled in.

Semicolons Join Clauses Separated by Conjunctive Adverbs or Transitional Expressions

Conjunctive adverbs are adverbs that are used as conjunctions to join independent clauses. **Transitional expressions** are expressions that connect one independent clause with another one.

> Use a semicolon to join independent clauses separated by either a **conjunctive adverb** or a **transitional expression.**

23.3.2 RULE

CONJUNCTIVE ADVERBS	*also, besides, consequently, first, furthermore, however, indeed, instead, moreover, nevertheless, otherwise, second, then, therefore, thus*
TRANSITIONAL EXPRESSIONS	*as a result, at this time, for instance, in fact, on the other hand, that is*

Place a semicolon *before* a conjunctive adverb or a transitional expression, and place a comma *after* a conjunctive adverb or transitional expression. The comma sets off the conjunctive adverb or transitional expression, which introduces the second clause.

EXAMPLE

He always wins; in fact, he runs faster than everyone.

Because words used as conjunctive adverbs and transitions can also interrupt one continuous sentence, use a semicolon only when there is an independent clause on each side of the conjunctive adverb or transitional expression.

EXAMPLES

He visited army bases in four states in only one week; consequently, he had no time to say good-bye.

We were very impressed, however, with Amy's knowledge of English history.

Using Semicolons to Avoid Confusion

Sometimes, semicolons are used to separate items in a series.

Use semicolons to avoid confusion when independent clauses or items in a series already contain commas.

When the items in a series already contain several commas, semicolons can be used to group items that belong together. Semicolons are placed at the end of all but the last item.

INDEPENDENT CLAUSES

The city, supposedly filled with food, was a fable; and the hungry, tired explorers would only find it in their dreams.

ITEMS IN A SERIES

On their holiday, my cousins visited their older brother, who lives in New Mexico; my sister, who lives in Texas; and my friend, Bill, who lives in California.

Semicolons appear commonly in a series that contains nonessential appositives, participial phrases, or adjectival clauses. Commas should separate the nonessential material from the words it modifies; semicolons should separate the complete items in the series.

APPOSITIVES

I went to the offices of Mr. Wills, the dean; Mrs. Monegro, the admissions director; and William Dee, the president.

PARTICIPIAL PHRASES

I acquired a love for cooking from television, watching live cooking shows; from home, watching my mother cook; and from magazines, reading about famous chefs.

ADJECTIVAL CLAUSES

The large truck that I bought has headlamps, which are very bright; a spot light, which has just been installed; and a powerful engine, which has been newly rebuilt.

Using Colons

The **colon (:)** is used to introduce lists of items and in certain special situations.

> **Use a colon after an independent clause to introduce a list of items. Use commas to separate three or more items.**

Independent clauses that appear before a colon often include the words *the following, as follows, these,* or *those.*

EXAMPLES | For my presentation, I had to interview the following experts: a senator, an assemblyperson, and a mayor.

> **Do not use a colon after a verb or a preposition.**

INCORRECT | Terry always orders: books, tapes, and DVDs.

CORRECT | Terry always orders books, tapes, and DVDs.

> **Use a colon to introduce a quotation that is formal or lengthy or a quotation that does not contain a "he said/she said" expression.**

EXAMPLE | Oliver Wendell Holmes Jr. wrote this about freedom: "It is only through free debate and free exchange of ideas that government remains responsive to the will of the people and peaceful change is effected."

Even if it is lengthy, dialogue or a casual remark should be introduced by a comma. Use the colon if the quotation is formal or has no tagline.

A colon may also be used to introduce a sentence that explains the sentence that precedes it.

> **Use a colon to introduce a sentence that summarizes or explains the sentence before it.**

 RULE 23.3.7

See Practice 23.3A
See Practice 23.3B

EXAMPLE Her explanation for being late was believable : She got lost and had to stop to ask for directions.

Notice that the complete sentence introduced by the colon starts with a capital letter.

> **Use a colon to introduce a formal appositive that follows an independent clause.**

RULE 23.3.8

EXAMPLE I had finally decided on a sport : running.

The colon is a stronger punctuation mark than a comma. Using the colon gives more emphasis to the appositive it introduces.

> **Use a colon in a number of special writing situations.**

 RULE 23.3.9

SPECIAL SITUATIONS REQUIRING COLONS	
Numerals Giving the Time	10 : 30 A.M. 7 : 15 P.M.
References to Periodicals (Volume Number: Page Number)	*Scientific American* 32 : 16 *Time* 24 : 19
Biblical References (Chapter Number: Verse Number)	Esther 4 : 14
Subtitles for Books and Magazines	*A Field Guide for Aquatic Life* : *Sea Creatures and Their Habitats*
Salutations in Business Letters	Dear Mr. Jones : Dear Madam :
Labels Used to Signal Important Ideas	**Warning** : NO Trespassing

PRACTICE 23.3A **Adding Semicolons and Colons to Sentences**

Read each item. Then, rewrite each item, adding a semicolon or colon as needed.

EXAMPLE It would seem like sound advice however, I must consider the source.

ANSWER *It would seem like sound advice; however, I must consider the source.*

1. The following animals are marsupials kangaroos, koalas, and opossums.
2. The judge ordered "Court is adjourned."
3. Nora lost her compass as a result, she'll have to borrow one.
4. The answer is clear Lower ticket prices.
5. Spiro works days Mindy works nights.
6. Calvin disagreed with the council's decision nevertheless, he supported the council.
7. Janet had written a list of groceries lettuce, tomatoes, cereal, and bread.
8. Dear Ms. Mayor
9. Fred's trip went through several cities Atlanta, New York, Boston, and Chicago.
10. Don't forget the bus leaves at 800 A.M. sharp.

PRACTICE 23.3B **Using Semicolons and Colons**

Read each sentence. Then, rewrite each sentence, replacing the incorrect comma with a semicolon or a colon.

EXAMPLE The movie starred a famous actor, Paul Newman.

ANSWER *The movie starred a famous actor: Paul Newman.*

11. Due to the foggy conditions, visibility was low, therefore, traffic was slow.
12. The departing time is 4,30 P.M.
13. Joan brought all the decorations, streamers, lights, posters, and confetti.
14. The elephants ran to higher ground, the monkeys climbed back up their trees.
15. The book was written by a prolific writer, Isaac Asimov.
16. Substituting olive oil for butter is beneficial, The olive oil has no cholesterol.
17. The host welcomed his guests, "Please come in and make yourselves at home."
18. The air was cold, in fact, snow was falling.
19. We stopped in Cheyenne, Wyoming, Louisville, Kentucky, and Savannah, Georgia.
20. Guyana is in South America, Ghana is in Africa.

SPEAKING APPLICATION

With a partner, read aloud the sentences in Practice 23.3A. Then, read your corrected sentences aloud. Discuss whether it is easier or harder to read the sentences that have the semicolons and colons. Explain your answer.

WRITING APPLICATION

Write a short story about a kid who finds a good-luck piece. Use colons and semicolons to combine sentences in your story.

23.4 Quotation Marks, Underlining, and Italics

Quotation marks (" ") set off direct quotations, dialogue, and certain types of titles. Other titles are **underlined** or set in *italics*, a slanted type style.

Find It/FIX IT

6

Grammar
Game Plan

Find It/FIX IT

18

Grammar
Game Plan

Using Quotation Marks With Quotations

WRITING COACH

Online

www.phwritingcoach.com

Grammar Practice
Practice your grammar skills with Writing Coach Online.

Grammar Games
Test your knowledge of grammar in this fast-paced interactive video game.

Quotation marks identify spoken or written words that you are including in your writing. A **direct quotation** represents a person's exact speech or thoughts. An **indirect quotation** reports the general meaning of what a person said or thought.

> A **direct quotation** is enclosed in quotation marks.

RULE

23.4.1

DIRECT
QUOTATION

"When I learn to play piano," said the girl, "I'm going to practice every day."

> An **indirect quotation** does not require quotation marks.

RULE

23.4.2

INDIRECT
QUOTATION

The girl said that when she learns to play the piano, she'll practice every day.

Both types of quotations are acceptable when you write. Direct quotations, however, generally result in a livelier writing style.

Using Direct Quotations With Introductory, Concluding, and Interrupting Expressions

A writer will generally identify a speaker by using words such as *he asked* or *she said* with a quotation. These expressions, called **conversational taglines** or **tags,** can introduce, conclude, or interrupt a quotation.

Quotation Marks, Underlining, and Italics   593

Direct Quotations With Introductory Expressions

Commas help you set off introductory information so that your reader understands who is speaking.

RULE 23.4.3

> **Use a comma after short introductory expressions that precede direct quotations.**

EXAMPLE   My neighbor cautioned , "If you use the pool, you'll be liable for your safety. "

If the introductory conversational tagline is very long or formal in tone, set it off with a colon instead of a comma.

EXAMPLE   At the end of the week, Bill talked about his idea : "My desire is to advance the cause of feeding hungry children. "

Direct Quotations With Concluding Expressions

Conversational taglines may also act as concluding expressions.

RULE 23.4.4

> **Use a comma, question mark, or exclamation mark after a direct quotation followed by a concluding expression.**

EXAMPLE   "When you received the ticket , you were responsible for paying it on time , " the judge stated .

Concluding expressions are not complete sentences; therefore, they do not begin with capital letters. Closing quotation marks are always placed outside the punctuation at the end of direct quotations that are followed by concluding expressions. The concluding expressions generally end with a period.

Divided Quotations With Interrupting Expressions

You may use a conversational tagline to interrupt the words of a direct quotation, which is also called a **divided quotation.**

> **RULE 23.4.5**
>
> Use a comma after the part of a quoted sentence followed by an interrupting conversational tagline. Use another comma after the tagline. Do not capitalize the first word of the rest of the sentence. Use quotation marks to enclose the quotation. End punctuation should be inside the last quotation mark.

EXAMPLE "When you received the ticket**,** " the judge stated**,** "you were responsible for paying it on time**.** "

> **RULE 23.4.6**
>
> Use a comma, question mark, or exclamation mark after a quoted sentence that comes before an interrupting conversational tagline. Use a period after the tagline.

EXAMPLE "You received the ticket**,** " stated the judge**.** "You are responsible for paying it on time**.** "

Quotation Marks With Other Punctuation Marks

Quotation marks are used with commas, semicolons, colons, and all of the end marks. However, the location of the quotation marks in relation to the punctuation marks varies.

> **RULE 23.4.7**
>
> Place a comma or a period *inside* the final quotation mark. Place a semicolon or colon *outside* the final quotation mark.

EXAMPLES "Georginna was a great monkey**,** " sighed Father.

We just learned about his "archaeological find"**;** we are very excited.

> **RULE 23.4.8**
>
> Place a question mark or an exclamation mark inside the final quotation mark if the end mark is part of the quotation. Do not use an additional end mark.

EXAMPLE Mike wondered**,** "How could I lose the race**?** "

Place a question mark or exclamation mark outside the final quotation mark if the end mark is part of the entire sentence, not part of the quotation.

EXAMPLE   Don't you dare say "I don't know"!

Using Single Quotation Marks for Quotations Within Quotations

As you have learned, double quotation marks (" ") should enclose the main quotation in a sentence. The rules for using commas and end marks with double quotation marks also apply to **single quotation marks.**

RULE 23.4.10

Use **single quotation marks (' ')** to set off a quotation within a quotation.

EXAMPLES   "I remember Shane quoting Tanya, 'If summer comes, can fall be far behind?'," Ken said.

"The instructor said, 'You may begin'," the student explained.

Punctuating Explanatory Material Within Quotations

Explanatory material within quotations should be placed in brackets. (See Section 23.7 for more information on brackets.)

RULE 23.4.11

Use brackets to enclose an explanation located within a quotation. The brackets show that the explanation is not part of the original quotation.

EXAMPLE   The council person said, "This law is a link between two generations [young and old]."

PRACTICE 23.4A **Using Quotation Marks**

Read each sentence. Then, rewrite each sentence, inserting quotation marks where they are needed.

EXAMPLE   He said, I may not remember a name, but I never forget a face.

ANSWER   *He said, "I may not remember a name, but I never forget a face."*

1. Sure, said Fareed. I'll get it for you.

2. Pam interjected, Pick me!

3. How many songs are on the CD? asked Mike.

4. The reporter said, The grateful mother repeated, Thank you, several times.

5. Shyly, Sarah asked, Can I help?

6. Keri thought that Jill said, I can't make it; so Keri went to the library alone.

7. The machine answered, Record your message at the beep.

8. Winnie answered the phone, but no one responded when she said, Hello.

9. Taylor groaned, Not again!

10. Please don't turn off the computer, Miss Patel, the librarian requested.

PRACTICE 23.4B **Revising for the Correct Use of Quotation Marks**

Read each sentence. Then, rewrite each sentence, correcting the misuse of quotation marks.

EXAMPLE   "The river, said Virginia, is rising fast."

ANSWER   *"The river," said Virginia, "is rising fast."*

11. "The principal addressed the students: Stay in your classes until the bell rings."

12. When Ed says, "I'll be there," I believe him, I explained.

13. "Dan continued, Then, the horse jumped the fence and galloped across the field."

14. Ellen said, "I'll be right back," Marcos claimed.

15. "The article stated, The recent news leaked to the press [about the new train station] is false."

16. Oh well! said Robert, "That's the end."

17. "How much time is left to complete the exam? Myra asked."

18. "That's the best I can do, the salesman said." It is my final offer.

19. "You know, my mother said, you should really wear a coat. It is cold outside."

20. "The dessert," said Nina, is too sweet for me."

SPEAKING APPLICATION

Take turns with a partner. Say sentences that are direct quotations. Your partner should indicate where quotation marks would be needed if your sentences were written.

WRITING APPLICATION

Write five additional sentences that contain misused quotation marks. Exchange papers with a partner. Your partner should correct the misuse of the quotation marks.

Properly Punctuating Quotations With Opening Taglines

Read each sentence. Then, rewrite each sentence, adding an introductory tagline to the beginning of each quotation. Be sure to use correct conventions of punctuation.

EXAMPLE   "Things were better in the old days."

ANSWER   *My uncle always says, "Things were better in the old days."*

1. "Quarks and leptons are small particles that make up matter."

2. "Beauty is in the eye of the beholder."

3. "I'll be studying in the library."

4. "Honesty is the best policy."

5. "Red is the new black—again."

6. "Don't play that song again!"

7. "Can you keep a secret?"

8. "My dog ate my homework, but he coughed it up whole."

9. "The goal of this organization is to provide food and shelter for the needy."

10. "The earthquake made our house shake!"

Properly Punctuating Quotations With Interrupting Taglines

Add an interrupting tagline to the middle of each quotation. Be sure to use correct conventions of punctuation.

EXAMPLE   "If at first you don't succeed, try, try again."

ANSWER   *"If at first you don't succeed," my mother says, "try, try again."*

11. "The tornado did not touch down in our town."

12. "You should attend a school at which you'll be happy."

13. "His dog ran away, but then it returned home."

14. "You should start practicing the drums more often."

15. "I forgot my umbrella at home, and it rained the entire afternoon."

16. "He told a ghost story around the campfire, and my little cousin got scared."

17. "You should try learning a new song to play on the piano."

18. "My trip to Alaska was full of surprises."

19. "Do you know the way home from here?"

20. "I hit the golf ball so far that I could not see where it landed."

SPEAKING APPLICATION

Taking turns with a partner, quote a proverb or a common expression. Your partner should add a tagline to the quotation and tell the punctuation that follows the tagline.

WRITING APPLICATION

Write a fantasy story that includes dialogue between two animals. Include a variety of introductory and interrupting taglines.

PRACTICE 23.4E **Properly Punctuating Quotations With Closing Taglines**

Add a closing tagline to the end of each quotation. Be sure to correctly use conventions of punctuation.

EXAMPLE   "Winters were colder when I was young."

ANSWER   *"Winters were colder when I was young," my uncle always claims.*

1. "You left the window open last night."

2. "The basement flooded after yesterday's storm."

3. "She works many hours in her garden."

4. "He planted tomatoes, corn, and green beans this year."

5. "If you climb the tree you may get hurt."

6. "Turn left at the next traffic light."

7. "I built a tree house for my younger sister."

8. "Sing the song you learned in chorus practice yesterday."

9. "Can you believe his dog weighs 100 pounds?"

10. "Please turn off the lights when you leave the room."

PRACTICE 23.4F **Revising to Correctly Punctuate Quotations**

Rewrite each of the items, adding, deleting, or changing punctuation and capitalization where necessary.

EXAMPLE   "You have met me too late" said James Joyce.

ANSWER   *"You have met me too late," said James Joyce.*

11. "One had better die fighting against injustice," argued Ida B. Wells. "Than die like a dog or a rat in a trap."

12. Victor gave a dramatic reading of verses from "Song of Myself;" I was impressed.

13. "I'll meet you in the morning;" I e-mailed Ty; then I added, "Unless I stay up reading."

14. Alice said My mom always finds something.

15. How many podcasts have you downloaded this week? queried my sister.

16. The teacher insisted, I've already said, "Time's up. Post your papers now."

17. No! my father said. "I can't believe it."

18. "I've been called many things, boasted Tallulah Bankhead, but never an intellectual."

19. My favorite short story is "The Necklace;" Fran commented. What's yours?

20. The Greek philosopher Diogenes said I am a citizen of the world.

SPEAKING APPLICATION

Working with a partner, quote a proverb. Your partner should add a tagline at the end of the proverb and tell you each mark of punctuation that the complete sentence requires.

WRITING APPLICATION

Search the Internet for famous quotations. Copy two that are interesting and add to each a closing tagline that identifies the speaker. Be sure to correctly use conventions of punctuation.

Using Quotation Marks for Dialogue

A conversation between two or more people is called a **dialogue.**

RULE 23.4.12

> **When writing a dialogue, begin a new paragraph with each change of speaker.**

The sun slowly set over the western edge of the ski resort, as the people watched the sky turn pink.

Beth looked at the heavy snow and talked with her sister about her plans.

"I'm going south," said Beth. "I think I'll like the sunny weather better; you know I don't like the snow."

"Have you packed yet?" asked Meg. "Can I have your blue snow jacket?"

"It's all yours," said Beth. "It is fine with me if I never see it again."

RULE 23.4.13

> **For quotations longer than a paragraph, put quotation marks at the beginning of each paragraph and at the end of the final paragraph.**

John McPhee wrote an essay about a canoe trip on the St. John River in northern Maine. He introduces his readers to the river in the following way:

"We have been out here four days now and rain has been falling three. The rain appears to be ending. Breaks of blue are opening in the sky. Sunlight is coming through, and a wind is rising.

"I was not prepared for the St. John River, did not anticipate its size. I saw it as a narrow trail flowing north, twisting through balsam and spruce—a small and intimate forest river, something like the Allagash. . . ."

Using Quotation Marks in Titles

Generally, quotation marks are used around the titles of shorter works.

> Use quotation marks to enclose the titles of short written works.

WRITTEN WORKS THAT USE QUOTATION MARKS	
Title of a Short Story	"To Build a Fire" by Jack London "The Fairy Box" by Louisa May Alcott
Chapter From a Book	"The Boy Who Lived" in *Harry Potter and the Sorcerer's Stone*
Title of a Short Poem	"Mending Wall" by Robert Frost
Essay Title	"Nature" by Ralph Waldo Emerson
Title of an Article	"Tear Down This Wall" by Patrick Symmes

> Use quotation marks around the titles of episodes in a television or radio series, songs, and parts of a long musical composition.

ARTISTIC WORK TITLES THAT USE QUOTATION MARKS	
Episode	"The Loneliest People" from *60 Minutes*
Song Title	"What's Love Got to Do With It" Tina Turner
Part of a Long Musical Composition	"Spring" from *The Four Seasons* "E.T. Phone Home" from the *E.T. The Extra-Terrestrial* soundtrack

> Use quotation marks around the title of a work that is mentioned as part of a collection.

The title *Plato* would normally be underlined or italicized. In the example below, however, the title is placed in quotation marks because it is cited as part of a larger work.

EXAMPLE　　"Plato" from *Great Books of the Western World*

Using Underlining and Italics in Titles and Other Special Words

Underlining and **italics** help make titles and other special words and names stand out in your writing. Underlining is used only in handwritten or typewritten material. In printed material, italic (slanted) print is generally used instead of underlining.

RULE 23.4.17

> **Underline or italicize the titles of long written works and the titles of publications that are published as a single work.**

WRITTEN WORKS THAT ARE UNDERLINED OR ITALICIZED	
Title of a Book	*Frankenstein*
Title of a Newspaper	*The Boston Globe*
Title of a Play	*Death of a Salesman* *Hamlet*
Title of a Long Poem	*On Time*
Title of a Magazine	*Time*

The portion of a newspaper title that should be italicized or underlined will vary from newspaper to newspaper. *The New York Times* should always be fully capitalized and italicized or underlined. Other papers, however, can be treated in one of two ways: the *Los Angeles Times* or the Los Angeles *Times*. You may want to check the paper's Web site for correct formatting.

RULE 23.4.18

> **Underline or italicize the titles of movies, television and radio series, long works of music, and works of art.**

ARTISTIC WORKS THAT ARE UNDERLINED OR ITALICIZED	
Title of a Movie	*Jaws, E.T. The Extra-Terrestrial*
Title of a Television Series	*Seinfeld, The Simpsons*
Title of a Long Work of Music	the *Jupiter* Symphony
Title of an Album (on any media)	*Yellow Submarine*
Title of a Painting	*Flying Machine, Battle*
Title of a Sculpture	*Crouching Woman* *Young Mother with Child*

> **Do not underline, italicize, or place in quotation marks the name of the Bible, its books and divisions, or other holy scriptures, such as the Torah and the Quran.**

RULE 23.4.19

EXAMPLE   Betty read from James in the New Testament .

Government documents should also not be underlined or enclosed in quotation marks.

> **Do not underline, italicize, or place in quotation marks the titles of government charters, alliances, treaties, acts, statutes, speeches, or reports.**

RULE 23.4.20

EXAMPLE   The Taft-Hartley Labor Act was passed in 1947.

> **Underline or italicize the names of air, sea, and space craft.**

RULE 23.4.21

EXAMPLE   My aunt sailed on the *Queen Mary II* .

> **Underline or italicize words, letters, or numbers (figures) used as names for themselves.**

RULE 23.4.22

EXAMPLES   Her *i's* and her *I's* look too much like *1's* .

Avoid sprinkling your speech with *like* .

> **Underline or italicize foreign words and phrases not yet accepted into English.**

RULE 23.4.23

EXAMPLE   "*Buenos dias* ," she said, meaning "good day" in Spanish.

PRACTICE 23.4G **Using Punctuation in Titles and Dialogue**

Read each sentence. Then, rewrite each sentence, adding the correct punctuation where needed. If any words need to be italicized, underline those words.

EXAMPLE   I just finished reading The Grapes of Wrath, said Oscar.

ANSWER   *"I just finished reading The Grapes of Wrath," said Oscar.*

1. Let's go to the movies, Diane suggested.

2. I can't said Tony. I have to pick up my uncle at the train station. Want to come along?

3. Diana replied immediately, Sure.

4. It's going to be cold. Bring a warm sweater. Tony told Diane.

5. Whoever thought said Diego that the race would end in a tie?

6. Joe replied, Yeah, that's really unusual.

7. Kelly asked Who wrote the book Emma?

8. Trina answered, Jane Austen wrote that book; she also wrote Sense and Sensibility.

9. Julian asked, Who are the main characters in the short story The Gift of the Magi?

10. I think they're James and Della Young, said Jerome.

PRACTICE 23.4H **Revising Punctuation in Titles and Dialogue**

Read each sentence. Then, rewrite each sentence, revising the use of quotation marks. If any words need to be italicized, underline those words.

EXAMPLE   "My book report is on Frankenstein by Mary Shelley, said Louise"

ANSWER   *"My book report is on Frankenstein by Mary Shelley," said Louise.*

11. "My report Carl said is on The Canterbury Tales."

12. Isn't that about a group of people telling stories while on a trip? "asked Carmen."

13. "Yes. My favorite character is the clerk, replied Carl."

14. "Joanna chimed in I wrote my report on the Odyssey."

15. "Me, too, said Wayne"

16. "Who was your favorite character?" Joanna asked. Mine is Odysseus.

17. "Wayne replied, I liked Circe, the siren."

18. "Louise added, "I felt sorry for the Cyclops."

19. "What's a cyclops? Carmen asked"

20. "A creature with one eye," Wayne answered. Odysseus outsmarted him."

SPEAKING APPLICATION

Take turns with a partner. Say sentences that contain both dialogue and titles. For each sentence, your partner should indicate which words would be put into quotation marks and/or italicized if the sentences were written.

WRITING APPLICATION

Write a short dialogue in which two characters discuss their favorite works of literature. Use at least three titles and five lines of dialogue.

23.5 Hyphens

The **hyphen** (-) is used to combine words, spell some numbers and words, and show a connection between the syllables of words that are broken at the ends of lines.

Find It / FIX IT

19

Grammar
Game Plan

Using Hyphens in Numbers

Hyphens are used to join compound numbers and fractions.

> **Use a hyphen when you spell out two-word numbers from twenty-one through ninety-nine.**

RULE 23.5.1

EXAMPLES   fifty-five centimeters   sixty-eight meters

> **Use a hyphen when you use a fraction as an adjective but not when you use a fraction as a noun.**

RULE 23.5.2

ADJECTIVE   The recipe calls for one-half cup of milk.

NOUN   Three quarters of the convention is over.

> **Use a hyphen between a number and a word when they are combined as modifiers. Do not use a hyphen if the word in the modifier is possessive.**

RULE 23.5.3

EXAMPLES   The members took a 20-minute break.

The team put twelve weeks' work into the report.

> **If a series of consecutive, hyphenated modifiers ends with the same word, do not repeat the modified word each time. Instead, use a suspended hyphen (also called a dangling hyphen) and the modified word only at the end of the series.**

RULE 23.5.4

EXAMPLE   The eleventh- and twelfth-grade students came.

Using Hyphens With Prefixes and Suffixes

Hyphens help your reader easily see the parts of a long word.

Use a hyphen after a prefix that is followed by a proper noun or proper adjective.

The following prefixes are often used before proper nouns: *ante-*, *anti-*, *mid-*, *post-*, *pre-*, *pro-*, and *un-*.

EXAMPLES   post - Renaissance   mid - March

Use a hyphen in words with the prefixes *all-*, *ex-*, and *self-* and words with the suffix *-elect*.

EXAMPLES   self - employed   mayor - elect

Many words with common prefixes are no longer hyphenated. Check a dictionary if you are unsure whether to use a hyphen.

Using Hyphens With Compound Words

Hyphens help preserve the units of meaning in compound words.

Use a hyphen to connect two or more words that are used as one compound word, unless your dictionary gives a different spelling.

EXAMPLES   merry - go - round   on - site

father - in - law   five - year - old

Use a hyphen to connect a compound modifier that appears before a noun. The exceptions to this rule include adverbs ending in *-ly* and compound proper adjectives or compound proper nouns that are acting as an adjective.

EXAMPLES WITH HYPHENS	EXAMPLES WITHOUT HYPHENS
a well-made pair of gloves	widely held beliefs
the bright-eyed hikers	Grand Canyon hikers
an up-to-date map	Eastern European languages

When compound modifiers follow a noun, they generally do not require the use of hyphens.

EXAMPLE   The backpacks were **well made.**

However, if a dictionary spells a word with a hyphen, the word must always be hyphenated, even when it follows a noun.

EXAMPLE   The message was up-to-date.

Using Hyphens for Clarity

Some words or groups of words can be misread if a hyphen is not used.

> **Use a hyphen within a word when a combination of letters might otherwise be confusing.**

RULE 23.5.9

EXAMPLES   hi-fi, high-tech, re-elect

> **Use a hyphen between words to keep readers from combining them incorrectly.**

RULE 23.5.10

INCORRECT   the well known-actress

CORRECT   the well-known actress

PRACTICE 23.5A **Using Hyphens Correctly**

Read each item. If an item needs a hyphen or hyphens, add them. If an item does not need hyphenation, write *correct*.

EXAMPLE   editor in chief

ANSWER   *editor-in-chief*

1. happy go lucky
2. easy going nature
3. outgoing person
4. twenty first passenger
5. sister in law
6. bright young lady
7. never say never attitude
8. post Civil War
9. ever quickening pace
10. 2 liter bottle

PRACTICE 23.5B **Revising Sentences With Hyphens**

Read each sentence. Then, rewrite each sentence, correcting any error in hyphenation as needed. If the sentence is correct, write *correct*.

EXAMPLE   She likes wearing old-fashioned-clothes.

ANSWER   *She likes wearing old-fashioned clothes.*

11. There is an exhibit on man eating sharks at the city-aquarium.
12. Charlotte stared-longingly at the blue green sports car.
13. The forest is full of three hundred-year-old trees.
14. Happy Housing is a Detroit-based-organization.
15. The salesman was trying his best-to-sell me his state of the art product.
16. Jillian's mother is a board-certified-physician.
17. A government issued photo-ID is needed to enter the Pentagon.
18. My literature professor assigned us an award winning novel to read for-next-week.
19. This-is-a-time sensitive issue.
20. The meeting was for Native-American people to tell about their experiences with self employment.

SPEAKING APPLICATION

Take turns with a partner. Say words or phrases that may or may not need to be hyphenated. Your partner should indicate where the hyphens would occur in the words or phrases if they were written.

WRITING APPLICATION

Write ten sentences that include words that should be hyphenated. Exchange sentences with a partner. Your partner should correct your sentences by adding hyphens where needed.

Using Hyphens at the Ends of Lines

Hyphens help you keep the lines in your paragraphs more even, making your work easier to read.

Dividing Words at the End of a Line

Although you should try to avoid dividing a word at the end of a line, if a word must be broken, use a hyphen to show the division.

> **If a word must be divided at the end of a line, always divide it between syllables.**

23.5.11 RULE

EXAMPLE

In the middle of the day, we antici‑

pated having dinner at five P.M.

> **A hyphen used to divide a word should never be placed at the beginning of the second line. It must be placed at the end of the first line.**

23.5.12 RULE

INCORRECT

The teachers and students plan to sup

‑port this principal as long as he is here.

CORRECT

The teachers and students plan to sup‑

port this principal as long as he is here.

Using Hyphens Correctly to Divide Words

One-syllable words cannot be divided.

> **Do not divide one-syllable words even if they seem long or sound like words with two syllables.**

23.5.13 RULE

INCORRECT	mo‑ose	clo‑wn	thro‑ugh
CORRECT	moose	clown	through

Do not divide a word so that a single letter or the letters *-ed* stand alone.

INCORRECT	a-lert	bus-y	e-rode	accept-ed
CORRECT	alert	busy	erode	accepted

Avoid dividing proper nouns and proper adjectives.

INCORRECT	Ste-wart	Span-ish
CORRECT	Stewart	Spanish

Divide a hyphenated word only after the hyphen.

INCORRECT   I saw the ocean with my best friend and her sis-ter-in-law last year.

CORRECT   I saw the ocean with my best friend and her sister-in-law last year.

Avoid dividing a word so that part of the word is on one page and the remainder is on the next page.

Often, chopping up a word in this way will confuse your readers or cause them to lose their train of thought. If this happens, rewrite the sentence or move the entire word to the next page.

See Practice 23.5C
See Practice 23.5D

PRACTICE 23.5C Using Hyphens to Divide Words

Read each word. If a word has been divided incorrectly, rewrite the word, putting the hyphen(s) in the correct place, or writing it as one word if it cannot be divided. If a word has been divided correctly, write *correct*.

EXAMPLE   butt-on

ANSWER   *but-ton*

1. gigg-le
2. mon-itor
3. spac-ious
4. destin-y
5. spark-le
6. Jes-sica
7. demo-cratic
8. let-hal
9. semi-tran-sparent
10. fo-reign

PRACTICE 23.5D Correcting Divided Words at the End of Lines

Read each sentence. Then, rewrite the incorrectly divided word at the end of each sentence so that it is divided correctly. Or, if it cannot be divided, write it as one word.

EXAMPLE   Flowers are brightly color-
ed to attract insects and birds.

ANSWER   *Flowers are brightly col-
ored to attract insects and birds.*

11. Hybrid cars, wind turbines, and solar-po-
wered houses are environmentally friendly.

12. Lulu had to show a valid driver's license when she went to buy the tickets.

13. Yesterday, I spent the entire day reorgani-
zing the garage by myself.

14. Because her father was a diplomat, she lived in many different countries.

15. After hitting the game-winning run, Tyler celebrated with his teammates.

16. On a hot summer day, jumping into a swimming pool is a great idea.

17. Rain, snow, sleet, and hail are forms of prec-
ipitation.

18. Dan, a tennis champion, serves more a-
ces than any other player that I know.

19. Mr. Potts recited lines from William Shakespeare's *Romeo and Juliet*.

20. At the close of the ceremony, fireworks brigh-
tened the sky.

SPEAKING APPLICATION

Take turns with a partner. Say six words not found in Practice 23.5C. Your partner should tell where each word can be divided.

WRITING APPLICATION

Write a paragraph, using at least four correctly divided words at the end of four lines.

23.6 Apostrophes

The **apostrophe** (') is used to form possessives, contractions, and a few special plurals.

Using Apostrophes to Form Possessive Nouns

Apostrophes are used with nouns to show ownership or possession.

RULE 23.6.1 Add an apostrophe and -s to show the possessive case of most singular nouns.

| EXAMPLES | the scales of the alligator | the alligator's scales |
| | the hat of the boy | the boy's hat |

Even when a singular noun already ends in -s, you can usually add an apostrophe and -s to show possession. However, names that end in the *eez* sound get an apostrophe, but no -s.

EXAMPLE The Ganges' source is in the Himalayas.

For classical references that end in -s, only an apostrophe is used.

EXAMPLES Hercules' strength   Zeus' crown

RULE 23.6.2 Add an apostrophe to show the possessive case of plural nouns ending in -s or -es.

EXAMPLE the color of the leaves   the leaves' color

RULE 23.6.3 Add an apostrophe and an -s to show the possessive case of plural nouns that do not end in -s or -es.

EXAMPLE   the suits of the men

the men's suits

> Add an apostrophe and **-s** (or just an apostrophe if the word is a plural ending in **-s**) to the last word of a compound noun to form the possessive.

APOSTROPHES THAT SHOW POSSESSION	
Names of Businesses and Organizations	the Central High School's main office the Washington Monument's spotlight the Wong and Associates' office
Titles of Rulers or Leaders	Catherine the Great's victories Louis XVI's palace the head of the department's decision
Hyphenated Compound Nouns Used to Describe People	my brother-in-law's skis the secretary-treasurer's chair the physician-assistant's patient

> To form possessives involving time, amounts, or the word *sake,* use an apostrophe and an **-s** or just an apostrophe if the possessive is plural.

APOSTROPHES WITH POSSESSIVES	
Time	a year's vacation five days' vacation a half-hour's walk
Amount	one quarter's worth ten cents' worth
Sake	for Luke's sake for goodness' sake

RULE 23.6.6

To show joint ownership, make the final noun possessive.
To show individual ownership, make each noun possessive.

JOINT
OWNERSHIP
I enjoyed Patricia and Tom's dinner party.

INDIVIDUAL
OWNERSHIP
Liz's and Meg's coats are hanging here.

Use the owner's complete name before the apostrophe to form the possessive case.

INCORRECT
SINGULAR
Jame's phone number

CORRECT
SINGULAR
James's phone number

INCORRECT
PLURAL
two girl's dresses

CORRECT
PLURAL
two girls' dresses

Using Apostrophes With Pronouns

Both indefinite and personal pronouns can show possession.

RULE 23.6.7

Use an apostrophe and -s with indefinite pronouns to show possession.

EXAMPLES
somebody's rain coat

each other's houses

RULE 23.6.8

Do not use an apostrophe with possessive personal pronouns; their form already shows ownership.

EXAMPLES   her shoes   our pool   his red sports car

its doors   their house   whose report

Be careful not to confuse the contractions *who's*, *it's*, and *they're* with possessive pronouns. They are contractions for *who is*, *it is* or *it has*, and *they are*. Remember also that *whose*, *its*, and *their* show possession.

PRONOUNS	CONTRACTIONS
Whose homework is this?	*Who's* answering the phone?
Its tires were all flat.	*It's* going to be cold and windy.
Their dinner is ready.	*They're* going swimming today.

Using Apostrophes to Form Contractions

Contractions are used in informal speech and writing. You can often find contractions in the dialogue of stories and plays; they often create the sound of real speech.

> **Use an apostrophe in a contraction to show the position of the missing letter or letters.**

23.6.9 RULE

COMMON CONTRACTIONS				
Verb + *not*	cannot	can't	are not	aren't
	could not	couldn't	will not	won't
Pronoun + *will*	he will	he'll	I will	I'll
	you will	you'll	we will	we'll
	she will	she'll	they will	they'll
Pronoun + *would*	she would	she'd	I would	I'd
	he would	he'd	we would	we'd
	you would	you'd	they would	they'd
Noun or Pronoun + *be*	you are	you're	I am	I'm
	she is	she's	Jane is	Jane's
	they are	they're	dog is	dog's

Still another type of contraction is found in poetry.

EXAMPLES   e'en *(even)*   o'er *(over)*

Other contractions represent the abbreviated form of *of the* and *the* as they are written in several different languages. These letters are most often combined with surnames.

EXAMPLES O'Hare

d'Italia

o'clock

l'Abbé

Using Contractions to Represent Speaking Styles
A final use of contractions is for representing individual speaking styles in dialogue. As noted previously, you will often want to use contractions with verbs in dialogue. You may also want to approximate a regional dialect or a foreign accent, which may include nonstandard pronunciations of words or omitted letters. However, you should avoid overusing contractions in dialogue. Overuse reduces the effectiveness of the apostrophe.

EXAMPLES "Hey, ol' buddy. How you feelin'?"

"Don' you be foolin' me."

Using Apostrophes to Create Special Plurals

Apostrophes can help avoid confusion with special plurals.

> **Use an apostrophe and -s to create the plural form of a letter, numeral, symbol, or a word that is used as a name for itself.**

EXAMPLES *A*'s and *an*'s cause confusion.

There are five *3*'s in that number.

I don't like to hear *if*'s or *maybe*'s.

Form groups of *5*'s and *6*'s.

We have two *?*'s in a row.

See Practice 23.6A
See Practice 23.6B

PRACTICE 23.6A ▷ Identifying the Use of Apostrophes

Read each sentence. Then, tell if each apostrophe is used to form a *possessive*, a *contraction*, or a *special plural*.

EXAMPLE   Randy always crosses his *t's* and dots his *i's*.

ANSWER   *special plurals*

1. The fabric and buttons on my mother's old wedding dress have turned yellow.

2. There's the book of stamps from the 1920s.

3. With Paul and Donovan's help, this year's fundraiser will raise the most money yet.

4. Elijah got straight *B*'s in music class last year.

5. I can't leave until eight o'clock.

6. The chair's legs were cracked and warped.

7. Cindy's daughter told us that she'd meet us for lunch.

8. Count by *2*'s.

9. The girl's dress's skirt had ribbon trim.

10. In a month's time, we'll be traveling to Aunt Vanessa's house.

PRACTICE 23.6B ▷ Revising to Add Apostrophes

Read the sentence. Then, rewrite each sentence, adding apostrophes as necessary.

EXAMPLE   Julians jacket was too small for him this year.

ANSWER   *Julian's jacket was too small for him this year.*

11. Gus birthplace is Lockhart, Texas.

12. Johns and Petes lockers are around the corner from mine.

13. The childrens boots were jumbled in a big mess by my sister Susans front door.

14. Mrs. Robinsons student teacher said I use too many *!*s in my writing.

15. The Department of the Interiors budget wasnt cut in half this year.

16. The mens hockey team couldve won second place at the state championship.

17. Carol Anns mothers brother is Carol Anns uncle.

18. This sweatshirt could be anyones.

19. Its so funny to see a dog chase its own tail.

20. Rufus made a point to say "No *ifs*, *ands*, or *buts* are acceptable."

SPEAKING APPLICATION

Take turns with a partner. Say different sentences with words that indicate possession, contractions, and special plurals. Your partner should tell how each word uses an apostrophe.

WRITING APPLICATION

Write a paragraph, using at least six words with apostrophes. Not all of the words with apostrophes should be contractions.

23.7 Parentheses and Brackets

Parentheses enclose explanations or other information that may be omitted from the rest of the sentence without changing its basic meaning or construction. Using parentheses is a stronger, more noticeable way to set off a parenthetical expression than using commas. **Brackets** are used to enclose a word or phrase added by a writer to the words of another.

Parentheses

Parentheses help you group material within a sentence.

RULE 23.7.1

Use parentheses to set off information when the material is not essential or when it consists of one or more sentences.

EXAMPLE   The test of driving the car **(** as he learned from his friends **)** did require great skill and knowledge.

RULE 23.7.2

Use parentheses to set off numerical explanations such as dates of a person's birth and death and around numbers and letters marking a series.

EXAMPLES   Jose Sanchez invented a version of water tag with the help of his father, Juan Sanchez **(** 1825–1900 **)**.

Go to the store and pick up these items for dinner: **(** 1 **)** sauce, **(** 2 **)** pasta, **(** 3 **)** bread.

Which team won the Super Bowl you saw: **(** a **)** Giants, **(** b **)** Steelers, or **(** c **)** Cowboys?

Although material enclosed in parentheses is not essential to the meaning of the sentence, a writer indicates that the material is important and calls attention to it by using parentheses.

When a phrase or declarative sentence interrupts another sentence, do not use an initial capital letter or end mark inside the parentheses.

23.7.3 RULE

EXAMPLE   Steve took the furniture **(** it was beautiful **)** and delivered it as promised.

When a question or exclamation interrupts another sentence, use both an initial capital letter and an end mark inside the parentheses.

23.7.4 RULE

EXAMPLE   Jack **(** He is one strong man **!** **)** lifted the box on his shoulder.

When you place a sentence in parentheses between two other sentences, use both an initial capital letter and an end mark inside the parentheses.

23.7.5 RULE

EXAMPLE   Italy is known for its incredible art and artists. **(** See the Sistine Chapel as an example **.** **)** Italian art is staggering to behold.

In a sentence that includes parentheses, place any punctuation belonging to the main sentence after the final parenthesis.

23.7.6 RULE

EXAMPLE   The school board approved the construction **(** after some debate **)** **,** and they explained the new parking rules to the students **(** with some doubts about how the changes will be followed **)** **.**

Special Uses of Parentheses

Parentheses are used to set off numerical explanations such as birth and death dates and numbers or letters marking a series.

EXAMPLES   William Shakespeare **(**1564–1616**)** was an English poet and playwright.

Chelsea's phone number is **(**919**)** 777-1532.

His research will take him to **(**1**)** China, **(**2**)** Korea, and **(**3**)** Thailand.

Brackets

Brackets are used to enclose a word or phrase added by a writer to the words of another writer.

RULE 23.7.7

Use brackets to enclose words you insert in quotations when quoting someone else.

See Practice 23.7A
See Practice 23.7B

EXAMPLES   Cooper noted: "And with **[***E.T.'s***]** success, 'Phone home' is certain to become one of the most often repeated phrases of the year **[**1982**]**."

"The results of this vote **[**35–5**]** indicate overwhelming support by the board," she stated.

The Latin expression *sic* (meaning "thus") is sometimes enclosed in brackets to show that the author of the quoted material has misspelled or mispronounced a word or phrase.

EXAMPLE   Michaelson, citing Dorothy's signature line from *The Wizard of Oz,* wrote, "Theirs **[**sic**]** no place like home."

PRACTICE 23.7A Using Parentheses and Brackets Correctly

Read each item. Then, write a sentence in which you enclose the item in either parentheses or brackets.

EXAMPLE   the protagonist

ANSWER   *In the novel Pride and Prejudice, Elizabeth Bennett (the protagonist) is an intelligent, good-natured young woman.*

1. the youngest son

2. a bright, sunny day

3. sic

4. in the next three weeks

5. the former state senator

6. where it was lost

7. I couldn't believe my eyes

8. my best friend

9. a friendly dog

10. in the morning

PRACTICE 23.7B Revising to Add Parentheses or Brackets

Read each sentence. Then, add parentheses or brackets wherever they are appropriate.

EXAMPLE   We took the early bus 7:45 A.M. into the city.

ANSWER   *We took the early bus (7:45 A.M.) into the city.*

11. Water is a compound made from different atoms hydrogen and oxygen.

12. Benjamin Franklin 1706–1790 did not invent electricity, but he did invent the lightning rod.

13. Cecilia calls her grandmother *"Abuela"* which means "grandmother" in Spanish.

14. The mayor said, "The building will be renamed in honor of Mr. Byrd the retired post master."

15. During our trip, we went fishing for trout.

16. Baby dolphins calves stay with their mothers for five to seven years.

17. Mozart's first symphony written at age eight is *Symphony No. 1* in E-flat major.

18. A low-pressure system a storm is forecasted.

19. The trees obscured our view from the terrace.

20. The report stated, "The brige sic is in need of repairs."

SPEAKING APPLICATION

Take turns with a partner. Say four phrases. Your partner should use the phrases in sentences, indicating if the phrases would be appropriate in parentheses or brackets.

WRITING APPLICATION

Write two paragraphs in the form of a newspaper article about any topic of your choice. Include sentences that contain parentheses and brackets.

23.8 Ellipses, Dashes, and Slashes

An **ellipsis** (. . .) shows where words have been omitted from a quoted passage. It can also mark a pause or interruption in dialogue. A **dash** (—) shows a strong, sudden break in thought or speech. A **slash** (/) separates numbers in dates and fractions, shows line breaks in quoted poetry, and represents *or*. A slash is also used to separate the parts of a Web address.

Using the Ellipsis

An **ellipsis** is three evenly spaced periods, or ellipsis points, in a row. Always include a space before the first ellipsis point, between ellipsis points, and after the last ellipsis point. (The plural of *ellipsis* is *ellipses*.)

RULE 23.8.1

> Use an **ellipsis** to show where words have been omitted from a quoted passage.

ELLIPSES IN QUOTATIONS	
The Entire Quotation	"The Black River, which cuts a winding course through southern Missouri's rugged Ozark highlands, lends its name to an area of great natural beauty. Within this expanse are old mines and quarries to explore, fast-running waters to canoe, and wooded trails to ride."—Suzanne Charle
At the Beginning	Suzanne Charle described the Black River area in Missouri as having " . . . old mines and quarries to explore, fast-running waters to canoe, and wooded trails to ride."
In the Middle	Suzanne Charle wrote, "The Black River . . . lends its name to an area of great natural beauty. Within this expanse are old mines and quarries to explore, fast-running waters to canoe, and wooded trails to ride."
At the End	Suzanne Charle wrote, "The Black River, which cuts a winding course through southern Missouri's rugged Ozark highlands, lends its name to an area of great natural beauty . . . "

> **Use an ellipsis to mark a pause in a dialogue or speech.**

EXAMPLE   The director shouted, "Scene...and...cut!"

Dashes

A **dash** signals a stronger, more sudden interruption in thought or speech than commas or parentheses. A dash may also take the place of certain words before an explanation. Overuse of the dash diminishes its effectiveness. Consider the proper use of the dash in the rule below.

> **Use dashes to indicate an abrupt change of thought, a dramatic interrupting idea, or a summary statement.**

USING DASHES IN WRITING	
To indicate an abrupt change of thought	The book doesn't provide much information on Europe—by the way, where did you find the book?
	I cannot believe how many free throws the players missed—oh, I don't even want to think about it.
To set off interrupting ideas dramatically	The house was built—you may find this hard to believe — in two weeks.
	The house was built—Where did they get the money?—in two weeks.
To set off a summary statement	A lifetime of practice, ambition, and excellent teachers—if you have these, you may be able to get a job as a professional musician.
	To see her name on her diploma after four years—this was her greatest dream.

RULE 23.8.4

Use **dashes** to set off a **nonessential appositive** or modifier when it is long, when it is already punctuated, or when you want to be dramatic.

APPOSITIVE	The cause of the damage to the antique paint and the chrome—a rare form of rust—went undiscovered for weeks.
MODIFIER	The garden book editor—bored with writing about flowers and vegetables—quit after her last book.

Dashes may be used to set off one other special type of sentence interrupter—the parenthetical expression.

RULE 23.8.5

Use **dashes** to set off a **parenthetical expression** when it is long, already punctuated, or especially dramatic.

EXAMPLE	Today, we visited a gourmet restaurant—What a delicious meal!—set in the city.

Slashes

A **slash** is used to separate numbers in dates and fractions, lines of quoted poetry, or options. Slashes are also used to separate parts of a Web address.

RULE 23.8.6

Use **slashes** to separate the day, month, and year in dates and to separate the numerator and denominator in numerical fractions.

DATES	The date listed on the tickets was 11/05/10.
	Randy left for Chicago on 4/17/08.
FRACTIONS	3/4 2/5 1/3

> **Use slashes to indicate line breaks in up to three lines of quoted poetry in continuous text. Insert a space on each side of the slash.**

23.8.7 RULE

EXAMPLE I used a quote from William Blake, "Tyger! Tyger! burning bright. **/** In the forests of the night," to begin my paper.

> **Use slashes to separate choices or options and to represent the words *and* and *or.***

23.8.8 RULE

EXAMPLES Choose your color: pink **/** aqua **/** yellow.

Each lifeguard should bring a board and whistle **/** binoculars.

You can bat and **/** or bunt the next throw from the pitcher.

> **Use slashes to separate parts of a Web address.**

23.8.9 RULE

EXAMPLES http: **//** www.fafsa.ed.gov **/**
(for financial aid for students)

http: **//** www.whitehouse.gov **/**
(the White House)

http: **//** www.si.edu **/**
(the Smithsonian Institution)

See Practice 23.8A
See Practice 23.8B

PRACTICE 23.8A ▶ **Using Ellipses, Dashes, and Slashes Correctly**

Read each sentence. Then, rewrite each sentence, adding ellipses, dashes, and slashes where they are needed.

EXAMPLE   Jed yelled, "On your mark, get set, go!"

ANSWER   *Jed yelled, "On your mark . . . get set . . . go!"*

1. Yarn crafts including knitting and crocheting are becoming a popular hobby again.

2. The paintings have been cleaned restored and are ready to be exhibited.

3. We saw a flock of flamingos they really are pink at the botanical gardens.

4. The Gettysburg Address begins "Four score and seven years ago."

5. The waiter entertainer at the new restaurant sings while he serves food.

6. My mother adds a secret ingredient to her prize-winning chili peanut butter.

7. The vase made of red clay is a historic find.

8. The recipe lists 1 2 cup of vegetable oil.

9. The game-show host took forever to say, "And the winner is Alex Bailey!"

10. A positive attitude and friendliness these things will help you make friends.

PRACTICE 23.8B ▶ **Revising Sentences With Ellipses, Dashes, and Slashes**

Read each sentence. Then, correct the misused punctuation in each sentence to show the correct use of ellipses, dashes, and slashes.

EXAMPLE   Cody said, "I bought tomatoes, rice, eggs wait, I forgot the eggs!"

ANSWER   *Cody said, "I bought tomatoes, rice, eggs — wait, I forgot the eggs!"*

11. During archery class, I think to myself, "ready/aim/shoot."

12. The recipe calls for 2 — 3 cup milk.

13. Shannon ate soup, salad, a sandwich, and fruit. / I would burst if I ate that much for lunch.

14. The best part of the movie/ actually the entire film was good… was the opening scene.

15. Leah timidly replied, "I um — can't make it."

16. The next meeting is on 3 — 12/10.

17. The oboe is part of the woodwind family / by the way, Mrs. Dixon is giving oboe lessons.

18. You may read a book — magazine while you wait.

19. Your resume, cover letter, and referrals/these are the items you need/to apply for the job.

20. The book began with, "I couldn't wait to see."

SPEAKING APPLICATION

With a partner, reread the sentences in Practice 23.8A and your corrections for the sentences. Discuss how adding ellipses, dashes, and slashes changes each sentence.

WRITING APPLICATION

Write a paragraph. Your paragraph should include sentences that contain ellipses, dashes, and slashes. Use each of these types of punctuation at least two times.

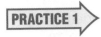 **PRACTICE 1** > **Using Periods, Question Marks, and Exclamation Marks**

Read the sentences. Then, rewrite each sentence, adding question marks, periods, and exclamation marks where needed.

1. Push the table to the other side of the room, so we have more space

2. Are you responsible for the grocery shopping

3. That was the most delicious and lavish meal I have ever eaten

4. How remarkable that he was able to complete all of those arduous tasks in one day

5. She budgeted her time well and finished the exam with a few minutes to spare

6. Yen wanted to attend both parties

7. Did you collect all of the water samples that you will need for your project

8. Wow That goal was amazing

9. So as not to get him confused with his father, we simply called Thomas, Tommy Jr

10. Write an article for the school paper on the dangers of polluting our environment

PRACTICE 2 > **Using Commas Correctly**

Read the sentences. Then, rewrite each sentence, adding commas where needed. If a sentence is already correct, write correct.

1. Struggling with the homework assignment Ted signed up for a tutoring session.

2. Emma gathered her books pens and notebooks together and headed home.

3. "The next holiday is on October 10 2009" Rebecca told us.

4. He and I waited patiently for the bus and discussed where we wanted to eat.

5. Who wrote, "To be, or not to be?"

6. She lives at 45 East Main Street Apartment B Brookfield New York 12345.

7. The conversation was a stimulating interesting break from our usual talk.

8. I needed to cancel this appointment yesterday, not today.

9. Robert made a friendly speech at every luncheon and this one would be no exception.

10. He responded "Yes I will review those figures."

PRACTICE 3 > **Using Colons, Semicolons, and Quotation Marks**

Read the sentences. Then, rewrite each sentence, adding colons, semicolons, and quotation marks where needed. If a sentence is already correct, write correct.

1. It didn't occur to him to notice the new paint in fact, he never noticed it!

2. For his project, Dan reviewed Mowing by Robert Frost Dan considered it a classic work of poetry.

3. Val told us to bring the following items to rehearsal: instruments, music, and pencils.

4. Caution Floors are slippery when wet.

5. The tickets were expensive however, we got a discount.

6. I was late for class, Shauna said, because my alarm was set for 1000.

7. The curry was hot I love Indian food.

8. We surveyed the destruction after the storm the wind had toppled our boat.

Continued on next page ▶

9. Marjorie announced her decision The vote stands.

10. Jack claimed that he had everything under control indeed, he finished his project on time.

PRACTICE 4 ▷ Using Apostrophes

Read the sentences. Then, rewrite each sentence, adding apostrophes where needed. If a sentence is already correct, write *correct.*

1. Deirdres new apartment is located just south of the train station.

2. Oh, for Pete's sake, just take Kevins keys.

3. The politician was described as the peoples choice; he couldnt let them down.

4. I went to Mel and Randys house yesterday.

5. We usually carried each others books when we didnt have that many of our own.

6. His first year of college, he read many of John Keatss works.

7. The vice-chancellors order was to reduce the budget by one-third.

8. James's doctor told him to get more sleep.

9. Whos going to come? Isnt it late?

10. Its time to have a talk; lets meet at 4 oclock.

PRACTICE 5 ▷ Using Underlining (or Italics), Hyphens, Dashes, Slashes, Parentheses, Brackets, and Ellipses

Read the sentences. Then, rewrite each sentence, adding underlining (or italics), hyphens, dashes, slashes, parentheses, brackets, and ellipses where needed.

1. Reading War and Peace was difficult, but in the end, it was very rewarding.

2. Duncan he is president of the student body always comes to meetings well prepared.

3. She read that 700 page book if you can believe it in three days.

4. The film is set during World War II 1939–1945.

5. In her address, she told the people, "It the economy can no longer be ignored."

6. The recipe called for 1 2 cup of flour and 1 3 cup of sugar.

7. The twelfth graders all the seniors had to take the exit exam.

8. The runners took their positions, and the referee yelled, "On your mark get set go!"

9. They needed fifty thousand dollars $50,000 to launch the project.

10. Each member of the committee the committee leaders as well as the regular members should attend.

PRACTICE 6 ▷ Using Capital Letters Correctly

Read the sentences. Then, rewrite each sentence, using capital letters where needed.

1. isis is the egyptian goddess of motherhood.

2. the mcteagues took a yearly trip to puerto rico, and last year they visited san juan hill.

3. jen inquired, "in which language are you most fluent—french, swedish, or german?"

4. buckingham palace is in london, england.

5. the department of the treasury is headquartered in washington, d.c.

RESOURCES FOR Writing COACH

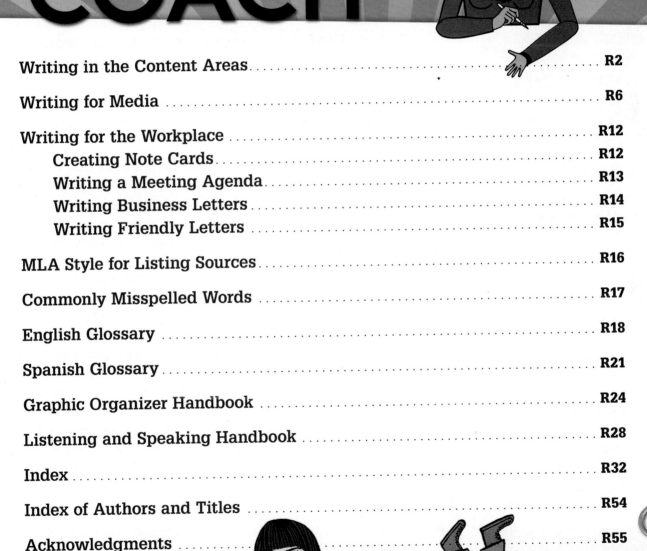

WRITING IN THE
Content Areas

Writing in the content areas—math, social studies, science, the arts, and various career and technical studies—is an important tool for learning. The following pages give examples of content area writing along with strategies.

FORMS OF MATH WRITING

Written Estimate An estimate, or informed idea, of the size, cost, time, or other measure of a thing, based on given information.

Analysis of a Problem A description of a problem, such as figuring out how long a trip will take, along with an explanation of the mathematical formulas or equations you can use to solve the problem.

Response to an Open-Ended Math Prompt A response to a question or writing assignment involving math, such as a word problem or a question about a graph or a mathematical concept.

Writing in Math

Prewriting

- **Choosing a Topic** If you have a choice of topics, review your textbook and class notes for ideas, and choose one that interests you.

- **Responding to a Prompt** If you are responding to a prompt, read and then reread the instructions, ensuring that you understand all of the requirements of the assignment.

Drafting

- **State Problems Clearly** Be clear, complete, and accurate in your description of the problem you are analyzing or reporting on. Make sure that you have used technical terms, such as *ratio, area,* and *factor,* accurately.

- **Explain Your Solution** Tell readers exactly which mathematical rules or formulas you use in your analysis and why they apply. Clearly spell out each step you take in your reasoning.

- **Use Graphics** By presenting quantitative information in a graph, table, or chart, you make it easier for readers to absorb information. Choose the format appropriate to the material, as follows:

  ✔ **Line Graphs** Use a line graph to show the relationship between two variables, such as time and speed in a problem about a moving object. Clearly label the x- and y-axis with the variable each represents and with the units you are using. Choose units appropriately to make the graph manageable. For example, do not try to represent time in years if you are plotting changes for an entire century; instead, use units of ten years each.

  ✔ **Other Graphs** Use a pie chart to analyze facts about a group, such as the percentage of students who walk to school, the percentage who drive, and the percentage who take the bus. Use a bar graph to compare two or more things at different times or in different categories. Assign a single color to each thing, and use that color consistently for all the bars representing data about that thing.

  ✔ **Tables** Use a table to help readers look up specific values quickly, such as the time the sun sets in each month of the year. Label each column and row with terms that clearly identify the data you are presenting, including the units you are using.

Revising

- **Ensure Accuracy** For accuracy, double-check the formulas you use and the calculations you make.

- **Revise for Traits of Good Writing** Ask yourself the following questions: *How well have I applied mathematical ideas? Does my organizational plan help readers follow my reasoning? Is my voice suitable to my audience and purpose? Have I chosen precise words and used mathematical terms accurately? Are my sentences well constructed and varied? Have I made any errors in grammar, usage, mechanics, and spelling?* Use your answers to help you revise and edit your work.

Writing in Science

Prewriting

- **Choosing a Topic** If you have a choice of topics, look through class notes and your textbook, or conduct a "media flip-through," browsing online articles, or watching television news and documentaries to find a science-related topic.

- **Responding to a Prompt** If you are responding to a prompt, read the instructions carefully, analyzing the requirements and parts of the assignment. Identify key direction words in the prompt or assignment, such as *explain* and *predict*.

- **Gathering Details**
  ✔ If your assignment requires you to conduct research, search for credible and current sources. Examples of strong sources may include articles in recent issues of science magazines or recently published books. Confirm key facts in more than one source.
  ✔ If your assignment requires you to conduct an experiment, make sure you follow the guidelines for the experiment accurately. Carefully record the steps you take and the observations you make, and date your notes. Repeat the experiment to confirm results.

Drafting

- **Focus and Elaborate** In your introduction, clearly state your topic. Make sure you tell readers why your topic matters. As you draft, give sufficient details, including background, facts, and examples, to help your readers understand your topic. Summarize your findings and insights in your conclusion.

- **Organize** As you draft, follow a suitable organizational pattern. If you are telling the story of an important scientific breakthrough, consider telling events in chronological order. If you are explaining a natural process, consider discussing causes and the effects that follow from them. If you are defending a solution to a problem, you might give pros and cons, answering each counterargument in turn.

- **Present Data Visually** Consider presenting quantitative information, such as statistics or measurements, in a graph, table, or chart. Choose the format appropriate to the material. (Consult the guidance on visual displays of data under "Use Graphics" on page R2.)

Revising

- **Meet Your Audience's Needs** Identify places in your draft where your audience may need more information, such as additional background, more explanation, or the definition of a technical term. Add the information required.

- **Revise for Traits of Good Writing** Ask yourself the following questions: *How clearly have I presented scientific ideas? Will my organization help a reader see the connections I am making? Is my voice suitable to my audience and purpose? Have I chosen precise words and used technical terms accurately? Are my sentences well constructed and varied? Have I made any errors in grammar, usage, mechanics, and spelling?* Use your answers to revise and edit your work.

FORMS OF SCIENCE WRITING

Lab Report A firsthand report of a scientific experiment, following an appropriate format. A standard lab report includes a statement of the hypothesis, or prediction, that the experiment is designed to test; a list of the materials used; an account of the steps performed; a report of the results observed; and the experimenter's conclusions.

Cause-and-Effect Essay A scientific explanation of the causes and effects involved in natural or technical phenomena, such as solar flares, the digestion of food, or the response of metal to stress.

Technical Procedure Document A step-by-step guide to performing a scientific experiment or performing a technical task involving science. A well-written technical procedure document presents the steps of the procedure in clear order. It breaks steps into substeps and prepares readers by explaining what materials they will need and the time they can expect each step to take.

Response to an Open-Ended Science Prompt A response to a question or writing assignment about science.

Summary of a Science-Related Article A retelling of the main ideas in an article that concerns science or technology, such as an article on a new medical procedure.

Writing in Social Studies

FORMS OF SOCIAL STUDIES WRITING

Social Studies Research Report
An informative paper, based on research, about a historical period or event or about a specific place or culture. A well-written research report draws on a variety of sources to develop and support a thoughtful point of view on the topic. It cites those sources accurately, following an accepted format.

Biographical Essay An overview of the life of a historically important person. A well-written biographical essay reports the life of its subject accurately and clearly explains the importance of his or her contributions.

Historical Overview A survey, or general picture, of a historical period or development, such as the struggle for women's right to vote. A successful historical overview presents the "big picture," covering major events and important aspects of the topic without getting lost in details.

Historical Cause-and-Effect Essay An analysis of the causes and effects of a historical event. A well-written historical explanation makes clear connections between events to help readers follow the explanation.

Prewriting

- **Choosing a Topic** If you have a choice of topics, find a suitable topic by looking through class notes and your textbook. Make a quick list of topics in history, politics, or geography that interest you and choose a topic based on your list.

- **Responding to a Prompt** If you are responding to a prompt, read the instructions carefully, analyzing the requirements and parts of the assignment. Identify key direction words in the prompt or assignment, such as *compare*, *describe*, and *argue*.

- **Gathering Details** If your assignment requires you to conduct research, consult a variety of credible sources. For in-depth research, review both primary sources (documents from the time you are investigating) and secondary sources (accounts by those who analyze or report on the information). If you find contradictions, evaluate the likely reasons for the differences.

Drafting

- **Establish a Thesis or Theme** If you are writing a research report or other informative piece, state your main point about your topic in a thesis statement. Include your thesis statement in your introduction. If you are writing a creative piece, such as a historical skit or short story, identify the theme, or main message, you wish to convey.

- **Support Your Thesis or Theme** Organize your work around your main idea.

  ✔ In a research report, support and develop your thesis with well-chosen, relevant details. First, provide background information your readers will need, and then discuss different subtopics in different sections of the body of your report. Clearly connect each subtopic to your main thesis.

  ✔ In a creative work, develop your theme through the conflict between characters. For example, a conflict between two brothers during the Civil War over which side to fight on might dramatize the theme of divided loyalties. Organize events to build to a climax, or point of greatest excitement, that clearly conveys your message.

Revising

- **Sharpen Your Focus** Review your draft for sections that do not clearly support your thesis or theme, and consider eliminating them. Revise unnecessary repetition of ideas. Ensure that the sequence of ideas or events will help reader comprehension.

- **Revise for Traits of Good Writing** Ask yourself the following questions: *How clearly have I developed my thesis or my theme? Will my organization help a reader follow my development of my thesis or theme? Is my voice suitable to my audience and purpose? Have I chosen precise and vivid words, accurately using terms from the period or place about which I am writing? Are my sentences well constructed and varied? Have I made any errors in grammar, usage, mechanics, and spelling?* Use your answers to revise and edit your work.

Writing About the Arts

Prewriting

Experience the Work Take notes on the subject of each work you will discuss. Consider its mood, or general feeling, and its theme, or insight into life.

✔ For visual arts, consider the use of color, light, line (sharp or smooth, smudged or definite), mass (heavy or light), and composition (the arrangement and balance of forms).

✔ For music, consider the use of melody, rhythm, harmony, and instrumentation. Also, consider the performers' interpretation of the work.

Drafting

Develop Your Ideas As you draft, support your main ideas, including your insights into or feelings about a work, with relevant details.

Revising

Revise for Traits of Good Writing Ask yourself the following questions: *How clearly do I present my ideas? Will my organization help a reader follow my points? Is my voice suitable to my audience and purpose? Have I chosen precise and vivid words, to describe the works? Are my sentences varied? Have I made any errors in grammar, usage, and mechanics?* Use your answers to revise and edit your work.

Writing in Career and Technical Studies

Prewriting

Choosing a Topic If you have a choice of topics, find a suitable one by looking through class notes and your textbook or by listing your own related projects or experiences.

Drafting

Organize Information As you draft, follow a logical organization. If you are explaining a procedure, list steps in the order that your readers should follow. If they need information about the materials and preparation required, provide that information first. Use formatting (such as headings, numbered steps, and bullet points), graphics (such as diagrams), and transitional words and phrases (such as *first, next,* and *if… then*).

Revising

Revise for Traits of Good Writing Ask yourself the following questions: *Have I given readers all the information they will need? Will my organization help a reader follow my points? Is my voice suitable to my audience and purpose? Have I chosen precise words, using technical terms accurately? Are my sentences well constructed? Have I made errors in grammar, usage, and mechanics?* Use your answers to revise and edit your work.

FORMS OF WRITING ABOUT THE ARTS

Research Report on a Trend or Style in Art An informative paper, based on research, about a specific group of artists or trend in the arts.

Biographical Essay An overview of the life of an artist or performer.

Analysis of a Work A detailed description of a work offering insights into its meaning and importance.

Review of a Performance or Exhibit An evaluation of an artistic performance or exhibit.

FORMS OF CAREER AND TECHNICAL WRITING

Technical Procedure Document A step-by-step guide to performing a specialized task, such as wiring a circuit or providing first aid.

Response to an Open-Ended Practical Studies Prompt A response to a question or writing assignment about a task or concept in a specialized field.

Technical Research Report An informative paper, based on research, about a specific topic in a practical field, such as a report on balanced diet in the field of health.

Analysis of a Career An informative paper explaining the requirements for a particular job, along with the responsibilities, salary, benefits, and job opportunities.

WRITING FOR
Media

New technology has created many new ways to communicate. Today, it is easy to contribute information to the Internet and send a variety of messages to friends far and near. You can also share your ideas through photos, illustrations, video, and sound recordings.

Writing for Media gives you an overview of some ways you can use today's technology to create, share, and find information. **Here are the topics you will find in this section:**

Blogs

A **blog** is a common form of online writing. The word *blog* is a contraction of *Web log*. Most blogs include a series of entries known as posts. The posts appear in a single column and are displayed in reverse chronological order. That means that the most recent post is at the top of the page. As you scroll down, you will find earlier posts.

Blogs have become increasingly popular. Researchers estimate that 75,000 new blogs are launched every day. Blog authors are often called bloggers. They can use their personal sites to share ideas, songs, videos, photos, and other media. People who read blogs can often post their responses with a comments feature found in each new post.

Because blogs are designed so that they are easy to update, bloggers can post new messages as often as they like, often daily. For some people blogs become a public journal or diary in which they share their thoughts about daily events.

Types of Blogs

Not all blogs are the same. Many blogs have a single author, but others are group projects. These are some common types of blog:

- **Personal blogs** often have a general focus. Bloggers post their thoughts on any topic they find interesting in their daily lives.

- **Topical blogs** focus on a specific theme, such as movie reviews, political news, class assignments, or health-care opportunities.

 WEB SAFETY Using the Internet safely means keeping personal information personal. Never include your address (e-mail or physical), last name, or telephone numbers. Avoid mentioning places you go to often.

Never give out passwords you use to access other Web sites and do not respond to e-mails from people you do not know.

Anatomy of a Blog

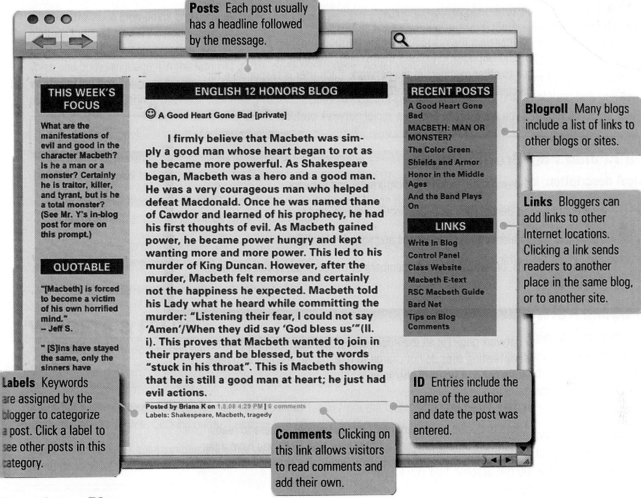

Posts Each post usually has a headline followed by the message.

THIS WEEK'S FOCUS

What are the manifestations of evil and good in the character Macbeth? Is he a man or a monster? Certainly he is traitor, killer, and tyrant, but is he a total monster? (See Mr. Y's in-blog post for more on this prompt.)

QUOTABLE

"[Macbeth] is forced to become a victim of his own horrified mind."
-- Jeff S.

" [S]ins have stayed the same, only the sinners have

ENGLISH 12 HONORS BLOG

☺ A Good Heart Gone Bad [private]

    I firmly believe that Macbeth was simply a good man whose heart began to rot as he became more powerful. As Shakespeare began, Macbeth was a hero and a good man. He was a very courageous man who helped defeat Macdonald. Once he was named thane of Cawdor and learned of his prophecy, he had his first thoughts of evil. As Macbeth gained power, he became power hungry and kept wanting more and more power. This led to his murder of King Duncan. However, after the murder, Macbeth felt remorse and certainly not the happiness he expected. Macbeth told his Lady what he heard while committing the murder: "Listening their fear, I could not say 'Amen'/When they did say 'God bless us'" (II. i). This proves that Macbeth wanted to join in their prayers and be blessed, but the words "stuck in his throat". This is Macbeth showing that he is still a good man at heart; he just had evil actions.

Posted by **Briana K** on 1.8.08 4:29 PM | 6 comments
Labels: Shakespeare, Macbeth, tragedy

RECENT POSTS

A Good Heart Gone Bad
MACBETH: MAN OR MONSTER?
The Color Green
Shields and Armor
Honor in the Middle Ages
And the Band Plays On

LINKS

Write In Blog
Control Panel
Class Website
Macbeth E-text
RSC Macbeth Guide
Bard Net
Tips on Blog Comments

Blogroll Many blogs include a list of links to other blogs or sites.

Links Bloggers can add links to other Internet locations. Clicking a link sends readers to another place in the same blog, or to another site.

Labels Keywords are assigned by the blogger to categorize a post. Click a label to see other posts in this category.

Comments Clicking on this link allows visitors to read comments and add their own.

ID Entries include the name of the author and date the post was entered.

Creating a Blog

Keep these hints and strategies in mind to help you create an interesting and fair blog:

- Focus each blog entry on a single topic.

- Vary the length of your posts. Sometimes, all you need is a line or two to share a quick thought. Other posts will be much longer.

- Choose font colors and styles that can be read easily.

- Many people scan blogs rather than read them closely. You can make your main ideas pop out by using clear or clever headlines and boldfacing key terms.

- Give credit to other people's work and ideas. State the names of people whose ideas you are quoting or add a link to take readers to that person's blog or site.

- If you post comments, try to make them brief and polite.

Social Networking

Social networking means any interaction between members of an online community. People can exchange many different kinds of information, from text and voice messages to video images. Many social network communities allow users to create permanent pages that describe themselves. Users create home pages to express themselves, share ideas about their lives, and post messages to other members in the network. Each user is responsible for adding and updating the content on his or her profile page.

Here are some features you are likely to find on a social network profile:

Features of Profile Pages

- A **biographical description**, including photographs and artwork

- **Lists of favorite things**, such as books, movies, music, and fashions

- **Playable media** elements such as videos and sound recordings

- **Message boards**, or "walls," on which members of the community can exchange messages

Privacy in Social Networks

Social networks allow users to decide how open their profiles will be. Be sure to read introductory information carefully before you register at a new site. Once you have a personal profile page, monitor your privacy settings regularly. Remember that any information you post will be available to anyone in your network.

Users often post messages anonymously or using false names, or pseudonyms. People can also post using someone else's name. Judge all information on the net critically. Do not assume that you know who posted some information simply because you recognize the name of the post author. The rapid speed of communication on the Internet can make it easy to jump to conclusions—be careful to avoid this trap.

You can create a social network page for an individual or a group, such as a school or special interest club. Many hosting sites do not charge to register, so you can also have fun by creating a page for a pet or a fictional character.

Tips for Sending Effective Messages

Technology makes it easy to share ideas quickly, but writing for the Internet poses some special challenges. The writing style for blogs and social networks is often very conversational. In blog posts and comments, instant messages, and e-mails, writers often express themselves very quickly, using relaxed language, short sentences, and abbreviations. However, in a face-to-face conversation, we get a lot of information from a speaker's tone of voice and body language. On the Internet, those clues are missing. As a result, Internet writers often use italics or bracketed labels to indicate emotions. Another alternative is using emoticons—strings of characters that give visual clues to indicate emotion.

:-) **smile** *(happy)*   **:-(** **frown** *(unhappy)*   **;-)** **wink** *(light sarcasm)*

> *Use these strategies to communicate effectively when using technology:*
>
> ✔ *Before you click Send, **reread your message** to make sure that your tone is clear.*
>
> ✔ ***Do not jump to conclusions**—ask for clarification first. Make sure you really understand what someone is saying before you respond.*
>
> ✔ ***Use abbreviations** your reader will understand.*

Widgets and Feeds

A **widget** is a small application that performs a specific task. You might find widgets that give weather predictions, offer dictionary definitions or translations, provide entertainment such as games, or present a daily word, photograph, or quotation.

A **feed** is a special kind of widget. It displays headlines taken from the latest content on a specific media source. Clicking on the headline will take you to the full article. Many social network communities and other Web sites allow you to personalize your home page by adding widgets and feeds.

Multimedia Elements

One of the great advantages of communicating on the Internet is that you are not limited to using text only. When you create a Web profile or blog, you can share your ideas using a wide variety of media. In addition to widgets and feeds (see page R9), these media elements can make your Internet communication more entertaining and useful.

GRAPHICS	
Photographs	You can post photographs taken by digital cameras or scanned as files.
Illustrations	Artwork can be created using computer software. You can also use a scanner to post a digital image of a drawing or sketch.
Charts, Graphs, and Maps	Charts and graphs can make statistical information clear. Use spreadsheet software to create these elements. Use Internet sites to find maps of specific places.

VIDEO	
Live Action	Digital video can be recorded by a camera or recorded from another media source.
Animation	Animated videos can also be created using software.

AUDIO	
Music	Many social network communities make it easy to share your favorite music with people who visit your page.
Voice	Use a microphone to add your own voice to your Web page.

Editing Media Elements

You can use software to customize media elements. Open source software is free and available to anyone on the Internet. Here are some things you can do with software:

- **Crop** a photograph to focus on the subject or brighten an image that is too dark.
- **Transform** a drawing's appearance from flat to three-dimensional.
- **Insert** a "You Are Here" arrow on a map.
- **Edit** a video or sound file to shorten its running time.
- **Add** background music or sound effects to a video.

Podcasts

A **podcast** is a digital audio or video recording of a program that is made available on the Internet. Users can replay the podcast on a computer, or download it and replay it on a personal audio player. You might think of podcasts as radio or television programs that you create yourself. They can be embedded on a Web site or fed to a Web page through a podcast widget.

Creating an Effective Podcast

To make a podcast, you will need a recording device, such as a microphone or digital video camera, as well as editing software. Open source editing software is widely available and free of charge. Most audio podcasts are converted into the MP3 format. Here are some tips for creating a podcast that is clear and entertaining:

- **Listen to several podcasts by different authors** to get a feeling for the medium.

- **Make a list** of features and styles you like and also those you want to avoid.

- **Test your microphone** to find the best recording distance. Stand close enough to the microphone so that your voice sounds full, but not so close that you create an echo.

- **Create an outline** that shows your estimated timing for each element.

- **Be prepared** before you record. Rehearse, but do not create a script. Podcasts are best when they have a natural, easy flow.

- **Talk directly to your listeners**. Slow down enough so they can understand you.

- Use software to **edit your podcast before publishing it**. You can edit out mistakes or add additional elements.

You can change the information on a wiki, but be sure your information is correct and clear before you add it. Wikis keep track of all changes, so your work will be recorded and can be evaluated by other users.

Wikis

A **wiki** is a collaborative Web site that lets visitors create, add, remove, and edit content. The term comes from the Hawaiian phrase *wikiwiki*, which means "quick." Web users of a wiki are both the readers and the writers of the site. Some wikis are open to contributions from anyone. Others require visitors to register before they can edit the content. All of the text in these collaborative Web sites was written by people who use the site. Articles are constantly changing, as visitors find and correct errors and improve texts.

Wikis have both advantages and disadvantages as sources of information. They are valuable open forums for the exchange of ideas. The unique collaborative writing process allows entries to change over time. However, entries can also be modified incorrectly. Careless or malicious users can delete good content and add inappropriate or inaccurate information. Wikis may be useful for gathering background information, but should not be used as research resources.

WRITING FOR THE
Workplace

Writing is something many people do every day at work, school, or home. They write letters and reports, do research, plan meetings, and keep track of information in notes.

Writing for the Workplace shows you some models of the following forms of writing:

- **Note Cards**
- **Meeting Agenda**
- **Business Letter**
- **Friendly Letter**

Creating Note Cards

Whether you are working on a research report or gathering information for another purpose, it is helpful to keep your notes on individual cards or in note files on a computer. You will need to make sure that you note your sources on your cards. You can organize information many different ways, but it is most helpful to keep notes of one kind together.

> You can name the **source**, as shown here, or refer to the source by number (e.g., Source 3) if you are using source cards.

> The **topic** is the main focus of the notes.

Topic: Octopus

Source: PBS Web site Accessed 10/15/2010
http://www.pbs.org/wnet/nature/episodes/ the-octopus-show/
a-legend-of-the-deep/2014/

- Acrobatic and shy animals
- Can squeeze into very small spaces to hide or catch food
- Talented swimmers
- Can change color
- Live in all kinds of environments

> In the notes section focus on the ideas that are most important to your research. Note that these ideas may not always be the main ideas of the selection you are reading. You do not need to write in full sentences. However, you may want to use bullets to make your notes easier to read.

Writing a Meeting Agenda

When you have a meeting, it is helpful to use an agenda. An agenda tells what will be discussed in the meeting. It tells who is responsible for which topic. It also provides a guide for the amount of time to be spent on each topic.

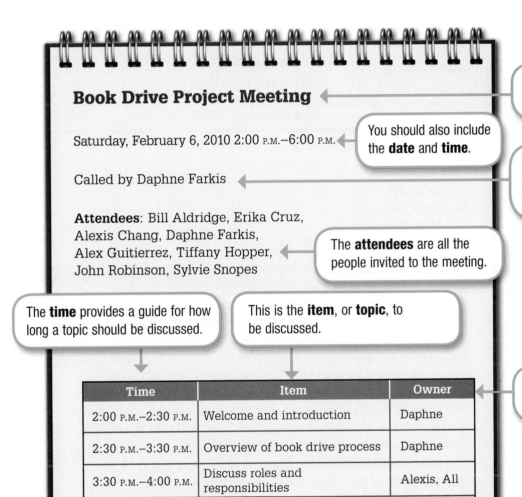

Book Drive Project Meeting

> Your meeting will need a **title** that explains the purpose of the meeting.

Saturday, February 6, 2010 2:00 P.M.–6:00 P.M.

> You should also include the **date** and **time**.

Called by Daphne Farkis

> This is the person who **called** the meeting. The person often, but not always, leads parts of the meeting.

Attendees: Bill Aldridge, Erika Cruz, Alexis Chang, Daphne Farkis, Alex Guitierrez, Tiffany Hopper, John Robinson, Sylvie Snopes

> The **attendees** are all the people invited to the meeting.

> The **time** provides a guide for how long a topic should be discussed.

> This is the **item**, or **topic**, to be discussed.

> The **owner** is the person who will lead each section of the meeting.

Time	Item	Owner
2:00 P.M.–2:30 P.M.	Welcome and introduction	Daphne
2:30 P.M.–3:30 P.M.	Overview of book drive process	Daphne
3:30 P.M.–4:00 P.M.	Discuss roles and responsibilities	Alexis, All
4:00 P.M.–4:30 P.M.	Break	All
4:30 P.M.–5:00 P.M.	Brainstorm session for flyer ideas	Erika, All
5:00 P.M.–5:30 P.M.	Next steps and deadlines	Daphne, All
5:30 P.M.–6:00 P.M.	Recap and adjournment	Daphne

Writing Business Letters

Business letters are often formal in tone and written for a specific business purpose. They generally follow one of several acceptable formats. In block format, all parts of the letter are at the left margin. All business letters, however, have the same parts: heading, inside address, salutation, body, closing, and signature.

The **heading** shows the writer's address and organization (if any).

The **inside address** indicates where the letter will be sent and the date.

A **salutation**, or **greeting**, is punctuated by a colon. When the specific addressee is not known, use a general greeting such as "To Whom It May Concern."

The **body** of the letter states the writer's purpose. In this case, the writer requests that the class participate in the book drive.

The **closing**, "Sincerely," is common, as are "Best regards," "Yours truly," and "Respectfully yours."

Oscar Diego
Community Book Drive
P.O. Box 34535
Middletown, NY 10941

February 10, 2010
Yin Wallenez
English Teacher
Marsden School
1515 Main River Drive
Middletown, NY 10940

Dear Ms. Wallenez:

We are writing to you to encourage you and your class to join in this year's Community Book Drive. We really appreciated your participation last year and hope you will join us again. As you know, the Community Book Drive gathers books for hundreds of children who otherwise could not afford them. Last year we gathered more than 1,500 books!

Participating this year is simple. Just nominate two members of your class to serve as the book drive leaders. They will post flyers about the book drive around the school and other community areas. They will also be responsible for letting the book drive team leaders know when the drop boxes at your school are getting full.

Please let me know if you are interested. I sure hope that your class will be able to make this year's drive as much of a success as the last! Thanks for your time and consideration.

Sincerely,

Oscar Diego

Oscar Diego • Co-Coordinator, Community Book Drive

Writing Friendly Letters

Friendly letters are less formal than business letters. You can use this form to write to a friend, a family member, or anyone with whom you'd like to communicate in a personal, friendly way. Like business letters, friendly letters have the following parts: heading, inside address, salutation, body, closing, and signature. The purpose of a friendly letter might be:

- to share news and feelings
- to send or answer an invitation
- to express thanks

> The **heading** includes the writer's address and the date on which he or she wrote the letter. In some very casual letters, the writer may not include his or her address.

345 Whitehall Dr.
Beaverton, OR 97005
July 20, 2010

Dear Grandma and Grandpa,

Thank you so much for the journal you sent me. I can't wait to write in it. The cover is gorgeous. Did you know that red is my favorite color? I also love the pen—I can't believe that it is erasable. How cool!

> The **body** of the letter is the main section and contains the message of the letter.

I am having a great summer. I've played soccer a lot and read a lot of books. It sure is hot here, though. Yesterday it was 90 degrees! I know that is nothing compared to summers in Texas, but it is sure hot for us.

Mom says that you are planning a visit for the early fall. I'm really looking forward to it. Maybe you can come watch me play soccer.

Thanks again for the terrific journal.

> Some common **closings** for friendly letters include "Best wishes," "Love," and "Take care."

Love,

Rhonda

MLA Style for Listing Sources

Book with one author	London, Jack. *White Fang.* Clayton: Prestwick, 2007. Print.
Book with two or three authors	Veit, Richard, and Christopher Gould. *Writing, Reading, and Research.* 8th ed. Boston: Wadsworth-Cengage Learning, 2009. Print.
Book prepared by an editor	Twain, Mark. *The Complete Essays of Mark Twain.* Ed. Charles Neider. New York: Da Capo, 2000. Print.
Book with more than three authors or editors	Donald, Robert B., et al. *Writing Clear Essays.* 3rd ed. Upper Saddle River: Prentice, 1996. Print.
A single work from an anthology	Poe, Edgar Allan. "The Fall of the House of Usher." *American Literature: A Chronological Approach.* Ed. Edgar H. Schuster, Anthony Tovatt, and Patricia O. Tovatt. New York: McGraw, 1985. 233–247. Print. [Indicate pages for the entire selection.]
Introduction, foreward, preface, or afterward in a book	Vidal, Gore. Introduction. *Abraham Lincoln: Selected Speeches and Writings.* By Abraham Lincoln. New York: Vintage, 1992. xxi–xxvii. Print.
Signed article in a weekly magazine	Walsh, Brian. "Greening This Old House." *Time* 4 May 2009: 45–47. Print. [For a multipage article that does not appear on consecutive pages, write only the first page number on which it appears, followed by a plus sign.]
Signed article in a monthly magazine	Fischman, Josh. "A Better Life with Bionics." *National Geographic* Jan. 2010: 34–53. Print.
Unsigned editorial or story	"Wind Power." Editorial. *New York Times* 9 Jan. 2010: A18. Print. [If the editorial or story is signed, begin with the author's name.]
Signed pamphlet	[Treat the pamphlet as though it were a book.]
Audiovisual media, such as films, slide programs, videocassettes, DVDs	*Where the Red Fern Grows.* Dir. Norman Toker. Perf. James Whitmore, Beverly Garland, and Stewart Peterson. 1974. Sterling Entertainment, 1997. DVD.
Radio or TV broadcast transcript	"Texas High School Football Titans Ready for Clash." *Weekend Edition Sunday.* Host Melissa Block. Guests Mike Pesca and Tom Goldman. Natl. Public Radio. KUHF, Houston, 18 Dec. 2009. Print. Transcript.
A single page on a Web site	U.S. Census Bureau: Customer Liaison and Marketing Services Office. "State Facts for Students: Texas." *U.S. Census Bureau.* U.S. Census Bureau, 15 Oct. 2009. Web. 1 Nov. 2009. [Indicate the date of last update if known or use "n.d." if not known. After the medium of publication, include the date you accessed the information. You do not need the URL unless it is the only way to find the page. If needed, include it in angled brackets at the end, i.e. <http://www.census.gov/schools/facts/texas.html >.]
Newspaper	Yardley, Jim. "Hurricane Sweeps into Rural Texas; Cities Are Spared." *New York Times* 23 Aug. 1999: A1. Print. [For a multipage article that does not appear on consecutive pages, write only the first page number on which it appears, followed by a plus sign.]
Personal interview	Jones, Robert. Personal interview. 4 Sept. 2006.
Audio with multiple publishers	Simms, James, ed. *Romeo and Juliet.* By William Shakespeare. Oxford: Attica Cybernetics; London: BBC Education; London: Harper, 1995. CD-ROM.
Signed article from an encyclopedia	Askeland, Donald R. "Welding." *World Book Encyclopedia.* 1991 ed. Print. [For a well-known reference, you do not need to include the publisher information, only the edition and year, followed by the medium used.]

Commonly Misspelled Words

The list on this page presents words that cause problems for many people. Some of these words are spelled according to set rules, but others follow no specific rules. As you review this list, check to see how many of the words give you trouble in your own writing.

absence	benefit	conscience	excellent	library	prejudice
absolutely	bicycle	conscientious	exercise	license	previous
accidentally	bought	conscious	experience	lightning	probably
accurate	brief	continuous	explanation	likable	procedure
achievement	brilliant	convenience	extension	literature	proceed
affect	bulletin	coolly	extraordinary	mathematics	pronunciation
agreeable	bury	cooperate	familiar	maximum	realize
aisle	buses	correspondence	fascinating	minimum	really
all right	business	courageous	February	misspell	receipt
allowance	cafeteria	courteous	fiery	naturally	receive
analysis	calendar	criticism	financial	necessary	recognize
analyze	campaign	curiosity	foreign	neighbor	recommend
ancient	canceled	deceive	fourth	niece	rehearse
anniversary	candidate	decision	generally	ninety	repetition
answer	capital	defendant	genuine	noticeable	restaurant
anticipate	capitol	definitely	government	occasion	rhythm
anxiety	career	dependent	grammar	occasionally	sandwich
apologize	cashier	description	guidance	occur	schedule
appearance	category	desert	height	occurred	scissors
appreciate	ceiling	dessert	humorous	occurrence	theater
appropriate	certain	dining	immediately	opinion	truly
argument	changeable	disappointed	immigrant	opportunity	usage
athletic	characteristic	distinguish	independence	parallel	valuable
attendance	clothes	effect	independent	particularly	various
awkward	colonel	eighth	individual	personally	vegetable
bargain	column	embarrass	intelligence	persuade	weight
battery	commercial	enthusiastic	judgment	physician	weird
beautiful	commitment	envelope	knowledge	possibility	whale
beginning	condemn	environment	lawyer	precede	yield
believe	congratulate	especially	legible	preferable	

A

achievement (ə chēv´mənt) *n.* something that has been accomplished or done very well

accurate (ak´yər it) *adj.* without errors; true

aesthetic (es thet´ik) *adj.* relating to beauty; artistic; pleasing to the senses

analysis (ə nal´ə sis) *n.* the process of looking at something closely in order to understand its meaning, structure, or parts

analytical (an´ə lit´ik əl) *adj.* relating to, or using, logical reasoning

analyze (an´ə līz) *v.* to look at something carefully to understand its meaning or structure

anticipation (an tis´ə pā´shən) *n.* the act of being prepared for something to happen

application (ap´li kā´shən) *n.* a form that one fills out to make a request or to apply for something

apply (ə plī´) *v.* to make a formal request for something

assertion (ə sʉr´shən) *n.* a strong statement of fact or belief about a subject

assumption (ə sump´shən) *n.* statement which is taken as true, without proof, sometimes incorrectly

B

ballad (bal´əd) *n.* a song-like poem that tells a story, often of love and adventure

bias (bī´əs) *n.* a point of view about a topic

C

category (kat´ə gôr´ē) *n.* a group or division of people or things which are seen as having similar characteristics

character (kar´ik tər) *n.* a person (or animal) who plays a part in the action of a story, play, or movie

characterization (kar´ik tər i zā´shən) *n.* the act of creating and developing a character in a story

compelling (kəm pel´ing) *adj.* (of an argument) very convincing; demanding attention; drawing interest, admiration, or attention in a powerful way; forceful

complex (käm pleks´) *adj.* not easy to understand or analyze; made up of many parts, complicated

complexity (käm pleks´ə tē) *n.* the state of having many complicated parts

conflict (kän´flikt´) *n.* the struggle between people or opposing forces which creates the dramatic action in a play or story

context (kän´tekst´) *n.* the part of a sentence which surrounds a word and which can be used to shed light on the word's meaning; the situation in which something occurs which can help that thing to be fully understood; the setting or environment

convention (kən ven´shən) *n.* a standard way of doing something; a method or practice

convincing (kən vins´ing) *adj.* (of an argument) strong enough to be able to make someone agree or believe something is true; believable, powerful

correspond (kôr´ə spänd´) *v.* to match, agree, or have a close likeness

D

demonstrate (dem´ən strāt´) *v.* to make a fact clear by giving proof or evidence

develop (di vel´əp) *v.* to explain or build an idea or example bit by bit

dialogue (dī´ə lôg´) *n.* a conversation between two or more people in a book, play, or movie

discrepancy (di skrep´ən sē) *n.* a lack of agreement between two or more pieces of information

divergent (dī vʉrj´´nt) *adj.* (of two roads, ideas, or other things) branching apart from each other; different from each other, or from a standard

E

effective (e fekt´iv) *adj.* successful in getting the desired results

embedded (em bed´əd) *adj.* placed firmly in the middle of something; (of a quotation) placed inside a sentence, not set apart from the rest of the text

emotion (ē mō´shən) *n.* a feeling, such as love or joy; feelings and automatic response, as opposed to logical thoughts and conclusions

engaging (en gāj´ing) *adj.* something which draws in and interests (engages) the reader; charming, interesting

essay (es´ā) *n.* a short piece of non-fiction writing on a particular subject

ethics (eth´iks) *n.* a set of moral principles or beliefs about what is right and wrong which guide how a person or group lives

evaluate (ē val´yü āt´) *v.* to look into something carefully so as to assess and judge it

evidence (ev´ə dəns) *n.* anything that gives proof or shows something to be true

F

factual (fak´chü əl) *adj.* correct; containing no errors; provable as true

figurative (fig´yər ə tiv´) *adj.* (of language) writing that is full of metaphors and images, where the words are very descriptive but not meant to be taken literally

formal (fôr´məl) *adj.* reflecting language that is traditional and correct, not casual

formatting (fôr´mat´ing) *adj.* related to the arrangement of text, images, and graphics on a page

free verse (frē vʉrs) *n.* a style of poetry that does not have a specific format or rhyme

I

imagery (im´ij rē) *n.* descriptive language that paints pictures in the mind or appeals to the senses

imply (im plī´) *v.* to indicate something indirectly, by inference, rather than stating it outright; to strongly suggest

importance (im pôrt´'nts) *n.* the state of being of great value or significance

impression (im presh´ən) *n.* an idea or feeling about a person or thing that is formed quickly, without a lot of thought

interpret (in tʉr´prət) *v.* to decide on and explain the meaning of something

L

literal (lit´ər əl) *adj.* the most basic meaning of a word or words, without metaphor or other figurative language; without any exaggeration or distortion

literary (lit´ər ar´ē) *adj.* of or relating to books or other written material

M

mood (müd) *n.* the atmosphere or overall feeling of a piece of writing as created by the author

N

non-stereotypical (nän ster´ē ə tip´i kəl) *adj.* not conforming to a pre-existing, simple idea of how something should be or how someone should act; unusual, unconventional

O

opinion (ə pin´yən) *n.* a belief or view that is not necessarily based on facts

organization (ôr´gə ni zā´shən) *n.* a way something (such as a poem or essay) is structured or arranged

P

paraphrase (par´ə frāz´) *v.* to reword information into one's own words

perspective (pər spek´tiv) *n.* a particular way of seeing or thinking about something; a viewpoint, point of view, or opinion

point of view (point uv vyü) *n.* the perspective from which a story is told; an attitude, position, standpoint, or way of looking at a situation; an opinion

precise (prē cīs´) *adj.* exact, accurate; careful about details

primary (prī´mer´ē) *adj.* (of sources, documents, or information) firsthand (such as newspapers, diaries) or direct; first in order or importance; basic

Q

quotation (kwō tā´shən) *n.* a group of words copied exactly from a speech or piece of writing

R

reader-friendly (rēd´ər frend´lē) *adj.* easy for an audience to read and understand

realistic (rē´ə lis´tik) *adj.* when people or events in a story or movie are shown in a way that is true to real life

refute (ri fyüt´) *v.* to prove to be untrue

relevant (rel´ə vənt) *adj.* closely connected, important, or significant to the matter at hand

reliability (ri lī´ə bil´i tē) *n.* the degree to which something or someone can be trusted and counted on to be consistent

resolution (rez´ə lü´shən) *n.* what happens to resolve the conflict in the plot of a story

rhetorical (ri tôr´i kəl) *adj.* related to a special use of language, such as a simile or a metaphor

rhetorical devices (ri tôr´i kəl di vī´səz) *n.* strategies and techniques, for example metaphor and hyperbole, used by writers to draw in or persuade readers

S

schema (skēm´ə) *n.* a diagram representing an organizational plan or outline

secondary (sek´ən der´ē) *adj.* (of sources, documents, or information) not direct but second hand, derived from primary sources; less important, of second rank or value

sensory (sen´sər ē) *adj.* relating to the senses

setting (set´ing) *n.* the time and place of the action in a story or other piece of writing

sonnet (sän´it) *n.* a poem of fourteen lines, often with a set pattern of rhymes

source (sôrs) *n.* (in research) a book or document that can be used as evidence in research, or when making an argument and trying to prove a point; a place, person, or thing which supplies information or other things; the place something begins, the origin

stanza (stan´zə) *n.* a group of lines of poetry, usually with a similar length and pattern, separated from other lines by spaces

statement (stāt´mənt) *n.* something written or said which presents information in a clear and definite way

statistics (stə tis´tiks) *n.* facts and data expressed in numbers

stereotype (ster´ē ə tīp´) *n.* an oversimplified and fixed idea about a type of thing or group of people

strategy (strat´ə jē) *n.* in a piece of writing, a literary tactic or method (such as flashback or foreshadowing) used by the writer to achieve a certain goal or affect

style (stīl) *n.* a way of doing something; a way of writing, composing, painting, etc., special to a period in history, a group of artists, or a particular person

stylistic (stī lis´tik) *adj.* of, or relating to, artistic or literary style

substantial (səb stan´shəl) *adj.* important, large or weighty; real and not imaginary; well-constructed

suspense (sə spens´) *n.* a feeling of anxiety and uncertainty about what will happen in a story or other piece of writing

T

technical (tek´ni kəl) *adj.* related to technology, computers, or applied sciences

theme (thēm) *n.* a central message, concern, or purpose in a literary work

thematic (thē mat´ik) *adj.* relating to a particular theme or subject or series of subjects

theory (thē´ə rē) *n.* an idea about something that has not been proven

thesis (thē´sis) *n.* an idea or theory that is stated and then discussed in a logical way

tone (tōn) *n.* the feeling expressed in a piece of writing

transition (tran zish´ən) *n.* the change from one part, place, or idea to another

U

unreliable (un´ri lī´ə bəl) *adj.* unable to be depended upon

V

validity (və lid´ə tē) *n.* the quality of being reasonable, logical, or acceptable as true

vivid (viv´id) *n.* producing clear images in the mind; very clear and detailed; colorful, bright; lively

Spanish Glossary

A

accurate / correcto *adj.* sin errores; verdadero

achievement / éxito *s.* algo que es muy bien realizado o hecho

aesthetic / estético *adj.* perteneciente a la belleza; artístico; agradable a los sentidos

analysis / análisis *s.* el proceso de examinar algo detenidamente para entender su significado, su estructura o sus partes

analytical / analítico *adj.* perteneciente a o utilizando el razonamiento lógico

analyze / analizar *v.* examinar algo detenidamente para entender su significado o estructura

anticipation / anticipación *s.* el acto de prepararse para la ocurrencia de algo

application / solicitud *s.* un formulario que se llena para pedir o solicitar algo

apply / solicitar *v.* pedir algo formalmente

assertion / aseveración *s.* una declaración fuerte de un hecho o creencia sobre un tema

assumption / suposición *s.* un hecho o declaración que se interpreta como la verdad, sin pruebas, y a veces equivocadamente

B

ballad / balada *s.* una canción poética que cuenta una historia, muchas veces del amor y la aventura

bias / predisposición *s.* un punto de vista sobre un tema

C

category / categoría *s.* un grupo o división de personas o cosas que tiene características comunes

character / personaje *s.* un individuo (humano o animal) que tiene un papel en la acción de un cuento, una obra de teatro o una película

characterization / caracterización *s.* el acto de crear y desarrollar un personaje en un cuento

compelling / convincente *adj.* (de un argumento) muy persuasivo; que exige atención; que atrae interés, admiración, o atención de un modo poderoso; contundente

complex / complejo *adj.* difícil de entender o analizar; hecho de muchas partes, complicado

complexity / complejidad *s.* el estado de tener muchos componentes complicados

conflict / conflicto *s.* la lucha entre personas o fuerzas opuestas que crea la acción dramática en una obra de teatro o un cuento

context / contexto *s.* la parte de una oración que rodea una palabra y que se puede usar para determinar el significado de la palabra; la situación en la que algo ocurre que puede facilitar la comprensión de la cosa; el escenario o entorno

convention / convención *s.* un modo estándar de hacer algo; un método o práctica

convincing / convincente *adj.* (de un argumento) suficientemente persuasivo para que alguien se ponga de acuerdo o crea que algo es verdadero; creíble, poderoso

correspond / corresponder *v.* encajar con, concordar, parecerse a

D

demonstrate / demostrar *v.* aclarar un hecho por dar pruebas o evidencia

develop / desarrollar *v.* explicar o exponer poco a poco una idea o ejemplo

dialogue / diálogo *s.* una conversación entre dos personajes o más en un libro, obra de teatro o película

discrepancy / discrepancia, inexactitud *s.* una falta de concordancia entre dos o más datos

divergent / divergente *adj.* (de dos caminos, ideas u otras cosas) bifurcándose; diferente del uno al otro, o de una convención

E

effective / efectivo, eficaz *adj.* exitoso en producir los resultados deseados

embedded / colocado *adj.* metido firmemente en medio de algo; (de una cita) insertada dentro de una oración, no separada del resto del texto

emotion / sentimiento *s.* una sensación emotiva, como el amor o la alegría; los sentimientos en general, opuestos al razonamiento y la lógica

engaging / interesante *adj.* algo que le atrae y le interesa al lector; encantador, interesante

essay / ensayo *s.* una obra escrita breve de no ficción sobre un tema particular

ethics / ética *s.* principios morales o creencias sobre lo que es correcto e incorrecto que guían cómo vive una persona o grupo

evaluate / evaluar *v.* investigar algo cuidadosamente para analizarlo y valorarlo

evidence / pruebas *s.* cualquier cosa que demuestre o indique que algo es cierto

F

factual / fáctico *adj.* correcto; sin errores; que se puede verificar

figurative / figurado *adj.* (de lenguaje) escritura que está repleta de metáforas e imágenes, donde las palabras son muy descriptivas pero su significado no debe ser interpretado literalmente

formal / formal *adj.* que refleja el lenguaje tradicional y correcto, no informal

formatting / formateo *s.* la colocación de texto, imágenes y gráficos en una página

free verse / verso libre *s.* un estilo de poesía que no tiene un formato específico ni rima

I

imagery / imágenes *s.* lenguaje descriptivo que crea dibujos en la mente o atrae los sentidos

imply / insinuar *v.* señalar algo indirectamente, por deducción, más que declararlo abiertamente; hacer una fuerte sugerencia

importance / importancia *s.* el estado de ser de gran valor o significado

impression / impresión *s.* una idea o sentimiento que se forma rápidamente sobre una persona o cosa sin mucho pensamiento

interpret / interpretar *v.* determinar y explicar el significado de algo

L

literal / literal *adj.* el significado más básico de una palabra o palabras, sin metáfora u otro lenguaje figurado; sin exageración o distorsión

literary / literario *adj.* perteneciente o relativo a los libros u otros materiales escritos

M

mood / ambiente, tono *s.* el ambiente o sentimiento general de una obra escrita creado por el autor

N

non-stereotypical / no estereotípico *adj.* que no se ajusta a una idea preexistente y simple de cómo debe ser algo o cómo debe comportarse alguien; poco común o convencional

O

opinion / opinión *s.* una creencia o perspectiva que no es necesariamente basada en los hechos

organization / organización *s.* la manera en la que algo (por ejemplo un poema o ensayo) se estructura o se arregla

P

paraphrase / parafrasear *v.* formular información utilizando sus propias palabras

perspective / perspective *s.* una manera de interpretar o pensar algo; un punto de vista tu opinión

point of view / punto de vista *s.* la perspectiva de la cual se cuenta una historia; una actitud, postura, o manera de interpretar una situación; una opinión

precise / preciso *adj.* exacto, certero; cuidadoso con detalles

primary / primario, primordial *adj.* (de fuentes, documentos o información) de primera mano (por ejemplo periódicos, diarios) o directo; primero en orden de importancia; básico

Q

quotation / cita *s.* un grupo de palabras copiadas exactamente de un discurso o texto

R

reader-friendly / fácil de leer *adj.* no complicado, fácil de entender y leer

realistic / realista *adj.* cuando se presentan las personas o los eventos en un cuento o una película conforme a la realidad

refute / refutar *v.* probar que algo es falso o incorrecto

relevant / relevante *adj.* conectado estrechamente, importante o significante al asunto en cuestión

reliability / fiabilidad, consistencia *s.* el grado al que se puede fiar de algo o alguien o que se puede contar con su consistencia

resolution / resolución *s.* lo que ocurre para resolver el conflicto en el argumento de una historia

rhetorical / retórico *adj.* perteneciente o relativo al uso especial del lenguaje, como un símil o una metáfora

rhetorical devices / técnicas retóricas *s.* estrategias y técnicas (por ejemplo, metáfora e hipérbole) utilizadas por los escritores para atraer o persuadir a los lectores

S

schema / esquema *s.* un diagrama que representa un plan de organización o un borrador

secondary / secundario, de segunda mano *adj.* (de fuentes, documentos o información) no directo, que no viene de primera mano, derivado de fuentes primarios; de menos importancia, rango o valor

sensory / sensorial *adj.* perteneciente o relativo a los sentidos

setting / escenario *s.* el lugar y el momento de la acción en un cuento u otra obra escrita

sonnet / soneto *s.* un poema de catorce versos, muchas veces con un patrón determinado de rima

source / fuente *s.* (en la investigación) un libro o documento que se puede usar como pruebas en una investigación o cuando se expone un argumento para demostrar un argumento; un lugar, una persona o una cosa que da información u otras cosas; el lugar en el que empieza algo, el origen

stanza / estrofa *s.* un grupo de líneas de poesía, normalmente con un patrón y extensión similar, separado por espacios de otras líneas

statement / declaración *s.* algo escrito o dicho que presenta información de una manera clara y definitiva

statistics / estadísticas *s.* hechos y datos que vienen de analizar información expresada en números

stereotype / estereotipo *s.* una idea fija y demasiado simplificada sobre una clase de cosa o grupo de personas

strategy / estrategia *s.* en un texto, una táctica o método literario (como el *flashback* o el presagio) empleado por el autor para lograr un objetivo o efecto específico

style / estilo *s.* una manera de hacer algo; una manera de escribir, componer, pintar, etc. que es especial a una época de la historia, a un grupo de artistas, o a una persona particular

stylistic / estilístico *adj.* perteneciente o relativo al estilo artístico o literario

substantial / considerable *adj.* importante, grande o pesado; real y no imaginario; bien construido

suspense / suspenso *s.* una sensación de ansiedad e incertidumbre sobre lo que va a pasar en una historia u otra obra escrita

T

technical / técnico *adj.* perteneciente o relativo a la tecnología, la informática o las ciencias aplicadas

theme / tema *s.* una idea, asunto, o propósito principal de una obra literaria

thematic / temático *adj.* perteneciente a un tema o serie de temas en particular

theory / teoría *s.* una idea sobre algo que todavía no ha sido verificado o probado

thesis / tesis *s.* una idea o teoría que se expone y que se discute de una manera lógica

tone / tono *n.* carácter o modo particular de la expresión y del estilo de un texto según el asunto que trata o el estado de ánimo que pretende reflejar

transition / transición *s.* el cambio entre partes, lugares y conceptos

U

unreliable / poco fiable *adj.* que no se puede fiar de la información

V

validity / validez *s.* la cualidad de ser razonable, lógico o aceptable como verdadero

vivid / vívido, vivo *s.* que produce imágenes claras en la mente; muy claro y detallado; colorido, brillante; alegre

Meeting Agenda

Meeting Title: _____

Date: _____

Time: _____

Called by: _____

Attendees: _____

_____

Time	Item	Owner

Cause and Effect Chart

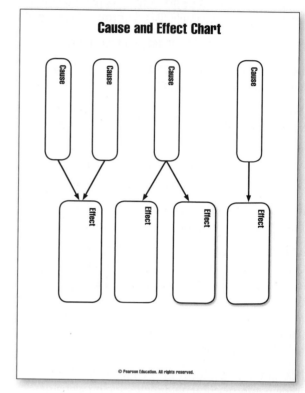

Cluster Diagram

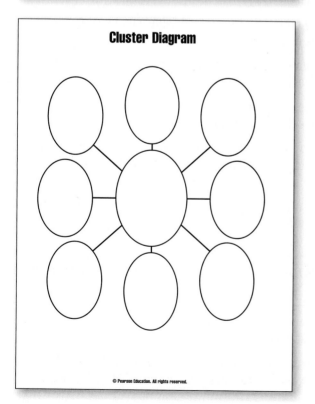

Five Ws Chart

Use these questions as you read, and write important details. Remember, you may not need to answer every question.

Who?

What?

When?

Where?

Why?

KWL Chart

Topic:

What I Know	What I Want to Know	What I Learned

Main Idea and Details Web

Use these questions as you read, and write important details. Remember, you may not need to answer every question.

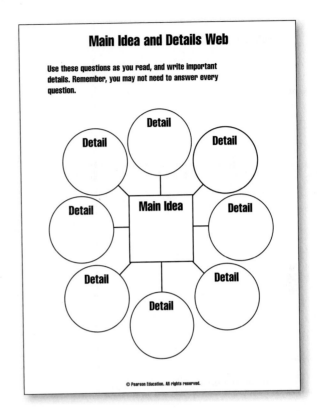

Meeting Notes

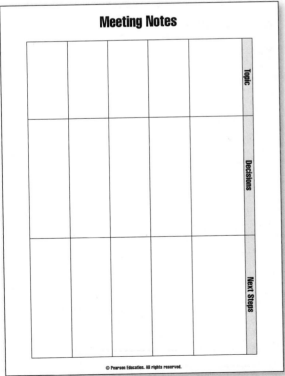

Topic

Decisions

Next Steps

Note Card

Topic:

Source:
-
-
-

Topic:

Source:
-
-
-

Graphic Organizer Handbook   **R25**

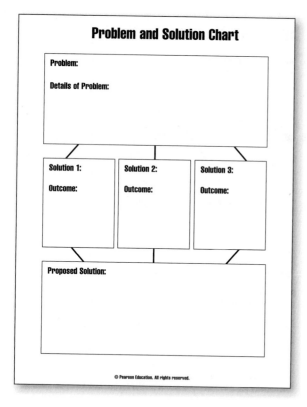

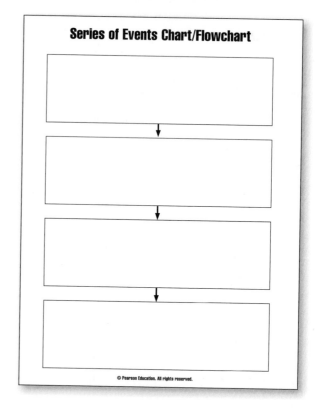

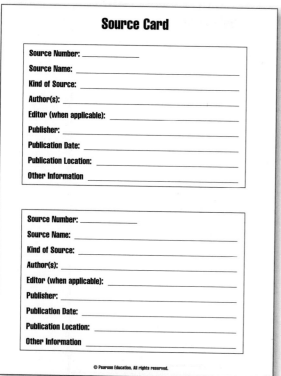

Outline

Steps in a Process Chart

Steps	Details
Step 1:	
Step 2:	
Step 3:	
Step 4:	
Step 5:	

Storyboard

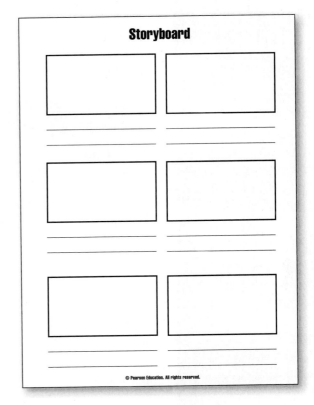

Timeline

Venn Diagram

Listening and Speaking Handbook

Communication travels between people in many forms. You receive information by listening to others, and you convey information through speaking. The more developed these skills are, the more you will be able to communicate your ideas, as well as to comprehend the ideas of others.

If you improve your listening skills, it will become easier to focus your attention on classroom discussions and to identify important information more accurately. If you develop good speaking skills, you will be better prepared to contribute effectively in group discussions, to give formal presentations with more confidence, and to communicate your feelings and ideas to others more easily.

Listening

Different situations call for different types of listening. Learn more about the four main types of listening—critical, empathic, appreciative, and reflective—in the chart below.

Types of Listening		
Type	**How to Listen**	**Situations**
Critical	Listen for facts and supporting details to understand and evaluate the speaker's message.	Informative or persuasive speeches, class discussions, announcements
Empathic	Imagine yourself in the other person's position, and try to understand what he or she is thinking.	Conversations with friends or family
Appreciative	Identify and analyze aesthetic or artistic elements, such as character development, rhyme, imagery, and descriptive language.	Oral presentations of a poem, dramatic performances
Reflective	Ask questions to get information, and use the speaker's responses to form new questions.	Class or group discussions

This handbook will help you increase your ability in these two key areas of communication.

R28   Listening and Speaking Handbook

Using Different Types of Questions

A speaker's ideas may not always be clear to you. You may need to ask questions to clarify your understanding. If you understand the different types of questions, you will be able to get the information you need.

- An **open-ended question** does not lead to a single, specific response. Use this question to open up a discussion: "What did you think of the piano recital?"

- A **closed question** leads to a specific response and must be answered with a yes or no: "Did you play a piece by Chopin at your recital?"

- A **factual question** is aimed at getting a particular piece of information and must be answered with facts: "How many years have you been playing the piano?"

Participating in a Group Discussion

In a group discussion, you openly discuss ideas and topics in an informal setting. The group discussions in which you participate will involve, for the most part, your classmates and focus on the subjects you are studying. To get the most out of a group discussion, you need to participate in it.

Use group discussions to express and to listen to ideas in an informal setting.

Communicate Effectively Think about the points you want to make, the order in which you want to make them, the words you will use to express them, and the examples that will support these points before you speak.

Ask Questions Asking questions can help you improve your comprehension of another speaker's ideas. It may also call attention to possible errors in another speaker's points.

Make Relevant Contributions Stay focused on the topic being discussed. Relate comments to your own experience and knowledge, and clearly connect them to your topic. It is important to listen to the points others make so you can build off their ideas. Work to share the connections you see. For example, say whether you agree or disagree, or tell the goup how your ideas connect.

Speaking

Giving a presentation or speech before an audience is generally recognized as public speaking. Effective speakers are well prepared and deliver speeches smoothly and with confidence.

Recognizing Different Kinds of Speeches

There are four main kinds of speeches: informative speeches, persuasive speeches, entertaining speeches, and extemporaneous speeches.

Consider the purpose and audience of your speech before deciding what kind of speech you will give.

- Give an **informative speech** to explain an idea, a process, an object, or an event.

- Give a **persuasive speech** to get your listeners to agree with your position or to take some action. Use formal English when speaking.

- Give an **entertaining speech** to offer your listeners something to enjoy or to amuse them. Use both informal and formal language.

- Give an **extemporaneous speech** when an impromptu occasion arises. It is an informal speech because you do not have a prepared manuscript.

Preparing and Presenting a Speech

If you are asked to deliver a speech, begin choosing a topic that you like or know well. Then, prepare your speech for your audience.

To prepare your speech, research your topic. Make an outline, and use numbered note cards.

Gather Information Use the library and other resources to gather reliable information and to find examples to support your ideas.

Organizing Information Organize your information by writing an outline of main ideas and major details. Then, before you deliver your speech, write the main ideas, major details, quotations, and facts on note cards.

When presenting your speech, use rhetorical forms of language and verbal and nonverbal strategies.

Use Rhetorical Language Repeat key words and phrases to identify your key points. Use active verbs and colorful adjectives to keep your speech interesting. Use parallel phrases to insert a sense of rhythm.

Use Verbal and Nonverbal Strategies Vary the pitch and tone of your voice, and the rate at which you speak. Speak loudly and emphasize key words or phrases. Avoid consistently reading your speech from you notes. Work to maintain eye contact with the audience. As you speak, connect with the audience by using gestures and facial expressions to emphasize key points.

Evaluating a Speech

Evaluating a speech gives you the chance to judge another speaker's skills. It also gives you the opportunity to review and improve your own methods for preparing and presenting a speech.

When you evaluate a speech, you help the speaker and yourself to learn from experience. Listed below are some questions you might ask yourself while evaluating another person's speech or one of your own speeches.

- Did the speaker introduce the topic clearly, develop it well, and conclude it effectively?

- Did the speaker support each main idea with appropriate details?

- Did the speaker approach the platform confidently and establish eye contact with the audience?

- Did the speaker's facial expressions, gestures, and movements appropriately reinforce the words spoken?

- Did the speaker vary the pitch of his or her voice and the rate of his or her speaking?

- Did the speaker enunciate all words clearly?

Listening Critically to a Speech

Hearing happens naturally as sounds reach your ears. Listening, or critical listening, requires that you understand and interpret these sounds.

Critical listening requires preparation, active involvement, and self-evaluation from the listener.

Learning the Listening Process Listening is interactive; the more you involve yourself in the listening process, the more you will understand.

Focus Your Attention Focus your attention on the speaker and block out all distractions—people, noises, and objects. Find out more about the subject that will be discussed beforehand.

Interpret the Information To interpret a speaker's message successfully, you need to identify and understand important information. You might consider listening for repeated words or phrases, pausing momentarily to memorize and/or write key statements, watching non-verbal signals, and combining this new information with what you already know.

Respond to the Speaker's Message Respond to the information you have heard by identifying the larger message of the speech, its most useful points, and your position on the topic.

Index

Index of Authors and Titles

Acknowledgments

Grateful acknowledgment is made to the following for copyrighted material:

Dutton Signet, A division of Penguin Group (USA), Inc.

From *Beowulf,* translated by Burton Raffel, copyright © 1963 renewed © 1991 by Burton Raffel. Used with permission of Dutton Signet, a division of Penguin Group (USA) Inc.

HarperCollins Publishers, Inc.

From *An American Childhood* by Annie Dillard. Copyright © 1987 by Annie Dillard. Used by permission of HarperCollins Publishers.

Brad Kollus

"Cats and Seniors: A Loving and Healthy Relationship" by Brad Kollus. Originally published in *Cat Fancy Vol. 50 No. 3 March 2007.* Copyright © Brad Kollus. Brad is a freelance cat writer. He lives in NJ with his wife Elizabeth, son Dylan and their 3 cats. All rights reserved. Used by permission.

Estate of Howard Moss

"Shall I Compare Thee to a Summer's Day" by Howard Moss from *A Swim Off the Rocks: Light Verse.* Copyright © 1976 by Howard Moss. All rights reserved. Used by permission of Richard Evans.

National Council of Teachers of English (NCTE)

"Mistakes are a fact of Life: A National Comparative Study" by Andrea A. Lunsford and Karen J. Lunsford translated from *bcs. bedfordstmartins.com/lunsford/PDF/Lunsford_article_Mistakes. pdf.* Copyright © NCTE. Used by permission of National Council of Teachers of English (NCTE).

Russell & Volkening, Inc.

From *An American Childhood* by Annie Dillard. Copyright © 1987 by Annie Dillard. From *Beowulf,* translated by Burton Raffel, copyright © 1963 renewed © 1991 by Burton Raffel. Used by permission of Russell & Volkening as agents for the author.

Salem Press Inc.

"Arthur Conan Doyle" by Robert W. Millett. Published in *Critical Survey Of Short Fiction, Pages 1298–1299.* Copyright © 1981 Salem Press. Reproduced by permission of the publisher.

Viking Penguin, Inc., A division of Penguin Group (USA) Inc.

"Trinity Place" by Phyllis McGinley from *Times Three.* Copyright © 1937 by Phyllis McGinley. Used by permission of Viking Penguin, a division of Penguin Group (USA) Inc.

Note: Every effort has been made to locate the copyright owner of material reproduced in this component. Omissions brought to our attention will be corrected in subsequent editions.

Image Credits

Illustrations
   Maria Raymondsdotter

All interior photos provided by Jupiter Images. Except

95, 96: Courtesy of The Library of Congress; 118: © Corbis/age fotostock; 170: © i love images/age fotostock; 227, 241, 250: Courtesy of The Library of Congress; 156: © Purestock/age fotostock